The Spacesuit Film

ALSO BY GARY WESTFAHL
AND FROM MCFARLAND

*Science Fiction and the Prediction of the Future:
Essays on Foresight and Fallacy*
(coeditor, with Yuen and Chen, 2011)

*Science Fiction and the Two Cultures:
Essays on Bridging the Gap Between the Sciences
and the Humanities* (coeditor, with Slusser, 2009)

Hugo Gernsback and the Century of Science Fiction (2007)

The Spacesuit Film
A History, 1918–1969

Gary Westfahl

Foreword by Michael Cassutt

McFarland & Company, Inc., Publishers
Jefferson, North Carolina, and London

LIBRARY OF CONGRESS CATALOGUING-IN-PUBLICATION DATA

Westfahl, Gary.
The spacesuit film : a history, 1918–1969 /
Gary Westfahl ; foreword by Michael Cassutt.
p.   cm.
Includes bibliographical references and index.
Includes filmography.

ISBN 978-0-7864-4267-6
softcover : acid free paper ∞

1. Science fiction films — History and criticism.   2. Space flights in motion pictures.   3. Outer space in motion pictures.   4. Astronauts in motion pictures.   I. Title.
PN1995.9.S26W47 2012   791.43'656 — dc23   2012007550

BRITISH LIBRARY CATALOGUING DATA ARE AVAILABLE

© 2012 Gary Westfahl. All rights reserved

*No part of this book may be reproduced or transmitted in any form
or by any means, electronic or mechanical, including photocopying
or recording, or by any information storage and retrieval system,
without permission in writing from the publisher.*

Front cover design by David K. Landis (Shake It Loose Graphics)

Manufactured in the United States of America

*McFarland & Company, Inc., Publishers
Box 611, Jefferson, North Carolina 28640
www.mcfarlandpub.com*

To my son, Jeremy Westfahl,
who has actually seen a few
films discussed in this book,
and is the only member of my family
who just might watch the others.

Table of Contents

Foreword: Don't Leave Earth Without It (by Michael Cassutt) 1
Introduction: Pre-Flight Briefing 3

1. FIRST FLIGHTS: THE EARLY FILMS 9
    Himmelskibet (A Trip to Mars) (1918) 12
    Frau im Mond (Woman in the Moon) (1929) 14
    Kosmicheskiy Reys (The Space Voyage) (1935) 17

2. THE TRUE FRONTIER: THE CLASSIC FILMS 20
    Destination Moon (1950) 20
    Spaceways (1953) 27
    Project Moon Base (1953) 32
    Riders to the Stars (1954) 35
    Gog (1954) 39
    Conquest of Space (1955) 41
    Disneyland: "Man and the Moon" (1955) 45
    Satellite in the Sky (1956) 47
    Destination Space (1959) 51
    Men into Space (1959–1960) 54

3. WILD ADVENTURES: THE MELODRAMATIC FILMS 74
    Television Programs of the Early 1950s 75
    Captain Video: Master of the Stratosphere (1951) and *Radar Men
        from the Moon* (1952 81
    Rocketship X-M (1950) 85
    Flight to Mars (1951) 88
    Cat-Women of the Moon (1953) 92
    Forbidden Planet (1956) 94
    World Without End (1956) 95
    Missile to the Moon (1958), *Queen of Outer Space* (1958), and *Nude
        on the Moon* (1961) 96

From the Earth to the Moon (1958) and *First Men in the Moon* (1964) 102
The Twilight Zone (1959–1964) 108
12 to the Moon (1960) 109
The Phantom Planet (1961) 113
Robinson Crusoe on Mars (1964) 115
Lost in Space (1965–1968) 117
The Time Tunnel: "One Way to the Moon" (1966) 121
In Like Flint (1967) and *You Only Live Twice* (1967) 123
The Terrornauts (1967) 126
Star Trek: "The Tholian Web" (1968) 127
Barbarella (1968) 131
Moon Zero Two (1969) 132
Döppelganger (*Journey to the Far Side of the Sun*) (1969) 134

4. SHIPS OF FOOLS: THE HUMOROUS FILMS 140
   Situation Comedies of the 1950s 141
   Abbott and Costello Go to Mars (1953) 144
   Space Ship Sappy (1957), *Outer Space Jitters* (1957), and *Have Rocket, Will Travel* (1959) 147
   Man in the Moon (1960) 149
   Moon Pilot (1962) 151
   The Road to Hong Kong (1962) 153
   The Mouse on the Moon (1963) 155
   Situation Comedies of the 1960s 158
   Sergeant Dead Head (1965) 162
   Way...Way Out (1966) 164
   Jules Verne's Rocket to the Moon (*Those Fantastic Flying Fools*) (1967) 167
   The Reluctant Astronaut (1967) 169

5. SPACE FRIGHTS: THE HORRIFIC FILMS 175
   The Quatermass Experiment (1953) and *The Quatermass Xperiment* (1955) 179
   Quatermass II (1955) 183
   King Dinosaur (1955) 185
   20 Million Miles to Earth (1957) 186
   It! The Terror from Beyond Space (1958) 187
   First Man into Space (1959) 189
   The Angry Red Planet (1959) 193
   Journey to the Seventh Planet (1961) 195
   The Crawling Hand (1963) 197
   The Outer Limits (1963–1965) 198

The Wizard of Mars (1965) 205
Mutiny in Outer Space (1965) 207
Space Monster (1965) 209
Frankenstein Meets the Spacemonster (1965) 211
Mission Mars (1968) 214
The Green Slime (1968) 216

6. PARALLEL FLIGHT PATHS: THE FOREIGN-LANGUAGE FILMS 220
   • The Soviet Union and Eastern Europe • 221
      Doroga k Zvezdam (*Road to the Stars*) (1957) and *Luna* (*The Moon*)
         (1965) 221
      Nebo Zovyot (*The Sky Calls*) (1959) and *Battle Beyond the Sun* (1962) 224
      Die Schweigende Stern (*First Spaceship on Venus*) (1960) 230
      Baron Prášil (*The Fabulous Baron Munchausen*) (1961) and *Automat
         na Přání* (*The Wishing Machine*) (1967) 232
      Planeta Bur (*Planet of Storms*) (1962), *Voyage to the Prehistoric Planet*
         (1965), and *Voyage to the Planet of Prehistoric Women* (1967) 236
      Ikarie XB-1 (1963) and *Voyage to the End of the Universe* (1964) 240
      Mechte Navstrechu (*A Dream Come True*) (1963) and *Queen of Blood*
         (1966) 243
      Tumannost Andromedy (*The Andromeda Nebula*) (1967) 245
   • Italy and Western Europe • 246
      Totò nella Luna (*Totò in the Moon*) (1957) 246
      La Morte Viene dallo Spazio (*The Day the Sky Exploded*) (1958).......... 249
      Space Men (1960) 251
      Il Pianeta degli Uomini Spenti (*Battle of the Worlds*) (1961) 254
      Terrore nello Spazio (*Planet of the Vampires*) (1965) 255
      Dos Cosmonautas a la Fuerza (*002 Operazione Luna*) (1965) 257
      I Criminali della Galassia (*The Wild, Wild Planet*) (1965) and
         I Diafanoidi Portano la Morte (*War of the Planets*) (1966) 258
      Il Pianeta Errante (*War Between the Planets*) (1966) and *La Morte
         Viene dal Pianeta Aytin* (*The Snow Devils*) (1967) 262
      Raumpatrouille: Die Phantastischen Abenteuer des Raumschiffes Orion
         (*Space Patrol*) (1966) 265
      2 + 5: Missione Hydra (*Star Pilot*) (1966) 266
      ...4...3...2...1...Morte (*Mission Stardust*) (1967) 268
   • Egypt and Mexico • 270
      Rehla ilal Kamar (*Journey to the Moon*) (1959) 270
      Conquistador de la Luna (*The Astronauts*) (1960) 272
      Gigantes Planetarios (*Planetary Giants*) (1965) and *El Planeta de las
         Mujeres Invasoras* (*Planet of the Female Invaders*) (1966) 274

- Japan and Western Asia • 277
    - *Chikyu Boeigun* (*The Mysterians*) (1957) and *Uchû Daisensô* (*Battle in Outer Space*) (1959) 278
    - *Kyojin to Gangu* (*Giants and Toys*) (1958) 281
    - *Yosei Gorasu* (*Gorath*) (1962) 282
    - *Kaijû Daisensô* (*Godzilla vs. Monster Zero*) (1965) and *Kaijû Sôshingeki* (*Destroy All Monsters*) (1968) 284
    - *Taekoesu Yonggary* (*Yongary, Monster from the Deep*) (1967) 286
    - *Uchû Daikaijû Girara* (*The X from Outer Space*) (1967) 287

7. FROM REEL TO REAL: THE REBIRTH AND DEATH OF THE FILMS 290
    - *Countdown* (1968) 291
    - *Marooned* (1969) 294
    - *2001: A Space Odyssey* (1968) 299
    - Television Coverage of the *Apollo 11* Moon Landing (1969) 307

8. RETURN TO EARTH: FILMS AFTER 1969 313

A Filmography of Spacesuit Films 323
Chapter Notes 341
Bibliography 345
Index 351

Foreword: Don't Leave Earth Without It
by Michael Cassutt

The time is the winter of 1965-1966, the place, a basement in a small town in Wisconsin. The weather outside is, as the song says, frightful. Gray skies, wind, temperatures below zero, snow as high as the windows ... or so memory tells me. It could be the surface of Europa.

But in this basement, boxes, blankets and chairs have been arranged to replicate the cockpit of a spacecraft — not a capsule, but a four-seat arrangement later to be replicated on the Space Shuttle's flight deck.

And the crew — two eleven-year-old boys, one nine-year-old lad and one five-year-old girl — are not pretending to launch or even to shoot at space pirates.

They are arguing about spacesuits. Why do we need them? Even if we have helmets, which are sort of cool, why do we need gloves?

The imperious commander sneers at his crew of conscripts, telling them they'll die if they dare to venture into space unprotected.

His arguments are unconvincing. The space crew goes into full mutiny, abandoning the craft in search of chocolate milk and a *Sons of Hercules* movie on television.

Not that this will be a surprise, but that commander was me.

Nineteen sixty-five was the year that spacesuits began. Yes, prior to that time I watched *Men into Space* and *Destination Moon*. I had seen pictures and footage of Mercury astronauts and Vostok cosmonauts. (Loved the silvery Mercury suits with the sleek lines and smaller helmets; thought the Soviet guys looked funny with their fishbowls.)

But it was the twin spacewalks — first by cosmonaut Alexei Leonov in March 1965, then NASA's Ed White in June — that turned me into a spacesuit person. During that year I also read Robert A. Heinlein's *Have Space Suit—Will Travel*, the best (and possibly only) novel dealing with the design of such a garment. But it was Ed White's EVA, complete with its soon-to-be-iconic photo of the astronaut in his brilliant suit, reflective gold visor and blue Earth background that permanently imprinted one idea on me:

You can't go into space without a spacesuit.

From that point on, whenever the grim Midwestern weather drove me, my brother and other playmates indoors to be astronauts rather than soldiers, I insisted that we had to have spacesuits, complete with helmets and gloves.

For some players, this meant using plastic U.S. Army–style helmets. My brother Mark had a Steve Canyon Air Force helmet.

I, however, had been given an honest-to-God Colonel McCauley *Men into Space* helmet. So I felt equipped.

The others ... not so much. None of them appreciated the cold reality of space travel, the bitter fact that you could not open the hatch and go outside without being sealed into a suit that provided you with your own atmosphere and protected you against extreme temperatures. They thought suits made them look stupid.

Years later, having become a writer and producer in Hollywood, I wound up fighting the same battle.

Hollywood hates spacesuits, too.

This hatred isn't rooted in political or technical antipathies, but aesthetic ones not far removed from those of my playmates in 1965: Spacesuits wrap you up and hide you.

For a business based on the large-screen display of actresses and actors of uncommon physical beauty, this is a problem. What good is having Scarlett Johansson in your space movie if she's stuffed into a rigid fabric balloon whose silhouette makes her indistinguishable from, say, Shia LaBeouf?

And the helmets are even worse! Even a transparent fishbowl causes reflections and degradation of image. The standard faceplate helmets are a complete disaster for a cinematographer, enveloping a star's head (goodbye to those raven tresses, perky ears, lovely neck) in plastic and putting that star's handsome or beautiful face in permanent shadow.

It's enough to make filmmakers pine for the days of Edgar Rice Burroughs and a planet Mars that had a breathable atmosphere, and temperatures warm enough to justify bikinis. (One genius director's solution? He added internal helmet lights that allowed star visages to shine at close to their ideal wattage.)

Knowing this, having lived this, I read Gary Westfahl's *The Spacesuit Film* with astonishment and great pleasure. As a sci-fi and space boomer geek, I knew most of these films and TV series — or thought I did. But Gary has gone far beyond memory: He's produced a thorough and highly readable history of the spacesuit on the big and small screen, following it from unpromising and unlikely beginnings to the age of Cameron.

Which means that *The Spacesuit Film* is also a story about the ultimate victory of science and rationality over ignorance and laziness ... and that's a rare gift.

Michael Cassutt
Los Angeles

Michael Cassutt is a novelist, short story writer and television writer as well as the author of several books and articles about human spaceflight. He is an adjunct professor at the University of Southern California's School of Cinematic Arts.

Introduction: Pre-Flight Briefing

From one perspective, it is only the clothing people need to travel in space — spacesuits, thick and airtight enough to protect against an icy vacuum — and hence never seemed important to science fiction film scholars. Yet the spacesuit functions as an icon that generates, and identifies, a significant film subgenre which has never been fully recognized or appreciated.

To explain why this subgenre emerged, one notes that, throughout the history of western literature, the discovery and habitation of new environments tended to create new literary genres. The American frontier spawned the western; the development of ships which could circumnavigate the globe inspired a general tradition of sea stories and a particular subgenre about pirates; nineteenth-century European ventures into African jungles generated a genre of jungle stories; and other stories set in recently explored places, like deserts, deep caverns, and polar regions, regularly appeared while never solidifying into recognized genres. Thus, it is unsurprising that, as humans first dreamed of someday traveling into space, then began working to achieve space travel, a genre appeared, eventually labeled science fiction, dominated by space stories. True, the genre included other sorts of fantastic narratives, but space travel was its most common trope, and for many, its defining trait.

When authors crafted adventures set in exotic terrestrial environments, they brought varying degrees of knowledge to the task. Some actually lived in those realms, or conducted research, so stories could be persuasively authentic; others relied upon second-hand information, common sense, and previous stories to write exciting tales that might be deemed implausible by those more familiar with their settings. Yet variations in the content and tone of the stories could not justify an attempt to establish narratives based upon facts, and narratives based upon fancy, as separate categories. Thus, H. Rider Haggard spent years in Africa, while Edgar Rice Burroughs never visited there, yet Haggard's Allan Quatermain stories and Burroughs's Tarzan stories remain similar enough to both be considered jungle stories. Considering stories and films about space travel, scholars might in parallel fashion observe that some authors and filmmakers are knowledgeable about space, while others are not well informed, but discern no reason to anticipate significant differences in their stories.

Yet the nature of space, I contend, widens the gap between the informed and ignorant. Authors may have lacked first-hand knowledge or data about the American frontier or jungles, but they still wrote about a familiar environment, the surface of Earth, providing their stories with a basis in certain universal truths. Space, however, is entirely unlike any place humans ever inhabited. It lacks three attributes of all terrestrial locales: normal gravity, breathable air, and protection from dangerous cosmic radiation. Further, while less hospitable regions on Earth may be gradually lethal to unprotected people, none cause instant death, as occurs when people without spacesuits are exposed to the vacuum of space or surface of an airless world.

And though other images suggest the strangeness of space — arrays of stars in a pitch-black sky, spaceships or space stations against that background, objects floating in spaceships without gravity to restrain them — spacesuits most comprehensively and powerfully indicate that humans are within a novel realm. As icons, spacesuits communicate that space is a dangerous environment, requiring unprecedented sorts of protection, and simultaneously demonstrate that humans are frail, weak creatures, unprepared for life beyond the cradle of Earth. As forms of disguise, they make people look odd and frightening, suggesting that people venturing into space may in some fashion be abandoning their humanity. Yet spacesuits also symbolize human strength and durability, proving that people have mastered technology so they can survive in adverse conditions and, in effect, make themselves larger and stronger with the protective garments they so ingeniously devise. Thus, spacesuits intimate that humans will be profoundly challenged and fundamentally altered by space, but also convey that they have the capacity to conquer this daunting new territory.

Authors and filmmakers who recognize the true nature of space, and understand the full implications of wearing spacesuits, will necessarily tell different kinds of stories about space travel than someone who is unaware of, or is indifferent to, the realities of this environment and the adjustments it demands. Thus, one discerns two distinct categories of space stories. First, some narratives ignorantly assume that conditions in space are largely identical to conditions on Earth and may include scientific absurdities, like people surviving in space wearing only helmets or humans inhabiting a Moon or Mars depicted as Earthlike; these may simply be called space films, and the subcategory of such films which minimally feature spacesuits, reflecting a desire to appear authentic with no intent to be authentic, can be described as pseudo-spacesuit films. Second, other films reflect a thorough knowledge of the characteristics of space and other worlds and rigorously adhere to scientific facts in all aspects of their adventures, so they must foreground characters in spacesuits; I call these the true spacesuit films.

To careful observers, the visual and kinetic differences between these types of space stories are particularly sharp, since a dedication to scientific accuracy both alters the nature of filmed narratives in significant ways and provides resulting portrayals of space and other worlds with special power. One point relates to C.S. Lewis's observation about why characters in science fiction often seem flat and one-dimensional: "[T]he more unusual the scenes and events of [a writer's] story are, the slighter, the more ordinary, the more typical his persons should be.... To tell how odd things struck odd people is to have an oddity too much: he who is to see strange sights must not himself be strange" ("On Science Fiction" 64–65). Since space and other planets, correctly rendered, are "strange sights" indeed, this explains why spacesuit films often feature stoic, uncommunicative heroes, characters lacking the depth and complexity to inspire audiences to care about their fates. Since compelling protagonists are usually considered essential in conventionally entertaining films, this engenders frequent complaints about the absence of satisfactory characters in two noteworthy spacesuit films, *Destination Moon* and *2001: A Space Odyssey*, and suggestions that this purported flaw makes them inferior to other space films.

One may also argue that, in film, the true viewpoint character is not the protagonist but the camera, so filmmakers may feel impelled to plant cameras in the position of stationary observers and display the wonders of space in long, unadventurous shots — like images of the space station in *2001*— that disappoint critics who prefer more creative filming techniques, like tracking shots and unusual camera angles. And, as if working in tandem with the bland characters and camera positions, space, if accurately portrayed, is disappointingly monochromatic, dominated by black sky, pinpoints of white light, the grayness of metallic spaceships and spacesuit fabrics, and barren terrains on lifeless worlds. Touches of color must be brought to space by humans, one reason why films like *Destination Moon* and *2001* feel obliged to offer brightly colored spacesuits.

Another seemingly minor but noticeable change in spacesuit films is that realistic stories about space travel follow their own unusual rhythm, with long passages of very slow movement interrupted by bursts of rapid action. When wearing bulky spacesuits, people must move slowly and clumsily, and in the vacuum and weightlessness of space, where even the slightest wrong movement can have disastrous consequences, astronauts also must be especially careful and deliberate in their movements. Paradoxically, though, if something goes wrong, it goes wrong in an instant. Thus, in *2001*, Dave Bowman spends several minutes meticulously setting up his desperate effort to enter the airlock of his spaceship by briefly exposing himself to the vacuum of space without a helmet; but his expulsion from the pod and perilous journey into the airlock take only a few frantic, confusing seconds. On the surface of alien worlds, lower gravity similarly imposes different styles of travel: astronauts can make great leaps, but must also be exceedingly cautious to avoid precipitous landings which might cause fatal leaks in their spacesuit. As one result, spacesuit films may seem slow-moving and undramatic; in *Project Moon Base*, for example, an astronaut struggles to subdue a saboteur, but due to sudden acceleration, the fight proceeds in eerie slow motion, disappointing audiences accustomed to more frenetic fight scenes.

Third, while most narratives — particularly those for mass audiences — involve conflicts between people, the overwhelming dangers of space necessarily engender stories about the conflict between humans and their environment, also contributing to what is perceived as inadequate characterization. Some spacesuit films, like *Destination Moon* and *Countdown*, may begin with personal dramas prior to liftoff, but later focus exclusively on protagonists overcoming the perils of space. Other films may carry ordinary sorts of conflicts into space but are driven to downplay them: In *Project Moon Base*, the saboteur is fought and overcome, but once the ship makes an emergency landing on the Moon, the former combatants must become teammates to set up an antenna to contact Earth and obtain desperately needed supplies. Space travelers in *Spaceways* venture into space solely to clear the name of an accused murderer, but once in space that motive is forgotten as they confront a potentially fatal crisis caused by a faulty rocket. And in *Conquest of Space*, crew members who reach Mars are first divided regarding the death of their maddened captain, but common struggles against a harsh Martian environment drive them into a harmonious working relationship.

Fourth, typical adventure stories celebrate the exploits of individual heroes who overcome adversaries and solve problems by relying solely upon their own abilities and acumen. However, the strange environment of space poses so many complex challenges that astronauts must rely upon information and advice constantly relayed to them from people on Earth monitoring their mission. As observed most clearly in *Riders to the Stars*, stories about space travel can be awkwardly divided narratives shifting back and forth between two sets of protagonists: actual space explorers, and technicians on the ground telling them how to deal with various crises. As proof that one can be a hero in both roles, Colonel McCauley of the series *Men into Space* is usually the astronaut in space confronting problems, but sometimes is an advisor on the ground, helping other astronauts. Such collaborative heroism defies age-old conventions of storytelling and again makes space adventures unsettling.

Finally, because space is so unrelentingly deadly and different from normal human experience, a story in that setting suggests that humans live in a hostile, alien universe where all their comforting assumptions may turn out to be illusions, where beings and phenomena may be utterly inexplicable to humans. Truly conquering this environment, then, may require fundamental changes in the very nature of humanity. Pondering such possibilities strikes at the heart of humanity's narrative traditions, all grounded in human experiences and expectations, and has the potential to make spacesuit films uniquely profound and disturbing. It is rare for science fiction stories, and even rarer for science fiction films, to venture into such sobering speculations; arguably, while *Men into Space* pioneered in offering intriguing indications of genuine alien presences in space, as opposed to the implausibly human villains and colorful monsters of lesser films, only *2001* really explores this issue to a significant extent. But when the captain in *Conquest of Space* develops the insane belief that God opposes human space travel, he suggests the disquieting thoughts that may occur to people when personally confronting the mysterious void of space.

More than the simple issue of scientific plausibility, which critics might deem unimportant, these sorts of differences justify the distinction in this argument. Films that are simply space films, and the subcategory of pseudo-spacesuit films, are identifiable because they avoid placing heroes in spacesuits whenever possible, freely ignore the peculiarities of space, move at a conventional pace, and follow familiar patterns — conflicts between appealing heroes and despicable villains or hideous monsters — allowing heroes to triumph solely through their individual efforts, and steering clear of disquieting ideas about unique mysteries in the universe. In contrast, genuine spacesuit films regularly place heroes in spacesuits, acknowledge the unusual and perilous nature of space, and necessarily neglect in-depth characterization, follow their own stilted rhythm, emphasize conflicts between humans and their environment, validate assistants on Earth, and fitfully ponder the awesome implications of an inhospitable cosmos.

This distinction between the forms is occasionally recognized by commentators, at least when discussing science fiction films of the 1950s, but only in a limited manner that marginalizes spacesuit films. Specifically, spacesuit films of the 1950s are described as "documentary-style" space films — and everyone knows that documentaries are boring, which is how these films are dismissed in critical surveys of science fiction films that devote more time to other, more conventional films. This may be the first time the fascinating history of spacesuit films is receiving the extended consideration it has long merited.

Briefly, this is its story: First, amidst other films that made minimal efforts, at best, to be realistic, three pioneering silent films establish models for later creators of spacesuit films: Holger-Madsen's *Himmelskibet* (*A Trip to Mars*), Fritz Lang's *Frau im Mond* (*Woman in the Moon*), and Vasili Zhuravlev's *Kosmicheskiy Reys* (*The Space Voyage*), the latter two made with the assistance of renowned space scientists. However, the genre of spacesuit films truly emerges in the early 1950s, due to improved scientific knowledge about space, the influence of a literary genre of science fiction mandating scientific accuracy, and the beginnings of actual space programs in the United States and the Soviet Union. In response, a small number of American and British filmmakers, like Lang and Zhuravlev, sought expert advice from scientists and science fiction writers, carefully considered the realities of space, and endeavored to develop, however clumsily, a new sort of film to acknowledge and deal with those realities while also providing entertainment; later, a few films along these lines appeared in the Soviet Union. Still, despite the box-office success of the first film of this nature, *Destination Moon*, the films and television programs that followed were regarded as financial and artistic failures, even as they ventured into genuinely novel territory to develop and present significant messages: that space travel was possible; that there were compelling reasons for nations to venture into space, including military advantage, vast resources, and scientific knowledge; that space would prove a strange, forbidding environment; and that despite this, or perhaps because of this, space travel would drive participants back to familiar values and lifestyles. However, exploring such themes did not allow filmmakers to include fistfights, explosions, romances, or rubber-suited aliens, all representing the preferred form of entertainment for audiences at the time (and learned critics today).

So it was that, almost from the beginning, profit-hungry filmmakers chose to produce films that paid lip service to the traditions of spacesuit films, with introductory scientific explanations and occasional spacesuits, but otherwise ignored the unsettling implications of the genre to focus instead of conventional adventures. The pioneer in this parallel genre of pseudo-spacesuit films was *Rocketship X-M*, but many others would soon follow, along with two serials and several television series. Despite a veneer of novelty, these filmmakers essentially fell back upon three tried-and-true narrative patterns: the melodrama of virtuous heroes battling despicable villains, the comedy of slapstick and banter, and the horror of monsters or disfigured humans. In these tired and unthreatening stories, spacesuits were minor props at best.

Still, traditional spacesuit films survived fitfully until the 1960s, when competition from active space programs appeared to make realistic spacesuit films unnecessary; thus, films like *Robinson Crusoe on Mars* and *Frankenstein Meets the Spacemonster* began like authentic tales of space travel but eventually collapsed into predictable stories about alien menaces. Still, as the 1967 deaths of the *Apollo 1* astronauts and Soviet cosmonaut Vladimir Komarov reminded the world that space travel could indeed be hazardous, and as Americans prepared to land two men on the Moon, the form staged a comeback with the films *Countdown* and *Marooned*, which are particularly interesting because, in describing events in the near future that might have occurred at the time of filming, they apparently move spacesuit films away from science fiction and toward realistic drama, though they were still considered science fiction. Most spectacularly, *2001* stunningly revealed the true potential of spacesuit films with an epic adventure that both summarizes the genre's history and sketches out bold new directions.

Yet a full renaissance of spacesuit films did not occur, largely due to two major events that occurred in 1969. First, when Neil Armstrong and Buzz Aldrin landed on the Moon in July, 1969, their landing module came with a camera; thus, when they stepped onto the lunar surface, countless millions of viewers watched on television what was effectively the most popular spacesuit film of all time. Yes, I am sure it really happened, rejecting conspiracy theories alleging it was all staged on a Hollywood set. However, the astronauts' sojourn on the Moon was carefully scripted by NASA officials, including Armstrong's first words and a telephone call from President Nixon, and there is evidence that the people who planned this production were aware of previous films in its tradition. Television coverage of the *Apollo 11* landing, then, was merely a spacesuit film that happened to be filmed on the Moon featuring actual astronauts. Five other films of its kind would follow, featuring crewmen from *Apollo 12*, *Apollo 14*, *Apollo 15*, *Apollo 16*, and *Apollo 17* and all shown on worldwide television.

Immediately after the *Apollo 11* landing, the second important event occurred when the television series *Star Trek* ended its network run. This series had masterfully deployed a strategy previously observed in films like *Forbidden Planet*, which was to eliminate spacesuits from space films by employing faster-than-light travel, combined with miraculous teleportation or shuttlecrafts, to transport heroes from impregnable spaceships to Earthlike planets throughout the galaxy so they would never need cumbersome spacesuits. Under these conditions, there were no barriers to comfortably familiar narrative patterns transplanted from the dark alleys and western prairies of Earth to spaceship corridors and alien worlds. And even as Americans turned away from monotonous footage of actual astronauts on the Moon, they enthusiastically embraced the fraudulent space travel of *Star Trek*, as the series finally reached a wide audience by means of daily appearances in syndication at times that attracted young viewers. The American space program would carry on, with the space shuttle and other cautious, budget-conscious initiatives, and genuine spacesuit films would occasionally appear, but filmgoers had essentially rejected the harsh realities of space; instead, in their fascination with *Star Trek*, *Star Wars*, and similar dramas, they embraced comforting illusions about space.

In telling this story for the first time, I adopt certain policies to thoroughly explore the history of spacesuit films while keeping the manuscript to a reasonable length. In literal-minded fashion, I consider as "spacesuit films" every film and television program I am aware of in which spacesuits appear or are mentioned, however fleetingly. Granted, there may seem no significant difference between a film like *Queen of Outer Space*, wherein one astronaut is ready to "break out the pressure suits" before being reassured that conditions on an alien world are Earthlike, and *Fire Maidens from Outer Space*, wherein astronauts disembark upon an Earthlike planet without referring to spacesuits; but the first film, however minimally, acknowledges that space travel might involve inhospitable conditions, while the second film does not. This commitment to thoroughness forced a decision to emphasize films and television programs up until 1969, with only a brief survey of more recent productions.

With similar literal-mindedness, I define "spacesuits" to refer only to garments that provide protection and oxygen for humans in a vacuum; thus, the silvery bodysuits worn by space travelers in television series like *My Favorite Martian* and *Lost in Space* are sometimes called "spacesuits," but while they look futuristic, these flimsy outfits would not help people survive in space (though characters in *Lost in Space* occasionally don genuine spacesuits over their shiny pajamas).

In this study, I freely mingle films and television programs, believing that as we move toward an era when all filmed entertainment will be viewed primarily via computers, the circumstances of a work's original production will be increasingly irrelevant. The film *Conquest of Space* and television series *Men into Space* are both significant examples of genuine spacesuit films, just as the film *The Green Slime* and an episode of *The Outer Limits*, "Specimen: Unknown," are equivalent examples of horrific spacesuit films; separating them for purposes of analysis seems pointless. However, to focus on fictional films most likely to convey insights about space, I exclude certain types of productions—animated films and documentaries—except when documentaries incorporate extended fictional sequences, like the *Disneyland* episode "Man and the Moon" and the Russian documentary *Doroga k Zvezdam* (*Road to the Stars*). The book concludes with a comprehensive bibliography of spacesuit films from 1918 to 1969, accompanied by a less comprehensive bibliography of more recent spacesuit films. In sum, I am breaking significant ground, while also leaving much territory to be explored more thoroughly by other scholars.

So, having completed this pre-flight briefing, I invite readers to fasten their seat belts and prepare for an interesting and illuminating journey through space; and I hope you enjoy the trip as much as I have.

— 1 —
First Flights: The Early Films

There are two reasons why realistic space films, or spacesuit films, did not become a significant tradition until after 1950: a lack of knowledge, and a lack of motivation.

First, during the first fifty years of film, scientists gradually accepted that, despite previous theories, no substance called "ether" filled the space between worlds that might render that environment habitable. This invalidated earlier, playful accounts of humans flying through space without protection and demonstrated that space travelers would need airtight spaceships and spacesuits. Knowing this, rocket scientist Hermann Oberth accurately advised Fritz Lang, director of *Frau im Mond*, to have a sturdy spaceship travel to the Moon through a space properly depicted as black and airless. Still, one might regard the nature of space as an unsettled question, which might explain why most films about space travel avoided outer space and had voyagers swiftly travel from Earth to other planets.

Further, throughout this period, one could still posit that the worlds usually targeted by imagined space travelers, the Moon and Mars, might possess breathable atmospheres and hospitable climates, allowing for stories of humans who visit those worlds in street clothes; thus, Holger-Madsen's *Himmelskibet* was one of many films envisioning an Earthlike Mars, while Oberth allowed Lang to assume that, on the far side of the Moon, there could exist deep valleys with breathable air. But by 1950, research showed beyond reasonable doubt that the Moon had no atmosphere, Mars had only a very thin atmosphere, and both worlds were extremely cold—firmly invalidating such comforting scenarios. As for other possible destinations in the solar system, all were visibly barren except the cloud-covered Venus, and there was growing evidence—confirmed by 1962—that Earth's "sister planet" was much too hot for human survival. Once these facts were accepted, it was obvious that space travelers would need spacesuits to protect them during voyages through space and on the surfaces of other worlds.

In addition to improving scientific knowledge, the 1940s also brought significant developments in technology. For much of the twentieth century, many learned scientists sincerely thought that space travel was impossible and said as much; for this reason, an overriding concern of early spacesuit films was simply to argue that human space flight could be accomplished, making this the first theme foregrounded in the genre. However, while the theoretical work of Konstantin Tsiolkovsky in Russia, and the experiments of Robert Goddard in America, provided some support for efforts to conquer space, the pioneering work of the German Rocket Society during the 1920s and 1930s, culminating in the V-2 rockets that rained on Britain during the final months of World War II, most powerfully proved how practical, and important, advanced rockets could be. After the war, impressed by these achievements, both the United States and the Soviet Union recruited German rocket scientists to design rockets which could travel into space; and there began appearing books and magazine articles describing these efforts and envisioning coming achievements like orbital flights, space stations, and journeys to the Moon and Mars. Thus, by the 1950s, when scientists finally knew what space and other worlds were really like, and finally deemed it possible to venture into those realms, filmmakers were fully prepared to produce realistic films about space travel.

Just because something is possible, however, does not necessarily mean it will come to pass, and filmmakers with the potential to be realistic also needed a motive to be realistic. And before the 1950s — except for *Himmelskibet*, *Frau im Mond*, and Vasili Zhuravlev's *Kosmicheskiy Reys*—films displayed no concern for scientific realism. If audiences are entertained by nonsense, the makers of the Flash Gordon serials might have argued, why should anyone worry about scientific accuracy?

This impulse to be scientifically accurate, then, did not develop within the film industry, but was imported from the emerging genre of science fiction. Hugo Gernsback, who in the 1920s began promoting science fiction, insisted from the get-go that science fiction stories had to present and respect the realities of science. (In instructions to contestants in a story contest, for example, he insisted all stories "must contain correct scientific facts."[1]) Soon, his energetic proselytizing inspired some writers to ardently believe in the overriding importance of scientific accuracy in their stories, while forcing other writers to grudgingly accept a need to pay lip service to scientific accuracy. Then, in the 1950s, when American and British filmmakers realized that they could profit by making science fiction movies, and acknowledged they knew little about the genre, they regularly recruited science fiction writers like Jerome Bixby, David Duncan, Robert A. Heinlein, and Curt Siodmak to help with screenplays, and they brought with them the enthusiastic or minimal attentiveness to science they had long internalized. This devotion to scientific accuracy never became as central to science fiction film as it was to science fiction literature, but it did have an influence, particularly on spacesuit films.

While interesting in their own right, most films about space travel before 1950 merit no attention in a survey of spacesuit films. While perhaps modestly realistic in describing the construction of spaceships and preparations for launch, they made little effort to depict space travel in a serious fashion and never employed spacesuits. Nevertheless, two brief observations about these films are relevant here.

First, while making no contributions to spacesuit films, the early space films did provide narrative models for pseudo-spacesuit films, since their less-than-realistic approaches were well suited for less-than-realistic filmmakers. Melodramatic spacesuit films, focused on adventures in Earthlike environments involving aliens who are identical to humans, were foreshadowed by Yakov Protazanov's *Aelita: Queen of Mars* (1924), wherein a human traveler to Mars romances a beautiful Martian queen while crewmates participate in a Communist-style uprising against an oppressive Martian regime. Better known, and more influential, were the space serials *Flash Gordon* (1936), *Flash Gordon's Trip to Mars* (1938), *Flash Gordon Conquers the Universe* (1940) and *Buck Rogers* (1939), all re-edited as feature films for television and videocassettes. Invariably, heroes flew to habitable planets resembling Southern California to be menaced by hostile human aliens while they allied themselves with friendly human aliens, amidst fistfights and chases in every chapter. These patterns were closely followed in science fiction television series of the 1950s and influenced many later films and TV programs, including the *Star Trek* and *Star Wars* franchises.

What was probably the first film about space travel, George Méliès's 1902 *Le Voyage dans la Lune* (*A Trip to the Moon*), can be seen as a precursor of humorous spacesuit films, since it was clearly designed to delight and amuse audiences. Other early silent films involving journeys into space, including Méliès's *Le Voyage à Travers l'Impossible* (*The Impossible Voyage*) (1904), Walter Booth's *The ? Motorist* (1906), and Segundo de Chomón's *Excursion dans la Lune* (*Excursion to the Moon*) (1908), had a similar intent and tone.[2] The first sound film with space travel, *Just Imagine* (1930), was a comedy as well, and its story about men traveling to Mars to humorously interact with a friendly Martian woman, her evil twin, and other good and bad identical Martians clearly anticipates the later antics of space travelers Abbott and Costello and the Three Stooges.

But it is hard to discern ancestors of horrific spacesuit films. True, the threatening Selenites of Méliès's *Le Voyage dans la Lune* are monsters of a sort, and *The Invisible Ray* (1936), while involving no space travel, does feature a menace from space: a meteorite that transforms a scientist into a deadly killer. But since few people of the era took space travel seriously, they rarely worried about dangers in space or from space, except evil but understandable alien villains like Ming the Merciless, whose schemes were harmful but not horrifying.

The second contribution of two early space films was to articulate a case for human space travel. In genuine spacesuit films of the era, people flew to other worlds for practical reasons, like discovering gold or simply to demonstrate it could be done and earn acclaim for the achievement. But a stronger argument surfaces in, of all places, *Just Imagine*, when inventor Z-4 (Frank Albertson) tells hero J-21 (John Garrick) why it is important for people to travel to Mars:

> Z-4: Thousands of years ago, man wondered what was across the river. Then he went over and found out. Later, Columbus wondered what was across the ocean, and he went over and found out. Since then, men have sought for and learned every secret of the Earth — on the land, in the water, in the air. But there is one secret, the greatest of all, that remains a mystery.
>
> J-21: And that is...?
>
> Z-4: The planet Mars!

Briefly serious in tone, the film advocates space travel as a natural continuation of humanity's ancient quest to learn about new and distant realms.

Similar sentiments, more eloquent and more renowned, come in William Cameron Menzies's *Things to Come* (1936), with a screenplay by H.G. Wells. After chronicling humanity's future descent into ruinous warfare before achieving a utopian state, the film concludes with efforts to launch a spaceship with two passengers to circumnavigate the Moon. After its launch, the magisterial Oswald Cabal (Raymond Massey) debates the value of space travel with a man who questions the initiative, Raymond Passworthy (Edward Chapman), ending with stirring sentiments:

> PASSWORTHY: Is there never to be any rest?
>
> CABAL: Rest enough for the individual man — too much, and too soon — and we call it death. But for Man, no rest and no ending. He must go on, conquest beyond conquest. First this little planet with its winds and ways, and then all the laws of mind and matter that restrain him. Then the planets about him and at last out across immensity to the stars. And when he has conquered all the deeps of space and all the mysteries of time, still he will be beginning.
>
> PASSWORTHY: But ... we're such little creatures. Poor humanity's so fragile, so weak. Little ... little animals.
>
> CABAL: Little animals. If we're no more than animals, we must snatch each little scrap of happiness

and live and suffer and pass, mattering no more than all the other animals do or have done. It is this, or that. All the universe, or nothingness. Which shall it be, Passworthy? Which shall it be?

More expansively than Z-4 in *Just Imagine*, Cabal's words effectively equate space travel with human progress itself, envisioning any argument about its merits as a choice between the fulfillment of human destiny or eternal stagnation. No other space film would ever build a case for space travel on such genuinely cosmic grounds.

Himmelskibet (*A Trip to Mars*) (1918)

Viewed today, *Himmelskibet* (*A Trip to Mars*) seems a transitional film. On one hand, it embraces the comforting Victorian notion that space travel would take people to Earthlike worlds inhabited by humans, the increasingly discredited idea rejected by Lang and Zhuravlev in favor of more realistic visions. On the other hand, while no evidence suggests that director Holger-Madsen brought strong concerns for scientific accuracy to this project, and while he lacked expert advisors like those of Lang and Zhuravlev, his film reflects an awareness of the genuine scientific and technological challenges that a voyage to another world would entail, including the daunting distances involved and (for the first time in film) the probable need for spacesuits on such journeys.

Opening scenes introduce protagonist Avanti Planetaros (Gunnar Tolnaes), who triumphantly returns from a scientific expedition seeking "new tasks." His astronomer father, Professor Planetaros (Nicolai Neiiendam), tells him, "In space, there are thousands of unsolved mysteries," including "Planets that we long for ... and that long for us." These comments suggest the primary purpose of space travel should be new scientific knowledge, but the idea never resurfaces; instead, as Avanti stares at a painting of Columbus, he seems primarily motivated by the sheer challenge of the task and glory to be obtained from its completion. Now desiring to "build a bridge between the planets," Avanti speaks to a scientist friend, Dr. Krafft (Alf Blutecher), who loves Avanti's sister Corona (Zanny Peterson), and asks, "Will you help me build a ship, a spaceship that can fly through the stratosphere?"

Interestingly, the film then anticipates *Things to Come* by introducing a fierce opponent of space travel: When Avanti and Krafft tell Avanti's father about their plans, Planetaros's colleague, Dr. Dubius (Frederik Jacobsen), immediately responds with scornful laughter. Two years later, after the laborious and briefly glimpsed process of building the spaceship, Avanti addresses a meeting of a scientific society to describe his coming flight and recruit volunteers, but Dubius disrupts the gathering by declaring it "a meeting in a mad-house." One might assume that Dubius believes space travel is impossible, like many scientists of his day; yet one comment, expressing amazement that Avanti and Krafft accomplished in two years what he had dreamed about for a lifetime, suggests the true reason for his skepticism is envy and personal spite that someone else might achieve what he sought to achieve himself. That theory is reinforced when Dubius gazes up at Avanti's departing spaceship and exclaims, "Avanti, I hate you!" The character was clearly introduced to provide dramatic conflict in a film often lacking that element, and by making his motive personal jealousy, not purely scientific doubts, Holger-Madsen could avoid the logical result of scientific objections, earnest arguments about the practicality of space travel that, as becomes apparent, were peripheral to his priorities.

Dismissing Dubius's caustic remarks by saying, "Anyone who has broken new ground has been scorned," Avanti recruits his crew, which will unusually consist of men from all over the world. (Such an explicitly international crew of pioneering space travelers would not appear again until 1960's *12 to the Moon*.) In the version I watched,[3] the men's nationalities are not identified, though one man, apparently supposed to be Asian, says he is from "the East," while another, David Dane (Svend Kornbech), looks and acts like an American.

The spaceship, named the *Excelsior*, disappointingly looks like a large enclosed airplane, complete with propellers, and it quietly takes off at daybreak and flies through the atmosphere like a conventional plane. We are told it will reach Mars because of some "power" enabling it to fly 12,000 kilometers per hour, considerably less than the needed escape velocity of 40,320 kilometers per hour. However, there *was* some scientific thinking behind that figure, because the men take off when Mars is closest to the Earth, which is about 55 million kilometers away; a flight of that distance, at 12,000 kilometers per hour, would take about 191 days, or slightly over six months, the length of the *Excelsior*'s flight to Mars.

In portraying this flight, *Himmelskibet* seems most prophetic, since no other journeys to Mars before 1950 accurately indicate that such a trip would take a long time. True, the film makes no attempt to depict weightlessness, or even an awareness that this occurs; but after six months in space, crewmen become restless, unsettled by the "endless night of space," "that brooding darkness around us," and an apparent lack of progress toward Mars. And unlike the unrealistically spacious spaceships of most spacesuit films, the *Excelsior* has very cramped quarters, contributing to the men's unhappiness. Oddly, though the men look out the window at space, Holger-Madsen makes no effort to show audiences what they see; there is only one brief shot, later, of the *Excelsior* flying through starry blackness while nearing Mars. This disinclination to fully display the vast darkness of space, observed in *Frau im Mond* and *Kosmicheskiy Reys*, suggests filmmakers were not yet comfortable with the realm's realities and preferred to focus on spaceship interiors and the surfaces of alien worlds.

Himmelskibet is also the first film to suggest space travel might lead to mental instability: During the flight, Dane returns to his "old addiction to drink" and encourages others to drink the bottles of wine he managed to bring along. Dane also announces, "We cannot bear to live anymore in this flying Hell," and plans a mutiny to return the spaceship to Earth. He takes out a gun, and Avanti, warned of possible unrest, arms himself as well; he is also looking a bit deranged himself, as if entertaining his own doubts about the mission's success. Later, guns are actually fired, though this would actually be suicidal in a spaceship, since bullets might make deadly holes in the hull. Fortunately, at the moment when armed conflict breaks out, astronomers on Mars observe the approaching spaceship (through telescopes that show hexagonal images instead of round images, a unique way to indicate that they are of alien design) and decide to "bring in the spaceship." By unexplained means, they draw the ship toward Mars. The Earthmen notice that they are traveling ten times normal speed: "We are approaching the goal. At last!"

Another theme introduced during this sequence, which surfaces in later spacesuit films, is religious piety: At his time of greatest despair, Avanti conspicuously prays, and when crew members realize they will reach Mars safely and gather around Avanti to thank him, he responds, "You should not thank me, but divine providence," and they all kneel down. However, while male Martians wear robes bearing the Egyptian ankh, a cross with a circle on top sometimes seen in Christianity, there is only one further reference to a divine being, though Martians do believe in life after death.

Preparing to land on Mars, the men "get out their oxygen masks," and there is a brief scene of them dressed in bulky clothing and wearing dark masks that cover their entire faces, except for two glass-covered openings for the eyes. These outfits, which are arguably thick and airtight enough to protect against a vacuum, can be regarded as the first spacesuits in a space film. They do not appear again, however, because one man immediately goes to the spaceship's open door, now "within the atmosphere of Mars," takes off his mask, and declares, "We can easily breathe in this atmosphere." Indeed, Mars looks exactly like Earth, with grass-covered hills, and they are greeted by human men and women wearing white robes recalling the togas of ancient Rome.

The rest of the film has little to do with space travel, as the director's true intent — providing a powerful anti-war message at the height of World War I — comes to the forefront. After initial conflicts caused by the Earthmen's offer of canned meat and use of a firearm (which appalls the vegetarian, pacifist Martians), visitors repent and resolve to henceforth behave in the manner of Martians. While Avanti falls in love with a Martian woman, Marya (Lilly Jacobson), Krafft longs for Corona and urges the Martians to send a message to let the people on Earth know they are all right — inspiring them to set off several flares that, when viewed from Earth, line up to form an image of the constellation Corona Borealis. This proves to the observing Corona and her father that they are alive. This recalls the old idea of communicating with other worlds by digging huge trenches and filling them with fires to form huge symbols that would be visible from space. After staying for several months, the Earthmen, accompanied by Marya, finally begin their return flight.

One might imagine the film would quickly draw to a close, but there is more drama as the *Excelsior* approaches Earth. The ever-spiteful Dubius pays another visit to taunt his "friend" with a journal article describing Avanti's presumably doomed flight as a "scientific fraud," almost driving Planetaros to suicide until Corona intervenes. The *Excelsior* is briefly endangered by a severe storm, but its only victim is Dubius, for as he stands on a hilltop to gesture angrily at the vehicle, he is struck by lightning and falls to his death, a crude act of divine comeuppance. The crew lands to be greeted by a rapturous crowd, and Avanti takes Marya, "the flower of a superior civilization," to meet his father and sister.

From the perspective of spacesuit films, *Himmelskibet* can be praised as the first to present space travel as a serious possibility and correctly depict a flight to another world as a lengthy enterprise that might require spacesuits. Yet Holger-Madsen was not prepared to portray the environments of space and other planets realistically, instead falling back on the comforting convention that such worlds and their inhabitants would closely resemble Earth and its people. Other filmmakers, assisted by scientific experts, would face this next challenge.

Frau im Mond (*Woman in the Moon*) (1929)

Fritz Lang's *Frau im Mond* is a film in three parts.[4] First, a lengthy sequence of Earth-bound melodrama establishes the personalities and motivations of characters who will travel to the Moon: elderly scientist Georg Manfredt (Klaus Pohl), who once proposed a lunar voyage to obtain the vast amounts of gold he theorized were there, only to be ridiculed by colleagues; engineer Wolf Helius (Willy Fritsch), who now plans to fulfill the professor's dream and fly to the Moon; his partner Hans Windegger (Gustav von Wangenheim), who is engaged to beautiful astronomy student Friede Velten (Gerda Maurus), a development which devastates Helius because he is secretly in love with her; Helius's friend Gustav (Gustl

Gstettenbaur), a boy who loves reading outlandish stories about space travel and later stows away on the rocket; and a man calling himself Walt Turner (Fritz Rasp), villainous agent of a powerful cabal determined to maintain control of the world's gold supply. Turner engages in theft and sabotage to pressure Helius and others to add him to the crew so he can effectively command the mission.

While this prelude, much lengthier than preliminary scenes in *Himmelskibet*, may strike viewers with an interest in space flight as tedious, it inspires audiences to feel strong emotions about the characters who will journey to the Moon, something other spacesuit films do not always accomplish. The most noteworthy feature of these scenes, to modern eyes, may be the colorful science fiction magazines that Gustav reads, perhaps making this the first science fiction film that explicitly refers to science fiction. It also represents Lang's acknowledgment that science fiction plays an important role in inspiring the men and women who will work to make space travel a reality. (In space films of the 1950s, such metaliterary references to science fiction become relatively common.)

The second part of the film depicts the launch of the spaceship and its flight to the Moon — and to contemporary audiences, a stilted silent film suddenly comes to electrifying life. Unlike most spacesuit films prior to 1960, wherein spaceships took off without spectators or elaborate procedures, *Frau im Mond*, under Oberth's expert guidance, predicts almost precisely what an actual launch would look like: A large audience sits in bleachers; the spaceship is slowly rolled from inside a hangar into position for liftoff; a backwards numerical countdown leads to the moment of takeoff, a convention of all American space flights introduced in this film; and the ship is a two-stage rocket that jettisons one stage after its fuel is exhausted. Only two aspects of this sequence differ from real rocket launches: Instead of supporting beams, later withdrawn, to maintain the spaceship in a vertical position for launch, Oberth immerses the ship in water to keep it upright; and the spaceship takes off with immediate swiftness, unlike genuine spaceships which rise slowly before gradually accelerating. Still, the scene impressively demonstrates a key message which dominates early spacesuit films: that human space travel would be possible, given sufficient resources and careful planning.

Once the spacecraft is launched, we see the ship's interior, and except for its spaciousness, everything again is meticulously plausible. Astronauts are strapped into couches while experiencing the tremendous pressure of liftoff, making this the first of many films to show faces of space travelers contorted in agony while enduring almost unbearable pain. Soon, the spaceship approaches the velocity requiring that the rocket engines be turned off. To prevent the ship from flying past the Moon into the depths of space, Helius must slowly stretch with great difficulty, battling the tremendous pressure, to pull a lever to shut off the engine. This is a standard moment of drama in later spacesuit films: an astronaut's struggle to reach an essential control mechanism, hampered by the pressure of acceleration. (True, intelligent spaceship designers would not position an important switch where it would be difficult for crew members to reach and manipulate, but providing spacesuit films with moments of drama can be challenging, explaining why this device is frequently employed.)

Once the pressure is gone, crew members awaken, not yet weightless. (At the time, some believed that weightlessness would only occur when a ship passed from Earth's gravitational field into the Moon's field.) In later scenes they employ straps on the floor to walk about in weightlessness, and Gustav floats in the air. A frustrating attempt to drink a beverage is dealt with by scattering the liquid into floating bubbles which astronauts catch in their mouths. In these ways, the film introduces another recurring theme of spacesuit films: that space is a strange new environment, unlike any place on Earth.

When the stowaway Gustav is discovered, we observe, hanging on the walls, the spacesuits the travelers have brought just in case (though they believe and will confirm that the valley where they will land has a breathable atmosphere), another intimation of the daunting dangers of space. The flight concludes with what becomes another familiar drama: approaching the Moon and endeavoring to slow down the ship to avoid a crash landing.

This part of the film disappoints in only one respect. On several occasions, travelers go to large windows to see the Earth, Moon, and star-filled blackness of space; in one scene, Manfredt gestures passionately toward the window to convey his powerful emotions upon finally seeing at close range the Moon that has so long been the focus of his dreams. Yet space glimpsed in a small window has little impact; one brilliancy of *Destination Moon*, imitated in later films, was to contrive a crisis to force astronauts to don spacesuits and actually venture out into space, to stand in awe at its magnificent vastness.

The third part of the film concerns the travelers' adventures after reaching the Moon. In contrast to the gripping realism of the previous sequence, these scenes are a letdown. Upon landing, crew members implausibly get bogged down in an argument about whether they should immediately depart, and Windegger reveals that he is selfish and cowardly, and hence does not deserve to marry the virtuous Friede. Understandably impatient, Manfredt puts on a spacesuit (which looks exactly like a standard diving suit of the era), and lowers himself to the surface and begins walking around. Thus, while astronauts in *Himmelskibet* donned spacesuits while still in their spaceship, Manfredt is the first cinematic space traveler to wear a spacesuit on another world, and on a realistically rendered lunar landscape where such apparel seems necessary. Once he is on the surface, however, Manfredt successfully lights three matches, concludes this area of the Moon has breathable air, and removes his helmet. Knowing it is safe, all his crewmates step onto the lunar surface in street clothes. Thus, like *Himmelskibet*, *Frau im Mond* contrives to get characters out of spacesuits as quickly as possible. (Oberth was probably unhappy about the decision to provide lunar valleys with an atmosphere, but in a silent film, actors must fully display their faces and have complete freedom of movement to convey emotions and actions.) Still, the lunar surface looks authentic, and it was reasonable to assume the Moon was covered with large layers of dust; surprisingly, no effort is made to convey the Moon's low gravity (in contrast to later films of imagined and actual space travelers making tremendous leaps, higher and longer than jumps on Earth).

The drama that unfolds on the Moon is predictably melodramatic. Manfredt is thrilled to discover the huge chunks of gold that he predicted, but accidentally falls into a crevice and dies. While Helius and Gustav look for Manfredt, Turner finds out about the gold, returns to the vicinity of the ship, captures and ties up Windegger, and attempts to board the ship (presumably to fly off with news of the gold and abandon his crewmates to die), only to be forcefully kept out by Friede. In a gun battle, Helius kills Turner, but a bullet accidentally hits an oxygen tank, cutting their supply of oxygen in half, meaning that one crew member must remain on the Moon (though the available air and water, and stacks of supplies, suggest that the person will easily survive until a relief expedition arrives). Helius and Windegger draw straws three times to determine who will stay behind; Windegger loses, but Helius altruistically drugs Windegger and Friede to stay behind instead, instructing Gustav to launch the rocket. Once the rocket is launched, Helius discovers to his delight that Friede elected to stay on the Moon with him, choosing him over the unworthy Windegger.

These contrived developments remind viewers of another curious omission. *Frau im Mond* opens with an inspiring quotation — "'Never' does not exist for the human mind ... only 'Not Yet'" — suggesting that the film, like later ones about space travel, will include statements about humanity's grand destiny to overcome all obstacles and conquer space as an expression of our fundamental drive to explore and progress — exactly the sentiments conveyed in the speeches of *Things to Come*. Surprisingly, the film presents no thoughts of this kind. The sole reason people want to go to the Moon, it seems, is to get its gold, with no grander motives evident.

Still, there is an advantage to these threadbare thematic underpinnings: These very human motives enhance the development of very human characters, and by the end, audiences have come to know and care about Helius and Friede more than they ever come to know and care about, say, the protagonists of *Destination Moon* or *Conquest of Space*. For when noble thoughts about humanity's basic nature are in the forefront, characters behave like representatives of the entire race, not distinct individuals, diminishing their attractiveness as likable personalities. Yet at the end of *Frau im Mond,* one can *only* be happy that Helius and Friede are finally together; there is nothing to inspire any broader exhilaration about the amazing achievement of humans venturing into space and walking on the surface of the Moon. To achieve its emotional impact, then, *Frau im Mond* diminishes its merits as a spacesuit film.

Kosmicheskiy Reys (*The Space Voyage*) (1935)

Vasili Zhuravlev's *Kosmicheskiy Reys: Fantasticheskaya Novella*, though of comparable quality in its realism and special effects, is less well known, and harder to locate, than Lang's film; the only version of the film I found is a slightly edited version (65 minutes, not 70 minutes long), posted on YouTube with untranslated Russian subtitles. The film is officially based upon Tsiolkovsky's novel *Beyond the Planet Earth* (1920), but has little relationship to Tsiolkovsky's saga of scientists from six countries who launch and inhabit a space station before traveling to the Moon and Mars. In a sense, the film anticipates *Destination Moon* in being purportedly based upon a novel that it actually ignores to provide a realistic story about a pioneering flight into space. The film might be better regarded as a Russian version of *Frau im Mond*, also focusing exclusively on one nation's successful effort to launch a manned rocket to the Moon and return it to Earth. The three members of Zhuravlev's crew even resemble characters from Lang's film: an elderly scientist, Pavel Ivanovich Sedikh (Sergei Komarov); his beautiful blonde assistant, Marina (K. Moskalenko); and Andryusha Orlov (Vassili Gaponenko), a boy stowaway. But there are no counterparts to Lang's leading man, his romantic rival, or the corporate villain, so this film, unlike *Frau im Mond*, offers no onboard drama — surely because the film was made in Josef Stalin's Soviet Union, where as a matter of official policy all petty conflicts between citizens had been eliminated.

Even on the ground before takeoff, a traditional arena for interpersonal disputes in other spacesuit films, there are only mild personal tensions, chiefly involving an overly cautious bureaucrat who wants to prevent the elderly Sedikh from going on the flight and some comedy involving Sedikh's wife as she packs her husband's bags. (Modern viewers may be surprised to see she is unconcerned about her husband's decision to fly to the Moon in the sole company of a beautiful woman, but infidelity may be another bourgeois vice purportedly eliminated in the Soviet Union.) An experimental rocket is also launched with a cat on board, strikingly anticipating what actually occurred in the Soviet and American space programs (Russia first launched a dog into space, while America began with a monkey).

Whereas Lang launched his spacecraft from a watery chamber, Zhuravlev employs a long, gradually rising track to get the ship off the ground, though water figures in the launch because he has space travelers immerse themselves in water to alleviate the pressure of liftoff. Once in space, crew members primarily occupy themselves by relishing the freedom of weightlessness, blissfully flying back and forth through the spaceship's immense chambers in scenes recalling a stage production of J.M. Barrie's *Peter Pan* (1904). The joys of zero gravity, in fact, outweigh any interest in contemplating the vastness of interplanetary space; repeatedly, cosmonauts open a spaceport to glimpse the blackness of space, but instead of staring out in awe like Lang's scientist, they quickly return to leaps and bounds. Thus, while *Himmelskibet* briefly mentions garnering scientific knowledge, and *Frau im Mond* focuses on obtaining wealth from space, *Kosmicheskiy Reys* places more emphasis on the pleasures of escaping from Earth's gravity to enjoy weightlessness. This effort to depict space as both strange and wonderful is an early intimation that achieving personal freedom might be one reason to venture into the cosmos.

Once they land on the Moon, crew members don spacesuits, again closely resembling diving gear, the difference being four oxygen tubes extending from both sides of the helmet. One suspects that Lang simply borrowed diving suits for his film, but Zhuravlev actually designed these suits, and since these are worn throughout the sojourn on the Moon, there are grounds for regarding this as the first genuine spacesuit film. Unlike Lang's space travelers, they occupy themselves on the surface of the Moon by leaping about in the low gravity, again stressing the exhilarating possibilities of life in space.

To provide a modicum of drama during their visit, two problems arise which are readily resolved. First, after fretting about their dangerously low supply of oxygen, crew members discover there is frozen oxygen on the lunar surface which can replenish their supplies. Second, the scientist is briefly trapped by falling rocks, but succeeds in attracting attention by firing the boy's pellet gun and is soon rescued. Lang and Zhuravlev's films both indicate that travelers to alien worlds face two principal threats: the absence of an essential supply (oxygen, water, or food) that cannot be found in their vicinity, and an accident that, while inconsequential on Earth, could be fatal to a spacesuited visitor.

The travelers' triumphant return to Earth has one noteworthy feature: As an uplifting conclusion, the woman reveals that they rescued the cat that was launched to the Moon (though how they safely retrieved the cat from the probe without a feline spacesuit is not explained). Apparently, realizing the survival and return of his one-dimensional characters might generate little emotional response, the director appealed to animal lovers by making an adorable cat the centerpiece of their arrival back on Earth. And this imbues the ending with a heartwarming glow it would otherwise lack. (Introducing a cute animal to augment interest in wooden astronauts is a strategy observed in later spacesuit films like *Robinson Crusoe on Mars*.)

There were no immediate successors to *Himmelskibet*, *Frau im Mond*, and *Kosmicheskiy Reys* in America or other countries, in part because the advent of sound temporarily shifted filmmakers' attention away from special effects extravaganzas to cloistered, talky melodramas and flashy musicals. Then, when filmmakers could again produce visually ambitious films, most nations were drifting toward war and lacked the resources, or desire, to make futuristic films. As for America, while Gernsback vainly campaigned to persuade Hollywood to make more science fiction movies, the only common examples were horror films like *Frankenstein* (1931) and *Island of Lost Souls* (1932).

There were also particular historical reasons why these films had little impact. The director of *Himmelskibet* was more interested in opposing war than exploring space, explaining why he made no further films about space travel, and the film itself was long considered lost, represented only by a few clips, until a version was rediscovered in 2006. The husband-and-wife team of director Lang and writer Thea von Harbou broke up in the early 1930s, as Lang fled to America to escape Nazi Germany while von Harbou stayed behind to become its loyal propagandist, so they could not collaborate on further science fiction films along the lines of *Frau im Mond* and *Metropolis* (1927). And *Frau im Mond* was long suppressed because the Nazi government, having recruited former members of Oberth's Rocket Society to construct rockets for military use, feared its realistic scenes of rockets might assist potential competitors. As for *Kosmicheskiy Reys*, it was released when most nations had lost interest in silent films, even those with impressive visual effects, and it probably never appeared outside the Soviet Union.

Hence, it is unclear whether the creative forces behind the next spacesuit film, Robert A. Heinlein and George Pal, had seen, or were even aware of, these predecessors. However, even if unknowingly, they would follow in their footsteps as they and others established the genre of spacesuit films in the 1950s.

— 2 —

The True Frontier: The Classic Films

While *Himmelskibet*, *Frau im Mond*, and *Kosmicheskiy Reys* represent important pioneering spacesuit films, they have little to say *about* space. True, they convey the key message that space travel is feasible, and establish that space is an unusual environment with unique characteristics. But broader questions are unaddressed: *Why* should humans travel into space? What is it really like to inhabit space for long periods of time? What perils lie in space travel, and how can they be confronted? How will humans be changed after life in space? For answers to such questions, one turns to the films of the 1950s which created the subgenre of spacesuit films: six films—*Destination Moon*, *Spaceways*, *Riders to the Stars*, *Gog*, *Conquest of Space*, and *Satellite in the Sky*; one episode of a television series (*Disneyland*'s "Man and the Moon"); two failed television pilots repackaged as films (*Project Moon Base* and *Destination Space*); and a television series, *Men into Space*, which both summarized its predecessors and ventured into new territory.

These films command attention because they calmly and confidently confront something genuinely unknown—the authentic experience of space—while pseudo-spacesuit films only present the human villains, comic misadventures, and terrifying monsters long familiar in humanity's history and legends. As spacesuit films knowingly or unknowingly built upon their predecessors, all had new things to say about space and space travel; despite idiosyncratic lapses, all strived to be realistic in describing what space travel would be like; and all were sufficiently plausible as to anticipate aspects of actual space flights. But despite their fascinating qualities and undeniable importance, all have been unjustifiably ridiculed or ignored.

Destination Moon (1950)

When co-author Robert A. Heinlein, director Irving Pichel, and producer George Pal began planning *Destination Moon*, they had the same priority that governed *Himmelskibet*, *Frau im Mond*, and *Kosmicheskiy Reys*: to depict a flight to the Moon as realistically as possible, making the film a true work of science fiction. In his article "Shooting *Destination Moon*," Heinlein explains his commitment to authenticity above all else. After noting the first problem in science fiction filmmaking is sufficient funding, he continues: "The second biggest hurdle to producing an accurate and convincing science fiction picture is the 'Hol-

Venture into the Void: Film's first spacewalkers — Sweeney (Dick Wesson), General Thayer (Tom Powers), and Jim Barnes (John Archer) of *Destination Moon* (1950) — are distracted from their contemplation of the cosmos since they must rescue a drifting colleague by riding on an oxygen tank.

lywood' frame of mind — in this case, people in authority who either don't know or don't care about scientific correctness and plausibility." Fortunately, director Pichel was willing to make the film "as accurate as budget and ingenuity would permit" (118–19).

What Heinlein does not discuss is the first step he took to achieve the goal of being "accurate and convincing" in depicting space travel: jettisoning the plot of his novel *Rocket Ship Galileo* (1947), the purported basis of the film, to replace it with a different story about a pioneering lunar flight. In writing *Rocket Ship Galileo,* his first juvenile, Heinlein had not yet learned to create stories that would both appeal to young readers and meet his normal standards of plausibility; instead, his scenario was basically silly. An atomic engineer believes he can modify an existing rocket to reach the Moon, but his company will not support the effort, so he quits and looks for assistance elsewhere. Observing his teenage nephew and two friends testing a tiny rocket, he recruits them to help him prepare his ship and fly to the Moon with him. After landing on the Moon, they discover that the satellite has been settled by scientists from Nazi Germany seeking to establish the Fourth Reich. Though their own ship is destroyed, they outwit the Nazis and return to Earth in a German spaceship.

Only scattered traces of this story are discernible in *Destination Moon*. Both novel and film involve four astronauts traveling to the Moon; the leader of the novel's expedition is Donald Cargraves, while the film's mission is headed by Charles Cargraves (Warner Anderson); in both works, a man appears before the flight with a court order to stop the launch, though it is fraudulent in the novel and legitimate in the film (but nonetheless ignored); and both crews, upon reaching the Moon, claim the satellite as a possession of the United States (though the novel's speech also references the United Nations).

However, everything else in the novel was eliminated from the film because, along with a desire to create an entertaining movie, Heinlein and his collaborators had two other goals: to educate the public about the realities of space and genuine possibility of space travel, and encourage policymakers and voters to support efforts to reach the Moon. For this particular project, then, if not his other works, Heinlein embraced the three purposes of science fiction articulated by Gernsback: to entertain, provide scientific education, and inspire actual inventions. And his testimony in "Shooting *Destination Moon*" directly links the written genre's concern for scientific accuracy, long expressed in pulp magazines and inculcated in writers like Heinlein, and the similar concern embedded in the tradition of spacesuit films.

Furthermore, to make a film to achieve those goals, Heinlein abandoned his usual, more sophisticated approach to storytelling and co-authored a screenplay that recalled the fiction of Gernsback, with scientists and engineers as protagonists and a narrative regularly interrupted by long didactic passages explaining scientific principles and posited technological devices. Hence, this Heinlein film seems unlike the stories he became famous for; but perhaps science fiction must always take a clunky approach when seeking new audiences. Thus, just as Gernsback's *Ralph 124C 41+: A Romance of the Year 2660* (1911–12, 1925) and later editorials strived to introduce true science fiction to magazine readers, *Destination Moon* strives to introduce true science fiction to filmgoers.

To construct a new story for the film, Heinlein essentially heeded the advice of a character in his novel, Mr. Jenkins, who objects to Donald Cargraves's scheme by exclaiming, "Space flight is not a back-yard enterprise. When it comes it will be done by the air forces, or as a project of one of the big corporations, not by half-grown boys" (*Rocket Ship Galileo* 38). So, when Charles Cargraves learns that the government will stop supporting his rocket research, he meets with executives from major companies to obtain funding for a flight to the Moon. During his presentation, Cargraves offers the first extended argument for human space travel, starkly contrasting with the thirst for glory in *Himmelskibet*, the greed in *Frau im Mond*, and the quest for freedom in *Kosmicheskiy Reys*. His argument is rooted in Cold War politics: A nation gains a military advantage with a presence in space — seizing the high ground, as it were — and if the United States does not establish a beachhead in this realm, its enemy — the unnamed Soviet Union — certainly will, threatening national security. With this appeal to patriotism, Cargraves wins the support of initially skeptical businessmen.

His other challenge is to explain to them (and audiences) how space travel will be achieved, to convince them it is feasible — a major theme in early spacesuit films. Demonstrating a lack of confidence in the scientific acumen of his listeners, he does so primarily with an animated cartoon featuring Woody Woodpecker boarding a rocketship to fly to the Moon. Still, despite the incongruity of an animal protagonist, the cartoon is in other respects scientifically accurate; Woody even wears a realistic spacesuit.

While *Himmelskibet*, *Frau im Mond*, and *Kosmicheskiy Reys* said little about spacesuits, *Destination Moon* pays considerable attention to them. This reflected Heinlein's background since, as H. Bruce Franklin notes, he worked during World War II on constructing "high-altitude pressure suits" (Franklin 14), so he was both qualified and motivated to ponder the similar challenge of crafting a practical spacesuit. His later juvenile *Have Space Suit—Will Travel* (1958) incorporates a detailed and loving description of a spacesuit, and even *Rocket Ship Galileo* devotes several paragraphs to the subject (54–55). For his film, Heinlein faced a special challenge in creating spacesuits for men on wires, but developed a solution:

> Did you ever try to wire a man who is wearing a spacesuit? The wires have to get inside that suit at several points, producing the effect a nail has on a tire, i.e., a man wearing a pressurized suit cannot be suspended on wires. So inflation of suits must be replaced by padding, at least during wired shots. But a padded suit doesn't wrinkle the same way a pressurized suit does and the difference shows.... To get around the shortcomings of padded suits we worked in an "establishing scene" in which the suits were shown to be of two parts, an outer chafing suit and an inner pressure suit. ("Shooting *Destination Moon*" 120)

Now, learning a scene was added simply to explain a film's spacesuits, some critics will discern misguided priorities: Why burden a film with such dull sequences? Such attitudes lead to judgments like that of Phil Hardy, who said *Destination Moon*'s "script is colourless and wooden; the dominant concern of those involved was to make the journey to the Moon realistic rather than dramatic" (*Encyclopedia of Science Fiction Movies* 125). Yet commentators ignore two considerations. First, some viewers might prefer a technical discussion of spacesuits to yet another chase scene or fistfight; such people, from the beginning, were enthusiastic science fiction readers, and today they subscribe to *Analog: Science Fiction/Science Fact,* the leading magazine of "hard science fiction." Simply because something does not interest Hardy and other critics does not mean it is uninteresting to everybody. Second, even viewers bored by such scenes receive a message that may heighten their interest in later scenes: If these people take such pains with their spacesuits, that indicates they are preparing for an extremely dangerous environment, requiring flawless protection at all times. Thus, when watching astronauts in spacesuits venture into space or onto the Moon, they better recognize that they are, at all times and quite literally, a few inches and few seconds away from death. In contrast, films that pay little attention to the technical challenges of space travel suggest those involved in the mission are not concerned about the hazards of space and invite audiences to be similarly unconcerned about their safety.

Still, in a ninety-minute film, one cannot indefinitely hold audiences' attention simply by stressing that spacesuited travelers constantly face the threat of an equipment failure or accident which would expose them to the lethal vacuum of space; instead, conflicts, problems, incidents, and/or crises must keep the story moving. Crafting such moments of drama, while remaining true to the goal of scientific plausibility, becomes a recurring challenge for everyone making spacesuit films.

The easy solutions are aliens — ranging from humanoid scoundrels to extravagant monsters — or human villains — such as saboteurs, traitors, or space pirates — creating what I categorize as pseudo-spacesuit films. Yet, seeking realism in all respects, Heinlein and Pichel rejected these options. They knew the frigid, airless Moon was lifeless, so astronauts could not discover humanoid aliens or monsters there. They reasoned that people planning to fly to the Moon would take reasonable precautions to prevent saboteurs from slipping aboard the spacecraft before takeoff and exclude passengers likely to become deranged (though later makers of spacesuit films like *Project Moon Base* and *Conquest of Space* would include such developments, contrived as plausibly as possible). Further, the makers of *Destination Moon* clearly thought that antagonists on board their spaceship or on the Moon, engaging in fisticuffs or gun battles, would detract from the story they wanted to emphasize: the inspiring first journey of humans across space to reach the surface of another world. So, the film only involves minor elements of human villainy before the launch: The explosion which ended Cargraves's government project may have been caused by enemy sabotage, and there is that brief, last-minute effort by concerned citizens to stop the flight.

With aliens and human villains out of the picture, the remaining options to provide drama are interpersonal squabbles or misunderstandings that do not rise to the level of open conflict, natural disasters, or accidents, and this is how *Destination Moon* strives to be dramatically involving. One device to enliven shipboard life is to include a character who was not supposed to be part of the crew; in both *Frau im Mond* and *Kosmicheskiy Reys*, a boy stows away on the spaceship to bring unexpected youth and inexperience to the mission. More realistically, *Destination Moon* has one crewman get sick at the last minute, requiring the substitution of radio man Sweeney (Dick Wesson), who is good at his craft but otherwise knows little about space travel. Unlike the crew's savants, Sweeney can serve as a representative Everyman to ask questions or make comments to provoke scientific explanations actually aimed at the audience. He is also allowed to display a sense of humor.

Regarding other sorts of drama, there are no genuine catastrophes in the film, though a brief image of a meteor passing the spaceship provides a frisson of drama. (Meteors, then regarded as a major threat to all space flights, would regularly cause problems in later spacesuit films.) And two accidents inspire the most dramatic sequences in the film: First, because the ignorant Sweeney mistakenly lubricates the ship's antenna, causing it to freeze in the chilly vacuum of space, astronauts must don spacesuits and go outside their ship to release it; later, since the pilot unexpectedly needed extra fuel for a difficult Moon landing, the crew is advised by ground monitors they must remove as much mass as possible so the ship will be light enough to take off with less fuel. The fact that they must rely upon expert guidance from Earth to achieve the right amount of reduced weight briefly introduces another theme of spacesuit films which becomes central to *Riders to the Stars* and the series *Men into Space*: that due to the difficulties of space travel, it will always be, to an extent, a collaborative effort involving both voyagers in space and advisors on Earth who provide astronauts with information and advice.

The first sequence is of greater significance because it addresses a problem observed in *Frau im Mond* by bringing space travelers into direct contact with the awesome void of space. In developing this scene, Heinlein undoubtedly recalled his story "Ordeal in Space" (1948), which I argue elsewhere is the film's second, unacknowledged literary source.[1] In a narrative set further in the future than *Destination Moon*, spaceman William Cole, on a routine flight to Mars, must go outside his spacecraft to replace a broken antenna — perhaps the first recorded instance of a scenario that repeatedly occurs in spacesuit films — and looks out at his surroundings:

> The wrench slipped as he finished tightening the bolt; it slipped from his grasp, fell free. He watched it go, out and out and out, down and down and down, until it was so small he could no longer see it. It made him dizzy to watch it, bright in the sunlight against the deep black of space.
> [Then, when Cole loses his lifeline and finds himself clinging to the handhold,]
> He looked down — and regretted it.
> There was nothing below him but stars, down and down, endlessly. Stars, swinging past as the ship spun with him, emptiness of all time and blackness and cold [121].

While not the sort of language one normally associates with Heinlein, the author unusually strives for an emotional impact, attempting to communicate how huge, hostile, and inhuman

Superfluous Spacesuits: It may look like astronauts Thayer (Tom Powers) and an unidentified crewmate in *Destination Moon* (1950) are preparing to do their lunar laundry, but they are actually disposing of their spacesuits as part of a desperate effort to make their spaceship light enough for a successful liftoff.

the depths of space would seem to a single, vulnerable man in a spacesuit. Soon, Cole loses his grip, begins falling endlessly through space and, after being rescued, develops a severe case of acrophobia requiring him to retire from space flight. Later, he conquers his fear of heights by rescuing a kitten on a ledge, inspiring a return to space with his newfound companion.

In the film, the scene of astronauts repairing the antenna arouses the response Heinlein wanted from readers of his story. First, three men don space helmets; pushing a button, one man watches as a light announces "VACUUM"; the airlock door slowly opens to reveal the starry blackness of space; the camera shows them emerging from the spacecraft *upside down*, a striking visual reminder that in space there is no "up" and "down"; and, still upside down from the audience's perspective, they pause to gaze at the awe-inspiring immensity of space. Proceeding to work, they walk around the hull, using magnetic shoes to remain attached to the ship, and gradually vanish from view as they walk over the ship's "horizon." Here, *Destination Moon* achieves the effect that Lang vainly sought with Manfredt's gestures at the window into space, as the majesty and alienness of space are dramatically conveyed to audiences.

Soon, one man loses contact with the spaceship and begins drifting away into space — the crisis in "Ordeal in Space" — but a rescue is effected more quickly: Another crewman employs an oxygen tank as a rocket to maneuver to the man and, with a rope, guides him to the ship. In later spacesuit films, astronauts lost in space for longer periods, drifting further into the void, would be icons of the hugeness and hostility of space.

Once crewmen land on the Moon, they step onto its surface and, in a scene that resembles actual footage of Armstrong and Aldrin walking on the Moon for the first time, they unfurl a flag to claim the Moon with a stirring speech: "By the grace of God, and in the name of the United States of America, I take possession of this planet on behalf of, and for the benefit of, all mankind." The men then explore a realistic lunar landscape and engage in inevitable horseplay: large leaps across the surface recalling similar scenes in *Kosmicheskiy Reys* and suggesting the freedom to be gained in space travel, and a carefully staged photograph of Sweeney in which he appears to hold Earth in his palm like a latter-day Atlas. When Sweeney notes that no one will recognize him while wearing his spacesuit, he anticipates the humorous moment in *2001: A Space Odyssey* when spacesuited visitors to the lunar monolith pose in front of the object, like typical tourists, though they are similarly unrecognizable. And this is another reason why filmmakers dislike spacesuits: They make it difficult for filmgoers to distinguish the individual characters viewers presumably must like and identify with to enjoy the film. Unwilling to emulate *Frau im Mond* in minimizing the use of spacesuits, *Destination Moon* puts characters into spacesuits of different colors to help audiences keep track of which astronaut is which.

In a film that devotes so much attention to spacesuits, it is interesting that its final crisis involves a spacesuit: After crewmen remove every possible object on the spaceship to reduce its weight, scientists on Earth inform them they still must remove a little more. There is an obvious answer: One astronaut could volunteer to remain behind, the way a similar dilemma was resolved in *Frau im Mond,* and Sweeney volunteers to do so. But in *Destination Moon,* the other crewmen devise a way to avoid this unpalatable solution (since Sweeney, unlike Helius, will clearly die if he remains behind). This is the problem: They could achieve the right weight by jettisoning their last spacesuit, but the last person on the Moon must wear that suit to safely board the ship. Their solution is to have Sweeney drill a small hole in the airlock (presumably meaning the air would only leak out slowly, though it would probably rush out quickly), get into the airlock and close it, quickly remove his spacesuit before all the air leaks out, and attach the suit to a line that goes through the hole with an oxygen tank attached to the other end. Then, after Sweeney enters the ship and closes the other door of the airlock, the weight of the tank will pull the spacesuit out of the airlock; and when it falls to the ground, the ship will be light enough to take off. This is the sort of improvised, jerry-built solution that would keep the *Apollo 13* astronauts alive, but it is hardly the stuff of conventional drama — nervously waiting to see if a spacesuit will fall in the right manner — again suggesting such films may not appeal to audiences seeking more action-packed thrills.

Still, in its time, *Destination Moon* was a successful film: A colleague of mine recalls eagerly standing in a long line outside a theatre to watch it when first released, it garnered respectable profits, and it earned an Academy Award for special effects. Still, its influence on later films was limited: While a few strived to emulate its rigorous concern for authenticity, others paid only minimal respect to scientific accuracy while indulging in crowd-pleasing implausibilities. And this dichotomy between serious films like *Riders to the Stars* and *Conquest of Space*, and silly films like *Rocketship X-M* and *Cat Women of the Moon*, is observed through the history of spacesuit films.

Spaceways (1953)

Since the nations of Europe and Asia suffered much more than America from World War II, they unsurprisingly took longer to begin making films about space travel, which involved certain expenses and technical challenges. With the release of *Spaceways* (1953), after several American space films already appeared, Britain produced its first genuine spacesuit film, which endeavored in its own way to follow the example of *Destination Moon* to tell a realistic story about a first flight into space without humanoid aliens or similar absurdities. There was even a science fiction writer involved, since the film was a loose adaptation of a radio play by British author Charles Eric Maine — though unlike Heinlein, he was notoriously a writer more inclined to pay lip service to scientific accuracy than adhere to it. (John Clute and Peter Nicholls's entry on Maine in *The Encyclopedia of Science Fiction* delicately explains that his works manifest "a disinclination to argue too closely scientific pinnings that are often shaky"—a tendency that "is particularly visible in stories featuring Hard-SF themes like space travel" [768].) Still, in part because of a business decision made before filming, *Spaceways* is also a film that oddly reinforces negative stereotypes about the British and questions their ability to become space pioneers, contrasting with the boundless American optimism of *Destination Moon*.

The problem was that Hammer Films, which produced *Spaceways*, yearned for profitable American releases, yet feared that their films could not appeal to American distributors and audiences with all–British casts. It might help to choose a subject that was popular in America, like space travel, but Hammer also deemed it prudent to recruit an American star as a lead player to attract American filmgoers. Further, since the very purpose of this figure was to make the film seem more American, the imported actor could not adopt a British accent or play a British citizen; rather, the script had to be modified to explain the prominent presence of an American in an otherwise British enterprise. For *Spaceways*, producer Michael Carreras and director Terence Fisher chose Howard Duff, star of some Hollywood B-movies, to portray rocket scientist Dr. Stephen Mitchell, working for the British space program "on loan" from the American government. However, since the Americans would not assign a top rocket scientist to assist a foreign government, even a friendly one, the unfortunate implication is that the British are relying on a second-rate American scientist, just as producers relied on a second-rate American actor.

Still, whatever its merits, the British space program in the film was at least launched with unusual clarity about its purposes, presented early in the film in a neatly organized conversation involving the scientist heading the program, Professor Koepler (Philip Leaver), its military overseer General Hayes (Anthony Ireland), and a visiting government minister (David Horne). After establishing that constructing a space station is the program's ultimate goal, Koepler calls it "an observatory that will at last pierce the secrets of space."

Hayes immediately answers, "It will keep every part of the globe under constant surveillance."

With the ball back in his court, Koepler calls the space station "a stepping stone to the Moon, to the planets, to whole new worlds."

Hayes adds, "And if necessary, a launching platform for atomic weapons."

Then, when Koepler protests, "I hope we shall never have to use it for that purpose," Hayes replies, "No, but it will be available if necessary."

As articulated by these emblematic characters, two competing visions of the purpose of space travel are presented: the scientist's dream of gaining new scientific knowledge about the universe by observing the stars and traveling to other worlds; and the general's desire to achieve a military advantage on Earth by monitoring terrestrial activities and launching attacks from space "if necessary." While *Destination Moon* made the general's case, *Spaceways* may be the first spacesuit film to explicitly argue in favor of conquering space strictly for benign, peaceful purposes. However, the film's final position on the purpose of space exploration, as summed up by the minister, is that both men are correct: "I too share Professor Koepler's hope that our space station will only serve peace. But we've been spending tremendous amounts of our defense budget on your work, Koepler, and we must be prepared for both peace and war."

Even if its motives are clear, the film immediately puts the British space program in a negative light. A small spacecraft has crash-landed, and scientists led by Mitchell rush to the scene of the crash, which seems dramatic enough and generates some suspense regarding why they are so desperately anxious to reach the site. It comes as a considerable anticlimax to learn their chief priority is ascertaining the fate of the white mice on the rocket, and to hear a scientist sadly lament that one mouse, "poor little Minnie," died due to the "intense heat" of the flight. True, it makes sense to send animals into space as experimental subjects before attempting human flight, which is what the American and Soviet programs would do; but American pilots of spacesuit films in the 1950s willingly risked space travel without furry predecessors, so the scene mildly suggests the British are approaching the challenge of space rather timidly, employing animals instead of humans, a theory to be spectacularly buttressed later in the film.

The film then spends considerable time on the ground, laying the groundwork for the singular developments that will prod the British to approve a manned flight. Mitchell's wife Vanessa (Cecile Chevreau) is unhappy because her husband, dedicated to space travel, refused a lucrative job offer from private industry. Further frustrated by being confined to the military base where he works, she is having an affair with biologist Philip Crenshaw (Andrew Osborn). While later American films usually feature wives and girlfriends who are unfailingly supportive of their partners' determination to reach space at all costs, this is the first film to suggest this obsession might also engender spousal resentment and domestic disharmony.

As a further blow to British credibility, we also will learn that the greedy Crenshaw betrayed his country to work as a Soviet spy in tandem with Vanessa; thus, her bitterness over being neglected in favor of spaceships led her to become not only an adulteress, but a traitor. (True, while this makes the pair the film's villains, such enemy espionage is not entirely unreasonable, since the general planning to build the space station envisions it primarily as "a launching platform for atomic weapons.") Stephen knows of his wife's affair, but is not concerned because he no longer loves her and is instead attracted to the project's brilliant mathematician, Lisa Frank (Eva Bartok), who shares his devotion to space.

All this leads to a crisis when the next experimental flight, upon jettisoning its second stage and using its remaining fuel to achieve a projected orbit some 1000 miles away from Earth, unexpectedly fails to reach the desired height and instead settles into an orbit only 633 miles up, high enough to remain orbiting for several decades but now destined to eventually fall back to Earth. At the same time Crenshaw and Vanessa have vanished, which seems impossible since all exits from the base are constantly patrolled by veteran guards. Dr. Smith (Alan Wheatley), an investigator from Scotland Yard who improbably worked previously as a biologist, is assigned to simultaneously replace Crenshaw and determine what happened to Crenshaw and Vanessa. Noting that the rocket's low orbit could be explained if someone had drained away some fuel, and that Mitchell was the last person with access to the tanks, Smith announces a bold theory: Learning of his wife's affair,

Mitchell murdered his wife and her lover, drained two rocket tanks, and stuffed their bodies inside, thus effecting the perfect crime, since the incriminating bodies could not be recovered for several decades, if ever. Lisa later theorizes that another problem in the spacecraft could have caused its improper orbit, but she unaccountably only tells Mitchell about her ideas, leaving Smith's theory unchallenged.

In response to this accusation, Mitchell proposes the British space program's first manned mission, with a unique purpose: Mitchell will fly the AS-2 to rendezvous with the orbiting AS-1, use magnets to attach it to his spacecraft, and return to Earth with the AS-1 in tow to prove there are no bodies stashed therein and that he is innocent. In other words, he argues, the British government's massive and expensive program must alter its plans solely to help one person, who is not even British, get out of a jam. In the context of spacesuit films, the proposal is disheartening. While films of the 1950s usually associate space travel with the sorts of noble goals previously explained by the scientist and general, Mitchell returns to the theme of *Frau im Mond*, that human space travel will be primarily motivated by purely selfish concerns.

Still, as if sensing his personal needs might seem insufficient grounds for rushing a human into space, Mitchell links his suggestion to broader goals: "Isn't this the greatest thing we're doing — making the age-old dream of all men come true?" He argues that the program always had "one idea in mind" — "to design the first rocketship to contain a human being" — and that "until a human being, a trained human being, makes the first rocket flight, we're at a standstill as far as future developments are concerned." Presumably, Mitchell's statements relate more to Koepler's goals of peaceful scientific progress than to Hayes's pursuit of military superiority, but his very vagueness in articulating precisely why space travel has been an "age-old dream" suggests that these sentiments are insincere, and he remains primarily interested in clearing his name.

After Mitchell makes his proposal, one might expect Smith to protest that sending the accused murderer into space to retrieve the spacecraft makes no sense, since he might have a chance to dispose of the bodies in space and destroy the evidence that would convict him. And officials in charge of a program financed and controlled by the British government would presumably prefer to have a British citizen, not an American, earn the honor of becoming the first human in space. But these objections are not raised. Instead, Mitchell is opposed solely on the grounds that the flight would be too dangerous. "We're not ready to think about" a manned flight, Koepler sputters, because "our spacesuits are still experimental" and "we don't know the effect of pressure acceleration on the human body organism." But Mitchell protests that, since the British already experimented with animals in space, it is time to send a human into space. He further insists he is the right person to take the chance because he is an accused murderer; his point, one guesses, is that such a life is less valuable than the life of an upright British citizen and a life that people might more willingly risk. Seemingly impressed by his astounding courage in volunteering to become the first person in space, everyone finally agrees to let him make the flight.

At this point, an uncharitable person might theorize that the British people working on the program are simply *afraid* to go into space, as also suggested by their focus on sending up only experimental animals, and hence are happy to let their American colleague take on the onerous task of venturing into the unknown. Sad to say, the film provides this unflattering notion with substantive support. Determined to assist the man she loves, Lisa decides to accompany Mitchell into space, since his work will be easier with a crewmate. Recognizing, without needing to explain, that Koepler would never allow a woman to go into space, she approaches Mitchell's associate, Toby Andrews (Michael Medwin), and asks him to volunteer to go with Mitchell. Noting the distressed look on his face, Lisa reiterates that she is only asking him "to volunteer"—not to actually do it. Andrews then understands her plan: He will volunteer to go along, Koepler will agree, and Andrews will let Lisa take his place at the last minute. Later, when Andrews is suited up and Lisa comes to replace him, he announces a change of heart and says he actually wishes to join Mitchell. But Lisa persuades him to follow the original plan, and he lets her don his spacesuit.

It is hard to believe this plot twist was devised by a British writer and approved by a British director, since it reflects so poorly upon British manhood. Given a compelling reason to travel into space and risk his life — to help a friend and colleague — Andrews nonetheless allows a *woman* to take his place and risk *her* life. In the context of attitudes in his day, Andrews, representing the typical British man, proves a cad and coward. Further, while her nationality is not stated, Lisa is portrayed by an actress who was born and raised in Hungary and speaks throughout the film with a heavy accent, establishing that she is not British by birth and perhaps not even a British citizen. A film about a British effort to place the first humans into space, one thinks, would feature British astronauts; instead, *Spaceways* literally depicts the British staying on Earth to watch an American and a Hungarian conquer space. It is as if filmmakers were predicting, despite a story featuring an envisioned British space program, that the British would not have the drive or fortitude to confront the challenges of space travel; the task would instead be accomplished by Americans, or people from another European country (which turned out to be the Soviet Union, not Hungary).

Hearing of Lisa's scheme, one might also wonder: How will a woman contrive to take the place of a man without anyone noticing? The answer lies in the peculiar design of the film's spacesuits, which have helmets resembling welder's helmets that cover the entire face, save for a narrow slit for the eyes. One hardly needs to point out this design is impractical, since astronauts in space or on the Moon will need to see all around them, instead of being limited to seeing a small area directly in front of them. From a filmmaker's perspective, such helmets are also unappealing, since they entirely conceal the faces of space travelers. But such helmets must be worn so the helmeted Lisa can board the AS-2 while everyone thinks she is Andrews.

The success of Lisa's scheme also requires an odd policy in the way astronauts wear spacesuits: While it might make sense to have them fully suited during takeoff, in case something catastrophic occurs, astronauts in spacesuit films rarely board a spaceship already wearing space helmets. But this must happen to maintain Lisa's secret until the ship is launched. Then, to explain why she keeps her space helmet on after the spaceship reaches orbit, Mitchell says something about turning on the "air conditioning" before removing his helmet, suggesting somehow that the spaceship's air was previously not breathable without "air conditioning" and thus required astronauts to wear spacesuits.

All things considered, the filmmakers, if they wanted to launch a spaceship with a handsome hero and his girlfriend aboard, should have cast a British actress in the part and made her the sort of plucky woman we will see in *Project Moon Base* who could persuade, or force, authorities to let her come along openly. Such an assertive, courageous British woman would boost British pride without compromising the film's appeal to American audiences and allow for more realistic, and more realistically deployed, spacesuits. But perhaps only Heinlein was sufficiently ahead of his time to envision such a character; the only way these filmmakers could see to get a woman into the crew was to make her a conniver, with the help of questionable technology.

The film's story, unaccountably, continues to foreground British bumbling. Smith, having provoked this unnecessary flight with his ingenious but incorrect theory, belatedly and accidentally finds out that one of the base's guards was a recent arrival who has left his position. Calling himself a fool for not having investigated these matters earlier, Smith immediately realizes that this new guard might have treacherously arranged to allow Crenshaw and Vanessa to leave the base undetected. He tries to find the guard, but can only talk to his wife, who reports that her husband recently died in a car accident; but she mentions a friend who was in the car, named Philip, and she recognizes him from a photograph as Philip Crenshaw. From her testimony, Smith determines that Crenshaw and Vanessa are staying in a house by the sea, awaiting the arrival of a boat to take them away. As Smith rushes to the scene, Crenshaw and Vanessa are in the house arguing: Vanessa is upset because Crenshaw promised to take her to America, but now proposes to go to the Soviet Union, which is unnamed but unmistakably their destination, since she describes it as a prison with 200 million people. Because Vanessa knew her paramour was a Soviet spy, she was foolish to believe he could take her to America, but one might answer that she is never presented as particularly bright. When she refuses to go, Crenshaw shoots her dead, precisely when Smith and his men burst in to seize him. Her death is convenient, of course, because it frees Mitchell to settle down with his true love, Lisa. To make amends for his blunder, Smith tries to contact the base and cancel the flight — but phones are disconnected. He frantically drives his car to the base to deliver his message in person — but is delayed by a long train crossing the road. By the time he arrives, Mitchell's ship is already in space. The British, it seems, can never do anything right.

The same point is further underlined when Mitchell and Lisa get into space. Upon jettisoning the final stage, the spaceship is jolted by an explosion, the air inside the craft becomes foggy, and Mitchell discovers that the controls are jammed. The ship is out of control, seemingly destined to either drift through space forever or crash into Earth; and while Lisa only makes the point later, it seems clear she had been right: There was a design flaw in the British ship that led the previous spaceship into an incorrect orbit and is dooming this one. The notable scientific lapse here is that scenes of Mitchell and Lisa in space make no effort to depict zero gravity.

When the crisis occurs, one might imagine that, since the film borrowed a little footage from *Rocketship X-M* (a film discussed below), *Spaceways* might also borrow its conclusion and have its lovers embrace as their spaceship crashes and kills them both. Certainly, this is what Lisa expects, since she announces, "There is no way back," and radios Earth to inform them about the problem they must correct: "Replace the final section lining with stronger absorbent." To vindicate their flight, she says, "Someone else must follow us so that all this won't have been in vain." However, a last-minute happy ending occurs when Mitchell improbably discovers that the controls are no longer jammed, allowing him to guide the vessel safely back to Earth.

Overall, it is difficult to reach a judgment about the merits of *Spaceways*. The movie is realistic enough to qualify as a genuine spacesuit film; it is unusually strong in presenting the reasons for humans to venture into space; and, more so than other spacesuit films, it presciently argues that the greatest perils facing astronauts in space may stem from seemingly minor flaws in spaceship design, a point tragically proven by the fates of the *Challenger* and *Columbia* space shuttles. Yet *Spaceways* also seems a very Earthbound spacesuit film: Almost all the action takes place on Earth, and despite protestations to the contrary, protagonist Mitchell primarily ventures into space not to move humanity into new territory, but simply to restore the status quo on Earth by allowing him to clear his name and return to his work. In the conversation between Koepler, Hayes, and the minister, there are intimations of humanity's glorious future in space, taking the form of a functioning space station in Earth orbit. However, while a drawing of a space station prominently figured in posters, the film itself never shows audiences such a station — not even a model. The conspicuous absence of this projected conclusion relates to the film's curious and unsatisfying pessimism: This British film predicts a British space program while simultaneously suggesting in multiple ways that the British are not well suited to conquer space and are unlikely to do so.

This conclusion, which proved correct in real life, is observed in the subsequent history of British science fiction films. Though another company, the British division of Warner Brothers, would attempt a spacesuit film, *Satellite in the Sky*, the general tendency of British space films would be to either surrender to silliness, as in *Devil Girl from Mars* (1954), *Fire Maidens of Outer Space* (1956), and *Man in the Moon* (1960), or veer toward horror, as in *The Quatermass Xperiment* (1955), *Quatermass II* (1957), and *The Trollenberg Terror* (1958), generally letting the Americans handle the real business of space travel, precisely as observed in *Spaceways*.

Project Moon Base (1953)

Project Moon Base, co-written by Heinlein, was not intended to be a film; rather, it was the pilot for a television series Heinlein hoped to launch which would present different science fiction stories each week, some original (like *Project Moon Base*) and others based on published stories by Heinlein and others. When no one wanted the series, producer Jack Seamans repackaged the pilot as a film, explaining why the film was shorter, and had a smaller budget, than Heinlein's previous effort, and why it was less prominent and successful.

Still, *Project Moon Base* is arguably more interesting than *Destination Moon*, despite its deficiencies.[2] Most prosaically, this film provides an updated vision of humanity's future in space. While previous spacesuit films posit that the first space flight would travel directly to the Moon, *Project Moon Base* reflects the emerging scientific consensus of the 1950s: that there would first be orbital flights, followed by construction of an Earth-orbiting space station, before a lunar flight would use the station as a starting point. Thus, to feature a mission to the Moon, the film must venture farther into the future, when space flight is already established, with professional military pilots replacing the *ad hoc* crews of earlier films. In addition, American authorities plan, as a cautious next step into space, a flight that after stopping at the station will simply orbit the Moon. Commander Colonel Briteis (Donna Martell) brashly suggests a landing, but her superiors regard the idea as overly bold. Thus, the film anticipates the actual course of the Apollo space program, which twice sent astronauts to orbit the Moon before having them land. Here, it is only due to a mishap involving the discovery of a saboteur that the first spaceship to orbit the Moon becomes the first spaceship to land on the Moon.

Project Moon Base also commands attention because it intriguingly explores issues of space travel that the more straightforward *Destination Moon* ignored. First, as was true of *Destination Moon*, people in *Project Moon Base* primarily wish to go to the Moon to gain a military advantage over the Soviet Union. However, officials also recognize that such blatant military objectives, which might rally support in some quarters (like captains of industry), would be resisted elsewhere and might harm America's image abroad. So, as General "Pappy" Greene (Hayden Rorke) confides to the mission's second-in-command, Major Bill Moore (Ross Ford), Americans must play "the science angle" by including a scientist on the flight and pretending its purpose is to obtain scientifically valuable photographs of the hitherto-unseen far side of the Moon. This makes *Project Moon Base* the first spacesuit film to acknowledge public support as an essential element in a space program, as opposed to merely convincing a few government officials or businessmen, and the first American film to echo the argument in *Spaceways*, albeit without conviction, that garnering scientific knowledge is a significant reason for space travel. As another concession to public opinion, Greene is pressured by the president to grant a last-minute interview to journalist friend Polly Prattles (Barbara Morrison), who as her name suggests is amiable but ditzy. This sets up a scene, comparable to the cartoon in *Destination Moon*, wherein Greene can explain the mechanics of space travel to possibly ill-informed audiences — while saying nothing about the military motives behind the mission.

Their purported scientific objectives, however, do not fool enemy agents, who recognize that America's space program, and in particular its space station, improve America's military position and harm their own; hence they plot to sabotage the flight by replacing scientist Dr. Wernher (Larry Johns) with an identical duplicate who will use the spaceship to destroy the station. To modern eyes, successful execution of their plot may only seem a way to kill time before sending protagonists into space, recalling the similarly lengthy Earthbound prologue in *Frau im Mond*, though it is more entertaining than the interpersonal conflicts that achieved the same purpose in the previous film. Further, the ease with which they accomplish the substitution may seem unrealistic, for today, anyone assigned to a space flight, particularly one with a covert military agenda, would surely be under close guard the day before the launch. Still, a saboteur on board generates additional suspense, and provokes a struggle in space, arguably making this the most involving of the early spacesuit films.

As another virtue, despite its limited budget, *Project Moon Base* imaginatively depicts the strangeness of space in the sequence when Briteis, Moore, and the saboteur visit the space station. Interestingly, unlike the elaborate wheels in the sky described or observed in films like *Gog* and *Conquest of Space*, this station is a nondescript disc, which is not only more practical but also eliminates the standard pretext that a rotating space station could simulate Earth's gravity to avoid disquieting (and expensive) depictions of zero gravity on the station. Thus, once the crew enters the station, they immediately encounter a crewman walking past them in the opposite direction *upside down*, establishing that there is no gravity on the station. They also observe a sign stating "Please do not walk on the walls" and confer with three station personnel who are seated, from their perspective, in chairs on a wall. More so than the brief scene of upside-down astronauts in *Destination Moon*, then, the film demonstrates that people living in weightlessness will abandon conventional notions about "up" and "down" and freely interact in ways which would be bizarre and impossible on Earth. These scenes earned the film rare praise in Bruce Lanier Wright's *Yesterday's Tomorrows*: "[S]equences set on the zero-gravity space station are rather nice ... anticipating similar scenes in *2001*" (28).

Also, while other films of the era often assume without discussion that space travel must be exclusively reserved for men, *Project Moon Base* singularly features a woman, Briteis, as both the first person who flew into space and commander of the first lunar mission (though her colleague and future husband Moore displays little respect for his superior officer by constantly calling her "Bright Eyes"). Actually, as Heinlein realized, female astronauts make sense for two reasons: first, since the critical problem in rocket launches is minimizing the mass of the rocket, to reduce the amount of fuel needed, smaller astronauts are an asset; second, since precise movements are more important than brute strength in weightlessness, a woman's dexterity might be more advantageous than a man's musculature. However, the true reason that a woman played these important roles is only revealed in the final scene, showing that the president who made the assignments is a grandmotherly woman clearly seeking to advance the interests of women (also explaining why the president had a friend like Prattles).

This aspect of the film may be why executives rejected this pilot. In the 1960s, NBC disliked Gene Roddenberry's first *Star Trek* pilot, then called "The Menagerie" and now referred to as "The Cage," in part because a woman was the *Enterprise*'s second-in-command. A decade earlier, in even less enlightened times, this story's protofeminist touches surely were even more disturbing — here, women commanded both a spacecraft and the entire nation — and observers may have feared additional series episodes would be equally heterodox in having future women disconcertingly exercise power over men.

As for the film's depiction of space travel, there are no problems during the flight from Earth to the station — since such flights are routine — but the flight to the Moon is imperiled when Briteis and Moore belatedly discover that Wernher is an imposter. The key clue for Moore is that the Brooklyn-born Wernher did not seem aware of baseball's Brooklyn Dodgers, proof positive that he was a phony. (Science fiction could imagine many strange things in the future, but never, it seems, the possibility that the Brooklyn Dodgers might relocate to another city, since another spacesuit film, *Conquest of Space*, similarly references the Brooklyn Dodgers.) Moore's struggle to subdue him, carried out in eerie slow motion due to acceleration, further conveys the strangeness of conditions in space — but more importantly to the plot, disrupts the flight and requires an emergency landing on the Moon.

After landing, the crew confronts two familiar problems: an accident, and lack of resources. Now allied against a common adversary — the harsh lunar environment — Moore and the fake Wernher scale a lunar mountain to set up an antenna and notify Earth about their situation. While descending the slope, the saboteur falls, cracks his helmet, and dies, becoming the first space traveler buried on the Moon. When Greene hears from Briteis and Moore, he quickly arranges to have a rocket sent to their location with supplies. However, he also conveys some limitations of the military mind; initially flabbergasted to hear that their circumlunar flight became a Moon landing, Greene and his colleagues recover their composure and rename the mission "Project Moon Base," bureaucratically reclassifying a failure as a success and restoring a sense of orderliness to an unexpected event.

Then, again displaying the concern for public opinion that this film emphasizes as a major element in space operations, Greene hastily pressures Moore to propose to Briteis to avoid the scandal of an unmarried couple living together on the Moon. Briteis accepts the proposal on the condition that the president promotes her future husband to the rank of general so he, not she, can command America's first moon base. The president herself presides by television over a long-distance marriage ceremony, arguably making her the first official who attempts to gain a political advantage by associating herself with a successful space mission and anticipating President Nixon's similarly motivated telephone conversation with the first astronauts on the Moon. *Project Moon Base* also introduces another idea that becomes more prominent in *Men into Space*: that the experience of traveling into the environment of space will not encourage astronauts to adopt new strange lifestyles to match their strange new home, but instead drive them back to the domestic conventions of traditional American life.

Having re-established male supremacy on the Moon, the film concludes with astronauts who will remain there indefinitely until scientists can devise a way to get them back and, one assumes, replace them with other residents for Project Moon Base. In this way, the film again reflects contemporary scientific opinion by projecting a permanent lunar colony as an eventual objective of a proper space program. Also, while the film offers no hint of this outcome, Moore and Briteis might become parents to the first child born on another world — yet another way in which *Project Moon Base* may be both the most limited, and most visionary, spacesuit film of the 1950s.

Riders to the Stars (1954)

With the remarkable and prophetic *Riders to the Stars*, the spacesuit film moves into new and more disturbing territory. For despite some problems, those who previously traveled in cinematic space generally had it easy; this is the first film to graphically suggest just how challenging and dangerous space travel might actually be.[3] Perhaps creators were influenced by *Spaceways*, since there are superficial similarities in their stories: Both films involve space programs led by an elderly scientist and include a young female scientist who falls in love with an astronaut about to fly into Earth orbit. However, *Riders to the Stars* devises a stranger and more elaborate motive for space travel than a desire to prove oneself innocent of murder.

The problem with the film is that it contrives to be prophetic by means of a premise which, while ingenious, is nonsensical. Scientists sending rockets into space discover that cosmic ray bombardment completely alters the structure of metal, making it shatter to the touch and apparently rendering human space travel impossible. Noting that meteors reach Earth's surface without being transformed, scientists Donald Stanton (Herbert Marshall) and Jane Flynn (Martha Hyer) hypothesize that meteors have some sort of coating that protects them from cosmic rays but burns away as they approach Earth. Thus, they must send astronauts into space to scoop up meteors before they hit the ground, to examine them and determine the nature of their coating.

Yet none of these ideas withstands scrutiny. While the particles making up cosmic rays might over time weaken the strength of metals, the radiation could not conceivably have the immediately devastating effect this film posits. Further, since meteors mostly consist of leftover debris from the primordial cloud of matter that engendered the planets, it is hard to imagine a natural mechanism that would imbue them with a protective coating, or a substance powerful enough to withstand the purportedly destructive cosmic rays but flimsy enough to burn away due to the frictional heat of penetrating Earth's atmosphere. Next, the extreme difficulties involved in rendezvousing with another object in space, complex enough to serve as the subject of future Apollo astronaut Buzz Aldrin's doctoral dissertation, ensure that no astronauts could possibly approach and seize meteors by the process outlined in this film: namely, sending astronauts in rockets to the vicinity of a swarm of meteors and instructing them to look out their windows, find suitable candidates, and visually maneuver their ships in their direction to grab them. And there is the awkward, unanswered question of how the meteor-chasing astronauts will survive the mission, since their own spaceships will be exposed to the same deadly radiation that disabled other rockets.

Nevertheless, all this idiocy serendipitously enables *Riders to the Stars* to achieve genuine drama by depicting astronauts who soar briefly into the fringes of space, instead of flying directly to the Moon, making this the first film to anticipate how the American space program actually began—with suborbital flights by Alan Shepard and Gus Grissom. Further, the flight's purpose, as was true of the Mercury flights, is primarily to ensure that regular space travel will be feasible. Astronauts fly in tiny, cramped spaceships resembling the space capsules of the 1960s, not the unrealistically large vehicles of other films. Strangely, working from absurd premises, producer Ivan Tors, writer Curt Siodmak, and director Richard Carlson created the most realistic, and most genuinely prophetic, of all the early spacesuit films.

One striking feature is that, while *Project Moon Base* implies that its astronauts are systematically selected and trained, *Riders to the Stars* actually shows audiences this process. To find suitable candidates for the mission, the scientists survey the computerized records of 150 million people (on the punchcards that computers then used) and, applying rigorous criteria, winnow the data down to a list of twelve men who seem capable of becoming successful astronauts. (For added personal drama, one of them is Stanton's son.) Not all of the selection criteria are specified, but they are all male (scientist Flynn admits to dreaming about space flight, but knows that, for some reason, this cannot be allowed) and unmarried (presumably, unattached men would be best suited for a potentially fatal flight); it is further clear that they possess considerable scientific knowledge, can pilot aircraft, and are relatively young and in good physical condition. In all respects except marital status, then, this film anticipates the criteria NASA applied in choosing its first astronauts. Interestingly, while NASA first chose only military personnel, these scientists select three civilians, perhaps because only civilians possessed the extensive scientific background they deem necessary.

Yet paper qualifications are insufficient; the candidates, once summoned to the base in lengthy sequences that establish the characters of two eventual astronauts, Dr. Richard Stanton (William Lundigan) and Dr. Jerry Lockwood (Carlson), must be subjected to a series of demanding tests, though only two are actually shown. The first test is ingenious—and devious: Finalists are escorted to a room and told they will be called in a few minutes; then, they are forced to wait for over two hours while finding themselves locked inside the room. When one man cannot stand the wait, starts screaming, and attempts to leave the room, he establishes to the satisfaction of an observing psychologist that he is not suitable for space travel, because he lacks the essential quality of patience. This is important because, as noted, one requirement of space flight is an ability to remain calm while slowly and meticulously carrying out certain procedures. (Another candidate is identified as a potential problem because he constantly paces and chain-smokes, but is allowed to remain. Once selected, however, he reveals he was indeed unsuitable by rejecting the assignment.)

The second test involves no deception: Candidates are strapped in a rotating chair and spun around to simulate heightened gravitational force and determine if they can withstand pressures of up to twelve times normal gravity (twelve Gs) without blacking out. After one candidate unsteadily emerges from the chair, demonstrating that he cannot bear the strain, Stanton passes the test in a sequence that also suggests a burgeoning romantic relationship between him and Flynn, who monitors the test and displays great concern for his well-being.

While she never ventures into space, Flynn is a dominating presence in the film, a key player in all decisions, and portrayed by an actress who was both beautiful and had genuine acting ability (a rare quality in these films). She inexorably becomes the center of attention of every scene she appears in (though Marshall is also an unusually capable performer). Viewers may actually care about the fate of an astronaut in a spacesuit film, because a talented actress shows that she cares, making him seem more like a real person.

Flynn's crucial role is signaled during the opening credits, which are accompanied, for the first time in spacesuit films, by a theme song. While the history of science fiction films offers many tawdry theme songs recalled today only for occasional ridicule, producer Tors clearly regarded this song as something important. To provide lyrics for the ethereal melody written by film composer Harry Sukman, he hired professional lyricist Leon Pober (later known for composing Don Ho's "Tiny Bubbles"), and recruited a respected jazz vocalist, Kitty White, as its singer.

Its lyrics, likening space travel to romantic love, anticipate a conversation when Flynn describes her secret desire to fly into space:

FLYNN: I dream of it almost every night.
STANTON: What?
FLYNN: Flying.
STANTON: In a rocket?
FLYNN: Of course. Speed, 18,000 miles. And then I look back on the Earth, huge round ball. As I fly toward the ionosphere, I can see the Gulf of California and the Pacific Ocean.... Cities are like hazy stars below me, and when I look up, why, there's the Sun, and myriad of stars no human eyes have ever seen before. We do live in a dark hole down here on Earth, like blind moles. I envy you going up there.

Here, for the first time in a spacesuit film, someone aspires to go into space not to become wealthy, achieve a military advantage, or gather scientific knowledge; rather, she relishes the

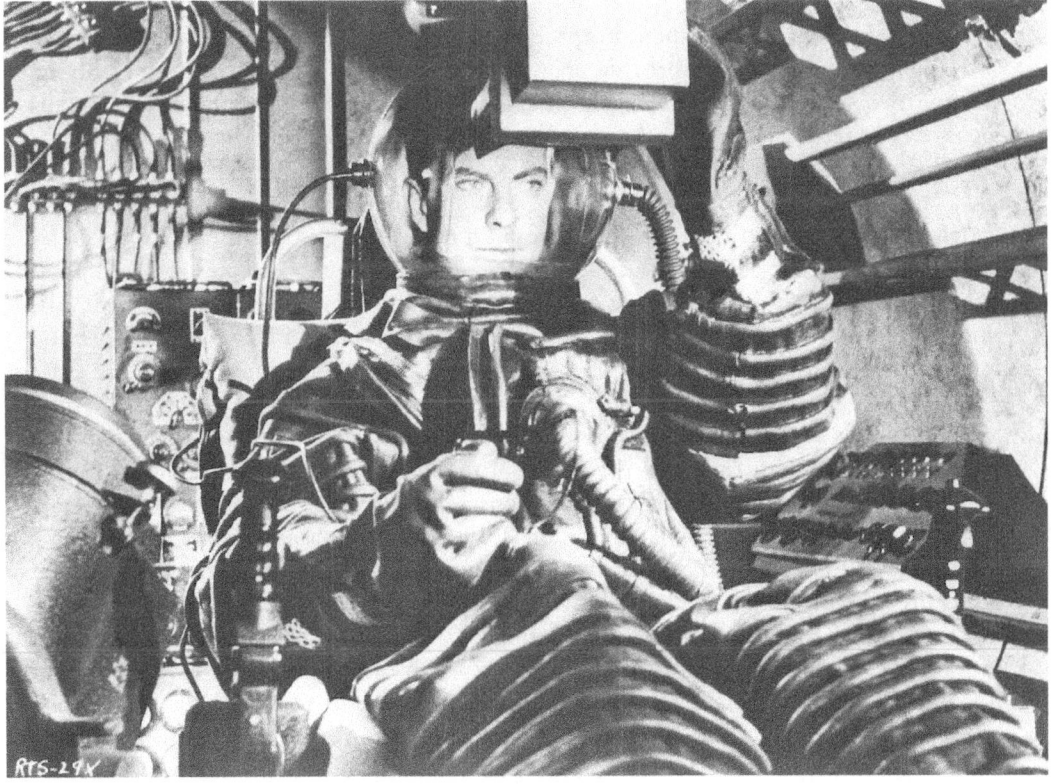

Maiden Voyage: As astronaut Richard Stanton, William Lundigan dons his first spacesuit in *Riders to the Stars* (1954); it will later become his regular uniform when he stars in the series *Men into Space* (1959–1960).

envisioned experience of traveling at great speeds and enjoying a spectacular view of Earth below and stars above. While Lisa Frank went into space because she loved a man, Flynn wishes to go into space because she loves space itself. Space travel, in other words, is desired primarily as a pleasurable sensual experience — something like falling in love, as in the song. Significantly, a woman introduces this notion that it might simply be *fun* to go into space. While it is hard to posit that women have a special capacity to appreciate such experiences, they may be more willing to express such feelings, in contrast to stoic males who often pretend their careers are driven by practical concerns or patriotic duty. The contrast is observed both on film and in real life, for after dozens of male American astronauts said little if anything about the sheer joy of space travel, America's first female astronaut, Sally Ride, memorably likened her space shuttle flight to an E-ticket ride at Disneyland. So that song appears to be more portentous than one might suppose.

In any event, the irony in this film is that, after Flynn speaks of space travel as a dream come true, the subsequent experiences of the astronauts, to an extent unparalleled in the short history of spacesuit films, prove genuinely nightmarish — emphasizing as never before the terrible dangers. If anything will ameliorate the perils they will face, it is that they will not face them alone; for as astronauts fly their separate ships into space, we see, for the first time on film, the necessarily collaborative nature of realistic space flight. True, the crews in *Destination Moon, Spaceways,* and *Project Moon Base* occasionally spoke to colleagues on Earth, and in the American films they depend upon guidance from Earth when facing a crisis; during journeys, however, they were generally left to their own devices. In this film, as was the case with actual American space flights, astronauts are continuously in contact with monitors on Earth who provide updated information, issue orders, and give advice, creating two sets of heroes: astronauts in space, the handsome men audiences naturally focus on, and technicians on Earth, who guide their actions and share responsibility for the success or failure of their missions.

These bifurcated dramas, interestingly, play out differently on film and in reality. To match audience expectations, films must establish the primacy of heroic space travelers by having them at some point refuse orders and act on their own to achieve some desirable result, for which they are duly celebrated (as occurs in this film). During actual space missions, astronauts who disobey orders or ignore advice from Earth are considered fools, and those few who dared to behave in this manner were immediately removed from the space program.[4]

The drama of the astronauts' suborbital flights, scheduled to last only fifteen minutes, for once proceeds with the rapid pace that conventional drama demands. But after they survive the grueling pressures of liftoff and approach the meteor swarm, everything starts to go wrong. One astronaut, Walter Gordon (Robert Karnes), rashly decides to scoop up a meteor that is too large for his craft, causing his spaceship to explode. What happens next is literally stunning: When Lockwood investigates what happened to his colleague, he looks out the window to see Gordon's body floating in space, his face inside the space helmet transformed into a desiccated skull. This represents an early intersection of the spacesuit film and horror film; for the image of his dead comrade is so unsettling that Lockwood effectively goes insane, fires his rocket in a desperate attempt to avoid a similar fate, and sends his craft deeper and deeper into space, dooming him as well. While previous space travelers experienced major mishaps, this film represents the first time an astronaut faces tragedy due to insanity induced by space travel — a problem in later films like *Conquest of Space.*

With one astronaut killed and another about to die, people on Earth understandably order the third astronaut, Stanton, to abandon his mission and return immediately, and at first he agrees. However, spotting a suitable meteor along the way, he decides he might as well capture it, and monitors reluctantly provide information enabling him to scoop it up. A less than smooth landing provides a final moment of suspense, but his father and Flynn find him unharmed inside the damaged spacecraft, and an inspection of the meteor yields the elusive secret of their invulnerability to cosmic rays — a coating of "crystallized carbon," or diamond. This discovery provides a happy ending, since scientists now know how to protect spacecraft from the hazards of space — but at what cost? One hates to spoil the celebration with a dose of economic reality, but the huge expense of covering every rocket with a diamond coating would appear to forever preclude a vigorous space program just as effectively as lethal radiation.

Still, one must overlook everything that *Riders to the Stars* gets wrong to acknowledge that, for the most part, it got the future of America's space program right. Until the actual space flights of the 1960s, no other film would so precisely show what human space travel would really be like. So, the fact that commentators like David Wingrove generally describe it as "dull, lecturing ... poor movie-making" is sadly telling (193).

Gog (1954)

After making a film that was mostly about preparations for space flight, Ivan Tors then produced another film, *Gog*, that was *entirely* about such preparations, concluding only with the launch of an unmanned satellite and promise of an eventual space station. Thus, more so than other spacesuit films, *Gog* conveys the important point that space travel will require extensive and time-consuming research in several fields to be successful, and it explores initiatives that other films never consider.

Interestingly, two areas of research in the film's vast underground laboratory in New Mexico, devoted to building the station, involve efforts to avoid the use of spacesuits. Initially, Dr. Hubertus (Michael Fox), using a chimpanzee as his subject, experiments with a technique to freeze and revive human beings. According to project head Dr. Van Ness (Herbert Marshall), Hubertus "believed that by pre-freezing the pilot we'll be able to conquer space. A man kept frozen and refrigerated could avoid the danger of space flight — cosmic rays, meteors, lack of weight and oxygen, the pull of gravity." (Presumably, by "pull of gravity" he means the pressures of a spaceship's liftoff, since the normal "pull of gravity" is harmless.) This idea resurfaces in *Space Men* and, of course, *2001: A Space Odyssey*. Another scientist, computer expert Dr. Zeitman (John Wengraf), wants to avoid sending humans into space altogether. In the room where he monitors NOVAC, the immense computer controlling all mechanisms in the laboratory, he shows investigators David Sheppard (Richard Egan) and Joanna Merritt (Constance Dowling) multi-armed robots that move on wheels, Gog and Magog, and says, "Our robots will pilot our rockets into space" because "Man's inadequate body will never be able to leave the Earth."

Sheppard notes that his is a minority opinion, and other work demonstrates that there are still plans to send unfrozen human astronauts into space. First, there is a chamber where people in metal suits, surrounded by magnets, can practice movements in low or zero gravity. The experimental subjects are a man and woman, obviously professional acrobats who compulsively turn to the audience and smile after every maneuver; they take turns tossing the other person around, and the woman even elevates the man in a standing position by holding him in one hand. Also, to provide power for station residents, scientists are developing a special mirror to harness solar energy that could also be employed to beam destructive rays as a weapon. (Indeed, this feature of the station — graphically illustrated when the mirror destroys some buildings in a model city — seems, even more so than in *Spaceways*, to make enemy efforts to sabotage the project justifiable. But no one in this film, at the height of the Cold War, sees things that way.)

Finally, and making *Gog* relevant to this study, an experiment involves spacesuits. A scientist tells Sheppard and Merritt, "I've got to test two new pressure suits," and we see two astronauts in blue spacesuits, seated on opposite sides of a small revolving centrifuge. He tells them to "check your oxygen," turns a dial to "evacuate the air from the chamber," and starts the centrifuge, which spins faster and faster as he works them up to the force of ten gravities to ensure that their spacesuits will protect them in such conditions. There is an especially evocative moment when the camera points to the observers watching the astronauts, and we see superimposed on them an image in the glass of the revolving astronauts, as if they represent the dreams of space pioneers.

Reading about these experiments, one might imagine that *Gog* is a dull movie indeed, but Tors keeps things lively with several mysterious murders which Sheppard is investigating, the pretext for his visits to the research facilities. The murders begin when Hubertus and his assistant separately step into the refrigeration chamber, the door closes and locks itself, and the refrigeration machinery turns on to freeze them to death. Later, the small, experimental space mirror begins shooting deadly rays at a scientist, and the mechanism controlling the centrifuge jams, keeping the astronauts revolving at high speeds for too long and killing them — which functions as a warning about the dangers of space travel though no actual space travel was involved. Only the acrobats miss out on becoming the object of attempted murder.

As for the robots, the title of the film indicates that they will turn menacing. A robot not only strangles Zeitman and his assistant but also, as the final crisis, attempts to remove the control rod in an atomic power generator and cause a nuclear explosion. At the same time, Sheppard puts together clues to figure out how the murders were committed: an enemy rocket plane, flying above the range of the laboratory's radar, is sending instructions to NOVAC by means of a secret receptor installed when the computer was assembled in a neutral country, directing it to kill scientists. Since they evidently knew how to blow up the entire facility, one wonders why America's enemies unwisely began with isolated murders that only made residents aware of the threat and determined to find its cause. But the laboratory escapes destruction due to Sheppard, who alerts authorities, enabling them to dispatch planes that shoot down the enemy aircraft, while Sheppard disables the robots with a flame thrower. Then, the surviving scientists immediately perform an important operation — launching a tiny model of the station into orbit — so this "baby space station" can function as a "flying television set" to monitor all activities on Earth and, among other things, prevent further plots against the American space program. A concluding image of a moonscape underneath the words "The End" suggests further initiatives in space to come.

Unlike *Riders to the Stars*, which assumed without discussion that space travel would be an all-male activity, *Gog* is explicitly open to both male and female astronauts. Observing the male and female acrobats doing their routines, Merritt comments, "Women are better suited for space travel than men," given their smaller size and agility (a point also conveyed by *Project Moon Base*), and when the female acrobat holds the male acrobat in her hand,

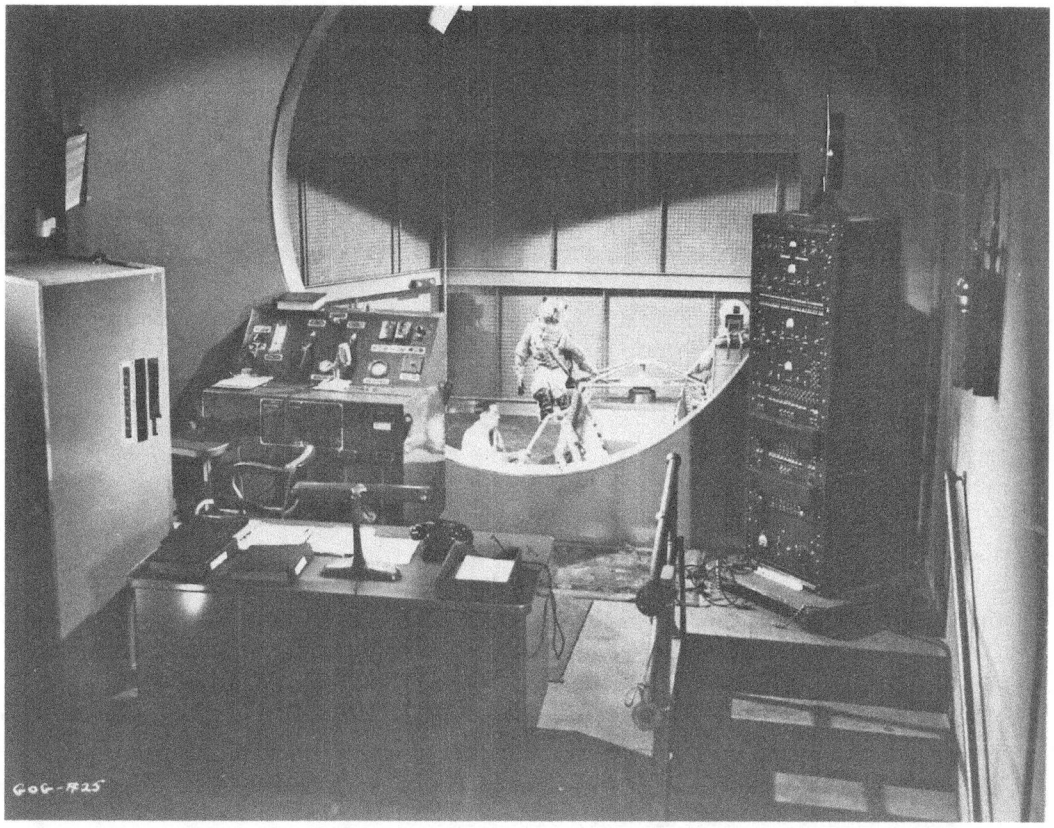

Spinning Out of Control: Preparing for the pressures of space flight by spinning in a centrifuge, two unidentified astronauts in *Gog* (1954) will soon be killed when their laboratory's deranged computer makes the centrifuge spin too fast, crushing them with simulated gravitational force.

she notes, "In space there's no such thing as a weaker sex." More significantly, one spacesuited subject killed in the centrifuge was a blonde-haired woman, seen only from behind, indicating they are training women to serve on the station. In addition, about half the scientists in this laboratory are women, another fact making *Gog*, at least in the area of women's liberation, an unusually enlightened spacesuit film — though none of its characters reach space.

Conquest of Space (1955)

Conquest of Space was planned as the crowning masterpiece of the spacesuit film — a tour of the solar system with lavish special effects in glorious color. As budgetary constraints came into play, however, the film was reduced to a flight to Mars, and when it proved a box-office failure, the film brought the embryonic tradition of spacesuit films to a halt, at least in America, though it reemerged on television in the TV pilot *Destination Space* and the series *Men into Space*.

One readily sees why *Conquest of Space* failed to attract large audiences, since it is not only superficially undramatic like previous spacesuit films but also sometimes unpleasant to watch. Building upon the premises of *Riders to the Stars*, the film suggests with even greater force that space travel may be too much for most people to bear. Still, one reason for the mental problems exhibited by its astronauts may be that everyone involved in training and selecting the crew for humanity's first expedition to another world is seemingly making a deliberate *effort* to drive crew members crazy.

If the statement seems extreme, consider how General Samuel T. Merritt (Walter Brooke) treats prospective crewmates. First, he arranges for all personnel to serve on board an all-male space station for extended periods of time, unable to have any contact with women — frustrating, among others, Merritt's son Barney (Eric Fleming), who understandably wishes to return to Earth and see his new wife, from whom he has been separated for three years. But his father refuses to grant him leave, citing the urgency of the upcoming mission. Then, as part of their training, potential crewmen must subsist on a diet of pills; as a purported gesture of sensitivity toward their feelings, Merritt forbids all mention of food on board the station. Yet when meal times come around, potential crewmen enter a large mess hall, filled with numerous men working on the station eating normal food, endure verbal taunts about their diet, and embarrassingly sit at one table to conspicuously dine from a plate of pills — a policy that would only increase their frustration and unhappiness about their unpalatable regimen.

Further, possible crewmen are constantly observed while going through drills, knowing that even the slightest lapse will disqualify them from the mission. When Roy Cooper (William Redfield) is momentarily paralyzed during one drill, Merritt immediately removes him from consideration. And how does he "sensitively" inform him about this decision? When Cooper sits at the crewmen's table, settling down to another meal of pills, a man brings him a tray with normal food and urges him to start eating — abruptly informing Cooper, and everyone else on the station, that he will not be part of the flight despite years of training and his passionate desire to do so.

Asked to defend his apparently sadistic behavior, Merritt might respond that, given the extraordinary pressures of space travel, he must test potential crewmates as severely as possible to ensure the men he selects can handle the daunting experience. Yet observers might also conclude that he simply treats his men the way he is treated by his own superiors, who similarly seem intent upon driving *him* mad. Merritt is obviously under extreme pressure to complete preparations for the mission by a certain date, as evidenced by the fact that he periodically sedates himself with medication from a secret compartment; at one point he himself has a fainting spell. He also displays an obsession about constantly reading the Bible in a manner suggesting psychological problems. Further, Merritt learns that, all along, he was kept in the dark about the mission's true goal: Believing he is preparing a ship and crew to go to the Moon, he is suddenly informed, a few days before departure, that be will actually command a flight to Mars, a lengthier and more complex flight which he is completely unprepared for. This is not a revelation likely to improve one's mental stability, so it is unsurprising that, during the flight, Merritt goes completely insane, developing from Bible readings the singular notion that humans going to Mars constitute a violation of God's will.

This shift in a spacecraft's destination from the Moon to Mars — earlier observed in *Rocketship X-M* (1950) — has no place in serious films about space flight, since anyone making such a film should know the tremendous difference in the distances involved. The Moon is about 238,000 miles from Earth, whereas Mars, even at its closest, is 36,000,000 miles away. Deciding at the last minute to go to Mars instead of the Moon is literally comparable to planning a boat trip from Los Angeles to Santa Catalina Island — about 26 miles off-shore — then deciding to sail to Japan — about 5500 miles away. This represents the film's "idiosyncratic lapse" in scientific logic.

Of course, Merritt is not the only member of the crew who seems mentally unbalanced. Longtime associate Sergeant Mahoney (Mickey Shaughnessy) is so determined to join his beloved general on the mission (though Merritt insists he is too old) that he stows away on the spaceship and almost gets himself killed by enduring the brutal force of initial acceleration without being strapped in a protective chair; after landing on Mars, he displays extremely poor judgment in evaluating Merritt's demented actions. And the Jewish Andre Fodor (Ross Martin), by placing his hand comfortably on Cooper's shoulder upon realizing that his friend has been eliminated from the crew, signals by the iconography of the era that he is homosexual, which in the 1950s would be considered a mental disorder. The suggestion that he is gay is reinforced by the scene where Brooklyn-born Jackie Siegle (Phil Foster), the film's version of *Destination Moon*'s Sweeney, receives a final message from a two-timing girlfriend, while Fodor hears from his aged mother in Austria, calling him a "good boy" and indicating that he is a momma's boy who suspiciously has no girlfriend to wish him goodbye.

Other than its recurring suggestions of mental instability, *Conquest of Space* breaks new ground in its rationale for space travel. By envisioning a future when space travel is sponsored by an international agency of cooperating nations, the film cannot argue that space travel is necessary for the United States to gain an advantage over its enemies. Ignoring other ideas that surfaced in *Spaceways*, *Project Moon Base*, and *Riders to the Stars*— garnering scientific knowledge, or simply having a good time — *Conquest of Space* argues that humans must venture into space to obtain needed resources. This is explained at length when Merritt announces to assembled candidates the three men he wants, along with himself and his son, to join the crew — Fodor, Siegle, and the Japanese Imoto (Benson Fong). To justify his decision to volunteer for the mission, Imoto makes a long, awkward, and frankly bizarre speech wherein he likens humanity's decision to enter space to Japan's decision to launch World War II. While explicitly not defending Japan's initiatives, Imoto explains that, at the time, the Japanese felt compelled to act because the country lacked vital natural resources which could be obtained from other nations; now, he says, humanity faces a similar shortage of resources, requiring them to seek new supplies available in space. Presumably, though this is not stated, there are no moral issues involved in this because, unlike Japan, humans will exploit regions without indigenous inhabitants who claim the desired resources as their own. Still, at a time when World War II had ended only a decade ago, and innumerable Americans had painful memories of loved ones killed by Japanese soldiers, it seems extraordinarily inappropriate to validate humanity's first mission to another planet by comparing it to the Japanese attack on Pearl Harbor.

After the spaceship is finally on its way to Mars, there occurs, as in *Destination Moon*, a mid-flight crisis which forces crewmen to don spacesuits and venture outside; but what happens to them conveys more strongly that space is indeed very dangerous. First, instead of enjoying a placid moment to gaze in awe at a vast, peaceful cosmos, astronauts immediately cower in fear as a glowing red asteroid flies past their ship, narrowly avoiding a disastrous collision. Then, instead of the minor problem of an astronaut briefly drifting away from the ship, Fodor is suddenly struck by a meteor which penetrates his spacesuit, causing his immediate death. Unlike *Riders to the Stars*, the film offers no horrifying close-up of Fodor's ghastly corpse; however, providing the first image of a tradition previously mentioned in the serial *Radar Men from the Moon*, and later observed in films like *Star Trek II: The Wrath of Khan* (1982), surviving crewmen provide Fodor with a stirring space funeral. Some might regard Fodor's fate as the era's harsh punishment for implicit homosexuality; in a mission for manly heroes, there is no place for sissies who will get all touchy-feely at critical moments. However, as a matter of holding viewer interest, killing off Fodor eliminates the film's most talented actor and sympathetic character.

The death of Fodor finally drives Merritt over the edge. As they approach Mars, he reveals his unique interpretation of the Bible: Since the book never mentions other worlds, only Earth, it is evident that God intended humans to forever remain only on Earth. Since the Bible also fails to mention other things that Merritt is not disturbed about — including the advanced science that led to the space station he constructed and inhabited — there is no logical defense for this argument, but the obviously insane Merritt is beyond the realm of logic. One understands why filmmakers dealt with the character of Merritt in this fashion: To generate conflict on board a spacecraft staffed by carefully chosen and trained astronauts, one must either introduce a villainous stowaway, as in *Project Moon Base*, or have a crew member go insane, as in *Riders to the Stars* and this film.

Still, portraying Merritt's madness as a matter of skewed religious beliefs probably contributed to the failure of *Conquest of Space*. For better or worse, Merritt functions as this film's representative of Christianity, and though depicted as mentally unbalanced, he still suggests that devout Christians improperly cling to antiquated beliefs and oppose beneficial scientific progress. One travels into space, it is tacitly argued, in opposition to Christianity, not in harmony with it. Surely, Christians who supported space travel were a major portion of the film's audience, and they cannot have been pleased by Merritt's pronouncements and subsequent actions. The film's treatment of Christianity as a potential roadblock to space travel also contrasts with the behavior of later astronauts, like those in the "Christmas on the Moon" episode of *Men into Space* and actual American astronauts, who regularly refer to their Christian faith and present space travel as a natural way to learn more about God's universe. (The *Apollo 8* astronauts read Bible verses to the world on Christmas Eve while orbiting the Moon.)

Convinced that reaching Mars is blasphemous, Merritt attempts to sabotage the landing, and once they land, tries to drain all the mission's water to ensure the crew will die, defending himself by brandishing a gun and threatening to shoot anyone who interferes with him. When his son attempts to stop him, the gun accidentally fires and Merritt is killed. Mahoney, too blindly loyal to his mentor to properly interpret what he sees, insists that the younger Merritt deliberately murdered his father and promises to have him court-martialed upon their return to Earth. Ongoing tension between Mahoney and Merritt, who takes command of the mission, is not the only thing making the crew's lengthy sojourn on Mars an ordeal: Merritt's actions force them to survive on severely rationed water during the months they must wait until Mars reaches the proper position for an expeditious return flight. Observing the deaths of two crewmen and subsequent misery of survivors, one might detect bitter irony in the film's title: instead of conquering space, it seems, these men are being conquered *by* space.

Eventually, however, they receive good news: On Christmas Day, a threadbare celebration is energized when they see snow falling around them, a white Christmas that provides ample water for the rest of their stay. This unexpected Christmas present could have been presented as a rebuttal to Merritt's fears of divine punishment for landing on Mars, as God's way to bless this mission and demonstrate His approval, but no one makes this point, which might have softened the film's apparent condemnation of Christianity. Later, as the crew prepares to depart, there is another uplifting moment when Imoto, who planted a seed when they arrived, sees it has sprouted, a sign that crops can grow on Mars and sustain a population of colonists. Still, though discovering vast new areas for agriculture might fall into the category of obtaining new "resources," Imoto's rationale for the mission, the film puzzlingly makes no reference to efforts to seek the sorts of mineral resources that usually motivate space travelers. Perhaps, borrowing from *Frau im Mond*, filmmakers might have had the crew find gold or, given the era's fascination with atomic energy, listen to Geiger counter beeps revealing deposits of uranium, both of which would be more consistent with the stated goal of obtaining new resources.

Finally, to tie up the plot's loose threads, Mahoney reconciles with Merritt by offering him a deal: If all crewmen join in providing a false story about how General Merritt heroically died to save them during their difficult landing, thus preserving his reputation, he will abandon efforts to have Barney Merritt court-martialed. The problem with this "happy ending" is that the people planning future space missions need accurate information about what transpired during this flight, to properly anticipate and deal with the probability of mental instability in space. Incorrectly believing that nothing went amiss during humanity's first flight to Mars, officials might launch another mission with a pressured commander on the brink of a nervous breakdown who, without precautions in place to hinder him, might cause more tragedy.

Overall, it seems appropriate that *Conquest of Space* temporarily ends the American tradition of spacesuit films, since it offers this presumably unintended message: Space travel represents an enormous challenge that many people are not ready to face. More so than preceding spacesuit films, it depicts space as a realm of menaces and madness, and its inability to craft even a minimally appealing story out of its premise, in the manner of *Destination Moon* and *Riders to the Stars*, further suggests that space is a genuinely alien environment which defies conventional expectations. If critics are not entertained by this film, it is unfortunate that they respond by dismissing it instead of exploring the unsettling reasons why they are not entertained. But this represents precisely the sort of failure of imagination observed before, and to be observed again, in analyzing the history of spacesuit films.

Disneyland: "Man and the Moon" (1955)

As documentary-style films about near-future space travel appeared, unsurprisingly there were also actual documentaries, drawing upon the best available scientific expertise to describe the probable future of humanity in space. Some early examples include three episodes of the series *Disneyland*: "Man in Space" (aired March 9, 1955), "Man and the Moon" (aired December 28, 1955), and "Mars and Beyond" (aired December 4, 1957). Generally, documentaries fall outside the scope of this study, and the first and third of these relied solely on animation to depict the spacecraft and space travelers of tomorrow. However, "Man and the Moon" merits attention. Its first segment is merely a historical survey of how the Moon figures in human history and folklore, illustrated by crude animation, and its second segment is a lecture by scientist Wernher von Braun about how humans would someday construct a space station as a base to explore the Moon. However, its third segment employs live actors and special effects to describe the first orbital flight around the Moon, effectively making it a short narrative film about space travel that is comparable to other spacesuit films, in both the quality of its effects and the flat acting style of the four actors

(Frank Gerstle, Richard Emory, Frank Connor, and Leo Needham) who portray the spaceship's crew. It also breaks new ground in the tradition of spacesuit films.

The groundwork for the narrative is provided by von Braun's discussion of the new type of spacesuit needed to assemble a station in Earth orbit. It resembles a huge white top, with a crystal globe on top for an astronaut's head (to provide visibility), and seven mechanical arms around its sides which astronauts manipulate to perform operations in space. While this device (more like a small spaceship than a spacesuit) figures in the story, astronauts also wear normal spacesuits and space helmets when their flight takes off from the station. They remove the helmets once the engines stop firing.

As their long flight to the Moon proceeds, astronauts relax by reading, eating, and playing cards, and while they themselves do not float around in weightlessness while strapped in their chairs, a few objects float around them. This moment of calm is interrupted by the obligatory crisis: Emergency lights come on and alarms sound when a fuel tank is struck by a tiny meteor (about one-sixteenth of an inch in diameter). To repair the leak, one crewman gets inside the new spacesuit, moves it into position, and uses a mechanical arm to stick a specially prepared patch into the breached hull, sealing the leak. No further problems disrupt the flight, though there is an interesting moment near the end when the spaceship turns itself around to use rockets to slow down for the approach to the station. Now we see all astronauts upside down in their cabin, carrying on with their business, reminding us there is no "up" or "down" in the weightlessness of space.

The flight's most stunning development comes when it flies around the Moon and crewmen observe its dark side for the first time in human history. They first spot an enormous crater, so deep that its depth cannot be determined by their "contour mapper." Then, after high levels of radioactivity are detected in one area, an astronaut notes the mapper's detection of a "very unusual formation" in its vicinity, and a flare is launched at the dark surface to observe the phenomenon more clearly. When the flare lands, we see, etched on the surface of the Moon, what looks like an enormous drawing of a human-like figure, its head surrounded by a circle suggesting a space helmet, with one hand extended outward and holding a large box of some kind. Alternatively, one might interpret the markings as the ruins of a settlement, as also suggested by unusually circular rings in its vicinity. No comments are made about this discovery, but this is manifestly the work of intelligent beings. If intended as an image, writers may have recalled the large stick drawings on the plateaus of Nazca, Peru, visible only from the air. Since the moon has no atmosphere, the image, or ruins, could also be extremely ancient, though the deep crater might represent the entrance to an underground realm where intelligent aliens could be living today.

Previously, unlike frivolous films that introduced human-like aliens and horrible monsters, spacesuit films avoided all mention of the possibility of intelligent life in space. In broaching this subject for the first time in a spacesuit film, however, the documentary remains within the realm of plausibility; for while it is extraordinarily unlikely that humans in the near future will encounter living aliens, we might find evidence of their existence in the form of fossils, artifacts, or radio transmissions. And "Man in the Moon," to my knowledge, is the first film involving this sort of alien encounter, distinguished by an elusiveness and air of mystery that properly reflects the challenging novelty of space.

What the men observe naturally provokes interesting questions. If it is a figure of some kind, the fact that it was constructed on the dark side of the Moon suggests it was intended for visitors from other planets, not observers on Earth. And since its builders were clearly intelligent and capable of deducing conditions of Earth, this might indicate that lunar inhabitants have a physiology vastly different than that of Earth's inhabitants — so different as to make it impossible for them to imagine Earth might become the abode of life. As another theory, the image or ruins may date from billions of years ago, when the Moon had not yet settled into its present-day orbit and builders had no way of knowing which direction it would someday face; and in such ancient times, the Moon might have had an atmosphere and Earth might have been a molten cauldron, which could also explain why it faces away from Earth. One has no idea how deeply writers thought about these matters when they had astronauts make this discovery, but it is proper for spacesuit films to inspire weighty ruminations without providing definitive answers.

Granted, the entire incident is only a brief moment that is never spoken about, so it will be left for the series *Men into Space* to delve more deeply into the question of how human space travelers might detect and respond to signs of alien life in the universe. Still, that enigmatic image on the Moon earns "Man and the Moon" a prominent place in the history of spacesuit films.

Satellite in the Sky (1956)

Pondering the failure of *Conquest of Space*, producers might conclude that straightforward stories of spacesuited astronauts, struggling to survive in the harsh environment of space, were insufficiently exciting, so something more dramatic was needed. If not quite ready to introduce aliens or monsters, and abandon any pretense of realism, they might devise adventures involving threats not only to the lives of space travelers, but the lives of everyone on Earth. Such hypothetical reasoning might have inspired the British film *Satellite in the Sky*, which represents a hybrid of sorts: not silly enough to be a pseudo-spacesuit film, yet founded on such scientifically shaky premises as to distinguish itself from other, more plausible spacesuit films.

As one questionable aspect, *Satellite in the Sky* describes plans to enter space not with a spaceship, but rather an advanced airplane, launched from an underground chamber on a slanted ramp to gradually rise 1000 miles above Earth. For *faux* authenticity, producers turned to British aircraft manufacturers Folland Aircraft Co. and A.V. Roe, Ltd., thanked in the credits for the models they employed. Yet this approach had already been rejected by scientists in the 1950s, who universally envisioned the vertically launched spaceships observed in other films. It is especially difficult to imagine this film's large, spacious craft, which accommodates a crew of six with ample room to spare, being lifted into orbit by this method.

The purported reasons behind this flight are explained schematically (in a manner recalling *Spaceways*) by two characters: a supporter, Commander Michael Haydon (Kieron Moore), and a skeptical opponent, reporter Kim Hamilton (Lois Maxwell). While Project Stardust is announced as a "purely scientific venture," Haydon expands upon the point: After the mission, he says, man will "know a little more, be a little less ignorant, about the universe and our place in it."

Yet Hamilton, noting two men already died in experimental flights preparing for the mission, describes the project as "completely unnecessary" and "suicidal." When Haydon reiterates the theme of garnering knowledge ("Someday men are going to explore the universe"), she asks, "What are you going to find up there that's worth so much?"

"Perhaps a new world," he answers, additionally suggesting the possibility of someday colonizing space.

Later, while showing her the spaceship, Haydon tests another argument: "We're just doing something that's never been done before," presumably worth doing for that reason.

Her immediate riposte is, "Is there any point in trying to do something just because it's never been done before?"

Getting testy now, Haydon answers, "You want to stand still and the world can't and doesn't"; scientific advances of this kind, by this argument, are inevitable. In this conversation, three purposes for the flight are articulated: gaining scientific knowledge; possibly finding new homes for humanity; and taking the next inescapable step in humanity's steady progress. That space travel is a matter of destiny is also suggested by a quotation from Nostradamus opening the film:

> And man
> Having conquered the Earth
> Shall rise into the skies....
> And reach the stars.

One thinks the film would seek to validate Haydon's position, but further doubts about the project are soon expressed, strangely, by one of its leaders: When the spacecraft takes off, and someone calls this event "the first step into space," the official muses, "Here

A Bomb Too Far: Observed by crewmates Larry Noble (Jimmy Hanley) and Professor Merrity (Donald Wolfit), Commander Michael Haydon (Kieron Moore) suits up to go into space to deal with a problematic bomb that is defying the laws of physics in *Satellite in the Sky* (1956).

we are, dashing out in space ... before we've even thought about the problems we might have to meet." Like characters in *Spaceways*, he seems reluctant, even fearful, to send humans into space, which might reflect a characteristically British sense of caution. (It does not increase one's confidence in the project that the office where this exchange occurs has a globe decorated with images of zodiac signs — mythological people and animals — instead of stars.)

Even more strangely, we eventually learn that, unbeknownst to Haydon and his crew, advancing scientific knowledge and human progress are not the actual reasons for the flight. Rather, its true purpose involves scientific gobbledygook right out of the Saturday afternoon serials: a new sort of amazingly powerful atomic bomb, fueled by the element Tritonium, will be taken into orbit by Haydon's spacecraft and detonated in space, to demonstrate the futility of war and achieve world peace. The obvious notion that other nations might regard Britain's explosion of a devastating new weapon as more threatening than salutary, astonishingly, occurs only to Hamilton, who upon hearing about the bomb sarcastically comments, "You used to think of the first space travelers landing on planets and planting flags.... Now, I suppose the first thing they do is explode an atomic bomb."

During the long lead-up to the flight (which occupies about two-thirds of the film), we also revisit another theme of *Spaceways*, that dedication to space travel might be harmful to one's marriage. Barbara Noble (Thea Gregory), wife of Haydon's assistant Larry (Jimmy Hanley), is distressed because his work constantly takes him away from her side; when he cannot accompany her to a party the night before the flight (because he is summoned to the base to learn about the bomb), she attends the party herself and flirts with another man (though she repents and recommits herself to her husband upon learning his life is imperiled). Granted, the notion that astronauts' wives might stray is not entirely absent from American films, since we observe an unfaithful girlfriend in *Conquest of Space* and encounter wives attracted to other men in *Destination Space* and the soap opera *The Clear Horizon*; but the general tendency, seen in *Riders to the Stars* and later films like *Countdown*, is to assume that wives and girlfriends are staunchly supportive. In contrast, British films are inclined to suggest that such wives will feel neglected and seek other male companions.

As another implausible development during flight preparations, Hamilton, after repeatedly criticizing the mission as pointless, for some reason decides to sneak on board the space plane. One might celebrate her courage in seeking to obtain a valuable scoop and become an astronaut, but her status as a liberated woman is compromised when, after being discovered, she assumes her proper, womanly position by serving coffee to male crew members. Further, both her dislike for space travel, and perverse resolve to engage in space travel, are eventually explained in a condescending manner: Her father died in an explosion while testing potential rocket fuels, and her brother died in an experimental flight aimed at achieving space flight. This simultaneously accounts for her opposition to the flight and determination to participate in the flight: She is bitter about the deaths of her father and brother but nevertheless is subconsciously driven to become a space traveler because, as Haydon notes, "it's in your blood."

As a final bit of silliness, because the bomb requires capable supervision to be "primed" and prepared for detonation, a scientist, Professor Merrity (Donald Wolfit), joins the crew at the last minute. (Bizarrely, the cover story is that he is being added as a "meteorologist," though such expertise would be useless 1000 miles above Earth, far away from the atmosphere.) Since he is not trained for space travel, this predictably leads to difficulties, as Merrity complains about the stress of liftoff, is constantly disagreeable and, when fearing death, panics and attempts to land the spaceship all by himself. While again suggesting space might drive people mad, this also conveys a theme that comes up elsewhere in spacesuit films, notably in *Men into Space*, that space travel is a difficult business best left to military men, since civilians will likely run into or cause problems (though the other untrained civilian on the flight, Hamilton, remains calm throughout the crisis).

Once the crew achieves orbit, there is a brief acknowledgment of the airlessness of space when Hamilton holds up an oxygen mask and asks, "Will we need these masks?" and Haydon replies "No," because the spacecraft is "completely pressurized." Otherwise, only dubious science is on display. We observe no effects of zero gravity because, "to maintain gravity inside the ship," Haydon says a crewmate must "set two jets firing" every five minutes or so, though how such intermittent force would function to simulate constant Earth gravity is not explained. Then Merrity begins to prime the bomb to explode in nine hours and supervises the process of moving it outside and setting off its rockets so it flies a safe distance away from the spacecraft before exploding. Unfortunately, the rockets fail and the bomb drifts back to the spacecraft. To dislodge it, Haydon dons a spacesuit and goes outside to push it away, but it again moves back and sticks to the craft's hull. The incredible explanation is that, since there is no gravity in space, the "mutual magnetic attraction of two metal objects" makes the bomb keep returning, and since its rockets do not work, nothing can be done to keep it away before it explodes.

Since science fiction writer J.T. McIntosh was one screenwriter, one wonders how this scientific nonsense found its way into the script. First, metal objects are not naturally magnetic, so there is no reason to suppose that two metal objects in space would be magnetically attracted to each other; in addition, since the gravitational pull of a spaceship is minuscule, any object pushed away from it would not drift back but continue on its path indefinitely unless deflected by some other force or object. This is the problem facing the astronaut in *Destination Moon* who lost contact with his spaceship and would have drifted away forever if colleagues had not retrieved him. Thus, even with malfunctioning rockets, the bomb would keep moving away from the spacecraft.

The problem now is that the spacecraft cannot land with a deadly bomb in tow, and since the bomb cannot be dislodged or disarmed, the crew seems destined to continue orbiting Earth until the bomb explodes and kills them all. It is briefly suggested that their deaths could be averted by last-minute American assistance, in the form of an experimental plane that might rescue the crew, but the possibility is soon forgotten. Instead, the space travelers are saved solely because Merrity, apologetic after his moment of panic, decides to redeem himself at the cost of his life. He gets another crewman who is distraught about the recent death of his wife, "Lefty" Blake (Barry Keegan), to join him in donning spacesuits to go outside the spacecraft, grab the bomb, and use propulsion units on the backs of their spacesuits to fly away with it, allowing the other crew members to return to Earth while they remain in space until being killed by the bomb's explosion (the film's final image). A more enterprising crew, one imagines, would strap two unused spacesuits to the bomb and turn on propulsion units so the bomb could be driven away without loss of life. Such improvisations are standard in American spacesuit films, but they are seemingly beyond the ability of the British, who before the professor's heroism simply sit in their spacecraft, passively waiting to die.

Still, one must praise *Satellite in the Sky* for excellently rendered scenes of the spacecraft in orbit against a deep blue, but not black, backdrop of stars. The three astronauts who emerge from the craft to deal with the bomb are generally observed from a great distance, so their small size makes a statement about humanity's weakness and frailty in contrast to the enormity of space. These images compensate for the spacious familiarity of the spacecraft's interior, an ideal place to sip coffee and discuss one's personal history.

All things considered, while less insulting to British pride than *Spaceways*, *Satellite in the Sky* is also the story of a British space mission that fails, due to a problem in its design, and its happy ending is only that most crew members come back alive. Cynics might note that the film further suggests that the British lack not only the engineering skill, but the basic scientific knowledge, needed for successful space flights. Thus, it seems appropriate that the next time we observe a British space program is in the American series *Men into Space*, where the British, as in *Spaceways*, must rely on expert American assistance to deal with problematic situations.

Destination Space (1959)

The launch of Sputnik in 1957, and subsequent Russian and American space initiatives, sparked renewed interest in space travel and new space films; however, perhaps recalling the failure of *Conquest of Space*, major studios did not make them. Instead, smaller companies produced, for the most part, space films that were exploitative and silly, and the tradition of American spacesuit films continued, briefly, only on television.

Based on available evidence, this is my theory as to how the pilot film *Destination Space* and series *Men into Space* came into being. Some time in 1958, CBS let it be known they wanted to air a serious, realistic series about space travel; two studios — Paramount Pictures and United Artists — responded by producing pilots. The Paramount effort was rejected and its pilot *Destination Space* was shelved and forgotten before being dusted off for DVD release; the United Artists effort was accepted and engendered the series *Men into Space*. Support for the theory comes from the fact that the credits for *Destination Space* identify it as a joint production of Paramount and CBS — verifying it was a pilot for a CBS series, though there is otherwise virtually no information available about this film.

In creating a series about space travel, Paramount clearly sought to build on existing tradition of spacesuit films. To produce the pilot and write the screenplay, they recruited a co-author of *Destination Moon*'s screenplay, Rip Van Ronkel, who possibly developed the pilot's similar title, and re-used footage of a space station and spaceship from their own *Conquest of Space*. Both decisions, however, were unwise; Van Ronkel had no experience in writing science fiction other than *Destination Moon*, and his *Destination Space* teleplay was, to say the least, unimaginative. Using footage from *Conquest of Space* required the series to begin at a relatively late stage in the process of conquering space, with a space station already constructed and routine travel to and from Earth orbit already a reality. Thus, the series could not address earlier stages in the conquest of space — like the first human flight into space and construction of the first space station — that were depicted in *Men into Space*. Further, there were visible differences between old footage from *Conquest of Space* and new footage for the pilot, especially when station head James Benedict (Harry Townes) and observer Kurt Easton (Edward Platt) are about to jump from their spaceship to the station: It is painfully apparent that their spacesuits, and those worn in *Conquest of Space*, are dissimilar in design.

However, the main reason why *Destination Space* was rejected, while *Men into Space* was accepted, is most likely that the pilot for *Men into Space* depicts an actual accomplishment in space, whereas *Destination Space* is a long story in which nothing really happens.

With a plot apparently constructed to maximize the recycling of footage from *Conquest of Space*, the film depicts people in an orbiting space station supervising the launch of the first spaceship to orbit the Moon — to use *Conquest of Space* footage of a huge wheel in the sky next to a spaceship. The first attempt to launch the flight is aborted when a meteor hits the station — to use *Conquest of Space* footage showing the station disrupted by electrical problems. And men later return to the station for a second launch attempt — to use *Conquest of Space* footage of astronauts floating from a spaceship to the station. These conspicuous cost-cutting measures may have contributed to CBS's displeasure with this pilot.

After the first failure, there is a long interlude when Benedict is summoned to Earth to face a Senate committee and answer hostile questions from a Senator who is not opposed to space travel, but believes flights could be carried out more cheaply and efficiently without the expensive station (nicknamed "Benedict's Billions" because of its huge cost). The Senator's argument is that, if the lunar flight had not been so dependent upon the station, it could have successfully launched despite problems caused by the meteors. In response, Benedict defends the station as a facility serving multiple purposes, including weather forecasting, astronomical observations, radio and television relaying, and numerous military uses such as global reconnaissance. He concludes with a passionate speech calling upon America to maintain a vigorous space program: "Let us go forward in the American way, pioneering new frontiers without fear, taking pride in accomplishment, yet facing dangers and disappointments with resoluteness, and without qualms and complaints." (Incidentally, this speech, written and filmed two years before President John F. Kennedy spoke in support of the space program, may represent the first time space was described as a "new frontier," albeit obliquely, though since the pilot never aired, it could not have influenced Kennedy.) A reference to the "enemy," recalling a previous comment from Benedict's assistant Colonel Matthews (John Agar) to the effect that critics from Earth "couldn't help the enemy more if they were paid agents," fleetingly conveys that, as in *Destination Moon*, the Moon mission is a major priority because of Cold War politics making an American military presence in space vital to national security.

Another complication in Benedict's life emerges during his trip on Earth: He has dinner with his patient girlfriend Jane Kramer (Whitney Blake) and Kim Reynolds (Gail Kobe), wife of spaceship commander Dave Reynolds (Charles Aidman), and Reynolds fumes at Benedict ostensibly because his obsession with space travel keeps her husband away from her. However, as Benedict prepares to return to space, Reynolds reveals that she actually loves Benedict and is upset because he does not respond to her affections. This odd subplot of a romantic triangle involving a potentially adulterous wife, middle-aged bachelor, and his girlfriend contrasts to the relentless domesticity of *Men into Space*, which may have made that series more reassuring to CBS than *Destination Space*. Also, despite the film's purported focus on space travel, these dull scenes on Earth occupy most of the running time, perhaps due to budgetary limitations, yet another reason why CBS may have found this pilot unexciting.

The Senate agrees to keep the station in operation, but dispatches Easton to accompany Benedict to observe what occurs on the station and report back to Earth. Initially skeptical, he becomes convinced of the space station's value. To provide final drama, the next effort to launch the lunar flight is threatened when its nuclear-powered engine malfunctions, almost leading to an atomic explosion before Reynolds can break away the ice that formed on one component, the cause of the problem. This is the only scene that conveys the strangeness of space, albeit slightly, since Reynolds's rescue mission requires Benedict to depressurize the station, forcing the crew to don spacesuits, and since the approach to the dangerous component shows crewmen floating in the weightlessness of the spaceship. (As in *Conquest of Space*, all scenes on the station, without explanation, show people experiencing normal gravity.) Also, as Reynolds goes through the tube leading to the component, he is filmed from two directions, so he sometimes appears to be rising and sometimes appears to be descending, demonstrating that space offers no real "up" or "down." After the credits, some final footage from *Conquest of Space* shows a spaceship actually being launched, undoubtedly to provide an upbeat ending indicating that eventually, if not now, the Moon mission would succeed.

If accepted as a series, the story of *Destination Space* would presumably have continued along the usual lines envisioned by science fiction, with a successful flight around the Moon following by other missions like a lunar landing and construction of a moon base (both goals mentioned by Benedict), with regular encounters with hostile politicians and/or romantic intrigues on Earth. But along with its obdurate uneventfulness, the pilot reveals several flaws in plans for the series. First, by accepting the convention that space travel would necessarily be an all-male activity, the series could only depict women in occasional scenes of visits to Earth — unlike *Project Moon Base*, which kept things entertaining in part with a woman as part of the mission, and *Men into Space*, which despite its title eventually brought two women into space. Also, while both projected series embraced the logic of *Riders to the Stars* by depicting space travel as a collaboration between astronauts and monitors who stayed behind to inform and guide astronauts, *Men into Space*, following the pattern in *Riders to the Stars*, employs an astronaut as its protagonist, only occasionally relegating him to the role of ground-based advisor, so monitors facing no dangers are secondary characters. However, *Destination Space* made sedentary administrator Benedict the protagonist, with astronauts as infrequently observed supporting players, setting up a pattern wherein episodes would primarily involve people in a space station or on Earth communicating with the men actually conquering space. For that reason alone, *Men into Space* might have seemed the more attractive option.

Finally, the role of John Agar is puzzling. Though easily the best-known member of the cast, as Shirley Temple's ex-husband and hero of several minor films, his character Colonel Matthews has few lines and nothing to do. He sits next to Benedict in space station scenes, ostensibly as his assistant, but contributes nothing to the story and does not accompany Benedict to Earth. Was the character added to the script at the last minute to work a star — of sorts — into its cast? Or was Agar belatedly inserted as a potential replacement for Townes (an actor generally noted for portraying frail, nervous characters), who might not appeal to CBS executives?

Still, for all its flaws and foibles, *Destination Space* makes two significant contributions to the dialogue concerning humanity's future in space in spacesuit films of the 1950s. First, while the decision to depict a planned flight to the Moon twice delayed by problems — a meteor and a mechanical problem — seems a dramatic weakness, it conveys that space travel may prove more difficult than was the case in previous films, where problems did not require postponing or abandoning missions. Second, while previous films with a space station — *Project Moon Base* and *Conquest of Space*— implicitly presented the facilities as useful and necessary, *Destination Space* foregrounds the question of whether a station would be essential, especially in light of the show's realistic estimate of how much it would cost, and explicitly defends its utility. The debate interestingly, and perhaps un-coincidentally, occurred at a time when American officials and engineers were pondering how the space program should proceed, and one focus of ruminations was whether, or when, to build a space station. In the end, Kennedy rejected the option of a space station as insufficiently dramatic and committed American energies to landing humans on the Moon. But by making a space station a matter of public debate, *Destination Space* represents the first sign that such a decision might be made, contradicting previous predictions that space stations would be inevitable elements in the conquest of space.

Men into Space (1959–1960)

Though *Men into Space*, like most series of its era, was produced quickly and cheaply, it is nonetheless the culminating epic of the spacesuit film's first decade, as its thirty-eight episodes constitute a sixteen-hour film which recapitulates its predecessors, fills in gaps in the story of humanity's conquest of space, and moves in significant new directions.[5]

Specifically, the series first stresses, with unprecedented thoroughness, a key point in all spacesuit films — that space travel is possible — addressing not only the basic question of flights to another world but also delving into specific problems that space travelers must confront and overcome, ranging from refueling a spaceship in flight to transporting sick personnel. The series also emphasizes the theme of *Riders to the Stars* that space flights will necessarily be collaborative efforts requiring both astronauts in space and advisors on Earth, though it only briefly comments on the high costs of ventures into space. Recalling past films, episodes illustrate the dangers of space travel, while touching upon the strangeness of this new environment and the joys of experiencing it. There are recurring suggestions that life in space will be stressful, perhaps even maddening, while more forcefully than before, the series indicates that space travel will drive participants toward traditional domesticity, back to the values and lifestyles of the past. With lingering references to terrestrial conflicts, *Men into Space* generally presents future space travel as an international enterprise, focusing on scientific research. Most significantly, *Men into Space*, for the first time in genuine spacesuit films, thoroughly explores how humans in space might realistically encounter alien life — or at least evidence of its existence. Rarely eloquent or dramatically involving in a conventional fashion, this stolid program nonetheless is a work which, as Brian W. Aldiss said of Daniel Defoe's *Robinson Crusoe*, "lumbers to real greatness" (*Billion Year Spree* 71).

While previous spacesuit films dealt exclusively with one pioneering achievement in space, the extended and episodic nature of television allows *Men into Space* to also portray the numerous small steps that would necessarily precede and follow such breakthroughs. It recognizes that long-term success in space travel demands continual improvements which must be tested, while realizing that occasional crises would bring to light minor problems requiring quick, improvised fixes as a prelude to permanent solutions. In other words, *Men into Space* suggests the full array of issues that must be resolved during humanity's conquest of space and optimistically conveys that challenges can be met through the efforts of innovative researchers and stalwart astronauts like Colonel Edward McCauley (William Lundigan, no doubt chosen because of his capable performance in *Riders to the Stars*), and various colleagues.

The first episode, "Moon Probe" (aired September 30, 1959), addresses a basic question — how to accomplish a flight to the Moon — and correctly posits that this would require a multi-stage rocket, with bolts to detach each stage when its fuel was exhausted and it was no longer needed. In contrast to the improbably spacious spacecraft of previous films, this episode, and later episodes, show space vehicles that are small and cramped, similar to the space capsules developed for the Mercury, Gemini, and Apollo programs, a necessary concession to the need to reduce the weight of crafts that are boosted into space. Next, though *Project Moon Base*, *Conquest of Space*, and *Destination Space* display completed space stations, "Building a Space Station" (aired October 21, 1959) innovatively addresses the question of how such a large facility might be assembled: by first launching pieces of the structure into orbit, then having astronauts employ tools to lock them together, roughly predicting the actual techniques employed to construct the current space station. The potential need for creative metallurgy comes up in "Burnout" (aired December 9, 1959), wherein McCauley helps to test a new alloy designed to allow spaceships to safely re-enter Earth's atmosphere at a steeper angle and land with more accuracy. "Tankers in Space" (aired January 6, 1960) has McCauley conduct an experiment to perfect a technique that will someday be necessary — refueling a spacecraft while in flight. When the bending hose they use causes a crisis, McCauley concludes that an inflexible hose would be better. "Into the Sun" (aired August 24, 1960) tests a proposed method for disposing of nuclear wastes: by hurling them into the Sun. And "The Sun Never Sets" (aired August 31, 1960) takes McCauley to Britain to observe and contribute to its test of a new, more powerful rocket which, if used as a spaceship's second stage, would enable space explorers to reach remote destinations like Venus or Mars.

Improvised answers to pressing crises first appear in "Water Tank Rescue" (aired October 28, 1959), addressing the question of how to safely transport frail personnel who cannot withstand the stress of acceleration during liftoff. When a crewman has a heart attack on the Moon, McCauley realizes that the pressures of the return trip launch will kill him. An expert on Earth suggests a possible solution, based upon an idea previously observed in *Kosmicheskiy Reys*: If the victim could be immersed in water during liftoff, it might provide sufficient protection against the force of acceleration. Using a water-filled enclosure jerry-built from two storage tanks, McCauley brings the man safely home. Another issue — the need for emergency shelters to protect endangered people on the Moon — comes up in "Moon Trap" (aired June 1, 1960), when three astronauts crash-land on the Moon. Though one man dies, another implements a plan to take a cached oxygen tank into a cave, seal the cave, and release the oxygen to create a temporary shelter with breathable air until they can be rescued by McCauley.

Episodes of *Men into Space* also present a solution to a problem evident since *Destination Moon*— that all people in spacesuits look identical. While a concern for filmmakers, who want audiences to know which character is which, this could also cause confusion among astronauts themselves, who might sometimes need to immediately recognize particular colleagues. The way the issue was addressed in *Destination Moon*— placing characters in spacesuits of different colors — was not possible in the black-and-white *Men into Space*, and in any event was not a long-term solution when there might someday be dozens of astronauts on the Moon who could not all be clad in different hues. The series instead developed the convention that astronauts' helmets have their names printed in large capital letters above their faceplates; thus, one always identify McCauley because the top of his helmet reads MCCAULEY. Even the issue of two different astronauts with the same surname arises in "First Woman on the Moon" (aired December 16, 1959), where a married couple is on the Moon; as the solution, the wife's helmet reads MRS. HALE.

Contributing to the series' overall aura of authenticity were the various agencies and experts listed in each episode's closing credits. *Men into Space* always acknowledged the

Department of Defense, United States Air Force, Air Research and Development Command, Office of the Surgeon General, and School of Aviation Medicine, and specifies that spacesuits were provided by the United States Navy. To ensure that the spaceships and lunar landscapes looked realistic, the series employed space artist Chesley Bonestell, who drew upon his experiences working for *Destination Moon, Cat-Women of the Moon,* and *Conquest for Space* to provide "Space Concepts." Listed as technical advisors for different episodes were USAF Colonel Frank P. Ball, Air Force Major Charles A. Berry from the Office of the Surgeon General, and Lawrence D. Ely of the Air Force Ballistic Missile Division.

Even in "Moon Probe," *Men into Space* emphasizes that successful space travel would always involve two teams, astronauts in space and experts on Earth; for when McCauley is lost in space, crewmates must rely upon information relayed from Earth to locate and retrieve him. However, unlike *Destination Space*, this series makes the people who are actually in space its center of attention. Though the episodes "Lost Missile" (aired November 4, 1959), "Burnout," "Emergency Mission" (aired May 4, 1960), and "The Sun Never Sets" initially show McCauley playing the role of earthbound observer, a crisis leads him to travel into space to resolve a problem. Both "Lost Missile" and "Asteroid" (aired November 25, 1959) also show a spacefaring McCauley receiving advice from Earth, though of minimal utility: A monitor on Earth flips a coin in "Lost Missile" to help McCauley make a decision, while a general in "Asteroid" issues an order which McCauley ignores.

The series only pays minimal attention to the issue that dominates *Destination Space*—the anticipated expense of space travel—since the subject only comes up in "Asteroid," when an official planning McCauley's trip to an approaching asteroid comments that using it as "a building site for a space station" would "save a real bundle," suggesting that constructing Space Station Astra proved rather expensive.

Men into Space also provides a thoroughgoing survey of various dangers associated with space travel, some previously observed, others never considered previously. Several episodes involve accidents in space that might threaten the lives of space travelers in two familiar ways: instant death due to exposure to the vacuum of space, or gradual death due to insufficient oxygen. As indicated, "Moon Probe" essentially replicates the scenario of the spacewalk sequence in *Destination Moon*: After McCauley ventures outside his spacecraft to detach the second stage of the rocket, he is sent careening into the cosmos by a freed bolt. While crewmates in *Destination Moon* quickly retrieve their colleague, the solitary McCauley drifts for a considerable period of time, with the real chance he will not be rescued until he runs out of oxygen. Men from his spaceship, aided by international observers on the ground, maneuver into his vicinity and toss him a rope to be pulled into the spaceship. An entire spaceship faces the same peril in "Emergency Mission," when a mechanical problem sends a ship racing into deep space, dooming its crew. McCauley employs an experimental ship that allows him to overtake the runaway spaceship and rescue its crew.

The deadly possibility of exposure to a vacuum, which kills space travelers in *Project Moon Base, Riders to the Stars,* and *Conquest of Space*, arises in "Building a Space Station" when a man assembling the station gets his sleeve caught between two sections as they are joined and McCauley fears that his suit is punctured, so he would die instantly should the pieces be taken apart to free him. McCauley uses a risky maneuver to clamp the suit while he cuts the man free from the station and returns him to the spaceship. In "Space Trap" (aired November 18, 1959), a piece of spacecraft equipment malfunctions, causing a buildup of carbon dioxide which renders crewmen unconscious, so McCauley must rendezvous with the ship to pump in oxygen. "Edge of Eternity" (aired December 2, 1959) features a familiar problem in spacesuit films, a meteor, which strikes McCauley's spaceship and releases most of its oxygen. Improbably, McCauley extracts oxygen, in both liquid and gaseous form, from the engine to obtain enough to survive. In "Christmas on the Moon" (aired December 23, 1959), a rain of meteors threatens McCauley, who constantly dodges them while crossing the lunar surface on a rescue mission. (Given the episode's emphasis on dangerous meteors, its director was interestingly Richard Carlson, the actor who memorably saw a crewmate killed by a meteor in *Riders to the Stars*.) As a unique variation on the pattern, an astronaut deliberately exposes himself to space and sacrifices his life in "A Handful of Hours" (aired January 20, 1960), since crewmates need the wrench inside his spacesuit to access needed oxygen in a tank.

Problems with faulty equipment are relatively common. In "Sea of Stars" (aired January 13, 1960), "Emergency Mission," "Into the Sun," and "The Sun Never Sets," space travelers are imperiled by malfunctioning rockets in their spacecraft, and as noted, "Space Trap" features a problem with the machinery that maintains a spaceship's oxygen supply. In addition, without explicitly making the point, two episodes convey that fundamental design flaws can create hazards. In "Lost Missile," the process of disabling the unmanned rocket that is about to explode is needlessly problematic, first of all, because of the device McCauley must employ to reduce the criticality of its nuclear engine: There is a wheel to turn, but it must be turned sometimes to the left and sometimes to the right. To determine the proper direction, one experimentally turns the wheel in one direction, observes a dial to see whether criticality is increasing or decreasing, and concludes which direction is correct. Unbelievably, as another error in design, the dial is bizarrely placed in a position where the wheel turner *cannot see it*, which means that two men are needed to complete the task (one to watch the dial, the other to turn the wheel); thus, when the second man faints, McCauley must randomly guess the direction. In "A Handful of Hours," astronauts stranded on the Moon appear safe because they have a spare canister of oxygen to keep them alive until they can reach a safe haven; but they cannot access the oxygen without a wrench, so as noted a man must sacrifice his life to provide one.

Other episodes focus on more novel dangers in space and occasionally seem eerily prophetic. In "Sea of Stars," a wayward satellite is on a collision course with Space Station Astra, prompts McCauley and his crew to send out a spacecraft to destroy it. Today, increasing amounts of space debris in Earth orbit are recognized as an ongoing danger to the space station; though there have been no catastrophic collisions, on several occasions the station engaged in evasive maneuvers. In "The Sun Never Sets," a malfunctioning experimental rocket causes a spaceship to start tumbling uncontrollably, requiring McCauley and another astronaut to make a tricky rendezvous with the spacecraft to rescue its helpless crew. Precisely such a problem occurred during the *Gemini 8* flight, though commander Armstrong corrected it without outside assistance. An out-of-control rocket also causes Space Station Astra to begin spinning too fast, threatening to destroy the station, in "Voice of Infinity" (aired April 20, 1960). In "Mission to Mars" (aired May 25, 1960), a Russian spaceship to Mars veers off course and explodes, leaving its spacesuited crew clinging to life in their damaged craft until McCauley comes to their rescue. In real life, a similar explosion imperiled the *Apollo 13* astronauts, though they survived by entering the attached lunar module.

Some *Men into Space* dilemmas have not yet occurred in real life, but seem eminently possible. Positing there will be innumerable missions to the Moon involving large numbers of men and various exploratory expeditions, the series predicts several problems that might afflict astronauts walking across the Moon. (Neither this series, nor other spacesuit films of its era, anticipate that astronauts might bring wheeled vehicles to the Moon to drive around in.) As in *Frau im Mond*, a man falls into a lunar crevice in "Moonquake" (aired November 11, 1959); astronauts also fall into a deep hole in "Caves of the Moon" (aired February 3, 1960) and into a crater in "Moon Cloud" (aired February 17, 1960); in all cases, the man's spacesuit is not damaged by the fall so he can be rescued. "Quarantine" (aired December 30, 1959) features a man who gets seriously ill on Space Station Astra, prompting McCauley to place him in quarantine; as discussed in my *Islands in the Sky*, other science fiction stories depict the extreme threat of virulent illness in a space station. The emergency landing leading to the crisis in "A Handful of Hours" is provoked by a "solar electrical disturbance" that disrupts communication, an early recognition that powerful solar flares might become a hazard to space travel (though the radiation unleashed by a solar flare would not only affect radio broadcasts, but might actually endanger the lives of astronauts). The possibility of not having enough fuel to successfully lift off, which generates the final drama in *Destination Moon*, is a minor factor in "Moon Landing" (aired October 7, 1959), since astronauts also spend their last moments on the Moon frantically discarding excess equipment so their ship can safely launch. They achieve this goal without extraordinary effort; it is a greater worry in "Flight to the Red Planet" (aired September 14, 1960) when a fuel leak forces a premature departure from the Martian moon Phobos so liftoff can occur before too much fuel is gone. Concerns about having enough fuel did arise during the descent of *Apollo 11*: The landing was almost aborted because Armstrong came close to using too much fuel while searching for a suitable landing site.

Men into Space also repeatedly emphasizes, plausibly enough, that the stress of space travel might lead to medical emergencies, though this seems more of a threat to the presumably frail scientists who venture into space than stalwart military astronauts like McCauley. In "Moon Landing," the acceleration of liftoff causes the scientist on the first flight to the Moon to have a broken rib, leading to a punctured lung and his later death because he refuses to tell anyone about his condition, to avoid preventing a successful lunar landing. (The dying scientist tells his colleagues, "Leave me here," and they honor his wishes with a lunar burial, like the spy in *Project Moon Base*; thus, the first two men buried on the Moon were both civilians.) "Water Tank Rescue," as noted, depicts efforts to save a man who had a heart attack on the Moon. In "Lost Missile," the visibly delicate scientist helping McCauley prevent a rocket from exploding (Harry Townes, the visibly delicate protagonist of *Destination Space*) suddenly faints, forcing McCauley to guess the best way to stop the explosion. Whether it was provoked by the rigors of space travel is hard to say, but the crisis in "Christmas on the Moon" involves a scientist who develops appendicitis while visiting the Moon.

Finally, demonstrating that no prophets have perfect records, the series shows a few space hazards that seem highly unlikely, if not impossible. Despite worries about ubiquitous, dangerous meteors observed in other spacesuit films of the 1950s and the episodes "Edge of Eternity" and "Christmas on the Moon," we now know that the chances of dangerous collisions with meteors are extraordinarily small. The titular disaster in "Moonquake" appears impossible, since the Moon is not geologically active, though the impact of a large natural or artificial object might cause a similar upheaval. The crisis in "Earthbound" (aired January 27, 1960) involves a man who, like the boy in *Frau im Mond*, stows away on a spaceship, and his extra weight damages the ship's power system. But this has proven an implausible scenario because, with effective security measures logically implemented, and limited space on all spacecraft, no one ever stows away on actual space missions. In "Asteroid," an astronaut is blinded because he looks directly into the Sun without using his protective visor; however, while sunlight might appear more intense in a vacuum, it is unlikely to provoke temporary blindness. "Flash in the Sky" (aired April 6, 1960) actually involves two improbable crises: First, McCauley is trapped in lunar dust, requiring a crewmate to rescue him by using oxygen to blow away the dust; however, while many once posited that portions of the Moon might be covered by hazardous dust (provoking the drama of a buried lunar craft in Arthur C. Clarke's 1961 novel *A Fall of Moondust*), actual explorations of the Moon failed to detect signs of this problem. Later in the episode, an unmanned rocket orbiting Venus somehow picks up an electromagnetic charge from Venus's atmosphere, making it difficult for McCauley and a crewmate to approach the craft and retrieve its valuable data. If a probe did come near enough to Venus's atmosphere to pick up an electrical charge, the friction would surely make it decelerate and plunge to the surface.

While diligently thorough about various dangers of space travel, *Men into Space* was less energetic in depicting the strangeness of this new environment, or the sheer joy to be had from visiting it. As a convenient by-product of realistically cramped spacecraft, wherein astronauts were tightly strapped in chairs, the series avoids the problem of showing weightlessness within space vehicles. Even when astronauts are not confined, as in "Lost Missile" or episodes taking place on Space Station Astra, there is little effort to show them moving about any differently than they would on Earth. Only occasional scenes, in the episodes "Building a Space Station," "Tankers in Space," and "Flash in the Sky," feature astronauts floating in space. The most impressive of these sequences was probably the one in "Moon Probe," where the image of McCauley drifting helplessly through the void powerfully conveys how vast and threatening space could be. But only "The Sun Never Sets" makes the point conveyed by upside-down astronauts in *Destination Moon* and *Project Moon Base*—that there is no "up" and "down" in space—in scenes of astronauts madly spinning around in an out-of-control spacecraft. There are only sporadic efforts to convey the Moon's low gravity; at times, astronauts make jumps that would be impossible on Earth, but more frequently, they walk and act as they would here. Since depicting weightlessness or reduced weight requires special effort and concealed wires, cost-conscious producers may have deliberately kept such scenes to a minimum. For whatever reason, with few images of astronauts extravagantly cavorting in zero or low gravity, the series does little to convey that space travel would bring new freedom to humans, the main message of the leaps and bounds observed in *Kosmicheskiy Reys*. Perhaps, American astronauts are too focused on their duties to waste time with pointless calisthenics.

There are also, in the entire series, precisely two comments suggesting that space is an unusual place. In the opening scenes of "Asteroid," a woman asks McCauley, "What's it like out there in space?"

His first response—"It's cold and black"—is exactly the sort of dull, literal description one might expect from the stolid McCauley. Then, as if sensing that such a response is inadequate, he says more: "It's kind of hard to explain. It's something to be experienced, not described. I tell you one thing, though: No man can feel very important once he's been out there." McCauley thus indicates that there is something essentially indescribable, and very daunting, about the environment of space. And in "Beyond the Stars" (aired May 11, 1960), there is one unusual speech when McCauley, recording a radio message for later broadcast, asks a crewmate to describe the Moon. His startling response: "I see nothing but desolation. It is a devil's nightmare. Not a blade of grass, not a tree, nothing moves out there. This is a land of death." McCauley scolds the man for saying things that could frighten children, and he says he was only trying to be dramatic. Still, the speech serves as a reminder that, though humans visit the Moon many times during the series, it remains forbidding and dangerous.

As for appreciations of the joys of space travel, this is predictably left for rare women astronauts to express. In "First Woman on the Moon," the "experimental" female astronaut, Renza Hale, is going stir-crazy because a protective McCauley insists she remain inside the moon base at all times. Eventually she decides to go for a walk on the lunar surface by herself; by sitting down to relax with her radio turned off, she provokes a frantic search. Thus, while male astronauts don spacesuits and venture into the lunar vacuum only to perform important work, Renza becomes the first person who does so solely as a leisure activity. The series' other female space traveler, the astronomer who visits Space Station Astra in "Dark of the Sun" (aired March 9, 1960), is also unusually willing to acknowledge the pleasures of space travel, as she comments, "It's the most exciting thing I've ever known."

Several episodes emphasize that space might prove such a stressful environment as to provoke interpersonal conflicts, poor decision-making, or even flirtations with insanity. Civilians seem more susceptible to these problems, but even military men and McCauley himself are not immune. "Quarantine," "Moon Cloud," and "Dark of the Sun" focus on two scientists who cannot get along, though space travel, at best, only exacerbates conflicts unrelated to space travel: The feuding scientists of "Quarantine" and "Moon Cloud" disliked each other for other reasons before the episodes begin, while the astronomers of "Dark of the Sun" are competing for the affections of a third astronomer, a beautiful woman.

There are also inklings of a theme that emerges in *Space Men* (1960)—natural conflicts between veteran space travelers and neophytes—since the problems that McCauley confronts regularly involve the misbehavior of first-time visitors, like the stowaway in "Earthbound," a deceitful journalist in "Dateline: Moon" (aired February 10, 1960), the scientist smuggler in "Contraband" (aired March 2, 1960), a frustrated wife in "First Woman on the Moon," and those quarreling scientists.

Ongoing crises on Earth contribute to mental instability in space in two episodes. In "Moonquake," an astronaut named Farrow is vital to the survival of colleagues on the Moon, since he is the only man who can repair the spaceship's mangled radio to contact Earth and allow a rescue mission to locate them; but Farrow's wife, just after takeoff, was injured in a car accident, making it difficult for Farrow to concentrate. And "Verdict in Orbit" (aired March 16, 1960) explicitly suggests that space might drive men insane, as a colleague explains that "a man's thinking can go haywire" in space. However, the reasons why McCauley and scientist Dr. Rawdin go haywire are understandable enough, in light of what happened on Earth: McCauley is upset because his son was struck by a hit-and-run driver while riding his bicycle and is now in critical condition, and Rawdin is consumed with guilt because he was the hit-and-run driver, rushing to belatedly attend a pre-flight briefing. When McCauley learns that tire tracks identify Rawdin as the perpetrator, and that Rawdin has taken a spacesuit and left the station, he uncharacteristically refuses to authorize a rescue mission, preferring to let the guilty man die. A subordinate assumes command on the grounds that McCauley is too upset to function as a proper commander. Soon, McCauley comes to his senses, and when a crewmate cannot persuade Rawdin to return, McCauley himself saves him by convincing the scientist that his actions did not result from immorality, but only fear.

Extreme situations may also drive astronauts to uncharacteristically disobey orders; thus, at the start of "Flash in the Sky," McCauley orders a scientist to return to the base and seek help when he is buried in lunar dust, but the man refuses and instead uses oxygen to dispel the dust and free McCauley. An indignant McCauley immediately sends the man back to Earth due to his insubordination. Yet McCauley himself disobeys orders for the same reason in "Asteroid": A general on Earth orders McCauley to return to his spaceship instead of rescuing a blinded colleague, but McCauley offers the transparently dishonest excuse that he could not hear the order because of "too much static."

"Voice of Infinity" focuses most clearly on the problem of madness in space and how to prevent it. Worried about overstressed astronauts making mistakes that endanger themselves and colleagues, a scientist arrives on Space Station Astra with a new invention: equipment that monitors the stress levels of all personnel and reveals when a man has reached his critical level and should be replaced. After one crewman refuses to stop working when told he must be relieved of duty, he makes an error which causes the space station to spin faster and faster, threatening to tear it apart. Though monitors indicate that he himself is too stressed to make good decisions, McCauley makes an accurate guess as to when and how long to fire the station's retro-rockets and stabilizes the station, calling upon the "voice of infinity" in all people that allows them to keep functioning in moments of need despite overwhelming pressure. Thus, the episode simultaneously suggests that life in space can be too stressful for humans to handle, and that extraordinary individuals like McCauley might be able to handle that stress.

There is finally the suggestion that even McCauley might be becoming mentally imbalanced in "From Another World" (aired April 27, 1960). Just before ending a mission to explore an asteroid, McCauley reports seeing the fossilized imprint of a prehistoric bird, then faints. Back at the ship, a doctor believes that the overworked McCauley was hallucinating. Since as one man notes, discovering evidence of alien life is McCauley's "favorite dream," the purported image is dismissed as delusional wish fulfillment, and McCauley is grounded for six months to rest and recuperate. However, as discussed below, a later return to the same asteroid confirms the accuracy of his initial observation.

In depicting the general feasibility, the collaborative nature, the dangers, strangeness, joys, and mental stress of space travel, *Men into Space* largely replicates points already made in previous spacesuit films, albeit in a more thorough and variegated fashion. To discuss areas where the series breaks new ground, one first acknowledges an unprecedented, forceful emphasis on conventional domesticity. True, *Spaceways, Riders to the Stars, Conquest of Space*, and *Destination Space* involve earthbound romances as subplots, and *Project Moon Base*, while featuring a female commander, concludes with a marriage and re-establishment of male superiority. But space travel had otherwise been an all-male affair, with a military aura and minimal female involvement (Briteis in *Project Moon Base*, and female stowaways in *Spaceways* and *Satellite in the Sky*). But along with two female astronauts and references to others, *Men into Space* literally smothers astronauts with wives, children, and all the accoutrements of conventional suburbia, making these aspects of their lives seem just as important as space missions.

One reasonably assumes that this resulted, in large part, from network pressure. While the pilot "Moon Probe" shows McCauley's wife Mary (Angie Dickinson) and son Peter (Charles Herbert) amidst a crowd of dignitaries observing his flight, the episode otherwise focuses on all-male heroics, in space and on the ground. While CBS executives were pleased enough with the pilot to purchase the series, they may have worried that the series would be insufficiently appealing to 50 percent of its potential audience, namely, women. Hence, the edict went out: henceforth, each *Men into Space* must begin and end with extended sequences on Earth featuring astronauts' wives, children, and spacious homes, presumably pleasing female viewers while not overly disturbing men who tuned in to watch a space adventure. (An issue in early episodes — the awkward absence of Mrs. McCauley, presumably because rising star Angie Dickinson left the series — was addressed by recasting the role.) As further evidence that the scenes were the network's idea, not the producers', one notes that in the final episodes, presumably filmed after the series' cancellation, framing domestic dramas were largely abandoned, suggesting that the producers, no longer caring about keeping CBS happy, reverted to their own preferences to focus exclusively on the masculine business of space travel.

For the most part, these domestic vignettes are obviously superfluous, since they are rarely related to anything else that happens. Indeed, since all astronauts are young and handsome, all wives are beautiful, and all children are adorable, they are almost interchangeable and tend to blur together in one's memory. Thus, unlike the introductory sequence in *Frau im Mond*, which individualizes characters and makes their subsequent fates more involving, these sequences are pointless. There are only minor variations in astronauts' home lives: One episode shows an astronaut with a fiancée; another features an astronaut whose wife is about to give birth to their first child; and an astronaut in "Beyond the Stars" is an unmarried playboy, juggling several girlfriends. What audiences generally observe, then, could be characterized as an almost ritualized tradition that crewmen of an upcoming mission must come together with families for social gatherings before and after their flights, so they can exchange pleasantries while drinking cocktails in comfortable living rooms, sitting by pools, or anticipating backyard barbecued steak dinners. Wives may joke about the travails of being married to an astronaut — in "Burnout," a wife smilingly comments that the major "occupational hazard of space" is "happy marriages" — but they evidently are all committed to their spouses and their unusual careers, and willing to stoically endure their long absences. And though the men seem equally devoted to their wives and families, we never hear them talk about them when they venture into space. In "Edge of Eternity," a general hosting a pre-flight party for astronauts and their wives presents his men with photographs of their wives to take with them to the Moon and comments, "No matter what you find up there, the good things are here on Earth." Cynics might say the general gives them the pictures so, for once, astronauts might actually remember and refer to their wives while on a mission, to connect their domestic interludes and assignments in space.

To be sure, there are times when terrestrial and celestial dramas intertwine. In "Moonquake" and "Verdict in Orbit," as noted, astronauts on the Moon are stressed because family members on Earth were injured in traffic accidents, and the former episode unusually interrupts its lunar narrative to show the astronaut's stricken wife lying in a hospital bed, more concerned about her husband's fate than her own. A scientist in "Caves of the Moon" is distraught because he just learned that his son on Earth has drowned. And at least one pair of introductory and concluding vignettes have an emotional impact due to events in space: At the beginning of "A Handful of Hours," McCauley and another astronaut, Kelly, supervise their sons racing go-karts; subsequently, on the Moon, Kelly is the astronaut who sacrifices his life for that wrench; and in final scenes, the two boys again race go-karts, but now, only McCauley is there to watch them.

Still, while the series' framing domestic scenes and main narratives are frequently unrelated, these homey sequences are not entirely irrelevant; for since they take up a substantial amount of time in each episode, it was perhaps inevitable that, eventually, depictions of conventional happiness on Earth would begin to influence adventures in space. The process

Honoring a Space Hero: Illustrating that he was not entirely forgotten, someone resolved to celebrate the first fifty years of William Lundigan's *Men into Space* (1959–1960) by preparing and stamping a special commemorative envelope.

began, one can argue, with a striking episode explicitly involving a representative of the home front invading the realm of space.

"First Woman on the Moon" is painful for modern viewers to watch, due to timebound and condescending attitudes toward women. Its premise is that, as an experiment to determine whether space can be colonized, officials will select an "average housewife" to visit the Moon for ninety days to see if she can endure the daunting experience. After examining some astronauts' wives, they determine that an unremarkable woman named Renza Hale is an ideal choice, so she and husband Joe Hale, along with McCauley and other astronauts, are soon living on the Moon. At first, the poor woman visibly struggles with the rigors of lunar life: She breaks into tears upon first surveying their cramped quarters, is frustrated by the difficulties of "atomic cooking" and humiliatingly burns the meat for one dinner, and goes stir-crazy because McCauley, as noted, confines her to the moon base. The drama of the episode involves the question of whether the woman can survive, as the narrator comments, when she is forced to live with "no telephone, no shops, no female companionship, and the extremely small quarters of Moon Base." However, her unauthorized walk on the Moon prods the protective McCauley to grant her more freedom to move around. Though a feud with her husband provokes a demand that she return to Earth immediately, the two are quickly reconciled, and Renza completes her mission, concluding with an elaborate candlelight dinner she prepares using supplies she secretly brought along with McCauley's assistance.

This cloying story could be dismissed as a feminist's nightmare. If the intent was to open space to women, they could have found more qualified candidates, like *Project Moon Base*'s Briteis or the female scientists of *Rocketship X-M* and *Flight to Mars*; and in light of modern sensibilities, it is risible to suggest that a woman in space would demand special attention and coddling from male companions and would be obsessed with issues like cooking a tasty dinner for the men every night.

Still, if one considers this episode not in isolation, but in the context of the entire series, it is evident that Renza in her own way takes control of the Moon, and of the series, effecting a permanent transformation in the way *Men into Space* depicts life in space. As one result of her presence, this is the first episode that involves no threats to the lives of astronauts, which in the iconography of the time means that space has been de-masculinized; the point is that the long-term habitation in space will not only demand constant efforts to rescue colleagues from danger, the characteristic activity of men, but will also mean establishing and adjusting to the uneventful daily routines of life, the special talent of women like Renza. She is also the first astronaut who ventures to the surface of the Moon not because of a pressing assignment, but because she simply wants to go for a walk; at one point, she stops and sits down, turns off her radio, and relishes the experience of being on another world. She thus insists upon another essential element of space life which the series neglected: that the experience must include pleasure as well as business. The message is emphasized by a later scene in which Renza and her husband enjoy a quiet, romantic moment on the Moon, which incidentally explains one reason why producers wish to avoid characters in spacesuits: The natural ending of the scene would have the reconciling lovers kiss each other, but because of spacesuits, all they can do is embrace.

Her seemingly trivial concerns about learning to cook on the Moon, and providing companions with an elegant, atmospheric dinner, are also relevant to a determination to make space a more pleasant experience. After a hard day of work, why shouldn't people on the Moon enjoy a palatable, congenial meal? All in all, in an understated fashion, Renza imposes a new and important priority on those who venture into space: While they have important jobs, astronauts also need time for relaxed dining and casual conversations. To succinctly explain the significance of the episode, Renza succeeds in domesticating space; she imports the values of 1950s suburbia, previously observed only before and after sojourns in space, into the actual environment of space.

While this character is not seen again, which is the pattern in the series for all characters except McCauley and his family, the impact of her visit to the Moon is felt in later episodes. "First Woman on the Moon" shows viewers the first dinners in space; later episodes regularly show astronauts eating on the Moon or in Space Station Astra. Characters on the Moon will soon be playing cards, playing chess, and singing songs while strumming on a guitar. If the final episodes, as noted, tend to exclude the framing domestic interludes on Earth, an alternate explanation would be that they are no longer necessary, since astronauts are now empowered to enjoy social interludes in space. As one example, "Mission to Mars" takes place entirely on the Moon and in space, but begins and ends with pleasant meals: First, the Russians invite the Americans to a dinner where vodka is served; then, after McCauley rescues the Russians from a mission that failed due to insufficiently careful preparation, the Americans reciprocate by inviting the Russians to dinner and serving lemonade — not so subtly suggesting that while many pleasures from Earth should be brought to space, alcohol is perhaps not one of them.

Given that the "experiment" conducted in "First Woman on the Moon" was a success (Renza's Moon visit lasted a full ninety days), one expects the Americans would continue with additional "experiments" of this kind, and that is what we are told in "Moon Trap": When an astronaut's tomboy kid sister says she wants to go the Moon, she argues, "Several women have been to the Moon," but McCauley responds that they were only there "on an experimental basis." However, "Dark of the Sun" actually involves another female astronaut onscreen, and while she is very unlike Renza, Dr. Gallagher (Carol Ohmart) ultimately has a similar impact upon life in space. In this case, she is eminently qualified to be taken into space, since she is one of the nation's top astronomers, chosen by a computer as one of three excellent candidates to join McCauley in observing the Sun from deep space during an eclipse. (We never learn her first name because the name generated by the computer only gave her initials, so McCauley is surprised to discover that Gallagher is a woman.) Like her predecessor Renza, she is unusually willing to acknowledge the pleasures of space travel, and hers is also an adventure that does not involve a matter of life and death. Instead, when the three finalists are brought to Space Station Astra for tests to determine which two astronomers should be chosen, Gallagher becomes embroiled in an implausible conflict: She is unmarried and attractive, and the other two astronauts happen to be unmarried men who fall madly in love with her, generating the episode's tension as they constantly feud over which man should have the right to propose to her. Gallagher endeavors to end the argument by pretending to faint during a spacewalk to disqualify herself from the mission; when she explains her actions by saying, with a note of resignation, "Space belongs to men," McCauley indignantly replies, "Space belongs to the men *and women* who have the courage to conquer it" and insists that she remain a candidate. Thus McCauley, skeptical about bringing women into space in "First Woman on the Moon," is now willing to accept their presence. She then decides to pretend to fall in love with the ship's doctor to end the men's dispute, although it transpires that they are actually in love. Having previously ascertained that he has the right, as commander of the space station, to marry a couple in space, McCauley nevertheless cannot perform the ceremony because, as he later reports, he forgot the marriage vows. But thanks to her experience, the possibility of marriages in space has been confirmed.

A capable woman ready and able to do a man's job in space, Gallagher is clearly more like Briteis than Renza. Such women evidence no particular interest in cooking or home décor. However, like Briteis, she threatens conventional values as an unmarried woman in close company with men, requiring that she get married and thus bring terrestrial domesticity into the new realm of space. While Briteis's marriage was merely a coda to a story that was otherwise thoroughly masculine in spirit, involving conflict with a sinister spy and the peril of being stranded on the Moon without sufficient supplies, "Dark of the Sun" foregrounds its romantic triangle, suggesting that such concerns might sometimes be just as important to space travelers as the dangers posed by saboteurs or hazardous environment of space. Not since *Frau im Mond* have we observed a central drama in spacesuit films that is so similar to typical dramas that take place on Earth.

One necessarily has a mixed reaction to the aura of domesticity that came to characterize *Men into Space*. On one hand, these touches may reflect the simple reality that, as humans venture into space, they will invariably bring terrestrial values and terrestrial concerns with them, and will invariably strive to make their homes in space resemble, as much as possible, their homes on Earth. On the other hand, all this undermines what should be a central focus of the spacesuit film, the idea that space is a strange environment, without precedent in human history, requiring significant adjustments in the ways humans behave and perceive their surroundings. Perhaps the series' limited efforts to portray zero gravity and low gravity stem not only from budgetary concerns but also from a desire to make space seem as comfortingly familiar as possible, in keeping with its increasing emphasis on domesticity. If we have not yet arrived at the homey, shirt-sleeve environment of *Star Trek*, we are at least moving in that direction.

The other episode of *Men into Space* which most visibly brought terrestrial values into space was the one that immediately followed "First Woman on the Moon," "Christmas on the Moon." Here, producers follow what was once a standard policy for television series — a December "Christmas episode" that bends the series format to provide holiday cheer and an uplifting Christian message. The episode begins with a premature Christmas celebration in McCauley's house, since he and other astronauts will be on the Moon on Christmas Day, observing an approaching comet. The scenes also introduce a Scrooge figure: an astronaut who calls for Christmas to be abolished and seems to doubt God's existence, stating, "The most beautiful thing on Earth is knowledge — knowledge based on science, not faith." This man predictably receives his comeuppance when a crisis occurs at a remote moon base: a scientist (Whit Bissell) has appendicitis, requiring the doctor at the main base to join a colleague in a perilous walk during a meteor shower to save the man's life. When they get lost and their arrival is delayed while McCauley looks for them, the aforementioned astronaut is saddened because he knows he must keep the scientist cool until the doctor comes, but lacks a way to find or create ice for that purpose. Though he previously scorned Christmas, he now prays for divine assistance. He then realizes that the passing comet may have deposited a large piece of ice on the Moon and immediately leaves his base to find just such a piece only a few feet away, which he interprets as divine intervention, allowing him to keep the patient cool so the doctor can perform a life-saving operation. For additional resonances with the Christmas story, when McCauley appears escorting the other two astronauts, they are likened to the Three Wise Men — now bearing "the gift of life"— and the astronaut who prayed for help discovers that his first child, a son, was born prematurely on Christmas Day.

One might say that this episode merely recapitulates a sequence in *Conquest of Space*, wherein other astronauts struggling to survive on Christmas appear to receive help from above; but whereas the religiosity of that event is understated, this episode brings it to the forefront, presenting events as proof that a benign God exists. Still, while the values of "First Woman on the Moon" penetrate into other episodes, "Christmas on the Moon" stands alone in endorsing Christianity, since the subject never comes up in other episodes.

As another major innovation, *Men into Space* offers a new perspective on how space travel might foster a spirit of international cooperation. In previous spacesuit films, American space efforts were generally portrayed as extensions of the Cold War, with Americans striving to conquer space to maintain military superiority over adversaries and occasionally encountering active resistance from spies or saboteurs; only *Conquest of Space* envisioned future space travel conducted by an international agency, suggesting that formal agreements between nations might precede significant initiatives in space. But in 1959 and 1960, even while tensions between the United States and the Soviet Union remained high, *Men into Space* predicted — correctly — that space travel would be a matter of peaceful competition between America and Russia, increasingly characterized by a sense of teamwork and cooperation among different nations.

This was evident even in the first episode, "Moon Probe." While McCauley helplessly drifts through space, his supervisors on Earth call for help from monitors all over the world to keep track of the lost astronaut so crewmates can locate him before his radio stops functioning; and people shown providing helpful information about his whereabouts include men from Asia, from France, and (I believe) from Russia. Indeed, in a final discussion of lessons learned from the mission, McCauley emphasizes the importance of international assistance: "For one half-hour, the entire world made one human life more important than anything else." Further suggesting that America's space program would involve only peaceful exploration that could properly garner broad international support, "Moon Landing" conspicuously fails to have its pioneering astronauts plant an American flag on the Moon, like astronauts in *Destination Moon*, and claim the Moon as American territory. Indeed, it is later established that other nations have reached the Moon: "Contraband" refers to astronauts from "other nations" said to have visited the American moon base, and both "Mission to Mars" and "Flare Up" (aired August 17, 1960) involve a Russian moon base near an American base. A British space program comes up in "Burnout," and McCauley visits Britain to assist that nation's efforts in "The Sun Never Sets."

The episode that works hardest to counter feelings of competitiveness in space is "Mission to Mars," though it opens with the United States and the Soviet Union essentially racing to be the first to reach Mars. Both nations are preparing to launch missions from the Moon, to take advantage of Mars's favorable position in relation to Earth, and McCauley's younger colleagues are patriotically anxious to leave as soon as possible to "beat the Russians." However, concerned about safety, McCauley insists upon waiting until last-minute improvements in the spaceship can be completed. Inviting their American colleagues over for a prelaunch dinner, the Russians confide that they will go ahead without any changes. McCauley's caution is rewarded when his ship has a successful launch, while the Russian spacecraft immediately veers off course and explodes, leaving its two astronauts clinging to life in their spacesuits inside their devastated craft.

At this point, McCauley abandons his Mars mission to rendezvous with the Russian craft and rescue its astronauts. When he is then instructed to not return to the Moon, but instead proceed directly to Earth, he fears punishment for his decision. Instead, upon reaching Earth, he is brought to meet the president of the United States, who praises McCauley for his actions: "You have at one stroke done more to make the American position clear than anything else that has been done in the last fifty years." McCauley thus demonstrates to the world that, at least for Americans, helping others in space is more important than advancing purely national interests.

Even an episode with a Russian villain, "Flare Up," ultimately validates cooperation in space endeavors. After a Russian commander's craft crash-lands on the Moon and his crewmates are killed, the commander so fears being blamed for the crash that he hatches an elaborate cover-up scheme: He claims to superiors that the crash was caused by American sabotage — purportedly the ship's radar was jammed — and attempts to destroy the ship's flight recorders, since they would prove he was lying. He then hides himself when a rescue party from a remote moon base, led by McCauley, arrives at his crashed ship. The Russian sneaks into the moon base while they are gone, kills the one American who remained and tries to prevent McCauley and his crewmates from re-entering so they will run out of oxygen and die as well. He figures that with all Americans dead, he can maintain his cover story, but McCauley tape-records his incriminating remarks and announces that he will take the tapes to America's main moon base (though, in truth, he would not have enough oxygen to get there). The fooled Russian leaves the moon base hoping to shoot McCauley, but McCauley and his men grab him. Significantly, despite the commander's inflammatory charge, both the Americans and Russians proceed cautiously and reserve judgment, since both sides wish to avoid major incidents. When the Russians recognize their commander was in the wrong, they have no complaints about McCauley's efforts to thwart his plans. The episode ends with McCauley and a Russian officer calmly discussing the situation. The point, obviously, is that although one Russian engaged in hostile acts, the Russians should not be regarded as villains, but rather as colleagues. All things considered, it seems remarkably enlightened for its times.

So, if the American space program in *Men into Space* is not motivated by a desire for military superiority over the Russians, what is its main purpose? The answers are not unusual, but they are answers surprisingly overlooked in previous spacesuit films. In "Moon Landing," the scientist on the first lunar mission suggests that space travel represents a natural continuation of the development of life on Earth: "Life began in the sea, then groped out onto the land; with intelligence and time it staggered into the sky. Now we're leaping into space. We are ready. Space flight is only a natural, inevitable step in evolution." Implicitly, he envisions humanity colonizing space just as sea creatures colonized the land. This goal is clearly stated in "First Woman in the Moon," since the reason for the woman's visit to the Moon is to investigate whether ordinary citizens will be able to live there. Still, the most frequently expressed purpose behind space travel is to carry out scientific research. True, the lunar flight of *Project Moon Base* includes an astronomer to observe the dark side of the Moon, but he was only there to play the "science angle" and solidify public support for a space program really focused on military objectives; and true, scientists played major roles in the space flights of *Destination Moon* and *Riders to the Stars*, but their primary interest was achieving or improving space flight itself, not garnering knowledge about the universe. In sharp contrast, those running the American space program in *Men into Space* seem sincerely interested in science, and the experts they transport into space represent many disciplines.

Men into Space's first scientist in space (in "Moon Landing") is an astronomer observing Mars, and another astronomer visits the Moon in "Christmas on the Moon." However, the scientist brought to the lunar surface in "Space Trap" seems to be a biologist or geologist, since he brings back "spores" from the Moon. Also on the Moon, two scientists are among those imperiled by a lack of oxygen in "A Handful of Hours"; "Caves of the Moon" involves a scientist seeking frozen water within the Moon's extensive caves; in "Moon Cloud," two scientists search for radioactive material to generate atomic energy; in "Contraband," four scientists who visited the Moon are suspects when a lunar crystal is sold on the black market; in "Flash in the Sky," a scientist accompanies McCauley to retrieve an unmanned rocket that orbited Venus and obtain its data; and in "Moon Trap," a scientist is in the crew that crash-lands on the Moon.

However, scientists are also regular visitors to Space Station Astra; indeed, in "Quarantine," we are told the facility's main purpose is to serve as a research center, and the two feuding scientists in that episode are a biologist studying viruses and a physicist working with high frequencies. In "Verdict in Orbit," the hit-and-run driver is a scientist taken to the station to test samples of Venus's atmosphere to see if it can be converted into breathable oxygen, suggesting plans to land humans on Venus; and "Voice of Infinity," as noted, focuses on a scientist's efforts to monitor station residents to ensure that no unwise decisions are made by overly stressed astronauts.

Finally, venturing to other regions of space, a scientist comes with McCauley to the unmanned rocket about to explode in "Lost Missile"; as noted, three astronomers visit Space Station Astra to be trained for a mission to observe an eclipse from space in "Dark of the Sun"; a scientist accompanies McCauley on his return visit to the asteroid where he saw a fossil in "From Another World," and an astronomer is part of the mission to the Martian moon Phobos in "Flight to the Red Planet." Granted, all these scientists may be there in part to serve as characters who, unlike professional military men, can generate drama by feuding, disobeying orders, or developing health problems; but the series nevertheless conveys the clear message that transporting and supporting scientists engaged in groundbreaking research would be a significant part of America's space program.

This series' emphasis on space as a spur to renewed domesticity, international cooperation, and scientific advances go further than any predecessors, but its messages in these areas are not entirely innovative. One aspect of *Men into Space* is more original: its thorough examination of how human space travelers might search for extraterrestrial life.

Aliens were commonplace in other science fiction films of the 1950s, though they tended to look and act just like humans, or humans with funny makeup. But spacesuit films strived to be plausible and realistic in envisioning humanity's near future in space, and by the 1950s, scientists knew that planets and moons in the Solar System were too inhospitable to support organisms resembling humans or other terrestrial lifeforms, and the immensity of the universe made it improbable that spacefaring aliens from elsewhere would happen to visit at this time. Thus, bound to reflect the best scientific knowledge of the day, producers of spacesuit films felt obliged to assume that human space travel in the near future would necessarily involve cold, lifeless environments where astronauts would never encounter other living beings.

Still, as noted, there remained the realistic option that humans venturing into nearby space might discover tantalizing *evidence* of the existence of alien life in the form of radio messages from distant alien civilizations, a fossil of an ancient lifeform, or an artifact left by aliens who visited the Solar System thousands or millions of years ago. In the previous history of the spacesuit film, the discovery of such evidence occurred solely in a brief sequence of "Man and the Moon": however, the search for knowledge of alien life would become a recurring theme in *Men into Space*.

In early episodes, true, there were only brief references to any concerns about such discoveries. In "Moon Landing," the astronomer who gave up his life to make the first observations from the Moon comments that such data will finally allow humanity to learn whether the canals of Mars are natural or artificial, possibly demonstrating that the planet was once home to an advanced civilization. In "Space Trap," a scientist returns from the Moon with "spores" that might provide proof, we are told, that there was or is life on the Moon — an odd assertion, since one assumes something called a "spore" was already identified as an embryonic living organism. (Perhaps the identification was provisional and later discredited, since there are no other comments in the series about lunar lifeforms.) In "Asteroid," an astronaut jokes about getting his wife's permission to travel into space: "All I had to do was promise I wouldn't flirt with any female Martians we might run into."

However, even if only because they were running out of ideas, the makers of *Men into Space* brought the issue of possible extraterrestrial life to the forefront in eight later episodes. In doing so, they even established that this quest is McCauley's central motive for traveling into space. In "Dateline: Moon," after the discovery of a purported alien artifact that turns out to be a hoax, McCauley confides that, despite his doubts, "Somehow I wanted to believe it," adding, "Man has always wanted to know if there are intelligent beings, or at least life, in the universe." In "From Another World," as noted, finding evidence of alien life is called McCauley's "favorite dream," and in "Mystery Satellite" (aired September 7, 1960), McCauley confesses, "Someday a human being is going to make contact in space, and when it happens, it's going to be the greatest thing in the history of mankind. I have to admit that I'd kinda like to be that man." In the various ways McCauley seeks to fulfill this dream, *Men into Space* confirms its status as the most profound spacesuit film to date: for on one hand, the evidence McCauley encounters is, in keeping with the spirit of the series, plausible in light of current science; on the other hand, it remains tantalizingly unconfirmed or incomplete, conveying again that space is a strange new environment without precedent in human history, filled with daunting mysteries.

In its fleeting image of a figure on the Moon, "Man and the Moon" did not address the question of how such evidence should be evaluated. In contrast, the more extended accounts of such discoveries in *Men into Space* would require consideration of that issue. The series insists that potential evidence of alien life must be approached with a balance of openness and skepticism and carefully examined before jumping to unsustainable conclusions. There are always three possible explanations: The evidence is fraudulent, is a natural phenomenon being misinterpreted, or is authentic. There is also the chance that it will prove impossible to determine whether the evidence is genuine or not. Episodes of the series presented all these possibilities.

A case of fraud occurs in "Dateline: Moon." Chosen by lottery to be one of the first two journalists to visit the Moon, sleazy reporter Jimmy Manx (Harry Lauter) is not content to chronicle what McCauley describes as the "awesome and terrible beauty of the Moon" or the activities of human explorers. Instead, seeking a spectacular scoop, he has someone construct a small rectangular object with strange markings, takes it to the Moon, and plants it where he knows an astronaut will retrieve it. A skeptical McCauley insists that no announcement of the discovery be made until experts examine the object, but during a live television broadcast, Manx describes and displays the object. Knowing his hoax will be revealed if it is returned to Earth for thorough scrutiny, Manx next tries to hide it on the lunar surface, but a suspicious McCauley catches him in the act, proving it was all a hoax — as later confirmed by scientists on Earth. This desire to find evidence of aliens will problematize efforts to prove their existence, because not only will it create opportunities for self-serving deception, as in "Dateline: Moon," but it may also lead overactive imaginations to detect signs of alien life when none exist. Even the level-headed McCauley eventually falls victim to this tendency.

Still, in "Shadows on the Moon" (aired March 30, 1960), McCauley is not fooled by apparent indications of the presence of intelligent aliens on the Moon. When crewmates point out that a large outcropping of rock looks like a smiling human face, McCauley correctly argues that it was not carved by aliens, but is a natural formation that coincidentally resembles a face. An astronaut then observes what appear to be signal lights on the face — but they are nothing more than reflected sunlight. Finally, a crewman panics and runs away when he thinks he sees a large ambulatory being — but McCauley discovers he only saw his own distorted reflection in a slab of obsidian glass. In rejecting their outlandish claims, McCauley tells colleagues, "The only enemy is the Moon itself," insisting that there could be no alien beings in its forbidding environment.

Yet McCauley himself is briefly convinced by bogus evidence of alien life in two later episodes. In "Lunar Secret" (aired April 13, 1960), his crewmate on a lunar mission takes a photograph which, when examined later, apparently reveals an object of artificial origin. Follow-up photographs further indicate that the object has somehow shifted its position, deepening the mystery. However, when they finally climb the difficult slope to examine the object at close range, they find the moving object is actually two objects in different positions that happened to be alternately undetectable in the photographs; and the objects are the helmets of dead American astronauts, members of a failed lunar mission whose fate had been unknown. And in "Mystery Satellite," McCauley's spaceship is approached by a vehicle which assumes a parallel course, meaning that it must be guided by intelligence. After another spaceship burns up in the atmosphere while pursuing this vessel, McCauley chases it, and when it again positions itself near his spaceship, he flies directly to the Moon and changes course at the last minute, hoping to get the object to crash into the Moon — which it does. McCauley then lands and determines that the pursuing vehicle is only an old robot satellite of human origin.

Having dealt with one hoax, and three cases of mistaken identity, *Men into Space* nonetheless argues that skepticism about evidence of alien life is not always appropriate, balancing these four episodes with two episodes illustrating the third possibility — that the signs of alien life or intelligence are genuine — along with two episodes that leave the authenticity of the signs as an open question.

In "Is There Another Civilization?" (aired March 23, 1960), a rocket returning to Earth is struck by a small meteor made of an artificial alloy unknown on Earth. McCauley leads a follow-up mission to the swarm of meteors where it was encountered, retrieves a large object that was obviously part of some space vehicle, and returns it to Earth, whereupon scientists determine that the fragment came from a spaceship that is 500 years old, establishing that it was constructed by aliens. And in "From Another World," McCauley reports that while visiting an asteroid, he observed the fossilized imprint of a prehistoric bird just before he fainted and had to be returned to the ship. Knowing of his desire to detect alien life, superiors assume that the overworked McCauley imagined the imprint as a form of wish fulfillment and ground him for six months. Later he is allowed to return to the asteroid on a mission that, due to the asteroid's eccentric orbit, can only last one hour. McCauley and another scientist search for the imprint but are finally forced to return to their ship. Yet the camera shows viewers that, just beyond where he stopped, the fossil (closely resembling the famed fossil of the archaeopteryx) is clearly visible. Still, McCauley is vindicated when a rock retrieved by the scientist turns out to conceal an image of a claw — not a fossil, but more provocatively, the work of a "primitive artist" — evidence of not only life, but *intelligent* life.

(One might argue that both episodes ignore other possible explanations: Perhaps there existed, centuries ago, a secret society of advanced human scientists capable of building and launching a spaceship; perhaps the asteroid was a fragment from Earth, hurled into space by some fantastically powerful volcanic explosion. However, these theories seem even more unlikely than posited alien intelligence, so it is logical to maintain that, barring additional revelations, the existence of alien life is the best explanation of the phenomena.)

Finally, in the first of two episodes where matters are left unresolved, "Beyond the Stars," we interestingly observe (for what I believe is the first time on film) what many suspect will be the actual way we establish the existence of extraterrestrial intelligence: radio astronomy. While McCauley and other crewmen are on the far side of the Moon, using a radio telescope to scan space, they record one man's improvised song about being on the Moon. ("Darling to you I sing from the Moon / Into the void of sky. / Hear from the stars, forever my love / Words that will never die.") After the singer has an accident, he deliriously says he wants to hear sounds from the stars. When McCauley listens to what the radio telescope is receiving, he hears a pattern of sounds seemingly conveying a message ("one-two, one-two, one-two-three-four; one-two-three, one-two-three, one-two-three-four-five six") which he interprets as aliens saying two plus two is four, and three plus three is six. In response, he broadcasts to the star where the sound originated a spoken message and a recording of the man's song. However, since that star is two hundred light years away, it will be four hundred years before the aliens can demonstrate their existence by responding to McCauley's odd message.

The series' final episode, "Flight to the Red Planet," similarly concludes with an unresolved mystery. After McCauley and a crew fly to Phobos to set up observational equipment and determine the feasibility of landing on Mars, a scientist reports that he observed green areas around the Martian canals, suggesting that there is life on Mars, and that its canals were designed by intelligent beings for irrigation. Naturally, the episode ends with the scientist looking forward to an actual landing on Mars "next time," but McCauley responds, with a sardonic expression on his face, "Next time? Maybe."

There are two ways to interpret this episode. First, contemporary television audiences are accustomed to series that end their seasons with a cliffhanger episode designed to leave viewers in suspense until the next season's first episode completes the interrupted story. Thus, many might assume that "Flight to the Red Planet" was designed to make people eagerly anticipate a second season of *Men into Space* in which McCauley and colleagues would land on Mars and encounter life — exotic plants, strange creatures, perhaps even intelligent beings. However, I am skeptical of this theory, for two reasons. First, it was not the habit of television series of the 1950s and 1960s to end their seasons with unresolved dramas. Second, given the leisurely pace of the television business around 1960, when low-rated series were usually allowed to complete their seasons even when networks had no intention of bringing them back, it seems certain that, when they filmed their final episode, producers of *Men into Space* already knew their series was cancelled and there would be no second season — making McCauley's "Next time? Maybe" a bitter in-joke. In other words, if they wanted McCauley to land on Mars and meet some Martians, they would have done so in this episode, since it was their final opportunity.

Instead, I submit, the producers of *Men into Space* knew exactly what they were doing in crafting this final episode, and provided their series with the only appropriate ending for a realistic film about space travel involving evidence of alien life. For if intelligent aliens actually exist, they will almost certainly be truly alien, and humans will be fundamentally unable to anticipate their nature and behavior. If human writers attempt to portray aliens in detail, then inevitably, as Stanislaw Lem argues, they will do little more than create distorted mirror images of humans like themselves. Instead, to convey even a marginally authentic picture of what humans can expect when coming into contact with aliens, writers must restrict themselves to offering tantalizing hints of strange and poorly understood aliens, suggesting a genuinely alien presence without any futile effort to provide specifics. This is precisely what Lem himself would do in his most famous novel, *Solaris* (1961), twice adapted as a film (1972, 2002); it is also what we observe in *2001: A Space Odyssey*, wherein the alien manipulators of humanity remain unseen and mysterious.

Thus, while not a work of similar quality, *Men into Space* intelligently took the same approach, offering only scraps of information about aliens who built spaceships, drew images of ancient birds, and perhaps constructed canals on Mars but never attempting to go further in depicting alien life. Ending the series with humans on Phobos, speculating about evidence of possible advanced life on Mars, was therefore the only proper way to conclude the series.

In the decades since *Men into Space*, as desires to detect signs of extraterrestrial intelligence moved out of science fiction into mainstream culture, all the scenarios predicted by the series were realized. We have seen fraudulent "evidence" of alien life, including the notorious video of the Roswell "alien autopsy" and numerous faked photographs of alien spacecraft. There have been cases of misinterpreted data, the most spectacular example being a real-life replay of the storyline from "Shadows on the Moon": that photograph of the "face on Mars" apparently carved on the surface by intelligent humanoids which, when re-examined in higher-resolution photographs, turned out to be an ordinary, and un-facelike, Martian mesa. There has been one discovery of seemingly authentic evidence of alien life, a Martian meteorite (found in 1984) which, it was announced in 1996, contained signs of microorganisms, though doubts have emerged as to whether the evidence is definitive. Finally, there has been at least one case where a possible message from intelligent aliens has been neither confirmed nor denied: a strange radio burst from space, received at Ohio State University on August 15, 1977, which remains unexplained to this day. And people have generally responded to these findings in the manner of McCauley: keenly interested, but reluctant to believe until careful study eliminates any chances of fraud or misinterpretation.

Overall, then, *Men into Space* can be described as the first spacesuit film which suggests the full potential of the subgenre as a consideration of the strange and unprecedented environment of space and its possible impact upon visiting humans. Even today, more than fifty years after its last episode aired, few science fiction films have matched or exceeded its accomplishments. Instead, many more films — to be examined — garnered more attention and critical praise by scrupulously avoiding the realities that *Men into Space* confronted and instead offering comforting, conventional fantasies.

Assessing these spacesuit films and television programs collectively, one sees that they accomplished a great deal in describing and characterizing space travel. Despite their usual attachment to large, spacious spacecraft as the vehicles of choice, rather than the smaller capsules that were actually used, they otherwise depict future space travel in a reasonably realistic manner and argue successfully that it would be scientifically and technologically possible. They present reasons for humans to venture into space: achieving military superiority, expanding our scientific knowledge, gaining access to new resources, supporting a spirit of international cooperation, and perhaps, just having a good time. And they forcefully convey that space represents a genuinely strange and threatening environment that might lead some travelers to madness, while driving others back to familiar beliefs and lifestyles from humanity's past, and further intimate that space travelers might encounter provocative signs of alien life and intelligence.

Despite all these virtues, these works failed to achieve one goal: attracting a sufficient number of viewers as to generate healthy profits. The disappointing response to most of these spacesuit films might in itself explain why the subgenre essentially vanished for several years during the 1960s. But another event was also a factor: On April 9, 1959, NASA chose seven pilots to serve as America's first astronauts and began publicizing plans for their upcoming space flights in Mercury space capsules. Soon, all Americans could follow the training and exploits of actual space travelers, celebrated in the pages of *Life* magazine and featured on live television broadcasts whenever they were launched into space; thus, producers had little incentive to attempt to compete. Instead, any appealing drama about space travel would seemingly have to offer viewers something that magazine articles and television coverage could not provide, such as the dastardly villains, amusing antics, or terrifying monsters that were staple features of the pseudo-spacesuit films already commonplace in the 1950s. For a long time, those were the only traditions that remained viable patterns for films, and only in the late 1960s, when the *Apollo 1* disaster and America's impending moon landing temporarily revived interest in a space program that had degenerated into monotonous routines, would there be a revival of the true spacesuit film, as discussed below.

— 3 —
Wild Adventures: The Melodramatic Films

Pseudo-spacesuit films — addressed in the next three chapters — may begin like standard spacesuit films, with earnest narration, speeches filled with scientific information, and realistic-looking scenes of spaceship launches. However, unlike spacesuit films, they soon betray their true nature by descending into nonsense. In particular, they characteristically find a pretext for ensuring that characters wear spacesuits as little as possible, or not at all, as they follow three strategies to steer stories away from the daunting realities of space and into familiar territory. Some, which I call the melodramatic spacesuit films, typically take heroes to alien worlds that are much like Earth and focus on conflicts with human villains, or aliens resembling humans in both appearance and behavior, generating stories that are identical to conventional adventures set on Earth. Others are outright comedies which resemble other comedies save for the accoutrements of space travel. Finally, what I call the horrific spacesuit films contrive either to introduce alien monsters or transform human astronauts into monsters, creating stories about destroying or escaping monsters that are identical to conventional horror films.

The odd combination of elements often found in pseudo-spacesuit films — an introductory effort to seem realistic, followed by expedient silliness — suggests a simultaneous desire to appeal to audiences seeking plausible stories about space and hedge one's bets by emphasizing the fistfights, pratfalls, and thrills that are proven crowd-pleasers in other film genres. Thus, disguising themselves as genuine spacesuit films, they mislead viewers about tales actually told many times before, in more familiar settings, justifying the descriptive term of pseudo-spacesuit films. Beginning with melodramatic spacesuit films, I first discuss television programs and serials of the early 1950s before turning to relevant films of the 1950s and 1960s, generally in chronological order (though a few related films are discussed in thematic groups).

While terms like "pseudo-spacesuit film" and "melodramatic spacesuit film" inevitably convey the critical attitude these films often deserve, they are not always entirely without merit. They may offer an insight or two amidst the general absurdity of their wild adventures. Indeed, the environment of space may be so overwhelmingly unprecedented in human experience that even filmmakers determined to ignore its realities may be affected, and disturbed, by minimal efforts to acknowledge the novelty of space travel by briefly introducing spacesuits.

Television Programs of the Early 1950s

As space travel figured in more and more films of the 1950s, interest in the subject naturally emerged in two related media, one just being born, the other about to die: television series and Saturday afternoon serials. These efforts, even more so than their cinematic counterparts, were direct descendants of the 1930s Flash Gordon and Buck Rogers serials, with most of the same features, though television series were usually set in the near future and serials were usually set in the present. But there were invariably intrepid teams of adventurers, generally including a handsome hero, plucky sidekick, beautiful woman, and elderly scientist, who travel in not-particularly-realistic spaceships to other planets (identical to Earth) and encounter entirely human friends and enemies wearing exotic clothing recalling the styles of ancient Egypt and Rome, enlivened by purportedly futuristic touches like lightning-bolt or rocketship insignias. Then, usually with the help of newfound allies, the heroes successfully thwart the sinister schemes of alien evildoers by besting them in extended fistfights, fooling them with obvious tricks, or — rarely — deploying a bit of scientific magic accompanied by laughable gobbledygook. The only difference is that in the 1950s, since knowledge of true conditions in space was universal, producers could not entirely ignore the dangers of space and hence sometimes felt obliged to introduce, or refer to, spacesuits.

The television series should be discussed first, since in one case they actually preceded *Destination Moon* in depicting space travel. Ignoring peripheral examples (like 1953's *Johnny Jupiter*, a children's puppet show purportedly about a television show broadcast from Jupiter), there were eight series of the era that regularly involved space travel: *Captain Video and His Video Rangers* (1949–1955), *Space Patrol* (1950–1955), *Tom Corbett, Space Cadet* (1950–1955), *Buck Rogers* (1950–1951), *Rod Brown of the Rocket Rangers* (1953–1954), *Flash Gordon* (1954–1955), *Rocky Jones, Space Ranger* (1954), and *Commando Cody: Sky Marshal of the Universe* (1955). Detailed evaluation of these series is difficult, first, because most were broadcast live, not filmed, and their episodes were usually not considered worth preserving; hence, it appears there are today no extant episodes of *Buck Rogers* and *Rod Brown*, and only a limited number of episodes of *Captain Video*, *Space Patrol*, and *Tom Corbett*. In addition, the poor-quality kinescopes that survive may have gaps, distorted images, and/or inaudible or unsynchronized soundtracks. The following analyses are based on episodes located and viewed after a reasonable amount of research, either on DVD or online; future researchers may reach different conclusions from more extensive data. Generally, the viewable science fiction series fall into three categories: completely silly (*Captain Video and His Video Rangers*), usually silly (*Space Patrol, Flash Gordon*, and *Rocky Jones, Space Ranger*), and almost plausible (*Tom Corbett, Space Cadet*).

Based on three untitled episodes available at the Internet Archive, there is little to say about the first, and probably worst, of these, *Captain Video and His Video Rangers* (1949–1955). This live series, airing five or six days a week, generally offered continuing, slow-moving dramas, advanced by much conversation and little action, involving the efforts of Captain Video (first Richard Coogan, later Al Hodge) and colleagues to oppose the schemes of various villains on Earth and other worlds. The series' most incongruous feature was that, in an obvious effort to kill time, the action periodically stops to show excerpts from old westerns. In one episode that did show a crew on board a spaceship, they wore only the caps and goggles of aviators, not spacesuits (and it is particularly ridiculous to wear goggles, designed to protect aviators' eyes from being buffeted by high atmospheric winds, to travel through airless space). Granted, the episodes I saw were from the first two years of the series, and later episodes may have been better, perhaps inspired by the marginally better serial *Captain Video*; still, it seems reasonable to assume that spacesuits rarely if ever figured in its adventures.

The successful series *Space Patrol* did feature characters in spacesuits and occasionally offered viewers accurate information about space.[1] For example, in "The Exploding Stars" (aired November 13, 1954), Commander Buzz Corry (Ed Kemmer) shows Cadet Happy (Lyn Osborn) how vast space is by having him place a thumbtack on a photograph of the Milky Way and noting that the thumbtack covers up our entire solar system. Still, there remained two reasons why these series had a strong incentive to regularly ignore scientific realities. First, since they were, like serials, aimed at young viewers, producers naturally focused on struggles between heroes and villains and adventures in familiar-looking environments, not dramas with spacesuited astronauts making repairs in space. Thus, "Threat of the Thormanoids" (aired May 25, 1952), "The Laughing Alien" (aired March 28, 1953), and "The Atomic Vault" (aired February 26, 1955) feature alien enemies who look exactly like humans. The second reason was practical: Live broadcasting meant limiting adventures to indoor sets representing spaceships, headquarters, or dwelling places, and avoiding spacesuited characters in space or on airless planets. Preparing such sets and backgrounds would be expensive and technically difficult, and without lengthy interruptions, it might take too much time for characters to don and remove spacesuits while still appearing at all necessary times.

Thus, "The Space Patrol Code Belt" (aired October 20, 1951) only refers to spacesuits. Corry suspects that a spaceship captain is stealing supplies and has Happy hide on his ship to investigate. When Happy is captured, the captain plans to kill him by leaving him on the Moon, "where there's no oxygen ... and without a spacesuit!" But Corry rescues Happy before this occurs.

A later episode, "Hit by a Meteorite" (aired February 9, 1952), actually shows Corry and Happy in spacesuits. The story is filled with implausibilities: As they return to Earth with female passengers Carol Carlisle (Virginia Hewitt) and Tonga (Nina Bara), there are intense meteor showers, and their spaceship is struck by a meteorite which lodges in the hull and disables their power supply. Strangely, this causes no breathing problems, though the mechanisms that kept air circulating are presumably not working, and such a meteorite would in any event surely penetrate the hull. But when Happy reports, "We're not losing any oxygen," Corry responds, "That's the least of our worries." What concerns him is that, when their spaceship enters Earth's atmosphere, the meteorite will become a fireball due to friction and burn up the ship. Yet one imagines that a spaceship already insulated to guard against atmospheric friction could also withstand the added heat of a vaporizing meteorite nearby. Be that as it may, Corry and Happy don spacesuits and go outside to dislodge the meteorite and weld a patch over the hole — a process that also, improbably, results in no loss of air within the craft. They finish right before the ship enters Earth's atmosphere.

A third series, *Flash Gordon*, benefits from being filmed and having better special effects, but otherwise remains difficult to take seriously. As in the serials, the stars are space pilot Flash Gordon (Steve Holland) and his colleagues, beautiful Dale Arden (Irene Champlin) and scientist Dr. Zarkov (Joseph Nash). But the premise is entirely different: These individuals now live twelve hundred years in the future; they work as agents for the Galaxy Bureau of Investigation; their spaceship *Sky Flash* takes them all over the galaxy and even to other galaxies; and Zarkov has invented a time machine so they occasionally venture into the past. But storylines remain depressingly similar, with Flash battling human villains from other planets and usually defeating them in furious fistfights.

Still, the series did not entirely ignore the fact that some planets lack breathable atmospheres and require visitors to wear spacesuits. In "The Breath of Death" (aired November 26, 1954), spacesuits are only mentioned: first, Flash and Dale visit a prison planet so Dale can repair the oxygen purification equipment needed to maintain the facility's air supply; then after an escaping convict commandeers Flash's spaceship, he forces them to land on the planet Ariel, where he can get a supply of fuel. Dale resists this idea because, she says, Ariel has "the most deadly atmosphere in the galaxy. One breath means death. Even space helmets are no protection." But the criminal has a cunning scheme: He and Flash will hold their breath for a few minutes to find and retrieve the fuel (and he notes that because "gravity pressure is low," the fuel tanks will be "light enough" to carry, a rare reference to a planet with gravity different from Earth's). Dale's statement about "space helmets" qualifies as a reference to spacesuits, but if holding one's breath provides sufficient protection against the lethal atmosphere, it is hard to see why a space helmet would not be equally effective. In any event, Flash predictably resolves his problems by getting into a fight with the criminal. One potent punch pushes him to the ground and makes him scream, forcing him to breathe and killing him.

In "The Claim Jumpers" (aired November 12, 1954), Flash and other characters wear spacesuits, since the story involves visits to not one but two asteroids said to be "barren and airless." On one of them, miner Planetoid Pete (Erich Dunskus) discovers a valuable ore that will make him and daughter Marie (Wera Frydberg) rich. Meanwhile, Flash and Dale spot a space pirate spaceship on another asteroid; Flash lands to plant a homing device on the spaceship that will allow Earth authorities to locate the main pirate base. But Dale notes, "We can't stay out there too long, even with our radiation-resistant spacesuits." While Flash dons a spacesuit with a clear cylindrical helmet to carry out his errand, two pirates, wearing similar spacesuits, enter the *Sky Flash*, tie up Dale, and knock Flash unconscious when he returns. To avoid being connected to their deaths, the pirates leave Flash and Dale to die from radiation instead of killing them; they then take off in their own spaceship, though instead of going to the pirate base they stop at Pete's asteroid, since he just filed his claim via radio.

Flash and Dale escape death when Dale loosens her bonds to revive Flash so they can take off before succumbing to radiation. Their device tells them the pirates have landed on Pete's asteroid, where they confront Pete and his daughter and announce they will kill them and seize their claim. Flash reaches Pete's home and overcomes the pirates. All things considered, this might be the most realistic episode of *Flash Gordon*, since it unusually features no Earthlike planets, human-like aliens, or fantastic technology.

The science fiction series *Rocky Jones, Space Ranger* is probably most familiar to contemporary viewers, not because it was the most popular (it ran only one season), and certainly not because it was the best. However, since *Rocky Jones, Space Ranger* was filmed, like *Flash Gordon*, all episodes remain available; further, producers wisely had the series mostly consist of three-part episodes which could be re-edited as "films" for later television appearances. I viewed eleven episodes—two on a videocassette, three at the Internet Archive, and six in the form of two re-edited films—which will be taken as representative of the series.

To its credit, this series shows characters in spacesuits at least twice; however, reflecting a strange combination of the realistic and ridiculous, those sequences are scientifically absurd. The initial three-part episode "Beyond the Curtain of Space" (aired April 10, 17, and 24, 1954) displays a minimal concern for scientific accuracy by explaining why their characters in spaceships never experience zero gravity; for when the *Orbit Jet* reaches Earth's exosphere, Rocky Jones (Richard Crane) tells assistant Winky (Scotty Beckett) to "switch on artificial gravity." Then, when a meteor penetrates the hull of Rocky's spaceship, the *Orbit Jet*, it causes an improbably slow leak of the craft's air supply. At first, Rocky addresses the problem by sealing off the room where the leak occurred, but when he discovers that crewmate Vena Ray (Sally Mansfield) is still in the room, he employs an acetylene torch to open the sealed door and rescue her. Realizing that this will imperil his entire crew, Rocky tells Winky, "Get out the oxygen helmets. Once I cut through, the ship will be dry of air." Soon, the three space travelers don spherical glass helmets which they wear for the duration of the flight. The problem is that an actual leak in a spacecraft hull would not only drain its air in a matter of seconds, not minutes, but would also expose passengers to the chilly vacuum of space, quickly killing them if they only wore space helmets instead of complete spacesuits. After this incident, the episode descends into typical nonsense, as Rocky and his crew face intrigue and adventure on an alien world which, aside from inhabitants who speak a foreign language (a rare acknowledgment that not everyone in the galaxy speaks English), is so similar to Earth as to have automobiles driving down two-lane highways.

In the similar "Escape into Space" (aired May 1, 1954), a villain fleeing from Earth finds that his spacecraft was damaged by meteors and its air is, again, leaking out in an impossibly slow manner. To save him, Rocky maneuvers the *Orbit Jet* right next to his spaceship and, somehow remaining inside his own ship, he dons a spacesuit and uses his acetylene torch to open a door to the villain's spaceship. We are thus asked to believe that a spaceship could somehow latch on to another craft and seal one of its rooms to its hull. A theory to explain this scenario would be that the original script had Rocky floating in space while he cut that opening, but the budget would not allow for filming Rocky against the black void of space, and producers figured their young viewers would not notice the essential impossibility of what their hero was doing. Then, upon completing the opening, Rocky enters the craft and brings the man to the safety of the *Orbit Jet*.

Spacesuits are mentioned in the three-part episode "Bobby's Comet" (aired April 6, 13, and 20, 1954), when Rocky lands on the Jovian moon Fornax. To ensure their safety before leaving their spacecraft, Winky deploys a "mechanical canary" to test the atmosphere (recalling how coal miners used a canary to ensure that the air deep inside coal mines was always safe). While doing so, he fulfills his role as comic relief by saying to the device, "If you tell me that I've got to put on a spacesuit, I'm going to pluck out all your tail feathers one at a time." Fortunately for Winky, the world (like all other worlds in this series) is Earthlike, so spacesuits are not required.

If there is genuine novelty in *Rocky Jones, Space Ranger*, it lies in the unusual sexual dynamics of the series. Constantly on board the *Orbit Jet* is navigator Vena Ray, a beautiful woman and presumably Rocky's romantic interest, though he conveys no feelings for her, preferring to spend his free time in the company of male crewmate Winky, possibly a coded homosexual relationship (though Winky is observed in "Escape into Space" unsuccessfully approaching several women about a date). Rocky and Vena are usually accompanied by a symbolic "son," Bobby (Robert Lyden), officially described as the ward of elderly scientist and occasional crewmate Professor Newton (Maurice Cass) while displaying no particular affection for or connection to the man except in the initial episode introducing the characters. Bobby is also, strangely, the only successful Lothario in the cast, since he regularly pairs up with attractive girls his own age on alien worlds. Possibly, one might argue, this suggests that the novel environment of space might inspire novel sorts of family relationships, though the real explanation is surely that producers were endeavoring to introduce as much subdued sexual tension as possible into a series that was intended for children.

Finally, in sharp contract to other series, *Tom Corbett, Space Cadet* (1950–1955) visibly strives for a high degree of realism, and one could argue that it represented a genuine contribution to the tradition of spacesuit films. The series had a distinguished precursor, being vaguely related to Heinlein's 1948 novel *Space Cadet*, and a well-qualified technical advisor, science writer and occasional science fiction writer Willy Ley, who apparently had a significant influence on the series. Its star Frankie Thomas also had an interest in astronomy and worked to avoid scientific errors. Thus, while the series was only barely plausible, based on the science of its time, in presenting Mars as a habitable desert planet and Venus as a world of jungles and swamps, it accurately depicted Mercury and several asteroids as airless worlds which required visitors to wear spacesuits; even the opening credits for its final season, with a model "Kraft cameraman" filming rocketships on the Moon, have the cameraman outfitted in a spacesuit with a spherical helmet. (In fact, one unseen episode that is probably lost, "Suit Up for Death" [aired January 8, 1955], even focuses on spacesuits, as it involves a conflict between Tom and a quartermaster over the safety of the space cadets' spacesuits.) In addition, the series avoids encounters with humanoid aliens to instead feature stories about rescuing colleagues from space accidents and natural disasters and opposing the schemes of human villains. Its spaceship crews were businesslike and all-male, eschewing the children, beautiful women, and elderly scientists of other space films and television programs.

Still, the demands of live television, and a desire to appeal to very young viewers, imposed certain restrictions on *Tom Corbett, Space Cadet* that weaken its authenticity: To account for why space travelers never experience weightlessness, the episode "Assignment: Mercury" (aired February 26, 1955) has a crewman turning the ship's "gravity generators on," indicating that their ship, like the *Orbit Jet*, employs some magical form of artificial gravity. A voyage to Sirius in the episode "Pursuit of the Deep Space Projectile" (aired April 30, 1955) is accomplished by use of an otherwise-unexplained "hyperdrive." Even if peripheral elements in stories, these lapses into pseudoscience consign *Tom Corbett, Space Cadet* to the category of pseudo-spacesuit films.

In addition, certain plot developments, while technically possible, seem unrealistic; for example, in "The Runaway Rocket" (aired May 22, 1954), Tom prevents an out-of-control spaceship from plunging into the Sun essentially by running into it and knocking it off course — a maneuver obviously likely to cause ruinous damage to one or both ships. Finally, and more broadly, the basic premise of the series — that youthful cadets still being trained for space duty would regularly receive important assignments in space, with only minimal supervision of adult commanders — defies common sense. As spacesuit films like *Riders to the Stars* argue, space travel is so difficult and challenging that it will necessarily require trained, experienced adults. In sum, while *Tom Corbett* seems mature and realistic in contrast to other television series of its day, it remains, when contrasted to genuine spaceship films, juvenile and unrealistic.

Nevertheless, spacesuits do regularly figure in episodes, though appearances are brief, and they often talk about spacesuits without actually displaying them. As one dramatic example, the episode "Ambush in Space" (aired May 21, 1955) shows Tom outside his spaceship, confronting an escaped criminal who is attempting to evade capture by leaving Space Beacon #12, and both men wear authentic-looking spacesuits. However, all viewers see is the men standing and facing each other for a few seconds before the criminal leaps out of camera range. Then, we learn the villain floated away from the spaceship, and "when his oxygen gives out, he'll just drift around out there forever"; thus, he confronts the problem that threatened astronauts in *Destination Moon* and the first episode of *Men into Space*, but there is no stirring footage of the man drifting through space. One also senses this conclusion only represents a strategy to keep the criminal's fate unresolved so he could return to oppose Tom in later episodes.

In other cases, there are efforts to avoid the introduction of spacesuits. Earlier in "Ambush in Space," an explosion arranged by the criminal "ripped our antenna loose," so Tom's crewmate says, "I'll have to go out on the hull and see if I can fix it." This would have been a replay of another sequence in *Destination Moon*, but we never observe a man in a spacesuit trying to repair an antenna because Tom decides to instead go to Space Beacon #12 and make the repairs there. Another instance of unseen spacesuits occurs in "Fight for Survival" (aired June 4, 1955): When Tom and his colleagues abandon a spaceship that is about to crash on Venus, he tells them, "Get into your spacesuits — we got to bail out," but the next time we see them, they are already on the surface of Venus and have removed their spacesuits. However, unlike the hapless astronauts of *Cat-Women of the Moon*, they are provident enough to carry their spacesuits as they trek through the jungle — because these space travelers, obviously, appreciate the daunting challenge of space travel sufficiently to understand the importance of spacesuits.

Though all episodes are lost, a survey of science fiction programs of the early 1950s should mention *Rod Brown of the Rocket Rangers*, which might have proven just as interesting as *Tom Corbett, Space Cadet*. While plot summaries suggest regular appearances by colorful aliens, the series was otherwise said to be a close imitation of *Tom Corbett* (which provoked the legal action which may have inspired the destruction of all its kinescopes); there is a photograph of star Cliff Robertson in a spacesuit, holding a transparent spherical space helmet, so spacesuits were definitely employed in the series; there was even an episode, "The Suits of Peril" (aired July 18, 1953), in which Rod tests a new type of spacesuit, a rare story focused on spacesuits. However, barring some surprising discovery, scholars will never examine this series to properly evaluate its merits as a depiction of future space travel.

Finally, an early science fiction series aimed at adults, the anthology series *Tales of Tomorrow* (1951–1953), sometimes involved space travel. However, producers seemingly imagined their mature viewers would resist the whole idea and accordingly crafted stories that consistently cast space travel in a negative light. One episodes featuring human space travel, "Flight Overdue" (aired March 28, 1952), describes an aviatrix resembling Amelia Earhart, Paula Martin (Veronica Lake), who is driven by unhealthy ambition to join the crew of a secret flight to the Moon. Later, when her husband, who believed the cover story that she was lost over the Pacific, learns that she died when her spaceship crash-landed, he is happy to be free of her baleful influence. In "Appointment on Mars" (aired June 27, 1952), three astronauts who fly to Mars solely to find minerals and become rich are manipulated into killing each other by unseen Martians. And in "Test Flight" (aired October 26, 1951), unscrupulous businessman Wayne Crowder (Lee J. Cobb) is motivated to build a spaceship both by megalomania — as he dreams of "controlling not just one world, but all worlds" — and greed. He tells a colleague, "There's money, there's more wealth, more minerals, more — than anything we've dreamed of up there." Planning a test flight, he is tricked by a Martian scientist who directs the ship to take both men to Mars.

Unsurprisingly, these cheaply made dramas, broadcast live, did not bother with spacesuits: Paula Martin's Moon flight is only described, never seen; astronauts in "Appointment on Mars" are only observed on Mars, normally dressed in its breathable atmosphere; and the men of "Test Flight" do not wear spacesuits during their flight. One other episode, "Plague from Space" (aired April 25, 1952), fleetingly mentions a spacesuit, as men at a military base, opening a mysterious spacecraft that landed there, observe a figure inside "sucking oxygen through a metal mask," suggesting that the writer intended to have the alien wear a spacesuit. However, when removed from the craft, the alien simply looks like a normal human adorned with silver paint. (The creature is a sort of pet to the craft's actual occupants, intelligent Martian bacteria intent upon invading Earth. They are destroyed when an atomic bomb is dropped on the base.)

By 1955, all these science fiction series were cancelled. Another anthology series, *Science Fiction Theater* (1955–1957), endured until 1957, but that series rarely dealt with space travel and to my knowledge never featured spacesuits. Younger viewers, it seemed, had tired of science fiction and preferred westerns. Only the emergence of an American space program in the late 1950s would inspire television to offer a few series, like *Men into Space* and *The Twilight Zone* (1959–1964), that again brought space travel into America's living rooms.

Captain Video: Master of the Stratosphere (1951) and *Radar Men from the Moon* (1952)

When the makers of Saturday afternoon serials returned to space adventures with new energy in the early 1950s, they unsurprisingly displayed little interest in probing the realities of space travel and pondering its possible impact on the human experience. Rather, for them, rocketships and aliens only represented novel pretexts for the good-guys-versus-bad-guys stories they had long offered young filmgoers, filled with fistfights, car chases, and gun battles to keep things exciting. Serials like *Flying Disc Man from Mars* (1950) and *Zombies of the Stratosphere* (1952) take place entirely on Earth and involve evil aliens intent upon conquering our planet; unsurprisingly, the aliens look exactly like humans and evidence no need to wear spacesuits in Earth's atmosphere. Two other serials, *Brick Bradford* (1947) and *The Lost Planet* (1953), feature space travel, but it is not presented realistically. In *Brick Bradford*, the primary means of reaching the Moon is stepping through a "crystal door" that instantly teleports people to the dark side of the Moon, which has an atmosphere and resembles Southern California. In *The Lost Planet*, characters fly from Earth to the titular world, which is similarly Earthlike, in an ordinary airplane! Only two serials, *Captain Video: Master of the Stratosphere* and *Radar Men from the Moon*, deal with space travel slightly more seriously by minimally acknowledging the genuine dangers of space by introducing, if only briefly, plausible-looking spacesuits.

While based upon a ludicrous television series, *Captain Video: Master of the Stratosphere* had slightly better special effects (even if spaceships were usually, and obviously, animated cartoons) and a storyline involving significant amounts of space travel. Vultura (Gene Roth), dictator of the roving planet Atoma, seeks to take over both the peaceful planet of Theros and Earth as a prelude to conquering the universe. His nefarious activities on Earth are handled by an associate, scientist Dr. Tobor (George Eldredge), whose treachery is blatantly obvious even in the first chapter, "Journey into Space," though Captain Video (Judd Holdren) gives him free rein because he lacks "proof" of his crimes. The action occurs on three planets — Earth, Atoma, and Theros — which are color-coded so viewers know where they are (Earth scenes are standard black-and-white, Atoma scenes are tinted red, and Theros scenes are tinted green).

In the first chapter, believing several disasters on Earth were caused by people on Atoma, Video sets off in his spaceship, accompanied by a youthful companion identified only as "Ranger" (Larry Stewart) and wearing no special clothing. When Vultura attacks his spaceship with manipulated comets, Video and Ranger save themselves (as revealed in the second chapter, "Menace of Atoma") by retreating to a special "safety compartment" and donning large masks that cover their faces, presumably to breathe, though Video oddly says the helmet "neutralizes the atmospheric pressure density in the cabin." (The serial is so filled with so pseudo-scientific gobbledygook that in the sixth chapter, "Astray in the Stratosphere," Ranger listens to one example and asks Video, "Does that double-talk make any sense?" Video replies, "No.") After their diverted ship lands on the unknown planet Theros, Ranger begins to remove his helmet and Video barks, "Don't take that off. Wait until I check the outside atmospheric content. Remember we're on a strange planet."

"It has air, hasn't it?" Ranger asks.

"I hope so," Video replies, "but there may not be oxygen enough to sustain life." Upon checking the readings, Video determines that the planet is like all other planets in pseudo-spacesuit films: "The atmospheric content is almost identical to that of Earth." But at least, unlike others, he checks before getting out of his spaceship.

After teaching the peaceful people of Theros how to steal the Atomans' weapons to resist their incursions, Video and Ranger travel to Atoma, where they "rescue" the visiting Tobor (who claims he was abducted and taken there though he actually went voluntarily at the behest of Vultura). When they return to Earth in the third chapter, "Captain Video's Peril," Tobor attempts to kill them by first pretending to be ill (Video theorizes it is "a touch of air sickness," though the proper term would be space sickness), then retreating to a back chamber to turn a conveniently located oxygen supply gauge down to zero and remove the air from Video and Ranger's compartment. In the fourth chapter, "Entombed in Ice," they are saved when the spaceship reaches Earth's atmosphere, which replenishes the ship's air supply (though, since the spacecraft is airtight to keep out the vacuum of space, it would also keep out any surrounding atmosphere). Despite these silly elements, the serial unusually conveys that space is airless, and that having enough air to breathe is a major challenge in space travel.

Returning to Earth, Video and his team deal with new acts of sabotage caused by sinister robots from Atoma, which are controlled, Video discovers in the fifth chapter, "Flames of Atoma," from what is literally a "space platform"—a small round surface where two Atomans sit on chairs in the open air (since, despite its name, it appears to hover in the upper atmosphere, with clouds in the background). But while they do not seem necessary within Earth's atmosphere, these men wear actual spacesuits with transparent helmets. Using super-science, Video forces it to land, and he and Ranger put on the men's spacesuits to fly the space platform to Atoma. There then comes a brief, stunning scene that almost makes the entire serial worthwhile: Video and Ranger sit on the platform, rising through the blackness of space, and look around at the stars in a manner suggesting awe and appreciation. Since pseudo-spacesuit films so often strive to avoid space as much as possible, this represents a rare moment when characters actually confront the reality of this cold, challenging environment. As if recognizing the unique power of this scene, producers use it as one scene shown in the background during the opening credits of each episode.

Any hopes the serial will shift toward more scientific authenticity are dashed by blatant absurdities in later episodes: In the sixth chapter, when Video and Ranger are about to be incinerated on the planet Atoma, they remained unharmed because, Video explains, "here on Atoma, fire apparently has no effect on us because of the differences in our chemical properties." Needless to say, this "explanation" is senseless. Then, in the eighth chapter, "Invisible Menace," an Atoman on Earth wearing only street clothes rushes to the space platform, puts on a helmet, and blasts off into space, though an unprotected man would be quickly killed by exposure to the vacuum even if wearing a helmet to provide breathing air. Worse, he takes along an unconscious Video, wearing no protective gear at all, and pushes him off, seemingly dooming him to instant death in space. On Earth, Video's assistant Gallagher (Don Harvey) exclaims, "He's floating in stellar void" (though we observe him falling with clouds in the background, indicating that he is within the atmosphere). And how does Gallagher rescue Video from this peril? "I'll see if I can increase the Earth's gravitational pull." Then, when Gallagher accomplishes this impossible feat and the enhanced gravity attracts Video toward Earth, he does not crash-land, but hits the ground softly, due to a "gravitational decelerator."

The rest of the serial mostly takes place on Earth. Video contrives to prove Tobor is a traitor, stop efforts to destroy vast regions of Earth with a mysterious new metal, gain access to a massive lens that will enable Earth to monitor Vultura's actions on Atoma, and dodge a "flying disc" that attempts to destroy his aircraft. In the last chapter, "Video vs. Vultura," there is a final space journey, as Video first brings a new weapon to Theros, a "psychomatic" gun to temporarily turn the Atomans into idiots (an uncharitable viewer would say this weapon is unnecessary), then travels to Atoma and defeats Vultura. This delights his subjects, who are happy to be free of his tyranny and plan to establish a democracy, warming the hearts of patriotic American boys in the audience.

As for *Radar Men from the Moon*, its story recalls that of *Captain Video* and other serials: sinister aliens from a dying world endeavor to conquer Earth. A key difference is that these aliens are inhabitants of the Moon, a world with known properties that limited how it could be portrayed. As its key gimmick, this serial takes the flying rocket suit introduced in a previous serial that did not involve space travel, *King of the Rocket Men* (1949), and gives it to a new character, Commando Cody (George Wallace), who also has a spaceship ready to fly to the Moon. In the first chapter, "Moon Rocket," authorities ask Cody to make the trip after Earth experiences several destructive explosions caused by atomic weapons deployed by aliens from the Moon. However, despite the ensuing flight, space travel is only a minor element in a serial mostly occurring on Earth.

Employing the *Flash Gordon* model, and ignoring what scientists had figured out about how to break free of Earth's gravity, Cody's cylindrical spaceship takes off and lands horizontally; there is also a borrowing from *Flash Gordon* in the periscope Cody uses for observation. Once on the Moon, Cody dons his flying suit — which, with its helmet covering his face, apparently also serves as a spacesuit, though it has no oxygen tanks — and is invited to meet the Moon's ruler, Retik (Roy Barcroft), who obligingly explains that the Moon men are, in fact, behind the attacks, which represent their effort to damage Earth's defenses before launching a full-scale invasion. When asked why they want to invade the Earth, Retik answers, "Because the atmosphere on the Moon has become so thin and dry, it is impossible for us to raise food, except in pressurized greenhouses. None of us could move outside without helmets." This is at least a half-hearted attempt to correctly characterize the Moon's harsh environment, positing that it has a thin atmosphere instead of no atmosphere, but this is undermined because the Moon is depicted as a barren desert underneath a bright (and presumably blue) sky with clouds. Also, while wearing his rocket suit on the Moon, Cody is later shown with bare hands, which would be fatal on an almost airless, and frigidly cold, Moon.

After Cody escapes from Retik's underground chamber (naturally, by besting the Moon men in a fistfight), he absurdly declines to immediately return to Earth and instead undertakes to steal an atomic ray gun for examination by Earth's scientists, a feat accomplished by pumping nitrous oxide into the Moon men's headquarters to knock them out. However, he loses the ray gun when he and his crewmate are pursued by two Moon men driving a tank of sorts and, oddly enough, wearing actual and reasonably authentic spacesuits with oxygen tanks, presumably left over from a previous production. (Director Fred C. Brannon clearly had access to only two spacesuits, since we never see more than two on the screen at one time.) But Cody's companion Ted Richards (William Bakewell) stays alive simply by donning a helmet identical to the one on Cody's flying suit, though he also has no oxygen tanks.

Returning to Earth in the third chapter, "Bridge of Death," Cody and colleagues remain there for a while to deal with various crises instigated by the Moon man directing Earth operations, Krog (Peter Brocco), and two human henchmen, Graber (Clayton Moore) and Daly (Robert R. Stevenson). They need more money to produce another ray gun and

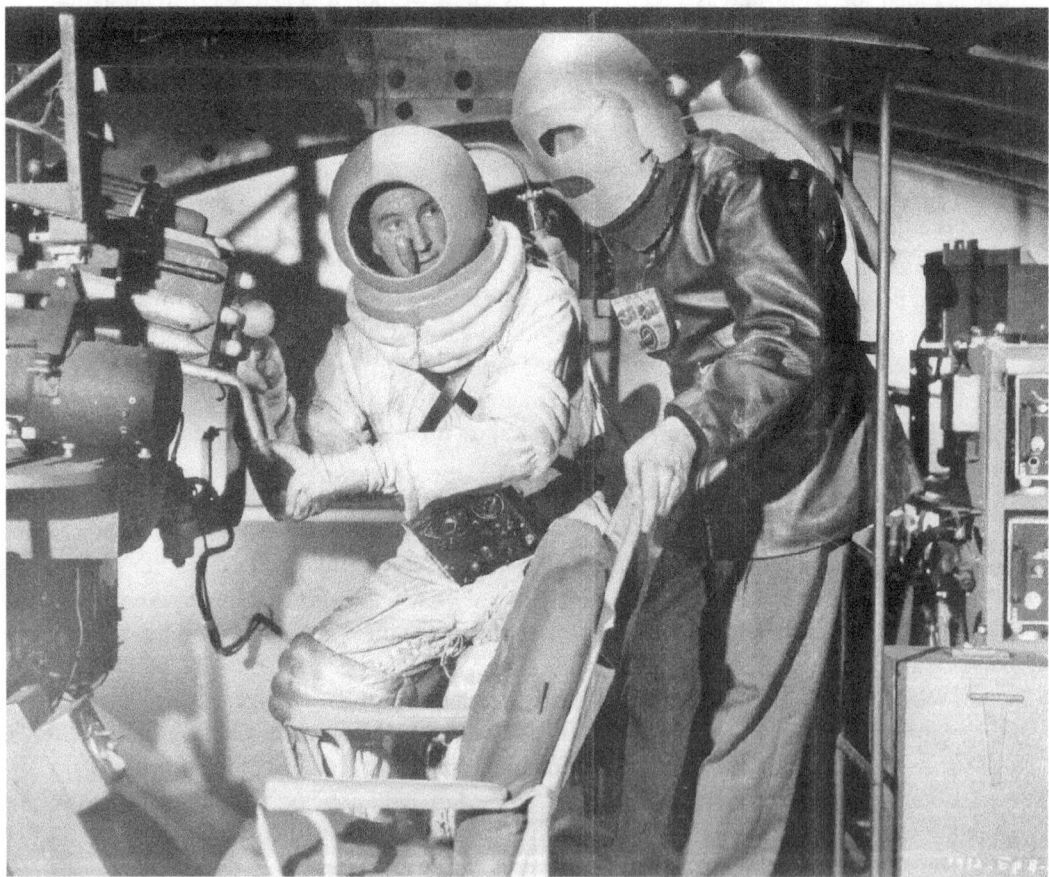

Second-Hand Spacesuits: In the serial *Radar Men from the Moon* (1952), Commando Cody (George Wallace) at left, briefly dons a genuine spacesuit, borrowed from an earlier film, while conferring with his assistant Ted Richards (William Bakewell), who is temporarily wearing Cody's "rocket suit" (and ersatz spacesuit), first seen in the serial *King of the Rocket Men* (1949).

resume their sabotage, requiring Graber and Daly to attempt a bank robbery, kidnapping, and payroll theft. Theoretically, one might applaud this recognition that the business of invading another planet might require economic resources as well as scientific acumen, but this is visibly a device to kill time with economical Earthbound escapades like car chases and gun battles. The most interesting development comes in the sixth chapter, "Hills of Death," wherein Moon men seek to drop an atomic bomb into a volcano and make it erupt to provoke torrential rainfall, causing destructive floods and striking another blow at Earth's defenses — all presented, for the most part, by means of stock footage.

Cody and his crew return to the Moon in the eighth chapter, "The Enemy Planet," this time seeking a supply of the magical radioactive element Lunarium, which powers the Moon men's atomic weapons, so Earth scientists can also build such weapons; and the story briefly addresses the genuine problem of having enough oxygen to breathe on the Moon. First, when Cody overpowers a Moon man in a spacesuit to find out where Lunarium is stored, he defeats him by temporarily cutting off his air supply; then, after Ted puts on the Moon man's spacesuit and drives a stolen tank to get Lunarium to the spaceship, a blast from a ray gun knocks him down and apparently damages his spacesuit, since we observe him unconscious and hear a hissing noise, providing the chapter's cliffhanger conclusion. In the next chapter, though, Cody arrives and pulls Ted to his feet, apparently all right; perhaps, as also observed in television series of the early 1950s, it was only an impossibly slow leak.

Cody's subsequent departure from the Moon begins with additional nonsense: Taking the captured Moon man with them as a prisoner, they make no effort to guard him, so he naturally starts a fistfight, grabs a gun, and eventually shoots himself; yet there is no damage to the spaceship hull. When they drag his body into the spaceship's other room, and Cody's assistant Joan Gilbert (Aline Towne) asks what will happen, Cody replies, "It's just like a burial at sea, Joan, only his body will float around in space forever." Of course, we do not observe this event, since depicting it would be beyond this serial's budget, but it is interesting that this iconic image of space tragedy, the burial in space, as impressively observed in *Conquest of Space* and *Star Trek II: The Wrath of Khan* (1982), was first discussed on film in this undistinguished serial. As for the rest of the serial, suffice it to say that after more adventures on Earth, including the arrival of Retik to take personal charge of the operations, all Moon men on Earth and their human allies are killed. Now equipped with ample supplies of Lunarium, authorities feel well prepared to handle future lunar invasions.

Based on such examples, it is difficult to lament the demise of the Saturday afternoon, serial by the mid–1950s, since they suggest that the genre had become hopelessly locked into tired patterns which made less sense than ever in the new context of space travel. In these adventures, all people, on both Earth and other planets, divide neatly into the categories of virtuous heroes and despicable villains; the evildoers' schemes combine advanced super-science and amazing stupidity; and the fate of the universe is invariably determined by who wins a fistfight. Imprisoned by such conventions from the past, the serials could not begin to contemplate predictable future realities.

Rocketship X-M (1950)

Kurt Neumann's *Rocketship X-M* technically qualifies as the first American spacesuit film, since it was actually released before *Destination Moon*, though its production started long after work on *Destination Moon* was underway (and it represented a crass effort to exploit publicity about that film by hastily completing and releasing a similar film). It begins soberly enough, with a leisurely press conference featuring the five astronauts who are scheduled, in less than twenty minutes (!), to begin a pioneering flight to the Moon. Scientist Dr. Eckstrom (John Emery) uses a chalkboard to draw diagrams as he explains how the flight will be accomplished, including realistic use of a multi-stage rocket. The military officer leading the conference also explains why the mission is important: Rejecting the notion that one might venture into space for "adventurous, fantastic reasons," he calls it the "first step toward practical interplanetary travel." A substantive motive emerges indirectly: Although the flight is "not strictly a military mission," he later adds that because of this initiative, someday an "unassailable base could be established on the Moon to control world peace." Though the idea is presented more circumspectly, then, it appears that this mission is, as in *Destination Moon*, primarily designed to guarantee American military superiority in space.

Even in opening scenes, there are signs that this film will not follow the documentary-style approach of *Destination Moon*; for along with obligatory scientist Eckstrom, handsome heroes (pilot Colonel Floyd Graham [Lloyd Bridges] and navigator Harry Chamberlain [Hugh O'Brian]), and comic relief (a stereotypical Texan, Major William Corrigan [Noah Beery, Jr.]), the crew includes a beautiful young woman, Dr. Lisa Van Horn (Osa Massen), whose presence is defended because she is the brilliant chemist who devised the rocket fuel mixture. One might wonder why the chemist who worked out the spaceship's fuel mixture would have to join its first flight, but *Rocketship X-M* does answer that question — albeit in a ridiculous fashion.

But first, the film must provide typical scenes of space travelers painfully enduring the stress of liftoff, a couple of evocative comments about how "it's hard to express" the experience of rising above Earth and how space offers only "eternal night," and a brief scare when the spacecraft almost collides with one of its detached stages. In addition, as further evidence that fidelity to scientific fact is not an overriding concern, the spaceship's transition to zero gravity is illustrated by a floating jacket and floating harmonica, among other items, but the astronauts remain firmly planted on the floor. (In actual zero gravity, both small objects and large objects would float, but lifting human actors with invisible strings may have been beyond this film's limited budget. And Neumann evidently did not know enough science, or care enough about science, to provide astronauts with magnetic shoes, like those in *Destination Moon*, to explain why his space travelers never leave the ground.)

As the first major crisis, the astronauts discover that the ship is not moving as fast as it should, leaving it stranded between Earth and the Moon. Eckstrom deduces what the problem is: "It must be the fuel mixture." It transpires that the ship is designed to travel at variable speeds by altering its fuel mixture; thus, since the ship is not traveling fast enough, Eckstrom and Van Horn must begin complex, time-consuming calculations to determine how to properly change the fuel mixture and achieve a higher velocity. Now, one might indeed travel at different speeds by using different fuel mixtures, but all spaceships in genuine spacesuit films, and real life, employ a much simpler method: firing rockets for briefer or longer durations to achieve less or more acceleration, and using smaller rockets mounted at various angles to change one's speed and trajectory. Thus, if an actual spaceship was moving too slowly, the crew would fire its rockets for a longer than anticipated period of time until the desired speed is reached. One would not have to do what this crew does: calculating a different fuel mixture, then manually moving around fuel tanks to achieve the new mixture.

And while engaged in this procedure, astronauts receive no assistance from Earth because, we are told, they moved out of radio range when nearing the Moon, though maintaining contact, as *Destination Moon* and later films recognize, would not be particularly difficult — another way in which the film seems unrealistic.

When the new fuel mixture is used, it is more forceful than anticipated (perhaps, it is intimated, due to an error in Eckstrom's calculation which he refuses to correct, though Van Horn's differing calculation suggests he is wrong). The sudden acceleration causes the crew to black out; when they awaken several days later, they have no idea where they are. There is additional tension when some "meteorites" rush pass the ship; the soundtrack provides a dramatic "whooshing" sound when they pass, though no sound can travel in the vacuum of space. This anticipates the notorious sound effects accompanying the *Enterprise* in the opening credits of TV's *Star Trek*.

Incredibly, the space travelers discover they are about to reach Mars. As indicated, using a rocket designed to reach the Moon to instead go to Mars is equivalent to launching a boat from Los Angeles to Santa Catalina and instead going to Japan, but when this occurs in *Conquest of Space*, at least the crew deliberately aims their ship at Mars; the chances that a spaceship randomly drifting between Earth and the Moon would, as a result of unexpected acceleration, somehow travel a precise course to the distant Mars are impossibly small. Even Eckstrom acknowledges that this turn of events is "unbelievable" and could only have occurred because "something infinitely greater assumes control." In other words, the film suggests that, for some reason, God Himself intervened to send the spacecraft to Mars.

What really occurred, of course, is that writer-director Neumann had the crew land on Mars instead of the Moon, no matter how implausible the method might be, for two motives that come to define the pseudo-spacesuit film. First, it enables him to keep characters out of spacesuits; in this case, once the spaceship lands on Mars, Corrigan happily notes, "I've been itching to get into one of these things," referring to the ships' spacesuits, and holds up what looks like a helmet from the suits worn by the pilots of high-altitude aircraft. But Eckstrom responds that "pressure suits" will not be needed because, unlike the Moon, Mars has an atmosphere. Instead, they can simply wear oxygen masks over their mouths. In 1929, *Frau im Mond* could still posit that deep valleys on the Moon might have an atmosphere to keep spacesuits out of the picture; but by 1950, it had been established that the Moon was airless, so Neumann, addressing an audience that included adults (unlike the makers of serials), felt obliged to send astronauts to Mars, known to have a thin atmosphere, to depict astronauts on the surface of an alien world without spacesuits.

Next, as astronauts emerge from their ship and begin walking across a barren Martian landscape (which again resembles Southern California), the real reason why God wanted these space travelers to visit Mars becomes apparent; there is, as one character says, "a lesson here for our world." It is first suggested by a ruined structure that the humans come upon, suggesting that a Martian civilization of "a high order of intelligence" existed there thousands of years ago, as well as signs of dangerously high levels of radioactivity, indicating that the civilization was destroyed by some sort of blast effect. Clearly, Martians engaged in self-destruction by waging atomic war.

Then, since static ruins are insufficiently exciting, the other characteristic feature of pseudo-spacesuit films is introduced: humanoid aliens, here bald men dressed like cavemen with strange scabs on their backs. They begin hurtling rocks at the astronauts, killing Eckstrom and Corrigan and severely wounding Chamberlain. (One beautiful cavewoman also makes a fatal brief appearance, since films aimed at the masses must introduce as many pretty women as possible.) Mars is therefore a world, as Eckstrom comments, that went from "atomic age to stone age," driven by war from advanced civilization back into savagery, and thus provides an important reminder to Earth that it must be wise enough avoid the same tragic fate. So, astronauts must return to Earth to "[t]ell them what we've found."

Needless to say, this "lesson" is insignificant, since scores of news articles, political speeches, and other science fiction stories had for years made the obvious point that a global nuclear war would have catastrophic effects and must be prevented at all costs. Perhaps, as Eric Leif Davin argues while introducing his interview with Neumann in *Pioneers of Wonder*, Neumann was indeed the first director to "put such a vision [of "nuclear holocaust"] on the silver screen" (319). But one does not need spacesuit films to illustrate oft-repeated warnings about human behavior on Earth; instead, their priority should be the more original work of exploring the probable characteristics of life in space. But diverting films about the strange environment of space into familiar territory — here, literally, the American Southwest — to provide familiar messages — here, a warning against nuclear war — becomes the usual pattern in most subsequent films involving journeys into space.

Still, in precisely one way, *Rocketship X-M* contributes to our understanding of the realities of space travel; for while three surviving crew members return to their spaceship and fly back to Earth, they do not have enough fuel to make a safe landing and hence are doomed to crash-land and die. The film acknowledges, in other words, not only that space travel will be dangerous, but that a single problem (in this case, insufficient fuel) would probably lead to the deaths of entire crews. That is, deaths featured in *Project Moon Base*, *Riders to the Stars*, *Conquest of Space*, and episodes of *Men into Space* only involve single individuals, and there is just one fleeting reference to a disaster that killed an entire crew — the crash landing on the Moon discovered in the *Men into Space* episode "Lunar Secret"; the crisis here singularly kills all persons on board a spaceship. (And this grim conclusion had been planned from the start, since Neumann's original title was *None Came Back*.) One might say, then, that the film was prescient in projecting that problems in space would likely cause the deaths not of one or two crew members, but of everyone on board a spacecraft (which actually occurred three times, once with the Soyuz and twice with the space shuttle).

Final scenes, however, put a positive spin on this tragic ending, as a general argues the flight produced "practical information which may well mean the salvation of our own world" and orders construction of a second spaceship. Perhaps, though this is not said, this second mission will, in light of knowledge gained about the Martians' fate, be less focused on military motives and more on achieving peaceful coexistence.

Flight to Mars (1951)

Just as *Rocketship X-M* represented the cheap imitation of *Destination Moon*, *Flight to Mars* invites consideration as the even cheaper imitation of *Rocketship X-M*. Director Lesley Selander and screenwriter Arthur Strawn were in a fashion remaking the Russian film *Aelita: Queen of Mars*, but signs of its influence are minimal: a Martian civilization that lives underground, a revolt of sorts against an evil government, and a beautiful Martian woman named Alita. Otherwise, little about this film's story resembles the earlier film, save that both flights to Mars involve space travelers who, anticipating an Earthlike Mars, do not bring spacesuits; like the astronauts of *Rocketship X-M*, they will only wear oxygen masks. When boarding their spaceship, they disconcertingly wear street clothes, acceptable in 1924 but wildly inappropriate in 1951. Yet this qualifies as a spacesuit film because, on Mars, they encounter humanoid *Martians* wearing spacesuits (strangely, the colorful spacesuits from *Destination Moon*), since Martians find the changed surface of their dying world uninhabitable; they emerge from underground, garbed in protective clothing, solely to greet visitors from Earth. (The next chapter discusses other films wherein aliens wear spacesuits when they are on Earth.)

Even before the ship takes off, this film conveys little concern for scientific accuracy, since its crew again includes a beautiful woman — physicist Carol Stafford (Virginia Huston) — who like Van Horn is called a brilliant scientist. However, she shows she is a real woman, by the standards of her time, with her obsessive, unrequited love for engineer Jim Barker (Arthur Franz). Another incongruous crew member is the first cinematic journalist in space, Steve Abbott (Cameron Mitchell), also the only non-scientist on board, who unusually functions as both hero and comic relief. Though the mission is controlled by "the Pentagon," as indicated by an opening heading, there is no indication of any military purpose for this pioneering flight; instead, the trip is repeatedly likened to climbing a high mountain, suggesting it is being undertaken solely as a stimulating challenge. While scientist Dr. Lane (John Litel) volunteers to tell Abbott all the "scientific reasons why I want to go," the journalist does not want to hear them, seeking a "human angle" on the flight for his dispatches. But later in the film, Stafford briefly refers to a desire to gain scientific knowledge from the mission, and on Mars, it is stated that the real "object of our flight" is obtaining "data or information about Mars."

There is also, from the beginning, an unusual air of pessimism about this film, since almost everyone on board seems convinced that they will not survive; one crew member, renowned scientist Professor Jackson (Richard Gaines), even comments, "Personally I feel this rocket is my coffin." Another depressing message is conveyed in opening scenes: Jackson agreed to a television interview, despite a prior agreement among all astronauts to give no interviews, because his lifetime devotion to science left him poor, so he must earn three thousand dollars to provide for his widowed daughter and grandchildren. (One could say, then, that the film offers the first indication that space travel might offer personal profits for space travelers, a point later made in the *Men into Space* episode "Contraband.") The final element introduced before the flight is a developing romantic triangle involving Stafford, Barker, and Abbott, who recognizes that Stafford loves Barker and tries to woo her away from the engineer and into his arms.

As for efforts to convey the strangeness of space, the film offers a promisingly disorienting shot, filmed from above, of astronauts climbing a ladder to get to their stations before liftoff, suggesting that the flight might similarly indicate there is no "up" and "down" in space. But this never occurs; in a radio message to Earth, Abbott notes that once in flight, "Carol Stafford floated up to the top of the rocket," but we observe no weightlessness because, he continues, "She kept bumping her head until we got the magnetic fluid stabilizer to equalize the gravitational pull." Since weightlessness by definition means the absence of "gravitational pull," and since no "magnetic fluid stabilizer" could have any effect on the force of gravity, the explanation is clearly little more than scientific gobbledygook, as Abbott himself suggests in his concluding comment: "And how do you like those for big words?" Later space films refer to some form of artificial gravity.

In the only worthwhile scene in the film, an interesting conversation begins with Stafford conveying some irritation (motivated, one gathers, by her fruitless passion for the engineer); she then apologizes, saying, "It's just that being confined like this has gotten on my nerves." After this brief intimation that space travel might be mentally upsetting, the talk turns more philosophical: Abbott looks at the receding Earth and comments, "The Earth seems so big when you're on it, from out here so small and nothing. It's like closing your eyes in the dark and suddenly there you are, alone with your soul."

Jackson then advances what is, for films of that era, a very cosmic idea: the theory that "the universe is a living, giant being, and that we, as human beings, made in its image, are miniature universes in ourselves." With objects in the universe likened to corpuscles making up our body, another crewman opines, "It makes this trip seem small and futile," then asks, "If we're simply going from one corpuscle to another in some giant being, what will we find?" The professor has a conventional answer about advancing human knowledge: "Crossing over may provide some of the answers to things man has wanted to know since the beginning of time." Briefly, in terms that science fiction readers might find trite, the film provocatively suggests that the experience of space travel might profoundly alter the way that humans perceive the universe.

This somber mood doesn't last; the film immediately shifts to the routine drama of a threatening swarm of meteors, forcing the spaceship to abruptly change course. After the meteors pass, a crewman is told to check for damage. This seems strange, because surely, if a meteor actually caused damage that could be detected from inside the spacecraft, it would

An Encore Appearance: The spacesuits from *Destination Moon* (1950), destined for many appearances in later films, first resurface on a group of unidentified Martians escorting Earthwoman Carol Stafford (Virginia Huston) in *Flight to Mars* (1951).

have penetrated the hull and caused a disastrous leak that everyone would notice. But somehow, it transpires, a meteor broke an important landing gear cable within a compartment without breaching the hull. This is impossible, but the film could not have astronauts experience an air leak because they had no spacesuits. Now, in a ship with broken landing gear that cannot be repaired, they must either turn back or crash-land on Mars. Because there is a chance they could obtain valuable data about Mars and return them to Earth, they resolve to risk landing.

Once they reach Mars, providentially surviving by "belly-landing" on snow which almost buries their spaceship before they escape, the film becomes completely silly. As in *Rocketship X-M*, travelers find ruins indicating that there was once an advanced civilization, and then encounter Martians who look and act exactly like humans. This time, while decadent in their own way (as we will learn), the Martians have remained civilized, wearing spacesuits to survive on their planet's now-barren surface and maintaining a scientifically advanced society in underground chambers fueled by the element Corium. The Martians also seem friendly, offering to shelter their visitors underground while helping them rebuild their spaceship. But their leader Ikron (Morris Ankrum) and a majority of the planet's governing council have evil plans: since their supply of Corium will be exhausted in ten years, dooming their race to extinction, they will seize the spaceship once it is repaired, kill the Earth people, construct many duplicates of the craft, and conquer Earth. Thus, the Martians resemble the sinister aliens observed in serials, a similarity reinforced by Martian costumes featuring childish lightning-bolt symbols and rocket symbols.

Fortunately, there are a few virtuous Martians, including elderly council member Tillamar (Robert Barrat), an engineer named Justin (Edward Earle), and Justin's beautiful daughter Alita (Marguerite Chapman), a scientist who falls in love with Barker, resolving the romantic triangle and allowing Stafford to pair up with Abbott. Together, the visitors and good Martians scheme to deceive the council about when the spaceship will be ready, enabling the Earth people to leave unexpectedly early. They will also bring along Alita (now set to marry Barker) and Tallimar to represent Mars on Earth in negotiating a more peaceful solution to their problems.

Everything goes smoothly until Ikron gets suspicious and summons Alita to the council chambers for questioning. When Barker rushes to the council to challenge him, Ikron orders the two of them to be confined and the spaceship to be seized immediately. At this point, the film's descent into serial-like melodrama is complete, as Barker punches the council head. He and Alita flee from the room, leading the evil Martians on a chase that ends when they barely manage to board the spaceship, slam the door in the face of a Martian at their heels, and join the others in blasting off for Earth. While the rock-throwing Martians of *Rocketship X-M* were ludicrous enough in their own way, this film officially introduces the fistfights and chase scenes of serials to feature films about space travel.

With an Earth woman joining the first expedition to Mars, and a Martian woman playing a key role in assisting its crew, one might praise *Flight to Mars* for featuring two strong female characters. But any proto-feminist aura is dispelled when the visitors enter their quarters beneath the surface of Mars. Stafford immediately asks where the kitchen is; but their female guide explains that, on Mars, all food is prepared by a central "food laboratory" which sends plates of cooked food to people's homes. And, when the guide presses a button and makes the food she had ordered appear, Stafford proclaims Mars is "a woman's paradise." To add to her bliss, she then learns she will not even have to wash the dishes, since that will be taken care of "mechanically." Stafford responds to this news by saying,

"Mars, I love you." Oddly, while there are brief references to miraculous alloys and a glimpse of flying vehicles in underground chambers, this is the only detailed discussion of advanced Martian technology. Thus, there is no need for a woman astronaut to domesticate a strange space environment; this planet, with its familiar heroes and villains and benevolent dining arrangements, is already domesticated and unthreatening. One can only cherish, then, the thought-provoking dialogue in this film which precedes its banal depiction of an alien world.

Cat-Women of the Moon (1953)

One would not expect scientific plausibility in a film entitled *Cat-Women of the Moon*, and the expectation is generally correct. Still, there are intermittent signs of a desire to deal with space travel seriously, and the film even breaks new ground. For one thing, this is the first spacesuit film to open with a lengthy narration, contextualizing its story within a broader narrative about an inexorable human drive to conquer space:

> The eternal wonders of space and time.... The faraway dreams and mysteries of other worlds, other life.... The stars, the planets.... Man has been face to face with them for centuries, yet is barely able to penetrate their unknown secrets. Some time, someday, the barrier will be pierced. Why must we wait? Why not now?

This stirring speech seems incongruous in a film where the "unknown secret" of the Moon is that it is inhabited by a race of beautiful, sultry women in black bodysuits; but its true significance may lie in what this narration replaces.

Specifically, this is the first spacesuit film that begins with its space travelers already in flight, on their way to the Moon. All previous films included prologues on Earth, designed not only to introduce main characters but to show audiences how space travel might actually be achieved, culminating in the dramatic image of the spaceship blasting off. The absence of such scenes in *Cat-Women of the Moon* might be attributed solely to a desire for economy in story-telling, instigated by the development of its subgenre: Since previous films had addressed the task of persuading audiences that space travel might be possible with preliminary sequences on Earth, the filmmakers may have reasoned that such material was no longer necessary. So, they could eliminate the preliminaries, replacing them with some brief narration about space travel, and begin the adventure at a more exciting moment, when people are already in space.

However, one can also say this film represents a crucial turning point in depictions of space travel: By showing space travelers both on Earth and in space, previous films asserted and maintained a connection to their home planet, indicating that space would only be a place to visit, not a place to live. But by presenting characters who are solely observed in space and on another world (since the film concludes with characters returning to Earth, but still in space), *Cat-Women of the Moon* arguably anticipates the day when seasoned space travelers would see themselves primarily as residents of space, not of Earth, creating a divide between ground-dwellers and space-dwellers. This theme would not surface in films until 1960, in *Space Men*, but it is a significant undercurrent in *2001: A Space Odyssey*.

Granted, all of this may overstate the significance of a film that, almost immediately, signals it will be the silliest of the early pseudo-spacesuit films. The spaceship crew is in a spacious room, with no indication of zero gravity, sitting in normal office chairs; once they endure the usual pressures of liftoff, the now-predictable beautiful woman on board, navigator Helen Salinger (Marie Windsor), picks up a mirror and begins combing her hair. This behavior seems so inappropriate during a space mission that her commander and boyfriend Laird Grainger (Sonny Tufts) feels obliged to remind his crew, "This is a scientific expedition, and not a stunt!" Later, when the inevitable meteor damages the rocket's atomic engine and starts a fire, a crewman dons what looks like a normal radiation suit and puts out the fire with a standard fire extinguisher.

The film becomes more impressive once astronauts land on the Moon, primarily because it employs persuasive moonscapes prepared by noted space artist Chesley Bonestell, who previously worked on *Destination Moon*. The first scenes of space travelers surveying and walking across the lunar surface are realistic and evocative. However, nothing else about their lunar sojourn can withstand scrutiny. First, though it was no longer possible to imagine a breathable atmosphere on the Moon, which led previous makers of melodramatic spacesuit films to shift the action to Mars, director Arthur Hilton and screenwriters Jack Rabin, Al Zimbalist, and Roy Hamilton essentially return to the scenario of *Frau im Mond*, either coincidentally or because they had seen the film: Astronauts land on the dark side of \the Moon, they find and enter a cavern, they suspect it has a breathable atmosphere, and a character proves this by lighting a cigarette and watching it burn, establishing that oxygen is present. (Yet in the Moon's low gravity, no atmosphere could be retained, either in a deep valley or underground.) The "scientific" explanation for this atmosphere is ridiculous: "a magnetic field on the dark side could exert gravitation pull—a special one" to attract and retain the air. Strangely, as a spectacular lapse in continuity, Grainger demonstrated, only a few minutes earlier, the dangerous heat just across the line separating the Moon's bright side from its dark side by throwing a cigarette on the bright side and let-ting colleagues watch it burn—which as the film notes, could not happen in the lunar vacuum.

Knowing they are not needed within the cave, astronauts entirely remove their spacesuits, leave them lying on the ground, and continue walking through the cave, since they are confident the Moon is uninhabited and their spacesuits will be undisturbed. That is a reasonable assumption, but this is not a reasonable film; these caves are actually home to both giant spiders (obvious puppets, as shown by unconvincing scenes of astronauts struggling with them) and beautiful women, survivors of a once-extensive lunar civilization now threatened with extinction due to a gradual loss of air. Employing their telepathic powers (which work only on women), they long had Salinger under their influence, prodding her to guide the spaceship to the place on the Moon's dark side where they could be led to the Cat-Women's cavern. These aliens steal the spacesuits, seize Salinger, plant a device on her hand which gives them complete control over her (except when she holds a man), and meet the astronauts, pretending to be friendly even as they intend to kill them, commandeer their spaceship, travel to Earth, and use their mental abilities to dominate Earth women and thus conquer Earth. None of this makes sense—one particularly wonders why, if their powers extend to Earth, they must travel there to effect their plan—but the plots of melodramatic spacesuit films rarely make sense.

As the space travelers are entertained by the Cat-Women, all the men seem overwhelmed by their beauty and implausibly persuaded they are friendly. All the men, that is, except Kip Reissner (Victor Jory), who strangely supplants *Cat-Women*'s ostensible star, Sonny Tufts, as the film's true hero. (Salinger is really in love with him, but the Cat-Women mentally force her to love Grainger because the latter can provide more useful information.) A detailed account of subsequent plot contrivances is unnecessary, save to note that the Cat-

Women are eventually defeated and the astronauts, except for one slain crewman, fly back safely to Earth. As the film concludes, crew members reestablish radio contact with Earth and are predictably asked, "What happened?" The response, a considerable understatement: "That is a long story."

Searching for serious comments to make about this absurd film, more or less on the level of a serial, one could note that when Salinger is asked why she sent a radio message to Alpha (the name of the chief alien, since they identify themselves by Greek letters), the mentally influenced navigator can only describe it as "a touch of space madness," which may be the first time this particular term came up in a space film and arguably anticipates later films like *Conquest of Space* wherein space travelers actually go mad. Inhabited entirely by women, this is another world that is already domesticated, since they provide "delicious" food for their guests. They also indulge in a bizarre modern dance.

But perhaps the film's most striking aspect is that spacesuits are an important part of the plot. Exploring an airless world, astronauts were foolish to abandon their spacesuits, even when there seemed no possibility of losing them, and after their spacesuits are taken, they realize they cannot return to their ship, and Earth, unless they retrieve them. Spacesuits are also important to the Cat-Women (who oddly have never built spacesuits of their own), since one woman must put one on to bring a smitten crewman to the spacecraft and obtain important instructions about flying the ship. Even while contriving to minimize use of spacesuits, *Cat-Women of the Moon* (like *Phantom from Space*, discussed below) acknowledges the importance of spacesuits in space travel, a point often evaded in other melodramatic spacesuit films.

While one of the worst spacesuit films of the 1950s, *Cat-Women* also qualifies as the decade's most influential spacesuit film — since it was not only remade in 1958 as *Missile to the Moon* but also inspired at least three similar films. It is as if producers were saying, science be damned, if we want audiences to buy tickets, we must send astronauts to planets inhabited exclusively by beautiful women in provocative outfits.

Forbidden Planet (1956)

Technically, *Forbidden Planet* qualifies as a spacesuit film on the flimsiest of grounds, but merits brief attention as a pioneering demonstration of strategies being developed to not only minimize the use of spacesuits in films, but eliminate them entirely. To be sure, other films of the 1950s had developed other techniques for avoiding spacesuits, such as *This Island Earth* (1955), wherein travelers to and from the world of Metaluna must undergo a process of "conversion," which involves being placed inside special chambers and bathed in radiation, to survive in the differing environments. But such mumbo-jumbo requires a certain amount of time to explain and illustrate, creating an incentive for simpler ways to keep characters out of spacesuits.

Forbidden Planet was more efficient. First, unlike the absurd television series *Rocky Jones, Space Ranger*, which place dozens of Earthlike planets and moons in the Solar System, more plausible stories must posit that future humans will develop faster-than-light travel, so space travelers can visit hypothetical planets of any nature instead of being limited to the known conditions of nearby planets and satellites. Second, stories require a policy that astronauts only land on planets resembling Earth, eliminating any need for spacesuits.

Thus, when Commander J.J. Adams (Leslie Nielsen) and his crew approach Altair IV, to investigate the fate of a mission that landed there twenty years ago, he already knows it is an Earth-type planet, so he tells crewmates that "no survival suits will be required upon landing." Here, then, while the verbal reference suggests that Adams and his men have spacesuits to be used when they land on an inhospitable planet, the adventure of this film conveniently does not require them, so spacesuits are never observed.

World Without End (1956)

Arguably, *World Without End* combines the stories of *Rocketship X-M* and *Flight to Mars*: The crew of a spaceship heading for Mars, upon landing, is first attacked by deformed savages (survivors of a devastating nuclear war), then encounters an underground race of normal, civilized humans with both friendly and hostile factions, engendering melodramatic conflicts before matters are resolved. The difference is that this spaceship actually lands on Earth in the future, making the planet's Earthlike environments and people entirely plausible.

The implausibility here lies in the way time travel is achieved: As the spaceship returns from its mission to orbit and observe Mars, it runs into an "exponential time displacement" which makes it accelerate rapidly, so their ensuing four-century journey seems like only a day. As a character notes, "If you go fast enough, time slows down," a rare instance of someone in these films providing correct scientific information, according to Albert Einstein's theory of relativity (though, bizarrely, the idea is attributed to a fictional scientist, not Einstein). Of course, such amazing speeds would also drive a spaceship many light years away from the solar system, so its unguided landing on Earth seems impossible. It is also unlikely that such a rapidly traveling spaceship would crash-land somewhere in the Rocky Mountains without harming its crew and causing only minor damage, a fortuitous outcome explained solely, as in *Flight to Mars*, by the fact that the craft landed in snow.

Not knowing where they are, the men display admirable caution when Herbert Ellis (Rod Taylor) advises crewmates to "break out the oxygen helmets and pressure suits — we may need them," which qualifies this as a spacesuit film. But John Borden (Hugh Marlowe) responds, "Feels to me as though we have plus gravity. It's normal." And since instruments indicate there is "plenty of oxygen," the four men then leave their spaceship in normal clothing, though they take the precaution of carrying handguns. At this point, Ellis conveys his knowledge of precisely what sort of film he is in: He tells his colleagues, "If this is Venus or some other strange planet, we're liable to run into some high-domed characters with green blood in them who'll blast at us with atomic death-ray guns." What they actually "run into" — two absurd giant spiders and mutated, one-eyed cavemen who attack them — is only slightly less silly.

When a retreat into a cave leads them to an entrance to the underground world of normal humans in 2508, events also recall *Cat-Women of the Moon*: All women are beautiful, and while there are men around, they are frail-looking — the descriptive term repeatedly used is "bloodless" — so the women are naturally attracted to the buff newcomers (particularly the sometimes shirtless Ellis) and begin throwing themselves at them. The group's aged leader, Timmek (Everett Glass), and other elders are friendly enough, but since Timmek's daughter Elaine (Shawn Smith) visibly lusts after the men from the past, the jealous Mories (Booth Colman), who wants her for himself, schemes to turn the others against them. But his plot is discovered and he is killed by mutants while trying to escape. Then the visitors, deducing the race is dying because people are cut off from the surface world and lack the "guts" to battle mutants, train them how to build and use weapons and lead a campaign to drive off mutants to establish a beachhead on the surface. The result, stated in the film's last line, is "the rebirth of the human race."

Unimportant as a spacesuit film, *World Without End* commands attention as a precursor of later science fiction films: It surely influenced George Pal's peculiar approach to his 1960 adaptation of H.G. Wells's *The Time Machine*, with one reversal: actor Taylor (the time traveler) now teaches passive people on the surface to battle aggressive mutants who live underground. The film further anticipates an episode of *The Outer Limits*, "The Man Who Was Never Born"—wherein another returning astronaut lands on a devastated future Earth—and the first two *Planet of the Apes* films: In the first (1968), returning space travelers again land accidentally on a future Earth after a destructive nuclear war, though this one left apes, not deformed mutants, in control of the surface; and in *Beneath the Planet of the Apes* (1969), astronauts encounter normal-looking humans who survived by moving underground. Displaying Hollywood's progress in dealing with an annoying problem, however, astronauts in these films never wear and/or mention spacesuits.

Missile to the Moon (1958), *Queen of Outer Space* (1958), and *Nude on the Moon* (1961)

As noted, *Cat-Women of the Moon* proved the most influential spacesuit film of the 1950s by inspiring at least four films with the same plot: male astronauts land on an alien planet inhabited mostly or entirely by beautiful women who alternately scheme against them and fall in love with them. The first, *Fire Maidens of Outer Space* (1956), is not relevant to this study: While astronauts "check the outside atmosphere" before disembarking on the newly discovered thirteenth moon of Jupiter, they never mention spacesuits and, anticipating an Earthlike environment, apparently did not bring them. But filmmakers were clearly imitating *Cat-Women of the Moon*, as is most evident in the alien beauties' extended dance routines.

Another film, *Missile to the Moon*, is not officially labeled a remake of *Cat-Women of the Moon*, and indeed the film goes to considerable trouble to provide a different sort of spaceship crew; yet it retains the key elements—discovery of a dying, all-female civilization beneath the surface of the Moon conspiring to seize the spaceship and conquer Earth. This time, however, the Moon women previously sent one of their few remaining men, scientist Dirk Green (Michael Whalen), to Earth, seeking data before the invasion. To return to the Moon, he works with scientist Steve Dayton (Richard Travis) to build a spaceship entirely powered by "solar energy"—which is odd, the Walrus told the Carpenter, because it takes off in the middle of the night. Displeased to learn that the government is preparing to take control of his project, on the grounds that all missile experiments should be government business, Green decides to immediately launch his spaceship, exploiting a fortuitous coincidence: Two escaped convicts, Gene Fennell (Tommy Cook) and Lon (Gary Clarke), just hid themselves inside his spaceship, and upon finding them, Green recruits them to become his crew on the hasty lunar flight. As they take off, Green does not realize that Dayton and his fiancée, June Saxton (Cathy Downs), also boarded the spaceship to investigate indications of recent activity. Through these complex maneuvers, *Missile to the Moon* achieves a crew roughly similar to that of *Cat-Women of the Moon*, four men and a beautiful woman, though only two people are really prepared for their assignment.

The more sympathetic of the two convicts, Fennell, reveals his intelligence when he asks Green before taking off, "Hey, do we need oxygen masks?" The scientist replies, "No, this control room's sealed, contains its own oxygen source." Dayton and Saxton, trapped in the spaceship's other room without oxygen, survive the liftoff because Dayton runs to a compartment and tells Saxton, "Here are a couple of spare face masks." Aside from the potential problem of not having enough air to breathe, the other peril encountered during the flight is a predictable meteor shower — termed a "meteor field" — which has only one unfortunate effect: a shelf falls and kills Green. First suggesting the film's links to *Cat-Women of the Moon*, the dying Green hands Dayton a medallion, insists the ship must land at his prearranged position (near the entrance to the Moon's underground civilization), and asks for forgiveness from "Lido," who we learn is the current leader of the Moon.

Upon landing on the Moon, Dayton announces, "It's a dream come true," what one might expect a rocket scientist to say. What Saxton exclaims is more surprising: "I'm so happy, I don't know what to say." Like women in *Riders to the Stars* and *Men into Space*, then, she seems especially attuned to the sheer pleasure of space travel. Next, after Dayton advises his crew to "break out the spacesuits," we get a new perspective on these garments when Fennell complains, "My head feels like it's in jail." Perhaps an escaped convict would be unusually sensitive to the confining aspects of a spacesuit, which explains why, once they are in the cave and discover it is filled with oxygen, they are eager to emulate their predecessors and quickly "get out of these suits." The fact that there are no indications of the Moon's low gravity is explained, minimally, when Lon says, "These gravitational shoes work like a charm." One novelty is that the astronauts do not immediately encounter giant spiders (they show up later), but are driven into a cave by an even more ludicrous menace — enormous "rock men" who slowly stalk across the surface of the airless Moon, but avoid the caves because they cannot stand oxygen. (This suggests they could easily be repelled by an enterprising astronaut opening the value of an oxygen tank to blast them with oxygen, but these space travelers are incapable of such ingenuity — after fleeing, they later defeat them by throwing grenades they obtained from the Moon women.)

After succumbing to knockout gas pumped into the cave, the astronauts awaken in the chamber of the Moon women, and we meet the ruler, the Lido (K. T. Stevens) — Lido is a title, not a name — who is now blind and assumes, because he wears Green's medallion, that Dayton is Green and addresses him accordingly, asking for the information he garnered from Earth. Dayton plays along, though he also learns to his distress that Green is betrothed to an associate of the Lido, the duplicitous Alpha (Nina Bara). Making these women seem less menacing, the Lido oddly explains that they no longer plan to invade Earth, having deemed the planet unsuitable, and will instead migrate to another, unspecified planet. Soon, determined to marry Dayton though he professes his love for Saxton, Alpha murders the Lido, assumes her position as leader, uses mental powers to enslave Dayton, and plans to marry Dayton and place the others in the "extermination chamber," where the means of death, in the tradition of *Cat-Women of the Moon*, will be an enormous, hideous spider. Fortunately, there is ample time to prevent these evil deeds because the marriage ceremony is delayed by a strange and interminable dance routine (another vestige of *Cat-Women of the Moon*, though there is only one dancer this time), allowing another woman, still loyal to the former Lido, to help the prisoners escape and free Dayton from his spell. As the Earth people leave, she throws a grenade to break open their underground chamber and expose it to the vacuum, dooming the Moon women.

Once back in their spacesuits and on the surface, Dayton, Saxton, and Fennell are again threatened by rock men, but keep them at bay with grenades while waiting for Lon to return. This less sympathetic convict is filling bags with lunar diamonds so he can be rich upon returning to Earth. When he belatedly appears and is surrounded by rock men, he refuses to drop his bags and run away; instead, he slowly backs into the direct light of the Sun, which instantly burns him up and reduces his body to a skeletal cinder. This brief, horrific image recalls the dead astronaut observed in *Riders to the Stars* and adds a touch of sobriety to an otherwise frivolous tale, vividly illustrating that space is a dangerous place, though this particular peril is wildly implausible. (Yes, an astronaut in the direct heat of the lunar day would experience discomfort and eventually die, without the cooling systems now included in spacesuits, but he would not burst into flames on the airless lunar surface and die instantly.) Still, despite its obvious weaknesses, this moment alone makes *Missile to the Moon* a better film than *Cat-Women*.

To account for another 1958 film about an alien planet inhabited solely by beautiful women, the story goes that famed screenwriter Ben Hecht attended a Hollywood party in the late 1950s, making sardonic comments about the sorts of outlandish stories now sought by producers; as an amusing example, he outlined an absurd scenario about male astronauts who fly to Venus and discover a race of beautiful women. A producer overheard him and, proving Hecht's point, promptly asked to purchase the story. I do not know whether the tale is true or not, but it remains the most plausible way to explain why Hecht is credited for the story of *Queen of Outer Space*.

Needless to say, the film is thoroughly ridiculous, though there are incongruous touches of accurate science, surely the work of screenwriter Charles Beaumont, a science fiction writer obliged to make Hecht's story into a film. Thus, upon reaching an unknown world that turns out to be Venus, astronauts note that its gravity is about 0.87 that of Earth's (Venus's actual surface gravity), so they know they are not on Mars, because that planet has only 0.38 Earth gravity (also accurate). There are also knowing references to other science fiction works: As they begin exploring, Professor Konrad (Paul Birch) speculates that the inhabitants of Venus "could be insects with tremendous mental powers," while Lieutenant Larry Turner (Patrick Waltz) says he "read one of throwaway dollar magazines" describing small green aliens with big heads and eyes on feelers.

Such aliens would have been more logical than the gorgeous models they actually encounter on Venus. Konrad, Turner, Captain Neil Patterson (Eric Fleming) and Lieutenant Michael Cruze (Dave Willock) are brought to Venus because, while flying to visit Earth's space station to investigate signs that Earth has unfriendly "neighbors," they see the station blown up by a mysterious ray; accelerating to avoid the same fate, they black out and awaken on Venus. Konrad explains the slim odds of their reaching Venus accidentally by saying that "all things are possible in space," though they may have been brought there deliberately. To explain why they survived a crash landing without damage, there is a reference to "automatic landing controls," and theirs is yet another spaceship that providently landed in snow to further cushion any blows. As one more bit of idiocy, we later learn that Venus has several moons, but they are unknown on Earth because they are concealed by the "cloud cover" (though in reality, no moons could remain in orbit close enough to their home planet to lie within the atmosphere).

Before venturing outside, one crewman says, "I'll break out the pressure suits," but these are never seen, since Konrad states, without scientific justification, "The gravity is so close to Earth's, the atmosphere should be breathable." A check of instruments reveals that he is right, so the crew "won't need the pressure suits or the oxygen." Then, after doing some exploring, they are captured by beautiful women wielding ray guns whose beams start fires; as an especially laughable touch, all women wear skimpy outfits and high heels. The men are brought before the ruler of Venus, the masked Yllana (Laurie Mitchell), who despises men because the destructive war that Venusian men waged against another world had devastating effects (like disfiguring her face with radiation burns). Afterwards, she led a revolt, took control of Venus, and killed or exiled all men; she now plans to destroy Earth, employing the same ray that blew up the space station. Yllana is attracted to Patterson, but he rejects her upon ripping off her mask and seeing her hideous features.

Fortunately for Earth, another Venusian woman, Talleah (Zsa Zsa Gabor), sympathizes with the Earthmen, in part because she has fallen in love with Patterson. She helps them escape and leads them through the jungle to destroy the machine that will emit the ray, dodging energy beams along the way. As a homage to *Cat-Women of the Moon*, they are briefly menaced by a huge spider in a cave, a development evidently so embarrassing to the cast that no one says a word about the encounter. Soon they are captured, but sabotage the machine anyway. Yllana is killed trying to make it work, and Talleah takes over Venus to establish peaceful relations with Earth, also asking Earth to order the men to remain on Venus for another year.

Despite its scientific implausibility, the appealing concept of a planet filled with beautiful, scantily clad women was too powerful to abandon, and it surfaces again in another film about Venus, the altered foreign film *Voyage to the Planet of Prehistoric Women* discussed below, long after science had proven humans could not inhabit the planet. But the next film in this dubious tradition was a pornographic variation on the theme, Doris Wishman's *Nude on the Moon*, which qualifies as a unique curiosity, and not simply because its beautiful women are topless.

Nude on the Moon stands out, first, as the second spacesuit film that begins with a theme song, "Moon Doll," sung by Ralph Young (later part of the singing duo Sandler and Young). While its significance only emerges later, it is obviously a song sung by an Earthman who visits and falls in love with a beautiful Moon woman, as suggested by its first line, "I'm mooning over you, my little Moon doll." The song accompanies an animated view of a lunar landscape beneath twinkling stars in an incongruous blue sky, also appropriate for this peculiar film.

As probably the first pornographic film to venture into space, *Nude on the Moon* appropriately mimics other pioneering space films by devoting a surprising amount of time to preparations for its Moon flight, instead of immediately introducing unclad women. Waiting to obtain government funding for his proposed mission, rocket scientist Jeff Huntley (Lester Brown) learns that he inherited three million dollars from his uncle and tells his colleague and mentor, "The Professor" (Walter Meyer), that he can now finance the project himself. In several scenes, the scientists work with test tubes filled with liquids producing vapors — presumably testing rocket fuel — and discuss the dangers involved in the flight; specifically, because the Moon experiences extreme changes in temperature, the Professor fears that constant contraction and expansion might have reduced its surface to rubble, preventing their rocket from taking off on a return flight. A subplot involves Huntley's secretary Cathy (Marietta), who secretly loves him, and the Professor's efforts to encourage Huntley to pursue a normal life with a wife and family; but Huntley responds, "Science is my life and nothing else." We learn from establishing shots that the scientists are based near Miami, Florida (where *Nude on the Moon* was filmed), perhaps making this the first film set in modern times to have its Moon flight take off from Florida.

Their spaceship takes off, and after a brief bout with the painful acceleration of liftoff, their flight is uneventful, as there is "first stage separation" for its multi-staged rocket and a glimpse of meteors that prove unthreatening. Oddly, while approaching the Moon, the men succumb to an irresistible impulse to sleep. When they awaken, they find that, somehow, they have made a safe landing on the Moon. This may be designed to cast their upcoming, highly implausible lunar experiences as a dream, though both men will remember everything that happened. As they land, there are images of a stark, traditional moonscape, which makes what they discover upon emerging from the spaceship doubly incongruous.

One startling thing is the unbelievable spacesuits the wear: outfits primarily made of a thin skintight fabric, red or green, which seems insufficient protection against a cold night in Florida, let alone conditions on the Moon. To bizarrely suggest more substantive garb, they have leather breastplates and codpieces. While they wear space helmets and gloves, their bare necks and bare wrists are visible, demonstrating that the spacesuits are spectacularly less than airtight. Huntley and the Professor do not immediately die, however, because they are somehow in a region of the Moon with a blue sky, lush green vegetation, and an atmosphere. To explain this, the Professor comments that they are at the "bottom of a crater," one of two possible references in the film to *Frau im Mond*, which also posits an lunar atmosphere in a depressed area. But Lang at least did not also provide a blue sky and plant life.

Despite all indications that this area is exactly like Earth, the men have oxygen tanks on their backs but they seem to breathe air from a tube near their mouths, and the Professor insists they have limited time to explore the Moon because of their "thirteen-hour supply of oxygen." It seems, then, that this territory has an atmosphere supporting plants identical to Earth plants, and scantily clad women identical to humans, but not breathable to men from Earth.

As they wander through this verdant landscape, the Professor picks up abundant nuggets of gold, a second possible borrowing from *Frau im Mond*. He explains he is merely "financing our next trip to the Moon," but Huntley angrily retorts, "We came here not for gold; we came here for science." He also asserts that their spaceship cannot bear the excess weight of these gold rocks, though they are only a few inches in diameter and could not weigh more than a few pounds, and speculates that there is no point in retrieving the gold, because the "radiation belt may alter the character" of the element. This is scientific nonsense, since no cosmic radiation could possibly transmute elements, but it indicates that director Doris Wishman, in her own way, wishes to follow the conventions of spacesuit films, which demand frequent discussion of scientific matters. The gold is forgotten as the men come upon a stone structure and ladder indicating that a "thinking entity" is somewhere on the Moon.

Upon climbing the ladder, Huntley raises his visor to get a better look at what he discovered: a small community of women and men, all wearing nothing but tight-fitting shorts, with the large bare breasts of the women as the obvious focus of attention. Everyone also wears decorative antennae which, the astronauts deduce, enable them to communicate with each other telepathically. Though women dominate the community, both in numbers and in political power, two men sneak up to capture the astronauts, and another woman wields a wand to tranquilize the visitors so they can be taken underground. This displeases their queen (also played by Marietta), who mentally tells the others she will convene a council to determine whether "these two strangers [are] friends or enemies." Despite scowls from one woman, who evidently distrusts the astronauts, the queen concludes that the men only "seek knowledge about the heavens" and orders their freedom. Talking to the queen, Huntley confirms, "We're here on a scientific expedition. We're friends," and he and the Professor proceed, strangely, to survey the surroundings, taking notes and photographs, displaying more interest in plants than the inexplicable English-speaking humans who surely represent their most unusual discovery.

It goes without saying that the primary purpose of these scenes is to show eager male audiences the breasts, and a portion of the bare behinds, of beautiful women; but there is thematic interest here as well. For like silent fantasies of space travel like *Himmelskibet* and *Aelita*, *Nude on the Moon* essentially posits that aliens on other planets will enjoy a utopian existence. Moon people never need to work; they spend all their time lounging beside pools of water, throwing balls around, or playing pranks on each other. Despite the slight suggestion of disagreement over how to handle the newcomers, there seems no significant discord among residents. Adding to the idyllic atmosphere, one woman is even accompanied by two small boys, evidently her children, and in one scene the cherubic boys sit by a pool without wearing the usual shorts, making them the only genuinely nude people in the film. Further, while the Professor remains intent upon taking pictures and notes, complimenting himself on the "highly useful data" he gathers, Huntley begins succumbing to the pleasures of lunar life. When the Professor complains that Huntley is "acting like a schoolboy," he responds, "I feel like a schoolboy." The Professor sternly reminds him, "Don't forget, we're scientists."

Attracted to the Moon's leisurely lifestyle, Huntley is also falling in love with their queen. In the strangest moment of all in this strange film, he announces, "I must sing to her," and while we never see his lips move, he approaches the queen while we again hear Young singing "Moon Doll," its meaning now abundantly clear. When the Professor warns that their supply of oxygen is running low, Huntley insists he is not going back because he is in love. "For the first time in my life," he explains, "I care for someone. It's strange, but it's wonderful." The domesticating power of space travel has never seemed stronger: Huntley's journey to another world only inspired him to feel that ancient human emotion, love, and he is now ready to settle down with a beautiful woman and, one supposes, eventually father his own lunar sons. However, sensing that the man she loves cannot survive in her atmosphere, the Moon queen thinks, "My heart does not wish you to go, but I know that you must leave," and she uses the tranquilizing wand to subdue Huntley so the Professor can escort him back to the spaceship for a safe departure.

Back on Earth, the men face harsh realities: Because they forgot to bring their camera, and have no specimens, they have no evidence to prove they went to the Moon. No doubt recalling their sleep before landing, the Professor even notes, "We really don't know where we went." And having spent his inheritance, Huntley now requires government funding for a second Moon mission, and the skeptical officials who inspect his spaceship do not believe the vehicle could have gotten off the ground. It is not logical, in light of everything we have seen, but we are again invited to consider that their entire experience was a dream. This is reinforced by a final scene when Cathy enters Huntley's office and, as if seeing her for the first time, he realizes that she looks exactly like the Moon queen; he even has a brief fantasy in which the conservatively dressed Cathy suddenly appears with breasts on display, like lunar residents. "You're here on Earth," he tells her, and they embrace, indicating that the smitten scientist will now be happy even if he cannot pursue his once-powerful desire to travel into space. An underlying message, presumably, is that if secretaries want to catch the eye of handsome bosses, they should walk around topless.

Overall, this once-shocking film, which will strike contemporary audiences as charmingly quaint, clearly has little to say about what humanity will likely find in space, but more so than other films of its type, it conveys how people might respond to space. Like Huntley and the Professor, they may refuse to accept the realities of space — the stark lunar landscapes that they approach — and instead indulge in fantasies of space — such as lush gardens filled with beautiful, undressed women. The film strikingly anticipates later works like the series *Star Trek* and *Döppelganger,* wherein space travelers again travel to strange worlds, only to encounter precise replicas of the people and places of Earth.

From the Earth to the Moon (1958) and *First Men in the Moon* (1964)

As major film studios lost interest in science fiction films during the late 1950s and early 1960s, one sort of project remained appealing: adaptations of famous novels by Jules Verne and H.G. Wells. Such films, while still involving fantastic subjects to attract science fiction fans, would also have a certain *gravitas,* due to their association with classic authors, making them seem more distinguished and dignified than other genre films. Amidst several other films based on Verne and Wells novels, including *The War of the Worlds* (1953), *20,000 Leagues Under the Sea* (1954), *Around the World in Eighty Days* (1956), *Journey to the Center of the Earth* (1959), *The Time Machine* (1960), and *Mysterious Island* (1961), filmmakers inevitably turned to their major novels about the trendy subject of space travel, Verne's *From the Earth to the Moon* (1865) and Wells's *The First Men in the Moon* (1901). Yet these adaptations faced a special challenge: To connect their stories to the older writers who inspired them, the films had to retain the novels' Victorian-era settings and style of technology; yet changes were needed to make these antiquated visions relevant to modern audiences. One alteration, deemed necessary in both cases, was adding a woman to the novels' all-male lunar expeditions. For further updating, *From the Earth to the Moon* inserts a contemporary issue, while *First Men in the Moon* surrounds Wells's adventure with a twentieth-century frame story.

To emphasize that it was a higher-class production than other space films, *From the Earth to the Moon* has opening credits printed in Gothic lettering on pages of a slowly turned book, unlike more *declassé* background images in other science fiction films' credits, like a spaceship or Saturn. The film retains the core elements of Verne's novel — two rival weapons manufacturers join forces to construct and fly a vehicle to the Moon — but otherwise took liberties with the story to please contemporary audiences, like a female astronaut. But it also references the scientific development other than space travel which dominated science fiction films of the 1950s, atomic energy: The film's Victor Barbicane (Joseph Cotten) initially wishes to fire a projectile to the Moon not merely as an interesting challenge, as in the novel, but to set off a spectacular explosion caused by his amazing discovery "Power X," which must be either a form of, or an analogy to, nuclear energy. He demonstrates its force by disintegrating a sheet of the hardest alloy devised by his bitter enemy, Stuyvesant Nicholl (George Sanders). Only after President Grant (Morris Ankrum) urges him to abandon this plan, since it would be viewed as a provocative American act of war, does Barbicane decide to send people, not explosives, to the Moon.

As a belated convert to the desirability of space travel, Barbicane advocates this new plan to associates by asserting that if they "explore the heavens [and] visit the Moon," they will "make man's oldest dream a reality," since such journeys are what man has "dreamed of ever since he dropped out of the trees." Yet such rhetoric, found in other spacesuit films, seems forced and unpersuasive here, since this was not Barbicane's original intent. As the crew for the proposed mission, the film eliminates Verne's French adventurer Ardan; instead, Barbicane will be accompanied by assistant Ben Sharpe (Don Dubbins) and Nicholl, who is involved because Barbicane needs his alloy to protect his projectile from friction when it reenters Earth's atmosphere. Nicholl's daughter Virginia (Debra Paget) stows away because she loves Sharpe and wishes to be part of his cosmic journey.

As another change, Barbicane hopes to actually land upon the Moon, requiring him to bring spacesuits. We see three of them when Virginia sneaks on board and conceals herself in one. In contrast to the spacesuits resembling old-fashioned diving suits observed in *Frau im Mond* and *First Men in the Moon*, these suits look anachronistically modern, if not quite sturdy enough to withstand a vacuum, and even sport the bright colors of the spacesuits in *Destination Moon*. Though these hanging spacesuits are seen two more times in the film, no one but Virginia puts one on, and even when the spaceship might be struck by a meteor, no one suggests donning them as a precaution; in fact, when there is later a gas leak, characters put on masks but not spacesuits. The final, fleeting appearance of the spacesuits is noteworthy because we see one spacesuit is adorned with the elegantly stylized initials "VB," for Victor Barbicane, meaning that the film anticipates *Men into Space* in having spacesuits identify wearers by name.

Despite the film's apparently generous budget, the special effects sometimes seem inadequate, as scenes of the liftoff depend heavily upon a standard shot of a bullet-shaped projectile, rising upward with flames coming out of its bottom, seen against a dark blue sky, an image incongruously repeated later when the vessel is supposedly deep in space. But somebody was evidently concerned about the major scientific flaw in Verne's scheme for manned space travel: the fact that humans shot from a cannon would be crushed to death by the force of acceleration. As if in response, Barbicane devises a complex way to protect himself and crewmates during the launch. First, passengers insert themselves into three linked cylindrical chambers; these chambers are filled with a special gas to reduce their heartbeats to five beats per minute; and as the ship takes off, the chambers spin rapidly, like test tubes in a centrifuge. These precautions, Barbicane asserts to a skeptical Nicholl, are essential for their survival, which is oddly inconsistent with Virginia's ability to survive the liftoff protected solely by her flimsy-looking spacesuit. As another touch of unusual science, the ship includes an enormous gyroscope which somehow provides artificial gravity, explaining why crew members walk about as if on Earth.

When the spaceship reaches space, there is a mildly impressive scene of Barbicane opening windows at the top of the projectile and displaying an expanse of black sky and white stars, and there are later images of the Earth and Moon seen from space. But the film focuses on a series of poorly explained mechanical problems, leading to various explosions, animated electrical flashes, and characters careening around the chamber. These were caused by Nicholl, who secretly sabotaged the spaceship before liftoff for reasons that drive home the connection between Power X and nuclear energy: Nicholl fears that if Power X is successfully demonstrated, and comes into use around the world, it will bring a destructive war and end all life on Earth. He even claims to act with divine support, saying that Barbicane's death will be the work of "the avenging hand of God Himself," which arguably makes him another example, along with *Conquest of Space*'s Merritt, of someone driven to religious mania by space travel, though his opinions were formed before the flight. Barbicane responds that widespread access to Power X would actually ensure world peace, which seemed to be happening in the 1950s, and further notes that even if his own work is thwarted, someone else will rediscover Power X. But characters have little time to debate such matters, with their attention constantly drawn to each new crisis.

Having been discovered and accepted as a crew member, Virginia predictably settles into a domestic role, cooking dinner for the men, and does not assist in repairing the spaceship. But she receives an unexpected tribute: As crew members contemplate what seems their certain death, Virginia observes that everyone is destined to die, and it is wonderful that they have the privilege of dying in a spectacular space explosion. Barbicane then notes that if he survives to lead other expeditions into space, he will always insist upon including "one woman — for courage." One might admire the film for this suggestion that women might be tougher than men in facing the challenges of space, though except for this speech, nothing about her actions supports the idea.

Eventually, though Nicholl never verbally recants his views, he changes his opinion about Barbicane, since he at one point advances through animated electrical flashes to pull a switch to save Barbicane and comments afterward, "I did one thing right." Barbicane then proposes an astounding solution to their predicament: By provoking an explosion, he tells crewmates, the spaceship will split into four separate vehicles, each with independent rockets and a capacity to make a safe landing. Ben and Virginia will remain in the more comfortable compartment likely to reach Earth, while Barbicane and Nicholl enter the other compartment likely to head toward the Moon. Nothing was previously said about these remarkable features of Barbicane's craft, which is strange, since one imagines that this plan would be the first thing that would come to his mind when he recognized that his spaceship was sabotaged. Soon, as Ben and Virginia approach Earth, they observe lights on the Moon's surface, indicating that Barbicane and Nicholl successfully landed on the Moon and are undoubtedly pleased, though their supplies will only last for several days. Any further information about characters' fates is withheld from audiences, as the film abruptly and unsatisfactorily ends with the sudden appearance of author Verne, whose enigmatic response to queries about Barbicane's mission is that he deals with "something much more real than facts," which is "imagination."

While *From the Earth to the Moon* remains exclusively in the nineteenth century, *First Men in the Moon* at first seems a radical updating of Wells's novel: a first flight to the Moon is occurring today, with a multinational crew under the auspices of the United Nations (the only way, realistically, for a British film in the 1960s to include a British astronaut); the mission follows the design then contemplated by NASA of a larger "mother ship" that stays in orbit while a smaller craft detaches to descend to the Moon; and the lunar surface is realistically depicted as stark and lifeless. There is one understated innovation in the landing procedure: Before emerging from their vehicle, astronauts pause to "decontaminate" themselves, presumably to protect the Moon from potentially harmful micro-organisms from Earth. The significance of this step only becomes apparent in the film's final moments.

After scenes of international celebrations and news broadcasts from America, Russia, Britain, and Japan, one astronaut makes a startling discovery: Lying on a lunar rock is a tattered Union Jack, along with a document bearing the name of Katherine Callender, from Dimchurch, England, claiming the Moon for Queen Victoria and Britain in the year 1899. United Nations investigators rush to Dimchurch to interview a befuddled old city registrar (Miles Malleson), who reminds them "this is a land of eccentrics" as he searches through dusty records for Callender's birthdate. Without finding her name, he remembers performing the marriage ceremony of Katherine and Arnold Bedford, and while she died ten years ago,

Benford is alive in a local nursing home. Greeted by investigators and curious journalists, Bedford (Edward Judd in old age makeup) is gratified to learn that his wild stories about going to the Moon, universally disbelieved, are finally vindicated, and he begins telling everyone what happened in 1899, an account that roughly follows Wells's novel.

As in the book, Bedford is a scoundrel: Hounded by creditors, he retreats to the country to write a play to earn enough money to pay his debts. He meets his neighbor, eccentric inventor Joseph Cavor (Lionel Jeffries), and soon helps him prepare a sphere that will employ his anti-gravity substance, Cavorite, to take them to the Moon. But there is a new character, Bedford's American fiancée Callender (Martha Hyer), who is skeptical about his plans to exploit Cavor's substance for financial gain. Since Cavor realizes that the Moon is airless, something equivalent to a spacesuit is part of his plan. He tries on a diving helmet, and when Callender asks about "those diving suits" hanging on the wall, Cavor replies, "What keeps water out, keeps air in." In fact, a diving suit of flimsy cloth, which is what we observe, would not sufficiently protect astronauts against a vacuum, but might represent precisely what a Victorian scientist would employ for a space flight.

As preparations for the flight proceed, Callender remains angry, but she brings live chickens to be placed inside the sphere, so the men can have fresh food to supplement Cavor's canned food. (Later, Bedford grows sick of eating sardines.) However, she now discovers precisely how sleazy Bedford is: Not only did he tell the old-fashioned Cavor that Callender is his wife, not his fiancée, but he is also lying to both persons in claiming to own the house he actually rents. Worse, to establish a profitable business relationship with Cavor, he draws up documents purportedly transferring ownership of the house to Callender, so she in turn can sell it to Cavor. Just as the sphere is about to be launched, Callender receives an ominous summons from the house's real owners, and when she indignantly rushes to the sphere to confront Bedford about his duplicity, the men must get her inside the craft so she will not be harmed by liftoff. When she understandably fumes at Bedford for rushing off to the Moon while leaving her in a legal mess, his lame apology is that he never thought that people would find out about his scheme so quickly. All this seems to make Bedford an unusual, interestingly, flawed hero for a spacesuit film, but the film does not exploit the idea; rather, Bedford and Callender are quickly reconciled, and on the Moon he settles into being a bland, typical hero.

The flight has a few noteworthy touches: When Callender begins floating inside the sphere, Cavor says, "I'll put magnets in your shoes"; one assumes that he and Bedford do not float because they already have such footgear. When Cavor learns that Bedford and Callender are not married, the morally offended man immediately tells Callender "Kindly leave the room" before everyone is reduced to laughter, recognizing that such a departure would be impossible during a journey through space. Cavor says a conventional prayer before an elaborately served meal of sardines, the film's only reference to religion. And to provide some improbable drama, Callender accidentally sends the craft toward the Sun before correcting their course. (Needless to say, the Sun is so vastly more distant than the Moon that any lunar spaceship diverted in its direction would take weeks, if not months, to get close enough to the Sun to be in danger.)

Although careful manipulation of the sphere's panels of Cavorite should have allowed for a soft landing on the Moon, the sphere tumbles roughly along the ground before coming to a halt at the slope of a lunar mountain. Briefly, everything is realistic enough: Cavor jauntily says, "Hello, Moon!"; the men take large leaps in the low lunar gravity; and after describing the Moon as "an empire Caesar never dreamed of," Cavor takes his Union Jack

Unwieldy Weapons: In the improbably breathable atmosphere of the lunar caverns, Victorian astronauts Arnold Bedford (Edward Judd) and Joseph Cavor (Lionel Jeffries) have seemingly hit upon a new use for space helmets — as weapons to stop an advancing Selenite monster in *First Men in the Moon* (1964).

and document and announces, "I claim the Moon in the name of our sovereign lady, Queen Victoria." But following Wells's story, they must implausibly stumble upon an immense, irising opening in the lunar surface. Upon falling into the hole they discover that the Moon has a "subterranean atmosphere" when Bedford loses his helmet but can still breathe. Cavor removes his helmet as well, but unlike the unwary astronauts of *Cat-Women of the Moon*, they keep their "oxygen suits" on and carry their helmets with them.

Carefully descending into the Moon's interior, they encounter its inhabitants, whom they call Selenites. While said to resemble ants or bees, stop-motion animator Ray Harryhausen's creations resemble humanoid crickets more than anything else. In the disparate reactions of Bedford and Cavor, we discern the first of a few remnants of Wells's social satire: Bedford assumes they are hostile and begins attacking them, while a disapproving Cavor, who wanted to communicate with them, complains, "You've certainly given them a taste of human violence." Returning to the surface, they find their sphere, with Callender inside, has been dragged underground by Selenites — a development that seems borrowed from another Wells novel, *The Time Machine* (1895), wherein subterranean Morlocks drag the Time Traveller's time machine underground.

Descending to search for the sphere, Bedford and Cavor are separated when they encounter, for no particular reason, a giant caterpillar. A captured Cavor discovers the sphere, which is being disassembled, as well as Callendar, kept in a chamber for observation (a sort of x-ray machine shows her skeleton). After joining her, he begins teaching one Selenite English. As another interesting element taken from Wells but left underdeveloped, three Selenites move near some motionless Selenites in cocoons; a translucent wall is lowered in front of them, and when it rises, they are in cocoons as well, while a Selenite explains that they will remain inactive until they are "needed." As in the novel, Cavor sees this as one solution to the problem of unemployment.

Having figured out that the Selenite empire is powered by solar energy, Cavor understands what is happening when a predicted lunar eclipse cuts off the Sun's rays, turns off the Selenite machines, and makes the Selenites stand motionless. When solar power returns, Cavor has an audience with the Moon's ruler, the Grand Lunarian, while Bedford and Callender frantically strive to repair the sphere. Cavor's comments to the Grand Lunarian (attempting to explain human war) faintly recall the more extensive satirical conversation that concludes Wells's novel, but he is dragged away by Bedford to assist in fixing a jammed panel on the sphere. As Selenites converge on the sphere, Bedford and Callender take off to return to Earth, but Cavor insists on staying behind, so he can continue studying and communicating with the Selenites.

Returning to the present, the elderly Bedford explains that he and Callender landed off the coast of Zanzibar, whereupon the sphere started sinking. After being rescued, they had no evidence to support their implausible story about visiting the Moon. The crowd around Bedford then turns to the television to watch live coverage of the international astronauts venturing into the lunar interior, further substantiating Bedford's account. While this film's lunar landing was not televised, these scenes of events broadcast from the Moon does make the film one of several science fiction stories that, contrary to reports, predicted television coverage of a lunar mission. However, the astronauts find no living Selenites, only evidence of ruin and decay; the most logical theory is that the Selenite civilization was wiped out by "some simple germ" humans brought to the Moon. To support this idea, Bedford concludes the film by commenting that Cavor "did have such a terrible cold." (This is not playing fair with audiences, since Cavor exhibited no signs of a cold during the film.) This is a second idea borrowed from another Wells novel, *The War of the Worlds* (1898), wherein common Earth bacteria wipe out invading aliens, and it also explains the importance of having the modern astronauts "decontaminate" before stepping on the lunar surface. Bedford, Cavor, and Callender did not decontaminate before contacting the Selenites, and hence doomed them. All this reflects a real concern, now reflected in actual efforts to remove micro-organisms from space probes, that humans might harmfully contaminate alien environments, and this may be the first film to raise the issue (though several horrific spacesuit films explore the danger of alien organisms contaminating Earth).

Overall, both *From the Earth to the Moon* and *First Men in the Moon* largely ignore the satire and social commentary in the novels to focus on adventure, with a handful of changes to make stories more acceptable to contemporary audiences. Strangely, in the context of other films based on Verne and Wells novels, they qualify as two of the most faithful. Perhaps, with the central trope of space travel as their attraction, filmmakers felt no need to further elaborate on the original narratives.

The Twilight Zone (1959–1964)

From its inception, Rod Serling's anthology series *The Twilight Zone* generally focused on fantasy, not science fiction, and even its science fiction stories, like its fantasies, primarily aimed to provide morality tales with an ironic twist, not realistic portrayals of future possibilities. In addition, its budgets were conspicuously low, allowing only for limited special effects. For these reasons, many episodes involving space travel, such as "The Lonely" (aired November 13, 1959), "And When the Sky Was Opened" (December 11, 1959), "Third from the Sun" (January 8, 1960), "Elegy" (February 19, 1960), "People Are Alike All Over" (March 25, 1960), "On Thursday We Leave for Home" (May 2, 1963), and "Probe 7 — Over and Out" (November 29, 1963), never show space travelers in spacesuits.

Indeed, only three episodes involve genuine spacesuits, and one only includes a brief reference. In "Death Ship" (February 7, 1963), astronauts Paul Ross (Jack Klugman), Ted Mason (Ross Martin), and Mike Carter (Fredrick Beir) see a glint of light on an alien world and land to investigate. While they immediately open a door to see the planet looks exactly like Earth, they do test the atmosphere, and after determining it contains sufficient oxygen, one man concludes, "We won't need helmets." For some reason, however, they don flimsy bodysuits that resemble traditional spacesuits, though there seems no need for them. From that point on, the episode becomes a fantasy: The light came from an exact duplicate of their spaceship (the flying saucer from *Forbidden Planet*) containing the dead bodies of men who look exactly like them. After pondering other theories, they realize that they discovered their own spaceship and bodies, and that they are ghosts, condemned to endlessly repeat the pattern of discovering their own corpses.

The classic "The Invaders" (January 27, 1961) at first seems a story about an alien invasion of Earth: In a farmhouse, an old woman (Agnes Moorehead) hears a strange sound and, upon investigating, discovers that a small flying saucer has landed on her roof. From this vehicle emerges a tiny figure in a spacesuit who brandishes a ray gun and later threateningly picks up a knife. The woman fights back furiously, beating one alien to death and driving the other back into the saucer, which she attacks with an ax. Then, right before his presumed death at her hands, the being inside sends a radio message, in English, declaring that he has discovered a dangerous planet of giants that must be avoided. After the saucer is destroyed, we see it bears the words "U.S. Air Force: Space Probe No. 1." The vehicle came from Earth; thus, "The Invaders" is actually a story about humans who visit another planet. Here, spacesuits disguise the fact that the tiny "aliens" are human and make them seem menacing, as in other films about aliens coming to Earth discussed below. At the same time, the small size of the astronauts, and the way they are easily overcome by a large woman, interestingly suggests that humans, rather than conquering the universe, may be overwhelmed by the universe, discovering through space travel that they are, in contrast to its wonders, weak and insignificant.

While "The Invaders" clearly occurs in humanity's distant future, Serling's usual pattern for space adventures, a third *Twilight Zone* episode with spacesuits, "The Parallel" (1963), was solidly based upon current events. It begins with the impending launch of a single astronaut, Major Robert Gaines (Steve Forrest), on an orbital flight around Earth; a colleague identifies him as a successor to Mercury astronauts John Glenn, Walter Schirra, and Gordon Cooper, who similarly orbited Earth. Like "Death Ship" and "The Invaders," but more subtly, the episode suggests from the onset that people venturing into space are fragile beings who face formidable challenges: In sequences before his launch, Gaines is made to appear entirely helpless, as technicians must put on his space helmet and place his body in the proper horizontal position for takeoff; and his helmet, intentionally or not, seems too large for his body, creating the effect of a child wearing an adult's uniform. (Arguably, this image was anticipated in Serling's opening narration, describing Gaines' coming flight as "one of the first faltering steps of man to sever the umbilical cord of gravity and stretch out a fingertip to the unknown"—likening Gaines to a newborn baby.) Neither does he do anything heroic during his flight: After routine checks, he loses contact with Earth, experiences a flash of bright light, and awakens in a hospital bed while an orderly examines his eyes— again, a person who is being acted upon, not a person who is acting.

"The Parallel" then develops the theme that space travel might drive men to madness, as both the officials who interrogate Gaines and members of his family, wife Helen (Jacqueline Scott) and daughter Maggie (Shari Lee Bernath), suspect he has become deranged. For one thing, he has no memory of what happened after losing contact with Earth, though he somehow managed the impossible feat of landing his capsule safely upon dry land. He begins noticing slight differences in the world around him: His superior officer, Colonel Connacher (Frank Aletter), insists he did not phone Helen before his flight, but Gaines is sure that he did; there is a picket fence around his house he does not recall, though Helen says it has always been there; and he is startled to find himself wearing the insignia of a colonel, not a major. Military psychiatrists are further disturbed by his confident assertion that the president of the United States is John Kennedy, a name they do not recognize. Audiences, of course, understand what Gaines gradually figures out: He landed not on our own Earth, but a parallel Earth, similar to ours but with various minor changes. Yet colleagues still believe he is merely suffering from unusual delusions and regard the plight as a logical reaction to the pressures of space flight.

Eventually, Gaines is vindicated when his space capsule is carefully studied, and several slight differences in its design are detected. At this time, Gaines mysteriously finds himself back in space, speaking to monitors on Earth as he prepares to land. He is gratified to learn that the president is Kennedy, proving that this time, he is landing on the right Earth. But after he is again observed in a hospital bed, having his eyes examined, his reports about landing on a parallel world again make others think he is losing his sanity. But they realize he might be telling the truth when a fleeting radio message is received from space, with the speaker identifying himself as Colonel Robert Gaines.

Pondering Gaines's strange experience, General Eaton (Philip Abbott) offers a concluding comment about humanity's ventures into space: "We're like little ants that have just made it to the desert, and now we say we've conquered the Sahara and we haven't conquered anything." Thus, after first suggesting that humans confronting space are like babies, they are now compared to ants. While the stories are vastly different, both "The Invaders" and "The Parallel" indicate that humans in space are tiny creatures who might be crushed by a hostile universe. This message, of course, represents a recurring theme of the series (fallible people doomed by implacable forces), not any particular concerns about space travel, which in *The Twilight Zone* is just another place where people who take one false step face serious trouble.

12 to the Moon (1960)

Few films discussed here begin as soberly, and end as absurdly, as *12 to the Moon*. The film's first thirty minutes promise an internationalized update of *Destination Moon*, while later events recall a Flash Gordon serial. Even as a child, watching the film in a theatre, I was thrilled by the realistic aura of its opening scenes and disappointed by its descent into nonsense (interestingly suggesting that the attitudes underlying this study were forming long before becoming a scholar).

One intriguing aspect of the film is that, except for the twice-heard voice of Francis X. Bushman as the "Director of the International Space Order," its only characters are the twelve astronauts constituting humanity's first mission to the Moon (with an unintentional exception to be noted). Perhaps this was only a cost-cutting device in a low-budget project, but such films can usually recruit actors to work for low wages; so this may represent a deliberate effort to suggest that, once in space, astronauts would be isolated from humanity more completely than anyone in history, so they must rely on each other for support and company. A unifying theme in the film is the way people forced into constant contact, facing common threats, tend both to form strong emotional bonds and become embroiled in personal conflicts.

From the start, *12 to the Moon* also emphasizes that this international mission is motivated primarily by a desire "to prevent national disputes" arising over the Moon in particular and, one infers, other subjects in general. This is a future world, then, where there is increased international cooperation, though separate nations and disagreements still exist. Its purpose explains why the flight has an unusually large crew of twelve, said to represent twelve different countries (though the nationality of Robert Murdock [Robert Montgomery, Jr.], who seems to be a second American, is unspecified). The diverse roster otherwise consists of American John Anderson (Ken Clark), Brazilian Luis Vargas (Anthony Dexter), British Sir William Rochester (Philip Baird), French Etienne Martel (Roger Til), German Erich Heinrich (John Wengraf), Swedish Sigrid Bomark (Anna-Lisa), Russian Feodor Orloff (Tom Conway), Turkish Selim Hamid (Tema Bey), Israeli David Ruskin (Richard Weber), Nigerian Asmara Markonen (Cory Devlin), and Japanese Hideko Murata (Michi Kobi). To illustrate the problem of national differences, one emerges between Orloff and Ruskin (who resents Russian domination of Poland, the country of his birth), but other crew members get along just fine.

The crew is already heading for the Moon as the film commences. Its members have only minimal contact with Earth. They are being monitored, in a sense, by Ruskin (who periodically speaks into a tape recorder) as the mission's chronicler. Endeavoring to assess their psychological condition, he first reports that crew members seem "artificially calm," though this is only "to cover up the real excitement of man's first trip to the Moon." Once on the Moon, he again notes that "the excitement is great," albeit "controlled because of its momentous importance." Indeed, in contrast to other space travelers who become mentally unbalanced in response to the challenges of space, these astronauts consistently remain not only artificially, but preternaturally, calm in response to extraordinary developments.

To veteran watchers of spacesuit films, there is nothing particularly unusual about the flight to the Moon. Their spacecraft is extremely spacious, even by the era's standards, and the film breaks new ground by showing a bathroom, distinguished by its "ultra-sound shower" (used by Hideko when Anderson barges in). Other passengers include two monkeys, a dog, and two cats named Mimi and Adolfo, brought to test whether "procreation" is possible on the Moon; one crew member looks forward to a "litter of moon kittens." The first sign of danger comes with detection of an unusual magnetic field, followed immediately by the inevitable "meteor clusters" on a collision course with the ship, though they are avoided without incident. Two crew members look down on Earth and remark, "She looks rather small and insignificant."

There is interesting dialogue when the spaceship lands on the Moon. After its Muslim astronaut exclaims, "Allah be praised," another responds, "Praise this ship—not Allah." This anticipates the exchange at the end of the *Star Trek* episode "Obsession" (aired December 15, 1967), wherein Montgomery Scott says, "Thank Heavens" when Kirk's life is saved, and Spock archly answers that "No deity was involved" in rescuing him. This also makes *12 to the Moon* a rare spacesuit film that appears to criticize religion, while other films endorse Christianity or avoid the subject.

When the crew members (except Martel) prepare to walk on the lunar surface, the dubious science begins. Ruskin dons his spacesuit and helmet, but instead of lowering a glass visor over his face, he reports that he activated the "invisible electromagnetic ray screen" to function as a "protective shield over our faces." This implausible technology may have been introduced at the last minute, after major filming was completed, when someone noticed it was all too visible that astronauts on the Moon had nothing covering their faces to protect from the vacuum. The theory is reinforced by the scene in which Hamid and Bomark enter a cave with a breathable atmosphere and do not deactivate their invisible shields, but rather remove their helmets.

After astronauts receive a congratulatory message from the director of the International Space Order (in a way anticipating Nixon's phone call to the *Apollo 11* astronauts), they disembark, plant their international flag (fulfilling their goal of preventing national conflicts), and proceed to the second part of their mission: scientific exploration. As another instance of questionable technology, they deploy "magnetic meteorite deflectors" to reduce the speed of falling rocks, which proceed to slowly descend all around them, as if being thrown by offstage prop handlers (which is absurd, since even in the Moon's low gravity, meteorites would still crash into the surface rapidly enough to create craters). As they explore, wisps of white smoke emerging from craters may create an eerie mood but are difficult to explain, given what we know about the Moon, though crew members do not notice the phenomenon. As one more incongruous touch, audiences can see a flash of motion in the background of one scene; one might charitably posit this was a subtle hint that the Moon is inhabited, but it is really a stagehand who was wandering around the set, inadvertently strayed into view during filming, and was never noticed by director David Bradley.

Since astronauts only have two hours of air for their initial survey, ridiculous incidents must occur rapidly. Dispatched to separately search for signs of life, Hamid and Bomark go into a cave, discover strange formations and minerals, and observe a burning rock, indicating that there must be air in the cave. Removing their helmets does enable them to engage in a passionate kiss before they retreat to a corner of the cave, presumably for a romantic interlude, whereupon a wall mysteriously forms to block them off. When crewmates later enter the cave, they can only follow the footprints to the wall, and never see them again. On the surface, liquid begins flowing from a small hill; one astronaut imprudently touches it and backs away screaming in pain, though whether the material was merely too hot or acidic is not explained. Finally, two men begin sinking into the "pumice dust" of the lunar surface. While one is pulled out in time, the other keeps sinking until only the upper part of an arm is visible, reaching up as if struggling; finally, the arm disappears as well, a striking sequence that evocatively illustrates the perils of exploring other worlds.

The eight remaining astronauts then return to their spaceship, not only because their air is low, but also because of "the necessity to normalize our bodily processes," whatever that means. At this point, the film lurches into risible melodrama. Astronauts find they cannot contact Earth, their ship darkens, and they begin receiving a message consisting of strange pictorial symbols. These in no way resemble Japanese or Chinese; if they look like anything at all, they vaguely resemble the Mayan alphabet. Yet Hireko (who is a doctor, not a linguist) can somehow translate them. "I speak for the Great Coordinator of the Moon," she reads. "We advise and warn you: Return to Earth at once!" To account for this hostility, the alien explains, "We are not enslaved by your earthly emotions," and they fear that human contact will "only contaminate our perfect form of harmony." They soon add one strange condition: that the humans "leave behind the two cats," which have a "most unusual feel to us" and "interest us almost as much as the two human beings who joined us"—making this the second film, after *Cat-Women of the Moon*, to link lunar inhabitants and felines. We also learn that the aliens communicate by thought, not speaking, though one must ask why they did not contact the astronauts via telepathy instead of symbols.

As astronauts leave in response to this warning, one might imagine that the film will soon end, since other films about pioneering missions to the Moon devote little or no time to the return flight. However, as if to artificially prolong the film, *12 to the Moon* now offers some trivial incidents on their spaceship: a glowing rock they brought from the Moon, "the Medea stone," bursts into flames, but crew members are fortunately alerted by their barking dog and extinguish the fire; then, there is more tension when it is announced, again, that there are "meteor clusters ahead." But these are mere preliminaries to the actual, incredible crisis that delays their return to Earth: Apparently determined to wipe out the flawed human race, the Moon's inhabitants unleash hitherto unrevealed powers and place all of North America in a deep freeze. The astronauts learn about these events by listening to a radio broadcast from Britain, featuring a reporter who amusingly announces that Europe lost all contact with an apparently frozen North America before concluding, "We now return to our regular programming." Since the complete devastation of an entire continent is insufficient provocation, one is left to wonder what magnitude of crisis would be required to cause this station to completely suspend regular programming.

Implausible scientific problems require implausible scientific solution, so the astronauts resolve to use elements of atomic energy from their spacecraft to create an atomic bomb—or "bomblets" (both terms are used)—to be dropped into a volcano to somehow reverse "the big freeze" that engulfed North America. As one more example of lingering national conflicts, there is a brief problem when Martel attempts to sabotage the bomb, telling crewmates that, with North America eliminated, people from their countries can dominate the world. After he is subdued, other male astronauts draw straws to determine which two men will pilot a shuttlecraft to carry out this kamikaze mission; they ironically turn out to be the Israeli Ruskin and his friend Heimrich, who we learned is the regretful son of a notorious German war criminal. While they complete the assignment before dying, the explosion they cause is not powerful enough to affect the frozen conditions.

Just as all hope seems lost, however, there comes another pictorial transmission from the Moon people. Impressed by Ruskin and Heimrich's deeds, they report, "We have seen your human strength in the way your people have sacrificed themselves to save others." Further, from observing the lovers they kidnapped (though the pair decided to remain behind voluntarily), they have learned that "all of your Earth emotions are not evil and warlike," and the humans "have come to us in peace." Now persuaded that humanity should survive, the Moon's inhabitants turn off the deep freeze—which, it turns out, did not kill anyone, but merely placed all people in North America into suspended animation. According to the next Moon transmission, "When you come back, you will be welcome."

It was perhaps appropriate that a mission intended to end conflicts between nations on Earth should conclude by ending a conflict between Earth and another world; but there remain unanswered questions about the Moon people's actions. Why did they rush to eliminate a huge region of Earth based on what turned out to be insufficient information? Why did they target North America, when at least ten of the twelve astronauts came from elsewhere? And if they possessed such immense powers all along, why did they deal with humans in such a meek fashion? Surely they could have removed the spaceship, and taken the cats, all by themselves, without asking the astronauts to cooperate. The real message to take from *12 to the Moon* may be that it is not simply humans, but also aliens, who can be driven insane by space.

The Phantom Planet (1961)

By 1960, with knowledge of true conditions on other worlds of the Solar System more discouraging than ever, it was more difficult to devise ways to depict astronauts in the near future reaching worlds where they would not need spacesuits. Two films of the 1960s, *The Phantom Planet* and *Robinson Crusoe on Mars*, could achieve this desirable goal only with bizarre contrivances. Thus, *The Phantom Planet* begins like a genuine spacesuit film, but with a touch of fantasy right out of *Gulliver's Travels*, its story begins to resemble *Flight to Mars*, with signs of the influence of *This Island Earth*: In 1980, two spaceships on routine missions are destroyed by a mysterious planet that appears out of nowhere and then vanish, so authorities send astronauts Frank Chapman (Dean Fredericks) and Ray Makonnen (Richard Weber) to investigate. While they find nothing unusual, there are a few comments about the nature of space travel: Makonnen notes, "It's quiet and lonely out here," while Chapman offers a striking analogy: "It's just the same as fishing. You gotta be patient and wait." Yes, in genuine spacesuit films, the slow, careful movements required, and stillness of space, might recall fishing.

Matters get more exciting with a swarm of meteors that damages the spaceship hull, causing a fuel leak. (Actually, the escaping material looks more like air, but astronauts determine that the cabin pressure is normal.) Donning spacesuits, the men go outside to effect repairs, incongruously using a wrench. Chapman is struck by a tiny meteor that damages his air supply. Makonnen maneuvers him back inside the spaceship, but another meteor hits him and sends him careening into the void toward certain death, since the unconscious Chapman cannot rescue him. By the standards of other depictions of astronauts drifting in space, the scene is not artfully staged, with a few medium long shots of Makonnen moving away from the spaceship, but there is a touch of poignancy when Makonnen is heard reciting the Lord's Prayer, indicating that he knows all too well he will soon die.

When Chapman wakes up, he finds his spaceship is somehow being guided toward an unknown world, but he still suffers from the effects of his accident. After managing to put his spacesuit back on and stagger out of his craft, he collapses onto the ground. At this moment, realism gives way to silliness, as the prone astronaut is approached by a band of men about six inches tall. (This is the only scene that recalls *Gulliver's Travels*, despite comments suggesting that it is an adaptation of Swift's novel.) Once Chapman is exposed to the world's atmosphere, he shrinks to the same size. There is an intriguing image of a tiny, naked Chapman peering out of his space helmet at the visitors before he is captured and taken away.

When Chapman awakens inside these people's underground chambers, he undergoes a quick "trial" on trumped-up charges that he harmed a citizen of Rheton (the planet's

Maimed by a Meteor: Astronaut Frank Chapman (Dean Fredericks) attempts to help crewmate Ray Makonnen (Richard Weber), who has been struck by a meteor, in *The Phantom Planet* (1961).

name). This device enabling inhabitants to "sentence" Chapman to lifelong residency on Rheton so he cannot return to Earth and reveal its existence. Their leader Sesom (Francis X. Bushman) then has the task of explaining the peculiar properties of his planet: With unusually heavy gravity, it also has a unique atmosphere that shrinks everyone who breathes it and amazingly allows the planet to pass in and out of normal space to avoid detection. Inhabitants seek to conceal themselves because they are menaced by an alien race, the Solarites, who covet the planet's peculiar attributes. We encounter one Solarite held in captivity, a rubber-suited monster played by Richard Kiel. The Solarite seems a thoughtless brute, though the Solarites possess enough advanced technology to later mount an attack on Rheton. Like Metaluna of *This Island Earth* and the Mars of *Flight to Mars*, Rheton is a decadent civilization, but here this is a matter of choice: Since advanced science made residents "lazy" and inclined to "fight among themselves," they voluntarily returned to primitive ways, retaining only the technology needed to make food and defend themselves.

Romance and conflict are essential ingredients in a melodramatic spacesuit film, and Chapman is soon involved in both. He is attracted to two beautiful women, Liara (Coleen Gray) and the mute Zetha (Dolores Faith). Herron (Anthony Dexter) loves Liara and challenges Chapman to a duel. After Chapman wins the duel but declines to kill Herron, the men become allies. Herron devises a scheme to help Chapman return to Earth and thus remove his rival from the scene. Thus, while those who supervised the trial and Herron both seemed hostile at first, they are ultimately revealed, like all residents of Rheton, to be nice people, unlike other decadent civilizations in these films which include both admirable and despicable characters. Perhaps, because these people were the size of toys, filmmakers made them especially lovable.

The focus shifts to the true villains, the Solarites. Soaring in from space, they unsuccessfully attack Rheton, and the captive Solarite escapes and menaces residents until being subdued. Then Herron completes his scheme: He maneuvers Rheton to be temporarily close to the Moon, so people from Earth can notice and visit the planet. Chapman is placed back in his spacesuit and, exposed to Earth's atmosphere, regains his normal size. The astronauts who find him view his comments about Rheton as delusional ravings, and as he sits in their spaceship, he knows his story will never be believed, though he has a tiny piece of evidence. All things considered, one might prefer to side with the rescuers and regard everything that happened to Chapman after he landed on Rheton as a dream, perhaps derived from the absurd films that this astronaut in 1980, now in his thirties, might have watched as a child back in the 1950s.

Robinson Crusoe on Mars (1964)

Robinson Crusoe on Mars might be regarded as an exercise in how to artfully transform a genuine spacesuit film into a melodramatic spacesuit film. Opening scenes promise a grim, realistic saga of human survival on a desolate Mars, recalling *Conquest of Space*; but the story becomes less and less plausible and eventually recalls *Flight to Mars*. Since science now ruled out the possibility of an Earthlike Mars with human inhabitants, the film must be incrementally devious to persuade viewers to accept precisely such a scenario.

Still, one can compliment the film for its beginning, with Commander Frank McReady (Adam West) and Christopher Draper (Paul Mantee) approaching Mars on a mission to orbit and study the planet, accompanied by a monkey named Mona. The monkey floats with McReady in one room of their spaceship, wearing its own spacesuit, and Draper enters to talk with McReady while upside down from the commander's perspective. After banter about the semi-solid food in squeeze tubes that is their steady diet, the astronauts encounter a familiar hazard, summarized in concise dialogue: "Meteor — massive — collision course!" Establishing the chain of command by telling McReady, "You're the boss," Draper watches as McReady orders evasive maneuvers to avoid the object (also called a "planetoid"). Afterwards, they find their spaceship is dangerously close to Mars, requiring them to eject in separate compartments. (Oddly, the abandoned spaceship will later be observed from the surface in an apparently stable orbit.) Draper leaves first, and as the story follows him to Mars, audiences first realize that he, not the more handsome McReady, will be the film's hero.

Draper lands upon a planet that seems hellishly alien: Huge firestorms rage around him, and he must constantly wear his spacesuit and helmet because the air is unbreathable. The film then follows an almost diagrammatic structure, as Draper must find, step by step, each element he needs for survival. First, he requires shelter, a problem solved when he enters a suitable cave; next, to generate warmth to endure cold Martian nights, he discovers that a yellow rock burns like coal. But obtaining other necessities — oxygen, water, and food — seems a daunting challenge, since Mars looks lifeless. Draper figures that by rationing resources from his ship, he can stay alive for a couple of days, when he expects to meet with McReady and, he suggests, take advantage of the ingenious solutions the more resourceful McReady will surely devise.

Climbing over a mountain, Draper spots McReady's ship and is disheartened to find he died in a crash landing. Since Mona's smaller body needs less oxygen, enabling her to survive in the thin Martian atmosphere (one assumes, because nothing is said about this), Draper can humanely appropriate her small oxygen tanks to stay alive a bit longer. But soon, just as his limited oxygen supply is running out, he serendipitously discovers that the rocks he burned for heat also emit oxygen, which he can breathe while in the cave and also pump into empty oxygen tanks to sustain him while walking outside. Then, noticing that Mona rarely wants water, he follows her and stumbles upon a large pool of potable water. Aquatic plants growing in the pool are edible and nourishing. Though Draper once seemed stranded on a barren, inhospitable planet, he now has ample oxygen, water, and food, so life on Mars is literally "a day at the beach," the phrase he uses to describe a plan to skinny-dip in the pool.

At this point, skeptical viewers might note that there was nothing about the stark environment Draper initially encountered to suggest this world had underground water or plant life; but the film subtly makes Mars seem more and more Earthlike. There are no further firestorms or intimations of inclement weather, and Draper abandons his spacesuit to walk about in street clothes, while still carrying an oxygen tank. Mars now looks less like an alien world and more like a desert on Earth (in fact, much of the film was filmed in Nevada's Death Valley). The only unusual touches are glimpses of the spaceship and the large glowing meteor that threatened it, both still orbiting Mars, and a brief but evocative image of two tiny crescent moons.

Draper also familiarizes Mars by introducing references to his native country. Outside his cave, he proudly displays an American flag, he whistles "Yankee Doodle Dandy," and after devising a bagpipe out of oxygen tanks, he plays "Dixie." He also resolves to explore Mars to find "canals," "green areas," and "polar ice caps" that would be more Earthlike than the barren landscapes he now traverses.

Only one more issue bothers Draper: loneliness, since Mona is of limited value in easing his sense of isolation. After a nightmare wherein a zombie-like, mute McReady enters his cave, he recognizes the problem and, speaking to hypothetical psychologists into his recorded diary, he exclaims, "A guy can lick the problems of heat, water, shelter, food — I know, I've done it. But here's the hardest problem of all — isolation. Being alone. Boy, here's where he'll crack. Here's where he'll go under." Fortunately, having provided bountiful resources to meet his other needs, this film's Mars will now completely abandon scientific logic to provide him with a human friend.

Draper discovers a headstone over the grave of a human skeleton with a metal bracelet; noting that the man was apparently murdered, he removes all signs of his presence outside the cave. Next, fast-moving spaceships, resembling those of director Byron Haskin's earlier film *The War of the Worlds* (1953), appear in the sky and emit destructive rays causing explosions on the surface. As Draper hides near the rim of the valley where the bombardment occurs, holding up a camera to film what is going on, he is confronted by a bare-chested man (Victor Lundin) wearing a headdress and kilt resembling those of ancient Egypt. Sensing he is fleeing from someone, Draper brings the man back to his cave. The film Draper took reveals the situation: Spacesuited aliens, also resembling humans, held ray guns on men dressed like Egyptians, evidently their slaves, working in a mining operation.

At least, one might say, the film does not assert that humans are indigenous to Mars, since both masters and slaves come from other worlds. (The man later reveals he comes from a planet circling a star in the constellation Orion.) But the scenario still makes little sense. If the aliens had advanced spaceships and destructive rays, they would have technologies more advanced than manual labor to gather and transport the ores they mined. It is also illogical that they would trouble to transport these slaves across a distance of many light years to Mars and then, before leaving, slaughter them as "expendable." And if they do not value these slaves, one wonders why they later engage in energetic efforts to track down one escapee. But like villains in more traditional melodramas, the aliens must be portrayed as evil, even if their motives seem irrational.

With this almost naked man casually walking by Draper's side, any sense that Mars is inhospitable vanishes; even Draper's oxygen tank becomes unnecessary, as his companion provides magical "oxygen pills" that supply all the oxygen he needs for an indefinite period of time. To make Mars even more domesticated, Draper (who previously imposed icons of American patriotism on his environment) now bonds with his new friend by means of another traditional value, religion. We previously heard him reciting the Lord's Prayer while trekking across Mars, and after the prescient Mona locates another source of water for the travelers as they move underground toward the Martian ice cap to escape the aliens, Draper exclaims, "Thank God for water." When his companion inquires about the meaning of "God," they discover that they both believe in a divine being, though the alien has a different name for this comforting presence.

The film also projects the colonizing attitude found in its purported source material, Daniel Defoe's *Robinson Crusoe* (1719): Having previously been subordinate to McReady within the confines of civilization, Draper now asserts his superiority over a savage, telling him "I'm the boss" and naming him "Friday—with apologies to Robinson Crusoe." To Europeans of earlier centuries, even an ordinary westerner must rule over non–Europeans. Yet one can also interpret these developments less politically as a sign of Draper's maturation: While he once felt inferior to the smoother and seemingly more capable McReady, his success in surviving on Mars boosts his self-confidence, so he is now assertive in dealing with Friday (who, perhaps not coincidentally, resembles a more swarthy West).

As if feeling guilty about introducing human-like aliens as villains, the film removes them from the scene when Draper succeeds in cutting off the bracelet that allows them to detect Friday, and it again becomes a story of survival in a harsh environment as they endure the explosive crash-landing of the meteorite, flowing lava, and, near the ice cap, a watery marsh that almost sucks them in. But there is a *deux ex machina* in the end, as Draper's radio picks up a human voice from a second mission approaching Mars that will land to rescue Draper and his companion. The film mercifully concludes before Draper must begin explaining what happened to him on Mars.

Lost in Space (1965–1968)

Regular viewers of Irwin Allen's *Lost in Space* will primarily remember silly stories on Earthlike planets featuring the comically duplicitous Dr. Zachary Smith (Jonathan Harris) and, as his straight men and foils, precocious little Will Robinson (Billy Mumy) and the deadpan Robot. Yet early episodes were more somber in their tone and did show characters traveling in spaceships, wearing spacesuits, and sometimes venturing into the vacuum of space. There is even evidence that this came at the urging of CBS executives.

There are two noteworthy differences between the series' original pilot, "No Place to Hide," and the series it spawned: The pilot omits the stowaway Smith and the Robot, who became the series' most prominent characters; but the pilot also takes the Robinson family almost immediately to the surface of an alien planet, to deal with issues ranging from a cold spell to a vicious giant. One can reasonably theorize, then, that in approving the series, CBS also recommended two changes: adding a character or two to offer more possibilities for drama and conflict, and stretching out the initial story to allow characters to actually spend some time lost in space. One also notes that the series, unlike the pilot, had opening credits featuring animated figures of the stars wearing spacesuits, floating in space while tethered to a lifeline, replicating a scenario that unfolds in the first two episodes. Someone at CBS, then, may have liked the idea of a space series with spacesuits. (It is also relevant that, after two seasons that mostly involved the Robinsons lingering on two alien planets, the third season had them travel more through space, in an evident effort to liven things up.)

The first episode, "The Reluctant Stowaway" (aired September 15, 1965), extensively borrows footage from "No Place to Hide" to establish the series' premise: Earth in 1997 is severely overpopulated, and humanity's only hope is to send people to live on other planets. Interestingly, then, this is one of the first films to introduce a new argument for space travel — to relieve overpopulation on Earth — which sounds appealing but is illogical, since calculations demonstrate that transporting the necessary millions and millions of people into space would never be practical. (This was also the rationale for a flight to Alpha Centauri in *Spaceflight IC-1: An Adventure in Space* [1965]; spacesuits did not figure in its plot.)

Thus, as a pilot project, the Robinson family — parents John (Guy Williams) and Maureen (June Lockhart) Robinson, daughters Judy (Marta Kristen) and Penny (Angela Cartwright), and son Will — along with pilot Don West (Mark Goddard), will fly the *Jupiter II* to a planet orbiting Alpha Centauri, though during the journey, they will be placed in suspended animation. While everyone prepares for the launch, enemy spy Smith sneaks into the spaceship to sabotage its equipment and reprogram its Robot to destroy the ship. But he is accidentally trapped on board when the ship launches, and after his excess weight drives the vessel off course, he panics and awakens the hibernating crew so they can return the spaceship to Earth. After dealing with the now-homicidal Robot, John decides he must venture outside the ship to make some repairs. (Of course, going into space to repair damaged equipment was already a tradition in spacesuit films.)

All things considered, the depiction of his spacewalk is reasonably well done: He dons a realistic-looking spacesuit, he moves slowly and carefully while struggling to stay attached to his ship, and at one point he floats upside down in space against a starry background, held in position by a lifeline. It is deflating, though, when he describes the experience of being in space by commenting, "I feel like I've been hit by a truck." The crisis occurs when the rope breaks and he begins to drift away from the spaceship. Because West must remain safely inside, as the only person who can pilot the spacecraft,[2] the others urge Smith to "suit up" and rescue him. Smith refuses to do so (to avoid a later spacewalk, he claims to suffer from a severe fear of heights). Maureen then bravely dons her own spacesuit and goes into space to save her husband from certain death, following in the footsteps of the professor's daughter in *Conquistador de la Luna* (discussed below) to become the second woman to walk in space. Her actions outside the spaceship are the epitome of caution: She clings to the hull and fires a rocket gun with a lifeline in John's direction, hoping he will grab it. Even this simple action, it seems, taxes her courage to the utmost, since she subsequently declines to move from her initial position throughout a lengthy sojourn in space. Still, she and her Mexican predecessor establish an interesting pattern regarding the different motives that stereotypical men and women have for confronting the vacuum of space: Men go outside to repair some piece of machinery, while women try to rescue their men.

As the episode reaches its cliffhanger conclusion, it seems Maureen's efforts are in vain, as John is unable to grab the lifeline; however, at the beginning of the second episode, "The Derelict" (aired September 22, 1965), he escapes oblivion in "the trackless void of outer space" by finally seizing the lifeline and pulling himself in, so the couple can enjoy a happy reunion on the hull of the spaceship. Then John slowly makes his way to the top of the spaceship to deal with the damaged equipment. After he finishes, a second problem emerges: When John attempts to open the airlock door, he finds it is jammed shut due to excess heat. West suits up to try opening it from the other side, but he cannot. To add a sense of urgency, a comet is approaching. John and Maureen lie motionless outside the spaceship, indicating that their oxygen is running out.

Fortunately, Will has the bizarre idea that spraying the door with a fire extinguisher will make it open, perhaps reflecting a confused notion that a device that puts out flames would also reduce heat, and this plan proves successful. When they are dragged inside, John recovers immediately, but the frailer Maureen arouses concern by briefly remaining unconscious until finally opening her eyes. As if unable to believe she really mustered the courage to enter space, she asks John, "Was I really — out there?" and he assures her she really did go "out there." The rest of the episode, involving their spaceship's capture by, and escape from, a spherical spacecraft containing enigmatic aliens, requires no summary here.

In the third episode, "Island in the Sky" (aired September 29, 1965), John takes another walk in space, though this time for a dubious reason: The *Jupiter II* is approaching what looks like a suitable planet to land on, but John wants to go outside and drift closer to the planet to, in effect, get a closer look at a potential new residence. While he again is momentarily upside down in space, the execution of this second spacewalk is more perfunctory, with a focus on dull, medium-range images of John moving from right to left across the screen to indicate that he is getting dangerously close to the planet. Sure enough, he is soon falling to the surface and, due to another act of sabotage by Smith, his "parajets"— presumably, jets to reduce his rate of descent as a sort of parachute — are not working, and the spaceship loses contact with him. All these incidents in space — the broken scanner, elusive lifeline, jammed door, broken jets — might be said to make the point that humans in space will constantly depend on properly functioning machinery to stay alive; but the only lesson the crew of the *Jupiter II* seem to learn is that they need to find an Earthlike planet, so they can start confront more colorful problems like giants and aliens. Symbolically, at least, this is precisely the plan John follows: He escapes from space and rushes to the safety of a planetary surface, luckily surviving because, we later learn, his parajets finally started working about one hundred feet above the ground, allowing for a reasonably soft landing. (In fact, a man falling through an Earthlike atmosphere with only a spacesuit for protection would burn up due to friction long before reaching that point, which is why an astronaut who attempts a similar feat in a genuine work of science fiction, Allan Steele's novel *Orbital Decay* [1989], succeeds only due to elaborate precautions.)

After the *Jupiter II* lands to search for John, more footage from the pilot episode is employed, and the situation of the first season is established: The Robinsons will remain on the planet to effect repairs while dealing with Smith's constant scheming, discoveries of strange devices and menacing robots, and implausible human and alien visitors. However, as if returning to the promise of the opening credits, or hoping to attract new viewers with space adventures, the series' second season began with the Robinsons, their spaceship repaired, leaving the planet to resume the journey to Alpha Centauri. In the episode "Wild Adventure" (aired September 21, 1966), they again don spacesuits to walk in space.

The first order of business is escaping a daunting menace — a approaching red mass in space — that provided the previous episode, "Blast Off into Space" (aired September 14, 1966), with its cliffhanger ending. To the Robinsons' amazement, their spaceship passes through the mass without ill effects, since it is only a harmless, gaseous cloud, which is why it did not register on their instruments until observed through the spaceship window. The problem, John concludes, is that "we trusted our eyes instead of our instruments," which might be taken as an apt observation that people must rely on technology, not their senses, to deal with the unfamiliar environment of space.

Other dramas in the episode are provoked, as usual, by the inept machinations of Smith, who is determined to return to Earth even though the Robinsons wish to proceed to their original destination. First, trying to reset the controls himself, he accidentally releases all the ship's fuel, requiring a quick trip to a nearby "fuel barge" that John improbably happens to know of. When West puts on his spacesuit for a brief, uneventful trip through space to retrieve the fuel, he reports a fleeting glimpse of some sort of being in space, which prompts Smith to berate him for apparently succumbing to derangement and demonstrating his incompetence; West had a "hallucination," he claims, because he suffered from "space rapture," a term that also surfaces in an episode of *I Dream of Jeannie*. The tables are predictably turned when Smith himself observes a beautiful green woman (Vitina Marcus) floating in space without a spacesuit, singing murmured syllables that soon mention Smith by name; naturally, no other crew members believe his story. But the alien will soon "hypnotize" Smith into putting on his spacesuit and joining her in space for a free-floating dance, as Smith now believes himself in love with her. Grumbling that "*some*body has to haul him back in," West dons his spacesuit. Unfortunately, this maneuver requires the Robinsons to give up their chance to set a course for Alpha Centauri. The alien is finally explained as one of many beings that live off energy and hence were attracted to the fuel barge and now seek fuel from the Robinsons' spaceship.

After visiting a world ruled by robots in "The Ghost Planet" (aired September 28, 1966), the Robinsons settle down on another planet in "The Forbidden World" (aired October 5, 1966). Initially, this world seems inhospitable to humans, as the Robot tells them that, despite oxygen in its atmosphere, the humans must wear "artificial breathing apparatus" to remain safe. However, after Smith wears a breathing mask to go outside and rescue the Robot, he and the others are soon doing perfectly fine without such gear, and they will spend the rest of the season on this planet, preoccupied with nonsensical adventures.

However, as if following a now-established ritual, they again blast off into space in the third season's first episode, "Condemned of Space" (aired September 6, 1967), and again engage in a spacewalk. Problems begin when Smith seeks to hurl a sort of message in a bottle into space and accidentally opens the airlock to send the Robot out into space. Leaving the door open for more than an instant, of course, would actually make all the air inside the spaceship rush out, but the Robinsons detect the loss of pressure, run to the airlock door, and close it without further incidents. John suits up to retrieve the Robot, but he is frustratingly unable to reach it; this may be the most emotionally involving of all the series' crises in space, since the way the Robot slowly drifts away from the spaceship, waving its flexible arms, conveys a special sense of the helplessness that persons truly lost in space would feel. (One can also argue the Robot is the series' most appealing character.) Further, the situation will apparently end tragically, since John must return inside, abandoning the Robot, so West can move the vehicle away from a supernova.

There then occurs what is arguably the most interesting predicament in the entire series: Due to damage from the supernova, sparks start flying from the instrumental panel, and John announces that the spaceship's hull might be breached. "Everybody — into your helmets!" he exclaims, but we actually observe characters putting on full spacesuits, with Will helping Smith don the garment. (Perhaps reflecting budgetary concerns, we never observe smaller-sized spacesuits for Will and Penny, only adult-sized spacesuits.) When Smith complains they need a "lifeboat," he is impatiently told, "Your spacesuit's your lifeboat." We are thus invited to expect a plausible disaster in space, as the spaceship's hull is damaged, air rushes out, and the Robinsons and their companions must drift in space, wearing spacesuits to survive, near the wreckage of their vehicle.

However, the expected problem never occurs, as the spaceship instead has a rendezvous with a large spaceship. By means of some sort of connection between the spacecraft, John, Will, West, and Smith can enter it without spacesuits. The Robot has also, in some unexplained fashion, returned to the spaceship on its own, as it pounds on the airlock door to gain reentry. Some standard melodrama then follows: The spaceship proves a prison ship filled with frozen convicts and patrolled by a hostile robot (Robby the Robot from *Forbidden Planet*). West is mistaken for a criminal and almost frozen, and Smith conspires with one thawed-out convict to seize control of the Robinsons' spaceship. John intervenes with an offer to repair the spaceship's errant timing mechanism so the convicts, who served their sentences, can be released.

Comparing the spacewalks that began each season, we observe a progression that reveals the series' shifting priorities: In the first crisis, the imperiled spacewalkers were John and Maureen, then envisioned as the series' main characters; but in the second season, Smith must be rescued, and in the third season it is the Robot, demonstrating that those characters had become the stars. Further, while the stories that foregrounded those characters were risible, explaining why the series did not enjoy lasting popularity, one must also admit that *Lost in Space*, on those occasions when the cast was not on a planet, addressed the realities of space travel more plausibly than the purportedly more mature *Star Trek*. Thus, while *Lost in Space* is rarely cherished, a more charitable re-evaluation of the series, acknowledging its scattered virtues as well as myriad flaws, would seem in order.

The Time Tunnel: "One Way to the Moon" (1966)

By the mid–1960s, one would think, filmed depictions of future flights to other worlds would be modeled on the current achievements and future plans of NASA, with astronauts traveling in small, separable space capsules, one to orbit its destination and the other to land on its surface. It seems incongruous, then, that an episode of another series produced by Irwin Allen, *The Time Tunnel* (1966–1967), "One Way to the Moon" (aired September 16, 1966), features a large, roomy spaceship that will fly directly from the surface of the Earth to Mars, an approach NASA rejected as impractical. The explanation is simple: The cost-conscious Allen, who reused footage from *The Lost World* (1960) for an episode of *Voyage to the Bottom of the Sea* (1964–1968), decided to reuse footage from *Destination Moon* for this episode, so its spaceship had to resemble the one in that film.

As if paying homage to its distinguished predecessor, the flight initially seems realistic enough, if one overlooks its dated design and the fact that time travelers Tony Newman (James Darren) and Doug Phillips (Robert Colbert) coincidentally materialize in the spaceship's unoccupied "service module" seconds before launch. But Newman and Phillips are soon floating upward, as Phillips comments, "We're coasting in zero gravity," and when they are again in normal gravity, he offers a reasonable explanation: "The capsule's spinning to create its own gravity." However, if the spaceship is built so that its manned compartment is the top floor and the service module its bottom floor, as seems apparent, spinning the spaceship would make people feel attracted to the walls, not the floor.

The inadvertent stowaways are discovered because their extra weight made it difficult for the spaceship to reach escape velocity. Despite Newman and Phillips' expectation that people in 1978 would know about a time travel project that was top secret in 1968, Commander Kane (Larry Ward) does not believe their story and imprisons them as probable enemy agents while he debates how to handle the problems caused by their presence. He decides to land on the Moon, if a landing is possible, obtain fuel from a storage area, and resume the flight to Mars.

A very 1950s-style crisis then occurs: The spaceship is struck by a meteor, causing an air leak in the service module. Newman and Phillips are told by a crewman, "Here — spacesuits, put 'em on quick!" and when the three men are safely suited up, we recognize the distinctive red, green, and blue spacesuits from *Destination Moon*. To repair the leak (and not incidentally, bolster their image for the skeptical commander), Newman and Phillips agree to accompany crewman Nazarro (Ben Cooper) on an expedition outside the spaceship to seal the leak. There follows the episode's only impressive footage, as the men emerge from the spaceship upside down, from the camera's perspective, and walk around the spaceship to stand amidst a sea of stars — footage taken directly from *Destination Moon*. The novelty is that they see an Earth based on recent photos taken from space, so it looks like a blue ball with wisps of white clouds. And while the men are there to fix the leak, Nazarro does say, "I'll take a look at the aft antenna" to "rig up something to restore communications," a possible tribute to the film it is stealing from (since repairing an antenna inspired the spacewalk in *Destination Moon*).

At this point, the story becomes a bit silly. For advice on how to assist the time travelers, the scientists who constantly monitor them in 1968 invite three NASA officials to observe their space flight; one is a younger version of Beard (James T. Callahan), a member of the Mars mission crew. He cannot explain why his future self expresses disbelief when Newman and Phillips say they are time travelers, since he would presumably remember his past encounter with the time-travel project; it is also odd that his future self confidently announces that, according to his calculations, the spaceship can land safely, when scientists in 1968 calculate that the ship will be unable to do so. The obvious explanation is that Beard, in the present and future, is an enemy agent, intent upon sabotaging NASA missions; he does not vouch for Newman and Phillips because he wants crew members to suspect them, not himself, if they notice his previous efforts to prevent the success of the Mars flight, and he misleads them about the results of his calculations because he wants the spaceship to crash and fail, even if that endangers his own life. Surprisingly, none of the time-travel scientists voice suspicions about Beard; even when informed by NASA that one observer is a spy, they simply decide to imprison them all while they investigate. To draw suspicion away from Beard, one supposes, another NASA official who is also a spy grabs a gun and brandishes it while he flees into other areas of the time-travel complex. Beard later tracks him down and shoots him, establishing his own loyalty and ensuring that he will someday be selected to join the Mars mission.

The future Beard also is up to no good: Upon realizing they cannot land safely, crewmen don spacesuits to protect themselves if the ship's hull is penetrated when they land roughly, leaving Newman and Phillips, who lack spacesuits, exposed to possible death. Fortunately, the ship remains intact, so the still-suspicious Kane sends Beard and Nazarro to get the needed fuel while he watches the interlopers. For no defensible reason, they must refuel and take off within twenty-two minutes or they cannot reach Mars. When the men reach the cache with the fuel, the four needed fuel tanks are very small, and look exactly like the oxygen tanks commonly attached to spacesuits — which makes no sense, since a spaceship flying to Mars would require large quantities of fuel, not tiny containers. Beard kills Nazarro by pulling out his air hose. Kane believes Beard's story that Nazarro is not responding because his radio is malfunctioning, but Newman and Phillips realize that foul play is involved. Newman leaves the spaceship to obtain the fuel and confront Beard.

In a ridiculous scene, Newman finds Beard and the two spacesuited men engaged in a clumsy struggle, illustrating that the conventions of melodrama do not translate well to authentic space settings. For neither spacesuit is damaged, and when Newman finally overcomes Beard and knocks him to the ground, he is momentarily stunned but not killed. Newman leaves with the fuel, but in the meantime, Phillips departs on his own to search for Newman. He finds Beard and has his own fight with the man, with similar results. Newman returns with the fuel and announces he will search for Phillips, telling Kane to blast off if the men do not return in time, which in fact occurs. In the end, Beard is left to die while Newman and Phillips are magically transported to another place and time, a collapsed coal mine in 1910.

While they subsequently encounter aliens from space in their past, and their future, Newman and Phillips never venture into space again, perhaps because Allen could not obtain footage from another space movie for such an adventure.

In Like Flint (1967) and *You Only Live Twice* (1967)

Following the unexpected success of the third James Bond film, *Goldfinger* (1964), glamorous spies employing ingenious equipment to combat secret organizations and mad scientists became increasingly common in films and on television, creating a competition to make each new story even more extravagant than its predecessors. By 1967, as a predictable consequence, spy adventures began including space travel, creating a new sort of melodramatic spacesuit film. In some cases, earthbound spies merely thwarted earthbound adversaries whose evil plans happened to involve astronauts or space vehicles; one lackluster example is an episode of the series *I Spy*, "Apollo" (aired November 20, 1967), which merely used NASA facilities and an impending rocket launch as a backdrop for a story about spies Kelly Robinson (Robert Culp) and Alexander Scott (Bill Cosby) trying to thwart saboteurs. But two films actually feature space travelers.

The farcical Derek Flint (James Coburn) became the first spy to reach space in his second film, *In Like Flint*. Since Flint was portrayed as a womanizer, like his cohorts, this story's gimmick is that its sinister secret organization is made up entirely of beautiful women. Using the Fabulous Face company as a front, and brainwashing female customers with modified hair driers, they seek to conquer the world, first by taking over the first manned space platform the Americans are launching. Watching its liftoff on television, the women imagine a new brand of cologne ("Blast Off— the Cologne That Sends You"), seeing an involvement with space travel as a way to make money as well as gain power. Soon, two female cosmonauts sent by the women board the space platform in a manner suggesting little concern for scientific accuracy: They open the hatch, enter the compartment, and immediately remove their transparent helmets. In actuality, opening the hatch would cause all the air inside to rush out, so the women could not breathe without helmets.

After this glimpse of space travel, the story shifts back to the ground for tedious intrigues: The president (Andrew Duggan) is replaced by an imposter, and he and ally General Carter (Steve Ihnat) conspire to discredit Flint's boss, Lloyd C. Cramden (Lee J. Cobb). Assigned by Cramden to investigate, Flint breaks into the headquarters of his organization, Z.O.W.I.E. Discovering that the facility is monitoring the heartbeats of female cosmonauts, he travels to Moscow and learns enough to realize that his next stop must be the Virgin Islands, where the Fabulous Face company is based. There, he finds that the phony president and Carter have rebelled against their female allies and are implementing "Project Damocles" by planning to launch nuclear bombs to arm the space platform. An incredulous Flint asks, "Project Damocles calls for nuclear energy to be used as a threat?" When the answer is "Correct," he announces, "That's a totally discredited idea." This demonstrates again, as first suggested in *The Road to Hong Kong*, that exploiting space for military purposes is, in the 1960s, regarded as irrational.

To carry out his scheme, Carter forcibly removes the two astronauts who were to fly in the spacecraft and dons a spacesuit to replace them, telling technicians monitoring the launch, now led by the rescued president, that they must let him take off or he will detonate the bombs immediately. In a rare touch of realism, a pursuing Flint tells them to stall Carter. He says, "Give me three minutes"—the time he needs to put on a spacesuit and board the ship. It is unusual for such a film to acknowledge that putting on a cumbersome spacesuit does require more time than putting on other clothes. When Flint enters the spaceship with seconds to spare, there is another authentic development: One expects that the foes would immediately start fighting, but instead they calmly sit next to each other in their couches to endure the pressure of liftoff. Only when they reach orbit can they begin their inevitable struggle.

The ensuing scene is also revelatory, because the fight is choreographed as one might actually occur in the weightlessness of space. Both Flint and Carter move slowly and awkwardly, making this climactic battle dramatically disappointing; it recalls the similarly slow-paced struggle in *Project Moon Base*. Again, recognizing the realities of space reduces a filmmaker's ability to offer conventional sorts of cinematic excitement; and one is surprised that, in a film where plausibility was not a priority, director Gordon Douglas did not ignore the effects of zero gravity and stage a standard, fast-moving slugfest.

The film promptly returns to scientific nonsense, for after Flint wins the fight and ties Carter down, he leaves the spacecraft, presumably because he correctly suspects it will be destroyed by American missiles, and happens to observe the space platform in the distance. Using a small propulsion device, he makes his way to the platform, and to safety, before the spaceship is blown to pieces. When monitors on the ground, after mourning Flint's death, suddenly hear his voice on the radio, one man exclaims, "He must be on the platform!" The immediate response—"That's impossible!"—is correct, because if a man left a spaceship that was off course, the odds he would happen to be near a small orbiting object are virtually nil.

In the final scene, Flint passionately kisses the cosmonauts on the platform, with only a small floating microphone to indicate zero gravity, and advises his superiors that there is no need to rush efforts to bring him back to Earth. As in humorous spacesuit films like *Totò nella Luna* and *The Road to Hong Kong*—and this film almost qualifies as a comedy—Flint is happy to stay in space indefinitely, as long as he can enjoy the company of a beautiful woman.

A few months after *In Like Flint*, the fifth James Bond adventure, *You Only Live Twice*, was released, and the story again involved space travel, though Bond (Sean Connery) never makes it into space. In the opening sequences, two spacesuited astronauts are in an orbiting space capsule called the *Jupiter 16*. After one astronaut exits for a spacewalk, still tethered to the ship by a lifeline, a large spaceship approaches the capsule, four panels open at its front, and the craft literally swallows the space capsule, in the process cutting the spacewalking astronaut's lifeline and sending him drifting off into space. In a tense meeting between American, Russian, and British officials, the Americans accuse the Russians of capturing the space capsule, but the Russians deny any involvement. When the British representative politely asks the American what possible motive the Russians could have for this action, he says it must be "a blatant attempt to gain complete and absolute control of space itself—for military purposes." Strangely, the British man does not respond that, by current thinking, that goal makes little sense.

Since the British determined that the abducting spaceship landed near Japan, they dispatch Bond to investigate, to be assisted by Japanese spy Tiger Tanaka (Tetsurô Tanba). After a Russian space capsule is similarly captured, with the Russians now accusing the Americans of malfeasance in space, the true situation is apparent: The evil head of SPECTRE, Ernst Blofeld (Donald Pleasence), is launching spaceships from a secret base beneath a Japanese island and seizing American and Russian space capsules so that the nations, blaming each other for the hostile acts, will launch a nuclear war. Then, a nation allied with Blofeld (implicitly Communist China) can dominate the world.

After several exciting incidents of little real importance, Bond and another Japanese spy, Kissy Suzuki (Mie Hama), discover the island base hidden underneath a phony lake in a volcanic crater. While Suzuki goes to get help from Tanaka, Bond slips inside the base and finds two American astronauts in a prison cell, a lapse in continuity since we previously observed one of the two Americans in orbit being left to die in space. (Perhaps we are intended to think that one man is a Russian cosmonaut, but since we saw two cosmonauts captured, there should then have been three men in the cell.) Freeing them to serve as allies, Bond intercepts an astronaut preparing to board the spaceship, takes his place, and walks alongside the other astronaut toward the spaceship hatch, wearing a spacesuit and helmet, without being noticed, exploiting the spacesuit as a form of disguise. He must assume that, like Flint, he can figure out how to fly a spaceship and prevent another capture of an American space capsule. However, he never gets the chance to fly into space, because by improperly carrying his "air conditioner" on board the spaceship, he reveals he is an imposter. Bond is removed from the craft and brought to Blofeld. Thus, he must stop the spaceship, and avert a nuclear war, while on the ground.

Helpfully, like other stupid villains, Blofeld lets Bond watch his impending triumph instead of killing him immediately. This gives Tanaka and his ninjas time to invade his headquarters and launch a chaotic battle to seize the control room. After some colorful mayhem, Bond reaches the control room and, with five seconds to spare, pushes a button to blow up the spaceship, save the space capsule, and prevent the war. In reality, a spaceship exploding near a space capsule would send debris hurtling into the capsule and cause significant damage, but this story bears little relationship to reality.

Perhaps the most significant thing about *You Only Live Twice* is that the film inspired Connery to abandon the role of Bond (the films were becoming too silly for him to tolerate). And in the 1970s, as Roger Moore settled into the role, Connery's fears came true, as Bond films grew more and more absurd. *Moonraker* (1979) would not only have the spy don a spacesuit but actually send him into space.

The Terrornauts (1967)

While frivolous and barely qualifying as a spacesuit film, *The Terrornauts* unusually involved two veteran science fiction writers — a source novel by Murray Leinster and a screenplay by John Brunner — so it has moments of interest. Most strikingly, it begins by depicting the most likely way humans might actually come into contact with alien life — by receiving a message using a radio telescope. (Only the *Men into Space* episode "Beyond the Stars" previously explored this possibility in film.) Astronomer Joe Burke (Simon Oates) leads a project to search for messages from the stars, though the facility's skeptical leader, Henry Shore (Max Adrian), eagerly awaits the imminent end of Burke's funding so the radio telescope can engage in more productive work. At this moment, Burke and colleague Ben Keller (Stanley Meadows) pick up a message sent from an asteroid.

Burke's reaction to the message is incredible: He *recognizes* it. He tells colleagues that, as a child, he visited his archaeologist uncle at a French site, where he was given a strange black box with a receptacle that, obviously of modern origin, did not interest the archaeologists. Later, he accidentally broke the box and, after touching blue material from its interior, had a dream featuring a planet with two moons and a strange signal — identical to what the radio telescope picked up. The experience also inspired him to seek evidence of extraterrestrial life.

A depiction of the dream, clearly connected to the plot, is the first indication that this seemingly sober account of first contact will soon become absurd; for after Burke's response is received by the asteroid — an automated space station — it dispatches a spaceship to Earth which lifts up the building containing Burke and carries it off into space. Its other occupants are Keller, their associate and Burke's romantic interest Sandy Lund (Zena Marshall), and two guests to provide comic relief: Mrs. Jones (Patricia Hayes), the simple-minded woman who brings them coffee, and Joshua Yellowlees (Charles Hawtrey), a timid accountant sent by the foundation supporting Burke to examine his records. During their journey, Burke notes that they enjoy normal gravity and a breathable atmosphere instead of floating in airless space, which means they are dealing with advanced aliens who can create "artificial gravity" and a "force field" to protect space travelers. Displaying an awareness of science fiction, Yellowlees worries that the aliens "might be monsters" and "could have tentacles."

But once inside the alien facility on the asteroid, Burke and his companions encounter no living beings, only an ambulatory robot that administers a few tests to demonstrate that they are intelligent. Then, after discovering the corpses of two green-skinned humanoids, Lund falls upon a platform and is teleported to an alien planet with two moons, the world in Burke's dream. She is attacked and seized by green-skinned aliens wielding bows and arrows, seemingly intent upon making her a ritual sacrifice. Burke follows her to the planet and rescues her. Fortuitously, Burke brings back a skullcap with wires which he deduces is the device necessary to access data from black boxes, identical to the one he received as a child, which are all over the station.

From the boxes, Burke learns that the green-skinned aliens, after searching the cosmos for intelligent life, encountered an evil race they call the Enemy. To protect themselves and similar beings, they established military bases in various solar systems, though the Enemy deploys a weapon against their world which reduces them to savages. Since they mastered teleportation, it is unclear why they, or the Enemy (presumably at the same level of development) would need or use spaceships, but the frenetic pace of the plot allows no time to ponder such questions.

Burke and the others now realize that the signal they received was a call for beings to man the station and use its weapons to fend off an impending attack. Frantically drawing information from the boxes, Burke begins launching missiles at an approaching armada of ten Enemy spaceships, locked in a triangular formation. As Burke begins to destroy them, they make no effort to engage in evasive maneuvers and continue on their preset paths, easy targets for the next missiles. It would have been an interesting nuance if someone speculated that the Enemy, like the race they opposed, had become extinct or mindless, so their battles are now pointless exercises involving automatic attackers facing automatic defenders, but no explanation is given for their senseless passivity in response to Burke's missiles.

As the one surviving Enemy spaceship crashes into the station, the plot takes its final ridiculous turn: Having somehow modified the teleportation platform, Burke and his companions teleport themselves back to Earth, where they find themselves at the same site where Burke received the alien box. As a noteworthy final twist, the returning space travelers are "attacked" by three boys wearing colorful green spacesuits and transparent visors suggesting space helmets — officially qualifying *The Terrornauts* as a spacesuit film — and Mrs. Jones responds indignantly to this interruption by exclaiming, "There's no such thing as spacemen anyway." While their own experiences appears to contradict this claim, it is, from another perspective, true that if space travelers enjoy access to artificial gravity, force fields, and teleportation, they will not be "spacemen" of the conventional sort requiring spacesuits to protect themselves. This odd encounter might convey Brunner's recognition that, as space films moved away from the realism of *Destination Moon* and toward the fantasy of *Star Trek* (which also featured artificial gravity, force fields, and teleportation), the spacesuited astronaut would become an anachronism, of interest only to children.

Star Trek: "The Tholian Web" (1968)

To this day, efforts to evaluate the original *Star Trek* series (1966–1969) are hampered by the mythology crafted by, and serving the interests of, series creator Gene Roddenberry. As the story goes, the series thrived during its first two seasons under Roddenberry's inspired control; then, when he retired as *Star Trek*'s producer to protest NBC's decision to move the series to an inappropriate time slot, Fred Freiberger took over and drove the series to ignominious mediocrity. Actually, while Roddenberry's key role in creating this imaginative and involving series must be praised, the successes of *Star Trek*'s first two seasons can mostly be attributed to producer Gene L. Coon, whose departure during the second season noticeably diminished its quality. While Freiberger did produce some terrible episodes, he also brought his own innovative energy to some of the series' finest moments.[3] As one unacknowledged contribution, he added to *Star Trek* a belated recognition that, even in the twenty-fourth century, space travelers might sometimes need spacesuits.

Originally, Roddenberry carefully designed his series so that spacesuits would never appear. The *Enterprise* was equipped with artificial gravity, a strong hull, and powerful energy "shields" to fend off enemy attacks, so crew members would have no concerns about the dangers of space. James Kirk (William Shatner) and his crew would solely visit "M-class" (Earthlike) planets, so they would never require special protection, and they would travel from their starship to these planets, and other spacecraft, using teleportation, entirely avoiding space. When "transporters" could not be used, crew members might travel in small shuttlecrafts, but these were evidently just as well protected as the *Enterprise*, since crews always wore normal uniforms.

Despite these stipulations, episodes of the series repeatedly presented situations that, to any intelligent viewer, demanded spacesuits, though none were employed. In "The Enemy Within" (aired October 6, 1966), several crew members are stranded on a planet steadily growing colder because of a transporter malfunction, making the point that even "M-class" worlds might sometimes have harsh environments demanding special protection. And several episodes involve suspenseful space battles when assaults from enemy "phaser beams" and "photon torpedoes" gradually weaken the all-important shields, which are sometimes about to fail completely; and if that occurs, the next attack would tear open the hull and expose the *Enterprise* crew to the vacuum of space. Yet during these crises, no one suggests breaking out the spacesuits; it seems the ship does not have such garments, though crew members regularly face the prospect of desperately needing them to survive. Thus, throughout the first two seasons, the closest thing to a spacesuit one observes is the bright red, protective garments worn by Mr. Spock (Leonard Nimoy) and another crewman in "The Naked Time" (aired September 26, 1966), when they visit a research station on a planet termed a "frozen wasteland." Yet they resemble outfits worn by firefighters, not by astronauts; cowls with transparent faceplates are draped over their heads, visibly not airtight, and Spock's companion casually pulls off his glove. Clearly, these garments would be of no use in space.

Reflecting the series' bias against spacesuits, the original teleplay for the third-season episode "The Tholian Web" (aired November 15, 1968) featured crew members wearing "personal shields," miniature versions of the force fields protecting the *Enterprise*, to protect them when they board a derelict starship. Such scientific magic would be Roddenberry's preferred solution in such circumstances. However, "shields" would not be sufficient to safeguard individuals in space, since they require not only a barrier between their frail bodies and the vacuum, but also a steady supply of oxygen. Somebody involved in the episode, presumably with Freiberger's blessing, clearly recognized that conventional spacesuits with oxygen tanks, even in the far future, would be the most practical garments for extra-vehicular activity.

Thus, when "The Tholian Web" begins with the discovery of the missing starship *Defiant*, apparently hovering lifelessly between this universe and a parallel universe, Kirk, Spock, Dr. McCoy (DeForest Kelley), and Chekov (Walter Koenig) stand in the transporter room wearing traditional spacesuits to be teleported to the potentially airless starship. (Just to be different, the outfits are called "environmental units.") On board the *Defiant*, they discover that all crew members are dead, apparently after attacking each other as if insane. Mr. Scott (James Doohan) then informs them that the *Defiant* is drifting away from our plane of existence, so they must return to the *Enterprise*. Only three transporter stations are functional, so Kirk orders his crewmates to leave while he stays on the vanishing starship.

What No Man Has Worn Before: To investigate a derelict starship, *Star Trek* crewmates Pavel Chekov (Walter Koenig), James Kirk (William Shatner), Mr. Spock (Leonard Nimoy) and Dr. McCoy (DeForest Kelley) don spacesuits for the very first time in the episode "The Tholian Web" (1968).

When Spock takes command, he orders that the ship remain in the vicinity of the *Defiant*'s disappearance, despite dangerously unstable conditions, to retrieve Kirk when the starship reappears in our space after two hours. As a complication, spaceships of the alien race, the Tholians, appear and the aliens aboard complain that the *Enterprise* has invaded their territory. Spock placates them by explaining that the humans are only staying temporarily to rescue a crewmate. But other problems emerge, as crew members begin acting in a crazed, violent manner, indicating that the disease that infected the *Defiant* has spread to the *Enterprise*. When the scheduled attempt to locate and save Kirk is unsuccessful, Spock sadly concludes that Kirk must be dead, because "his environmental unit can provide breathable air for no more than 3.62 hours." Spock then presides over a funeral service and seemingly assumes permanent command of the *Enterprise*.

These developments had a special impact when the episode was first aired. Today, one watches "The Tholian Web" and knows immediately it is all a mistake, that Kirk will be found alive and rescued before the episode ends. But at the time, even relatively youthful viewers knew that television stars occasionally had disputes with colleagues, fell seriously ill, or abandoned series for other opportunities, sometimes abruptly.[4] Thus, it was possible that "The Tholian Web" represented Shatner's final *Star Trek* episode, and that subsequent episodes would feature Spock as the *Enterprise* captain. No other episode of the series so forcefully suggested that space travel, even in the distant future, could be dangerous; and it is at least an interesting coincidence, and perhaps an unintended consequence, that this message came in the only *Star Trek* episode featuring a spacesuit, the genre's most powerful icon of the daunting hazards of space. "The Tholian Web" might be offered as evidence that the presence of a spacesuit indeed affects the story being presented, in this case taking *Star Trek* into territory it had vigorously endeavored to avoid.

To be sure, after briefly suspecting this was Shatner's curtain call, viewers could soon figure out he would return, because Uhura (Nichelle Nichols) sees an image of a spacesuited Kirk, drifting like a ghost. While this is dismissed as her wishful fantasy, others observe Kirk as well, indicating that he is still alive, somewhere in the other universe. But something else is different about his role in "The Tholian Web": In other episodes, Kirk is an active hero, leading his crew and working vigorously to defeat villains or overcome obstacles. Here, wearing a spacesuit, he is a helpless victim, floating in a parallel universe, unable to save himself. He is left to hope that, somehow, Spock and his crewmates can do something to rescue him. And this is another message about space travel embedded in the icon of the spacesuit that *Star Trek* rarely conveyed: that the awesome challenge of space can make human beings seem frail and insignificant, and dependent upon monitors for their safety. While advanced aliens previously made Kirk seem childish in the episode "Errand of Mercy" (aired March 23, 1967), it is now space itself that renders him powerless.

With the series' usual hero trapped in a spacesuit, other regulars handle the heroics. McCoy cures the space madness afflicting the crew; Spock outmaneuvers the Tholians, who attempt to ensnare the *Enterprise* in energy filaments; Spock positions the ship to rescue Kirk; and another crewman skillfully manipulates the transporter to bring Kirk back precisely when he is running out of oxygen. The episode concludes typically, with a conversation on the bridge involving Kirk, Spock, and McCoy that makes one more telling point about genuine space travel, and melodramatic space travel. Kirk tells his crewmates, "I had a whole universe to myself" while drifting in space; "There was absolutely no one else in it." Indeed, in the vastness of space, travelers in spacesuit films often feel profoundly lonely. But when Kirk continues, "I prefer a crowded universe much better," he identifies a standard priority of melodramatic spacesuit films: to fill space with aliens resembling humans and planets resembling Earth, creating a "crowded universe" where no one is ever alone. Placing characters in such familiar places, with an exception to be noted, remained *Star Trek*'s priority in later incarnations.

Barbarella (1968)

Summarized carefully, *Barbarella* (1968) seems a throwback to the serials of the 1930s and television programs of the early 1950s: A valiant hero travels to an Earthlike planet in another solar system, discovers human inhabitants ruled by an oppressive tyrant, forms an alliance with an underground movement opposing the tyrant, and succeeds in defeating the despot and freeing the planet's citizens. This sounds very similar to *Captain Video: Master of the Stratosphere.* The differences in this film, based on a French comic, are that its projected audience is not prepubescent males, but adult males; both hero and tyrant are beautiful young women; there are nude scenes and sexual encounters; and the story has an aura of tongue-in-cheek humor. Both *Barbarella* and a later spoof, *Flesh Gordon* (1974), seem failed efforts to update the melodramatic spacesuit film to attract more sophisticated viewers, but the juxtaposition of juvenile adventure and soft-porn sexuality proved incongruous. A more successful approach, unveiled in *Star Wars* (1977), would maintain the subgenre's chaste earnestness while improving production values and special effects.

Barbarella features spacesuits in two scenes, though in both cases they are deployed purely for humorous effect. During the opening credits, the lovely Barbarella (Jane Fonda) floats in her spaceship and slowly removes parts of it until she is completely undressed. Clearly director Roger Vadim thought that weightlessness and a spacesuit would entertainingly begin his film with a novel striptease. Oddly, after this sequence, Barbarella walks normally on the floor of her spaceship, now apparently enjoying artificial gravity, and no one in the film wears a spacesuit again.

A spacesuit, however, appears one more time, after the credits end and a still-naked Barbarella receives a television message from Earth's president (Claude Dauphin). While this far-future universe is a peaceful utopia, the president worries that a scientist named Durand-Durand (Milo O'Shea) has reportedly invented a powerful new weapon that might bring back war; hence, he assigns space pilot Barbarella to track him down. To assist in her search, the president displays the "only known photograph" of Durand-Durand, which shows some normally dressed people surrounding a man in a spacesuit. The spacesuited figure must be the scientist, because Barbarella comments, "I don't think I'm going to be able to recognize him"—a joke hearkening back to Sweeney's observation that his spacesuit makes him unrecognizable and reinforcing the idea that spacesuits depersonalize individuals.

After this moment, the film forgets all about spacesuits; for when Barbarella reaches the planet where Durand-Durand has gone, her computer analyzes its atmosphere and announces it is "terrestrial"; a relieved Barbarella says, "At least I'll be able to breathe." But if the atmosphere had proven non-terrestrial, Barbarella presumably could have breathed in her spacesuit—a garment she has seemingly forgotten about.

The rest of the story is a series of frivolous vignettes. After Barbarella is attacked by rogue children who send walking dolls to bite her, she meets a group of rebels that include scientist Professor Ping (Marcel Marceau) and winged angel Pygar (John Philip Law). Captured by the planet's Great Tyrant (Anita Pallenberg), she learns that its main city is built upon an immense pool of organic liquid that feeds upon and encourages evil. She is subsequently assailed by biting birds before being rescued by another rebel, Dildano (David Hemmings). Durand-Durand, secretly working as the Great Tyrant's concierge, attempts to overthrow her, leading her and Barbarella to become allies in resisting his efforts. While most scenes are played for laughs (with limited success), images of bloody wounds on Barbarella's body inflicted by the dolls and birds undermine the generally playful mood; it is not surprising that this uneven film was a box office failure. It is also not surprising, given Hollywood's ongoing struggle to come up with new ideas, that there are plans to remake the film in 2014.

Moon Zero Two (1969)

Sixteen years after *Spaceways*, Hammer Films finally produced another spacesuit film, seemingly endeavoring to follow in the footsteps of *2001: A Space Odyssey* and exploit public interest in the Moon landing. Yet *Moon Zero Two* was bizarrely incongruous, blending realistic scenes of spacecraft and astronauts with depictions of an implausible Moon City with a spacious airport, hotels, bars, and female dancers. Promoted as the first "space western," the film also falls back on a standard melodramatic plot—a stalwart space pilot opposing a corrupt businessman—and is weakened by a blaring, jazzy score at odds with any effort to portray the quietly lethal environment of space. The effect is like watching scenes from *Destination Moon* randomly mixed with scenes from *Barbarella*.

The film's recurring juxtapositions of contrasting elements are evident at the start: The credits, accompanied by a raucous theme song, show spacesuited astronauts from America and Russia flying to the Moon, planting their national flags, and fighting in the Moon Hotel before being thrown out like garbage. This might be interpreted as a capsule history of space flight from the 1960s to 2021, the year of the film, but this is far from clear. There follows a sequence with an air of documentary realism: An astronaut in a spacecraft resembling a lunar lander emerges in a white spacesuit to approach and grab a satellite, which he brings back as if engaged in space salvage. But the astronaut, William Kemp (James Olson), is then observed in a large enclosed area, evidently the terminal of a lunar airport, under a sign reading WELCOME TO THE MOON.

Next, there is mild comedy as Kemp confronts a woman seeking him when he emerges naked from a shower, but he immediately sees a man inscribing two names on a plaque with the dedication, "To the Memory of the Spacemen Who Died, That Mankind Should Live on the Moon." This somber reminder of the dangers of space travel is followed by scenes of beautiful female dancers in white costumes, entertaining lunar guests with an extended routine that recalls *Cat-Women of the Moon*. (They later perform two more dances in different costumes.) Kemp gives the woman a brief tour of the Moon, including a monument to Neil Armstrong and the "ice mines" that provide water and oxygen. The woman comments that the Moon is "so bleak." The mood shifts yet again as Kemp sits at a futuristic bar with a large drink dispenser, while rich lunar residents play Monopoly.

After another evocative comment from Kemp—that "we're all foreigners here," on the Moon—elements of the plot become clear. Kemp is approached by wealthy businessman J.J. Hubbard (Warren Mitchell), who discovered an asteroid with sapphires. Though it is illegal, he hires Kemp and his Russian partner, Korminski (Ori Levy), to visit the asteroid, attach rockets, and send it to the far side of the Moon, where the sapphires can be mined. As if to emphasize that the story is indeed modeled on western adventures involving disputes over valuable ore and jewels, another dance sequence features women dressed up like cowboys.

The film gets back to business as Kemp approaches the asteroid, and there are authentic-looking scenes of Kemp slowly attaching rockets to its surface; he is sometimes observed upside down. Returning to the spaceship, he comments, "It's a little lonely out here." But

Cosmic Couple: Demonstrating why tender scenes rarely include spacesuits, the romantically involved partners of *Moon Zero Two* (1969), William Kemp (James Olson) and Clementine Taplin (Catherine Schell), get as intimate as they can on the far side of the Moon.

the stark isolation one feels in space is quickly forgotten, as Kemp returns to Moon City and gets involved in a barroom brawl, rendered even more bizarre by his apparent decision to turn off the artificial gravity, which for some reason then makes everybody move in slow motion. While awaiting the asteroid's arrival, Kemp takes on another assignment: Clementine Taplin (Catherine Schell) wants Kemp to assist in determining the fate of her brother, who was working a mining claim on the Moon's far side. Kemp, Korminski and Clementine ride in his vehicle toward the brother's claim.

Amidst these developments, we learn some things about Kemp's background that could be regarded as prophetic. He became famous as the first man to land on Mars, but after a successful expedition to Venus, the people in charge of space travel abandon all efforts to further explore space, since they see no profit in it. Instead, they focus on developing the Moon and promoting its mining and tourism industries, so a disillusioned Kemp gives up the space program to become a pilot for hire on the Moon. Arguably, this is precisely what is happening today, as plans to revisit the Moon or travel to Mars are repeatedly postponed while private entrepreneurs plan to make money by taking tourists into space and/or building orbiting hotels.

The film's combination of authenticity and nonsense reaches its peak when Kemp and Clementine arrive at her brother's claim. There are comments about the grim realities of lunar life, as Clementine tells Kemp, "I see what you mean by 'We're all foreigners here,'" and Kemp acknowledges the suddenness of death in space by saying, "Nobody dies slowly on the Moon." Then, recalling a similar scene in *Riders to the Stars*, they come across his dead body, a skull visible through a space helmet, and determine that he died by wrongly using an empty tank of oxygen — "just a stupid mistake," as Clementine remarks. They are attacked by three astronauts in red spacesuits, inspiring Kemp to take out what looks like a typical handgun and fire at the assailants, causing a couple of deaths. After this silly gun battle, they flee into a cave, and Kemp shoots their remaining pursuer. They then ride the assailants' space buggy to Moon City through searing heat during a long lunar day, forcing them to remove items of clothing.

Upon returning to confront Hubbard, Kemp figures out the situation: The businessman arranged to have Clementine's brother buy an empty oxygen tank so he would die, allowing Hubbard to safely land his contraband asteroid on the site of his claim. A threat to kill Clementine forces an outraged Kemp to continue working for Hubbard, as Kemp, Korminski, Clementine, and Hubbard's men travel to the claim site to wait for the asteroid. To conclude the story, the good guys escape from the bad guys and safely fly into space, whereupon the asteroid crashes into the Moon, presumably killing the henchmen. It turns out not to matter, because the crime of murder means the sapphire will belong to the brother's sister, and not Hubbard.

Moon Zero Two is not particularly enjoyable or interesting, though it commands attention as a striking confirmation of this book's thesis: that portraying space travel realistically, and including characters in spacesuits, drive a film away from conventional narrative patterns into discomfiting territory. This is why most melodramatic spacesuit films contrive to keep characters out of spacesuits as much as possible, so as to unproblematically feature routine derring-do. What dooms *Moon Zero Two* is that director Roy Ward Baker, perhaps seeking to emulate the success of *2001*, had characters spend a lot of time wearing spacesuits, instead of keeping them within the Earthlike confines of Moon City. But these scenes unsettlingly suggest that the unforgiving environment of the airless Moon makes the machinations of criminals like Hubbard relatively unimportant; that both heroes and villains should focus on their common foe, space itself; that actions which are reasonable on Earth, like picking up a gun to shoot opponents, make no sense in space; and that the qualities characterizing a hero on Earth — firm convictions, quick thinking, and physical strength — may be irrelevant to the demands of space. Recurring activities in spacesuits, then, consistently contradict and undermine the main narrative of the film. Due to such complicating issues, it is unsurprising that, following the failure of *Moon Zero Two*, Hammer Films returned to the less challenging task of producing further Dracula and Frankenstein stories.

Döppelganger (*Journey to the Far Side of the Sun*) (1969)

One never expects excellence from Gerry and Sylvia Anderson, but *Döppelganger* may represent the best thing they ever did. They took great care in crafting plausible spaceships and special effects, and the film reflects an admirable intent to replicate both the stately gravitas and cosmic perspective of *2001: A Space Odyssey*. It is doubly unfortunate, then, that *Döppelganger* devolves into a mindless celebration of everything that makes melodramatic spacesuit films so risible.

First, while the slow pace of the film's space sequences might be said to reflect the necessary meticulousness of space travel, it more likely exposes an effort to extend to feature-film length a story that was told more economically in a one-hour episode of *The Twilight Zone*, "The Parallel" (which itself seemed padded). Certainly, the introductory scenes, wherein traitorous Dr. Hassler (Herbert Lom) steals secrets from the future's European Space Exploration Complex (Eurosec) with a camera concealed in a false eye, are superfluous. Their only arguable purpose is to add a sense of urgency to the agency's need to act upon a top-secret discovery from an unmanned space probe: There is another planet in the Solar System, in the orbit of Earth but on the opposite side of the Sun, so it is constantly blocked from our view. It seems illogical that this discovery did not occur until one hundred years from now, since unmanned probes were already studying the Solar System when the film was released, and the entire idea seems dubious, because no opposing bodies are in the orbits of other planets. But for a long time, this is as silly as the film gets.

The head of Eurosec, Jason Webb (Patrick Wymark), resolves to mount a manned expedition to the new world, particularly since word of its existence might have leaked out due to the now-assassinated Hassler's treachery. There are heated objections to the plan because of its enormous costs — three thousand billion pounds — which a German representative describes as "out of the question." This snag in the project's development indicates that the economic realities of human space travel were becoming apparent, but these concerns also primarily seem designed to kill time. Webb secures needed American support by agreeing to send American astronaut Glenn Ross (Roy Thinnes), along with scientist John Kane (Ian Hendry). This leads to further subplots that go nowhere: Ross arrives with wife Sharon (Lynn Loring), a raving bitch who complains in private conversations that radiation from previous space flights rendered him sterile and unable to have children. "You went up there a man," she concludes, "but you came back less than a man." Understandably upset, he confronts her with a package of female contraceptives — the real reason the couple has no children — and even strikes her. As for Kane, the frail-looking man submits to space pressure simulations, first in a rotating centrifuge, then an accelerating rocket car. There are concerns that he might be unable to endure the experience, though no health problems actually develop.

As a final exercise, Ross and Kane are ejected from an airplane and must walk back to Eurosec headquarters, apparently to test their survival skills, though Ross nonchalantly hitches a ride on a farmer's horse-driven carriage to avoid a long hike. During the journey, Ross and Kane have a potentially interesting conversation about space. Kane asks, "What it's like up there?"

"Lonely," is Ross's laconic reply.

"How lonely?" Kane inquires.

"Same as down here," Ross says, but "different." There is a long tradition, in film and life, of laconic astronauts who are reluctant to share their feelings about space travel; still, even in that context, Ross's comments about the loneliness of space seem unenlightening, and nothing about the rest of the film reinforces the idea that space travel might engender such emotions, since neither Ross nor Kane are ever alone.

After these tedious preliminaries, Ross and Kane are ready to fly, and there are familiar scenes of astronauts undergoing medical testing before their flight and technicians putting space helmets on them and positioning them in the spaceship for launching. As if anticipating problems that never occur, the men put down their visors before liftoff, but the only noteworthy event during the first part of their flight is some vibrations. Reflecting the influence of *2001*, their spaceship moves slowly and silently through space, as a refreshing alternative to the whooshing spacecraft of other films. The astronauts hook themselves up to intravenous tubes and are sedated so they sleep for the duration of their three-week flight. The experience is visually conveyed by fuzzy images of the Sun and strange, multicolored clouds, which seem to be this film's sedate version of *2001*'s "trip" sequence.

When the astronauts wake up, they orbit the new planet, determine that conditions are suitable for human life, and clamp down their visors so they can float in weightlessness toward their landing craft, all accompanied by slow, ethereal music that again recalls scenes from *2001*, this time initial images of the spaceship *Discovery*. There is then, finally, some excitement: As the landing vehicle descends, it begins spinning out of control, crashes into a cliff and bursts into flames. Ross and Kane escape from the ship before it explodes, though Kane soon falls unconscious, in keeping with his well-established frailty. Ross is left to confront a strange light in the sky, followed by the descent of a human-like figure wearing something like a spacesuit. This, however, is a reassuringly human rescuer who asks, "Do you speak English?" After carrying Ross up to his airplane, he tells him, "I will get your friend," conveying a friendly intent. (He is later described as part of a "Mongolian rescue team.") There comes a stunning revelation: Ross and Kane are back on Earth, facing hostile questions from Webb and his colleagues about why the astronauts "turned back" after three weeks, instead of completing their flight to the new planet before returning, a trip which would take at least six weeks. In an "interrogation room," Ross insists they did not turn back, rendering their return to Earth after only three weeks inexplicable.

Unable to get him to change his story, Webb allows Ross to go home with Sharon, whereupon the film's resemblance to "The Parallel" becomes all too apparent. For, just like Robert Gaines, Ross suspects that something is wrong as soon as he gets home: a room he expects to be on the left is on the right; a light switch he expects on the right side of the door is on the left side; and, looking at a bottle of cologne, he notices the words on the label are backwards, like a mirror image of correct writing. As the disturbed Ross breaks bottles in the bathroom, Sharon calls Eurosec authorities to have orderlies take him to the hospital. "Everything is reversed," he insists, and after Eurosec resorts to drugs to determine the truth, he relates the same story—conveyed by flashbacks intertwined with more images of brightly colored clouds and a huge eye, yet another visual echo of *2001*.

Ross explains his theory to Webb: The new planet opposite Earth is "physically connected" to our Earth as its exact double, its "döppelganger"; the only difference is that everything is physically reversed, like mirror images. Ross completed his mission and landed on the new planet to meet a Webb and Sharon who are not the people he knew, but their doubles on the other planet. Just as he offers this theory to Webb, he continues, the Ross they knew is on Ross's Earth, offering the theory to the Webb he once knew. Surprisingly, Webb accepts this outlandish theory—because they x-rayed the now-deceased Kane and discovered that the positions of his organs were reversed—like a mirror image of human anatomy.

The only way to confirm the theory beyond doubt, the men conclude, is to examine Ross's original spaceship, still in orbit, which seems another borrowing from "The Parallel" (in which Gaines's theory of a parallel Earth was accepted only when they studied his spaceship and noticed subtle differences in its design). Ross is allowed to fly a landing vehicle like his own to rendezvous with his ship, though there is concern that different "electrical polarities" will make the mirror-world's shuttlecraft and the original Earth's spaceship incompatible. These fears prove accurate, since Ross attempts to dock with the ship, only to be repelled, and subsequently falls back to Earth on a ruinous collision course with the Eurosec base, causing the complete destruction of his vehicle, a spaceship on the launching pad, and all evidence regarding his experience. We learn this in a brief coda, showing an elderly Webb in a nursing home, mumbling regrets that nobody believes his story about a duplicate Earth because there are no records to support it. As if maddened by thoughts of his double on the other Earth, he rushes toward a mirror image of himself to conclude the film.

For much of its length, *Döppelganger* appeared a genuine spacesuit film but, paradoxically, it is actually its complete antithesis. For if anything distinguishes true spacesuit films, it is their daunting insistence that space is an environment significantly different from Earth, in contrast to melodramatic spacesuit films, which reassuringly claim that conditions in space will closely resemble conditions on Earth. *Döppelganger*, therefore, is the ultimate melodramatic spacesuit film: Its astronauts do not merely discover another planet that is *similar* to Earth, but a world that is *identical* to Earth. The "aliens" they encounter are *exactly* like people on Earth, without even trivial novelties like pseudo–Roman garb or rocket insignias on their shirts. What sort of travel to another world could be more comforting, and less threatening, than this?

True, one could argue that the Earthlike destination of Ross and Kane's journey is not merely the result of naïveté, as in earlier films, but rather a device to comment on, and contradict, the classic spacesuit film. Building upon J.G. Ballard's famous observation, "The only truly alien planet is Earth," the film might be maintaining that all space travel, inevitably, will involve confronting and dealing with our human concerns, not discovering anything genuinely new; wherever human beings travel, they will always be confined to their own preoccupations. Thus, Ross can put on a spacesuit and travel to another planet, but he will remain obsessed with his shrewish wife, demanding boss, and suspicious colleagues, so the film's duplicate Earth merely reflects his inability to escape from his problems on Earth. By this reading, *Döppelganger* is a stinging refutation of spacesuit films for falsely promising novelty in space, and a ringing affirmation of the seemingly contrafactual assumptions underlying melodramatic spacesuit films.

Unfortunately, nothing in the Andersons' *oeuvre* suggests they are capable of crafting such a thoughtful message; rather, one is more inclined to believe that while desperately seeking some workable idea for their first feature film, they watched an old episode of *The Twilight Zone* and decided that, with cosmetic changes and padding, its story would suit their purposes. The fact that *Döppelganger* brings the saga of melodramatic spacesuit films to a spectacularly fitting conclusion, then, is probably only serendipitous, not deliberate.

All things considered, the difference between the tradition of genuine spacesuit films, and the tradition of the melodramatic spacesuit films, can be summed up in one sentence: True spacesuit films take space travelers into space, whereas melodramatic spacesuit films, in one fashion or another, take space travelers back to Earth. Literally true in films like *World Without End* and *Döppelganger*, it is figuratively true of all films with Earthlike environments and human-like aliens in space and on other worlds. Since nothing resembles Earth in our vicinity of space, all melodramatic spacesuit films, whatever their other virtues or flaws, are fundamentally absurd.

One response to melodramatic spacesuit films might acknowledge their occasional merits while otherwise regarding them as objects for amusing derision; and in discussing lesser examples of the subgenre, I sometimes emulate other commentators in adopting a lighthearted tone. Still, one can also argue that these films are evil, since they present a fundamentally dishonest and potentially dangerous picture of space that might mislead viewers into behavior that could lead to tragedy.

True, one cannot sanely suggest that officials planning a space mission might watch, say, *Radar Men from the Moon*, accept its picture of a Moon with an atmosphere as accurate, and accordingly plan a Moon flight without providing astronauts with spacesuits. One cannot possibly believe in a literal fashion anything these films say about conditions in space or on other planets. Still, these films cumulatively convey an impression that might have some subliminal impact, the suggestion that despite superficial differences, space is fundamentally a place that is as safe for humans to explore and inhabit as their own world, with potential problems that are identical to problems that humans have long dealt with on Earth. Repeatedly watching space films without spacesuits, like *Forbidden Planet* or episodes of *Star Trek*, one might develop the attitude that extreme caution is not necessary when sending humans into space, and act accordingly, with ruinous results.

Could works of science fiction really have such an influence? In 2003, when I suggested in "*Columbia*, and the Dreams of Science Fiction" that complacency about the dangers of space induced by science fiction might have contributed to the *Columbia* disaster, I faced fierce criticisms from members of the science fiction community, and admittedly, it might be difficult to establish a direct linkage between science fiction and the lack of concern about damage to heat-resistant tiles that led to that vehicle's destruction. But an earlier catastrophe that was on my mind when I wrote that commentary, the explosion of space shuttle *Challenger* in 1986, might better support my provocative claim, for the impact of one work of science fiction—*Star Trek*—upon its planning and execution is easier to detect.

True, some of the attitudes and decisions that led to the first loss of a space shuttle may never be known, but certain things can be established. We know that, in developing the space shuttle and recruiting its astronauts, NASA in the 1970s actively sought to exploit the popularity of *Star Trek*: The prototypical space shuttle (which never flew) was named the *Enterprise*, members of the *Star Trek* cast were invited to inspect that vehicle in a much-publicized visit, and the actress who played Uhura, Nichelle Nichols, was asked to appear in a film that encouraged women and minorities to become astronauts. We also know that the 1986 flight of the *Challenger* was explicitly planned as a showcase event for NASA: Its crew included the highly anticipated first "teacher in space," Christa McAuliffe, and during the flight, she was scheduled to offer a special lesson on space physics that would be broadcast on live television and watched in classrooms all over America. And while one can discount the discredited rumor that officials were anxious to launch the shuttle on the morning of Tuesday, January 28, so astronauts could be shown watching President Ronald Reagan's State of the Union address that evening, NASA was definitely embarrassed because this prominent flight had been repeatedly delayed, undoubtedly contributing to their special desire to get that shuttle into space before the president spoke. It is finally interesting to note that the mission's crew apparently was especially chosen to highlight the new diversity of NASA's astronauts and seemed similar to the cast of *Star Trek*: Along with three white males, the crew included two women, an African American, and an Asian-American.

Putting these factors together, a picture emerges: NASA envisioned this flight as its own version of *Star Trek*, an appealing program with a diverse cast that would repeatedly appear on network television and attract numerous viewers. And while Kirk and his crew might confront human villains or funny-looking aliens, they never worried about mere mechanical problems that might cause a ruinous explosion; such things never happened in series like *Star Trek*. So, with the script for their television program *Challenger and the Teacher in Space* completed and ready to go, NASA officials may have been less worried about problems involving cold weather and O-rings than when they oversaw more routine missions, with tragic results.

Substantiating this theory, to be sure, would require research of a sort that I am ill-suited to conduct, and I offer it merely as food for thought. Yet one thing is clear: When administrators cleared the *Challenger* for liftoff on January 28, 1986, despite expressed concerns about cold weather, they were thinking like James Kirk, not Edward McCauley. Fully confident in his invulnerable starship, Kirk was known for repeatedly "taking a big risk" (as McCoy observed in "Balance of Terror" [aired December 15, 1966]), and since his risks always paid off, his advice to NASA on that day would have been "full speed ahead." But the risk-adverse McCauley, thoroughly aware of the potential dangers of space and obsessed with safety, would have vetoed a launch in conditions that were less than ideal. And everyone involved in the *Challenger* decision was familiar with Kirk, but had probably never heard of McCauley.

Even if one rejects the argument, the fact remains that, as other examples suggest,[5] cinematic dramas can influence real-life actions; on those grounds, films and television programs that understand and present the genuine dangers of space travel, whatever their flaws, should be celebrated, and films and television programs that downplay or ignore those dangers, whatever their virtues, should be condemned.

Yet one sort of unrealistic space film is exempt from such criticism: Films that are openly and deliberately humorous, that never pretend their stories are anything other than contrived fantasies to provoke laughter. Yet these humorous spacesuit films will sometimes have their own, very serious points to make about the people most likely to conquer space.

— 4 —
Ships of Fools: The Humorous Films

In a sense, the genre of space films is rooted in comedy, since its pioneering works, the silent films of Georges Méliès and others, are comic fantasies, and the first sound film featuring space travel, *Just Imagine*, was a musical comedy. However, these films assumed that space travel was impossible, and hence a topic to address frivolously, as films mixed depictions of planetary surfaces with images of the Man in the Moon or posited fanciful space journeys on ladders or trains.

But as filmmakers like Holger-Madsen, Lang, and Zhuravlev gradually helped teach the world that space travel was possible and would require specific equipment to deal with its hazards, childlike fantasies became unacceptable; now, the Moon would have to resemble astronomical photographs, not a human face, and space travelers would have to use spaceships, not cars. The childlike comedy of early silent films was only appropriate in recreations of classic fantasies like *Baron Prášil*, *The Adventures of Baron Munchausen* (1988), and other Munchausen adaptations. Elsewhere, to amuse new generations of filmgoers, the emerging tradition of spacesuit films required a different sort of comedy.

This process involved two stages. In the 1950s, as more and more films and television programs involved space travel, comedians could make fun of these adventures, as observed in an early episode of *The George Burns and Gracie Allen Show*. Abbott and Costello and the Three Stooges also starred in comic space films. Then, in the 1960s, as actual cosmonauts and astronauts ventured into space, film comics could model their routines on their exploits. The later films are more realistic, but most humorous spacesuit films still embraced the premise of melodramatic spacesuit films—that the environments of other worlds would resemble Earth and aliens would look and act exactly like humans. But these films were sillier than their melodramatic predecessors, which featured trained astronauts as protagonists, in positing that complete incompetents, placed inside spaceships and rocketed into space, could somehow pilot vehicles to other planets and safely return to Earth.

True, reflecting minimal awareness of genuine spacesuit films, humorous spacesuit films might incorporate unexpected moments of seriousness or even brief scientific lectures, as if filmmakers felt some lingering obligation to be educational, even within absurd adventures. However, since these films, unlike melodramatic spacesuit films, generally strived to appeal to audiences of all types and ages, they may be most valuable to scholars not as commentaries on space travel, but as commentaries on public attitudes toward space travel. Instead of pilots and scientists, these films featured Everyman figures who, even amidst buffoonery, could represent typical filmgoers transported into space, reacting as ordinary individuals might react. This virtue of humorous spacesuit films is most evident in a later film, *The Reluctant Astronaut*, but is arguably an underlying theme in all its predecessors, and an aspect of the films that may add unexpected poignancy to the clownish antics.

Situation Comedies of the 1950s

Some of the earliest humorous responses to space and space travel may lie beyond critical scrutiny, since they occurred on television in the 1950s, when variety shows and situation comedies, like all programs, were usually broadcast live and only sporadically preserved for posterity. Relevant material might also be difficult to locate, since only the most obsessive researcher would examine detailed descriptions of every single variety program and comedy of the era, hoping to find a sketch or sequence involving space travel to search for; yet there seems no other way to locate such items. Still, because programs of the 1950s produced up to thirty-nine new episodes per season, constantly requiring new pretexts for comedy, the spaceships and spacesuits featured in films and television programs were surely, at least occasionally, a target for wisecracks.

The Red Skelton Show (1951–1971) dealt with space travel at least twice during in the 1950s: In "Queen of Mars" (aired February 1, 1955), Freddie the Freeloader is captured by aliens and taken to Mars, where its queen falls in love with him; and in "Clem and the Satellite" (aired October 7, 1958), Clem Kadiddlehopper rents his barn to a scientist (John Carradine) working on a rocketship and accidentally launches the scientist into space. One suspects that no significant insights about space travel could have been derived from this material. However, two surviving episodes of 1950s situation comedies involving space travel — an episode of *The George Burns and Gracie Allen Show*, "Space Patrol Kids Visit" (aired August 16, 1951), and an episode of *The Mickey Rooney Show*, "The Moon or Bust" (aired September 4, 1954) — might suggest how television in the 1950s was having fun with the new realm of space.

In "Space Patrol Kids Visit,"[1] Gracie's sister Mamie visits with her three daughters, who are fans of television space programs. Calling themselves the Rocket Patrol, they wear futuristic costumes while deploying "ray guns" that expel small balls, and one girl briefly dons a spherical glass space helmet. The tone of the comedy is set when Gracie asks why she is wearing a "goldfish bowl," and Mamie responds, "That's not a goldfish bowl, that's a space helmet."

Later, when George addresses the audience for his monologue, he uses the subject of his nieces' interest as the basis for jokes. He is bemused that he is now described in a new way, as an "Earthman," and continues, "And these things the kids play with today — spacesuits, rocketships, atomic ray guns, you know, they're so scientific their own fathers can't play with them. Yes, uh, those things the kids play with today, it's just simply fantastic." To show how children speak differently today, he describes a modern boy saying to another boy, "I bet my father can disintegrate your father," while another boy is unhappy because "we split an atom and he got the biggest piece." Recalling his childhood, George says, "I did have a spacesuit when I was a kid — it was my father's old suit. There was enough space in it for me and my two brothers." Returning to today's children, he says, "The games the kids play today, rocket patrol and space captain, I guess they get the idea from watching all these television shows. You know, to have a successful television show you've got to have something fantastic, something out of this world." Then, after hearing a typically lame-brained comment from Gracie — her advice to children that, because it is cold, they must wear a sweater if they go swimming — the audience gets the final joke: The unique Gracie represents this program's "fantastic," "out of this world" element.

These genial remarks, assembled in a seemingly offhand manner, actually have an intriguing structure. First, George conveys a sincere sense of alienation: Because children are interested in space travel, something foreign to older people, their parents can no longer play with them. Indeed, in addressing their uncle as "the Earthman," children even cast themselves as aliens, beings entirely different from their parents. Then he deals with this feeling by struggling in various ways to force new proclivities into familiar patterns: Children may have novel interests, he acknowledges, but still behave in the same way, only instead of bragging that their fathers can beat up other fathers, they brag their fathers can disintegrate other fathers, and instead of complaining they got a smaller piece of pie, they complain they got a smaller piece of an atom. Then he asserts that he had a spacesuit too, though it involved a different sort of "space," and in the person of his wife, he also has something that is "fantastic" and "out of this world" in his life. In these ways, he domesticates the strange new world of space by associating it with old, comforting things. This determination to liken the unfamiliar to the familiar, and thus cope with it, is also observed in Gracie's inclination to regard a space helmet as a goldfish bowl.

There is later a sardonic suggestion that George might be more open to new developments than his jokes indicate: As the episode proceeds, the girls become only one of several distractions preventing George from writing a speech he must deliver that night, as he is also disturbed by quarreling neighbors, a visiting school principal, and Gracie herself. As a solution to the problem, George dons his nieces' transparent space helmet, which is soundproof, allowing him to sedately work at his typewriter in the midst of noisy chaos. Essentially, George adopts the persona of a space traveler and metaphorically enters space to escape the petty annoyances of Earth. Yet this development is regressive in its own way: Usually envisioned as a way to explore new environments, space travel merely becomes a way to escape from old environments. Also, while other spacesuit films consider loneliness in space a potential problem, this comedy suggests it might sometimes be desirable.

One generally assumes that space films and television programs of the early 1950s were aimed at, and appealed to, little boys, so one would expect the "Space Patrol Kids" to be boys. Yet they are girls, and the oldest one calls herself the "space captain." Perhaps writers only thought it would be cute, or amusingly incongruous, to make the children who torment George adorable little girls; but it also might be one small indication, as later suggested by *Project Moon Base*, that space travel might undermine gender stereotypes and liberate women in new ways.

"The Moon or Bust" also addresses the influence of science fiction on everyday people, though its effects here are more substantive than some children's choices of games and playthings. Young Mickey Mulligan (Mickey Rooney) is first observed reading an issue of *Three Dimensional Space Comics*.[2] When his father (Regis Toomey) archly asks, "Aren't you a little bit old to be reading comic books?" Mickey defends this reading as "research." For, based on its information, Mickey and friend Freddy Devlin (Joey Forman) are constructing a rocketship to take them to the Moon. From one perspective, a work of science fiction is doing precisely what Gernsback once hoped — inspiring budding scientists to actually produce working inventions. When Mickey's old chemistry teacher, Professor Gordon (Maurice Cass), learns that his former student is studying what Mickey describes as "a science fiction magazine," he even endorses the procedure, noting that science fiction may be written by "reputable scientists" and citing the distinguished examples of Verne and Wells. Since the era's other references to science fiction involve the genre's proclivity for outlandish monsters, it is unusual to see science fiction treated with respect. But to show that old stereotypes are not entirely forgotten, Freddy later argues that a farmer cannot be a Moon man because he knows, from magazines, that Moon men have six arms instead of two.

Needless to say, Mickey and Freddy's rocketship will never demonstrate the effectiveness of science fiction in generating useful inventions. The very appearance of their vehicle — which resembles an airplane with a cockpit more than a spaceship — suggests their limited expertise. A failure to research their intended destination is revealed when Freddy asks, right before their first effort to launch the rocketship, "I wonder what kind of girls they got on the Moon." (Then again, this might be a reference to *Cat-Women of the Moon*, released in the previous year.) Next, after their first attempt to launch the rocket only causes an explosion, they decide without hesitation to use Gordon's experimental rocket fuel, said to be a form of liquid oxygen, though it looks like water and is casually carried in large cans (actual liquid oxygen must be stored in tightly sealed, refrigerated containers to remain at the necessary subzero temperature). Mickey also adds kerosene to the rocket's tank along with liquid oxygen. Mickey's mother (Claire Carleton) is understandably upset about her son's plan, though she cluelessly informs Mickey that he cannot go to the Moon simply because he has "no shots, no passport."

For their second attempt to launch their rocketship, the men take matters more seriously, since Freddy asks Mickey, "Should I get the spacesuits out?" This time, after they don standard-issue spacesuits (which they complain are "a little warm"), their rocketship actually takes off, just as Gordon and Mickey's parents come rushing up, concerned because Gordon has realized that he accidentally gave Mickey an overly powerful fuel mixture. When they land, audiences know they have returned to Earth, since they emerge from their spaceship onto a grassy field underneath blue skies. But Mickey and Freddy are sure they are on the Moon, so they keep their space helmets on until Mickey resolves to "test the atmosphere" by removing his helmet; finding it breathable, they remove their helmets. Then, recalling the protocol from previous stories and films like *Destination Moon*, Mickey pulls out an American flag and announces, "I claim the Moon for the United States of America." Even after observing a cow in a pasture, Mickey still asserts they are on the Moon, calling the cow a "Moon man."

A farmer and his wife (Roscoe Ates and Ellen Corby) rush to the scene because, in another reference to science fiction, the man believes he has seen a flying saucer. Seeing Mickey and Freddy, he screams, "They're men from Mars!" When they put their space helmets back on (they fear they are being approached by Moon men), the farmer exclaims that the aliens are "changing heads." The men and the couple then start talking gibberish to each other, both pairs thinking that the other people are aliens; even when the farmer mentions the name of the town they are in, Mickey and Freddy still think they are on the Moon: "They have a Glendale up here too?" Only after Mickey's parents and Gordon arrive on the scene do they finally understand that the rocketship only flew two miles before landing.

There is now a moment of poignancy, as Mickey is disappointed over his failure to reach the Moon and inability to recognize what had happened: "To think I claimed Glendale for the United States!" But Gordon consoles him by saying, "If there weren't any dreamers, there'd be no progress." Yet it is obvious that Mickey and Freddy's dreams will always remain just that — dreams; these exuberant but inept young men will never be the people who conquer space. While generally an inconsequential farce, then, "The Moon or Bust" anticipates a point made more clearly in later films: There is both something comical, and something sad, about inept bumblers who aspire to become space travelers.

Later in the 1950s, as Sputnik inspired tangible plans for American space travel, one might expect comedies to address the subject more often, but the one example I located — an episode of *Love That Bob* called "Bob Goes to the Moon" (aired April 1, 1958) — does not involve spacesuits. Instead, after Bob Collins (Bob Cummings) falsely tells a beautiful model he has volunteered to fly to the Moon, he is confronted by an eavesdropping admirer, homely Pamela Livingstone (Nancy Kulp), who professes her readiness to accompany him to the Moon as his wife solely by wearing an oxygen mask and aviator's helmet, indicating she is as ill-prepared for such a mission as the photographer she loves.

Abbott and Costello Go to Mars (1953)

During the late 1950s and early 1950s, the comedy team of Bud Abbott and Lou Costello made three films spoofing horror movies: *Abbott and Costello Meet Frankenstein* (1948), *Abbott and Costello Meet the Killer, Boris Karloff* (1949), and *Abbott and Costello Meet the Invisible Man* (1951). The new popularity of science fiction in the 1950s ensured they would also apply their talents to a science fiction spoof. And, just as their horror comedies sometimes offer a frisson of genuine horror, *Abbott and Costello Go to Mars*, amidst the silliness, includes some authentic touches in its space travel, including spacesuits.

This incongruous combination of elements is evident in the film's first scene, when handyman Orville (Lou Costello) is entertaining orphanage children with a toy airplane on a string. Questions about how airplanes work lead one boy to ask Orville, "How does a spaceship work?"

The simple-minded Orville does not know, but he tries to fake his way through an answer: "A spaceship? A spaceship. Well, first you gotta have a lot of space, and then, ya...." Then he changes the subject: "Want me to learn ya how to spin a top?"

When the persistent boy repeats the question, Orville says, "All you do is pull a string and away it goes!" In the context of the film, Orville is simply building on the example of the toy he is playing with, but the comment might also ironically refer to the way most films of the era visualized space travel — by filming model spaceships moved around by invisible strings. Indeed, as sharp-eyed observers may note, this is how this film's spaceship was depicted, since when the spaceship lands on Venus, one can briefly see its string.

When Orville's airplane hits a store window, he runs away and hides in a van driven by Lester (Bud Abbott), a menial worker delivering crates to the base where he works. There, a spaceship constructed by Dr. Wilson (Robert Paige) is ready to be launched to either Mars or Venus. Lester discovers his passenger and, convinced he is a spy, takes him to Wilson. Orville avoids punishment when Wilson's secretary Julia Howe (Martha Hyer) mistakes him for Dr. Orvilla (Joe Kirk), a scientist about to meet with Wilson and other scientists, leading to humorous conflict when Orvilla arrives and the two men compete to be accepted as the real scientist. While a blonde Hyer would adventurously dream of traveling through space in *Riders to the Stars*, this brunette Hyer is more traditionally cautious, as revealed in a conversation with her boss (whom she seems to be in love with, though this subplot is never developed). Wilson stares out a window at his spaceship and comments, "Beautiful, isn't it?"

"I think 'frightening' is a better word," she replies.

"Don't tell me you wouldn't like to spend your honeymoon on Mars."

"I'll still settle for Niagara Falls."

Wilson, who knows Orvilla, identifies Orville as the imposter, but tells Lester to hire Orville as a temporary worker until the spaceship takes off, to keep Orville on the base so that the spaceship's existence remains a secret. Their first assignment is to load supplies on the spaceship, which will take off the following day, after Wilson and others at the meeting decide whether to go to Mars or Venus and who will make up the crew. This leads to some business with the accoutrements of space travel that is mildly humorous, and mildly informative. First, while putting spacesuits in a locker, Orville asks, "What are they, football uniforms?"

"Certainly not," Lester replies, "they're spacesuits."

Next, Orville playfully puts on a space helmet and asks Lester, "Do I look like a piece of bubble gum?"

"Now put that back," says the exasperated Lester. "The doctor's crew are going to need those when they get up where there's no oxygen."

Finally, Lester has problems with magnetic boots; Lester explains, "The gravity plates on the soles of those boots are magnetized."

Like Burns and Allen, Orville attempts to relate to the unfamiliar technology of space travel to familiar items: Spacesuits are like football uniforms, and space helmets are like blown bubbles. (Later, Lester even recalls one of Gracie's jokes when he fills his space helmet with water and places goldfish in it, making it a goldfish bowl.) The scene employs the ignorant Lester, like Sweeney in *Destination Moon* and Polly Prattles in *Project Moon Base*, as a device to provoke scientific explanations audiences might need to understand later events.

Playing around with buttons, Orville accidentally launches the spaceship. After improbable antics in the lower atmosphere (including a trip through the Lincoln Tunnel), the two men land their craft near New Orleans. Believing they have landed on Mars, the men emerge wearing spacesuits. When Orville sees some grapes and begins taking off his helmet to eat them, Lester tells him, "Don't take that off! Mars might be just like the Moon, no atmosphere. And without oxygen, you'd drop dead!" Fulfilling his role as the team's serious member, Lester also declares, "I hereby claim Mars in the name of the United States of America." This moment, perhaps inspired by a similar moment in *Destination Moon*, oddly makes Orville the second human in a film to officially take possession of another world, albeit erroneously.

The reason the story brought them to New Orleans now becomes apparent: It is Mardi Gras time, and when the spacesuited Orville and Lester enter the city, they regard revelers wearing large *papier-mâché* heads as Martians. Later, they visit a restaurant, and there is some comedy involving Orville's reluctance to remove his space helmet because the smell of limburger cheese from a nearby table makes him think the Martian air is bad. In the meantime, two escaped convicts who resemble the pair, Mugsy (Horace McMahon) and Harry (Jack Kruschen), come upon the scene and exchange their striped prison uniforms for the spacesuits they find in the spaceship. Harry then contributes to the comedic familiarization of the spacesuit by asking his more knowledgeable companion, "We gotta wear these suits? You know, this thing don't do nothing for my figure." This is how a vain person might regard a spacesuit, as an unflattering outfit that makes one look heavier.

The film next refers to science fiction, conveying both an awareness of, and contempt

Spacey Pioneers: In posters for *Abbott and Costello Go to Mars* (1953) like this one, the first major comedy about space travel, Bud Abbott and Lou Costello were always portrayed wearing spacesuits.

for, the genre. On the spaceship, the convicts discover a gun that causes paralysis, which one explains: "Flash Gordon uses one of them.... You see him in the comic strips all the time." After the spacesuited criminals use the gun to rob a bank, they return to the spaceship and plan to force the returning "Martians"—Orville and Lester—to take them to Mars, prompting this description of Martians: "I seen pictures from there. They got big heads, four arms, and wireless aerials growing out of their ears." These comments suggest that science fiction is only colorful nonsense that deludes stupid people about scientific realities.

Escaping from the city, where people mistake them for the robbers, Orville and Lester reach the spaceship, confront the convicts, and accidentally make the spaceship take off again, this time toward Venus. At first the criminals, using their handgun, have the upper hand, and threaten Orville and Lester by saying the ship "could travel much faster if we get rid of the excess weight" by tossing them out into space. Instead, Orville and Lester gain control of the gun, and the situation. To show the effects of zero gravity, a hat slowly floats to the top of the chamber, because "there's no gravity left any more." There is also the unusual gimmick of lowering the pitch of the men's voices by playing the voices at low speed, some unexplained effect of being in space.

The spaceship lands on Venus, but Orville and Lester believe they are back on Earth, and hence Orville steps out of the spacecraft without wearing a spacesuit. Ironically, he wore a suit where it was not needed—in New Orleans—but does not wear a suit where it might be essential—on Venus. But the air is breathable, if a bit hazy. Asked where they are, Orville says, "Being as I can't see a foot in front of me, I say we're in Los Angeles," an early joke about the city's smog. Orville then runs into a cave to escape a giant dog and encounters the inhabitants of Venus—a race of beautiful women who exiled all their men four hundred years ago because the husband of their queen, Allura (Mari Blanchard), was unfaithful to her. Seeing these beauties in luxurious surroundings, Lester still believes he is in Los Angeles, telling them, "I didn't know this was a moving picture studio"—and, of course, it actually *was* in real life. Since this film was released four months before *Cat-Women of the Moon*, it is actually the first film to offer the attractive fantasy of a planet inhabited entirely by women.

The rest of the story demands little analysis: after Orville accidentally becomes king of Venus, he is romanced by the ever-jealous Allura but rejected when he is attracted to other women. The convicts attempt a brief revolt, and the queen finally orders that the spaceship be refueled so the men can return to Earth. They encounter a briefly threatening meteor shower during their flight home. Along the way, we learn that Venusians, like other denizens of future societies, consume pills as food, and a lie-detecting machine that Allura uses on Orville is said to contain a "positronic brain"; was someone involved in the film familiar with the works of Isaac Asimov, the only place anyone in 1953 would encounter that term? If so, it is odd that the film offers no other evidence of any knowledge, or appreciation, of science fiction.

Space Ship Sappy (1957), *Outer Space Jitters* (1957), and *Have Rocket, Will Travel* (1959)

After Abbott and Costello stopped making feature films in 1956, another aging comedy team, the Three Stooges, began dabbling in space travel with two shorts, *Space Ship Sappy* and *Outer Space Jitters*, which involved farcical trips to Venus with minimal references to spacesuits.

In the former, three bums, Moe (Moe Howard), Larry (Larry Fine), and Joe (Joe Besser), respond to what they believe is an advertisement for jobs as sailors and fail to recognize that the building at the given address is actually a spaceship, regarding it instead as avant-garde architecture. Once inside, Professor A.K. Rimple (Benny Rubin) and daughter Lisa (Doreen Woodbury) quickly hire them as their crew (without revealing their real plans) and launch their spaceship to Venus. When they land, Lisa announces, "The air test gauge shows the air outside to be the same as on Earth," so the professor declares, "We will not need space helmets." The Three Stooges then go exploring, are captured by three beautiful but cannibalistic women, and avoid being eaten when the women flee from a dinosaur. The men loosen their bonds and return to the spaceship, but upon opening the door they accidentally knock out the professor and his daughter. The Stooges try launching the spaceship themselves; when they are seemingly about to crash-land, the film cuts away to a scene showing the Stooges accepting an award from the Liar's Club, suggesting they made up the story of their trip to Venus.

Outer Space Jitters begins with the trio, along with Professor Jones (Emil Sitka), having already landed on Venus, entering a building while wearing transparent space helmets; however, they immediately take them off, since this Venus also has an Earthlike atmosphere with human inhabitants. The purpose of the helmets, presumably, was to inform audiences that the men had come from a spaceship without bothering to actually display a spaceship. The Venusian leader (Gene Roth) captures Jones and informs him that the Venusians plan to invade Earth with an army of zombies; in the meantime, the Stooges are entertained by three electrified women, leading to some comic business, and attacked by a zombie before they rescue the professor, disable the machine that would reanimate the zombies, and run from the building. The men are then shown finishing up a bedtime story for three babies, also portrayed by the Three Stooges, indicating that their adventure was again just a story — though the arriving babysitter looks exactly like the Venusian zombie. (It is interesting that both shorts, like the film *Robot Monster*, account for obvious implausibilities in their stories by finally suggesting they didn't really happen.)

After the launch of Sputnik in late 1957 made films about space travel more popular, it is not surprising that the Three Stooges made a feature film, *Have Rocket, Will Travel*, about yet another trip to Venus. (Noting that the first four avowedly humorous movies about space travel all feature Venus, one might theorize that this planet was preferred over Mars or the Moon because the absence of definitive data about its characteristics better justified depictions of a comfortingly Earthlike planet best suited for comedy.) Like the shorts, the film mixes typical Stooges slapstick and scientific nonsense. Perhaps as a humorous contrast to the shenanigans to follow, it begins with a stark image of space and somber narration:

> Stars beyond number, time without end. The universe stretches mysterious, unknown, demanding to be explored. Great institutions, mighty space vehicles, brilliant men and women. Science gathers its strength and stands ready to hurl a metal bird into the cold but inviting space beyond our tiny world. Following in the giant footsteps of the brave voyages of yesterday — Columbus, Magellan, Amundsen, Peary — are today's pathfinders, pathfinders to the planets, dedicated to the great adventure of discovery.

Since a similarly evocative passage opened *Cat-Women of the Moon*, it may be that only the silliest films feel a need to balance their idiocies with introductory sentiments of a solemn nature. The other noteworthy aspect of this passage is the reference to "brilliant men *and women*," anticipating the major role to be played in the film by a brilliant, beautiful scientist developing fuel for a rocketship, Dr. Ingrid Naarveg (Anna-Lisa). Yet she is far from a model of a liberated woman, since she happily makes coffee for her janitor friends Moe (Moe Howard), Larry (Larry Fine), and Curley Joe (Joe DeRita), and is later lured away from her obsession with space travel to fall in love with her enamored colleague Dr. Ted Benson (Robert Colbert), who employs the analogy found in *Riders to the Stars* to argue that being in love is "like being in another universe" and hence merits her attention just as much as her work.

The other serious aspect of *Have Rocket, Will Travel* is that upon landing on Venus, the trio displays appropriate caution by emerging from the spaceship wearing authentic-looking spacesuits (although, since they are accidental occupants of a spaceship earlier used to send a chimpanzee into space, it is hard to see where the spacesuits come from); they keep them on while fleeing from the first creature they encounter, an enormous spider. However, when one man falls and cracks his helmet without ill effect, they realize they "can breathe this air" and discard the helmets for the duration of their stay.

Everything else about this film is predictably ludicrous. Since Naarveg's inability to devise a powerful fuel caused a series of failures that may end the program and her job, the Stooges undertake to help her by brewing a fuel of their own; by accidentally mixing a cup of coffee and cup of fuel, they discover that adding sugar to the fuel gives it an extra kick. Then, after using a fire hose to pump the new fuel into the rocketship, they hide in the ship to evade the pursuing program executive, J.P. Morse (Jerome Cowan), who was awakened by their antics. When he ignites the hose, the fuel is ignited and the ship proceeds on an automatic course to Venus.

After escaping from the spider (which also hits them with a heat ray), the trio encounters a friendly talking unicorn, who takes them to a city ruled by an evil robot who destroyed all people on Venus by turning them into electrical energy. They are captured and shrunk by the robot, which feels lonely and in need of company. The robot next creates robot duplicates of the Stooges, but the originals escape and, with the unicorn, fly back to Earth to receive a heroes' welcome. All one can say is that the variegated lifeforms they find on Venus are preferable to the man-hungry, all-female societies ruling Venus in *Abbott and Costello Go to Mars* and *Queen of Outer Space*.

Five years later, to exploit ongoing interest in the space program, the title *The Three Stooges in Orbit* was chosen for another Stooges vehicle. However, its story had no space travel, instead focusing on the trio's misadventures with an eccentric scientist who invents a submarine-like vehicle that travels on land, in the sea, and in the air, and two Martians resembling Boris Karloff's Frankenstein monster who seek to steal his invention and conquer Earth. Needless to say, the Martians, who come to Earth in a teleportation chamber instead of a spaceship, do not need, or bother, to wear spacesuits.

Man in the Moon (1960)

Previously considered a real possibility in *Spaceways* and *Satellite in the Sky*, the British conquest of space, by 1960, could only be treated as a joke, which is one way to explain the farcical tone of *Man in the Moon*. Despite credits featuring dramatic music and a realistic image of the Moon, audiences immediately know this story will not be serious from its opening scene: William Blood (Kenneth More) wakes up in a bed on a grassy field, only to be startled by a beautiful woman in a flashy outfit with a feathered boa walking past him toward a rustic road.

Blood is a paid experimental subject in research conducted by the Common Cold Research Centre, and making him sleep outside presumably represented its effort to make him catch a cold. The woman, whom Blood keeps running into, is Polly (Shirley Anne Field), a stripper who fled from the amorous advances of a guest at a private party.

Blood is summoned to the office of the head of the facility and fired because of his persistent refusal, or inability, to catch a cold. He explains that his placid, unmarried lifestyle, and his refusal to worry about anything, renders him virtually invulnerable to any illness. This interests a visitor named Dr. Davidson (Michael Hordern), head of National Atomic Research Studies and Technological Development,[4] who thinks this "remarkably healthy young man" would be an ideal choice as the first person to be sent to the Moon. Recruiting Blood could be defended because such an individual (as demonstrated by subsequent tests) might be especially able to deal with some negative effects of space travel, like extreme temperatures and intense gravitational pressure, but the rationale given more emphasis seems absurd: As an "ordinary chap," he is deemed expendable, and hence a perfect guinea pig to gauge the safety of space travel before risking the lives of highly trained astronauts, the valuable products of five years of preparation. It is hard to understand why officials would devote considerable time to preparing certain men to fly into space, then hesitate to actually send them into space, preferring to begin with an untrained amateur; but it does make Blood, in contrast to previous incompetents who end up in spaceships by accident, the first such person deliberately chosen for a mission.

Blood makes a fool of himself in athletic exercises, but his "extraordinary tranquility of mind" makes him stand out in tests of endurance. Despite being locked in chambers that become freezing cold or boiling hot, Blood continues to calmly read a newspaper, and he survives pressures up to twenty times the force of gravity without ill effects. The film, then, presents an argument that seems stereotypically British: The key quality to seek in potential space travelers is sheer imperturbability, an ability to remain calm and functional in the face of adverse conditions, as opposed to other traits like courage, physical strength, or dexterity. Blood's subsequent exploits in space, however, do little to support this singular perspective.

But another relevant issue emerges during Blood's training: It is announced that the first person who reaches the Moon will receive a prize of £100,000, and the thought that a neophyte might earn this vast sum so upsets one astronaut, Leo (Charles Gray), that he effectively decides to murder Blood by sabotaging his equipment. This unexpectedly grim development underscores the point that a race to conquer space might be not only a competition between nations, but also a competition between individuals for glory and financial rewards that might drive one to desperate measures. But a comic tone is restored when the project's psychologist implausibly uses a sensory deprivation tank to reprogram Leo so he thinks of Blood as his best friend. An evening of drunken revelry leads to Blood's reunion with Polly, previously thwarted because Leo kept a letter she sent him. Preparing to marry Polly, the perpetually healthy Blood at times seems on the verge of a sneeze, presumably due to the stress of the relationship, but contrary to some summaries, he never develops a full-bodied cold, and nothing else occurs to prevent him from making the Moon flight.

Having traveled to the British rocket base in Australia, Blood has one more quintessentially British moment during final preparations when he insists that placing the space helmet on his head must be delayed until he finishes his tea. Once he is fully outfitted for space, Blood's essential helplessness is highlighted as he is never allowed to walk to his spacecraft; instead, he is lifted by an arm and propelled horizontally on a moving platform.

The film now oddly shifts its perspective to Davidson and the others, nervously waiting in the control room, and we never see Blood inside his spaceship or traveling through space. Instead, after telling Blood, "We shall be with you every inch of the journey," Davidson paradoxically notes that, for some reason, "we'll not be able to talk" during the three-day flight. With no news of Blood, the men on the ground "wait and pray for seventy-two hours"—which one man calls "the longest wait of my life"—until they re-establish contact with Blood once (they believe) he lands on the Moon.

After it is determined that Blood's blood pressure, temperature, and heartbeat are, as always, "normal," Blood briefly describes the experience of space travel in characteristically quotidian terms as "bloody hot!" He then emerges from his spaceship to confront what seems a reasonable approximation of a lunar landscape—a barren, rocky field underneath a dark sky. But after he is frightened by the appearance of some being wearing a strange helmet, a series of events make him realize where he actually is. His helmet falls off, but he can still breathe; he finds a can of Heinz Oven Baked Beans; he sees a kangaroo; and the figure that startled him is a human prospector frightened by Blood, whom he describes as "a man from the Moon." Recognizing that, somehow, his spaceship actually landed in Australia, Blood rushes in the man's dilapidated truck to the base to prevent the launch of Leo and two other astronauts, no doubt destined for the same errant fate. He tells Davidson and the others, "It's back to the old drawing board!"

The final joke of the film, in other words, is that the project which chose an incompetent as its first space traveler is an incompetent program, unable to send a spaceship any further than a few miles from its launching site. While Blood's stumbles after coming out of his spacecraft suggest he might not have been a capable astronaut, the failure of the mission had nothing to do with his shortcomings. What was implicit in the drama of *Spaceways* and *Satellite in the Sky*, then, is explicit in this comedy: The British will never conquer space. To underline the point, an epilogue shows Blood abandoning the space program to again work as an experimental subject, this time to sleep with new wife Polly in that outdoor bed as part of an evidently successful study in "Family Planning," since there are three cribs with babies nearby and a sign stating, "Experiment Completed." Thus, the pursuit of domestic bliss, elsewhere a consequence of venturing into the daunting realms of space, here is a happy alternative to space travel.

Moon Pilot (1962)

In retrospect, it seems curious that the Walt Disney Company, having examined future space travel in television documentaries, never attempted a genuine spacesuit film, though the genre embodied two of its priorities: family-friendly entertainment, and an aura of educational uplift. Perhaps there were concerns that these male-dominated adventures were not films that mothers would take their children to see, or that the drama of realistic space flight would not hold the attention of young filmgoers. In any event, Disney waited until actual astronauts ventured into space to offer its first space film, which was a light-hearted comedy mostly taking place on Earth, enabling filmmakers to follow standard comic patterns.

Moon Pilot broke new ground in one significant aspect: Though typical spacesuit comedies employ contrived circumstances to send obvious unqualified people into space (like Abbott and Costello, the Three Stooges, Bob Hope and Bing Crosby, and Don Knotts), this film innovatively suggests that even highly trained astronauts might be laughable figures.

The film begins as monitors on the ground nervously follow the progress of an astronaut called "Charlie" as he orbits the Moon; we see one image of Charlie from behind, wearing a spacesuit and space helmet and flicking a switch in his space capsule. When his capsule returns to Earth and is retrieved — unusually, by means of ropes in the middle of the air — the capsule is opened to reveal that Charlie is actually a chimpanzee. The grouchy general in charge of the space program, John Vanneman (Brian Keith), then holds a celebratory banquet for Charlie and asks one of the attending astronauts to volunteer to duplicate his mission. Displaying cowardice, none of them do so, until Charlie playfully pokes the astronaut taking care of him, Richmond Talbot (Tom Tryon), with a fork, making him stand up and inadvertently volunteer. From the start, then, the protagonist astronaut seems unusually unmanly (assigned the domestic chore of feeding Charlie, not brave enough to venture into space) and silly (a victim of slapstick who stammers a bit and will not explain the real reason he stood up so quickly).

Another person in these scenes, Senator Henry McGuire (Bob Sweeney), is also an object of ridicule. Recalling the common theme that politicians cannot really understand space travel, he responds with inappropriate concern when one official uses the phrase "space-drunk" to explain Charlie's diminished mental capacity in space, and he is sarcastically asked if he bothered to read the book they prepared, *Simple Science for Senators*. Unlike other spacesuit comedies, in which a few buffoons invade a space program otherwise run by reliable professionals, *Moon Pilot* singularly indicates that everyone involved in this project — the astronauts, commanders on the ground, and politicians overseeing the operation — are buffoons. With similar criticism of the Federal Bureau of Investigation (renamed the Federal Security Agency) to follow, this therefore qualifies as a subversive film, despite its lighthearted tone, which questions the competence of a broad range of government officials.

Pleased with Talbot's decision, Vanneman declares he is an ideal choice because he is "young, unmarried, physically fit," recalling the criteria governing astronaut selection in *Riders to the Stars*. When Talbot persuades the reluctant general to give him three days of leave to visit his mother and younger brother, another familiar bit of space humor follows: He is instructed to eat no solid food and instead receives a suitcase filled with tubes of food paste. Before he departs, absurdly, Talbot visits Charlie seeking advice about space travel, which the mute chimpanzee obviously cannot provide. The once-friendly animal is hostile to him, indicating "he got moonstruck" in some fashion. This apparent madness as an effect of space travel becomes a key element in the plot.

On an airplane to San Francisco, Talbot first encounters a mysterious woman named Lyrae (Dany Saval), who knows Talbot's name and his top-secret mission. She insists she has important information to give him to ensure a safe flight around the Moon but, to keep the story in motion, she cannot impart that information until later. Talbot's homecoming is an odd experience: Younger brother Walter (Tommy Kirk) cannot spend time with him because he has a date, while mother Celia (Sarah Selby) must host the regular Wednesday meeting of her bridge club. Left alone to wander down the street, Talbot whistles "There's No Place Like Home," accompanied by background music, but clearly this astronaut is a man who no longer feels welcome at home, indicating that it is time for him to move on to new experiences, like space and marriage (which are curiously linked in the film). After Lyrae makes another enigmatic appearance, Talbot worries she is an enemy spy and contacts Vanneman, who promptly orders the Federal Security Agency to send its best men to protect Talbot. But their chief operative, the blustering McClosky (Edmond O'Brien), proves unable to do the job, as Talbot has little difficulty in eluding his men in a San Francisco hotel and meeting Lyrae in a nearby park.

At this point, Lyrae finally provides the information Talbot needs: the formula for a special protective coating that will, she says, "protect you from the proton rays" and prevent him from going mad after returning to Earth. She further reveals that she is an alien from a planet orbiting the star Beta Lyrae: "We've been watching you for centuries," she reports, and "we want to be friends." With so many cinematic aliens intent upon preventing Earth from venturing into space, it is novel to find aliens who want to *help*. To bolster her story, Lyrae demonstrates an ability to read minds, and further displays the power to summon up projections from the future as she shows Talbot a three-dimensional image of the son they will someday have. These aliens will not only be our friends, then, but they can be lovers or even wives.

After Talbot contacts Vanneman and agrees to return if the general tests Lyrae's formula, there ensues more strange social commentary: Because Lyrae initially wore a tight-fitting purple blouse, the authorities somehow get the idea she was dressed like a "beatnik" (though contemporary viewers will struggle to discern how her stylish outfit could be regarded as counter-cultural). So, to locate the woman he believes to be a spy, McClosky orders the San Francisco police to round up all women who look like beatniks. Talbot and Vanneman are present at a series of police lineups with bizarre women: Some are relatively inactive, but others incongruously play guitars, recite abstract poetry, or engage in modern dance movements. There is the suggestion, then, of a natural link between Earth's misfits and aliens, which later becomes the theme of *Doin' Time on Planet Earth* (1988), though the only unusual thing about this film's alien is that she speaks with an unexplained French accent.

Only in the film's final few minutes is there actual human space travel, as we see Talbot lying horizontally in his capsule during takeoff, wearing a spacesuit and helmet. Once in space, he removes his helmet, gazes in awe as a crescent Earth in the distance, and confesses he feels "a little lonesome." He, however, will not have to endure the loneliness of space, since Lyrae immediately appears next to him, saying that "we have ways of doing things," and suggests they take a side trip to her home planet before returning to Earth. They even sing a risible song about her planet's seven moons.

Overall, *Moon Pilot* has disheartening messages to convey about human space travel which contrast with other space films of its era. First, the people of Earth will be incapable of conquering space, unless they receive assistance from helpful aliens. Second, despite the aura of domesticity often associated with space travel, *Moon Pilot* indicates that space will drive people away from conventional values, inasmuch as it is about a man who becomes disconnected from his home town and family, flies into space, disobeys his superior's orders, and marries an alien woman. Thus, while the film's poor performance at the box office can be attributed to its weaknesses as comedy, it is also a film at odds with the prevailing optimism about space travel common during the first years of the American space program.

The Road to Hong Kong (1962)

In 1962, while the Three Stooges lured audiences with the false promise of space adventures, another veteran comedy team — Bob Hope and Bing Crosby — actually traveled into space in their seventh Road film, *The Road to Hong Kong*. Extraterrestrial business is already prominent in opening scenes, as con men Harry Turner (Crosby) and Chester Babcock

(Hope) attempt to defraud investors by promising an "Interplanetary Spacecraft" from a new company, "Fly-It-Yourself, Inc.," when all they really plan is a phony demonstration flight in which Babcock (wearing a propeller cap and jetpack) will be hoisted upward by strings. The idea of making money from space travel will resurface when the men are about to crash into the Moon and Turner reassures Babcock by saying, "If we get to the Moon first, we'll clean up on real estate, boy."

When a crash ends Babcock's flight and makes him lose his memory, the men plan to fly to a Tibetan lamasery where, they are told, a person's memory can be restored. At the airport, Babcock is mistaken for a secret agent by Diane (Joan Collins), who works for an underground organization called the Third Echelon, and she gives him a recently stolen Russian formula for rocket fuel. After the lamasery's treatment gives him a photographic memory, Babcock tests his skills by memorizing the formula before the papers it is written on are destroyed. When Diane has Babcock and Turner taken to the Third Echelon leader (Robert Morley) and Babcock cannot recall the formula, the leader decides to have the men replace two apes (already observed putting on their spacesuits) on a spaceship about to orbit the Moon. The leader eventually reveals that he plans, with the help of the Russian fuel, to attack cities from space with destructive bombs and thus conquer the world. This reflects a shift in attitudes observed in other space films of the 1960s: A desire to employ space for military purposes, previously attributed to nations like the United States, Britain, and the Soviet Union, is now associated exclusively with secret conspirators and megalomaniacs.

When Turner and Babcock try to escape from the Third Echelon's subterranean headquarters, they come upon the apes' spacesuits, and predictable comedy ensues. Babcock comments that the shiny suit "looks like Liberace's underwear," while Turner decides they are "underwater diving suits" they can use to elude their pursuers. Instead, they are captured and placed on the spaceship. When Babcock asks, "Why do you suppose they're sending us up?" Turner provides one of the few funny lines in the film: "They want to find out if it's going to be safe for the apes," a reversal of standard procedure. After a takeoff makes the inexperienced astronauts jitter, the stress of acceleration is conveyed by distorted, flattened images of their faces, and they observe an asteroid passing their spaceship. Now the focus shifts to tedious comedy involving equipment designed for apes — a banana dispensing machine, face wipers, a water squirter, and a mechanical hand to scratch their sides.

When Turner and Babcock return to Earth, they are greeted as heroes, but as soon as his associate can extract the formula from Babcock's brain, the Third Echelon leader plans to kill the men to dissect their bodies and study the effects of space flight: "Their bodies will provide vital information to combat the hazards of future space travel." Appalled by this prospect, Diane helps them escape and, with additional assistance from old friend Dorothy Lamour (the other regular performer in the Road movies, added to the film at the last minute to placate angry fans), they storm the headquarters of the Third Echelon, along with police officers alerted by Diane, trying to prevent the launch of a second spaceship filled with bombs. Turner, Babcock, and Diane accidentally end up on board the spaceship, though they divert the craft from its mission of destruction and instead land on the Earthlike planet Plutonius, where they will be stranded for the rest of their lives — strangely, a fate similar to Pasquale's in *Totò nella Luna*, to be discussed.

The film's coda also features farcical cameo appearances by Frank Sinatra and Dean Martin, who are greeted with the comment, "The Italians have landed," another possible reference to *Totò nella Luna*. However, the real focus of the ending is Turner and Babcock happily accepting their fate because, like Pasquale, they will enjoy the company of a beautiful woman — the same woman. They even sing a song about sharing Diane's affections, at one point envisioning one man having her on Monday, Wednesday, and Friday while the other man has her on Tuesday, Thursday, and Saturday, with Sunday a day of rest for everyone. Here, albeit in a satirical manner, is a rare suggestion that the new environment of space might inspire new sorts of living patterns. One might even regard this conclusion as an anticipation of the group marriages that are standard on the inhabited Moon of Robert A. Heinlein's *The Moon Is a Harsh Mistress* (1966). Yet the film's final image, of Diane passionately kissing Turner while Babcock is lifted in the sky by "special effects," instead suggests that old habits will endure, and Diane will actually settle down with one man.

The Mouse on the Moon (1963)

In the 1950s, films like *Spaceways* and *Satellite in the Sky* could predict that Britain might pioneer in the conquest of space. By the 1960s, however, it was apparent that the United States and the Soviet Union would long be the only nations sending humans into space, so any envisioned British role in manned space travel would have to be played for laughs, as in *Man in the Moon*. This also explains *The Mouse on the Moon*, though the film was a sequel to the successful *The Mouse That Roared* (1959), and based upon the novel that was itself a sequel to the Leonard Wibberley book that inspired the first film.

The nation that farcically ventures into space here is not actually Britain, but the very British principality of Grand Fenwick, which faces a financial crisis because bottles of its wine, its chief export, inexplicably start exploding, causing sales to plummet. Thus, to garner funds to install indoor plumbing in his palace, Prime Minister Rupert Mountjoy (Ron Moody) requests a loan of $500,000 from the United States for the stated purpose of sending a rocket to the Moon, reasoning they would happily provide such a tiny sum as a good-will gesture while knowing this minuscule nation could never actually explore space. As one advisor tells Mountjoy, "We can't even build fireworks." Indeed, as a public relations ploy, the United States agrees to give Grand Fenwick a *million* dollars; and the Russians, seeking their own propaganda coup, send Grand Fenwick a leftover rocket. By mentioning precise sums of money, this film foregrounds an issue that only surfaced minimally in 1950s films but was now common knowledge: Space travel was very expensive. Everyone recognizes that a million dollars, a large sum by Grand Fenwick's standards, could not finance the research and engineering needed for space flight; one character jokes that the money "wouldn't even buy a second-hand spacesuit," and another character later repeats the comment. This is why only nations with enormous resources can realistically venture into space.

But comedies can be unrealistic, and the film falls back upon one implausible but common trope of science fiction films — the solitary inventor who achieves an astounding breakthrough — to enable Grand Fenwick to reach space. Studying the explosive wine, Professor Kokintz (David Kossoff) isolates an ingredient that will make an amazingly effective fuel to power a rocket from Earth to the Moon, albeit more slowly than conventional rockets. Then, while ostensibly focusing on indoor plumbing, Kokintz secretly works with Mountjoy's nerdish son Vincent (Bernard Cribbins) to launch the Soviet rocket, with himself and Vincent as its crew. This leads to comic depictions of their improvised efforts to "train" Vincent to be an astronaut. In one scene, he uses magnetic shoes to walk up a wall, prompting prospective girlfriend Cynthia (June Ritchie) to comment, "You really are completely crazy. Who ever wants to walk up walls?" Vincent answers, "Astronauts." Later, Vincent is hanging upside down in a tree, another attempt to acclimatize him to zero gravity. As launch time approaches, Vincent also wears a spacesuit, though it looks homemade and not tough enough to withstand the vacuum of space.

Not knowing that the professor and his son plan to fly into space, the prime minister seeks to earn sympathy, and additional funds, for Grand Fenwick by inviting dignitaries from nations like the United States and Soviet Union to watch the country's failed attempt to launch a rocket; he is dumbfounded when the rocket actually ascends into space.

The film humorously contrasts standard space procedures and the quirky routines of the professor's singularly slow ascent. The cabin is incongruously decorated like a Victorian drawing room, and the professor brings a chicken to provide food — eggs on the way to the Moon, cooked chicken on the way back. As the ship rises, Vincent panics and exclaims, "I'm not strapped in, professor. I've seen films of astronauts. And the blast-off and the gravitational pull is quite tremendous and that g-force is building up and...."

The professor calmly interrupts by offering him a cup of tea and asking him, "You take milk and sugar, don't you?"

The Mouse on the Moon might be classified, along with *From the Earth to the Moon*, *First Men in the Moon*, and the to-be-discussed *Jules Verne's Rocket to the Moon*, as "steampunk" stories of space travel, providing this modern activity with an absurd, old-fashioned look. Still, while the film provides a satirical portrayal of what a lunar mission launched by

A Mousy Scientist on the Moon: Grand Fenwick's greatest scientist, Professor Kokintz (David Kossoff), investigates lunar geology in *The Mouse on the Moon* (1963).

tradition-minded British citizens might be like, the film more directly assaults British pride. When a BBC news anchor announces the launch of Grand Fenwick's rocket, he notes that the mission involves the scientific expertise of Grand Fenwick, the financial support of the United States, and a Soviet rocket, but then states, as a matter of equal importance, that the astronauts wear British watches. Indeed, in contrast to cursory attention given to other nations' more meaningful contributions, he goes into extreme detail about the watches, purported evidence that Britain remains in the forefront of scientific progress. The real message is that the British can make no significant contributions to space travel.

Although Grand Fenwick's Moon flight is generally silly, the film is singularly prophetic regarding one reality of space travel: While slowly flying to the Moon, playing chess to keep themselves occupied, Vincent and the professor casually throw leftovers into space; these objects stay near the spacecraft as it approaches the Moon, and when they land, the trash falls all around them. The professor's sage conclusion is that "wherever civilization goes, garbage is sure to follow," and in fact, the debris from various orbital flights is increasingly regarded as a major problem for space travelers. And one recalls that Harlan Ellison described *Apollo* 11's "first activity on alien soil" as "dropping litter" ("That Moon Plaque," 189).

Needless to say, the American and Russian observers are appalled to see that their trivial assistance somehow enabled Grand Fenwick to potentially become the first nation to reach the Moon. Learning that the flight will take three weeks, both nations hastily launch their own missions to get there first. However, because Vincent accidentally hits a lever during the flight, the professor's spaceship unexpectedly accelerates and reaches the Moon before the other spaceships arrive.

When Vincent and the professor don spacesuits to walk on the Moon, the Professor seems displeased by the unusual surroundings, and even comments, "This Moon is a nice place to visit, but I wouldn't like to live here." But this film's Moon is more comfortably familiar than the Moon in more realistic films: It looks implausibly colorful, in contrast to the gray expanses usually observed. The sky is deep blue, not black, and despite the lunar vacuum requiring them to wear spacesuits, the film impossibly depicts sound traveling on the Moon: While Vincent brings out Grand Fenwick's flag to claim the Moon for their country, the professor holds an antique phonograph player blasting out patriotic music. Later, when the other ships land, and blue-suited Americans and red-suited Russians emerge to confront the astronauts from Grand Fenwick, they converse without using radio. But one aspect of their sojourn is realistic enough: Vincent enjoys huge leaps in the lower gravity, as observed long ago in *Kosmicheskiy Reys* and other films, and when asked to gather samples of Moon rocks — another prophetic element in this imagined lunar landing — he easily lifts an enormous rock.

Despite the silliness, the final scenes convey a serious message about a need for increased cooperation in space. While insisting that they reached the Moon first and claimed it for Grand Fenwick, the professor and Vincent invite the Americans and Russians to join them for a chicken dinner. However, when the professor remarks that the people who return to Earth first might receive more acclaim that those who reached the Moon first, the Americans and Russians hastily say goodbye and rush to take off; unfortunately, perhaps due to undue haste, their ships sink into lunar dust, so they must join the professor and Vincent for a return flight in their spaceship, which goes more slowly than ever due to its extra passengers. Having heard nothing for weeks, officials of the United States, the Soviet Union, and Grand Fenwick conclude their astronauts have died and gather in Grand Fenwick for a memorial ceremony. Attributing their supposed deaths to their competition to reach the Moon, the prime minister solemnly declares, "Never again shall man race to conquer the cosmos" and prepares to unveil a statue of the fallen astronauts with the Latin inscription "Per Harmoniam ad Lunum"—translated in a subtitle as "Togetherness—Moonwise." But the ceremony is disrupted when Grand Fenwick's spaceship appears and slowly lands.

While one might celebrate the film for embracing internationalism in the conquest of space, this was also, in a sense, a straight-faced counterpart to the humorous scene in which British watches were proclaimed as the nation's important contribution to the mission. For when your country is making significant strides in space travel, like the United States and the Soviet Union, your country's films can properly predict that your country will later achieve even greater triumphs. But when your country is not engaged in space travel, like Britain, one must call for an end to national rivalries, and collaborative efforts involving many nations, to envision a future in which someone, or something, from your country might share in the glory of future space achievements. Thus, films from nations like Italy and France (*La Morte Viene dallo Spazio*), East Germany and Poland (*Die Schweigende Stern*), and Japan (*Kaijû Daisensô*) may inevitably emphasize internationalism as a device to depict their people as deeply involved with space travel. In effectively aligning its nation with the Third World in attitudes toward space exploration, then, *The Mouse on the Moon* signals Britain's diminished stature in the world community.

Situation Comedies of the 1960s

As America's space program and astronauts became prominent news stories, these subjects unsurprisingly figured in situation comedies of the 1960s; shows now produced fewer episodes per season, but writers still needed new subjects for jokes and comic routines. The plots usually had no fantastic elements, as regulars simply met astronauts or participated in astronaut training programs.

As one example, consider "Nyet, Nyet, Not Yet," an episode of *Gilligan's Island* (aired November 18, 1965), wherein an errant Soviet space capsule with two cosmonauts accidentally lands on the castaways' Island. Having speculated the falling spacecraft might be a "flying saucer" with "men from Mars," Gilligan (Bob Denver) initially believes the cosmonauts, emerging in spacesuits, are alien invaders, though the Professor (Russell Johnson) realizes they are human astronauts. In an amiable conversation, cosmonauts Igor (Vincent Beck) and Ivan (Danny Klega) explain they accidentally landed off course but will soon be picked up by a Russian submarine; however, illustrating Cold War mistrust, the castaways suspect they came to the island deliberately to establish a Russian base, while the cosmonauts theorize the castaways are members of a secret American space program. Sneaking on board the capsule to investigate, Gilligan accidentally damages their radio, threatening their chances of escaping from the island. The Professor fixes the radio, and the cosmonauts hear the submarine will come at eleven o'clock the next morning. Reinforcing stereotypes about Russian drinking observed in the *Men into Space* episode "Mission to Mars," Igor brings out two concealed bottles of vodka so the men can celebrate. When his dubious colleague says, "Vodka—on spaceship?" Igor replies, "Only way to fly" (which could explain why Igor made the error that led to their off-course landing).

Though the cosmonauts now accept their new companions as real castaways, they fear their presence might get them in trouble when they are rescued, so they plan to use vodka to get the Americans drunk so they can be overcome and tied up. When Gilligan overhears their plan, millionaire Thurston Howell III (Jim Backus) suggests that Gilligan replace the contents of a marked vodka bottle with water, so the Americans can drink freely and remain sober while the Russians get drunk. Though the scheme succeeds, the castaways are not rescued, because Gilligan took the time from a Manila radio station in a different time zone; when the castaways arrive with their belongings, the submarine has already come and gone. A radio message indicates the Russians falsely claim the capsule landed in the Black Sea, showing that Americans of that era did not trust the Soviet Union to tell the truth about its space program.

Other episodes of this variety, all unseen, do not seem to merit detailed attention, although spacesuits may be fleetingly observed therein. "Spaceville," an episode of *The Many Loves of Dobie Gillis* (aired April 25, 1961), showed Army recruits Dobie Gillis (Dwayne Hickman), Maynard G. Krebs (Bob Denver), and a chimpanzee become subjects in an experiment, named Project Moonshot, requiring them to stay in a chamber for 30 days to simulate a long space flight. This scenario presumably highlights the psychological difficulties likely to arise in close quarters during lengthy space missions. "Lucy Becomes an Astronaut," an episode of *The Lucy Show* (aired November 5, 1962), similarly has Lucy Carmichael (Lucille Ball) and friend Vivian (Vivian Vance) participate in an experiment to simulate a space flight, this time only for 24 hours, which makes Lucy comically misbelieve that she has been chosen to become an astronaut. "Junior Astronaut," an episode of *Dennis the Menace* (aired January 13, 1963), shows its title character (Jay North) in a stamp-collecting competition, the prize being a vacation to Cape Canaveral to meet an astronaut. "McKeever's Astronaut," an episode of *McKeever and the Colonel* (aired January 20, 1963), involves a highly anticipated visit from an astronaut who turns out to be a chimpanzee. No plot summary is available for "José, the Astronaut," an episode of *The Bill Dana Show* (aired December 1, 1963), but presumably its star drew upon his famous comedy routine to have his bellhop character get mistaken for an astronaut or briefly endeavor to become an astronaut. "Robotic Astronaut," an episode of *My Living Doll* (aired February 3, 1965), had robot Rhoda (Julie Newmar) applying to become an astronaut. And Red Skelton returned to space travel with "Pop the Astronaut," an episode of *The Red Skelton Hour* (aired September 23, 1969).

There were also three comedy series involving space travel that could be regarded as science fiction. The unseen *It's About Time* (1966–1967) employs the familiar idea that astronauts might travel through time and land on Earth in a different era, but the astronauts come not to the future but the prehistoric past, where they humorously interact with cave people. Late in the series' run, in a switch designed to boost ratings, they return to the present with a few Stone Age companions.

Two other situation comedies featuring space travel, along very different lines, were more successful. *My Favorite Martian* (1963–1965) features a human-like Martian whose flying saucer crashes on Earth, temporarily stranding him in the company of a hapless journalist while he struggles to repair his spacecraft and return home. Its first episode, "My Favorite Martin" (aired September 29, 1963), has an interesting inconsistency. In the animated credits opening this and all future episodes, one observes a tiny Martian wearing a spacesuit in a spaceship resembling the flying cars of *The Jetsons* (1962–1963, 1985, 1987) to fly from Mars to Earth. In the episode itself, however, when reporter Tim O'Hara (Bill Bixby) first encounters the Martian he will call Uncle Martin (Ray Walston), he is in a more conventional spaceship; moreover, while he wears the silver bodysuit representing one common vision of space fashion (as also seen in *Lost in Space* and *Space: 1999* [1975–1977]), this visibly flimsy outfit, lacking a space helmet, cannot be regarded as a true spacesuit.

In later episodes, this silly series would occasionally include episodes wherein the stranded Martian attempts to fly back home, but I do not believe spacesuits were in view. One episode that does include a spacesuit, "How to Be a Hero Without Really Trying" (aired December 29, 1963), hearkens back to *The George Burns and Gracie Allen Show* by placing a space-obsessed child, not an actual space traveler, in a spacesuit. Little Stevie Richmond (Butch Patrick) likes to wear a space helmet and pretend he is from Mars because he is new in town and has no friends. Later, when an annoyed Martin vanishes to get away from Stevie so he can search for an ore he needs for his spaceship, the lonely boy wanders away and climbs up a dangerous mountain, forcing Tim to rely upon a Martian levitator to help him climb the mountain and rescue Stevie. As in the earlier situation comedy, then, a spacesuit illustrates one's alienation from society, though here it is a problem to be overcome by reaching out to the spacesuit wearer. This is the episode's narrative arc: When the boy is invited to come on a picnic with his older sister Jennifer (Kathy Kersh), Tim and Martin, he does not wear his spacesuit, and subsequent efforts by townspeople to rescue him surely convey to the boy that he is well liked by others in his community.

The second series, *I Dream of Jeannie* (1965–1970), features two working astronauts as regular characters, but its focus of attention was its titular star, a beautiful female genie, so the series was predominantly fantasy, not science fiction. In the first episode, "The Lady in a Bottle" (aired September 18, 1965), one does observe astronaut Tony Nelson (Larry Hagman) having a space helmet placed upon his head before an orbital mission (a scene reshown in later episodes), and later, upon landing on a desert island after a rocket failed and his flight ended prematurely, Nelson emerges from his downed space capsule wearing his spacesuit and carrying his space helmet. Yet as everyone knows, he soon discovers a bottle containing a genie named Jeannie (Barbara Eden), and the rest of the episode, like future episodes, is about Jeannie's magic, her efforts to become part of Tony's life, and the humorous complications that result.

While pondering the challenges of manned space travel was manifestly not a priority, some episodes did show Tony and fellow astronaut Roger Healey (Bill Daily) engaged in training activities or even traveling into space. For example, in the seventh episode, "Has Anybody Seen Jeannie?" (aired October 30, 1965), Tony's space mission will include America's first spacewalk (obviously inspired by the then-recent space walks of Soviet cosmonaut Alexei Leonov and American astronaut Ed White). Dubious about whether Tony is fit for space flight, due to unusual behavior caused by the antics of Jeannie, NASA physician Alfred Bellows (Hayden Rorke) conducts some tests on Tony, including one in which he is asked to don a spacesuit and engage in ergometric exercise on two pedals resembling those of a bicycle; however, having heard the spacewalk might be dangerous if the tether connecting Tony to his capsule is severed, Jeannie decides to prevent him from going by sabotaging the tests. However, after she hides in Tony's jacket to produce outrageous test results, Tony angrily tells Jeannie she is destroying his career as an astronaut. The genie then returns to Bellows's office and performs magic to make Bellows doubt his own sanity, so he will not trust his own judgment regarding Tony's fitness for the flight.

In an unusual coda, we actually observe a rocket containing Tony and other astronauts take off and see them in spacesuits within a cramped capsule. Then Tony stands up, opens the hatch, and pushes himself into space. While tethered to his spacecraft, he floats in the blackness of space, turning upside down at one point and proclaiming that he feels great. Fleetingly, the series portrays one joy of space travel, the freedom of weightlessness, and conveys one reason why Tony might fervently desire to be an astronaut, so he can continue to enjoy such experiences. Yet two aspects of the scene undermine its impact. First, clearly uninterested in portraying space realistically, producers do not bother to show any stars in the sky behind Tony, so he merely floats in complete darkness, failing to persuade viewers he is really in space and suggesting he is merely floating on wires on a set. Then, Tony's reverie in space is interrupted by Jeannie, magically able to survive in the vacuum of space. She approaches Tony to give him a kiss on his faceplate, leaving a red lipstick mark. To anyone trying to fathom the logic of this ridiculous story, it seems senseless that Jeannie worried about Tony's safety when she could visit him in space at any time.

The scene also has symbolic significance, since it essentially epitomizes the direction taken by the series: Tony is seduced away from his quest to explore space by the allure of pleasant domesticity with a spectacular trophy wife, as episodes focus less on space travel and more on his misadventures with Jeannie on Earth, eventually leading to their marriage during the series' fifth and final season. More broadly, this scene effectively delineates the story in this book of how filmgoers turned away from realistic depictions of space to be entertained by colorful fantasies. Why watch a man in a clumsy spacesuit, floating aimlessly in space, when one can be entertained by beautiful women and charmingly absurd events?

For the record, I did not watch all 139 episodes of *I Dream of Jeannie* for this study, seeking insights into cinematic depictions of space travel, though I watched several episodes which, based upon plot descriptions, seemed likely to feature space flight or spacesuits. "Happy Anniversary" (aired September 12, 1966) briefly shows Tony donning a spacesuit amidst a silly story: Jeannie transports Tony out of orbit to celebrate the anniversary of her discovery on the island where he found her bottle, but Tony finds another bottle containing the evil Blue Djinn (Michael Ansara), who briefly menaces the pair. In "Haven't I Seen Me Someplace Before?" (aired March 26, 1968), it's Roger's birthday, and a "birthday wish" mix-up results in Roger and Tony switching bodies. After typically lame comedy involving Tony in Roger's body and Roger in Tony's body, Roger learns that he is the only person who can reverse the switch. At first he resists, since he would like to go in Tony's place on a desirable mission, but eventually relents. When we observe Tony in orbit, Roger uses his replacement wish to join Tony in his capsule.

"Operation: First Couple on the Moon" (aired March 19, 1968) interestingly recalls the *Men into Space* episode "First Woman on the Moon" by having Tony selected for an experimental mission to live on the Moon with a woman. Due to a magically manipulated testing process, Jeannie's evil twin sister (also played by Barbara Eden) earns a position as Tony's partner, while Roger and a female scientist, Dr. Swanson (Kay Reynolds), will be their backups. But after Jeannie replaces her sister in the experimental chamber where Tony and his partner are being trained, her antics lead to Tony being disqualified. Roger then tells Tony the entire project has been cancelled by Bellows, ostensibly because of deep psychological issues preventing men and women from living together in space: "The American man and woman has [sic] deep-seated male-female hostilities, they have overly complicated libido problems, and they can't resolve the Oedipus complex." But the real reason is that Swanson's boyfriend, a linebacker, punched Bellows in the nose.

Finally, "Around the World in 80 Blinks" (aired March 24, 1969) also touches upon mental instability induced by space travel. Tony, Roger, and arrogant astronaut Wingate (Richard Mulligan) are on a mission to orbit the Moon. When Wingate returns from a spacewalk and Tony asks, "How was the walk?" he replies, "Exactly as I expected. You must remember, Nelson, that I have been here before." But Tony has a bad cold, and Jeannie, watching him on television, decides she must return him to Earth. Unfortunately, she mistakenly brings Wingate to Tony's house. When she then returns Tony, he tells Jeannie she must send him back, because one man cannot operate the spacecraft. Unwilling to risk Tony's health, Jeannie goes into space herself, where her inexperience briefly sends the spacecraft on a trajectory to Mars before Roger puts the ship back on course to orbit the Moon.

In the meantime, Tony must deal with the understandably befuddled Wingate, eagerly building upon his theory that he is having delusions brought on by space travel. Having heard of "raptures of the deep," Wingate says, he must now be experiencing the "raptures of deep space," a surprisingly evocative phrase considering its context. After Jeannie leaves to help Roger, Tony tries to make Wingate believe that he is still in space, though the men are actually in Tony's garage, hiding from Bellows's suspicious wife Amanda (Emmaline Henry). Though she eventually finds Tony, who has given Wingate tranquilizers, Jeannie is able to send him and Wingate back into space, right before Amanda can expose him to her husband and other NASA officials. Back in space, Wingate is eager to discuss his interesting hallucinations, considering them important to space scientists, but Tony and Roger convince him to keep quiet, or he will be disqualified for future space travel. While many episodes of the series dealt with Bellows's mistaken belief that Tony was becoming mentally imbalanced, this episode directly links space travel to potential madness, albeit in a farcical fashion.

The series' fourth season, from late 1968 to mid–1969, seemed to unusually emphasize space travel, as the aging series perhaps was striving to exploit heightened public interest in space as the lunar landing approached. But the series then employed another proven gimmick — having lead characters marry — to attract viewers during its final season, and space travel again became a background element.

Sergeant Dead Head (1965)

Since American International Pictures previously injected some novelty into its Beach Party movies by including an alien (Tommy Kirk as a Martian in *Pajama Party* [1964]), it might have seemed logical to further exploit public interest in space travel by actually sending Frankie Avalon into space. However, while *Sergeant Dead Head* employed other actors from those movies, a space comedy in the 1960s demanded radical changes in the teen-movie format. Earlier, teenagers might have stumbled upon an eccentric scientist building a rocket in his backyard and joined his expedition to the Moon; but now, a film must reflect current realities by depicting space travel as a government-sponsored activity led by the military. This meant not only that Avalon would have to play a soldier to board a spacecraft, but older characters, representing the authority figures in charge of the space program, would play larger roles. Beach Party films attracted young viewers with fun-loving teenagers enjoying freedom from adult supervision, with a few older people as easily defeated foils; *Sergeant Dead Head* may have failed because its true stars were veteran character actors dominating subservient youths in uniform.

Opening scenes establish the character of Sergeant O.K. Deadhead (Frankie Avalon), his name spelled that way in the film despite its title, as a childlike person in a world of adults. At a military base preparing to launch a chimpanzee into space, he plays with a toy rocket that comically explodes. While this suggests that he dreams of traveling into space, he never expresses any interest in doing so, and indeed protests angrily upon discovering that he was inadvertently launched into orbit. In a conversation between commander General

Rufus Fogg (Fred Clark) and romantic interest Lieutenant Kinsey (Eve Arden), we learn the purpose of this flight is to investigate a problem: "Something funny happens to personalities up there" [in space]; as one example, mice sent into orbit began chasing cats. Of course, other films express concerns about mental problems caused by space travel, but the idea of a complete personality reversal is manifestly only a premise for later comedy involving a transformed Deadhead.

After Deadhead is imprisoned for his rocket stunt, it transpires that he actually prefers such punishment in order to postpone his marriage to Airman Lucy Turner (Deborah Walley), meaning that, like other accidental astronauts in space comedies, he is a coward at heart. But another confined soldier (Harvey Lembeck) helps him escape, and he absurdly chooses the base's spaceship as a place to hide. Naturally, his presence goes undetected as the chimpanzee is placed on board and launched into space; only when Deadhead begins protesting via radio do Fogg and others on the ground realize what happened. With the aid of three visiting officers, Fogg devises a plan to depict this manned space flight as their real intent, with Deadhead presented as a "brave, heroic volunteer."

Though the film employs footage from actual space launches for an air of authenticity, no one involved sought to portray space travel realistically: Before liftoff, the chimpanzee puts on and takes off his helmet as he pleases, indicating that no one cares about his safety, and despite recycled images of a Mercury or Gemini capsule being recovered in the ocean, Deadhead and the chimpanzee are in a spacious room with no signs of weightlessness; the astronauts keep busy during their brief flight by playing checkers. But like the Three Stooges, also inadvertent passengers in a spaceship designed for a chimpanzee, Deadhead mysteriously acquires and wears his own spacesuit and space helmet.

Upon Deadhead's return to Earth, he experiences a "slight personality change," signaled by a moment during the flight when he gets a strange expression and demands a banana. However, the notion that he develops the personality of a chimpanzee is not well developed, since his newly developed character—brash, arrogant, and domineering—does not make him seem similar to a primate. The chimpanzee acquires an ability to talk, telling one interviewer, "That idiot Deadhead has made a mockery of my entire career," but other than one farcical scene, the chimpanzee is ignored. Instead, after confronting the transformed Deadhead, Fogg tells a colleague, "Congratulations, Dr. Frankenstein, I think you've created a monster," and frets about presenting him to the public as a hero. The improbable solution is to locate Deadhead's exact double, a Sergeant Donovan (also Frankie Avalon), and have him impersonate Deadhead.

There is no point in providing a blow-by-blow account of subsequent events in this thoroughly Earthbound film, as the aggressive Deadhead keeps escaping to temporarily replace the mild-mannered Donovan before he resumes his impersonation, constantly befuddling Turner, Fogg, and the others. The only point conveyed is that, by the 1960s, space travel has become almost entirely a matter of public relations: The only reason one sends astronauts into space, it seems, is so they can become heroes and bolster the careers of the people in charge. Fogg's bizarre machinations to prevent the unappealing Deadhead from appearing in public, which include persuading Donovan to actually marry Turner, demonstrate that promoting his own interests takes precedence over all other concerns, since no one bothers to ask Deadhead anything about his experiences in space or what, if anything, he might have learned. Even the president (Pat Buttram) seems solely interested in sharing in the glory of Deadhead's achievement, as he summons him and his new wife to the White House and eagerly accepts the gift of his space helmet, which he immediately dons (so he is briefly detained when guards mistake him for Deadhead). As for Deadhead, his original personality eventually returns. When he tells Turner, "When I kiss you, I go into orbit," as they flee the White House in a helicopter, it is apparent that, as in *Man in the Moon* and the to-be-discussed *The Reluctant Astronaut*, domestic bliss with a beautiful bride will serve as a consolation prize for someone who will never again be allowed to travel into space.

Way...Way Out (1966)

Since Abbott and Costello, the Three Stooges, and Hope and Crosby contributed to the genre, it was inevitable that another major film comic of the 1950s and 1960s, Jerry Lewis, would try his hand at a space adventure. Indeed, he already portrayed an alien visitor to Earth (who never wore a spacesuit) in an adaptation of Gore Vidal's play *Visit to a Small Planet* (1960). *Way...Way Out*, however, came when Lewis was striving to make more mature comedies. Along with pratfalls, the film also has serious messages about humanity's future in space.

The familiar problem driving the plot is the danger that space travelers, confined to

Calisthenics in the Craters: Lunar residents Pete Mattemore (Jerry Lewis) and his Russian neighbor Igor Valkleinokov (Dick Shawn) in *Way...Way Out* (1966) demonstrate the calisthenic possibilities in the Moon's lower gravity.

cramped quarters and surrounded by a deadly vacuum, might become mentally unbalanced. Near the beginning of the twenty-first century, both the United States and Soviet Union maintain two-man bases on the Moon, primarily to provide valuable data about weather on Earth — an early recognition that such observations might justify a human presence in space, though Earth's nations actually came to rely upon unmanned satellites for such information. One American on the Moon, Schmidlap (Howard Morris), is disturbing crewmate Hoffman (Dennis Weaver) with his erratic behavior, which includes periodically tying him up and attempting to kill him; Schmidlap also causes an international incident by attacking the female resident of the Russian base, Anna Soblova (Anita Ekberg). To achieve peaceful life at this "lonely, desolate post," the head of America's space program, Harold Quonset (portrayed by Robert Morley with an incongruous British accent), arranges a shotgun wedding between a male astronaut and female meteorologist, believing a married couple at the base will coexist harmoniously. The theory proves incorrect before it is implemented when the newlyweds begin fighting, disqualifying themselves for the assignment. In desperation, Quonset assigns backup astronaut Pete Mattemore (Jerry Lewis) to meet and marry one of the few available meteorologists. The marriage is deemed essential because Quonset, hearkening back to concerns expressed in *Project Moon Base*, thinks the American public would not tolerate the Russian pattern of assigning an unmarried man and woman to occupy their base.

There follows some tedious comedy involving Mattemore's efforts to woo the woman of his choice, beautiful Eileen Forbes (Connie Stevens). His inept efforts prove futile, and Quonset instead wants him to marry the unattractive Esther Davenport (Bobo Lewis). When Mattemore again seeks out Forbes, she confesses her desire to go to the Moon and agrees to the marriage, as long as it is "in name only." (As it happens, the idea that lengthy sojourns in space might inspire marriages of conveniences previously surfaced in science fiction stories like Heinlein's *Stranger in a Strange Land* [1961], but this may represent its first appearance in a film.) Ludicrously, due to an unrealistically tight schedule, they get married literally on their way to the spaceship, minutes before their flight. Then, signaling the genre's maturity, *Way...Way Out* devotes little time to the journey from Earth to the Moon, avoiding standard tropes like the painful acceleration of liftoff or zero gravity; the only joke comes when Mattemore and Forbes are unsettlingly told that their pilot was once suspended for drinking.

Approaching the Moon, they establish radio contact with Schmidlap and Hoffman, who are again fighting each other, sending one man soaring across the room in the low lunar gravity. (Earlier spacesuit films acknowledge the Moon's lower gravity only sporadically, but it is a recurring theme in this one.) Mattemore says they have "already gotten into our spacesuits," which they wear as they walk to the base, and later as Mattemore and Hoffman forcibly accompany Schmidlap to the spaceship, since he again misbehaves in his aroused reaction to Forbes.

The ensuing comic developments, more subdued than in most Jerry Lewis films, variously reference the history of the spacesuit film. As the couple prepares to sleep, they are visited by Soblova, who asks to spend the night; she is peeved with crewmate Igor Valkleinokov (Dick Shawn) because he will not follow the American example and marry her, another reflection of the desire for domesticity often expressed by space travelers. After Mattemore and Forbes are forced into the same bed by her presence, she makes an unusual speech describing her inevitable deflowering as the direct result of a chain of events initiated by the experiments of rocket pioneer Robert Goddard; strangely, this comedy may be the first spacesuit film that pays tribute to the American scientist whose work anticipated his nation's later space triumphs. Though she is obviously willing to consummate the relationship, Mattemore is too tired to take advantage of the opportunity. When Valkleinokov visits the next day, he reinforces the stereotype of hard-drinking Russians, observed in the *Men into Space* episode "Mission to Mars," by initiating a raucous party fueled by heavy consumption of home-made vodka. This spontaneous camaraderie of the Americans and Russians also supports the common theme that space travelers invariably transcend whatever national differences divide them, driven together by the shared experience of living in space.

After Mattemore and Valkleinokov are completely drunk, there is a telling indication that conventional behavior on Earth may not be appropriate in the novel environment of another world. Mattemore becomes upset because Valkleinokov dances too closely to his wife, and like other males in conflict, they step outside to settle their differences. On the Moon, though, this requires them to don spacesuits. There follows an odd scene in which one drunken man hits the other and sends him soaring through space in the low lunar gravity. The folly of this activity, which could cause a broken helmet and instant death, is all too apparent, and indeed undermines the humor of this scene. Even Mattemore's deranged predecessors had enough sense to confine their battles to the base's interior.

Some political humor surfaces in television programs featuring "elder statesman" Richard Nixon and a Southern Senator still demanding more time to adjust to integration, amusing suggestions that contemporary political phenomena might improbably endure into the next century. But there now occurs a political crisis overshadowing all domestic disputes on the Moon: Awakening from a two-day hangover (which also prevented him from warning Earth about disastrous weather conditions), Mattemore is told by blustering General Hallenby (Brian Keith, essentially playing the same role he played in *Moon Pilot*) that an apparent Russian incursion into a country within America's sphere of influence might ignite a nuclear war, and he assigns Mattemore to "secure the Moon." He does so by allowing Soblova to stay at the American base and hitting Valkleinokov over the head, rendering him unconscious. Yet by the time Mattemore reports the good news, Hallenby tells him the crisis has been resolved peacefully, and he fumes at him for possibly provoking an international incident.

Confirming the domesticating effect of life in space, Valkleinokov and Soblova are married by an official on Earth via television, in a ceremony that deliberately or unknowingly recalls the conclusion of *Project Moon Base*. It is also announced that Soblova is pregnant, apparently guaranteeing the Russians the propaganda coup of having the first baby on the Moon. However, Forbes delights a disappointed Quonset by saying, "I'm as pregnant as she is," so that an American baby might be born first. She then reveals to a baffled Mattemore the true meaning of her statement: Soblova is not really pregnant, but she lied to Valkleinokov (acting on Forbes's advice) to get him to marry her. Forbes concludes the film by telling Mattemore they must immediately get to work on beating the Russians to have the first child on the Moon. One readily imagines a coda to the film — or even a sequel — showing the two couples as new parents dealing with colicky babies and dirty diapers on the Moon, representing the ultimate domestication of space.

Strangely enough, *Way...Way Out* represents the most heterodox, proto-feminist vision of life in space since *Project Moon Base*, even though Forbes and Soblova, even more than Briteis, consistently act more like overgrown children than mature women. The men are not only equally childish, but are constantly controlled and manipulated by the women, effective masters of their lunar environment; and here the President does not intervene to re-impose male superiority on the Moon. More so than other films to date, *Way...Way Out* forcefully suggests that women will prove the superior sex in space.

Jules Verne's Rocket to the Moon (*Those Fantastic Flying Fools*) (1967)

Jules Verne's Rocket to the Moon, initially retitled *Those Fantastic Flying Fools* to exploit the popularity of *Those Magnificent Men in Their Flying Machines* (1965), is unlike other humorous spacesuit films, since it recalls the neo–Victorian space journeys of *From the Earth to the Moon* and *First Men in the Moon* and, despite its light tone, is not entirely farcical. Indeed, some of its nineteenth-century characters are working quite earnestly to reach the Moon, and their preparations convey an awareness of the genuine challenges of space travel.

This intermittent sobriety is not signaled by opening scenes, illustrating the follies of some main characters, accompanied by incongruously celebratory narration about the wonders of Victorian science. An inventor, the Duke of Barset (Dennis Price), constructs the first house in Britain entirely lighted by electricity, but after Queen Victoria (Joan Sterndale Bennett) pulls the switch, sparks fly and the house is consumed by fire. At the dedication of a suspension bridge designed by engineer Sir Charles Dillworthy (Lionel Jeffries), Victoria cuts the ribbon, and the bridge falls apart. We also meet swindler Sir Harry Washington-Smythe (Terry-Thomas), purchasing a crooked pool table with a magnet to attract steel balls, and American showman P.T. Barnum (Burl Ives), who slips away from creditors just as he learns he is ruined and flees to Britain.

Barnum joins a meeting of the Royal Society for the Advancement of Science just in time to hear a lecture by German explosives expert Siegfried von Bulow (Gert Frobe) about launching a projectile to the Moon. Most members laugh, but Barnum proposes to form a committee to actually accomplish that goal. The Duke of Barset and Dillworthy sign up, and Washington-Smythe is recommended as a financier. (Dillworthy is dubious because Washington-Smythe supplied the flawed materials that caused his bridge's collapse.) Since Barnum was already presented as a shady businessman, one might suspect he initiated this project solely as a crooked scheme to make money; however, while he later contrives to profit by selling tickets for a tour of the completed projectile, he is also portrayed as someone who sincerely believes the project can be completed. Thus, while he shows that greed might motivate space flight, Barnum also seems a sincere space enthusiast.

The other protagonist then appears — American scientist Gaylord Sullivan (Troy Donahue), enjoying a romantic moment with girlfriend Madelaine (Daliah Lavi), who insists she loves him, though she wears a wedding gown and is about to marry a wealthy Frenchman (who she also loves). Hearing of Barnum's project, he insists upon joining the team, since he has designed a unique projectile that (as he demonstrates) can not only travel to the Moon, but also return to Earth. He gets in a balloon to fly to England, Madelaine impulsively decides to join him, and they arrive in the midst of preparations for the flight.

The men replace the standard cannon with a large tunnel dug into a mountain, and use Sullivan's design instead of Dillworthy's. When Washington-Smythe is fired after embezzling much of the money raised for the project, both men have a motive for sabotaging the project, particularly since Washington-Smythe is taking bets, with long odds, on its success. Also, in a scene where Washington-Smythe faces the Duke of Barset's righteous anger, the con man attempts to deflect the crowd's hostility to the Duke by claiming he secretly took a bribe to have someone place an American flag on the Moon, making him a traitor to Britain. He intimates that space flight might be driven by a desire to seize new territory for one's country, though no one here thinks along such lines. When Victoria learns that Barnum's protégé, midget Tom Thumb (Jimmy Clitheroe), will be flying to the Moon, she expresses no concern about an American pilot and merely sends a congratulatory letter — which is how Tom Thumb learns of the plan and immediately refuses to go.

Sullivan agrees to take his place, and in an interesting scene is asked to jump up and down several times, wearing a spacesuit, to test how durable it will prove on the Moon. While this shows an awareness that the Moon is airless, the outfit otherwise looks strange and flimsy: a black body suit with a black mask entirely covering his face, except for two eyeholes, with a tube and a large black sphere above his head, presumably containing the oxygen he will need. He is also advised not to move too vigorously in his spacesuit because "you could fry out the circuits," suggesting that some electrical equipment is included. The projectile also features a unique device to protect him from the pressure of liftoff: a cushion to be lowered onto his body before launch. Removing it will not be a problem, we are told, because once Sullivan is in space, the cushion will float away due to weightlessness. As another indication of Barnum's desire to make money, we learn that the craft is equipped with chloroform — so Sullivan can subdue any creatures he finds on the Moon and return them to Earth, to be profitably exhibited by Barnum.

Before Sullivan finishes this training, Dillworthy and Washington-Smythe sneak on board and sabotage its rockets. When Madelaine observes their perfidy, they kidnap her and have her imprisoned in a peculiar "Home for Wayward Girls." Preparations for the flight are accelerated when an astronomer tells Barnum the projectile must be launched next Sunday to reach the Moon.

There is considerable time devoted to Madelaine's escape from captivity, her accidental discovery by Washington-Smythe and Dillworthy, and their frenzied pursuit of the woman. As a further complication, Barnum is warned by Colonel Scuttling of Scotland Yard (Allan Cuthbertson) that a Czarist spy will try to sabotage the flight, so when Madelaine arrives, she is arrested as a spy, and her reports about the real sabotage are dismissed.

As a crowd watches, the launch is delayed because Sullivan's arm is trapped by the lowered cushion and he cannot reach the launch switch. The spy, Joachim Bulgeroff (Joachim Teege), has also hidden on board, and when he is discovered he uses chloroform to subdue Sullivan. Thus, when he is removed from the projectile, he cannot tell anyone about the saboteur. At this point, Washington-Smythe and Dillworthy sneak into the projectile to make sure their own sabotage has not been undone due to Madelaine's testimony, and they inflict additional damage on the craft just to be safe. Bulgeroff then pulls the launch switch himself and the projectile takes off with the three men on board — to land in Russia, where Washington-Smythe and Dillworthy are imprisoned to receive their just punishment. (It is unclear whether Bulgeroff guided the projectile to his home country or if the projectile quickly fell to Earth because of the sabotage.) Barnum and his associates are not depressed by the apparently unmanned, and hence unprofitable, launch of the projectile, because its explosive liftoff unearthed large deposits of coal that will make everyone rich.

Perhaps *Jules Verne's Rocket to the Moon* would have been more successful if filmmakers had taken the idea of shady businessmen involved in a planned space flight to its logical conclusion and portrayed Barnum as a man who deliberately plans a phony trip to the Moon — a project he knows will fail — solely to fleece investors and enrich himself. It might have been, in other words, a film like Mel Brooks's *The Producers* (1968), where a Broadway producer attempts to profit by deliberately staging a surefire flop. Perhaps, as evidenced by occasional revelations about Barnum's less than honorable motives, this was the story's original thrust. But at a time when the United States and the Soviet Union were risking human lives in actual efforts to conquer space, with broad public support, it might have seemed inappropriate to openly question the motives of people behind a space project, to suggest it only represents a scheme to get rich quick.

Even if necessarily provided with an overlay of earnestness, the film has a point to make, now illustrated every day by the money NASA makes by giving tours of its facilities and selling souvenirs: People on Earth can indeed make a profit by sending other people into space.

The Reluctant Astronaut (1967)

Released at the same time as *Jules Verne's Rocket to the Moon*, *The Reluctant Astronaut* seems a throwback of another sort, to the raucous space comedies of the 1950s; as in earlier films, the story involves an inept buffoon's hapless misadventures in space. Yet while Don Knotts followed in the footsteps of Abbott and Costello and the Three Stooges, shoehorning such a story into the context of the actual American space program did make this a more serious film, and one that surprisingly deals with a significant subject that other spacesuit films downplay.

In the small town of Sweetwater, Missouri, mild-mannered Roy Fleming (Don Knotts) operates "Mr. Spaceman's Rocket Ride" at an amusement park. (While a tightly framed shot at first makes it appear he is a spacesuited astronaut in space, the camera moves back to reveal he is actually entertaining a group of children in a chamber which, from the outside, resembles a rocketship.) When he leaves the building, he must escorted down a small flight of stairs because of his severe fear of heights. His father, war hero Buck Fleming (Arthur O'Connell), wishes his son to continue his family's military tradition and hence sent in an application for him to become an astronaut. (One might think the man, obsessed with his World War II experiences, would want his son to become a soldier and fight in the Vietnam War, but his preference for the space program accords with a common perception of the time, that peaceful competition in space was becoming a desirable substitute for military conflict.) Roy also makes fumbling efforts to woo Ellie Jackson (Joan Freeman), who seems amenable to his advances while less than thrilled by his inability to be romantic.

When a letter arrives apparently indicating that Roy's application was accepted and inviting him to Houston, Roy's father is ecstatic and he assumes Roy is happy as well. Roy keeps trying to tell him he does not want to go, but he cannot interrupt his father's enthusiastic babbling. For much of the film, then, Buck Fleming seems a villain—an overbearing, arrogant man forcing his son into a role he abhors. Bowing to the inevitable, Roy travels to Houston, though in what becomes a recurring gag, his fear of heights prevents him from boarding the plane, and he instead takes a bus. Upon arriving, Roy is awestruck when given a ride by famed astronaut Fred Gifford (Leslie Nielsen, here a straight man not yet indulging in his flair for comedy), who inexplicably befriends him. When Roy finds the personnel office is closed for lunch, he wanders around the facility to nervously observe astronauts at work. One astronaut, in a chamber next to a lunar lander, practices a Moon walk; another rotates rapidly in a flight simulator; a third takes off for a brief flight using a rocket pack

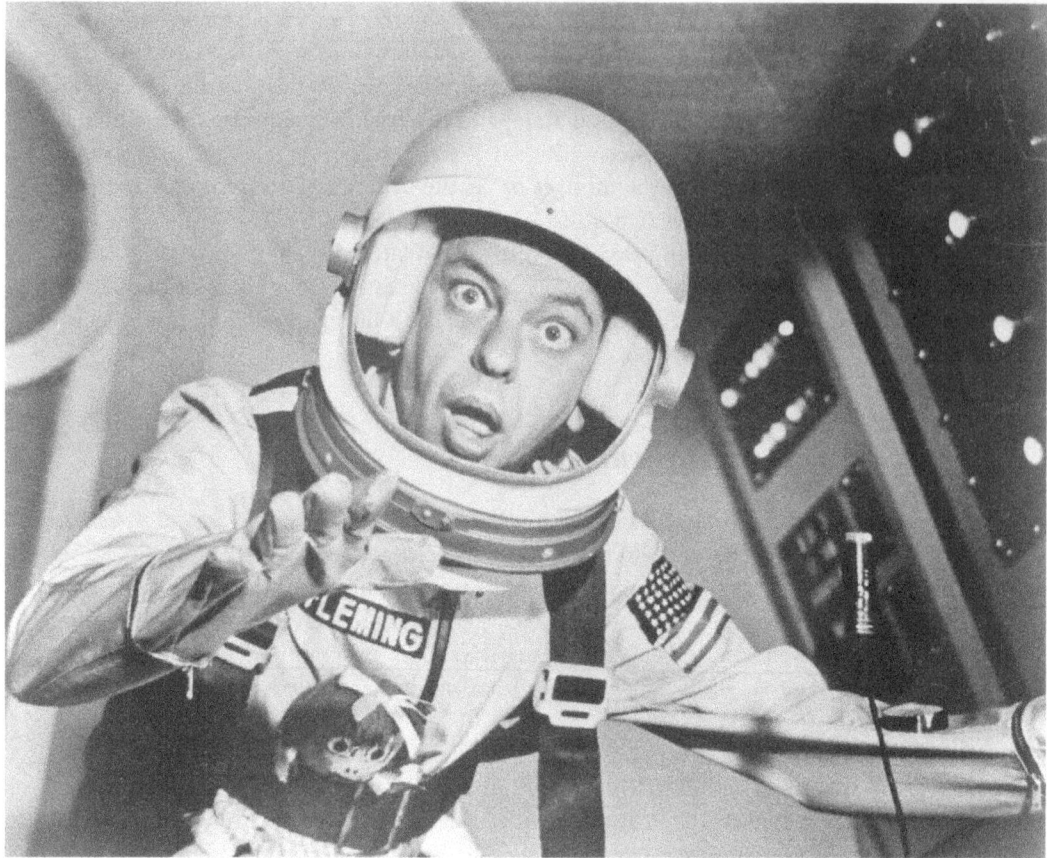

Far Out Space Knotts: The perpetually befuddled Don Knotts, as janitor Roy Fleming, both playfully and poignantly represents all of the people who should never be allowed to travel into space in *The Reluctant Astronaut* (1967).

on his back. When Roy attempts to attend a meeting of astronauts, he is sent to the personnel office to learn the humbling truth: He was hired to work for NASA as a janitor, not an astronaut, to be trained and supervised by the gruff Donelli (Jesse White).

The following scenes alternately suggest Roy is content to be a janitor while still longing to become an astronaut. Amusingly contrasting sequences show future astronauts being trained in procedures of space travel, and Roy and other future janitors being trained in procedures of cleaning. Roy also finds a space helmet, puts it on, and as if admiring himself for seeming worldly, he stands in front of a mirror and attempts to light a cigarette, which is cut off when the visor falls on it. Donelli perpetually fumes at Roy for his apparent unwillingness to focus on janitorial work, though Roy later reveals to friends from Sweetwater that he is learning how to keep the accoutrements of space travel clean. A chance encounter with Gifford leads to Roy being included in a photograph of NASA astronauts that appears in newspapers, further confirming to Buck and his friends that his son is now an astronaut.

Roy is then invited to a hometown celebration in his honor, though he again declines to fly home. The party features an annoying woman who repeatedly proclaims that she once changed his diapers, a large cake shaped like a rocketship, and a girl who gives him a talking doll and insists that he take it into space. Again attempting to explain his real status to his father, Roy finally conveys a half-truth: He plans to quit the astronaut program. In response, a distressed Buck makes a startling revelation: His stories about glorious exploits in World War II were lies; he actually spent the war years working in a library; and he earned a medal only because an encyclopedia fell on him. He urges Roy to remain an astronaut as the only way to salvage the family honor, and Roy cannot bring himself to refuse.

At this moment, a character previously portrayed as obnoxious and cruel suddenly seems vulnerable and sympathetic, and the true theme of *The Reluctant Astronaut* becomes apparent: This film is about people who are not strong enough, smart enough, or sophisticated enough to become astronauts. Unlike Gifford and other heroic astronauts, who journey into space and accomplish great things, these people are doomed to live in small towns, work at menial jobs, and enjoy the challenge of space travel only vicariously, by reading about astronauts in newspapers or watching them on television. In isolation, Roy Fleming would be just another clown, like Abbott and Costello and the Three Stooges; but juxtaposed with the figure of his pathetic father, fervently longing for his improbable success as an astronaut, Roy becomes a representative of all the decent, admirable people who lack the qualities that would allow them to become astronauts. Space travel effectively imposes a new class structure upon the world, elevating capable people like Gifford into an elite group of space travelers and relegating less competent people like Roy and his father to second-class status.

All this is reinforced by what happens next: Buck and a few friends visit Roy in Houston, and the startled Roy, desperately anxious to maintain the pretense he is an astronaut and avoid breaking his father's heart, puts on a spacesuit (though the men notice it bears another man's name) and gives them a tour of the training center, though his comments indicate he knows more about how various devices are cleaned than how they are used. But his thoroughgoing ineptitude indicates to audiences, if not the unperceptive visitors, that the bumbling Roy is completely unsuited to be an astronaut: He is temporarily rendered helpless by a malfunctioning air conditioner, gets trapped in a space capsule and must break a window to free himself, and foolishly straps himself into a rocket sled and turns it on, leading to a terrifying ride and a panicked ejection, setting off alarms as his parachute drifts toward the ground. An indignant Donelli rushes in, reveals that Roy is merely a janitor, and fires him on the spot. A dejected Buck leaves with his friends, but not before telling his son he should not be concerned because both of them are "losers," making his sorry fate inevitable.

The film then takes up the question: What do these people do when it becomes apparent that they will never be allowed to attain the desirable status of a space traveler? Buck goes home and, in a later scene, eagerly watches a movie about World War II, re-immersing himself in pleasant fantasies about imagined glories. But Roy's reaction is more disturbing: Walking around as if dazed, he enters a bar where patrons are playing a drinking game inspired by the space program. A man is handed a shot of liquor, those around him begin chanting "Ten — nine — eight — seven — six — five — four — three — two — one — ignition — blast-off!" and when they conclude, the man downs the entire glass. Roy joins the game as its central imbiber and soon gets extremely drunk. The disheartening point could not be clearer: For "losers" like Roy, an inebriated stupor is the closest they will ever get to the experience of "blasting off" into space.

Until this time, except for a few improbable coincidences, *The Reluctant Astronaut* was realistic enough, and it now reaches its logical conclusion: The unqualified people who aspired to become space travelers have been rebuffed, and they are left to reconcile themselves to their perpetual status as the people the space program will leave behind. But since a comedy requires a happy ending, there must now occur some unrealistic events to make Roy's impossible dream come true. In a meeting with Gifford and other astronauts, American officials reveal that the Russians are seeking a propaganda triumph: They will launch a completely untrained individual into space, to demonstrate that their space capsules are so advanced that they work perfectly well without capable guidance. The only way for America to beat Russia in this bizarre new competition is to hurriedly send someone into orbit who is even less qualified than the projected Russian cosmonaut, a dentist. After Gifford naturally says, "I have a suggestion," NASA officials track down Roy, still drinking in that bar, and persuade him to prepare for a space flight.

The film now, belatedly, becomes a complete farce in the manner of *Abbott and Costello Go to Mars* and *Have Rocket, Will Travel*. Escorted to a space capsule atop a tall rocket, Roy unwisely looks down and attempts to retreat. While other films strive to make astronauts seem childish by placing them in oversized spacesuits and having them strapped into seats like helpless children, Roy unquestionably seems the most childish astronaut of all, since he also clings to that girl's doll. After technicians leave, Roy tries to exit the capsule, but the platform next to the door has been removed, so he dangles precariously from the door's edge until he scrambles back inside and closes the door just in time for liftoff. While monitors on Earth note his regularly rising blood pressure and temperature, Roy then involves himself in typical sorts of spacesuit comedy. Upon seeing the first stage detach and fall off, he exclaims that his spaceship "broke"; he floats randomly around the capsule, at times upside down, and accidentally hits a switch to make the capsule start rotating. Asked to engage in "eating experiments," Roy tries to catch floating crackers and is disturbed when squirting a tube of peanut butter sends a large filament of peanut butter moving around him like a snake. The only original aspect of this business comes when Roy, to perform an important errand, begins swimming through space to reach his destination. (Isaac Asimov's "For the Birds" [1980] similarly makes the point that moving through an atmosphere in zero gravity is more like swimming than flying.)

Amidst these antics, though, a genuine crisis is developing, enabling the hapless Roy to briefly function as a genuine hero. He bumps into the rotating reels of computer tape that keep his mission running smoothly, and the tape completely unravels to float all around his capsule. Gifford instructs him to rewind the tape to allow the computer to work again. He botches the assignment, of course, by using crackers and peanut butter to put the tape back on the reels. Worse, he accidentally hits a panel that sets off sparks and disables his radio, so he cannot hear Gifford's instructions. Fortunately, he recognizes it is time to bring the capsule back to Earth and locates and turns a switch prominently labeled "Retro Rocket"; this allows his spacecraft to safely return to Earth and gently float toward a landing at sea, supported by a large parachute. For one more chuckle, the capsule actually lands on top of the aircraft carrier sent to pick him up, though the ever-befuddled Roy still opens the capsule, tosses out his inflatable raft, and begins rowing across the deck before recognizing where he is.

Despite this brief display of minimal competence, it is apparent to everyone as the film rushes to a conclusion that Roy has made his first and only trip into space; granted a one-time dispensation to experience space travel, he remains permanently excluded from the circle of regular space travelers. His consolation prize is that he finally marries Ellie Jackson, though in a final display of cowardice he cannot board the airplane taking them on their honeymoon, leaving Ellie to take the trip by herself. Despite his admirable qualities, then,

Roy is still a man one cannot count on; and such a man can never aspire to face the daunting challenges of space travel.

Overall, while they are just as misleading about the realities of space as melodramatic spacesuit films, it is hard to muster any indignation about humorous spacesuit films, since they label themselves as ridiculous fantasies. While one can imagine that *Star Trek* might have a subliminal impact on the thinking of space program officials, it is impossible to believe that films like *Have Rocket, Will Travel* or *The Road to Hong Kong* could have similar effects. But one can praise these films for inadvertently underlining some significant points about space travel that other films rarely emphasize.

The first is that space travel is a demanding business which requires qualified professionals. The extended training sequences in *Riders to the Stars* and *Gog* convey this message with positive examples of competent personnel being properly prepared for space, while the *Men into Space* episode "Earthbound" presents the negative example of an amateur space traveler whose sojourn might have catastrophic effects. One also recalls the hostility of space veterans to the visit of an untrained journalist in *Space Men* (to be discussed), since they similarly regard such individuals as useless at best and hazardous at worst. While the potentially lethal antics of Abbott and Costello and the Three Stooges in space never inspire real concern, the premise underlying the humor is the same: People must know what they are doing in space, and if they do not, they could kill themselves and their companions.

A logical consequence of this principle is that people incapable of meeting the demands of space travel must be permanently banned from space; and certainly, whatever their unexpected successes might have been, it is always clear that no one will ever allow the likes of Abbott and Costello or the Three Stooges into a spaceship again. In most films, this is not a problem, since the hapless bumblers who accidentally find themselves in space are unhappy, frightened to death, and delighted and grateful to return to Earth. *The Reluctant Astronaut* breaks new ground by portraying an incompetent who sincerely longs to venture into space, and despite his beautiful wife, Roy Fleming seems likely to end up like his father, a man perpetually sad and frustrated about his inability to become a true hero. But the harsh challenges of space virtually demand this new form of segregation: Those who are intelligent, physically fit, and thoroughly trained can travel into space, while those who lack those qualities must remain on Earth.

Interestingly, it seems that after two decades of space travel, NASA itself became aware of the problem, at least as a public relations issue: There were many capable astronauts for the public to admire, but as Americans lost interest in the space program, officials might have seen some value in recruiting some ordinary people as astronauts, suspecting that Americans might find them more appealing. This idea undoubtedly inspired the "Teacher in Space" program, which with great fanfare recruited thousands of teachers to apply to fly into space and, after a lengthy selection process, chose Christa McAuliffe to make the flight. And this Everyman figure in the 1986 crew of the *Challenger* helped to make the mission seem like a potentially popular television series. The tragic end of that flight, though, ended both the "Teacher in Space" program and a parallel project to have a "Journalist in Space."

Of course, no one blamed the *Challenger* explosion on its amateur crew member, who had no duties other than teaching science lessons from space, but it seems NASA did perceive potential problems in having unqualified people on board the space shuttle, since the backup choice for McAuliffe's slot, teacher Barbara Morgan, was only allowed into space, as a member of the 2007 crew of the *Endeavor*, after she resigned from her profession and went through the same training as every other astronaut. The only other unqualified people permitted into space have been a few multi-millionaires who paid vast sums of money to be "tourists in space." However, they had nothing to do and only remained in orbit for a few days. Presumably, the better-designed facilities they visited did not have any switches they could hit accidentally with ruinous results.

There are many science fiction stories that discuss in a celebratory manner how space travel will prove a weeding-out process for humanity, as the best and brightest confidently conquer space while their less qualified counterparts must drift into decadence on a doomed Earth. Since this idea is unpalatable to the general public, it is unsurprising that one rarely if ever finds an explicit version of the argument in films, which by their nature are a mass medium. Still, in the implicit contrast between people like Edward McCauley, and people like Roy Fleming, the same unsettling idea can clearly be deduced.

— 5 —
Space Frights: The Horrific Films

As noted, producers before 1950 were more comfortable with horror films than science fiction films, and after a flurry of interest in spaceships, astronauts, and flying saucers in the early 1950s, their science fiction stories began drifting back toward horror. In space films, common patterns were astronauts encountering monsters in space or on other worlds, bringing monsters back to Earth, or finding themselves transformed into monsters; and, given the lip service still paid to science, space travelers usually wore spacesuits, at least briefly. The latter two scenarios were particularly attractive since they led to films that, after prologues with space travel, took place entirely on Earth, offering a comfortingly familiar environment and reducing costs, since ready-made sets and locations could be used instead of constructing simulations of spacecraft, space, and alien worlds. In such films, space travel was only a marketing ploy to entice filmgoers seeking novelty into watching old stories, thinly disguised with scientific trappings.

Arguably, horrific spacesuit films are more realistic than melodramatic spacesuit films, since genuine aliens are more likely to look monstrous than to look exactly like humans, and since there are legitimate fears that encounters with alien organisms could have harmful effects, both in space and on Earth. Needless to say, the horrors depicted are invariably too outlandish to take seriously, and space monsters usually have predictable motives — like killing people or drinking blood — bearing little relationship to anything real aliens might do upon meeting an unknown species. The true horror of alien life will surely be not that they will want slaughter us, but that, as in *2001: A Space Odyssey*, they will be inexplicable to us.

One category of horrific spacesuit films is tangential to this book's concerns, since the films do not involve human travel into space, but rather alien visitors to Earth, generally with hostile intent. Such films merit attention because, in some cases, the aliens wear spacesuits. Placing aliens in spacesuits reflects a reality that science fiction writers had long realized: Since their planets would undoubtedly be radically different from Earth, requiring different physiologies, aliens would find conditions on Earth inhospitable and hence need spacesuits to survive. And while filmmakers came to expediently ignore this problem and have aliens visit Earth without special protection (like Steven Spielberg's *E.T.: The Extra-Terrestrial* [1982], who would have been much less adorable if garbed in a spacesuit), a few early films interestingly present spacesuited aliens.

One of these, *The Day the Earth Stood Still* (1951), is only briefly horrific: When the alien Klaatu (Michael Rennie) first emerges from his flying saucer in Washington, D.C., he frightens onlookers because his face is concealed by a shiny spacesuit of sorts. His protective gear is superfluous, since we learn that Klaatu is identical to a human and can easily survive on Earth wearing ordinary clothing. Further, his spacesuit seems illogical, since his people long studied Earth before his flight and would have deduced beforehand that the planet would be hospitable. Within the context of the film, one can only attribute Klaatu's spacesuit to an overabundance of caution, a way to protect Klaatu from unexpected hazards in terrestrial conditions until he ascertained that Earth was safe.

However, for the real reason behind Klaatu's spacesuit, one must step outside the context of the film to consider the filmmakers' interests, not the alien's. The spacesuit is needed to make the film's story work: Since Klaatu later pretends to be an Earthman and lives incognito in a boardinghouse, he cannot reveal his face during his initial appearance, and hence had to wear a suit and helmet to conceal his features. And since the helmet makes Klaatu seem mysterious and prompts a trigger-happy soldier to shoot him, the film conveys a relevant message about spacesuits: Among other things, they are forms of disguise, and might make others fear or mistrust the visitors wearing them.[1]

In addition, having a spacesuited alien step out of a flying saucer is more dramatic than having a normal-looking human emerge, a point also illustrated by a later, lesser film, *Teenagers from Outer Space* (1959). Like *The Day the Earth Stood Still*, it begins with a strange spacecraft landing on Earth, though this one lands in a deserted field. We next observe the top of the spacecraft being removed, followed by the emergence of a figure whose head is covered by a space helmet. However, the alien Derek (David Love) immediately removes the helmet to reveal that he looks exactly like a human teenager, and after he gets out, he is followed by similar colleagues who do not bother to wear helmets, indicating that they anticipated a suitable environment all along. The sole reason for the helmet, then, was to enhance the impact of the alien's first appearance. (The rest of the story, about alien efforts to use Earth as grazing grounds for creatures called "Gargons" and Derek's opposition to the plans, requires no attention here.)

While the briefly helmeted Klaatu and Derek turn out to be good, spacesuited aliens in *Earth vs. the Flying Saucers* (1956) are unquestionably evil, though their initial rhetoric sounds benign. Still, their dark, cumbersome garments, with huge opaque helmets entirely concealing their faces, virtually announce their villainous designs. As they periodically emerge from flying saucers to obliterate people with ray guns to persuade the people of Earth to surrender, one of them is strangely gunned down by an ordinary handgun, suggesting that despite their imposing appearance, the suits provide little protection, and this enables scientists to examine the suit. Finding the alien is "light as a feather" and physically weak, scientist Russell Marvin (Hugh Marlowe) concludes, "These suits must serve as an electronic and mechanical outer skin, to take the place of their atrophied flesh and muscle." Thus, it is actually what we now term an exoskeleton, designed to provide support for frail beings. Later, scientists discover that the helmet includes "a language-translating device" and improves vision and hearing in the manner of glasses and hearing aids. Perhaps it is incorrect to refer to these outfits as spacesuits, despite published references, since it seems their occupants must wear them at all times, not merely when they unsuccessfully try to conquer other planets.

Another strange use of a spacesuit — or part of a spacesuit — purely for dramatic effect occurs in the notorious travesty *Robot Monster* (1953). Unable to obtain a suitable and economical costume for "Ro-Man" (George Barrows), his robot invader from the Moon, director

5. *Space Frights*   177

An Intimidating Introduction: The helmeted Klaatu (Michael Rennie), accompanied by the robot Gort (Lock Martin), in *The Day the Earth Stood Still* (1951).

Phil Tucker had the character wear a gorilla suit, and in case that seemed insufficiently alien, he also wore a space helmet. (True, Tucker actually obtained a diving helmet, but it was clearly intended to suggest a space helmet.) His superior Ro-Man on the Moon, played by the same performer, looks exactly the same. Why the robot inhabitants of the Moon resemble gorillas, and why they require space helmets but not spacesuits to survive on Earth, is impossible to explain rationally, as commentators on this much-ridiculed film have long noted. However, the film's story, involving Ro-Man's efforts to kill the eight surviving members of a human race almost entirely exterminated by his death ray, is ultimately explained as the dream of a little boy named Johnny (Gregory Moffett), first observed in the film wearing a toy space helmet with air tubes, so one can argue that a child with space on his mind would naturally dream about aliens wearing space helmets.

In contrast to these unnecessary but dramatic spacesuits, the spacesuit and transparent helmet worn by *The Man from Planet X* (1951) is essential to his survival on Earth, since his home planet, now approaching Earth, has an atmosphere significantly different from our own. His dependence upon his suit enables humans to successfully oppose him, since there is a valve they can conveniently turn to cut off his supply of gas and render him helpless. The irony is that the short, large-headed creature, while somewhat monstrous in appearance, initially seems "friendly," as heroine Enid Elliot (Margaret Field) opines, visiting Earth solely to find some way to save his people, whose world is turning to ice. When first observed struggling with the valve and having breathing problems, he appreciates Enid's assistance in getting it to work and makes what appear to be friendly gestures. Unfortunately, the unscrupulous Dr. Mears (William Schallert), after tormenting the alien to extract scientific secrets, turns the alien against Earth and toward plans to invade our planet at the moment that Planet X, removed from its "natural orbit" by "scientific degravitation," is nearest Earth. The alien is aided by a mysterious ability to assume mental control of Earth people. Logically, aliens capable of moving planets around could also heat up a cooling world, but this shadowy movie, projecting an ambience of 1930s horror more than the brighter aura of 1950s science fiction, is uninterested in scientific plausibility.

Still, even when the alien must be killed to foil his plot, he remains a sympathetic figure, driven to evil by a desperate desire to help his people; and he seems likable largely due to his obvious frailty and vulnerability, his dependence upon his spacesuit. Thus, though spacesuits can make wearers seem menacing, they can also garner sympathy because they convey a certain helplessness in hostile conditions.

This is even more apparent in *Phantom from Space* (1953). After a spacecraft is observed approaching Santa Monica, reports come of a strange person in a sort of diving suit who kills two people and terrifies everyone who observes him. This, it transpires, is an alien who, with a physiology based on silicon, is somehow invisible to human observers (lamely explained by identifying silicon as "glass"), so everyone insists there is no head inside his helmet. This also means that, to avoid capture, the alien can remove his helmet and spacesuit and slip away without being noticed.

Yet this is only a temporary solution, because when scientist Dr. Wyatt (Rudolph Anders) and assistant Barbara Randall (Noreen Nash) examine the abandoned gear, they discover that the helmet contains a "breathing apparatus" providing its wearer with a mixture of gases including "eleven percent methane" and other, unidentified substances. The spacesuit "is conditioned to function above 63,000 feet ... where human blood would boil," "must withstand pressure and counter-pressure," and "must be so supercharged it can function in thin atmosphere." If the alien evolved, as this suggests, in weaker gravity than Earth and a different atmosphere, it should quickly die on Earth without protection; but Wyatt illogically argues that, "like a patient in an iron lung," the alien can temporarily survive for several hours without his spacesuit. As another senseless development, the spacesuit, previously shown to be impervious to knives and flames, spontaneously disintegrates, leaving only the helmet.

When the alien returns, as he must, to get his helmet for its breathing apparatus, he temporarily abducts Barbara but also uses scissors to tap out some sort of code (which he later sends out using a police car's radio). Barbara deduces that, since his helmet is running out of the gas he needs, he is striving to communicate the nature of the substance, hoping humans can provide it. When the alien, startled by a journalist's flash photography, drops the helmet, it also disintegrates, dooming the alien. After he is cornered inside the dome of Griffith Observatory, ultraviolet light reveals the alien is a naked humanoid who falls down and dies before similarly dissipating.

Even more than *The Man from Planet X*, this alien is ultimately sympathetic, since characters acknowledge he "may not be an intentional criminal" and only killed two people because they attacked him first. The scientist further insists they must try to see things from his angle: "He is in an alien world. No doubt we are as frightening to him as he is to us." *Phantom from Space* has interesting ideas, but screenwriters William Raynor and Myles Wilder and director W. Lee Wilder cannot render them interestingly in cinematic terms; as one example, the concept of an alien viewing Earth as "an alien world" might have been dramatized by filming humans from a distorted alien perspective, a device employed by a more skillful director, Jack Arnold, in *It Came from Outer Space* (1953). Still, despite dubious science and other flaws, this unusual film foregrounds its spacesuit and makes it integral to the story, establishing like a genuine spacesuit film that such protective gear is essential for space travelers of all kinds.

While not without occasionally interesting aspects, other films about aliens visiting Earth were not researched for this book, since its primary interest is human ventures into space. Yet most of Earth's visitors from beyond, like those in *Devil Girl from Mars* (1954) and *Stranger from Venus* (1954), apparently do not need or wear spacesuits, even briefly, and their ability to effortlessly survive on Earth is a particular implausibility accompanying the general implausibility of aliens from distant planets locating and landing on Earth. Realistically, one assumes humans will establish themselves in space long before contacting living aliens, justifying this study's focus on stories about the human experience in space.

The Quatermass Experiment (1953) and *The Quatermass Xperiment* (1955)

By 1969, NASA scientists realized that astronauts who visit another world might unknowingly return with alien microorganisms which could be dangerous if unleashed on Earth, so the *Apollo 11* astronauts were quarantined to check for such contaminants. Arguably, this precaution was inspired by the horrific spacesuit films of the 1950s, which repeatedly have space travelers bring back alien menaces. Yet as noted, the threats are so implausible that it is difficult to take the posited warnings seriously.

The first film of this sort was a television miniseries, *The Quatermass Experiment*, soon adapted as a feature film. Only the first two of its six episodes survive, but Nigel Kneale's script appeared in book form and was refilmed as a television movie in 2005. It is interesting that Kneale, though generally hostile toward science and the attitudes of science fiction, demonstrates an awareness of the genre and the tradition he joined in creating a filmed narrative involving space travel.

In the first episode, "Contact Has Been Established" (aired July 18, 1953), a British spaceship with three crewmen, launched from Australia, veers off course. The scientist supervising the project, Professor Bernard Quatermass (Reginald Tate), tells his associate, mathematician Judith Carroon (Isabel Dean) "Something went wrong.... Probably something as simple as valve failure." (Judith is the wife of one of the astronauts.)

Eventually, monitors detect the spaceship returning to Earth, and they separate its passenger component and bring it to a crash-landing in downtown London. As an improbability no doubt dictated by the demands of live television, it lands in the middle of a dwelling, doing absolutely no damage to its surroundings. After Quatermass and others gather around the spaceship, waiting for it to cool off, a knocking sound from inside indicates that someone is alive, so they open its hatch. Astronaut Victor Carroon (Duncan Lamont) staggers out, wearing a spacesuit and space helmet with two transparent panels for his eyes; he appears dazed and cannot speak, but the real puzzle is that the other two astronauts are not in the spaceship, though their spacesuits are there. Adding to the mystery, instruments show that the spaceship's hatch was never opened during the flight.

In the second episode, "Persons Reported Missing" (aired July 25, 1953), Quatermass speaks to a policeman (Neil Wilson) after Carroon is taken away for treatment. Revealing his (and Kneale's) awareness of science fiction, the policeman says, "That suit they wear — it is like they show in the comic magazines after all," reminding him of something he saw that could explain the fate of the missing astronauts: "I once saw a film about ... well, I suppose you'd call this a spaceship. The men opened the door and went out.... They seemed to float."

"That's quite correct," Quatermass replies. "In space, nothing has weight."

"One of them got lost. Could that happen in reality?"

"Yes, it could."

"Oh, by the way, when they went out in the film, they were wearing these ... uh, what do you call them?"

"Pressure suits."

"Yes, to get through that door alive, they'd have to use those, wouldn't they?"

"Yes."

"Then why is this here?" the policeman asks, indicating a spacesuit.

The conversation explains to audiences who may not be familiar with "comic magazines" or science fiction films precisely why the situation is so puzzling: Even if the instruments are wrong and the spaceship's hatch was opened, any departing astronauts would need spacesuits, to protect themselves in space, yet the missing astronauts' spacesuits are lying inside the craft. The passage also suggests Kneale had watched some spacesuit films, in particular *Destination Moon*; for, having studied all space films made up until 1953, I believe it is the only film featuring astronauts stepping out of a spaceship, astronauts floating in space, and an astronaut briefly lost in space. While there may be episodes of a television series with such events, Kneale was probably thinking about *Destination Moon* while writing this dialogue.

More language involving science fiction occurs in subsequent scenes. Speaking to Detective-Sergeant Best (Frank Hawkins), Detective-Inspector Lomax (Ian Colin) asks, "Do you read science fiction, Best?" Lomax asks.

"No, sir."

"Well, we've got to start to catch up on fast"—a statement supporting Gernsback's argument that science fiction prepares people for coming developments, as epitomized in his slogan, "Extravagant fiction today, cold fact tomorrow." Then when Louisa Green (Enid Lindsey), the wife of one missing astronaut, appears, she describes her husband by saying,

"In books, they like to make scientists absent-minded, untidy people," though her husband was nothing like that. In a film of the astronauts taken before launch, shown later in the episode, Carroon comments, "I've got a Union Jack, in case we happen to land on Mars," possibly referring to the astronauts who brought an American flag to the Moon in *Destination Moon*. In the same episode, German astronaut Ludwig Reichenheim (Christopher Rhodes), indicating his spacesuit, jokes, "How can anybody look at work wearing the spare parts of a vacuum cleaner?"— perhaps a jocular jab at the jerry-built special effects in cheap spacesuit films.

Despite these knowing references and comic relief, the second episode focuses on serious business. Reporter James Fullalove (Paul Whitsun-Jones), skeptical about the "spaceship jargon" spouted by Quatermass, describes such language as "Mankind trying to sound certain of himself, Jacko. That's because he knows that just beyond the air begins a new wilderness, pitch dark both day and night, empty and — cold." Just how strange and threatening this realm might be is conveyed when it is discovered, after showing Carroon that pre-launch film to restore his memory, that he now speaks German like Reichenheim. That is the first intimation of the astounding explanation of events expounded in the later, lost episodes — that Carroon's body was invaded by an invisible space being that absorbs tissue from other organisms and came to Earth intent upon invasion. However, to observe how the story might have continued in the 1950s, one must turn to the 1955 film.

Though based upon an earlier miniseries, Hammer's film adaptation, entitled *The Quatermass Xperiment*, can be viewed, serendipitously, as a key transitional film in the company's history, bridging the gap between a brief foray into science fiction (*Spaceways*) and its subsequent commitment to traditional horror fare, since it is literally the story of an astronaut who returns to Earth to become a menacing monster. Its misspelled title refers to the "X" (for adults only) British rating which producers correctly anticipated the film would receive. With an imported American actor, Brian Donlevy, portraying Quatermass (his American accent unexplained), the film also received American release as *The Creeping Unknown*.

Moving more quickly than the miniseries, it begins with the crash of a spaceship in rural Britain, which inspires what seems like a very slow-moving response from policemen and firefighters to an emergency situation. Upon the arrival of Quatermass (who constructed the rocket and launched it 15,000 miles into space with three astronauts on board without proper authorization), he explains their languor by maintaining that, because the ship is hot from the friction of re-entry, it will take several hours before it can be approached. However, upon receiving a radio response from the ship, indicating that someone is alive inside, he decides to expedite entry by having firefighters spray water on the ship as technicians open its hatch. As in the miniseries, Carroon (Richard Wordsworth), wearing a spacesuit and space helmet, immediately emerges, apparently suffering from shock, and utters one whispered word, "Help." In the ship, Quatermass finds two other spacesuits ("pressure suits") with "helmets still attached," but they are empty, and there are no signs of the other astronauts.

Maintaining the miniseries' mixture of science fiction and the police procedural, director Val Guest and co-screenwriter Richard Landau now introduce Kneale's police chief, Inspector Lomax (Jack Warner), since he regards the situation as the basis for a murder investigation, positing that the survivor may have killed the others. The earlier references to science fiction are condensed into a brief comment from Lomax, distancing himself from the story he is involved in: "I don't read science fiction. I'm a plain, simple Bible man." Unlike his television counterpart, he seems reluctant to examine material that might help him understand events that are very much matters of science fiction. The prickly Quatermass insists the case must be studied by scientists, not detectives, since everything about space is unknown: as he later observes, "There's a whole new world out there, a wilderness, uncharted." But he grudgingly agrees to cooperate with the inspector and provides detailed information about the astronauts. This leads the official to an unsettling discovery: Carroon, whose skin is already starting to look odd, now has fingerprints that look entirely alien.

The investigation leads to the film's most interesting scene, the showing of a recently processed film which, unlike the film in the miniseries, was taken during the mission, not before it. While television conversations between space travelers were commonplace in television programs of the early 1950s, this may be the first time a camera was trained upon a pioneering space flight, anticipating the coverage that became a regular feature of American space flights in the 1960s. The film shows the astronauts inside the main chamber while in space, with feet firmly planted on the floor, so it first seems that filmmakers, as in *Spaceways*, neglected to consider that a spacecraft thousands of miles away from Earth would experience zero gravity. But one astronaut then walks up the side of one wall and stands sideways, establishing that there is zero gravity on the ship and the astronauts wear magnetic shoes to remain attached to the floor or wall. This rare hint of the strangeness of space precedes events of greater interest to observers: The temperature in the ship rises; a bright, hazy light fills the spacecraft; and astronauts show signs of great distress.

After watching the film, Quatermass makes an astonishing (and frankly ridiculous) deduction regarding what occurred: "What if there is a form of life in space, not on some planet, just drifting," he muses. "Not life as we know it, with intelligence, yes, but pure energy, with no organic structure, invisible." He then posits, "It entered the rocket. If, even by accident, it could enter one of those structures [the humans on board], what a way to invade the Earth!" Thus, this invisible being from the vacuum of space somehow penetrated the spaceship's hull, reduced two astronauts to puddles of organic jelly (later discovered by investigators), and entered the body of the third astronaut to return to Earth, slaughter some people, and reproduce at a rapid rate to conquer the entire planet. Arguably, this absurd theory does acknowledge that life in the universe may take strange forms, and we later see that adapting to life in the vacuum of space might represent one ultimate goal of the spacesuit film. But here, a creature that achieved the power and freedom to survive in space, inexplicably, throws it away for the chance to resume an organic form and live inside a planet's gravity well.

Subsequent events validate Quatermass's amazing speculations: Carroon escapes from the hospital with the help of his wife Judith (Margia Dean) (here not a mathematician, but merely a housewife). He kills people with his mutated, enormous hand, and, by combining his human structure with other organisms, evolves into an enormous, tentacled creature, its presence betrayed because it leaves a trail like an enormous snail. The film's story becomes yet another saga about efforts to track down and kill a threatening monster, which is discovered in the rafters of an abbey where a television documentary is being filmed, so the monster can be observed at a distance on television monitors. Fearing it is about to reproduce, Quatermass orders all of London's electrical power diverted to destroy the creature, which is reduced to a burning mass of tissue. In the miniseries, the monster's destruction was assisted by an appeal from Quatermass to the lingering human presence within it, but that development was omitted in the film, making the monster completely inhuman and unsympathetic.

Since horror films are usually structured as cautionary tales, concluding with dire warnings about things that man is not meant to know, the predictable ending of *The Quatermass Xperiment* would feature solemn promises to avoid sending astronauts into space until some means of preventing future invasions by invisible space monsters can be devised. Instead, Quatermass forcefully strides away from the scene, ignoring comments from others until tersely announcing, "Gonna start again." And the film's final image is another rocketship blasting into space, with no indication that anything has been done to prevent a repetition of this film's events. Quatermass's stubborn determination to carry on with scientific progress, despite its dangers, is one aspect of the film that reflects the spirit of science fiction, not horror.

Quatermass II (1955)

After the success of *The Quatermass Experiment*, Kneale was invited to write a follow-up miniseries called *Quatermass II*. This was basically another horror story with a brief space flight, this time at the story's end, not its start. The other difference is that while *The Quatermass Experiment* features a monster, *Quatermass II* involves an equally common but subtler form of horror: humans with minds controlled by aliens.

In the first episode, "The Bolts" (aired October 22, 1955), Quatermass (now played by John Robinson, since Reginald Tate died shortly before the start of the miniseries) abandons his efforts to conquer space, since one of his two experimental nuclear rockets exploded during a ground test, killing several people. He becomes intrigued by the mystery of a top-secret government plant in England, purportedly designed to produce synthetic food; but noticing that the facility resembles his planned moon base, he determines it is actually a base for invading aliens. These beings, who cannot endure oxygen, are sent to Earth in embryonic form inside small meteorite-like objects launched from a nearby asteroid; the facility nurtures them in Earth's inhospitable environment until they can grow and eventually conquer the planet. The aliens can also take control of people's minds, a condition signaled by strange markings on their heads. One early victim is John Dillon (John Stone), the fiancé of Quatermass's daughter Paula (Monica Grey).

Though his investigatory efforts are repeatedly blocked by high government officials, evidently being manipulated by aliens, Quatermass ultimately convinces the plant's workers of its true, sinister purpose and puts it out of operation; but it is only one of several alien bases all over Earth. The only way to stop the invasion, then, is to destroy the recently discovered asteroid where the alien-bearing meteorites come from. To do so, Quatermass resolves to fly his other rocket into space, despite the risks. Alien sympathizers led by Dillon seize control of the launching area, but Quatermass appeals to the remaining humanity in Dillon and persuades him to temporarily call off the guards, so he and his colleague Dr. Leo Pugh (Hugh Griffith) can take off. At this point, during the sixth episode, "The Destroyers" (aired November 26, 1955), the miniseries suddenly becomes a spacesuit film.

Quatermass and Pugh are older than typical space travelers, and the doctor who examines them before takeoff acknowledges that, under ordinary circumstances, he would never approve them for space flight. But Quatermass insists upon flying his own creation, and Pugh must accompany him to perform essential last-minute calculations. Adding to the health risks, they must wear bulky spacesuits during the flight, which also concerns the doctor, who says, "Wearing these [spacesuits] the whole flight is going to increase the strain. Is it essential?"

"Yes," Quatermass replies. "We may be able to dispense with our helmets at certain periods, but more than that would be dangerous.... The rocket may suffer damage after takeoff."

"You mean," Paula asks, "retaliation?"

She guesses Quatermass's fear, that aliens will attack his spaceship to prevent him from destroying their base. But the aliens have another plan to thwart Quatermass: They secretly control Pugh's mind and will direct him to stop Quatermass at the crucial moment. Not recognizing this danger, Quatermass makes sure he and Pugh have their spacesuits on before taking off, and there is a bit of comedy when Quatermass attempts to embrace his daughter before he leaves: "Damn these things," he mutters, recognizing that spacesuits constitute a barrier to human intimacy (something discovered by Mr. and Mrs. Hale in an episode of *Men into Space*, "First Woman on the Moon").

Once in space, the miniseries both recognizes and ignores weightlessness in space. Quatermass advises Pugh to keep his feet on the floor so the spacesuits' "magnetic soles" can prevent them from floating; this is reasonable enough, but filmmakers usually illustrate weightlessness by having something like a pencil or notebook float around (though this effect may have been difficult during a live broadcast). By means of labored movements, the elderly astronauts also suggest they are stressed by the weight of their spacesuits, but even the heaviest of spacesuits would not be burdensome in zero gravity. For another frisson of drama, the spaceship is briefly imperiled by "a swarm of meteorites," but no damage is done.

Despite these lapses, this episode offers two authentic touches, indicating that writer Kneale knew his subject well. Quatermass and Pugh observe a sky full of stars, none of them twinkling, and Quatermass notes that there is "no atmosphere to deceive us — we're seeing them as they really are." Then, when Quatermass lands on the asteroid, Pugh rushes out of the spaceship and attempts to kill the pursuing Quatermass by firing a gun at him. However, since there is virtually no gravity on this small asteroid, the recoil from the gun instead sends Pugh hurtling outward into the void of space, slowing receding against a backdrop of black sky and scattered stars. This is both a rare acknowledgment that conventional guns would be problematic weapons in space, and a haunting image of the immensity and the dangers of space. The scene is even more effective because of the way it is filmed. Other films depicting astronauts lost in space and drifting toward their doom, like the *Men into Space* episode "Moon Probe" and *2001: A Space Odyssey*, tend to show astronauts from a side view, moving across the screen; but we see Pugh from the perspective of Quatermass, standing at his point of departure, so Pugh looks smaller and smaller as he moves further and further away and finally vanishes. The sequence makes space seem truly alien and is far more disturbing than the miniseries' humans with marks on their faces turned into evil automatons, or tiny, pulsating creatures representing immature monsters.

With Pugh out of the way, Quatermass detaches the ship's nuclear engine and takes off in its passenger section just before a nuclear explosion destroys the asteroid. One could argue that this miniseries, not *La Morte Viene dallo Spazio* or the "Asteroid" episode of *Men into Space*, first describes an effort to destroy a dangerous asteroid as it approaches Earth. However, Quatermass is not motivated by the usual concern, that the asteroid would smash into Earth and cause tremendous damage; rather, he seeks to defeat aliens using the asteroid as a base for an invasion — not something policymakers need worry about.

Like *The Quatermass Experiment*, this miniseries became a film, also called *Quatermass II* (1957), retitled *Enemy from Space* for American release; however, the film's action is totally

Earthbound, as Quatermass destroys the asteroid with an unmanned rocket. This may reflect budgetary concerns, or a need to shorten the miniseries' three-hour story to become an 85-minute movie. But it also makes *Quatermass II* a more conventional horror film, with alien-controlled humans joined by an enormous creature that emerges from the plant's dome. Such implausible threats, it seems, were deemed more entertaining than actual space dangers.

King Dinosaur (1955)

Monsters in horror films generally take two forms: humans wearing costumes to look grotesque, and enlarged animals presented by means of special effects. Of the latter, dinosaurs were long Hollywood's favorite oversized menace, so it was inevitable that space explorers of the 1950s would encounter a planet filled with dinosaurs — the story of *King Dinosaur*. Unfortunately, instead of employing the carefully rendered stop-motion animation of special effects artists Willis O'Brien or Ray Harryhausen, this film, like other Bert I. Gordon productions, relies on enlarged images of ordinary lizards spliced into footage of human actors. Here, while zoologist Ralph Martin (Bill Bryant) claims one alien dinosaur is like a Tyrannosaurus rex, the "king dinosaur" (justifying the film's title), anyone can see this long slender lizard, which moves close to the ground on four legs, bears no resemblance to that creature.

Unsurprisingly, the scientific background of Gordon's adventure is less than persuasive. The first twenty minutes of the film, using nothing but stock footage and narration, explain that a new planet named Nova, which seems much like Earth, has wandered into the Solar System, so scientists hastily prepare a spaceship to travel there, incongruously testing jet engines that would hardly be useful for space travel. Four scientists will be its crew: Martin, geologist Patricia Bennett (Wanda Curtis), physician Richard Gordon (Douglas Henderson), and chemist Nora Pierce (Patti Gallagher). As another indication of a low budget, we observe the rocketship taking off, flying through space, and landing on Nova, but never see its interior, a set that would be expensive to construct, so there are no scenes of astronauts strapped into padded couches and enduring the painful pressure of acceleration during liftoff.

Since astronomical observations confirm that Nova is Earthlike, one might imagine that astronauts would not bother with spacesuits, but producers of early films about space travel often felt obliged to include them, as a sop to scientific realism; and after several years of space films, spacesuits could now be rented or purchased for reasonable fees. Yet clearly the ever-stingy Gordon only obtained two of them, since when the spaceship lands, only two astronauts, Martin and Bennett, venture outside wearing bulky spacesuits with large transparent helmets and, incongruously, holding hands. (During the flight, the four scientists became two romantically involved couples.) They plan to conduct tests to "see if it's safe to remove our suits," and after an unusually thorough series of operations (again involving stock footage), they find the air is breathable (though with a higher oxygen content than Earth) and thankfully say, "Let's get out of our suits." The other two astronauts then emerge in normal clothing.

Exploring this verdant planet, they mostly find small and benign equivalents to Earth animals, though Gordon is attacked and injured by a crocodile and the party is menaced by a giant snake. Bennett is curious about a nearby island covered with jungle, so she and Martin row an inflatable raft to investigate while Pierce stays behind with her wounded boyfriend. Discounting advice from experts on Earth that they should never separate, Bennett sardonically says, "They all read too much science fiction," so they "probably thought we'd meet some kind of super-race up here or something." There are similar comments in *World Without End* and *The Quatermass Xperiment*; it is interesting that such reflexive, metaliterary references to science fiction are creeping into spacesuit films only a few years after the genre became popular. In that spirit, the problem with the experts' advice is they imagined they were sending astronauts into a melodramatic spacesuit film, where a super-race would be standard, and did not prepare them for the different experience of a horrific spacesuit film.

When they reach the island, the film is painful to watch, since its "dinosaurs" are so obviously enlarged lizards. There are also glimpses of a mammoth and giant turtle. When the "king dinosaur" traps Martin and Bennett in a cave, their distress flare brings Gordon and Pierce, who oddly do not rescue them, but simply watch as the two rescue themselves when the menacing monster is distracted by another dinosaur. Then, instead of merely fleeing from the island to return to their spaceship, and to Earth, Gordon decides to blow up the island with an "atom bomb" they happen to have. (In early scenes, this was explained as a portable power unit, powered by nuclear energy, which might become a bomb if improperly supervised; thus, its presence is slightly more plausible than other commentators suggest.)

Watching the explosion, Gordon announces that they've "brought civilization to planet Nova." When writers had Kim Hamilton of *Satellite in the Sky* complain that the first thing astronauts will now do upon reaching other planets "is explode an atomic bomb," they possibly were recalling this film. This ending may represent Gordon's effort to dignify his silly story with a bitter commentary on humanity's bellicose impulses; but it seems equally possible that the thrifty producer thought that stock footage of an atomic bomb explosion would provide his film with a dramatic conclusion.

20 Million Miles to Earth (1957)

20 Million Miles to Earth seems a straightforward variant on the plot of *King Dinosaur*: Instead of space travelers encountering dinosaurs on another planet, they bring a dinosaur to Earth. Since transporting an adult dinosaur would be a logistical problem, however, the astronauts instead carry an egg which promptly grows into a dinosaur, making this another film, like *The Quatermass Xperiment*, warning of dangerous contaminants from space. Innovatively, the film's monster, the Venusian Ymir, actually only resembles a dinosaur, since it is an imaginative mixture of human-like and lizard-like characteristics crafted by Ray Harryhausen, the era's master of stop-motion animation. In addition, since the story focuses on the Ymir's rampages on Earth and authorities' efforts to capture or kill the creature, the film pays little attention to astronauts, since they are solely a device to account for the presence of the menace.

Indeed, no space travel is depicted in the film, since it begins, like *The Quatermass Xperiment*, with a spaceship crashing into Earth — here, in the waters off the coast of Sicily — and there are no later scenes of astronauts in flight. Quickly, fishermen venture through a hole into the spacecraft, where they discover and retrieve one surviving astronaut, who wears what appears to be a space helmet with its visor up (though it might also simply be a motorcycle helmet). The ship's vital cargo, a metal cylinder containing the egg, washes ashore to be retrieved by a fisherman's son, Pepe (Bart Braverman), who sells it to local scientist Dr. Leonardo (Frank Puglia). He is excited when the egg hatches to reveal a tiny creature, which begins growing at a prodigious rate while he drives away with it and his daughter Marisa (Joan Taylor). The creature soon escapes.

In the meantime, officials speak to the astronaut and are anxious to track down the Ymir and keep it alive. Oddly, they do not wish to examine the creature to expand our knowledge of life on other worlds but have more practical motives. While on Venus, the astronauts contracted a deadly disease from the Venusian atmosphere, though they were protected by what scientists thought was "foolproof respiratory equipment"— presumably taking the form of spacesuits. Now, they must study the Ymir to determine how it stays alive in the Venusian air because Venus contains valuable minerals that Earth people need to mine, so they require protection. This elaborate explanation seemingly serves solely to generate time-consuming conflicts between the Italian police, who want to kill the Ymir, and the Americans, who want to keep it alive. To summarize the rest of the story, scientists use electricity to capture the Ymir, but the ever-growing creature escapes during a power failure and travels to Rome, where it fights an elephant in the Coliseum before being defeated by heavy-duty weaponry.

It! The Terror from Beyond Space (1958)

The novelty in *It! The Terror from Beyond Space* is that the monster brought back by astronauts never reaches Earth, but is instead confronted and defeated during the return flight, making the film an obvious precursor of Ridley Scott's *Alien* (1979). Since the menace, purportedly the decadent descendant of a once-advanced Martian race, is visibly a man in a rubber suit (Ray Corrigan), there is little to say about the story's scientific plausibility. Still, screenwriter Jerome Bixby, a science fiction writer who moved to California to pursue a Hollywood career, did provide the film with some touches of authenticity.

The backstory presented at the beginning is unusual: A spaceship crash-landed on Mars, and when a second ship arrived several months later to retrieve the survivors, they found only one man still alive, Carruthers (Marshall Thompson). The rescue mission interestingly includes two women, and while Ann Anderson (Shawn Smith) is a typically beautiful scientist, who later says she threw herself into science after a failed marriage, the other woman, Mary Royce (Ann Doran), is more realistically an older female physician. (These qualified women nonetheless know their place, as they demonstrate by serving coffee and food to male colleagues.) Commander Van Heusen (Kim Spalding) resolves to return Carruthers to Earth to be court-martialed for the murder of nine crewmates, believing Carruthers killed them to stay alive longer using the spaceship's limited supplies. They ridicule Carruthers' story that his space-mates were slaughtered by a mysterious monster, particularly since one crewman's skull has a bullet hole in it. (Carruthers theorizes that, when crewmen wildly shot at a creature dimly observed in a sandstorm, a bullet accidentally hit someone.) But viewers know the monster is real, since they see it slipping on board the spaceship before it blasts off.

Soon, the creature attacks three crewmen and kills one of them, draining his body of all oxygen and fluids, validating Carruthers' account of events. The ensuing efforts to kill the monster, by firing guns and exploding grenades, are scientifically ludicrous: no space travelers would risk using such weapons on a spaceship because they could penetrate the hull and expose passengers to the deadly vacuum of space. But miraculously, no damage occurs. To further add to the aura of unreality, the spaceship is amazingly spacious, crew members smoke cigarettes and set up gas grenades with no concerns about the air supply, and there is no zero gravity because, we are told, the ship has "artificial gravity." Another of the self-referential remarks becoming endemic in these films reveals that crew members are well aware of what sort of film they are in: One character jokes that they brought gas grenades just in case they "ran into any dinosaurs on Mars" — a possible homage to the film's undistinguished predecessor, *King Dinosaur*.

Gradually, crew members retreat upward through the spaceship, chamber by chamber, constantly fearing the creature will break through another sealed door and move higher. In the final moments, they are cornered in the uppermost chamber. But one crewman faces another, more understated menace: After encountering the monster, Van Heusen is afflicted by "alien bacteria" that attack his bone marrow, causing a leukemia-like condition that might prove fatal. Of course, such a disease, not a homicidal humanoid, is a peril astronauts on other worlds might actually confront, but it is only a subplot here, perhaps devised to remove Van Heusen from the scene so his former girlfriend, Anderson, can romantically connect with Carruthers.

To kill the monster, Carruthers and crewman Calder (Paul Langton) plan to go outside the spaceship, travel down to an airlock to sneak inside a chamber underneath the monster, and electrocute it with a surprise attack from below. This requires them to don spacesuits. When they emerge from their spaceship, they also step into another film genre, as a pseudo-spacesuit film briefly becomes a genuine spacesuit film.

When the men emerge from the airlock, they move slowly and awkwardly, establishing the rhythm of the spacesuit film. Apparently wearing magnetic shoes, they come to a standing position on the hull, standing sideways from the perspective of the camera and communicating there is no "up" or "down" in space. Then they carefully walk down the side of the spaceship to the lower airlock, against a background of black sky and accompanied by appropriately eerie music. It is surprisingly a sequence that would fit nicely into films like *Destination Moon* and *Conquest of Space*. The contrast between this scene, and those that precede and follow it, is nicely conveyed by two illuminated signs observed when they enter the lower airlock: As they close the outer door, the word "VACUUM" lights up, but when sufficient air fills the airlock, that light goes off and another one lights up, "NORMAL." And sure enough, after this stunning reminder of the unique nature of space, the story now gets back to normal (though astronauts keep their spacesuits on), with another effort to kill an implausible monster, this time by attaching cables to a ladder to provide enough electricity to kill thirty people — though the creature survives its journey down the ladder. Calder breaks both his leg and his faceplate struggling with the monster and so must remain, but he keeps the menace at bay with an acetylene torch while Carruthers re-enters the airlock and returns to his crewmates.

When the monster enters the room containing the spaceship's "atomic reactor," a delirious Van Heusen again attempts to kill the creature by opening the reactor and exposing it to intense radioactivity, a step vainly opposed by the women tending to the sick man because they correctly fear it might endanger Calder and another crewman who went down to rescue him. But the monster easily survives the intense radiation. Then, when Carruthers notices that the monster is reducing the ship's oxygen supply, evidently because its large lungs require a great deal of oxygen, he finally figures out how to kill the creature: They will let all air out of the spaceship (also the way *Alien*'s Ripley kills her alien). Recognizing this could kill all humans as well, Carruthers tells everyone to "get the spacesuits on quick."

Only when crew members are properly protected does Carruthers push a button to open an airlock, just as the monster enters the ship's highest chamber where the crew is now trapped.

There follows the film's other authentic moment, for in contrast to the absurdly slow leaks previously noted, Bixby's screenplay depicts precisely what would happen if there was an opening in a spaceship hull: All the air quickly rushes out, papers and loose objects flutter about the chamber, and crew members must hold railings to avoid being sucked out into space. With no air to breathe, the monster finally dies, and the crew can safely return to Earth, with Carruthers no longer suspected of murder. But this "terror from beyond space" has so spooked authorities that an official speaking to reporters in the final scene opines that humans, as they continue their space travels, may need to avoid Mars entirely because of its homicidal inhabitants. He ends his comments with an ominous pronouncement: "Another name for Mars is Death." This seems overly cautious, perhaps even cowardly, in contrast with the brash determination of Quatermass to carry on with space initiatives despite the dangers. One also imagines that, instead of staying away from Mars, scientists would wish to study this dangerous but intelligent remnant of a vanished Martian civilization. But a resolve to avoid seeking knowledge which might prove menacing, of course, is a traditional conclusion in a horror film.

First Man into Space (1959)

To succinctly describe *First Man into Space*, one might say "It's *Riders to the Stars* meets *The Quatermass Xperiment!*" For much of its length, to an extent that is unusual in pseudo-spacesuit films, the film offers a reasonably realistic picture of how a near-future space program might proceed cautiously into space with suborbital flights. Then, the film plunges into scientific idiocy, devolving into a story about efforts to kill an astronaut who was transformed into a monster. Still, before matters get out of control, *First Man into Space* has some intriguing intimations about humanity's future in space.

The opening sequence depicts the flight of experimental rocketship Y-12, launched by dropping it from a high-altitude aircraft and igniting its rocket engines to ascend, in this case, to a height of 300,000 feet, or about 57 miles, roughly half the altitude reached by Alan Shepard during his first suborbital flight. Like *Riders to the Stars*, and perhaps even more so, the film anticipates how actual space flights would be closely monitored, even controlled, from Earth: Pilot Dan Prescott (Bill Edwards), who wears a spacesuit and space helmet, remains in constant radio contact with his older brother on the ground, Charles Prescott (Marshall Thompson), while other individuals watch dials and indicators, including an African American man, a rare element of diversity in cinematic space flights of the era. Even the pilot's heartbeat and pulse are monitored, to ensure he is always all right. There is a bit of silliness, though, when Dan first passes through the "heat barrier," then the "controllability barrier" that, naturally enough, makes the craft difficult to control.

We then observe something that is unusual in spacesuit films, as Dan smiles broadly while his flight continues upward. Although women have expressed how enjoyable space travel might be, one might momentarily believe this pilot will be the first male in space who willingly acknowledges the sheer joy of the experience. However, his smile is supposed to be interpreted as a sign he is becoming mentally unstable due to weightlessness. As his medical mentor, Dr. Paul von Essen (Carl Jaffe) notes, "With release of pressures, judgment may be unsound for some seconds." To illustrate the problem, Dan briefly disobeys orders

First Monster into Space: Astronaut Dan Prescott (Bill Edwards) seems poised for the momentous maneuver that will make him the title character in *First Man into Space* (1959) ... and later, a murderous monster.

and flies higher than was planned, taking his rocketship out of its "preset orbit" and causing his craft to spin wildly, as shown with the film's better-than-average model. Interestingly, we also observe the rotation from the pilot's perspective, as the Earth below and space above are alternately in view.

In a state of panic, he reports he cannot reach the controls of the rocketship's stabilizers and cries out, "Tell me what to do." Von Essen issues several orders which calm him down and enable him to grab the proper handle, stop the spinning, and guide the ship to a safe landing. Recalling that disobedient astronauts in America's actual space program were immediately and permanently grounded, one might expect the same fate for Dan, but von Essen insists, "We do not yet understand the physiological conditions a man may have to endure at such heights" and calls his rebelliousness a physiological condition clouding his judgment: "For a few vital seconds, he was not himself." Previous spacesuit films suggest that people might go crazy in space due to its overwhelming strangeness, many dangers, or confined quarters; this film uniquely proposes that weightlessness itself might temporarily madden astronauts. Since he is deemed not responsible for his rash actions, Dan is assigned to the next flight, Y-13, which will go even higher into near space.

However, the way Dan acts upon returning to Earth indicates that, despite von Essen's theory, the real issue here is his brash personality. Those who find him say that he seemed "kind of high," and in an ironic anticipation of his eventual fate, one man says, "He looked like a man from Mars in that getup." (The next time he returns home, as will be discussed, he will actually look like an alien.) Instead of lingering to report on his flight, Dan rushes off for a romantic interlude with girlfriend Tia Francesca (Marla Landi), von Essen's assistant. When she complains about the risks he is taking with these flights, he says he is doing the best thing for both of them: "Who's gonna forget the first man in space? They don't forget Lindbergh, or the Wright brothers." Dan is driven, in other words, not by any patriotic duty or interest in advancing science, but purely by a desire for personal glory.

Dan's personality, and whether it is suitable for space travel, becomes a recurring issue in the film. Older brother Charles, the film's ostensible hero, is very responsible and always follows the rules—but, as Dan tauntingly points out, he is not a good pilot. His brother, in contrast, is an excellent pilot but seems unable to conform and always tries to excel. As Charles later recalls, "He was always climbing the highest tree, or swimming further than anyone else," and to explain his misgivings about Dan piloting the Y-13, he says, "I just don't think it's in his nature to stay inside any organized pattern."

But von Essen answers his objection: "It's not an unnatural characteristic to find in a man who risks his life for a new achievement." And he has a point: On Earth, many ventures into the unknown were undertaken by men who were willful and rebellious—genuine free spirits, or men like Lindbergh and the Wright brothers, one might say. But Charles also has a point, as conveyed by his immediate response: "Maybe so. But on a project such as this, I'd prefer to have someone more reliable." The key phrase, "a project such as this," references the attempted conquest of space, which represents an unprecedented human endeavor demanding different sorts of behavior. In space, successful adventurers must always follow the rules, and must be careful and cautious in everything they do, or they are doomed. In other words, they must be like Charles, or his soulmate Edward McCauley, always depicted as obsessively concerned with safety above all else. Such people may not be the traditional sorts of heroes favored by fiction and popular acclaim, like Dan, but they are the heroes that the special demands of space travel require. Thus, in true spacesuit films, we regularly observe dull but thoroughly "reliable" heroes like Charles Cargraves, Richard Stanton, McCauley, and Dave Bowman and Frank Poole; and the actual space program also preferred such men and weeded out colorful rebels. This film vindicates a preference for such stoic heroes, as Dan's later disobedience leads to tragedy, and the film's romantic interest, Francesca, deals with his apparent death by falling in love with brother Charles, underlining his status as the film's true hero.

Charles and von Essen resolve their dispute when von Essen agrees to provide Dan with the best psychological assistance to properly prepare him for the next flight; but he will remain unreliable and irresponsible. This time, he is scheduled to reach a height of 600,000 feet, or 114 miles, about the altitude attained by Shepard; this would, more so than the last flight, apparently qualify him as a genuine space traveler. But in this film, that is not quite high enough to represent space, so Dan refuses to reverse course, turns on the "Emergency Boost" for extra power, and announces to monitors, "I'm going straight up. First man into space!" He gets about 250 miles away from Earth, and possibly even further, before the predictable disaster strikes: He cannot turn his spaceship around, he is out of range of ground observers so they cannot control the ship, and he is buffeted by a strange cloud of meteorite dust. In desperation, he jettisons the passenger portion of his spaceship to return to Earth; monitors lose track of him, and when his craft is later located on the ground, arriving officials see that its canopy is shattered, meaning Dan must have died in space.

Up until this point, *First Man into Space* qualifies as a realistic spacesuit film and might have continued in the same spirit by having Charles make the next flight and, in doing everything by the book, prove himself more suitable for space travel than Dan. Yet by conventional standards, this would be a dull conclusion, so filmmakers instead introduce a murderous monster. Specifically, we soon learn that Dan actually survived the landing but was somehow transformed into a hideous creature that repeatedly attacks and kills people in a strange quest for human blood. (He also invades a blood bank.)

To explain this turn of events, characters offer several scattered ideas which, when assembled by alert viewers, seem wildly illogical. First, to account for Dan's new craving for blood, von Essen says the cause might be "cosmic rays we do not yet know or understand." Thus, far away from the protection of Earth's atmosphere, Dan may have been bathed in radiation that drained his blood and inspired a compulsion to seek out blood. This radiation also, it seems, had the effect of making Dan naturally suited for life at high altitudes, so when on the surface of Earth, he has difficulty breathing and cannot think clearly, until placed in a special chamber that duplicates conditions at high altitudes. Why he then immediately dies inside the chamber is something no one even attempts to explain.

But how did Dan survive exposure to the vacuum of space? Charles develops a theory: "Assume that there is life in outer space. It would have to create a protective coating in order to survive those destructive elements up there."

"You mean," von Essen replies, "like the primeval creatures that crawled out of the sea and grew skin to protect themselves against the sun?"

As it happens, some science fiction stories, like A.E. van Vogt's *The Silkie* (1969), explore the idea that organic creatures, by developing natural protection, might live in the vacuum of space without spacesuits; thus, these speculations are not entirely groundless. But it is further posited this sort of protective coating might, somehow, spontaneously form around someone or something in space. So, when struck by the meteorite dust, both Dan and his spaceship were covered with this coating, which enabled him to stay alive until he reached the ground. The added advantage of the coating, from the filmmakers' perspective, is that it makes Dan look horribly ugly, like a proper monster, and impervious to bullets, so he survives the inevitable gunfire of police officers.

Since explaining all these things at once would make for a long, slow-moving scene, and expose how senseless it all is, filmmakers structure this part of their film as a series of mysterious murders interspersed with scenes in the laboratory where Charles, von Essen, and/or Francesca discuss the latest discoveries. There is an attempt at poignancy in the final scene, since the chamber restores Dan's rationality and ability to speak, so he can confirm the basic accuracy of everyone's theories and acknowledge that hubris caused all his problems: "I just had to be the first man into space." But in the spirit of science fiction, everybody remains committed to carrying on with space travel: as Charles tells Francesca, "We're conquering a new world. The dangers have to be faced. Someone has to start." And future astronauts will be assisted by knowledge gained from Dan's tragic experience: "With a coating of this stuff, Y-14 will be able to go through that meteorite dust straight up. It will be able to go on forever." Thus, Dan did not die in vain.

Since the first part of the film is worthwhile, one might describe *First Man into Space* as a victim of its time. Five years earlier, producers might have had the courage to steer clear of absurdities and provide an honest, realistic look at the probable dangers of space and stimulating debate about the sorts of men that should be chosen for space flights. But by 1959, every film about space travel seemed to feature a colorful monster, and filmmakers may have felt pressured to contort their story to include a monster of their own. Increasingly, and unfortunately, the distinction to draw in space films will not involve distinguishing pseudo-spacesuit films from genuine spacesuit films, but distinguishing pseudo-spacesuit films that are entirely nonsensical from pseudo-spacesuit films that are serious for a while before surrendering to nonsense.

The Angry Red Planet (1959)

The Angry Red Planet was the Danish-born Ib Melchior's first venture into feature film science fiction, and while the story concocted by partner Sidney Pink mostly mixes familiar tropes — gigantic monsters resembling terrestrial creatures and grouchy aliens irked by humanity's childish violence — Melchior clearly strived, in his screenplay and direction, to make the film something special. The results are at least colorful and visually striking.

The film begins at the story's conclusion: Humanity's first spaceship to Mars, long out of contact with Earth, reappears near Earth. After hearing nothing from its occupants, authorities use automatic controls to bring it to a landing. They find only two of its four crew members: Thomas O'Bannion (Gerald Mohr), unconscious and infected with a mysterious disease, and Iris Ryan (Naura Hayden), alert but suffering from shock-induced amnesia. The ship's computer records have been mysteriously erased. Ryan is asked to tell her story from the beginning, and the film returns to the time the ship left Earth.

At first, the astronauts — O'Bannion, Ryan, older scientist Theodore Gettell (Les Tremayne), and the inevitable, Brooklyn-born comic relief, Sam Jacobs (Jack Kruschen) — find the flight uneventful, "not much different from the dry run" on Earth and likely to settle into a "boring routine." There is tension when a "radioactive meteor" appears, but it passes without incident. In subsequent scenes on board the typically spacious spacecraft, O'Bannion expresses a romantic interest in Ryan, whose responses are subdued but promising, and some comments reflect common themes in spacesuit films. Resenting the monitors on Earth, constantly checking on their progress, Jacobs describes them as a "mother hen watching over her four little chicks," and Ryan praises the awesome glory of space by saying it "makes Broadway look like a dark alley." Another glimpse outside inspires Jacobs to remark, "Here we are, between two dots. We could miss either one of them," acknowledging the immensity of space. Ryan offers the first intimation of the overwhelming fear that will dominate their thoughts when she observes (oddly, as she admits, since she is a scientist), "I wonder if some things aren't better left unknown."

Glimpses of their daily lives show Ryan working at a typewriter and a microscope, Jacobs using an electric razor to shave, and Ryan surreptitiously dabbing perfume behind her ear — a womanly gesture recalling the hair-brushing navigator in *Cat-Women of the Moon*. Finally, in an amusing reference to science fiction, Jacobs reads an actual science fiction magazine of the era —*Fantastic*— though he is finishing a story closer in spirit to science fiction comics than science fiction magazines, since it features a five-armed alien menacingly approaching an Earth woman.

After a realistically lengthy journey (forty-seven days), the spaceship lands on Mars. While Jacobs offers his obligatory joke — "Should we go out and claim the planet in the name of Brooklyn?"— Ryan and Gettell get down to business by conducting an unusually thorough check of conditions on Mars, including its "microbe count," "radiation," "atmospheric pressure," and "temperature." Looking outside, they see that nothing moves, as if "everything seems to

Seeing Red: In *The Angry Red Planet* (1960), the spacesuits worn by astronauts Thomas O'Bannion (Gerald Mohr), Iris Ryan (Naura Hayden), Theodore Gettell (Les Tremayne), and Sam Jacobs (Jack Kruschen) look realistic enough, but the fauna and flora they will soon encounter on the Martian surface do not.

be waiting." Despite this inexplicable sense of foreboding, crew members calmly prepare to venture outside, putting on spacesuits — though O'Bannion remarks that the garments are not flattering on a woman — and picking up handguns. It is particularly incongruous that Gettell keeps puffing on his pipe, the era's symbol of the scientist. The excitement comes when Ryan looks out the window and screams — which also brings her story to a temporary end and jolts us back to Earth, as Ryan cannot remember exactly what she saw. Only after drugs are administered can she describe what terrified her — a creature with a "huge distorted face with bulging eyes" — though her crewmates dismiss this report as a product of an overactive imagination.

The astronauts step onto the surface of Mars; its strange environment is portrayed by tinting the film red and overexposing images, giving the scenes an unearthly feel. These camera tricks also enable Melchior to unobtrusively insert evocative drawings into his tinted footage, enhancing the outré atmosphere — though the eye can easily distinguish between actual filmed objects and artwork. Entering a "jungle" of vegetation, Jacobs brings a weapon resembling a bazooka, a "freeze gun," and O'Bannion instructs everyone to "check your oxygen gauge," emphasizing another danger of Mars. As Ryan studies Martian plants, which have "no chlorophyll" and a "nervous system," she anticipates the menace she soon confronts — a huge carnivorous plant wrapping tentacles around her. O'Bannion cuts off the tentacles and Jacobs blasts the creature with his freeze gun.

On the astronauts' second day of exploring, they encounter an enormous, spider-like creature with a bat's face. Though the freeze gun cannot halt its progress, Jacobs uses the gun to blind the creature, enabling them to escape. Now ready to leave Mars ahead of schedule, they find they cannot lift their spaceship, which is held by some tremendous gravitational force, confirming that an inimical intelligence lurks somewhere on Mars.

With nothing else to do, the space travelers use an inflatable boat — a remarkable item to bring to Mars — and cross a Martian sea, where they see a towering city in the distance and, inevitably, see a third monster rising from the sea. This gigantic unicellular organism with one eye chases toward the astronauts, devouring Jacobs and taking an unusually long time to digest him. The others retreat to the safety of their spaceship; during these events, we also glimpse an intelligent Martian observing events. Inside the spaceship, the survivors are temporarily protected, but the creature entirely surrounds the vehicle and seems likely to break through soon.

To escape its deadly grip, O'Bannion sends a strong electrical shock through the hull. While this makes the giant amoeba withdraw, it also causes Gettell to have a heart attack (at least, he grips his chest to suggest a heart attack). With the spaceship now free of the force field, O'Bannion prepares to lift off, just as we hear a Martian voice beginning a message. The voyage home is grim: Gettell dies during the flight, and O'Bannion, having discovered that a piece of the creature attached itself to his body and infected him, falls unconscious, his body covered with green slime.

This brings us back to the framing story. A reinvigorated Ryan cures O'Bannion of his mysterious ailment. When Ryan, now looking glamorous, greets O'Bannion at his bedside and speaks about an upcoming date, officials enter to say they have found the Martian message recorded on a piece of tape. Its contents, to anyone familiar with science fiction films of the era, are predictable: The older, wiser Martians observed humanity for millennia, listening to radio broadcasts and learning our language, and are appalled by our proclivity for "destruction, war, and violence." They tolerated humanity's visit to Mars, and allowed astronauts to return, solely to deliver a warning: "Do not return to Mars," or Martians will destroy the Earth. They are, in other words, just another alien race in a long tradition which threatens genocide to keep the universe free from human violence.

Journey to the Seventh Planet (1961)

For their next joint project, Sidney Pink directed a screenplay he and Ib Melchior collaborated on, *Journey to the Seventh Planet*. Like other less-than-serious spacesuit films, it opens with incongruously serious narration: "There are no limits to the imagination, and man's ability to make reality out of his visions is his greatest strength. Through this skill, he has been able to conquer time and space." The irony here is that the story involves a sinister alien entity that attacks human space explorers by literally making reality out of their visions.

The innovative aspects of this film are its spaceship's destination — the planet Uranus — and the motive behind the flight: With the world now governed by the United Nations, there are no incentives for space travel involving national interests, so humanity's "great hunger now is for knowledge." However, since missions to Mercury, Venus, Mars, Jupiter, and Saturn found no signs of alien life, humans are turning to Uranus in their quest for evidence of extraterrestrial life. True, this was McCauley's obsession in *Men into Space*, but this is the first film to foreground this reason for exploring space.

Occupying a large, roomy spaceship utterly unlike the cramped capsules of current space missions, the all-male crew has an uneventful flight, with "no sign of meteors or other alien objects." Since they walk about normally, they evidently have artificial gravity, though it is not explained how this works, or why commander Eric (Carl Ottosen) tells his crew to "rig for weightlessness" and turn it off as they approach Uranus. After the men strap themselves into seats, we do see an apple hovering in space. While they are weightless, a strange being on Uranus, later said to be "from space and time itself," takes over their minds, extracts some memories, and intimates that he has sinister plans for his visitors.

Awakening after days of unconsciousness, the crew lands on Uranus, though scientists already knew the planet was a gas giant without a rocky surface. Before they can test conditions outside, their door mysteriously opens, and they find themselves in an Earthlike forest with breathable air, not the barren, cold place they expected. Since the youngest crew member, Karl (Peter Monch), recognizes this as a setting from his childhood, the alien obviously constructed this place from his childhood memories. The alien next provides the men with the company of beautiful women from their past. These events seem reminiscent of Stanislaw Lem's *Solaris* (1961), recently published and perhaps being imitated by someone working for this joint American-Swedish production who read Lem's novel; however, unlike Lem's enigmatic planetary organism, the monster here has obvious, and obviously evil, intentions.

Discovering that this temperate zone is surrounded by a permeable barrier, with freezing

Unrest on Uranus: In search of alien life on other worlds, astronaut Karl (Peter Monch) and his crewmates in *Journey to the Seventh Planet* (1961) surely did not anticipate fearful encounters with giant monsters.

cold conditions outside, the men don spacesuits, walk through the barrier, and enter the real, harsh environment of Uranus and, briefly, a real spacesuit film. Filled with mists and unusual bright colors, the scene looks unusually strange, recalling the bizarre Mars of the filmmakers' *The Angry Red Planet*, and contrasting with the Earthlike appearance of other alien planets in films. Their spacesuits also display some visual flair: They are bright blue with yellow trimmings, and their faceplates extend far forward and have a rectangular shape. In keeping with the new sobriety imposed by their spacesuits, perhaps, they encounter one peril that seems plausible enough — a sort of quicksand made of "ammonia snow" that almost engulfs one man. However, their attention soon shifts to a ridiculous menace — a rat-like monster created to frighten Karl, who has a fear of rats. The alien later conjures up a giant spider. To explain why this being is toying with the Earthmen instead of killing them, Eric theorizes that the creature wants "to find out what makes us tick." During visits outside, the astronauts also devise a novel way to deal with a common hazard of spacesuits: When Eric is wounded by a fall that tears open his suit, crewmates let the blood gush from the wound so it can freeze and seal the hole, keeping air in his spacesuit and protecting him from the vacuum. Given how quickly air would rush out of a penetrated spacesuit, and how bulky spacesuits are, one doubts this would really work, but it still qualifies as an interesting idea.

To kill the monster, the men build an enormous acetylene torch, using the convenient facilities of a blacksmith shop in the village the alien constructed for them. Though the being seemingly could thwart this plan in various ways, it actually sends a beautiful woman to sabotage the torch. When the men take it to the monster and find that it does not work, they use the liquid oxygen that powered it to freeze and destroy the monster (now said to require a certain amount of heat). Eric, who alternately told his crew to stay away from the dangerous female illusions and socialized with the dangerous female illusion from his own past, Ingrid (Ann Smyrner), takes his woman into his spaceship as they depart, but she vanishes, unable to exist when the being that created her is no longer alive.

Overall, since the monster lurking on Uranus is so patently evil, one cannot criticize the actions of those who encountered it; still, since the entire point of the mission was to discover evidence of extraterrestrial life, it seems ironic that, upon finally achieving this goal, they respond to the first alien they meet by killing it. If nothing else, someone could have suggested trying to keep the being alive to study it or learn from it, the natural response of scientists. Yet I recall no indications that crew members were scientists, and surely no scientists were consulted by the people who crafted this film.

The Crawling Hand (1963)

If nothing else, *The Crawling Hand* demonstrates that by the 1960s, the spacesuit film had become one of several cinematic patterns being recycled and combined by filmmakers seeking to inject novelty into tried-and-true formulas. This film seizes upon a familiar horror trope — the menacing, disembodied hand — and provides a science fiction twist by making it the result of a failed space mission, as in *The Quatermass Experiment*. The severe disconnect between the film's space-oriented prologue and the Earthbound horror story that follows conveys a point that more artful horrific spacesuit films conceal: that whatever else results from space exploration, a re-emergence of ancient hobgoblins of the human imagination is unimaginably implausible.

During opening credits, audiences see a spacesuited astronaut, Mel Lockhart (Les Hoyle), from the rear as he looks out his spaceship window at stars passing by; evidently distressed, he repeatedly says into his radio, "Can you read me?" and "Someone please come in." Those monitoring this second mission to the Moon, led by Steve Curan (Peter Breck) and Dr. Max Weitzberg (Kent Taylor), lost contact with Lockhart soon after he left the Moon and began returning to Earth — which is exactly what happened to the first lunar flight. When dials indicate that the astronaut is out of oxygen, Curan assumes he is dead, a victim of space, called "the strangest frontier of all." But a gaunt-looking Lockhart reestablishes contact and strangely asks Curan to press a button to destroy his spaceship, since he cannot do it himself. Curan reluctantly complies.

There are now unanswered questions: How did Lockhart stay alive with no oxygen? Why did he want his ship blown up, and why couldn't he push the button himself? Weitzberg theorizes that by introducing living beings and organic material, humans brought new elements into space that might engender bizarre new life forms combining terrestrial and ethereal ingredients. He rhetorically asks, "Does the living cell from Earth romance a cosmic ray and give birth to an illegitimate monster who makes its nest in Lockhart and Martin [the first lunar astronaut]?" Like other ludicrous theories in pseudo-spacesuit films (recall again *The Quatermass Experiment*), this one proves correct.

The drama shifts to Earth as one of Lockhart's arms lands on a beach, to be discovered by student Paul Lawrence (Rod Lauren) and girlfriend Marta Farnstorm (Sirry Steffen). Realizing the arm is in a spacesuit sleeve, Lawrence takes it to his house to inform space scientists about his find. The arm, animated by an alien entity, strangles Lawrence's landlady Mrs. Hotchkiss (Arline Judge). When it attacks Lawrence, he develops the same impulse to strangle people, though he retains some power to resist the alien influence and avoid killing intended victims. While *The Quatermass Experiment* explained its transformed astronaut's actions as an invasion attempt, *The Crawling Hand* says nothing about why a newly generated space creature would seek to kill everyone in its vicinity. But since this is now a horror movie, pure and simple, there is no need for logical explanations.

After local police, led by Sheriff Townsend (Alan Hale, Jr.), and the scientists try to cope with the problem, Lawrence is cured of his affliction because the alien presence cannot endure temperatures above 104 degrees. The hand itself, gnawed by cats, is placed in a box and sent to the proper authorities. But the final scene, wherein curious delivery men are about to open the box, suggests that the entity might become a menace again. The conclusion confirms that, even more than *The Quatermass Experiment*, this is a horror film, not a science fiction film, since its projected continuation involves the return of the monster, not a return to space.

The Outer Limits (1963–1965)

Unlike its obvious inspiration, *The Twilight Zone*, the anthology series *The Outer Limits* focuses exclusively on science fiction, and hence more frequently dealt with space travel. But producers faced one limitation: the series was sold to ABC with the understanding that every episode would feature a "bear," or monster, which steered stories toward horror, as shown by the five episodes featuring spacesuits: "The Man Who Was Never Born" (aired October 28, 1963), "Specimen: Unknown" (February 24, 1964), "Moonstone" (March 9, 1964), "Cold Hands, Warm Heart" (September 26, 1964), and "The Invisible Enemy" (October 31, 1964).

To be sure, other episodes involved space but lacked spacesuits. There were alien visitors to Earth who either looked and acted exactly like humans (as in "Controlled Experiment" [January 13, 1964]) and hence need no spacesuits, or are formidably monstrous, and hence need no spacesuits (as in "The Zanti Misfits" [December 30, 1963]). Sometimes, as in "The Galaxy Being" (September 16, 1963) or "The Mice" (January 6, 1964), aliens visit through teleportation or in the form of energy and do not even need spaceships. "Nightmare" (December 2, 1963) and "The Mutant" (March 16, 1964) briefly show space travelers who never wear spacesuits. Finally, episodes may depict research on Earth involving space that engenders horrors before space travel occurs, like "The Man with the Power" (October 7, 1963) and "The Brain of Colonel Barham" (January 2, 1965).

Though space travel is tangential to its story, "The Man Who Was Never Born" opens with the image of a man in a spaceship and this commentary: "Here, in the bright, clustered loneliness of the billion, billion stars, loneliness can be an exciting, voluntary thing, unlike the loneliness Man suffers on Earth. Here, deep in the starry nowhere, a man can be as one with space and time; preoccupied, yet not indifferent; anxious and yet at peace." This subject is quickly abandoned as astronaut Joseph Reardon (Karl Held) unknowingly enters a time warp while returning to Earth in 1963 and lands on Earth in 2148. Not believing the bleak landscape he sees is Earth, he carries his space helmet with him while emerging from his craft, fearing that the air is unbreathable.

He immediately encounters a hideous mutant, Andro (Martin Landau), who explains he is on a future Earth which was devastated by an alien micro-organism damagingly altered by scientist Bertram Cabot, Jr., whom Andro regards as a villain (though the effects of his work were unintentional). But Andro also blames all humanity for failing to anticipate this tragedy because people were "too busy going to the Moon" and "too busy" waging war. Interestingly, space travel harms the human race in two ways: by introducing a micro-organism which proved deadly, and distracting people from recognizing its dangers.

In a sense, the men then propose to use space travel to correct problems caused by space travel, as they will re-enter the time warp, return to 1963, and warn of the coming catastrophe. Reardon inexplicably vanishes after passing through the time warp, leaving Andro to land the spaceship and try to save humanity on his own. As an unlikely coincidence, he lands next to a boardinghouse that is home to Noelle Andresen (Shirley Knight), future mother of Bertram Cabot, Jr., who soon meets her fiancé, Bertram Cabot (John Considine). Andro, who makes himself look like a handsome man through "hypnotic suggestion," takes a room at the boardinghouse, figures out the situation, and begins striving to prevent Noelle from marrying Cabot. When a concerned Cabot insists on marrying Noelle immediately, a desperate Andro tries shooting him, causing the mutant to reveal his true appearance. Fleeing, he is pursued by a smitten Noelle, who has fallen in love with Andro and failed to see his hideous face. Ready to leave, feeling his mission failed, Andro is persuaded to take Noelle with him to the future to permanently prevent her from marrying Cabot.

The inexperienced Andro, who implausibly could safely land Reardon's spaceship, now displays the even more implausible ability to locate the time warp and again travel through time; but now *he* is a space traveler who vanishes, since by changing the future, he created a world in which he was never born. In a striking conclusion, the abandoned Noelle, still wearing her wedding dress, is observed as an object in space, gradually receding until she begins to blend in with the stars. Recalling other images of astronauts drifting into the void of space, this seems to visualize the extreme loneliness of space, returning to the theme of the prologue. Yet Reardon's loneliness was called "exciting" and "voluntary," while Noelle's isolation is tragic.

The seeming contradiction was avoided in the episode's original ending, described in David J. Schow and Jeffrey Frentzen's *The Outer Limits Companion* (133–34): after landing the spaceship, Noelle meets a man in a floating air-car, who says she is in a more idyllic version of 2148 and asks, "Are you lost?" "No, just alone," she replies. This better accords with the opening conceit that loneliness is forced upon people on Earth (like the abandoned Noelle) and chosen by people in space (like Reardon). The alternate ending also raises the intriguing possibility that, properly focused on improving life on Earth, these future people did not engage in space travel, helping to prevent the catastrophe that ruined Andro's world.

"Specimen: Unknown" involves a genuine concern in space travel—unknowingly bringing a dangerous alien organism back to Earth—illustrated by an absurd story. On Space Station Adonis (actually the recycled Space Station Astra from *Men into Space*), crewmen discover strange "dormant spores" on the hull. They wish to study them because, in the narrator's words, the station is a laboratory "dedicated to removing the unknown for future space travelers." When Rupert Howard (Dabney Coleman) places one in an incubator, it quickly grows into a large white flower which, when removed, shoots out tiny seeds and then emits a deadly gas. Recognizing that this alien plant is dangerous, Howard places it in a convenient "Outside Disposal Chute" which might represent an unusually prescient design feature included precisely to deal with such problems (though it may also be where crewmen dump their trash). Howard dies before explaining what happened to him, and his body is solemnly launched into space in the familiar ritual of space burial, with crewmates in spacesuits surrounding the wrapped body while a man offers comforting religious sentiments about "our Lord and Savior" and the promise of eternal life, another suggestion that religious faith might be strengthened by the challenge of space. Before the men leave the space station to be replaced by another crew, two other details are provided about their sojourn: One man sits under a sunlamp, replicating the common terrestrial experience of sunbathing unavailable in space, and a caged rabbit, clearly brought for research purposes, becomes another victim of the flowers.

Returning to Earth in what is termed a "shuttlecraft," the crew faces a problem with its "altitude stabilization control system." Discovering that one of the servos is malfunctioning, Captain Mike Dowling (Richard Jaeckel) announces he will have to leave the ship to correct it. There follows a slow-moving space walk, during which he repairs a "secondary servo break." One might praise the series for authentically presenting just how slowly and cautiously an astronaut would proceed while working in space. Actually, the film was slowed down solely because the episode came in five minutes short, and producers resorted to tricks to make it long enough. Meanwhile, the plants inside the shuttlecraft attack, leaving crewmates weak and groggy and making Dowling the only capable person on board.

Recognizing that they face a crisis they earlier discussed—the danger of contamination from an "alien virus"—Dowling recommends the shuttlecraft be destroyed to prevent the plants from reaching Earth. However, the commander on the ground, Colonel MacWilliams (Stephen McNally), is reluctant to sacrifice the crew's lives and instead orders Dowling to land his craft at a military base where, it is hoped, the organisms can be safely contained. Unfortunately, the ship goes off course and lands in a field, causing thousands of deadly white flowers to sprout. They threaten MacWilliams, Dowling's wife Janet (Gail Kobe), and others who arrive to rescue the crew. Having escaped death, but still menaced by the flowers around them, all MacWilliams can advise is another recourse to religion: "Thank God ... and pray." He particularly fears that humanity has reached the "end of the road" because a rainstorm is imminent, and he suspects the abundant water will allow the plants

Resourceful Researchers: Lunar scientists Lee Stocker (Alex Nicol) and Clint Anderson (Tim O'Connor) employ their special wagon for "Geological Expedition Samples" in the *Outer Limits* episode "Moonstone" (1964).

to multiply and spread even more rapidly. Instead, the water makes the plants dissolve, ending the danger.

This fortuitous development is hard to understand, since the plants looked much like Earth plants and flourished in the "synthetic Earth's atmosphere" of the station which presumably included water vapor; thus, these organisms should not find water deadly. Schow and Frentzen theorize that the ending was borrowed from a recent film, *The Day of the Triffids* (1963), which also concluded with menacing plants dissolved by water (114). In any event, despite their need to lengthen the episode, producers added no explanations regarding the origin or nature of the flowers; MacWilliams only answers Janet's question "Where did they come from?" by saying "I don't know.... Another planet, another time" (which is blindingly obvious, since "dormant spores" in space clearly did not come from present-day Earth).

Though the episode takes place entirely on the Moon, most of the action in "Moonstone" occurs inside a lunar base that resembles a typical laboratory. The opening sequence, one of three featuring spacesuited astronauts on the lunar surface, establishes one unusual convention of the episode: While on the Moon, everyone moves extremely slowly, perhaps motivated by extreme fear of a misstep that could damage a spacesuit. (The spacesuits, Schow and Frentzen inform us [138], are leftovers from *Men into Space*.) As three astronauts complete a survey of the Moon, there is a moment of realistic drama when one man falls through lunar dust into a hidden pit, requiring teammates to use ropes to extract him. There immediately follows the discovery leading to the inevitable monster: Emerging from the pit, the man notices and grabs a perfect white sphere, which astronauts return to the laboratory to be examined by Professor Diana Brice (Ruth Roman). Played by the episode's only recognizable star, Brice is unusually the central figure in the drama, and she reflects the era's conflicted attitude toward female heroes. On one hand, she is an intelligent and capable scientist, respected by male colleagues; on the other hand, as the only woman on the Moon, she becomes the center of a romantic triangle involving moon base commander Lee Stocker (Alex Nicol) and Clint Anderson (Tim O'Connor), who both covets Stocker's girlfriend and resents him for abandoning threatened citizens during the Korean War. Brice also offers the most extreme emotional reactions to Stocker's alleged betrayal and the plight of the aliens within the Moonstone.

These beings, periodically seen floating within the sphere, resemble both amoebas and human eyes, and they telepathically relate a predictably outlandish story: As virtuous beings with vast scientific knowledge, they fled from their tyrannical rulers, who would misuse their knowledge to conquer the universe. While an astronaut sets up an antenna to locate a promised rescue ship, the grateful aliens begin transferring their scientific data into moon base computers. But the rescue ship was seized, and the base is menaced by an immense sphere sent by the tyrants, announcing that the humans will die unless they surrender their visitors. Facing their overwhelming power, Stocker feels obliged to agree, in a situation that neatly parallels what he did to civilians during the Korean War, and he persuades Brice and Anderson that his actions were defensible.

For some reason, the tyrants' agents insist that the humans transport the Moonstone to a distant location, requiring another scene on the lunar surface wherein two astronauts slowly pull a wagon labeled "Lunar Probe 1: Geological Expedition Samples." Since Brice already commented that the Moonstone is lightweight, and since they are in the low gravity of the Moon, the men should not need a wagon to transport it, but in light of the episode's many illogical aspects, one might simply appreciate the offbeat suggestion that a wheeled wagon may sometimes be useful on the Moon. While Brice and the others watch on television, the sphere approaches the Moonstone, ready to capture it, but the beings inside instead blow themselves up, so their knowledge will be unavailable to the tyrants.

In its second season, a new creative team took over *The Outer Limits*, usually with inferior results, as evidenced by the first episode they produced, "Cold Hands, Warm Heart." At the core of the episode, though, is an intriguing idea: After a mission to Venus, astronaut Jeff Barton (William Shatner) begins feeling cold all the time. He resists telling superiors about his condition because he must prepare a presentation to secure funding for another project, a manned flight to Mars. His personal physician, Dr. Mike (Malachi Throne), finds that Barton's temperature has dropped to ninety-one degrees. As his condition worsens, he passes out in a super-heated steam room, and his hands become scaly. For some reason, his body is adapting to Venusian conditions.

Unfortunately, the episode does little to explain Barton's problems. Since his return, there has been some mystery about what happened to him during an eight-minute loss of radio contact while he approached Venus, and Barton remembers nothing about it. The answer comes in a nightmare: We see Barton in his spaceship, wearing a spacesuit and helmet, and there is a striking image of the stars he watches through the porthole. (A faint reflection of his helmet superimposed on the black sky suggests a man becoming one with the universe.) Descending into Venus' thick atmosphere for a landing, he again looks out the porthole and sees amidst wispy clouds a strange, plantlike creature gesturing at him. Somehow, audiences must infer, this being, while never contacting Barton, initiated the process of transforming him into a Venusian, presumably for some sinister reason. The way Barton is cured does not bear examination: Colleagues place a sedated Barton in a super-heated chamber, and an evening in these conditions purges him of his alien infestation and allows him to successfully argue for the Mars mission.

There is a striking speech when Barton explains to his wife Ann (Geraldine Brooks) why he is obsessed with space travel: "You married a man, not a headline. A man with certain peculiarities.... One day he broke through the troposphere, into the stratosphere, and right then, for the first time, he understood the purpose of his life. It was to lead the way to new worlds, new life, new knowledge." This defense of space travel anticipates the narration Shatner would provide for each episode of *Star Trek*, announcing that the *Enterprise*'s mission is to "explore strange, new worlds; to seek out new life, and new civilizations."

While generally as implausible as other episodes, "The Invisible Enemy" foregrounds a significant issue in spacesuit films: whether space missions should be governed by astronauts in space or monitors on the ground. (Perhaps this is because the script came from an experienced science fiction writer, Jerry Sohl, who recalled previous stories and films that raised the question.) In opening scenes, officials on Earth, contacting the the first two astronauts on Mars, are frustrated because of the three-and-a-half minute time lag in radio communication, limiting their ability to control astronauts' activities. (The figure is plausible since radio waves at the speed of light travel 39,000,000 miles in three and a half minutes, and when closest to Earth, Mars is about that distance away.) A general acknowledges the problem and comments, "I'd prefer more control down here." His position seems vindicated by what happens next: One astronaut, after going out in a spacesuit to explore Mars, suddenly screams and then is silent; the other astronaut immediately rushes out to rescue him and meets the same fate. Monitors, presumably, would have demanded greater caution and perhaps saved the second crewman's life.

Because of this mysterious tragedy, the second mission to Mars is carefully planned to avoid placing its four astronauts in danger. Not only can they regularly consult a computer, Tele, to receive the best possible advice, but a brand new system of communication, using a laser, allows instantaneous communication. (This is impossible because a laser beam, like radio waves, would be limited to the speed of light and could not travel from Mars to Earth in less than three minutes.) The general happily notes, "I can quarterback the entire operation right from my desk." Thus, upon reaching Mars, commander Charles Merritt (Adam West, surely chosen by director Byron Haskin due to previous service as a Mars-bound astronaut in *Robinson Crusoe on Mars*) endures constant micromanagement from the ground.

There is one novel feature of their flight: Aboard the spaceship before it lands, Merritt sits with his three crewmates at a table, playing cards, and his rueful remark, "Down three, doubled," indicates they were playing bridge, a logical activity for a four-man crew and an interesting change from the usual chess games. Once they land, Merritt consults his computer and learns that the Martian atmosphere will support life—"no helmets needed," which is odd, given that astronauts of the first mission constantly wore helmets. Perhaps Haskin inserted the line so these astronauts, the ones audiences would have to identify with, could appealingly show their faces at all times while confronting their Martian adversary.

Proceeding with his expedition, Merritt must acknowledge and follow Earth's precise instructions: One man, Jim Bowman (Anthony Costello), can go exploring, but Merritt keeps him constantly in view. When he briefly disobeys orders and moves behind a piece of wreckage from the first expedition to retrieve a piece of scarred metal, the Martian menace—a serpent-like creature that emerges from the Martian sands—promptly kills him. Annoyed because their careful guidelines were violated, monitors impose even more stringent conditions on a follow-up sortie to investigate the man's fate. Merritt watches from the spaceship as crewman Jack Buckley (Rudi Solari) explores, while another man armed with a bazooka, Frank Johnson (Robert DoQui), stands at an angle away from the ship to keep an eye on Buckley when he moves behind the wreckage to find out what happened to Bowman. Again, things do not go according to plan: As Buckley returns to the ship with the piece of metal, which is scratched and covered with blood, Merritt loses track of Johnson, who is slaughtered by the same monster.

The Earth monitors issue a new order: The two survivors must remain in their spaceship until the time is right to return to Earth. But Buckley, suddenly realizing that the expanses of Martian sand are like seas, and might harbor underground life, impulsively rushes outside to test the theory. Because he fails to bring his radio, Merritt must disobey orders to go out to find him. While both men avoid being killed by the monster, Merritt ends up stranded on an island of rock, surrounded by sand, and seems doomed. Earth relieves him of command and orders new commander Buckley to return to the ship and blast off before it is too late to return to Earth. Now Buckley disobeys orders, as he instead rushes onto the sand to serve as a decoy and allow Merritt to get back to the spaceship. Merritt in turn refuses to follow this plan and rushes out to retrieve Buckley. Somehow, the men get back to the safety of the rock, whereupon they use the bazooka to kill the monster. While Merritt and Buckley discover there are other monsters in the sand, it no longer matters, since they return to the spaceship and blast off for Earth with six minutes to spare. During their activities on Mars, there is a passing reference to a novel piece of technology—"sand shoes" (presumably designed for more efficient walking on the sands of Mars), which Buckley discards so he can move more quickly.

Oddly, once the men communicate that they will leave in time, the episode concludes with bland narration about this battle as a "painful step from the crib of destiny" without driving the obvious point home: that astronauts are better off if they make their own decisions, instead of following orders from Earth. After all, the brash actions of Buckley and Merritt enabled them to solve the mystery *and* return safely, while the Martian menace would have remained unknown if they obeyed orders and left Mars without investigation. At least the general might have said something like, "In light of events, be advised that plans for disciplinary actions have been cancelled"—a bureaucratic apology. Since Haskin, as quoted in Schow and Frentzen's *The Outer Limits Companion*, thought the story was "lousy"

(297), and both Haskin and story editor Seeleg Lester massively rewrote Sohl's script, it may be they never recognized that this story, despite its flaws, did have a significant message.

Generally, episodes of *The Outer Limits* were superior to their cinematic counterparts in the 1960s, since producers worked hard to offer intelligent stories, well-written dialogue, persuasive characterization, and effective actors. Still, the mandated appearances of monsters drove the series to emphasize a blunt, simplistic message about space travel: The universe is filled with grotesque, malevolent beings, and we must beware of them. The only variation permitted was that occasionally, as in "Moonstone," apparently menacing aliens might turn out to be benign, suggesting that in space, things are not always as they seem. And this is another area in which the series merits more attention than comparable films of its era.

The Wizard of Mars (1965)

Despite a title suggesting a science fictional update of L. Frank Baum's *The Wonderful Wizard of Oz* (1900) or the 1939 film adaptation, *The Wizard of Mars* bears little relationship to Baum's fantasy: There are again three men and a woman named Dorothy journeying across a strange realm upon a "golden road" to meet a wise old man who assigns them a task; and once it is completed, a conclusion suggests, as in the film, that their experience was only a dream. But the men are not clear analogues of the Scarecrow, Tin Man, and Cowardly Lion, and their adventures do not correspond to events in the novel or film. The most significant difference, which almost makes this film interesting, is that *The Wizard of Oz* is a fable of maturation and empowerment, as characters rise to challenges and get their wishes, while *The Wizard of Mars* conveys a somber message about the limitations of human ambitions.

The opening scenes establish that scientific plausibility is not a concern; for after we meet four astronauts on a mission to orbit and survey Mars — Steve (Roger Gentry), Doc (Vic McGee), Charlie (Jerry Rannow), and Dorothy (Eve Bernhardt) — they immediately face absurd problems: an approaching red sphere of "pulsating light" and a "magnetic storm" in space signaled by lightning bolts. To escape these phenomena, crew members detach their passenger compartment from the spaceship's main stage to attempt an unscheduled landing on Mars. The only realistic development is that the commander shouts, "Our pressure suits — quick! The hull may rupture on impact!" All astronauts are soon wearing realistic spacesuits and space helmets.

While their portion of the spaceship remains intact when they reach Mars, the astronauts have only limited amounts of oxygen and food. Since they are not sure if a rescue mission will arrive, they trek across Mars in search of their main stage, which contains ample supplies. While they have less than four days of oxygen, one man suggests they can "crack the intake valves" on their spacesuits and use the meager oxygen in Mars's thin atmosphere to augment their own supply and survive longer. Whether this procedure would actually help seems questionable — one thinks opening the valves would simply make them lose needed oxygen more quickly — and in any event, the idea is evidently forgotten, since they indicate in later dialogue that they have a four-day supply of oxygen and act accordingly.

The travelers begin their journey by floating down a Martian canal in two inflatable rafts, taking them underground. They continue on foot through a volcanic cavern with fiery outbursts of lava seemingly inspired by a similar underground hike in *Robinson Crusoe on Mars*. Despite efforts to generate suspense with narration suggesting that the humans are being watched, the only real drama during this lengthy sequence comes early, when the astronauts in rafts are assaulted by strange fish that resemble long rectangular boxes and look more laughable than menacing. Emerging onto the surface, they find themselves in a vast desert, about to run out of oxygen and unable to hear a signal from their main stage. Fortuitously, a sudden signal leads them to an old unmanned probe containing an oxygen tank that can resupply their own tanks. They then stumble upon bright yellow tiles, partially uncovered by shifting sands, which they identify as part of a "golden road" which they follow to reach a strange city covered by a red dome. One man's comment—"We've come to the end of the road"—indicates this is the equivalent of Baum's Emerald City, but the fact that it is not green suggests an essential indifference to the film's purported source material. And the Martian city, unlike the Emerald City, is a deserted ruin.

Entering a large building with interminable corridors, the humans find its air is breathable, so they immediately take off their spacesuits—which, as in *Cat-Women of the Moon*, proves an unwise decision. They become concerned when they see two black shadows on the ground, apparently the remnants of two Martians who were "cremated alive" while trying to break through a sealed door. The corridors are lined with what look like large wooden tubes; they brush off the covering on one tube to discover a white-faced, human-like figure beneath a clear dome containing a visible brain, suggesting a Martian mummy. However, the figure begins to move and, connecting its hand to one astronaut's hand, conveys a mental message in a strange, incomprehensible language. But the man somehow figures out from this contact that the Martians "mean us no harm" and only want the humans to travel to a meeting place, its location indicated by the turning of the figure's head.

After multiple ghostly images of the figure's face all rush toward this site, marked solely by a massive brain, the humans observe the face of an old man (John Carradine) materializing against a background of stars. Asked "What manner of life are you?" the face responds that he is a "composite being" representing all surviving Martians. He explains they were once a mighty race that "witnessed the birth and death of suns and worlds untold" and effectively conquered the galaxy. But they made a disastrous decision, "inquired into the very nature of the fabric of time itself," and "rose again to conquer death and pluck our city out of time." While this gave them immortality, they bitterly realized it also "kept us from our destiny," vaguely intimated to be a blissful life after death. Unfortunately, since Martians had become "incapable of physical action" (which is a strange claim, since we previously saw the body of a Martian moving around), they cannot "replace the sphere within the mechanism" that would restart time inside the city.

Since the face cannot maintain a presence, he says he cannot fully explain the amazingly complex procedure that must be completed, then vanishes. But it almost literally proves to be child's play. They stumble upon the needed sphere, which contains a replica of the Martian city, and deducing that the closed door they previously encountered leads to the appropriate "mechanism," they use a Martian version of an acetylene torch to open the door. There, they discover a golden pendulum with the face of the Sun as its base. Noticing a round opening at the place that attaches it to gears, they put the sphere in the opening and the pendulum begins moving at an ever-increasing rate. As falling debris indicates that the reawakening city is about to collapse, the humans rush to escape. Once outside, they collapse in the sand, presumably because they cannot breathe the Martian air, and appear destined to die; but they instead vanish, only to find themselves back on their spaceship, with the men having grown beards, and a radio report saying they have been out of touch for two minutes. With Carradine's voice repeating the point that "without death, life itself is meaningless," audiences must infer either that the whole experience was a dream, or that the Martians, while "incapable of physical action," somehow transported their guests back to the safety of their spaceship.

While the context of its message makes it almost impossible to take seriously, *The Wizard of Mars* is in its own clumsy manner arguing against the boundless human ambition explicitly linked to space travel in *Things to Come* and implicit in other films promoting space exploration, most prominently *2001: A Space Odyssey*. Perhaps humans can make themselves masters of the galaxy, the film asserts, but they will inevitably decline like the Martians. Further, should they attempt to avert their own demise, they will find their existence "meaningless" and seek to bring it to an end. It is also intimated, recalling the mad beliefs of *Conquest of Space*'s Merritt, that the conquest of space may violate God's will, since He instead wants beings to meekly die to transition into an afterlife of His design. The film's low quality, and haplessness of its performers, may even serve to strengthen this statement about the futility of human efforts to conquer space and make *The Wizard of Mars* more effective than a superior production with a similar theme, *Mission to Mars* (2000). But these are grandiose claims to offer about a film that, in most respects, is an aesthetic disaster.

Mutiny in Outer Space (1965)

Addressing the now-familiar scenario of a deadly organism from space, *Mutiny in Outer Space* treats this development more realistically than other films, almost qualifying as a genuine spacesuit film, and makes important points about the dangerous effects of prolonged life in space. Unfortunately, the way its menace is depicted and dealt with recalls more fanciful films, so the film ultimately seems more like "Specimen: Unknown" and *The Green Slime* than *Project Moon Base* and *Conquest of Space*.

Crew members of Space Station X-7 are awaiting the arrival of a spaceship from the Moon with two astronauts, Gordon Towers (William Leslie) and Dan Webber (Carl Crow), bringing frozen samples from the Moon's newly discovered "ice caves." Officials on Earth propose building a second lunar base, advantageously using water from the caves, but General Knowland (Glenn Langan) worries vaguely that "the human element" might complicate such plans, anticipating a key problem that will emerge at the station. Commander Frank Cromwell (Richard Garland) must deal with an old communication satellite that is dangerously nearing the station, requiring evasive maneuvers to avert a collision. Since Cromwell complains generally about having to cope with "so much junk up here" from the "early space years," this film anticipates what is now a major problem for astronauts, avoiding debris left over from decades of launching objects into space.

The film also introduces two beautiful women on board the station, clearly to appeal to male viewers: biochemist Faith Montaine (Dolores Faith), soon to marry Towers, and Connie Engstrom (Pamela Curran), secretly in love with Cromwell. A crew member refers to a famous science fiction character when he says, referring to Towers, that Montaine's "Flash Gordon's on his way." Though Towers and Webber were previously observed only in standard clothing in their spaceship, Towers tells his crewmate, as they approach the station, "Okay, Don, suit up," and the men are soon in spacesuits, ready to travel from their spaceship to the station. Their movements in space, the only time spacesuits are visible in the film, are striking because they essentially look like they are flying, like Superman, using their own muscles to propel themselves. But there is also scientific nonsense in the sequence, as the ship reaches the station's "landing platform" only when captured by what is alternately called a "gravitational beam" and "graviton beam."

Their arrival at the station brings some information about its routines: Visitors first go through what Engstrom describes as a "laundromat for people" to be thoroughly cleaned (though the process is not shown); they look forward to real food after subsisting on "synthetics" while on the Moon, and the station maintains "one half gravity," which they say "feels good" after the Moon's lower gravity. When Webber unexpectedly collapses after entering the station, people speculate he is suffering from "space raptures," a term for madness in space that later figures prominently in the plot. Speculation that he may have contracted an unknown disease from the ice caves inspires a noteworthy speech about the mysterious hazards of space: "Just when we think we have space under control, some new [variable] [?] looms up. There are things out there we may never understand — or live with."[2] To underscore the point, a subsequent alarm is assumed to be an "emergency drill" inspired by Cromwell's dedication to always being prepared to deal with "the unpredictable. The unknown dangers of space."

Actually, though, the station is on a collision course with a meteor shower. One meteor inflicts minor damage on the infirmary's hull, but a mechanism automatically seals the breach. Still, the order is issued to "Send a crew out to repair the outer wall."

Webber dies from "some kind of fungus" picked up in the ice caves, after being placed by Dr. Hoffman (James Dobson) in a special decompression chamber; we glimpse his grotesque corpse, covered with scaly growths, making him resemble the transformed astronaut of *First Man into Space*. Incredibly, Cromwell insists that nothing is wrong, orders that Webber's death be attributed to the sudden change in pressure upon reaching the station, and refuses to notify Earth about the true cause of his death. Obviously, Cromwell is now "on the brink of space raptures," having "become a very sick man" due to the effects of prolonged weightlessness, and he is making irrational decisions due to fears he might lose his command.

Because he fails to take immediate action, the problem of the fungus gets out of control, as Montaine finds herself menaced in the infirmary by huge growths of fungus creeping toward her. She is rescued by Towers. Now clearly insane, Cromwell still maintains that everything is fine, and when Towers tries to physically restrain him, the commander orders the imprisonment of Towers, Montaine, and Hoffman on the grounds of mutiny. It briefly appears he might retain command because he is supported by Engstrom, who controls communications to Earth, but she also realizes he is deranged when he tells her Towers held him at gunpoint. When she relays this conversation to Knowland and others on Earth, they realize as she did that he is suffering from hallucinations caused by space raptures, because "all weapons were ruled out of space as far back as 1970." While handguns are absurdly deployed in the space films *It! The Terror from Beyond Space* and *Moon Zero Two*, this film uniquely understands that such weapons, because they can breach a spaceship hull and cause fatal leaks, are senseless in space. (No one in the film explains *why* they were "ruled out.")

After showing restraint in presenting this deadly disease from space, and offering insights about life in space, *Mutiny in Outer Space* disappointingly goes over the top in depicting the results of the station's infestation. Since the mad Cromwell opened the door to the infirmary filled with fungus, huge filaments of fungus are all over the station's interior and exterior. This is a dramatic image but makes little sense, since Hoffman, now infected with the fungus himself, is developing the theory — which will prove correct — that the fungus can be killed by extreme cold. After all, the organism remained dormant in the Moon's ice caves and came to life only when transported to the warmth of a spaceship and space station. But nothing is colder than the vacuum of space, making the fungus's riotous growth outside the station virtually impossible. As if anticipating the objection, officials on Earth later explain that the fungus is thriving in space because of the heat of the Sun's rays beating on the station. But since the vacuum of space does not conduct heat, the fungus could live only when touching the station hull, though we actually see filaments of fungus extending from point to point, all over the station, like strands of a spider's web.

Once Cromwell is caught, restrained, and drugged, Towers and the others decide to don "survival suits" to protect themselves while reducing the temperature of the station and killing the fungus inside. One assumes he is referring to spacesuits, but the "survival suits" actually resemble garments worn by firefighters, made of thin fabric with a helmet. (They look exactly like the garments in the *Star Trek* episode "The Naked Time.") The presence of the suits is attributed to the admirable caution of Cromwell, but since these outfits cannot protect against the vacuum of space, one questions their utility to residents of a space station, where that would represent the major hazard. (One suspects the film could not afford more than two spacesuits and hence devised the "survival suits" as cheaper alternatives to be worn by several cast members.) The fungus outside the station remains, but authorities on Earth, after preparing to destroy the station should it approach Earth, now launch a rocket that unleashes an "ice crystal cloud" which improbably remains compact to surround the station and kill the fungus. A relief ship is sent to rescue the station's beleaguered crew.

Despite its lapses and excesses, *Mutiny in Outer Space* seems a jewel amidst the considerable dross of horrific spacesuit films, so it is disappointing that Phil Hardy dismisses it as "[r]outine fare" after providing a flawed summary suggesting he never watched the film (243). Thus, we observe again a paradox in critical responses to space films: Egregious scientific blunders are condemned, yet films striving to be realistic about space are derided as dull or "routine."

Space Monster (1965)

To defend horrific spacesuit films on practical grounds, one presumably must describe them as valuable warnings about potential dangers lurking in space, urging scientists and policymakers to proceed with appropriate caution in space initiatives. Such a message, though, would have little impact if a film presents menaces in space as inconsequential diversions, easily dealt with and quickly forgotten. Strangely, this pattern is observed in *Space Monster*.

One immediately lacks confidence in the scientific acumen of writer-director Leonard Katzman, since the opening narration conveys a confused understanding of astronomy seemingly derived from hasty glances at reference books:

> Beyond this and into infinity is man's last frontier. Over two billion light years of solar system reaching from the Great Clouds of Magellan to the galaxies of Andromeda and Triangulum. Through the eons of time, man has searched the heavens, peering incessantly into the vast millions of miles of universe, questioning every star, every planet. Can life exist? Like time itself, man's search for the answer never stops. He moves closer and closer to his final destiny, exploration of the heavens. And so his probes have taken him deep into space, past the planets of Mars and Jupiter, Saturn and countless others. Relentlessly he will seek new worlds to land on and always he will wonder if the next will be like the one before.

Katzman bizarrely describes the galaxies of the Local Group as a "solar system" (though the Local Group spans only about ten million light-years, not two billion) and thinks trips to other galaxies are the next natural step after humans reach Saturn; thus, his spaceship is flying to the Triangulum Galaxy (three million light-years from Earth) by 2000. He further sees nothing unusual about astronauts remaining in radio contact with Earth, with no transmission delays, despite the distances involved.

Before his spaceship takes off, an opening sequence depicts the tragic fate of another spaceship, the *Faith 1*: After a spacesuited man staggers inside a spaceship, he contacts Earth Control to inform them that some deadly gases penetrated suits, so "others [are] all dead"; he also says repeatedly to "please destruct" his spaceship using a mechanism for this purpose since his "whole ship may be infectious." With such a prologue, one imagines the next spaceship would be launched amidst discussion of new precautions to prevent dangerous gases from seeping into spacesuits or efforts to avoid the conditions that led to the other spaceship's destruction. But the incident is never mentioned again, the first instance of a peculiar amnesia regarding space hazards that characters display throughout this film.

We next meet the crew of the *Hope 1*, all standard figures: stalwart commander Hank Stevens (James Brown), beautiful scientist Lisa Wayne (Francine York), older scientist Paul Martin (Russ Bender), and the seemingly self-centered comic relief, John Andros (Baynes Barron). Scattered comments suggest their mission is to reach the distant planet Taurus (sometimes pronounced "torus" or "tyrus") to investigate whether it can support life, though this is oddly never brought to the forefront. To briskly explain why astronauts walk about normally, one man refers to the "artificial gravity that eliminates weightlessness," and there are mild interpersonal conflicts involving Wayne's presence: When Stevens reiterates his opposition to having a woman on board, Wayne puts him down with a joke involving spacesuits, saying that one reason the expedition cost billions of dollars was the money needed "to build a special helmet for that fat head of yours"; and when Stevens is irked by Andros's open lust for his female crewmate, Andros defends himself by saying, "You can't cuddle up to a spaceship on a cold winter's night," and asks Stevens to admit "she fills out a spacesuit a lot better than any of us." Incongruously, there is a reasonable scientific justification for Wayne's selection: She weighed less than the large man who was the only other person with the needed qualifications. (How much this would matter in an atomic-powered spaceship capable of traveling to another galaxy seems questionable.) Katzman's script also acknowledges, unusually, the importance of computers in space navigation, as Stevens complains: "The more we know about flight, the less there is for people like me to do. In the early days, the men flew the ships; now the ships fly the men."

Right after this comment, the first crisis occurs, as the crew spots a spaceship floating in space: Stevens announces, "John and I'll get our suits on" to investigate, and we soon see the men in spacesuits with clear spherical helmets, using jets on their backs to fly to the unknown vehicle, which has an open airlock; there is a brief but interesting shot of each astronaut floating toward the camera. Once inside the spaceship, filled with strange markings, the men suddenly see an alien (alive though it is not wearing a spacesuit) who resembles the evolved human in the *Outer Limits* episode "The Sixth Finger" (aired October 14, 1963). When he attacks Andros, Stevens feels obliged to shoot him, and they hurry back to their ship to retrieve a bomb and blow up the alien spaceship. Why this is necessary, when they could presumably remain safe simply by flying away from the vehicle, is far from clear, but the men note that the alien was "ugly" and a "nightmare" to seemingly justify their relentless hostility. Later, Stevens regrets they could not establish peaceful contact, though he made no effort to do so, but Andros responds that it was all for the best, since contact with aliens would give one group the status of a "minority" and lead to inevitable conflict. All in all, the film conveys one of the most unenlightened attitudes toward alien life ever depicted in film — aliens are ugly, and we'll never get along with them, so we might as well slaughter them now.

Another, more common problem then threatens the *Hope 1* — a "swarm of meteorites dead ahead"— and while they are easily avoided with a force field, this somehow causes the ship's computers to dangerously increase acceleration, forcing Stevens to turn off the computers to prevent the atomic reactors from exploding. Though near their destination, the Triangulum Galaxy, they must find another planet to land on to effect repairs, and such a planet miraculously appears. Unusually, the spaceship overshoots a land mass and lands underwater, though filmmakers (it becomes clear) had practical reasons for this novel development. As repairs begin, Wayne keeps the romantic subplot going by describing the work-obsessed Stevens as "Tom Swift and His Flying Machine" before passionately kissing him.

When the crew feels "an underground tremor," they discover another alien menace, as the submerged spaceship is surrounded by giant crabs — which, despite their size, look exactly like ordinary crabs. One now realizes that the underwater landing was contrived solely so Katzman could plant a toy spaceship in an aquarium and fill it with crabs to provide economical thrills. Fortunately, the force field that repelled the meteorites drives away the crabs, allowing Andros to put on a diving suit — which they brought for exploring Taurus — and swim to the surface to investigate conditions on land and obtain samples. One wonders why he did not don a spacesuit, but as if anticipating this issue, Andros says, "You can't wear a pressure suit underwater." (Why a garment designed to protect against the vacuum of space could not protect against water is not explained.)

As Andros swims through the alien ocean, we observe a humanoid sea monster, vaguely reminiscent of the *Creature from the Black Lagoon* (1954). Andros safely reaches shore just as it was poised to attack. After he fills his box with samples and returns to the water, the monster confronts him; his crewmates helpfully remind him via radio that he brought a torch which can drive it away. Still, he sustains fatal wounds and dies after entering the spaceship. His sacrifice is vindicated when Wayne announces that the samples prove this planet is "what we've been looking for," which is "a planet that's like Earth reborn." Now, after quickly finishing repairs and using the force field one more time to drive off a particularly huge crab, the crew members can take off for Earth, cancelling their trip to Taurus, to deliver the happy news they have found an ideal planet for humanity. Stevens announces that it will be named "Andros" to honor their deceased comrade.

Incredibly, no one suggests that a planet with an ocean filled with giant crabs and homicidal humanoids might not be a good place to settle, particularly since Andros's five-minute exploration of the land left open the possibility that similar menaces might lurk above the water as well. But humans in this film repeatedly encounter monsters, expeditiously conquer them, and entirely forget about them. *Space Monster*, then, can be appreciated for its novelty, if nothing else, as a singular horrific spacesuit film that conveys the characteristic message of melodramatic spacesuit films: Space can be comfortably like Earth, despite a few minor annoyances.

Frankenstein Meets the Spacemonster (1965)

As spacesuit films continued to decline during the 1960s, some filmmakers, as noted, were combining elements from earlier space films, perhaps incongruously, to make old stories seem new. Thus, *Frankenstein Meets the Spacemonster* (also known as *Mars Invades Puerto Rico* and *Duel of the Space Monsters*) might be described as a necessarily clumsy attempt to combine the plots of *Radar Men from the Moon, The Quatermass Experiment,* and *It! The Terror from Beyond Space*. In deference to its title, I consider this a horrific spacesuit film, but it can also be categorized as a melodramatic spacesuit film.

A spaceship from Mars is hovering near Earth and blasting destructive beams at our missiles, purportedly because the Martians regard them as threats. They also want to keep their existence a secret from the people of Earth (making their attacks counterproductive, but one cannot analyze the logic behind these Martians' actions). As an early indication this film will reflect a strange combination of disparate influences, most members of the crew wear spacesuits, but the commanders — Princess Marcuzan (Marilyn Hanold) and assistant Dr. Nadir (Lou Cutell) — do not, a pattern maintained throughout the film. There is a minimal attempt to explain this discrepancy: After Nadir reports, "The spectrographic probe indicates that the atmosphere [on Earth] is suitable to sustain us," the princess commands, "Instruct the landing party to wear pressure suits and breathing apparatus," presumably due to an abundance of caution about potentially hazardous conditions on Earth. Crewmen wear spacesuits, then, presumably because they may in the future, unlike the princess and Nadir, travel on the surface of Earth. This explanation is strained, to say the least, and one suspects that the true reason for the crewmen's spacesuits is that the film's Martians are depicted as having pointed ears (like Nadir), and dressing most of them in spacesuits eliminates the need to provide similar attachments for their ears.

To launch the plot's other thread, NASA officials on Earth hold a press conference to introduce astronaut Frank Saunders (Robert Reilly), who will shortly embark upon a solo flight to Mars. When he unaccountably freezes while answering a question, the conference is hastily concluded. In a subsequent discussion involving General Bowers (David Kerman) and scientists Adam Steele (James Karen) and Karen Grant (Nancy Marshall), we learn that Saunders was actually constructed by the scientists and called a "robot," though we would today call him a cyborg, an assemblage of human organs and a mechanical brain; he is still susceptible to atmospheric moisture, explaining his malfunction. Realistically, the scheme seems unworkable: at the conference, an experienced space journalist wonders why an astronaut he never heard of suddenly received this major assignment, and NASA could never employ a mystery astronaut without inviting intense scrutiny that would ultimately reveal the truth.

Still, the stated reasons why NASA is switching to a robot astronaut are interesting: One man notes, "We can control him," suggesting that this makes Saunders superior to less controllable human astronauts, and the information gathered by the robot brain can be easily downloaded. But the main motive appears to be that "[w]e can learn all we need to know about extended space travel without the loss of a solitary life." Albeit with the absurd pretext of a humanoid robot, the film touches upon what later becomes a genuine issue in space exploration: For reasons of safety and economics, should we shift to automated space probes instead of manned space flights? Even more provocatively, the film immediately identifies a major problem in relying too heavily upon mechanical intelligences in space: After Steele further extols his creation's virtues by noting, "We don't have to contend with the possibility of human error," Bowers responds, "That's fine, Steele, but what if the machine breaks? Or something goes wrong with his brain?" Strangely, this film anticipates *2001: A Space Odyssey* in depicting a space flight–leading robot that is driven insane by experiences in space and becomes a homicidal maniac; one can even say, to use a phrase in both films, that the root cause of the machine's eventual breakdown — here, an overly sensitive mechanism — is "human error." Unfortunately, the circumstances leading to this robot's problems and actions lack the logical foundation and understated power of HAL 9000's actions in *2001*: Everything here is the fault of those silly Martians.

To depict Saunders's launch, the film relies upon stock footage of an actual astronaut walking toward and boarding a space capsule; actor Reilly is only observed in one, repeated close-up shot showing part of his face, wearing a space helmet, within his spacecraft. We never see a full image of Reilly in a spacesuit because the film's spacesuits are noticeably unlike the spacesuits worn by actual Mercury and Gemini astronauts. Regarding Saunders's vehicle as just another missile to destroy, Nadir sends out a blast of energy causing a "malfunction in all electrical systems," forcing Saunders to abort the mission and make an emergency landing in Puerto Rico. Discovering that the "missile" was manned, and its astronaut survived and returned to Earth, the Martians decide to land, track him down, and kill him before he reveals their existence (though there is no reason to believe that Saunders actually knows what led to his craft's problems). As the robot staggers about the countryside, space-suited Martians blast him with a ray gun, leaving one side of his body hideously disfigured, but he escapes anyway.

By means of these events, the film can justify its titular reference to Frankenstein. First, due to either the energy blast or ray gun, Saunders loses his ability to reason, and he now looks like a monster. His creators speculate that, due to damage from his aborted mission, Saunders "could turn into a Frankenstein," and that is exactly what happens, as the deranged Saunders begins killing anyone he runs into. In its own way, then, the film shifts away from a focus on the effects of space travel to make Saunders just another man-made monster that turns upon its creator. True, one might say the same about HAL, but that computer gone mad was more evocative and genuinely frightening than a man in a rubber mask strangling people.

Fearing their presence will be revealed anyway, the princess resolves to move to phase two of her plan, which is completely ridiculous: Because the Martian race was devastated by atomic war, the survivors led by the princess have no women — except the princess herself, evidently uninterested in parenthood — so Martians must abduct Earth women to "acquire breeding stock" and replenish their race. In the aftermath of the 1964 findings of the Mariner 4 probe, revealing Mars is a barren planet with craters, it was inexcusable to posit that Mars might have human-like inhabitants, let alone beings able to interbreed with humans; yet both this film and *Mars Needs Women* (1967) ask viewers to take this scenario seriously. There follow scenes in which beautiful young women, usually wearing bikinis, are grabbed and taken to the Martian spaceship to be processed and prepared for breeding. If this is not risible enough, we also learn that the Martians have brought along a humanoid space monster in a cage — it resembles the monster of *It! The Terror from Beyond Space* — evidently for the purpose of disciplining errant crewmen or captives. One Martian that failed to kill Saunders is taken to the monster as an "example," and the monster later terrifies Karen.

Upon locating Saunders, evidently resting up after another murder, Steele calms him down and repairs his mechanical brain, again making him a trustworthy servant. In this respect, the film anticipates Arthur C. Clarke's sequel to *2001*, *2010: Odyssey Two*, by rehabilitating its errant machine to function as a reliable ally to human creators — though this diminishes whatever minimal impact the film has as a cautionary tale about the unintended effects of scientific progress. To wrap things up neatly, Steele sends Saunders to the Martian spaceship to rescue the women; he engages in a brief scuffle with the space monster, as dictated by the film's title; and when the Martians attempt to leave, Saunders uses a ray gun to destroy the spaceship and everyone on board. Karen enjoys a romantic motorcycle ride with her boyfriend during the closing credits.

Overall, to argue that horrific spacesuit films were simply efforts to retell traditional horror stories employing novel pretexts involving space travel, one could find no better example than *Frankenstein Meets the Spacemonster*, which makes no effort to conceal such intentions. And the ideal scenario for such projects was a returning astronaut transformed into a monster, a premise already employed in *The Quatermass Experiment, First Man into Space*, and *The Crawling Hand*.

Mission Mars (1968)

While released only a few months after *2001: A Space Odyssey, Mission Mars* seemingly seeks to follow in its footsteps, as it is also a slow, meticulous account of a future space mission involving the discovery of an enigmatic alien presence. Yet this cheap production is less interesting, largely because it devolves into a conventional monster movie.

Opening scenes may have been influenced by *Countdown* in focusing on the strained personal relationships between two astronauts scheduled to go to Mars, pilot Mike Blaiswick (Darren McGavin) and geologist Nick Grant (Nick Adams), and wives Edith Blaiswick (Heather Hewitt) and Alice Grant (Shirley Parker). The film begins with Edith's fragmented nightmare about an exploding spaceship and an astronaut drifting in space, but she remains supportive. In contrast, a bitter Alice feels that her husband is afflicted with a cosmic wanderlust that will inevitably cause his death. (After the spaceship takes off, there are additional scenes with the wives back on Earth, though their primary purpose seems to be killing time.) Early scenes also show Blaiswick, Grant, and a third astronaut, Duncan (George De Vries), passing a physical exam, intercut with extensive stock footage from American space missions, and the film establishes the annoying pattern of employing inappropriate pop-rock music to accompany key moments. The unusual aspect of the mission is that a supply rocket is launched first, so their initial task upon reaching orbit is to rendezvous with that rocket before beginning their nine-month flight to Mars.

The takeoff, with astronauts wearing space helmets that cover their entire faces (a conventional feature of spacesuits that seems more unusual in later scenes), involves the usual unbearable pressure; a trickle of blood emerges from Grant's mouth. Upon reaching orbit they remove their helmets and move around the cabin normally. Grant reports to the mission's ever-present ground monitor, Cliff Lawson (Michael DeBeausset), that weightlessness is "no problem," but the astronauts never experience any weightlessness. There is also a familiar bit of comedy involving space food: Duncan places pills in special containers that expand into omelets, but Grant pulls out a pastrami sandwich he brought as a more palatable alternative.

After docking with the rocket, the astronauts settle into a series of scenes that convey, with some success, how tedious a nine-month space flight might be. Several briefing sessions allow the astronauts to tell each other snippets of information they already know, for the benefit of the audience; astronauts engage in arm-wrestling and chess; one astronaut reads, for some reason, Jules Verne's *Twenty Thousand Leagues Under the Sea* (1869); and one astronaut gives another astronaut a haircut. There are only two moments of excitement, one of them a now-predictable meteor storm of dangerous particles that fly past the spaceship without doing any damage. The other, stranger development is a sudden glimpse of two motionless astronauts, drifting through space, obviously members of the mystery-shrouded Russian mission to Mars. The fate of its third cosmonaut remains unclear. Blaiswick speculates that the men were buried in space and notes they are not moving because they were "frozen in orbit." In light of previous depictions of doomed astronauts floating in the void of space, these scenes might have some emotional impact if it were not so obvious that the two cosmonauts are little toy figurines.

A difficult landing requires the astronauts to detach their rocket, but upon seeing the landscape outside, one man reports it was "like landing in the Arizona desert"— possibly a screenwriter's inside joke in anticipation that the frequently employed American Southwest would again stand in for an alien planet in this film (though *Mission Mars* was actually filmed in Florida). The astronauts then emerge from the spaceship in a new sort of spacesuit — all white outfits, not particularly sturdy, with faceplates extending over their faces but leaving their chins and necks exposed. Often derided as a laughable scientific error, the odd garments can be defended on the grounds that, since Mars has a thin atmosphere, complete protection against its environment is not necessary. But even if these spacesuits could provide the astronauts with sufficient oxygen (without having it all drift away), there remains the problem of the bitter Martian cold — which the film actually brings up: The astronauts discover the frozen, standing body of the third cosmonaut, whose fate is explained by the supposition that "his heating unit failed." Yet if Martian weather is cold enough to freeze humans lacking a heating unit, why would astronauts wear spacesuits exposing their necks to the bitter cold? At least, one expects they would wear scarves.

While the fallen cosmonauts add drama to the story, the film never discusses how they died. One guesses that their spaceship experienced an equipment failure that caused the deaths of two cosmonauts during the flight and required the survivor to dump their bodies into space; then, after he reached Mars, his efforts to explore the planet were thwarted when his spacesuit no longer provided him with heat (though his spacesuit was at least airtight). Even after the frozen cosmonaut improbably wakes up later on, lying inside the spaceship, he never says a word about what happened during his mission. This suggests that the film's failure to explain its major developments — the actions of strange creatures on Mars — did not result from a deliberate desire to keep the aliens mysterious, but rather a lack of interest in providing a satisfactorily cohesive plot.

The astronauts first suspect that aliens might be around when they reach their rocket and find a large hole burned in its hull and its contents scattered on the ground. Attempting to return to the spaceship, they notice someone or something removed the balloons they left suspended at various points as markers. Yet, as if fearing such tantalizing clues to an alien presence might be insufficiently entertaining to audiences, the filmmakers rush an actual alien onto the scene, as there suddenly materializes an elongated plantlike creature with arms ending with flat plates (later said to absorb solar energy) and a large head with one red eye, with the power to emit blinding rays of light. The astronauts discover they can fire at the eye to make the creature collapse and vanish.

The men rush to the spaceship to consult with Lawson, whose advice and instructions (unlike those in "The Invisible Enemy") are invariably welcome and helpful. They theorize that the creatures — called "Polarites," for some reason — are actually probes, controlled by and providing information to some unseen entity. Lawson orders the astronauts to take off immediately, but their spaceship is being held by a force, presumably emanating from a strange sphere that materialized nearby. When the sphere splits open, Duncan approaches it. After being first blinded and later killed by energy blasts, his body is dragged into the sphere. An emergency mission to the supply rocket, to obtain a supplemental rocket booster that might allow the spaceship to lift off, is facilitated when the surviving astronauts discover a creature apparently standing guard near their vehicle can be disabled by moving their antenna so its shadow cuts off the sunlight, which the creature depends on to remain active. Also, the frozen cosmonaut has somehow come to life, although he remains silent.

When the astronauts find that their spaceship is still locked in place even when they use the booster, they confront the sphere, which splits open again and first begins to echo, in a fuzzy deep voice, everything that Blaiswick and Grant say to them. But then it offers a sentence of its own, the nearest approximation to an explanation for its motives: "I want one of you, alive!" Grant decides to sacrifice himself to save his crewmate and voluntarily walks inside the sphere, which immediately explodes. Though Blaiswick witnessed the death of his crewmen, and the Russian experienced the same thing, they are inexplicably upbeat as they launch the spaceship back to Earth. To put the icing on this artificially happy ending, the film ends with Blaiswick receiving the happy news that his wife will have his baby.

The ultimate difference between *2001* and *Mission Mars* is that the former film's alien presence is carefully crafted so its plans and powers remain an ambiguous basis for thoughtful discussion; here, the alien entity is simply a monstrous menace that the astronauts must escape. The only patterns to be discerned in its arbitrary behavior involve an apparent desire to torment visitors in the process of studying them, like a boy pulling wings off of a fly. As will be discussed, Dave Bowman might also have complaints about the way he is treated by unseen aliens, but he emerges from his experience still willing to embrace the cosmos and its imponderable mysteries; but Mike Blaiswick, appalled by everything he observed, only wants to hurry home to the conventional domesticity of a wife and baby. Pondering the challenges of conquering space, he and his film, like many pseudo-spacesuit films, take the easy way out.

The Green Slime (1968)

The Green Slime involves yet another legitimate concern — that astronauts might unknowingly pick up dangerous alien lifeforms during their travels — dramatized in a risible manner. It most resembles the *Outer Limits* episode "Specimen: Unknown" since the deadly creatures first appear on a space station, with the primary concern being to prevent them from getting to Earth. But instead of the innocuous-looking flowers deemed suitable for television, the aliens featured in films must be large, ambulatory monsters.

As the film begins, an asteroid is detected on a collision course with Earth, due to hit in ten hours. Thus, *The Green Slime* stands with *La Morte Viene dallo Spazio* and the *Men into Space* episode "Asteroid" as a rare film of this era which recognized this potential hazard. To neutralize the threat, the retiring head of Space Station Gamma 3, Jack Rankin (Robert Horton), leads a hurriedly organized expedition to the asteroid to plant explosives and destroy it before it reaches Earth. Upon arriving, two teams of spacesuited astronauts drill holes and bury large boxes with explosives at what one assumes are precisely calculated places to achieve maximum damage. (The operation is not well explained, as if to announce it is merely a pretext to introduce the film's true menace.) Rankin's team drives a space buggy to their designated location, though this seems an ineffective vehicle for an asteroid's rugged terrain.

As they carry on with business, one astronaut notices a strange puddle of bubbling

Treacherous Terrain: Astronaut Jack Rankin (Robert Horton) and an unidentified colleague prepare to blow up an approaching asteroid imperiling the Earth in *The Green Slime* (1968).

green goo and picks up some of it. When he leaves to be safely distant when the explosives are detonated, Rankin is irritated to find that masses of green goo prevent the buggy from starting, requiring his men to abandon their equipment and run to their spaceship. To add drama, monitors on Gamma 3 report that the asteroid is impossibly accelerating, requiring the explosions to be advanced to a time when, the guarded language implies, Rankin and his men will still be close enough to be killed. But by pushing their spaceship to its limits, they get far enough away to survive.

Back at the station, domestic conflict briefly comes to the forefront, as new commander Vince Elliott (Richard Jaeckel) resents the brief reinstatement of his predecessor and is anxious to regain control. There is also tension between the men because Rankin's former girlfriend, physician Lisa Benson (Luciana Paluzzi), is now engaged to Elliott. Both Rankin and Elliott suspect she still loves Rankin. That Rankin, played by the film's major star, will prove the better man and win Benson's heart is virtually preordained, but there is an early signal of his superiority: Upon returning, Rankin insists that their equipment must undergo maximum decontamination, but Elliott, arguing the process takes too much time, vetoes this. Twenty minutes into a ninety-minute movie entitled *The Green Slime*, everyone in the audience knows Elliott's decision is disastrously wrong, especially since we repeatedly glimpse a glob of green goo on one man's folded clothing.

Soon, as a technician examines the returned equipment, the glob seethes and expands, and the man screams in terror as he is assailed. When Rankin and others rush to investigate, they spot a small green creature with tentacles. While this problem is dealt with, Benson's autopsy reveals that the man was somehow electrocuted, establishing that the aliens are deadly. Elliott then finds himself on the wrong side of another dispute: A concerned Rankin insists that all signs of alien infestation, which threatens to spread throughout the station, must be eliminated, while Elliott argues they should be preserved for scientific study as the first specimens of alien life that humanity has discovered. Science fiction filmgoers heard this argument long before, when it was central to *The Thing (from Another World)* (1951), and just as events thoroughly discredited that film's namby-pamby scientist seeking to study that film's lethal vegetable, and vindicated the soldiers seeking to kill it, attacks by larger monsters will discredit Elliott and vindicate Rankin. This becomes obvious more quickly in *The Green Slime*, however, since director Kinji Fukasaku, less skilled than *The Thing*'s uncredited director Howard Hawks, cannot sustain prolonged suspense regarding his monster's nature and appearance, and instead rushes to scenes featuring man-sized monsters, with green tentacles and one glowing red eye, menacingly advancing on station residents.

A certain monotony now sets in, as monsters keep appearing and men keep fighting them off using large ray guns. Rankin reaches the obvious conclusion: The station must be evacuated so it can be destroyed, to prevent the creatures from reaching Earth. He is again opposed by Elliott, who refuses to order the station's destruction until commanded to do so by superiors. By this time, all personnel on the station recognize Rankin as the better leader and effectively stage a mutiny, following Rankin's orders and ignoring Elliott. In these events, there is debatably an important point about life in space: Given the daunting challenges likely to confront space travelers, people must make hard decisions and face unpleasant consequences. Rankin, tough enough to handle space, is destined to triumph; Elliott, the weakest link, is destined to fail. To underline the point, Benson unambiguously chooses Rankin over Elliott.

As if filmmakers recognized that battles against monsters inside the station were becoming repetitive, Rankin discovers that his efforts to evacuate the station are being hampered by monsters who somehow got outside the station to surround its power source. This requires teams of men to put on spacesuits, go outside, and fly in space shooting ray guns at the creatures. Compared to the rest of the film, these scenes are actually exciting and suggest, long before *Crouching Tiger, Hidden Dragon* (2000) and similar films, that allowing combatants to defy gravity results in fascinating fighting sequences (though nothing resembling the artistry of Ang Lee's film is on display here). Later, as Rankin himself ventures out to attack monsters and let others escape, and seems to be sacrificing his own life, Elliott makes up for his poor decision-making by joining the fray. Melodramatic conventions dictate what happens next: The flawed Elliott dies, atoning for his errors, while the heroic Rankin survives. Everyone leaves and the station plunges to a fiery destruction in Earth's atmosphere, eliminating the aliens.

Unlike many films of this nature, *The Green Slime* involved a major company — MGM, also noted for producing *2001*. It was a joint American-Japanese production with a decent budget, and featured a reasonably prominent star, Robert Horton, who starred in two television series. The fact that the film was not much better than, say, *The Crawling Hand* or *Frankenstein Meets the Spacemonster* makes it a major disappointment. Not until Ridley Scott directed *Alien* (1979) would someone display sufficient talent to bring this tired storyline to life.

As repeatedly noted, horrific spacesuit films can be defended as helpful correctives to overly Earthlike portrayals of space and its inhabitants in melodramatic and humorous spacesuit films, warning that space should be cautiously approached as a strange, unknown environment harboring strange, unknown menaces. However, as the films are modeled on traditional horror films, that is not the real message they convey.

Horror films generally adopt the stance of blaming the victim, arguing that its monsters afflict society because somebody made a fatal mistake: An archaeologist entered a cursed tomb, or scientists sought to learn something Man Is Not Meant to Know. After the unleashed terror is defeated, the lesson learned is that no one should make the same mistake again, as the tomb is resealed and scientists vow to never again engage in forbidden research. These films, then, do not suggest that future space travelers should proceed with caution, but rather that humans should never venture into space again. Sometimes, as in films ranging from *The Day the Earth Stood Still* to *The Angry Red Planet*, humanity receives a blunt warning along these lines from hostile aliens. Other films may not explicitly advocate an end to space travel and may even conclude with brave talk about future space initiatives, as in *The Quatermass Xperiment* and *Space Monster*; but is space travel really portrayed as a hopeful option for humanity when its probable outcomes include being transformed into monsters or slaughtered by enormous predators?

Thus, melodramatic and humorous spacesuit films encourage people to travel into space because it is comfortingly familiar, whereas horrific spacesuit films urge people to shun space because it is disturbingly unfamiliar. They all prod people to embrace what they know and avoid what they do not know — space itself, accurately portrayed only in genuine spacesuit films.

— 6 —

Parallel Flight Paths: The Foreign-Language Films

After resisting the notion of isolating foreign-language spacesuit films after 1950 in a separate chapter, fearing the appearance of cultural chauvinism, I concluded there are both practical and philosophical reasons to discuss them separately. As a practical matter, American scholars face the realities that foreign-language films may be difficult to find, may lack subtitles or dubbing for those unfamiliar with their languages, or may only be available as versions edited or modified for American audiences. In such cases, their analyses, unlike analyses of Anglophone films, must be provisional.

As a philosophical matter, foreign-language films may be distinguished from American and English space films because they were not influenced by the priorities of American science fiction, as first articulated by Gernsback. While Anglophone films did not always involve accurate science and plausible predictions, as innumerable examples demonstrate, producers often felt obliged to pay lip service to science, explaining, for example why even the silliest space film might offer tidbits of correct science or briefly depict characters in spacesuits. In contrast, foreign science fiction filmmakers never faced such expectations, since their traditions of fantastic, futuristic literature never valued or demanded scientific accuracy or logic. Indeed, only in the Soviet Union does one encounter evidence of such concerns, perhaps due to the influence of science fiction writer and visionary Konstantin Tsiolkovsky and a government-sponsored film industry with a desire to promote the Soviet space program in documentary-style films. To articulate why foreign-language spacesuit films seem different, it is not simply that they are more inclined to lapse into scientific nonsense, but that they do so without any guilt or embarrassment; American and British filmmakers acknowledge their stories should be scientifically accurate, even when they have no interest in meeting that standard, but foreign filmmakers seem unaware of the issue.

None of this prevents a foreign-language spacesuit film from making important contributions to our understanding of space, as examples will demonstrate, but the impact of Gernsback's ideas did make American filmmakers especially well prepared to move beyond conventional patterns in exploring this new realm. The irony is that the impulse to make realistic space films came from foreign filmmakers who sometimes consulted scientific experts; yet films by their successors at best reflect their influence only sporadically, while a tradition of genuine spacesuit films emerged and evolved in America.

In addition, foreign-language space films belong to specific national traditions with specific recurring traits, and so are best discussed as three bodies of work: films from Eastern

Europe, dominated by the Soviet Union, which generally stress fidelity to scientific facts despite a later tendency to venture into more fantastic stories; films from Western Europe, dominated by Italy, which are usually comedies or melodramatic tales of space conflicts involving human-like aliens (also observed in films from the former European colonies of Egypt and Mexico); and films from Western Asia, dominated by Japan, which tend to be Earthbound dramas about alien invaders and giant monsters. Thus, there are foreign-language analogues to genuine spacesuit films (in Eastern Europe), melodramatic spacesuit films and humorous spacesuit films (in Western Europe), and horrific spacesuit films (in West Asia) — discussed in the order of the last three chapters to emphasize those parallels.

• THE SOVIET UNION AND EASTERN EUROPE •

Arguably, *Kosmicheskiy Reys* was the first genuine spacesuit film, since it first features spacesuits resembling the actual garments later developed, and first depicts conditions both in space and on the surface of another world accurately. Thus, it seems appropriate that the first films outside the Anglophone tradition that one might call genuine spacesuit films also came from the Soviet Union and, in one case, pay explicit tribute to Tsiolkovsky, who inspired *Kosmicheskiy Reys*. Unfortunately, the films are not as well-known or well-regarded as they should be, because two took the form of documentaries that mingled stunning footage of future space travelers with diagrammatic scientific explanations and propagandistic flourishes, and hence were never seen in America; and others were only available to foreign viewers in highly distorted American versions. Even today, some of these films have never been given English subtitles and thus remain poorly understood by Western commentators.

Doroga k Zvezdam (*Road to the Stars*) (1957) and *Luna* (*The Moon*) (1965)

The first noteworthy space films from the Soviet Union are Pavel Klushantsev's little-known documentaries; his *Doroga k Zvezdam* (*Road to the Stars*) seems a Russian equivalent to the *Disneyland* episode "Man and the Moon" as a documentary including fictional sequences of a future space flight. Both films first examine the history of space travel, present information about the science behind this endeavor, and conclude with future astronauts traveling to the Moon. However, while "Man and the Moon" employs animation for its history, followed by von Braun's lecture, *Doroga k Zvezdam* more interestingly opens by dramatizing the life of Tsiolkovsky (Georgi Solovyov). Another difference is that *Doroga k Zvezdam* features not one but three imagined ventures into space — an orbital flight, construction and occupation of a space station, and a landing on the Moon.

In several scenes, the schoolteacher Tsiolkovsky gradually figures out the principles of rocket design: He takes some boys to launch a balloon into the sky; then, boating with one student, he begins tossing objects out of the boat, making the boat move in the opposite direction and demonstrating the principle of recoil that is central to rocketry. Amidst images the scientist looking at the sky or sitting in his office, deep in thought, Tsiolkovksy sketches a cannon, leading to a vision (shown by animation) of a gun that could fire endless numbers of bullets. From this, he develops a diagram of a rocketship (also animated) employing a similar principle to reach space. But there remains the problem of flying fast enough to reach escape velocity; to achieve this goal, Tsiolkovsky first imagines three rockets on top of each other, and animated sketches of the rockets become an image of a multi-stage rocket. Unfortunately, the film notes that no one at the time was interested in his work; after Tsiolkovksy examines one of his publications outlining ideas for space travel, a later scene pointedly shows the document being used to wrap fish, illustrating how he is being ignored.

Throughout these developments, Tsiolkovksy ages to become an old man with gray hair; but the story continues with other researchers experimenting with rocket fuels and rockets launched into the sky. The trend in the scenes is that rockets get larger and larger, and more and more people are involved, so we finally see many scientists in a large laboratory, working to construct a rocket. Thus, as presumably reinforced by narration, audiences see how Tsiolkovksy's theories were gradually taken seriously, first by independent enthusiasts and later by the government.

After a few newspaper headlines probably announcing the launch of Sputnik, the film shifts to the near future with the first launch of a manned spaceship. As a crowd watches, three cosmonauts confidently stride to a spaceship, enter the vehicle, and strap themselves into horizontal couches. When launched into space, one cosmonaut releases his belt and floats upward, illustrating zero gravity and delighting crewmates. (An animated sequence of a man in an elevator explains why weightlessness occurs in space.) Initially, cosmonauts wear caps and jackets recalling the clothing of aviators, but when one man takes a spacewalk, he emerges from his craft upside down, wearing a persuasive spacesuit, and floats in space before reattaching himself to the ship and making his way around the vehicle. The spacewalk ends with an impressive long shot of a tiny cosmonaut standing on the spaceship as it flies past an enormous Earth. Finally, the spaceship returns, oddly landing horizontally on a body of water, and cosmonauts proudly ride to shore in a boat.

During this orbital flight, as if conveying an eventual goal, the film shows the Moon several times. But before that journey, several more rocketships being raised and readied for launch signal that something else must first be accomplished: constructing an orbital space station. A spacewalking cosmonaut apparently oversees the latching together of two pieces of this station and uses a small rocket to maneuver in space. This figure is attractive because, unlike the darker spacesuit of the previous spacewalker, his spacesuit has a bright golden color. Soon, the station is completed — a large golden torus containing a crew, three dishes resembling radio telescopes on one side, and an apparent lattice of propulsion units on the other side.

In several scenes depicting life on the station, the domestication of space is visibly portrayed; for the first time, we observe women (on the station they appear to outnumber the men), and one woman relaxes in private quarters, watching a ballet on television, while a cat lies next to a window, gazing out into space; another man converses via picturephone with someone on Earth, while others walk by a sort of botanical garden. A noteworthy scene shows a spacesuited astronomer in space, peering through a telescope, perhaps taking the pictures of Mars later discussed inside the station.

Attention shifts to a spacecraft attached to the station, ready to travel to the Moon. As it departs, a spacesuited figure in space waves goodbye, while station residents observe its progress through large windows. In what seems a hurried sequence, in contrast to depictions of previous space flights, this spaceship orients itself to land on the Moon, and a cosmonaut descends a ladder to the lunar surface. As he takes the first steps on the Moon, triumphant music swells. When he is joined by a comrade, the cosmonauts make exuberant gestures with outstretched arms and even embrace, conveying their delight upon achieving this amazing feat.

A later documentary from Klushantsev, *Luna* (*The Moon*), extends the story of *Doroga k Zvezdam* by depicting not only the first flight to the Moon, but humanity's gradual colonization of that world. The director begins with an extended discussion about the Moon. Since this is another film without English dubbing or subtitles, the nature of these opening sequences is a matter of conjecture, but multiple images of the lunar surface, intermingled with scenes of molten lava, suggest that features of the Moon are being explained as the result of volcanic activity. There follow several lectures from people one assumes are scientific authorities, who sit behind desks and talk about the Moon, again probably focusing on its geology. Then, a projected flight to the Moon is presented, solely relying upon animation of spaceships and astronauts, along with footage of Alexei Leonov's pioneering spacewalk.

Finally, the film becomes more interesting as we meet two cosmonauts on the Moon, portrayed by live actors. Unusually, they are a man and woman, who alternately narrate their experiences on the Moon. First, a woman hammers a nail inside a small chamber, presumably to show the low lunar gravity, as she drops the hammer and it falls very slowly. Then the cosmonauts are on the lunar surface, wearing large and bulky spacesuits making them appear fat and forcing them to move slowly and awkwardly, though the man playfully lifts the woman with one hand and tosses her a great distance, again illustrating the weak gravity. At one point, cosmonauts wear long slats resembling skis, probably to avoid sinking in lunar dust. Recalling the opening scenes, they seem especially interested in the Moon's geology, as they stick a probe into the ground, examine rock formations and jewels, and watch a lunar avalanche.

Advancing into the future, the film shows a huge vehicle resembling a metal spider, and people inside a large room surveying Earth; one also sees other equipment and a radar dish probably being used to examine Mars, as demonstrated by photographs of the planet. As in *Doroga k Zvezdam*, cosmonauts relax by watching a televised ballet, evidently Russia's preferred form of entertainment. Members of the growing lunar community mostly live in large spherical chambers positioned above the surface on spires, with interiors including lush gardens with plants and fruits — another link to the earlier documentary. There is also a rocket launcher that sends vehicles into space in a long cylindrical lattice, perhaps representing the "mass driver" space enthusiasts have long argued could economically transport minerals from the Moon to Earth.

A final scene is especially evocative: The man and woman are again in spacesuits, looking at the spherical chambers, but now they walk hand in hand with a little boy, also wearing a spacesuit, who must be their son. This, then, may be the first film to depict a child born on the Moon. To again connect these achievements to history, the film concludes with an image of a statue, perhaps Tsiolkovsky himself, standing near a rocketship.

Overall, *Doroga k Zvezdam* and *Luna* merit commendation for placing depictions of future space accomplishments within the context of a long historical struggle to achieve space flight; "Man and the Moon" had only done so to a limited extent with humorous animation, and other spacesuit films ignore earlier visionaries to portray pioneering space flights as the sole result of their heroes' work. The scenes of spaceships and cosmonauts are impressively authentic, and some images of life on the station and the Moon have a unique charm. Still, both films lack one important element, drama; even Disney's documentary includes an astronaut taking a spacewalk to fix a mechanical problem and unexpected signs of intelligent life on the Moon, and other spacesuit films have astronauts confront crises ranging from meteors to equipment failures. Thus, despite their virtues as visions of future space endeavors, one aspect of the films is completely unrealistic: the implicit claim that, during the conquest of space, nothing will ever go wrong.

Nebo Zovyot (*The Sky Calls*) (1959) and *Battle Beyond the Sun* (1962)

A comparison of *Doroga k Zvezdam* and *Luna* with *Nebo Zovyot* (*The Sky Calls*) shows that the dividing line between documentaries and dramatic films is not always clear. All three films begin with realistic sequences — Tsiolkovsky's life, lectures from experts, and a fictional but plausible present-day scientist — and all proceed to depictions of future space ventures that are frankly conjectural. The difference between the films is that the prophetic part of *Nebo Zovyot* is longer, with fully developed characters, and its status as a hopeful dream is communicated only at the conclusion.

In the prologue, writer Troyan (S. Filimonov) visits the laboratory of space scientist Kornev (Ivan Pereverzev) to learn about the "people who explore space." Kornev tells him, "There is nothing interesting. No romantic plots" involved, only "work, persistent work. Blueprints and mathematics." From the start, then, this film announces a determination to be realistic, rather than colorful, in depicting humanity's future in space. Kornev shows Troyan sketches and models of spacecraft, along with "letters from fans of space" with diverse backgrounds: "Doctors, pioneers, engineers and miners write. In a word, all ages and all professions." This enthusiastic interest demonstrates, as Kornev later says, that to fly into space represents the "eternal dream of humanity." A colleague also wears a prototypical spacesuit, "the latest space fashion," which "protects from the cold of space and the sun." Though it seems that human space travel lies many years in the future, Kornev and others then board a spaceship to fly to an orbiting space station. An epilogue suggests that the flight, and subsequent events, are only either Kornev's or Troyan's dreams of the future, but this is not made explicit at this time.

Sitting in comfortable seats on a spacious spacecraft, Kornev and others look through a porthole at the receding Earth and approaching station, a revolving wheel with a large deck. Such scenes occur in other spacesuit films, but here the reclining space travelers and large porthole are in the same shot, contrasting the size of their bodies with the perceived size of their distant origin and destination. As the spaceship docks at the station, several spacesuited figures stand on the deck to observe their arrival; it resembles the deck of an aircraft carrier, though why a space station would require such a deck is not clear. Later, astronauts move authentically in two ways: They walk slowly and stiffly on the deck, but an astronaut also leaps up on the deck and walks with a light skipping motion, suggesting zero gravity. (Oddly, while the astronauts' spacesuits look impressively authentic, they incongruously wear business suits inside spaceships and the station.)

Among other interesting touches, when the spaceship later departs on its flight to Mars, an astronaut on the deck holds a camera, filming the event for posterity, an early indication that people would desire moving images of major accomplishments in space; and there is a brief romantic interlude involving a man and woman strolling on the deck, though as was true in the *Men into Space* episode "First Woman on the Moon," the spacesuits prevent real intimacy. Finally, to explain why no one on the station appears weightless, there is a scene

Elder Spaceman: Scientist Kornev (Ivan Pereverzev, left), seen conferring with an unidentified colleague, may lack the youth and trim physique normally characteristic of astronauts, but he does bring a special gravitas to space travel in *Nebo Zovyot* (*The Sky Calls*) (1959). Its butchered American version was titled *Battle Beyond the Sun* (1962).

of a man from the spaceship, who just entered the station, wildly floating upward in a large chamber, telling colleagues, "Hello Earthlings, meet me," as they laugh and exclaim, "You've forgotten to wear your magnetic shoes."

Conflict arises when Kornev is contacted by two men, Klark (Konstantin Bartashevich) and Verst (Gurgen Tonuuts), requesting permission to visit the station; they are implicitly American, just as Kornev and his colleagues are implicitly Russian, though the film mentions no nationalities. Klark tells his companion, "I don't think they will be very pleased with our coming," for reasons that become clear during a subsequent dinner with Kornev and others at the station, where Verst announces, "Klark and I have decided to trek to Mars." Becoming the first to reach Mars would represent a victory for the Americans, at the expense of the Russians. But Kornev replies, "We are also flying to Mars," indicating that the nations are competing to get there first. (The American ship is named *Typhoon*, perhaps suggesting the Americans are bringing stormy discord into the peaceful realm of space.)

However, this Russian film understandably depicts Kornev as anxious to avoid any spirit of rivalry, enabling *Nebo Zovyot* to function as an argument about the purpose of space travel. Kornev surprises Klark and Verst by offering them a radio connection between Earth and Mars to make their journey easier; to explain, he announces the idealistic reasons that should motivate all ventures into space: "We have a great task. To open a path to other planets. To increase our knowledge of other worlds. To make space serve the people of Earth." He regrets that, instead of joining forces in order to achieve their common aim, "It's a pity that between us is a barrier and not friendship." Indicating that he does not care who gets there first, Kornev announces he will wait until next Wednesday to depart, since that is the most favorable time for a trip to Mars.

Klark and Verst feel differently, for even though the time is not yet ideal, they are pressured by commanders on Earth to leave the station immediately, though they may not have enough fuel for the presumably longer journey at an earlier time. They depart so quickly that they accidentally injure the astronaut Somov (V. Chernyak) who stood on the deck near their point of departure. Now he cannot be Kornev's co-pilot on the Mars flight and must be replaced by Andrei Gordienko (Aleksandr Shvorin).

And why are the Americans desperate to reach Mars first? Their motive is the excessive greed that, by Soviet doctrine of the day, drives all American capitalists. After they leave, we observe garish neon signs on busy city streets (including a Pepsi Cola sign), representing the Russian image of America, with announced breaking news about a "Sensation in space," sponsored by the "Mars Syndicate." Americans are urged to "Buy land on Mars. Ten dollars an acre," and to "Drink this space cocktail." Further, while they travel to Mars, Klark and Verst broadcast to Earth not news reports about discoveries in space, but commercials. After finishing one, Klark complains, "Damn the wiseguy who create these advertising transmissions." In light of the dangers involved in their early flight, this frenzied exploitation puzzles Kornev, who muses, "To risk for a sensation, I don't understand it." It is interesting to see how spacesuit films of the 1950s sought to reinforce negative stereotypes about the superpowers: American fears that the Soviet Union would seek a military advantage in space reflect a belief that the Russians were unrelenting warmongers, while Soviet concerns about the commercial exploitation of space emerge from an image of Americans as ruthless profiteers.

Later, when Kornev takes off on schedule, there is a brief sop to Russian patriotism when he and Andrei observe a passing satellite resembling Sputnik, said to have been constructed and launched by Kornev long ago — a reminder of the Soviet Union's first triumph in space. But the story becomes more dramatic, as the American rush to Mars predictably leads to a crisis. After finishing their commercials, Klark and Verst discover that their navigation system "has gone haywire," and instead of approaching Mars, "We are headed toward the Sun"; they are also threatened by "a meteor shower." Hearing their distress signal, Kornev immediately abandons his flight to Mars and instead aims to intercept the American spaceship and rescue its crew. These developments make little sense: Since a flight to Mars would begin with a prolonged period of rocket fire toward Mars, with small bursts of rocket fire for course corrections, it is difficult to see how even a "haywire" navigation system could cause the spaceship, after being launched toward Mars, to reverse course and head for the Sun. Also, this would not be an urgent crisis, since it would take a long time for a spaceship to travel from a space station in Earth orbit to the Sun, ninety-three million miles away; there should be plenty of time for a rescue effort without Kornev's immediate assistance.

Strikingly, the plot of *Nebo Zovyot* now seems much like the *Men into Space* episode "Mission to Mars," except that the national roles are reversed: In the American story, the Russians unwisely rush to reach Mars and end up imperiled, and the Americans abandon their own quest for Mars to rescue them. Since an authoritative reference — *The American Film Institute Catalog: Feature Films, 1961–1970* — states that *Nebo Zovyot* was released in

Russia in September 1959, the Russian filmmakers could not have been influenced by "Mission to Mars," which aired on May 25, 1960; but since foreign films were often privately screened in Los Angeles for audiences of filmmakers, it is very possible that someone connected with the series saw *Nebo Zovyot* in late 1959 or early 1960 and decided to use its story in an episode. (Roger Corman may have been in the same audience, inspiring him to purchase the rights to *Nebo Zovyot*.)

When Kornev maneuvers his spaceship near the *Typhoon*, we observe Andrei first standing upon his spaceship; then he is on top of the *Typhoon*, opening the hatch to take him inside, and he leads the Americans out of their own spaceship to board the Russian ship. What might have been the most impressive sequence — men floating from one spaceship to another — is oddly omitted. At this point, the Russian and American stories diverge: While McCauley rescues the Russians and returns home without incident, Kornev finds he does not have enough fuel to return to the station, so he lands on Ikar (Icarus), an actual asteroid with an orbit which takes it both near Mars and near Earth. Upon landing on Icarus, depicted as a dark blue, rocky object with tall pointed spires, the men set up radar screens so an unmanned rocket with fuel, sent from the station, can be guided to a landing. As Icarus approaches Mars, one American observes the planet and bitterly comments, "It's insulting. We have travelled a million kilometers and we are stopped right at the gate." In response, Kornev philosophically says, "Let this be a cruel but useful lesson about useless competitions."

After the unmanned rocket crashes into the jagged asteroid, the men seem doomed, because eventually "Ikar will go into the Sun" (which is not true). It is said that they have fallen into "a space mousetrap," and a joke about finding a "Space Friday" suggests that the men, like Robinson Crusoe, are stranded on a deserted island without hope of rescue. When an American denounces Earth for bringing them to this sad fate, Kornev insists he is still grateful because Earth "has given me wings to space" and "She teaches me to bring happiness to people." As station personnel debate how they might save the men, a now-recovered Somov develops a plan, shown after one stranded man has a dream involving a strange, brown-suited astronaut on Icarus, holding a sparkler; he awakens, looks out, and sees an actual astronaut staggering across a rocky outcropping before collapsing. It is Somov, who piloted another rocket with fuel to the asteroid at the cost of his own life.

Pondering his body, the men ask, "How did he manage to get here with an unmanned rocket?" But audiences will wonder why the trip was fatal. Summaries of the film say the rocket lacked the radiation shielding in spaceships intended for human occupants, so Somov died from overexposure to radiation. While this would be logical, the version I saw has a different, more puzzling explanation in a subtitle that is perhaps a poor translation: "Maybe he crossed the zone with an extreme explosion and literally burned it out." This suggests that Somov, rushing to rescue the men, propelled his unmanned rocket with an "extreme explosion" that damaged the spacecraft and caused his death.

Now refueled, Kornev's spaceship returns to Earth for an extended anticlimax. As crowds of admirers gather, the spaceship oddly lands on a platform in the ocean, perhaps to protect onlookers from fiery rockets. Kornev and the others ride a motorboat to the shore, where they are greeted by wives and mothers and make brief speeches. One American, acknowledging Kornev's kindly acts, notes, "I've realized that people on Earth are much better than I thought," while a Russian lauds Kornev because "You have made us believe in the power of human friendship." This probably inspired the more subdued scene in "Mission to Mars" when McCauley is praised by the president. But Kornev remains anxious

Hit-and-Run Space Drivers: Rushing to get a head start on their Russian competitors, the sinister Americans of *Nebo Zovyot* (*The Sky Calls*) (1959) injure Russian astronaut Somov (V. Chernyak), as observed by an unidentified crewmate, when they take off from the space station. The plot development was retained (with the nationalities of those involved now omitted) in the film's American version, *Battle Beyond the Sun* (1962).

to reach his original goal, since instead of taking a more traditional vacation after his adventure, he says his next vacation will be "on Mars."

Finally, the film abruptly returns to the scene of its opening sequence, with Kornev examining blueprints, and we realize that the film's story is only someone's dream. Underlining the point, Kornev says, "We are only spying on space. But after some time and people will own the space." He then looks directly at the camera and, with avuncular warmth, delivers the final line: "Safe journey, younger generation." *Nebo Zovyot*, in other words, was intended to inspire younger viewers to achieve the sort of space flight the film depicted. Arguably, all spacesuit films share this goal, but only this one states it out loud.

When Corman saw *Nebo Zovyot*, he realized that its impressive special effects would appeal to American audiences — as long as certain changes were made. In doing so, he ironically reinforces the film's unflattering perception of Americans as greedy profiteers, seeking money at the expense of all other considerations; for his version of the film, crafted by a young Francis Ford Coppola and retitled *Battle Beyond the Sun*, proved an exploitative butchering of an admirable film. *Battle Beyond the Sun* only occasionally duplicates the impact of the original.

First, it was necessary to alter the geopolitical underpinnings of *Nebo Zovyot*, which Coppola accomplishes with a new opening sequence, mostly consisting of clips from the original film, a few additions, and no dialogue, only voiceover narration. Eliminating any suggestion that the story is someone's dream, Coppola's narrator announces that the film takes place in 1995, after a worldwide nuclear war. The world is now divided between two nations, shown on a map that Coppola inserts: North Hemis, replacing the Soviet Union, and South Hemis, replacing the United States. Kornev, now called Andrew Gordon to suggest that he is American, again flies to his nation's space station, soon to embark on the first flight to Mars.

When Klark and Verst (who retain their names) contact Gordon to request permission to dock at the station, they now say that their spaceship needs repairs and have no plans to fly to Mars until Gordon announces his impending journey, inspiring them to take off immediately for Mars although recent repairs will make the flight risky. In these ways, *Battle Beyond the Sun* makes the story more like "Mission to Mars," where McCauley waited to make last-minute improvements in his spaceship while the Russians launched without such precautions. Just as one suspects someone from *Men into Space* saw *Nebo Zovyot* before writing "Mission to Mars," then, one suspects Coppola saw "Mission to Mars" before developing his version of *Nebo Zovyot*.

The story proceeds much as it did in the original film, though more quickly (all in all, Coppola's editing removed about half the original film), with an astronaut replacing the injured Somov, renamed Craig Matthews. However, when the ship lands on Icarus, Coppola's version, presumably to explain why the men see Mars at close range, idiotically describes Icarus as a "moon" of Mars, which is both factually incorrect and illogical: for if Gordon's ship had enough fuel to reach a Martian moon, it surely could have landed on the planet itself.

One final alteration is especially risible. In the original, the man who pilots the rescue mission dies for poorly specified reasons. However, Coppola preferred another, more crowd-pleasing development, and hence added brief footage of two ludicrous monsters to cause the man's death. Needless to say, no creatures like this could survive on a small, airless asteroid. Further, since there was little available footage to suggest that anyone on Icarus felt menaced by an approaching monster, Coppola had to use the brief scene of the dreaming man backing away from the brown-suited astronaut twice. Then, when the dying man is approached by men from the spaceship, Coppola offers dialogue about "creatures." The men on Icarus do not even bother to investigate as they retrieve the fuel and prepare for liftoff.

Still, Coppola retains most of the film's original ending, and even a bit of its spirit, when Gordon, now back on Earth, says he does not lament his failure to reach his original goal because a life "has more value than any goal man can strive for." The narrator provides a final inspirational speech suggesting that Gordon's rescue will inspire further cooperation between the superpowers: "A greater insight to the real problems of mankind had been achieved. The way was now open for both sides to begin working together in peace, and out of their combined knowledge and effort all men would come to know a better world in which to live, and one day, perhaps, the entire universe." It is ironic, though, that this glowing vision of American-Russian cooperation is expressed in an American film that brutally distorts an excellent Russian film.

Die Schweigende Stern (*First Spaceship on Venus*) (1960)

The East German–Polish *Die Schweigende Stern* has several alternate titles, including *Raumschiff Venus Antwortet Nicht*, *The Silent Star*, *Milczaca Gwiazda*, and *The Astronauts*, but is best known by its first American title, *First Spaceship on Venus*. Though American distributors cut 30 minutes and dubbed in English dialogue and narration, they added no footage to this most accessible version and left its story intact, which reflects the influence of several American films, including *Destination Moon*, *Rocketship X-M*, and *Forbidden Planet*.

In 1985, humanity has achieved a peaceful global utopia (something not fully conveyed in the American version's truncated opening, mostly employing narration). A recently discovered spool with an undeciphered message is traced to a spaceship that exploded near Earth in 1908 and caused the famed Tunguska event. When scientists determine that the spaceship came from Venus, an international crew is gathered for humanity's first flight to the planet (the Moon has been reached and colonized, as established by scenes of the "first space station on the Moon"). In the original, crew members are identified only by nationality and occupation; the American version adds names: a Japanese physician (Toko Tani), Sumiko Ogimura; an American physicist (Oldrich Lukes), Harringway Hawling; a Polish engineer (Ignacy Machowski), Orloff; an African communications expert (Julius Ongewe), Talua; a Soviet astronaut (Michail N. Postnikow), Professor Durand; an Indian mathematician (Kurt Rackelmann), Professor Sikarna; a German pilot (Günther Simon), Raimund Brinkman; and a Chinese linguist (Tang Hua-Ta), Lao Tsu. The American film sometimes misrepresents nationalities — Durand is French, Brinkman American — but the crew's multinational background cannot be concealed. It is particularly striking that, after decades of all–Caucasian space flight, except for one Japanese-American, there appeared three films in 1960 — this one, *Space Men* (discussed below), and *12 to the Moon* — that each could claim film's first astronaut of African descent.

The night before the flight, Sumiko interestingly places all astronauts, including herself, underneath panels to provide "artificially induced sleep" so they are well rested for takeoff, a sensible way to deal with pre-flight jitters; it is less clear why astronauts wear brown bodysuits with cowls. The journey to Venus consistently mixes logical extrapolations and dubious science: A crewman expresses delight upon reaching space by smiling and saying he is "riding the clouds," a rare sign of a man enjoying space travel, and one man convincingly floats in the weightlessness of space. But the commander then orders a crewmate to "switch on the artificial gravity field" so everyone moves about normally. (Oddly, Sumiko later hands crewmates bottles of liquid food to drink, deemed necessary because of the special problem of digestion in zero gravity.) The spaceship, we are told, is under robot control "because no human being could handle the immensely complex machines of the spaceship by himself"; yet during a crisis involving a swarm of meteorites, mere humans in fact control the spaceship. The meteorites inspire evasive maneuvers that make everyone lurch back and forth, anticipating the similar antics of the *Star Trek* crew whenever the *Enterprise* is attacked, and the almost comical effect is heightened by speeded-up footage.

Then, when the commander cannot decelerate to avoid further meteors because "a meteor fragment has damaged the deceleration unit," one crew member volunteers to go outside to try to repair it. The astronaut wears a realistic silver spacesuit with a glass faceplate. But it is not explained how a meteor could gouge a hole in the spaceship hull without threatening its oxygen supply, or how the astronaut repairs the damage simply by spraying something on the hole. The other unusual aspect of the space repair sequence is that the

Virulent Venusian: Unidentified astronauts help their female crewmate, physician Sumiko Ogimura (Toko Tani), get safely away from a blob-like alien menace in *Die Schweigende Stern* (*First Spaceship on Venus*) (1960).

astronaut moves around while inside a framework of sorts, perhaps inspired by the large spacesuits of "Man and the Moon."

Of the two other noteworthy aspects of the flight, one is its ninth crew member — a diminutive robot named Omega that looks and moves like a miniature tank, though rows of instruments suggest a face. Omega plays chess with Orloff and always wins, frustrating the scientist, until Durand provides the robot with a "heart" that inspires the robot to occasionally let Orloff win. While there were other robots in space before, including the villainous Tobor of the *Captain Video* television series and Robby the Robot of *Forbidden Planet*, this helpful, obedient robot embodies a realization that space travelers would require intelligent machines to succeed, with this one given a human face (and human personality) to make him accessible. Second is a significant new finding: Sikarna translates part of the spool's message, which describes a Venusian plan to conquer Earth. Instead of returning to warn Earth (since they are beyond the range of radio contact), the crew continues to Venus, now apprehensive about what the Venusians might do.

What makes the film impressive, and surely inspired its American release, was its stunning visualization of Venus. Since they determine that Venus's atmosphere is 27 percent carbon dioxide, 14 per cent formaldehyde, with no oxygen, making it poisonous, everyone wears spacesuits, and the posited surface of Venus looks like a truly alien world, a murky, dark-blue environment with enigmatic stylized structures. When Brinkman, scouting the territory with Omega, falls into a crevice, he finds "metallic insects"— Venusian information storage devices. After other crew members explore what is termed Venus's "petrified forest," they report, "Our spacesuits are so heavy that working outside the ship is difficult," though there are no visible signs of problems. Astronauts also travel in small vehicles, perhaps the first cinematic anticipation of the "moon rovers" that later Apollo astronauts drove on the Moon.

Gradually, using data from their survey and the "insects," they figure out that what they studied is a Venusian power plant, constructed to launch an atomic attack on Earth; but "a terrible catastrophe" occurred that wiped out all Venusians, leaving behind only shadowy images of humanoid figures on a wall (recalling similar images from Hiroshima). Lao Tsu finds plant seeds, indicating there still could exist life on Venus.

While these revelations are dramatic, they suggest no immediate dangers, so more aggressive, and less plausible, menaces must be introduced. First, a few astronauts are threatened by an enormous, pulsating organic mass, modeled on the monster from *The Blob* (1958). Cornered by this ominous goo, Durand fires a ray gun to make it retreat; this somehow triggers the alien mechanism, transforming mass into energy and causing an increase in local gravity, making it impossible to launch the spaceship. Lao Tsu figures out how to reverse the process; at the plant's control center, while Talua does the work, Lao Tsu announces, "My spacesuit — it's punctured!" and "my air's escaping." Crewmates tell him to try to hold on while Brinkman flies a small shuttlecraft to bring him oxygen. Lao Tsu remains alive for an improbably long time but eventually dies; right before dying he is heartened by news that his seeds are growing, offering the promise of colonizing and reviving the devastated planet. Then, the desired reversal of the process drives the spaceship away from the planet, because "the negative gravity's increasing," stranding Talua and Brinkman and leaving only five survivors to return to Earth. These developments seem illogical, to put it mildly, though arguably the Venusians, like the Krell of *Forbidden Planet*, developed science so advanced from humanity's perspective as to have, as stipulated by Clarke's Third Law, apparently magical effects.

Upon landing on Earth, astronauts announce that, like the space travelers of *Rocketship X-M*, they learned a valuable lesson from the Venusians, "destroyed by their own machines." And despite their losses, they also resolve to carry on with space travel: "We still have a grave task before us. We must use our other planets. We'll travel further and further — it's mankind's destiny." Thus, the film presents three reasons for humanity to conquer space: the discredited notion of military advantage, already rejected by this future society and further invalidated by the Venusian experience; a quest to learn about alien forms of life, the motive of the film's flight, rendered inoperative when the Venusians turn out to be extinct; and a concluding call for humanity to find new resources in space, as foregrounded in *Conquest of Space*, along with the suggestion that space travel represents our destiny. Regardless of what happens to space travelers, it seems, spacesuit films always seize upon some reason to continue exploration. In science fiction literature, stories that reject the notion of space travel are rare; in films, they seem nonexistent.

Baron Prášil (*The Fabulous Baron Munchausen*) (1961) and *Automat na Práni* (*The Wishing Machine*) (1967)

A standard argument about the difference between science fiction and fantasy — that science fiction focuses on humanity's future, while fantasy looks to its past — is supported by two fantasy films from Czechslovakia featuring characters in spacesuits. Yet the films share few other similarities; *Baron Prášil* (*The Fabulous Baron Munchausen*) pays homage to earlier fantasies about space travel, while *Automat na Přání* (*The Wishing Machine*) expresses nostalgia for an earlier human lifestyle.

To explain why humans feel impelled to travel into space, *Baron Prášil* begins, in the manner of *Disneyland*'s "Man and the Moon," with a symbolic history of flight featuring animated images of butterflies and birds, a man gliding with wooden wings, an early airplane, a modern passenger jet, and finally a spaceship headed for the Moon. Like other space travelers in less-than-realistic films, pilot Tony (Rudolf Jelinek) lands on the Moon to discover that conditions there are not what science indicated. He makes several odd discoveries — footsteps, a glove on the ground, an old-fashioned Victorola playing a phonograph record, and a large bullet-shaped capsule with a plaque bearing the title (in French) of Jules Verne's *From the Earth to the Moon*. He then meets five humans who are normally dressed despite the lunar vacuum: Verne's travelers Barbicane, Nicholl, and Ardan, Cyrano de Bergerac, and Baron Munchausen — all literary characters who voyaged to the Moon. They escort the spacesuited man to a table to toast him with glasses of wine, and express regret that he did not remove his helmet to join the drinking. Because of his unusual garb and habits, they speculate he is from Venus, Mars, or Jupiter before Munchausen decides he is an inhabitant of the Moon.

To show Tony what life on Earth is like, Munchausen offers to take him to Earth in a wooden ship carried by winged horses. During the flight, Tony finally accepts that, at least in the world he entered, he needs no spacesuit to survive, and takes it off and dons normal clothing while Munchausen hurls the empty spacesuit into space. Somehow, the men travel through both space and time, arriving on Earth in the eighteenth century to become involved in typical Munchausen adventures: Visiting a sultan, they rescue an imprisoned woman, Princess Bianca (Jana Brejchová), who falls in love with Tony. While escaping, Munchausen tricks pursuing ships into destroying each other. A ship containing Munchausen and Bianca is swallowed by a whale, whereupon they meet other swallowed sailors before the whale is harpooned and they reach land, where they meet up with Tony. Munchausen assists a general by riding on a cannonball to learn the positions of enemy soldiers and tells improbable tales about past romances, including one with the Mona Lisa.

During these escapades, space travel is not forgotten: Fascinated by the Moon, Bianca stares at it every night. (Munchausen calls the Moon "an enigmatic body" that is "as gray as its inhabitants.") More significantly, Tony draws a series of pictures for Bianca describing a princess confined in a tower and the lover who rescues her by putting gunpowder into a well, turning the tower into a spaceship that travels to the Moon. Bianca likes his story but says, "To travel to the Moon, to throw gunpowder down wells, that can never be more than a dream." Tony makes the dream come true: He takes the general's gunpowder and puts it down a well, and when he and Bianca elude palace guards by donning suits of armor, Munchausen tosses a candle into the well, and the explosion sends the lovers hurtling into space. Halfway through the flight, the suits of armor magically become modern spacesuits, and they reach the Moon.

In the final scene, the connection between Munchausen and spacesuits is articulated by Cyrano, who watches Tony and Bianca approach the Moon. "You have arrived at just the right moment," he says. "Till now the Moon has belonged to us, the poets, the dreamers, the visionaries, and the fantastic adventurers. And for ever and ever, the lovers." As he speaks, a spacesuited Tony charmingly hands a bouquet of flowers to a spacesuited Bianca. "Now," Cyrano continues, "I throw my hat into the starry void that it might fly to other worlds! That in our name it may salute those audacious ones who are already on the way" to other worlds.

Director Karel Zeman's message is clear: While the documentary *Doroga k Zvezdam* connects future space triumphs solely to the earlier work of scientists, Zeman celebrates a different set of predecessors: literary voyages to the Moon crafted by dreamers like Cyrano, Munchausen, and Verne. It was not simply practical researchers, but imaginative storytellers as well, who inspired humans to develop technologies like spaceships and spacesuits. These characters greet Tony when he comes to the Moon, and salute him when he returns with Bianca, in a spirit of passing the torch from the fantastic space travelers of the past to the real space travelers of the future. *Baron Prášil* thus presents itself as a transitional film, offering a nostalgic look at fabulous space journeys of previous centuries along with images of factual space journeys that will soon occur. Finally, the romance between Bianca, a character from a past fictional world, and Tony, a representative of humanity's future, suggests that the two concepts of space travel they embody, despite obvious differences, might harmonize better than one might expect.

Like *Baron Prášil*, *Automat na Přání* begins in the world of the near future before taking its own, more symbolic journey into the past.[1] Two boys, Honza (Vit Weingartner) and Vasek (Milan Zeman), skip school to visit a world's fair with various exhibits displaying the technological marvels of today and tomorrow. They collect various brochures and playfully photograph each other but also engage in regular mischief as they cut in line, plant stickers on unknowing strangers, toss a banana peel into a woman's food, and take rides on forklifts. When a boy seeks to be photographed next to an airplane, and they run from an exhibit to watch two helicopters, we understand that they are especially interested in human flight, as soon becomes apparent.

When the boys are back in school next day, describing the trip to friends, they have more fantastic stories to tell. While these are visualized, the framing device of the conversation invites us to regard these accounts as their inventions. First, they walk into an exhibit filled with eerie blue light that takes a few hummed notes and produces music, while a beautiful woman materializes from nowhere and hands a boy a clear rubber ball with colored filaments inside, which he shows to classmates as if it supported his story. Then a boy enters a clothing store, positions himself inside an upright boy-shaped mold, and has his casual clothes transformed into a formal suit.

A stern teacher (František Filipovský) interrupts the discussion to begin class. While he lectures, the boys indulge in a memory — or fantasy — of the visit that is even more extravagant. To a large crowd, a voice announces in several languages, including English, "The greatest invention in human history, achieved by pooling the genius of the world's scientists! the Automatic Wish Fulfiller!" As the boys sneak past the line to get inside, two other children enjoy the device, which looks like two boxes on stands behind two doors that open, with everything covered with blue lights. First, a girl wishes for an enormous dessert, the doors open, and she sticks her face into the treat. Then an older girl wishes for a horse, and the doors open to reveal the girl riding the horse on an expansive field.

When it is their turn, the boys wish for a flight to the Moon. After the doors open, they are seated in a spaceship, wearing blue spacesuits with helmets, with their belongings nearby on the floor. As a voice makes announcements about the impending launch and a digital clock displays the countdown, the boys don their helmets, though their nervousness causes the visors to fog up, requiring them to lift the visors to rub them — illustrating one potential problem with spacesuits. What frightens the boys is the revelation that, following the exact parameters of their wish, the spaceship will only take them on a one-way trip to the Moon. In response to their protests, the voice stops the countdown 2.8 seconds before liftoff and offers the boys a deal: If they discover something more beautiful than Earth in the next three days, they can take a round trip to the Moon.

After they hurriedly remove the spacesuits, don their clothes, and exit the spaceship, they fall into a haystack and find themselves in an idyllic rural setting, near the house of one boy's grandfather. As they ostensibly begin a frantic search for something beautiful to please the voice in the spaceship, they actually leisurely engage in typical pastimes of children in earlier times: They blow bubbles, look through a kaleidoscope, examine the mouse one boy has in his pocket, go fishing in a peaceful pond, and put on a helmet and bonnet in the grandfather's attic and pretend to be other people. Instead of dreaming about space travel in the future, it seems, they rediscover the simple pleasures of the past, a point reinforced by skillful cinematography that makes their surroundings seem a veritable utopia.

But their original wish is still on their minds: While they fish, one boy fantasizes about their return from a successful space flight, as fireworks go off, crowds of people parade through the town carrying posters of the spacesuited boys, and the boys are escorted to a podium where a man makes a laudatory speech and presents them with gold medals and a plaque. The dream ends when they catch a fish and delightedly jump into the water to claim their prize; but this is precisely when their pleasurable sojourn comes to an abrupt end: A policeman appears, intent upon arresting them for various crimes. They hurriedly dress and run into a greenhouse, but ever-increasing numbers of policemen pursue and apprehend them. Following a brief trial, in which the presiding magistrate tries to frighten the boys with a bear and skeleton, a cage drops on the boys. Dressed in conventional striped prison garb, they are taken to a cell and told that they will be executed tomorrow.

The meaning of this turn of events might be better analyzed by someone who knows Czech, but the timing of the policeman's appearance suggests this might represent punishment for their persistent dreams of space travel, when they are supposed to abandon fanciful aspirations for a new awareness of the joys of everyday reality. But the explanation I prefer is that the sequence is designed to balance the previously positive portrait of children's lives in the past, showing there were pains as well as pleasures for children of previous generations. In the past, children were punished for misdeeds, sometimes severely, whereas today, the adults around the boys tolerated their various acts of misbehavior. The deliberately antiquated appearance of the boys' prison garb and the prison where they are incarcerated may be designed to evoke the less pleasurable aspects of children's lives in earlier times; if children today have lost something in their ability to appreciate simple pleasures, they also gain by living in an era marked by both scientific and social progress.

Fortunately, the dark mood is lightened by the appearance of a childlike and incompetent guard, who leaves the door to their cell unlocked and is easily distracted when one boy helps him with his math, allowing the other boy to subdue him. They escape in a helicopter and fly toward the spaceship — but it takes off as they approach, denying them a possible trip to the Moon. A parachute falls from the spaceship with a note that asks, "Has your search for beauty taught you to distinguish between reality and fantasy?" Now reconciled to enjoying the world around them instead of obsessing about future possibilities, the boys run off through a green field to conclude the film.

Overall, despite the fact that the film's hoped-for flight to the Moon never occurs, it is hard to interpret *Automat na Přání* as an argument against space travel, or against dreaming about space travel. The film seems only to lament that today's youth are so enthralled by visions of conquering space that they neglect traditional activities of childhood which, even if associated with unenlightened times, remain worthwhile, nurturing experiences. The film might also represent writer-director Josef Pinkava's gentle proposal that people making children's films might profitably choose subjects other than space travel to focus instead on less trendy, but more enduring, sorts of realistic drama. But the final launch of the spaceship, even without the protagonists on board, still suggests there remains a place for space travel in today's society, though one perhaps less prominent than other science fiction films from Eastern Europe would suggest.

Planeta Bur (*Planet of Storms*) (1962), *Voyage to the Prehistoric Planet* (1965), and *Voyage to the Planet of Prehistoric Women* (1967)

Planeta Bur (*Planet of Storms*) was released in four versions: the original Russian-language version; a straightforward English-language version released in Britain as *Cosmonauts on Venus* (1962); another English-language version with added footage featuring Basil Rathbone and Faith Domergue, entitled *Voyage to the Prehistoric Planet*; and a third English-language version with different added footage featuring Mamie Van Doren and other actresses, entitled *Voyage to the Planet of Prehistoric Women*. The story remains the same, but the latter two versions add subplots to alter the tone and interestingly comment on the original film.

Planeta Bur is set in the near future, as the Soviet Union sends three spaceships on its first expedition to Venus; one is destroyed by a meteor before reaching its destination. The image of the spaceship suddenly exploding as the meteor hits, retained in all versions of the film, is a striking reminder that death in space can come swiftly and arbitrarily, though the film does little to drive the point home. In the wake of the disaster, it is decided that two men from one spaceship, Scherba (Yuri Sarantsev) and Kern (Georgi Tejkh), will land on Venus, accompanied by a robot, while the other crew member, female astronaut Masha (Kyunna Ignatova), will remain in their orbiting craft. By means of a goodbye kiss, which Scherba facilitates by lifting the faceplate of his spacesuit, we learn that Scherba and Masha are lovers, which explains why, later in the film, he is especially concerned about her fate. The men in the other spaceship, Ilya Vershinin (Vladimir Yemelyanov), Bobrov (Georgi Zhzhyonov), and Alyosha (Gennadi Vernov), initially plan to remain in space as observers, but after losing contact with Scherba and Kern on Venus, they land to search for their comrades.

On Venus, Scherba and Kern wear spacesuits with transparent helmets, though the atmosphere contains about four percent oxygen and, as is later established, they can survive for brief periods without helmets. The planet looks rather like Earth, but constant swirls of white fog and some exotic creatures are encountered, including hostile lizard men (played by men in rubber suits), an enormous carnivorous plant with tentacles, a dinosaur resembling a brontosaurus and a flying reptile identified as a pterodactyl in the Russian version (one of the few words I understood) but described only as a "flying reptile" in English versions. Scenes of Kern and Scherba shooting guns at attacking lizard men, and of Alyosha being ensnared by tentacles of the ravenous plant, do little to suggest this is a serious science fiction film, though arguably, if one grants that Venus might have a tropical environment (which scientists essentially ruled out by 1962), such inhabitants could be possible.

The character of John the Robot is more interesting. Shaped like a human, though larger, the robot possesses clawed feet to walk on unstable ground and is intelligent enough to carry on conversations. When Kern is suffering due to his torn suit (which means his spacesuit oxygen is being mixed with the less palatable Venusian atmosphere), members of the other party successfully instruct John by radio to take out a pill, pull open Kern's helmet, insert the pill in his mouth, and spray him with water to wash the pill down. Later, when the men are threatened by lava from an erupting volcano, they momentarily escape danger by climbing on the robot's back while it walks through the lava. However, it abruptly announces that, due to its self-protection mechanism, it will shortly have to reduce the excess weight it carries and drop Kern and Scherba into the lava — a danger they escape by disabling the mechanism. This suggests an awareness of Isaac Asimov's Three Laws of Robotics, which include a Third Law mandating that robots protect themselves. But in Asimov's system, that imperative would be overruled by the First Law (to preserve human life) and Second Law (to obey human orders), so astronauts would not be imperiled by an Asimovian robot; following the First and Second Laws, it would sacrifice itself to save humans.

There are also intriguing, if implausible, hints that Venus might have possessed, or even possesses today, intelligent inhabitants resembling humans. Members of the rescue party regularly hear a strange sound that Alyosha interprets as the voice of a woman, prompting discussion about the possibility that humans could adjust to the harsh environment of Venus. After the pterodactyl damages their hovercraft, the three men are forced to go underwater, leading to attractive scenes of the men walking on the bottom of the Venusian ocean. (Though spacesuits, built to withstand the vacuum of space, could readily protect people underwater, this film offers a rare glimpse of astronauts exploiting that feature.) They find strangely regular formations suggesting an ancient city's ruins and, more provocatively, a statue of a pterodactyl with a ruby eye, clearly constructed by intelligent beings, perhaps as an idol.

These suggestions of human-like Venusians are ultimately confirmed after the two parties unite and travel to the rescue party's spacecraft. During final preparations for departure, Alyosha uses a rock to break open a piece of equipment, and sees concealed in the rock the carved face of a beautiful woman, seemingly made of ivory, proving that humans once lived on Venus. They must take off and have no time to investigate, but after they leave, the film's closing image is of a Venusian pool in which the upside-down reflection of a human woman appears, gesturing upward. As the men speculated, the intelligent inhabitants of Venus stayed out of sight during their visit, perhaps regarding the visitors as monstrous intruders (which is how humans regarded spacesuited aliens in *The Man from Planet X* and *Phantom from Space*).

Given the quality of its special effects and a story with conventionally exciting moments, producers understandably discerned profits to be made by releasing the film in America, with dubbed English dialogue. Yet people marketing films to American audiences like to include an American actor or two, so it was logical to film new footage for *Planeta Bur* featuring American stars whose names could be displayed on theater marquees even though they make little more than cameo appearances. Thus, two actors were added to the retitled *Voyage to the Prehistoric Planet*, perhaps at different stages of production, since they are never seen together, and they separately address different perceived flaws in the original film.

Planeta Bur took place entirely in space: The story begins with spaceships already on their way to Venus, and ends when they are returning to Earth. Yet scenes of concerned characters on Earth can enhance the emotional impact of adventures in space, encouraging audiences to care about space travelers by showing people like them, in comfortably conventional terrestrial environments. Thus, as an additional narrative thread, *Voyage to the*

Prehistoric Planet introduces Professor Hartman (Basil Rathbone), who contributes nothing to the story but is regularly seen in a large monitoring station, sending anxious radio messages to inquire about the mission's progress. (Hoffman is based not on Earth, but the Moon, but only an occasionally glimpsed window displaying a lunar landscape indicates where he is.) Hoffman's message to audiences is clear: Here is an actor you recognize, in a place that looks familiar, conveying that he is worried about the astronauts on Venus, so you should worry about them too.

In addition, the character of Masha in the original film is almost always by herself, in the spaceship, communicating by radio with men on the surface. It would be easy, someone must have thought, to replace her scenes with new scenes featuring an American actress, who could attract audiences and deliver lines while her lips moved in the proper manner. Thus, to play the character renamed Marsha Evans, producers recruited Faith Domergue, recently seen only on television but known to science fiction fans for appearances in *This Island Earth* (1955), *It Came from Beneath the Sea* (1955), and *The Atomic Man* (1955). One potential problem was that Domergue, now forty-one years old, was visibly older than the actress she replaced and, by sexist standards of the era, unable to function as a romantic interest; it did not help that she sported a large beehive hairstyle that seemed completely inappropriate on board a spacecraft. Still, unlike the pointless Rathbone, she arguably improves the film: Not tied to one astronaut as a lover, Domergue's mature Marsha becomes a mother figure, with sufficient acting ability to suggest genuine affection for all the men on Venus. Like Jane Flynn in *Riders to the Stars*, she displays emotions that stoic male astronauts cannot show and inspires audiences to respond emotionally to their adventures.

Except for these additions, *Voyage to the Prehistoric Planet* is faithful to the original story, except for minor editing and, as a concession to American audiences, renamed characters: While Kern remains Kern, Scherba becomes Allan Sherman, Bobrov is Hans Walters, Ilya Vershinin is Brandon Lockhart, and Alyosha becomes André. Despite the generally American names, filmmakers cannot conceal the Russian words on the spacecraft.

It is a tribute to the quality of *Planeta Bur* that American producers decided to make a second American version, with new added footage and another new title, *Voyage to the Planet of Prehistoric Women*. To emphasize similarities between the two versions, one could say that, again, there were two sorts of new footage: Some scenes provide a broader context for the flight to Venus, while others heighten the film's appeal with a beautiful American actress. Yet the more unsettling additions here make this version very different from its predecessors.

To enhance the film's backstory, *Voyage to the Planet of Prehistoric Women* bizarrely borrows footage from *Nebo Zovyot*; thus, while narration describes how the spaceships heading for Venus first left Earth, then stopped at a space station for refueling, we see images of spaceships from the earlier film and its station with a platform where spacesuited astronauts observe an arriving spaceship. The fact that the spaceships from the two films look entirely dissimilar was evidently not regarded as important; to audiences, someone believed, all spaceships look the same. Even more strangely, one *Nebo Zovyot* scene of the spaceship nearing the rocky Icarus is described by the narrator as an approach to Venus, though the new film also includes footage from *Planeta Bur* showing Venus as a large, round world covered with clouds. It is hard to discern any purposes in these scenes; someone must have thought the effects from *Nebo Zovyot* were really neat and hence merited another appearance in a film for Americans.

What is more frequently noted about the film is its new scenes with voluptuous Mamie

Van Doren and other beautiful actresses as inhabitants of Venus, wearing seashells over their breasts and tight-fitting pants, who observe and (to an extent) interact with astronauts from the original film. Purportedly humorous commentators suggest it was the height of idiocy to introduce scantily clad women to a Venusian environment so inhospitable to humans as to require visitors to wear spacesuits, seemingly unaware that, in fact, a scantily clad woman is also shown on Venus at the original film's conclusion. Indeed, since *Planeta Bur* implies that such Venusians were always present, but stayed in hiding as men from Earth explored their world, it was perfectly justifiable for a new version of the story to actually show such Venusians watching their activities. The only valid complaint is that, by introducing the characters early in the film, instead of at the end, this revision of the story spoils the suspense of wondering whether such human-like Venusians actually exist.

Given that Venusians long ago built cities and carved images of themselves and pterodactyls, the planet's current inhabitants should be relatively civilized; yet the mentality of Van Doren (playing a woman named Moana) and her cohorts, as the title indicates, is definitely "prehistoric." The women, who evidently spend all their time sleeping on seaside rocks on a small island when not disturbed by visiting humans, worship the idol Ptera, modeled after the underwater idol in the original film. When the pterodactyl is accidentally killed by the men in the hovercraft, the women mourn its death and respectfully carry its body (the "body" is visibly pieces of cloth sewn together, not an actual dead reptile).

Angry because the men destroyed the flying reptile representing their god, the women pray to Ptera to send destructive fire to destroy the invaders, introducing scenes of the erupting volcano that menace Kern and Sherman. (This film retains the altered names from *Voyage to the Prehistoric Planet* and appears to take its footage directly from the American version, not the Russian original, since the retained dialogue is consistently identical.) When they discover that the men survived this menace, they ask Ptera to send horrible rain and are dismayed when this does not prevent their spaceship from taking off. This leads Moana to conclude that Ptera is a false god, since he could not kill the intruders, and as a better alternative, the women dig up the remains of John the Robot, covered with hardened lava, and make it their new god. Perhaps this is intended to recall the "cargo cults" created by primitive cultures that worshipped the artifacts of technologically advanced visitors, or even as a commentary on how scientific advances can lead to older deities being replaced by pseudo-scientific equivalents (as tales of angelic visitors are now largely supplanted by tales of visiting aliens). It suggests, more than the reflected image of the Venusian woman, that humans may tangibly affect Venusian culture.

But these scenes leave many things unexplained. Why do we only see young Venusian women, when one would also expect men, children, and old people? Why are these women so decadent, given that their people once possessed an advanced civilization? Perhaps we are supposed to imagine that, like the Martians of *Rocketship X-M*, the Venusians destroyed their society in a ruinous war that made them revert to primitivism; but filmmakers not only fail to explain why these women are the way they are, but seem unaware that there was a puzzling question to be answered.

As another logical lapse, *Voyage to the Planet of Prehistoric Women* is recast as a story told by André, who provides opening narration and announces he will recount what happened to him and his crewmates on Venus as a way to introduce the story. However, despite what is sometimes said about this film, André never actually observes or interacts with the Venusian women, so he could not tell anyone about them. He still finds the carved face, so he knows women once lived on Venus, but never learns that any are still alive. This film also omits the final image of the woman in the pool because this stately brunette, wearing a white gown, bears no resemblance to Van Doren and her companions.

Overall, one might defend both American versions by arguing that any account of the human experience, on Earth or in space, must include women, and that the Americans properly altered the film to enhance and expand the presence of women, in a way domesticating space more than the original story. Still, since few feminists would celebrate the introduction of Van Doren wearing seashells on her breasts as a tribute to women, one can also fall back on the idea raised by *Cat-Women of the Moon*, that pseudo-spacesuit films seek to include beautiful women, regardless of scientific accuracy, purely to appeal to adolescent males.

Ikarie XB-1 (1963) and *Voyage to the End of the Universe* (1964)

Significantly, Eastern European spacesuit films collectively convey an intent to gradually move farther and farther into the future of space travel while retaining an aura of realism; thus, after a documentary depicting a Moon landing, and films about pioneering trips to Venus and Mars, *Ikarie XB-1* involves the first expedition to another solar system. And unlike American films that usually posit faster-than-light travel to achieve such feats, this Czech production recognized that journeying to the nearest star, Alpha Centauri, would take a very long time, even moving at relativistic speeds, creating new issues for those who design the starship and select its crew.[2]

The film begins *in medias res* at a dramatic moment: A man on the ship with scars on his face, Michal (Otto Lackovic), has gone mad and threatens to turn the ship around, though he is told, "We can't go back now." Captain Vladimir Abajev (Zdenek Stepánek) thinks back to the time before the spaceship's launch. Docked to a space station, with two astronauts walking outside in spacesuits, the spaceship takes off, with passengers strapped down to experience the usual pressures of launch until it is announced, "Increased stress ended. Conditions normal."

Subsequent scenes move slowly, but that reflects the fact that the voyage will take fifteen years, from the perspective of Earth, and even passengers will experience a few years before reaching their destination, a "White Planet" orbiting Alpha Centauri. There is domestic drama: MacDonald (Radovan Lukavská) has a tense picturephone conversation with wife Rena (Svatava Hubenaková), who was left behind because she became pregnant (MacDonald later finds that the actual issue was her fear of space travel). He feels bitter upon learning that another passenger's wife, Steffa (Marcela Martinková), is also pregnant; but she came because no one knew of her pregnancy beforehand. A young man awkwardly romances the beautiful Eva (Ruzena Urbanova), with the secret assistance of Abayev (who automatically opens the door to her cabin when he nervously stands outside with a flower).

There are also moments of typical comedy: While others eat from trays with normal food, one man has a tray with a large pill, and another man being nagged by his wife to take his vitamins secretly feeds the liquid to his dog. An elderly passenger brings along a silly-looking humanoid robot, called "an antique." Other scenes quietly convey that a successful journey of such duration requires giving passengers lots of space and lots of things to do — as demonstrated differently in *Spaceflight IC-1: An Adventure in Space* (1965), wherein a small crew flying to Alpha Centauri is driven by stark, cramped quarters into fierce and sometimes physical conflicts, leading to three deaths. But conditions on this starship are more accommodating, as scantily clad passengers exercise with various pieces of equipment in a large room, play chess, watch movies, and play a grand piano. Finally, women don formal gowns to attend an elaborate dance, with couples making unusual, purportedly futuristic movements on the dance floor.

The event is interrupted by an alarm: The ship's computer has detected another spaceship approaching theirs. While one man insists the investigation should only employ robots, Abayev orders two men to don spacesuits and take a shuttlecraft to explore the vehicle. In the film's most interesting scene, the astronauts enter the spaceship and find several dead people, seated at tables with glasses of wine and seemingly interrupted abruptly while gambling and dining on fancy food. They were wealthy aristocrats who left Earth in the late twentieth century to escape from its turmoil; signs in English indicate they were Americans, and their decadent lifestyle is a clear critique of capitalism, though there is no blunt prop-

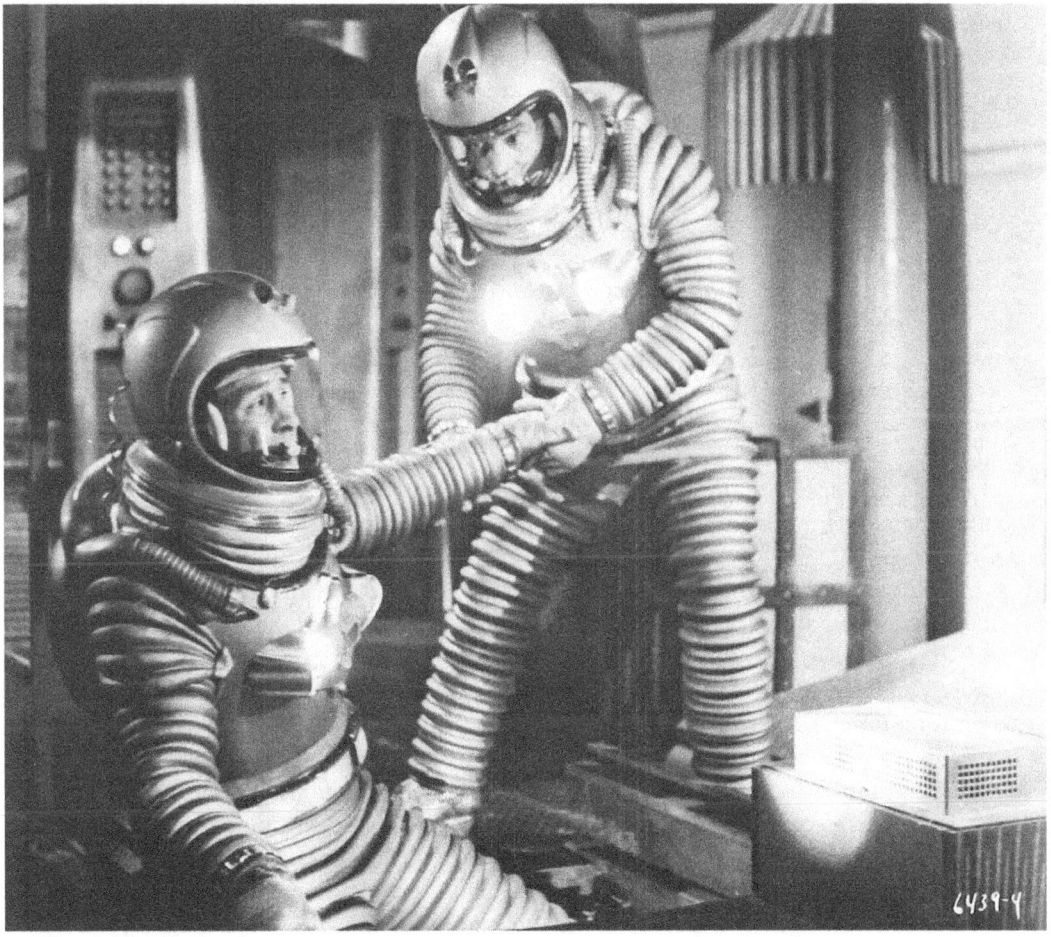

Socialist Spacesuits: Two unidentified crewmates on a Communist space mission don spacesuits to inspect a derelict spaceship for decadent capitalists in *Ikarie XB-1* (1963), reworked for American audiences as *Voyage to the End of the Universe* (1964).

aganda. As the most dramatic touch, an astronaut brushes against the face of one corpse and its decaying flesh falls away, showing a white skull.

The discovery of weapons on the spaceship suggests that something more sinister than a pleasure cruise might have been going on; the ship even contains nuclear weapons. When one is accidentally triggered, Abayev passionately urges his men to leave immediately, but it explodes before they can get away. A regretful Abayev says he should have heeded his crewmate's advice and sent robots instead.

Other problems then dominate everyone's attention: as if fulfilling a ritual obligation, passengers are briefly frightened by approaching meteorites, though they cause no damage. More gravely, after two astronauts in spacesuits go outside to install a spare rocket, everyone suddenly begins to experience "overwhelming fatigue," so much so that they must fight to stay awake. Abayev speculates this is an effect of radiation. After a rocket containing information from their flight is dispatched to Earth, so the expedition will not prove fruitless, passengers succumb to sleep, not expecting to wake up.

They are saved by residents of the White Planet, who are monitoring their flight and welcome the visit; they send out a force to dispel the effects of the radiation and revive the passengers. Now the astronauts who installed the rocket contract a disease that scars their faces. To oddly emphasize the disease's damaging effects, a woman comments, "Look what the radiation did to their spacesuits," and we see spacesuits covered with similar scabs. One man is calmly treated for his illness, but Michal goes on the rampage that opens the film. After destroying the robot with a ray gun, he is subdued by MacDonald and taken away to be cured. Soon, as the film's uplifting ending, Steffa's baby is born, the spaceship approaches the White Planet, and a glimpse of a gleaming white city suggests they will land in a pleasant utopia.

While not without unrealistic aspects, *Ikarie IX-B* merits praise for its unusual awareness of the true challenges involved in interstellar flight, as well as its recognition that, even in starships crossing the cosmos, there will remain a need for spacesuits. The story survives in its American version, *Voyage to the End of the Universe*, with some exceptions. First, the original theatrical version was cut to 64 minutes, eliminating the subplot of Steffa's pregnancy and birth. Second, some aspects of the plot are left unexplained: The origin and purpose of the derelict spaceship are not discussed, to eliminate any hint of criticizing American culture, and their recovery from fatigue is alternately theorized to have resulted from "some force," their "adaptation" to whatever radiation afflicted them, or "just luck."

Most importantly, the crew's destination is now the Green Planet, not the White Planet, and it is not described as orbiting Alpha Centauri. The reason for this becomes clear at the end, for when passengers near the Green Planet, they do not gaze upon a white city, but rather upon new footage of the skyscrapers of New York City and the Statue of Liberty, as seen from the air. This "surprise" ending, audiences must infer, means the passengers they have observed were not humans but aliens, whose lengthy journey was to Earth. This pointless change illustrates again that American producers of space films overwhelmingly prefer to take viewers to comforting, Earthlike places, instead of dauntingly different environments in space. Here, a pioneering voyage to a distant alien planet, its nature and inhabitants left unspecified, is transformed into a voyage to the most familiar environment imaginable, our own planet. Further, since people identical to humans are now depicted as aliens, the film adds the reassuring message that the aliens we encounter in space or on Earth will probably look just like us. It is surprising how a few seconds of additional footage — qualifying this as a separate film by my standards — can have such a broad transformative effect.

Mechte Navstrechu (*A Dream Come True*) (1963) and ***Queen of Blood*** (1966)

While my analyses of *Nebo Zovyot* and *Planeta Bur* were based on watching the original films, a person who only saw *Battle Beyond the Sun* and *Voyage to the Prehistoric Planet* could still claim familiarity with their foreign-language precursors, since the added footage does not unduly distort the original stories. The extent to which someone (like me) who only watched *Queen of Blood* can claim familiarity with its Russian predecessor *Mechte Navstrechu* (also known as *A Dream Come True* or *Encounter in Space*) is more debatable. True, the American film incorporates extensive footage from *Mechte Navstrechu* and follows its plot before crafting an utterly different conclusion; however, *Queen of Blood* effectively removes the original protagonists, except in long shots, replacing them with American actors, and includes far more original footage than other redactions of Russian films.

At the beginning of *Mechte Navstrechu*, the future Earth is a socialist utopia, and Andrei Sayenko (Boris Borisenko) sings a song he wrote about space travel to his girlfriend, cosmonaut Tanya Krilova (Larisa Gordeichik). This song is heard by aliens on the distant planet Centuria, who decide that a race capable of producing such music should be contacted at once. The aliens and their apparatus are impressively visualized: They wear strange transparent accoutrements on their heads, vaguely suggesting antennae, and their shadowy environs are filled with dark and glowing spheres of various sizes. Following the same stylistic motif, spaceships are also spherical, sometimes surrounded by glowing red tubes.

Their spaceship encounters difficulties, and the aliens must land on Mars, whereupon they send a capsule to Earth with video footage illustrating their plight. Earth immediately resolves to send a rescue mission which will include Krilova but not Sayenko. But the rescuers also face difficulties, as solar radiation damages their spaceship, and while they can land on Mars, they do not have enough fuel for a return flight. Exploring the barren Martian surface in spacesuits, they find a dead alien in a spaceship; knowing there were more aliens on board, the humans surmise that others left in another spaceship which must now be located to save potential survivors.

A second mission, headed by Sayenko, is hurriedly launched toward Mars. The spaceship releases observation satellites to assist in the search and lands on Phobos, where Sayenko discovers the alien ship and a living passenger—a beautiful alien woman wearing an elongated space helmet. She must be taken to Mars, but since the ship capable of making the journey can only carry two passengers, Sayenko altruistically stays behind, knowing he will die, so his comrade can escort the alien to safety. When they land, the cosmonaut begins an arduous trek across Mars, carrying the alien woman, but a massive sandstorm makes it difficult to locate the human spaceship. He and the alien woman seem doomed, as they collapse and become partially covered by the sand. But they are found and returned to the spaceship, which leaves for Earth, and there is a glorious, peaceful meeting between humans and the alien when they arrive.

A final scene showing Krilova and Sayenko beside a lake suggests the story may have only been Krilova's dream. Recalling that director Mikhail Karzhukov gave *Nebo Zovyot* the same sort of conclusion, one might see *Mechte Navstrechu* as an extension of the earlier film, as humans with an interest in space further envision a future in which divisions between nations are overcome, Mars is reached, and humanity achieves contact with aliens. However, since the alien is a beautiful woman who achieves effortless harmony with Earth, she suggests, like the woman at the end of *Planeta Bur*, that the impulse toward authenticity in the

Russian spacesuit film is being diverted toward the comforting idea that space, despite superficial differences, might be inhabited by beings whose appearance and proclivities resemble our own. However, nothing about its aliens and their behavior is quite as egregiously familiar as what is observed in its American version, *Queen of Blood*.

Asked to turn *Mechte Navstrechu* into an American film, director Curtis Harrington was surely impressed by its realistic depictions of spaceships and spacesuits, and evocative images of aliens and other planets (the Moon, Mars, and Phobos), since he employs many scenes with those special effects. But evidently unwilling to utilize footage of Russian actors with dubbed English dialogue, Harrington unusually replaces them with a new American cast, retaining only a few long shots of the original performers. More damningly, regarding its story of peaceful contact with aliens as insufficiently dramatic, he imposes a new ending which runs counter to the spirit of the original film.

Opening scenes of *Queen of Blood* recall previous spacesuit films more than *Mechte Navstrechu*, as Sayenko's replacement, astronaut Allan Brenner (John Saxon), tells this film's Krilova, Laura James (Judi Meredith), that he just completed a "high-G session," testing his ability to withstand the pressure of acceleration, and complains about the "exo-biologic" food eaten in space, which "tastes terrible." The one bad thing about space trips, he concludes, is "no banana splits." Their lunch is interrupted by an announcement from the space center's leader, Dr. Farraday (Basil Rathbone), that mysterious signals from space have been translated as a message from aliens soon to land on Earth. Their motive for visiting, which has nothing to do with a song, is only revealed at the end of the film.

Harrington follows the original story for a while, as a "video log" from the aliens reveals that their spaceship crashed on Mars, and a rescue mission is prepared that includes James but not Brenner. To his credit, the director tries to provide performers with spacesuits that are exactly like those in the Russian film, though discerning eyes can still tell the difference. Again, the spaceship with James, captain Anders Brockman (Robert Boon), and Paul Grant (Dennis Hopper) is threatened by a sunburst, causing Brockman to order crewmates to "put on your helmets" and "close your visors"; they also land on Mars, without enough fuel for the return trip, and find the spaceship with a dead alien. A second mission with Brenner and Tony Barrata (Don Eitner) launches observation satellites and lands on Phobos to find a spaceship with the alien woman.

At this point, the stories of *Mechte Navstrechu* and *Queen of Blood* begin to diverge. First, so as not to deprive James of her boyfriend's company, Brenner escorts the alien to Mars, and to avoid any hint of tragedy, Farraday specifies that another spaceship will arrive to save Barrata. More significantly, the alien woman has greenish skin, with speculations about a "chlorophyll content" in her anatomy making her more like a plant than an animal. Her nature is far from peaceful, as the always-silent woman, once the spaceship is returning to Earth, attacks Grant, using glowing hypnotic eyes to subdue him, and drains his blood, which improbably is her race's preferred food. Simply put, this alien from another solar system is a very common sort of terrestrial "monster," a vampire.

Arguably, the responses of people on the spaceship, and on Earth, are interesting, as Brenner's desire to kill the alien immediately is firmly rejected by others, who insist that humans should not judge the behavior of aliens and that the creature must be studied scientifically. One might admire these reasoned reactions to a murder, except it is painfully obvious that, as in *The Thing from Another World*, those advocating calm, rational treatment of the alien are naïve fools who fail to recognize the evil they are facing. Thus, after the alien is placated for a while by feeding her blood plasma, she kills Brockman and almost succeeds in killing Brenner. A distraught James, trying to stop her, scratches her, making her bleed green blood and revealing her fatal weakness — she is a "hemophiliac" who bleeds uncontrollably and soon lies dead near a pool of green blood.

While this seems to end the threat, Brenner and James discover, as they land on Earth, that the alien hid some bright red, pulsating eggs, and Brenner deduces why the aliens journeyed to Earth: to find a new home for their possibly dying race with ample victims to feed upon. But Farraday ignores Brenner's concerns, insisting that these valuable specimens will be treated with proper caution as he and others (including science fiction fan Forrest J. Ackerman) carry them out of the spaceship.

Overall, Harrington's film constitutes a grievous betrayal of the original film: An uplifting story about a harmonious meeting with aliens becomes a routine horror film, very similar to other horrific spacesuit films. Indeed, the film even works at cross purposes with itself, as the ethereally beautiful images of mysterious aliens taken from the Russian film hardly jive with the notion that they are predatory vampires. Noting that Coppola also felt compelled to add monsters to a Russian film, one speculates that confronting unfamiliar sorts of film, directors reacted the way many people react to the unfamiliar — they were horrified — and hence turned optimistic adventures into horror films. The impulse is often observed in American science fiction films, sometimes said to be haunted by paranoia, but rarely if ever in Russian films of the same period.

Tumannost Andromedy (*The Andromeda Nebula*) (1967)

Unlike earlier science fiction films from Russia, *Tumannost Andromedy* (*The Andromeda Nebula*) never received an American release with dubbed dialogue and added footage. In part this reflects its very nature: Intended as the first film in a two-part or multi-part series that never materialized, the film is unsatisfyingly incomplete, tends to be talky and slow-moving, and lacks spectacular effects. Its failure to reach American viewers was also a sign of changing times: As *Fantastic Voyage* (1966) indicated that Hollywood was again ready to produce major science fiction films, audiences grew less interested in watching dubbed foreign films with awkwardly interpolated footage of fading American stars. In any event, with no translated or subtitled versions available, *Tumannost Andromedy* remains obscure and elusive to American scholars, even those who watched it.

The film opens, surprisingly, with a lengthy depiction of a utopian future Earth that is visually uninteresting and, trusting reports of its bombastic propaganda, I suspect, dramatically uninteresting as well. Its citizens wear white clothing (signifying virtue), participate in stilted outdoor ceremonies, and otherwise spend their time wandering around or conversing in beautiful natural settings, with a particular inclination to linger near the ocean. These placid individuals communicate with other like-minded worlds by means of gigantic television screens, at one point watching an unusual dance involving colorful silhouettes of female dancers, and they follow the progress of starship *Tantra*, dispatched to explore the cosmos.

As the focus gradually shifts to the space explorers, we learn things are not going well. The *Tantra* was captured by the intense gravitational pull of the "Iron Star" (an ominously red sphere), forcing the spaceship to land on an inhospitable "dark planet." A passing reference to its atmosphere suggests that they tested this planet's air and found it unbreathable, for when they emerge from their spaceship, they all wear spacesuits. To solve the problem of spacesuits that obscure facial features, their suits have entirely clear helmets, showing their entire heads, and their cylindrical shape and flat tops seem more practical than the fishbowl designs in other films. Soon, the mysterious death of one crewman reveals that the planet is inhabited by invisible beings intent upon killing visitors. However, the humans can deploy huge searchlights to keep these deadly predators away.

Continuing to survey the planet, the crew members enjoy some technological advantages: a wheeled vehicle with a clear dome enabling them to travel around without wearing spacesuits, and a robot that can burn a circular hole through a spaceship hull. Their spaceship is extremely large and spacious, even including an indoor pool where one swimmer makes spectacular leaps suggesting some mechanism to counter gravity. But the mood remains grim as explorers come upon an abandoned spaceship, and a recorded message (ingeniously indicated by a revolving metal circle) apparently reveals that invisible aliens killed everyone on board. The subsequent death of a beautiful female crewmate hits the commander hard, and he dons a band with wires attached to a chair that seemingly represents a device to help him cope with the loss.

With the *Tantra* stranded on a hostile planet with little hope of escaping, Earth's people still remain optimistic, as the film ends by repeating the uplifting ceremony from its beginning, again showing a huge torch shaped like a raised hand, clearly intended to be inspirational. One assumes there is dialogue about the need to continue exploring space despite daunting setbacks.

Critics cannot confidently pass judgment on a film they do not fully understand, but its source material — Ivan Efremov's novel — and extensive scenes on Earth both suggest that pondering the mysteries of space is not its main priority, though its strange planet and enigmatic menaces convey that humans should be cautious in venturing into this new realm. Still, its luxurious spaceship, seemingly a microcosm of the idyllic future Earth (complete with its own tiny seashore), also indicates that human life in space can and should be similar to human life on Earth. Indeed, if one believes in the possibility of utopia, it is necessary to posit that an ideal state can be achieved both on Earth and in space, limiting one's ability to accept the fact that life in space can never be exactly like life on Earth.

• ITALY AND WESTERN EUROPE •

As was true in Russia, it took a while for the nations of Western Europe to recover from World War II, and since those nations, unlike the United States, Britain, and the Soviet Union, were not engaged in significant work to achieve space travel, they seemed uninterested in space films during the early 1950s. But the influence of American movies soon inspired Western European filmmakers, especially those in Italy, to make their own space films. Evidencing little concern for authentic visions of future space travel, these were generally modeled on the least challenging and most accessible of the American spacesuit films — melodramatic adventures and raucous comedies.

Totò nella Luna (*Totò in the Moon*) (1957)

Since aging American comedians like Abbott and Costello, the Three Stooges, Bob Hope and Bing Crosby, and Jerry Lewis turned to space travel to reinvigorate their careers, foreign comedians predictably employed the same strategy. Some of their efforts, like French comic actor Noël-Noël's *À Pied, à Cheval et en Spoutnik!* (1958), have no spacesuits,[3] but others at least briefly feature spacesuits as protagonists stumble into space. What may be the first European space comedy, *Totò nella Luna* (*Totò in the Moon*), unusually avoids the standard pattern of loosely structured stories featuring unqualified bumblers who inadvertently find themselves in space. Instead, Italian comic actor Totò offers a complex plot which makes serious points about prospects for human space travel, and the relationship between space travel and science fiction.

Mysterious aliens, represented only by animated circles suggesting either eyes or sound waves, are determined to sabotage human efforts to venture into space. While one alien describes plans to send "toys into space" as a "threat," they seemingly regard people in space more as an annoyance than a menace. By altering an important number on a page of calculations, aliens make an unmanned rocket go off course, forcing monitors on the ground to destroy it. The explosion awakens a sleeping publishing magnate, Pasquale Belafronte (Totò), whose complaints provoke a neighborhood debate about the value of space travel.

Standing at his window, Pasquale learns that the explosion was caused by a rocket, prompting him to exclaim, "I don't care about satellites, space, or the moon! ... I want to sleep." An employee in his own window, messenger boy and science fiction fan Achille Paolini (Ugo Tognazzi), is more supportive of space travel, but Pasquale sees no purpose in it: "Why? To conquer space? And I say what can they do with space? What can they do with it? What is space? It's nothing." Then, continuing to equate outer space with emptiness, he offers jokes based on the idea that space is really "air! Conquer air? If you want to conquer air, open the window!" Clearly viewing space travel as both pointless and impractical, he concludes by announcing, "Their space dreams will stay in the pages of comic books."

The film then unleashes several references to "comic books" and science fiction, as the focus shifts to Achille: Driving his vehicle, he simultaneously reads a science fiction comic book and fumes when the story refers to Hawkmen from Sirius because he knows (from Flash Gordon serials) that "Hawkmen come from Mongo." At Pasquale's office, he picks up a glass bowl and puts it over his head, humorously simulating a space helmet, while speaking to Pasquale's daughter Lidia (Sylva Koscina), who is Achille's fiancée. He asks her to type the final chapter of the science fiction novel he is writing, *The Rocket in Space*, which he dictates. Revealing a minimal awareness of scientific realities, the astronauts emerge from a spaceship "dressed in insulating spacesuits," but his story about a "big flying cockroach" is difficult to take seriously.

When Pasquale enters, he laughs at an illustration of a "vile octopus" on a comic book cover, prompting Achille to defend his own work by protesting, "It's not a comedy novel, sir. It's a science fiction novel." His defense of such colorful science fiction pertains to pseudo-spacesuit films: "In science fiction, the monsters, the Martians, create a thrill, an atmosphere." Implicitly, space stories do not involve something like a "big flying cockroach" are insufficiently thrilling or atmospheric. He then argues that these stories are better than other sorts of popular writing: "This doesn't talk about scandals, love intrigue, or scantily clad women. This doesn't talk about that nonsense." This interestingly echoes an argument made long ago by Gernsback, who regularly told readers that his magazine's genre represented a stimulating and wholesome "departure from the sex-infested novels and books that are so prevalent today" ("Results of $300.00 Scientifiction Prize Contest" 519).

Pasquale, who publishes a magazine featuring photographs of "scantily clad women," responds that science fiction has no appeal: "The public doesn't want to see monsters, swarms, spiders and the like, no! The public wants to see beautiful women, the more beautiful the better!" His position is temporarily vindicated when, after Achille secretly replaces a feature on a beautiful woman with part of his novel in the magazine's next issue, including a drawing of a "vile octopus," the issue sold poorly. Pasquale later describes Achille's sort of story as "science rubbish": "It doesn't exist!" In response, Achille calls him old-fashioned and medieval since "you ignore that civilization is only progressing to arrive in space!"

At this point, battle lines are clearly drawn between Achille and Pasquale. Yet surprising complications in their positions emerge. Ludicrously, scientists have determined that only beings with "glumonium" in their bodies can survive space travel; the substance is found only in monkeys, so humans can apparently never reach space. However, since Achille's father was a zookeeper who raised him in close proximity to monkeys, he is somehow the only human with glumonium in his system, making him the perfect candidate. The American space program sends two FBI agents to Italy to recruit Achille for an upcoming space mission, offering him vast sums of American money. Since the agents are not fluent in Italian, and Achille is not fluent in English, he believes they actually want to publish his novel and happily accepts their money. When Pasquale hears of this, he agrees to let Achille marry his daughter and arranges to publish the novel himself, so he can get some of the American money. When Pasquale learns the truth after the wedding, he is angry because he thinks publishing the novel was an enormous waste of money; however, since Achille is now his son-in-law, he urges Achille to accept the American invitation to fly into space.

Surprisingly, Achille refuses, primarily (it seems) because science fiction has taught him about the dangers of space, both real and fanciful, such as "meteors," "cosmic rays," "monsters," "swarms," and even "octopi." In response, Pasquale impatiently tells Achille to "Bring yourself an umbrella" to protect against such hazards, and he appeals to Achille's Italian heritage: "You have the chance to become the Christopher Columbus of Space. The Amerigo Vespucci of the rocket." The Italians, he says, "are a people of poets, or inventors, and above all, of navigators!" His arguments are futile, since Achille remains adamant about not going, even realizing this means humans may never conquer space; and the Americans calmly accept his decision. One normally assumes that people who love science fiction naturally support space travel; *Totò nella Luna* may be the first film to suggest this is not always the case, that someone fond of stories about adventurers in space may be unwilling to become one himself.

By means of further complications, Pasquale, not Achille, actually ventures into space. The Americans were followed by German spies, led by a scientist named von Braun (Luciano Salce), presumably to recall Wernher von Braun. Delighted to discover that Achille has glumonium, they kidnap him and Pasquale to make them the crew of their own, secret space flight. (Perhaps Pasquale will be used to test the theory that only humans with glumonium can survive space travel, but this is not specified.) To prevent this, aliens create "pod creatures," inspired by *Invasion of the Body Snatchers* (1956), to replace Achille and Pasquale. The duplicates emerge from pods entirely naked, and rather stupid, leading to comic business. Through a mix-up, the real Pasquale and duplicate Achille end up in the German spaceship.

Their flight is both similar to, and different from, depictions of space travel in more serious films. Like other astronauts, Pasquale and the duplicate Achille are strapped on padded couches to cope with the pressure of acceleration, but they lie on their stomachs, not their backs, a position perhaps intended to convey that they are victims, not volunteers. When Pasquale is unstrapped in space, he briefly floats upward, which is what would happen in zero gravity, but he unaccountably stops after a few feet instead of proceeding up to the ceiling. Following alien instructions, the duplicate Achille drives the spaceship off course, leading a despondent von Braun to call the mission a failure and describe space travel as impossible.

Aliens guide the spaceship to the Moon, where Pasquale and the duplicate Achille emerge in spacesuits. Seeing the lunar surface, the duplicate Achille smiles broadly, says, "Beautiful! Beautiful!" and does a brief dance — making him another rare man expressing how delightful space travel can be. However, since the character has been depicted as a simpleton, his joy, like that of Dan Prescott in *First Man into Space*, may instead be a sign of derangement. There ensues a comic reversal: Though wearing a spacesuit, Pasquale reports, "I can't breathe." The solution is for the men to remove their spacesuits and discover that the Moon has a breathable atmosphere. To Pasquale, this means that "All they write are fibs in science fiction books," though a lunar vacuum had been propounded more by scientists than science fiction writers, who as observed in earlier chapters would occasionally posit an atmosphere on the Moon.

An alien informs Pasquale that he must remain permanently on the Moon, so humans never discover that space travel is possible. When he protests that he needs female companionship, the alien transforms the duplicate Achille into a beautiful woman, who is readily accepted as suitable company. Indeed, with a "scantily clad woman" in the picture, Pasquale is now enthusiastic about the space travel he once scorned, as he exclaims, "I'll spend the rest of my life on Mars, on Saturn, and also on Mercury. Yes!" The alien shows Pasquale a glimpse of Earth: Achille works at a typewriter, surrounded by Lidia and some children, one of them on the back of the duplicate Pasquale. Told that these are his grandchildren, Pasquale is incredulous, but the alien says Pasquale's flight "lasted half an hour — but on Earth, ten years have passed, because you broke the space-time continuum." It is revealed that Achille's novel was a huge success, allowing him and his family to live comfortably, and the duplicate Pasquale replaced the original as a genial grandfather.

All things considered, this silly film is strangely prophetic. Uniquely, as this film concludes, human space travel has permanently ended, with no intimations of further progress, since both the Americans and Germans believe it is impossible. Instead, it seems, humanity has learned to be satisfied with science fiction stories about space, like Achille's implausible but well-received novel. This epitomizes what happened during the last forty years: Since the flight of *Apollo 17* in 1972, no humans ventured beyond low Earth orbit, so progress into space entirely stagnated; at the same time, unrealistic stories and films about space travel became enormously popular. Thus, *Totò nella Luna* is the first film to suggest that science fiction, instead of a device to promote space travel, might instead function as a palatable substitute for space travel.

La Morte Viene dallo Spazio (*The Day the Sky Exploded*) (1958)

Unlike most foreign-language spacesuit films, *La Morte Viene dallo Spazio* focuses solely upon a natural disaster in space: a massive object that, due to a mishap, is dangerously approaching Earth. Thus, it arguably addresses what scientists agree might someday be a real problem, an asteroid impact. However, if the 1961 English-language version is reasonably faithful, the film also offers some dubious science, weakening its power as a warning for humanity.

As announced by headlines from various newspapers, the Americans and Russians have worked together at a base in Australia named Cape Shark to launch an atomic rocket to circumnavigate the Moon, to be piloted either by an American, British, or Russian pilot. Nothing is said about the purpose of the flight, though its intent is surely peaceful. We learn that American John McLaren (Paul Hubschmid) was selected, though one suspects that versions of the film released in other countries may identify him as British or Russian. After he boards his spacecraft, a television camera shows his head as he sits at the controls, wearing a space helmet and lowering his transparent faceplate (though oddly, the faceplate does not entirely cover his face). The film, then, prophetically posits that pioneering flights into space may be filmed by onboard television cameras.

Once he is in orbit, the film remains realistic, as McLaren briefly converses with Earth monitors. Asked about meteorites, he reports only a "moderate quantity," presumably not enough to represent a threat, and in response to the question "Has the loss of weight affected you?" he replies "No, only the pencil," and displays a pencil floating in front of his face. Presumably, and economically, he is strapped into his seat so only the pencil shows the effects of zero gravity. During this exchange, McLaren also seems groggy, as if stressed by the experience of space travel, but no one comments on his unusual demeanor. Instead, happy monitors on Earth celebrate the mission's success by drinking champagne.

The crisis, along with the nonsense, begins when the rocket to place him in orbit around the Moon misfires and drives the spaceship off course. McLaren detaches his own compartment and returns to Earth, but the rocket proceeds to the "Delta asteroids," where it explodes. This atomic explosion somehow causes all the asteroids to merge together into a single mass that begins moving toward Earth. These absurd developments are followed by more absurd events: Animals on Earth begin premature migrations, as if sensing an impending disaster; the Earth's magnetic field is being drained; and the body's approach causes Earth's temperature to rise, provoking floods and numerous fires. In reality, a large object approaching Earth would cause none of these effects.

Fortunately, McLaren hits upon a solution: If nations fire all their atomic missiles at the approaching mass, they might destroy it before it reaches Earth. The plan might work if the missiles in question were designed to reach space; however, the atomic missiles of the 1950s, that only flew within Earth's atmosphere, would be too late to safely destroy a massive object already very close to the Earth. At best, such weapons might split an approaching asteroid into smaller pieces that would land with less disastrous effects, though the impacts would still cause destruction. But here, the improbable result is that "the mass of asteroids is now disintegrated," and "the remaining fraction of meteors have dispersed into space."

To extend its story, the film also offers melodramatic subplots: McLaren's wife becomes angry when he remains at the base to deal with the crisis and leaves with their son, but hesitates to board the flight and later returns to the base; an amorous technician tries to romance the cold but beautiful mathematician Katy Dandridge (Madeleine Fischer); and a scientist briefly goes crazy and attempts to sabotage efforts to calculate trajectories for the missiles, believing God wishes to punish the rash scientists who inadvertently caused the crisis. Indeed, the film seems to adopt the cautionary stance of horror films, as one scientist remarks, "Maybe there's a boundary we are not allowed to pass," which sounds much like "There are some things man is not meant to know." Also, unlike Anglophone films with disastrous outcomes like *Rocketship X-M* and *The Quatermass Xperiment*, this film ends with no indication that further space flights are planned.

Space Men (1960)

Space Men (also called *Assignment: Outer Space*), made in Italy, was unusually aimed at American audiences, explaining its English title. It is essentially a melodramatic spacesuit film which exemplifies the films that director Antonio Margheriti (also known as Anthony Dawson) would specialize in during the 1960s: settings further in the future than most spacesuit films, when space travel in the Solar System is commonplace; imaginative special effects, including authentic-looking hardware and regular use of spacesuits; handsome heroes and beautiful women; and ludicrous stories about threats to Earth's survival, usually involving sinister aliens. The novelty in *Space Men* is its menace, a runaway "electronic brain." While these films can be dismissed as trivial fluff, they have a certain charm, and occasionally offer a few insights.

On December 17, 2016 (the significance of the date emerges later), journalist Ray Peterson (Rik Van Nutter) is being taken by veteran pilot Al (Archie Savage) to visit a space station for his next story. Space travelers, "to overcome the earthly gravity," are placed in a form of hibernation by a "congealing process" to protect their bodies during liftoff. When the pilot awakens from his hibernation chamber, audiences observe that Al is played by an African American actor, also a noted Broadway dancer who worked on another Margheriti film as a choreographer. And, unlike the others who might be regarded as cinema's first African American astronaut, Asmara Markonen in *12 to the Moon* and Talua in *Die Schweigende Stern*, Al is a major character, described by station commander George (David Montresor) as the best pilot in the business. With "special magnetic boots" for weightlessness, he moves slowly and stiffly in a realistic manner.

When Peterson is awakened, there is another striking development: Though the men eventually become friends, there is immediate tension between seasoned spaceman Al and relative neophyte Peterson, who traveled to the Moon several times but never deep into space. While good-natured, Al describes Peterson as a "leech" and "parasite," using up resources in space without contributing to the mission. As Peterson prepares to leave the spaceship to float to the station and tells Al, "I know what to do," Al contemptuously responds, "You don't know anything yet."

When Peterson reaches the station, George is even more hostile to Peterson's presence, especially when he exits the station for unauthorized filming of a spaceship refueling operation and, while pushing another astronaut away from a meteorite, accidentally dislodges the hose and spills valuable fuel, apparently proving George's point that such an unqualified visitor is a liability. Others on the station, Archie (Alain Dijon) and the beautiful Lucy (Gabriella Farinon), are less antagonistic, though Archie does remark upon his arrival that Peterson "still smells Earthy," and Peterson later complains that everyone in space makes him feel like "an outsider." True, there were inklings of a coming split between Earth's residents and inhabitants of space dating back to films like *Cat-Women of the Moon*, which included no scenes of people on Earth, and tension between veteran astronauts and first-time visitors arose in the *Men into Space* episodes "Earthbound" and "First Woman on the Moon." Yet *Space Men* is the first film to clearly assert that those who live and work in space will come to see themselves as essentially different people, with attitudes and habits unlike people on Earth, engendering conflicts between the groups. A recurring theme in science fiction literature, the idea rarely surfaces in science fiction films.

Along with their familiarity with space routines, veteran astronauts differ from terrestrial counterparts in two other ways, though both represent clichés about future life found in old science fiction stories and films as early as *Just Imagine*. First, during their flight, Al hands Peterson a pill and says "Breakfast is served," conveying that astronauts subsist on food pills; second, people in space are primarily identified by alphanumeric codes, not names, so Al's official name is A15 and Lucy's is Y13. Indeed, Lucy was the astronaut Peterson rescued, but he had no idea because he only saw the Y13 on her spacesuit.

As Al's spaceship approaches the station, he remains distant, to maintain the station's stability, so visitors like Peterson must don spacesuits and float across two thousand feet to reach the station. Though his trip, mostly consisting of medium long shots of Peterson in space, does not visually convey the immensity of space, the film suggests how unsettling the experience is with Peterson's words: He speaks of "the terrifying void between us," describes the station as an "island in the sky," reports feeling "a sense of emptiness," and upon reaching the station says, "I have never felt so lonely." Al's solemn response is "Every baptism has his mystery," intriguingly suggesting that being alone in space for the first time represents a sort of rebirth.

Once Peterson is on board, minor dramas ensue: the incident with the fuel hose; Peterson's first conversation with Lucy, who gradually transfers her affections from George to Peterson; and another trip outside the station to watch passing asteroids. But a genuine crisis soon emerges: The men on the *Alpha II*, a spaceship returning from outside the Solar System, are dead, leaving the ship commanded by an electronic brain that, evidently deranged, is heading straight for Earth, which will be destroyed by the powerful force field extending 5000 miles around the spaceship. Precisely why such a spaceship would be constructed in the first place, and why it could not stopped by other spaceships of its kind, are questions never addressed. But this makes *Space Men* one of the first films to posit that advanced computers will become integral aspects of space travel, capable of piloting spaceships by themselves, and further suggests that such reliance upon machines might be hazardous—one theme in *2001: A Space Odyssey*.

To neutralize the threat, George, Al, Lucy, and Archie will take Al's spaceship to Mars and destroy the *Alpha II*; after Peterson appeals to superiors on Earth, they force an unhappy George to include him in the crew. When Lucy discusses fears that this "deadly mechanical monster" will eradicate people on Earth, Peterson attempts to console her by asking her what day it is. Her contradictory responses are "In space we don't count the days," and that today is the "359th rotation around the Sun."

This means, as Peterson says, "It's Christmas," and the soundtrack briefly and incongruously plays "Deck the Halls." We now understand why Peterson took off on December 17, eight days before Christmas, and he brings up the date presumably to remind Lucy that a divine being looking out for humanity will intervene to prevent disaster. However, since Lucy does not know it is Christmas, the major Christian holiday, space residents cannot be religious, another difference between them and people on Earth, though this is understandably not stressed in a 1960 from a Catholic country. Yet this moment provocatively contrasts with the more celebratory Christmases in *Conquest of Space* and the *Men into Space* episode "Christmas on the Moon," suggesting that space travel may drive people away from, and not back to, traditional values.

When the crew approaches Mars, the rogue spaceship destroys the space station, though two crewmen escape in a spaceship; one dies when it is destroyed near Mars, but the other leaps out to land on the Martian moon Phobos, presumably surviving the fall due to its low gravity. George lands on Phobos so crew members can put on spacesuits to rescue him. The moon is impressively rendered, though it improbably has pools of bubbling molten lava. George is then instructed to fly to Venus and again confront the menacing spaceship. The film's space geography seems inexplicable, since it is hard to see how a spaceship from outside the Solar System would first be near Mars, and then near Venus, while on a collision course with Earth, but this allows the crew to land on another barren world, Mars, and meet residents living under protective domes to survive its harsh conditions.

Back in space, George repeatedly fires missiles at the *Alpha II*, but they explode 5000 miles from the ship upon hitting its force field. But one penetrates further, supporting Al's theory that the force field actually consists of two separate "semispheres" (puzzlingly used instead of the more common "hemisphere"), creating a small "corridor" between the semispheres that a missile or spaceship might travel through to reach the *Alpha II*. To prove his theory, Al takes his spaceship through the corridor in hopes of reaching the rogue spaceship.

When George orders him to return because of the danger, Al says it is worth the risk because "if Earth were destroyed, we'd all be prisoners of space with no hope of return." Then, when Al's ship explodes after getting close to the *Alpha II*, a saddened George instructs the journalist to "Write this: He was never afraid, since man, even in space, changes his position but not his character. He is what he is wherever he lives." Despite previous indications that space residents have adjusted to their environment and regard themselves as a new race, Al asserts that there would be no point in living without a home planet, likening space to a prison, and George adds that people, wherever they are, always remain the same. Perhaps, one might theorize, being in the company of Peterson, and accepting him as a valued companion, make these space travelers better appreciate Earth's people and more inclined to see themselves as members of the same family. There is also the factor of a common threat that drives people together, since it is hard to see how humans in space could survive without support from Earth.

George then repudiates life in space entirely. As surviving crew members confront the apparently inevitability of Earth's doom, Lucy tells George, "I love you."

"I know," he replies.

"But love has no meaning any more, does it?"

"Perhaps it's the only thing that does matter," George answers, and delivers an extraordinary speech: "The world of human feelings has been much less explored than the whole of the universe put together. But now it's late. What have we been doing all these thousands of years? We've been congratulating ourselves on our progress in going faster and faster and faster, but in reality, we've only been getting further away from ourselves." Bluntly, he asserts, space travel was a horrible mistake. Instead of building spaceships and space stations, we should have focused on our emotions instead. To the extent that space travel accomplished anything, it only alienated people from their basic human nature. It also seems that the observed camaraderie of space residents, and calm acceptance of the unusual aspects of life in space, are only a pretense maintained by people who secretly long to return to Earth and reconnect with their true humanity. Thus, despite earlier indications to the contrary, *Space Men* ultimately confirms, like other spacesuit films, that the strange realm of space will make people yearn for the values and lifestyles of humanity's past.

Fortunately, as George wallows in despair, Peterson devises a plan to save the day: He will emulate Al and approach the rogue spaceship through the corridor, tossing small objects to the left and right as he goes to keep track of where the corridor ends and remain in the safe zone. He reaches and enters the spaceship, but when George instructs him by radio to turn off switches to disable the errant computer, he finds they are already turned off, evidently to no avail. He then uses wire-cutters to cut power cables and render the spaceship and its electronic brain inert, but the power loss means the spaceship's doors no longer open, so Peterson is trapped inside. Since he threw away his spacesuit's air regulator to stay inside the corridor, he is then threatened by an excessive "orgy of air" and feels "everything is spinning." But George disobeys orders and moves his spaceship into position to cut an opening in the powerless craft, rescue Peterson, and leave just before Earth's approaching atmosphere would have destroyed both vehicles.

Some argue that *Space Men* significantly influenced *2001*, based upon certain similarities: an inexperienced space traveler who visits a space station and travels to another world; space travelers kept in hibernation; and a lethal spaceship computer that must be disabled by human intervention. Yet Margheriti's story is a more conventional film, unwilling to fully explore such themes as the alienness of space, its transformative effects, and the dangers of overreliance on machines. Kubrick and Clarke would venture further into this unsettling territory.

Il Pianeta degli Uomini Spenti (*Battle of the Worlds*) (1961)

What makes *Il Pianeta degli Uomini Spenti* different from, and inadvertently more insightful than, other Italian science fiction movies is the fact that it stars Hollywood actor Claude Rains. To exploit this asset, the script was crafted to make him the star, though the elderly performer could not portray an astronaut on active duty. Thus, while his character briefly journeys into space, the film required a story that foregrounded scientists on the ground, not astronauts in space, conveying that terrestrial monitors may not simply be just as important as space travelers, but even more important.

If Rains's Benson seems unusually grouchy, it might be due to the risible "science" he must expound. Based on his calculations, he detects that a rogue planet, "the Outsider," wandered into the Solar System. He insists that the Outsider is from another galaxy, though how he knows this, and how this could be (since other galaxies are millions of light years away from Earth), are unexplained. Equally improbably, spaceships near Mars are being driven off course by this world's gravitation; there is a tense moment when one spaceship's crew must engage in radical maneuvers, causing their faces to show severe stress, to restore their correct flight path. Still, the film's astronauts, and the staff of a Martian base, are minor players, as the focus remains on Benson and scientists around him, including the officious Cornfield (John Stacy), whom Benson repeatedly berates. Benson's colleagues are concerned because they believe the Outsider will collide with Earth, but Benson remains calm, since his calculations indicate it will miss Earth by 95,000 miles.

When the Outsider goes into orbit around Earth at a distance of 95,000 miles, everyone congratulates Benson for his accurate conclusion — but Benson himself becomes alarmed and insists the Outsider must be immediately destroyed. For by orbiting Earth, something his calculations did not predict, the Outsider demonstrated that its movements are controlled by some intelligence, and its approach to Earth suggests it is being manipulated by alien residents with evil designs. None of this is spelled out, but it becomes evident when flying saucers emerge from the planet to attack spaceships. The scenes justify the English title *Battle of the Worlds*, though they are only a small element in the film. A downed saucer is found to contain no passengers, but a device from the craft enables Benson to begin figuring out what he terms the "music" of the beings behind the attacks.

There is now a reversal of roles: Having witnessed hostile saucers from the planet, authorities are more than willing to follow Benson's original advice and destroy the Outsider; but Benson also changes his mind and wishes to delay operations so the world can be scientifically studied. When permission is granted for a brief exploration before its destruction, Benson volunteers to join the crew. As crew members don spacesuits, we learn that astronauts generally wear two helmets: one fitting tightly over their skulls, presumably to guard against injuries, and a larger helmet with a glass visor for protection from the vacuum of space. Uncooperative as always, Benson refuses to wear the inner helmet.

When astronauts land on the Outsider, this stagnant film briefly comes to life. Entering a cavern, they walk past strange red filaments that must represent creations of the beings behind the saucers, and come upon remains indicating that the race that inhabited the Outsider is extinct. Finally, they reach what Benson declares is the "electronic brain" causing the saucer attacks. Delighted by the discovery, he insists upon staying behind, even as others recognize they must leave to get away from the Outsider before it is blown up. But Benson insists, "What importance does life have, young fella, if to live means not to know?" While Benson deduces the formula to force the Outsider to go away, his knowledge proves useless, as Earth proceeds to destroy the menacing planet.

All the film's events raise unanswered questions. The Outsider, one assumes, represents a sort of "Berserker"— like the deadly spaceships in Fred Saberhagen's stories, a machine programmed for the destruction of intelligent life, left behind by an extinct race that constructed it for unknown purposes. *Il Pianeta degli Uomini Spenti*, then, might be likened to *Space Men* and *2001* in depicting the danger of mechanical intelligences in space travel, since these can malfunction and become deadly. Yet since this out-of-control computer is of alien, not human, origin, the film also warns that the universe may be filled with unknown perils, requiring extreme caution in venturing into space, though the particular menace here seems unusually implausible: Logically, beings that could move planets through space could avoid extinction and develop destructive weapons far more powerful and effective than the saucers, which are not particularly formidable. Benson's death, and the planet's destruction, conveniently enable the film to avoid confronting these unresolved issues.

Terrore nello Spazio (*Planet of the Vampires*) (1965)

Often termed a precursor to Ridley Scott's *Alien*, *Terrore nello Spazio* (misleadingly retitled *Planet of the Vampires* for American release) is actually one of many science fiction horror films about sinister aliens who take control of human bodies, except that this story takes place on an alien world. And, in a minimal concession to scientific realities, the humans visiting the planet briefly wear spacesuits.

The film begins, apparently in the far future, inside a spaceship of palatial dimensions, one of two dispatched to the planet Aura, which sent out puzzling radio transmissions. As the ship approaches the planet, astronauts are inexplicably subjected to immense gravitational pressure, up to forty times Earth's gravity, which (as even they acknowledge) should have been fatal. While they somehow land safely, crew members immediately become deranged and start attacking each other, except for Captain Mark Markary (Barry Sullivan), who calms everyone down and snaps them out of their belligerent moods. When the one crewman who is still irrational, Dr. Karan (Fernando Villena), rushes out of the spaceship onto the steamy planetary surface, Markary prudently tells a crewmate, "We'd better get the helmets," and when they go outside, they wear helmets over their leather outfits, apparently well protected against an inimical environment. Despite the planet's strange appearance, its atmosphere is breathable: While Karan initially seems dizzy and falls to the ground, as if discomfited by unpalatable air, Markary and a crewmate bring him back to his senses without further signs of discomfort.

In all subsequent scenes, Markary and others do not wear helmets. Strangely, the film never explains why spacesuits are abandoned; one might expect Markary's companion to say, "Karan's all right, so I guess the air is okay," or to have someone on the spaceship report, "Instruments show the atmosphere is breathable." Instead, audiences must infer that the air is safe (though Karan's experience only shows it is briefly endurable). One suspects that the original intent was for actors to always wear space helmets while outside, but director Mario Bava quickly decided he did not like the way they obscured facial expressions, and instructed everyone to leave their helmets off, without bothering to add dialogue to explain the change. In light of Bava's characteristic proclivities, he seems someone who would sacrifice scientific accuracy to make his film more attractive.

This theory is supported by the peculiar way that space helmets are employed during the rest of the film. After Markary and others reach the other ship, they find its crew similarly went insane and actually managed to kill each other; but later returning to the spaceship, they do not find the four dead bodies they previously saw, but only four space helmets lying on the ground. This is senseless, because the dead crew members were not wearing space helmets when they were lying dead, but one admits that a space helmet is an effective visual symbol of a missing space traveler. In other scenes, space helmets regularly rest on consoles inside spaceships, as if astronauts have the habit of leaving them near their work stations at all times in case of emergencies. But during initial scenes, when the spaceship came in for a landing, no space helmets were visible inside the ship. The logical explanation for this, I believe, is that the production constructed or purchased large numbers of space helmets, to be worn by all cast members, but when Bava decided to have actors not wear the helmets, he figured he might as well get some use out of them, and began deploying them, in effect, as set decorations, to mark places where astronauts would usually be found.

The rest of the story unfolds conventionally, with a few interesting visuals and unexpected twists. When a man from Markary's crew goes missing, and a female astronaut sees a grotesque dead man walking around, Markary and the others realize that some force is bringing dead humans back to life and impelling them to attack the living. (Since they never evidence a desire for blood, "Planet of the Zombies" would be a more accurate English title.) The audience learns this from an eerie scene in which three jagged obelisks next to metal slabs are revealed as graves, which open to reveal dead crewmen, wrapped in plastic, who emerge alive from the wrappings. Later, Markary and others open the graves to find nothing but sheets of plastic.

After a few more incidents, one zombie calmly tells Markary that Aura is inhabited by energy beings who realize their world is dying and hence desperately tried to attract other intelligent beings to their planet, so they could take over their bodies and leave to find a new home. A wrecked alien spaceship that Markary and the others earlier discovered, now occupied solely by enormous, distorted skeletons (another nice visual), represented one earlier attempt to obtain host bodies. They maddened the approaching humans hoping they would all kill each other and make their bodies available; but they now ask Markary and his surviving crew to peacefully accept alien occupation. They will have to anyway, he concludes, because the zombies stole the all-important "meteor deflector" of Markary's spaceship, making it impossible for them to stay alive during a voyage through space.

Predictably, Markary rejects the aliens' demands and instead resolves to seize the meteor deflector and take off, which he improbably manages to do. Once in flight, however, Wess (Ángel Aranda) deduces that Markary and another crewmate are now controlled by aliens, and in a desperate attempt to prevent the parasites from reaching his home world, he damages the meteor deflector. Realizing they cannot continue their journey, Markary prepares to land on a nearby world that seems suitable for occupation, which surprisingly proves to be Earth in the twentieth century. In its final moments, then, the film is revealed to be precisely like its predecessors — a story about aliens who invade Earth intent upon taking over human bodies — except that it limits itself to describing events that occurred before the invasion actually began. The film also, in the manner of many pseudo-spacesuit films, contrives to take the action back to Earth.

Like other films, *Terrore nello Spazio* can be praised for its distinctively outré portrayal of an alien world, with low-lying mists, odd bursts of color, and evocative artifacts. That these noteworthy settings serve merely as a backdrop for a routine tale of humans battling zombies, then, is all the more regrettable. But this was not the first time, nor the last time, that striking special effects would be deployed for a lamentably silly story.

Dos Cosmonautas a la Fuerza (*002 Operazione Luna*) (1965)

The Italian comedy team of Ciccio Ingrassia and Franco Franchi recall Abbott and Costello — a tall straight man with a moustache partnered with a short, clean-shaven funnyman — and Franchi's propensity for mugging also reminds one of Jerry Lewis. As they made several films a year at their peak, they inevitably ventured into space, though most antics in *Dos Cosmonautas a la Fuerza* (the Spanish title) take place on Earth. Still, a few serious points lurk within the predictably contrived plot.

Oddly, the comedians also portray serious astronauts: In the first scene, Russian cosmonauts Colonel Paradowsky (Franco Franchi) and Major Borovin (Ciccio Ingrassia) approach a towering spacecraft carrying space helmets, which are placed on their heads by technicians, and they blast off into space. But as conveyed by conversations between a Russian bureaucrat and an officer, monitors lose contact with the cosmonauts, suggesting they are permanently lost. Since announcing their deaths would be a blow to Russian pride, they will find identical replacements for the cosmonauts and launch them into space, to return to a hero's welcome.

The scene shifts to Italy, where bumbling criminals Franco (Franco Franchi) and Ciccio (Ciccio Ingrassia) are breaking into a house. While they are busy, other criminals steal their car; then, when they discover its absence and abandon their stolen goods to get another car, the criminals return and take their loot. Franco and Ciccio soon find themselves pleading their innocence to a skeptical policeman. After they are arrested, their photographs appear in a newspaper. Soviet agent Leonidova (Linda Sini), manager of a woman's gym, notices their resemblance to the cosmonauts and realizes they would be ideal substitutes. When they are brought to the gym, a scientist escorts them into a chamber, evidently to gauge if they can handle the stress of space travel, as shown by distorted images of funny faces they are making, to show the effects of the pressures they are subjected to. To escape, they disguise themselves as women and are pursued through the gym. One recurring gag involves the efforts of various women to stick a needle in Franco's behind.

Eventually they are captured, tranquilized, and transported to Russia in a large box; still drugged, they are put into spacesuits and placed in a spaceship. After it takes off, they awaken in space, remove their helmets, observe the Moon from a window, and eat food from jars. Matters take a surprisingly grim turn as Francho observes the skeleton of a dog wearing a space helmet, floating through space, starkly illustrating the dangers of space travel, and they discover a note reading, "In case of danger, commit suicide." Franco takes a gun provided with the note and points it first to his head, then at his companion, as if taking the advice to heart, though they decide instead to go for a spacewalk. After donning helmets and emerging from the spaceship, they jump into space and maneuver around using swimming motions. There is another somber moment as the skeleton of an arm, followed by a skull, drift past them, but they embrace and seem to enjoy themselves in space. After re-entering the spaceship, a voice instructs them to push a button that will return them to Earth.

When the men land, they are rushed away by Russian officials who do not want reporters to hear the purported Russian cosmonauts speaking Italian. Before officials can congratulate themselves for their successful ruse, they receive a radio message from the real cosmonauts, who report they were out of contact because a meteor damaged their radio and are now returning to Earth. Meanwhile, the impostors, dressed in Russian military uniforms, meet the cosmonauts' wives, and their odd behavior is attributed to "space shock." After the real cosmonauts enter the house, the rest of the film involves various bits of business involving the real and phony cosmonauts alternately finding themselves in the company of confused wives and befuddling the Russian agents who arrive. Everything gets sorted out, and the final scene shows Franco and Ciccio resuming their careers as thieves, now breaking into a house in Moscow, with a Russian official standing watch — presumably fired for his role in the whole affair.

If nothing else, *Dos Cosmonautas a la Fuerza* argues that space travel may be most important as a matter of national prestige, since neither the real cosmonauts nor their impersonators ever attempt any scientific research during their flights; and there is again the suggestion that space travel might be appreciated simply as an enjoyable experience. But space manifestly had no real effects on Franco and Ciccio, as their cosmic journey is only another incident in their constantly troubled lives. Thus, their film suggests that space travel has been accepted as just another activity to be employed in standard comic routines.

I Criminali della Galassia (*The Wild, Wild Planet*) (1965) and *I Diafanoidi Portano la Morte* (*War of the Planets*) (1966)

Antonio Margheriti, previously noted for *Space Men* and *Il Pianeta degli Uomini Spenti*, agreed in the mid–1960s to make four science fiction films in rapid succession: *I Criminali della Galassia*, *I Diafanoidi Portano la Morte*, *Il Pianeta Errante*, and *La Morte Viene dal Pianeta Aytin*. Since all feature Space Station Gamma, these are called his "Gamma

Cosmic Construction Work: Anticipating the sorts of chores performed by actual astronauts in assembling the International Space Station, unidentified personnel in *I Criminali della Galassia* (*The Wild, Wild Planet*) (1965) move a girder on the deck of their space station. The scene was sufficiently impressive to merit being reused in *Il Pianeta Errante* (*War Between the Planets*) (1966).

Quadrilogy," though they are better characterized as two separate two-film series: The first two films feature Tony Russel as Mike Halstead and other characters, and the other two star Giacomo Rossi-Stuart as Rod Jackson with a different supporting cast. Other than recurring characters, there are few connections between the films' different plots, involving a human conspiracy, two alien invasions, and a natural disaster.

At the beginning of *I Criminali della Galassia* (literally "criminals of the galaxy" but released in America as *The Wild, Wild Planet*), a spaceship leaves Earth and approaches Space Station Gamma. As it pauses near the station, two astronauts emerge from the spaceship and launch themselves to the station, where they land on a platform where other astronauts manipulate a girder, perhaps engaged in construction work. The spaceship and space station are well rendered, the spacesuits seem authentic, and astronauts move slowly and awkwardly in the actual manner of space travelers, suggesting that *I Criminali della Galassia* will provide a realistic look at space travel in the future. But the film never shows spacesuits again, and other than two fleeting space flights, it takes place entirely on Earth or in enclosed environments identical to rooms on Earth.

Within the station, we learn that Commander Halstead is disgusted by biomedical research conducted there by Mr. Nurmi (Massimo Serato), saying it "makes me sick to my stomach," and is feuding with erstwhile girlfriend Connie Gomez (Lisa Gastoni), who is eager to go on vacation and escape what she terms the "circling merry-go-round" of the station. She also derides Halstead's doctrine of "woman's equal and full participation in space," calling it "junk," since she wants to be treated "as a lady, not as a buddy." These developments arguably convey insights about the value of scientific research in weightlessness (though there are no signs of weightlessness here), frustration caused by prolonged confinement on a space station, and space as an environment that might engender gender equality as well as resistance to gender equality. But none of these ideas surface again, as attention shifts to a convoluted plot on Earth and another planet.

Ever-increasing numbers of people on Earth are disappearing, to the bafflement of authorities. The abductions are carried out by beautiful woman accompanied by identical bald men, who also have four arms and glowing eyes that can see in the dark. The brutal assailants make some victims vanish and strangle others, including a little girl, making them especially despicable. Suspecting that Nurmi is involved, Halstead apprehends him at a strange dance performance (choreographed by Archie Savage, the veteran astronaut of *Space Men*), but bureaucratic superiors protect Nurmi and confine Halstead to quarters. Freed by crewmates Lieutenant Ken (Carlo Giustini) and Lieutenant Jake (Franco Nero), Halstead investigates a facility of Nurmi's company on Earth, discovering bodies in cylinders and several duplicates of the bald men. Meanwhile, Gomez unwisely agrees to accompany Nurmi on a vacation to an unknown destination; they are glimpsed in a spaceship without spacesuits. But they actually travel to the company's experimental station Delphus (depicted as a red planet), where she learns of his horrific work and becomes his prisoner.

Halstead and his men fly to Delphus (in the spaceship, they wear aviators' helmets but not spacesuits), but upon arriving they are promptly captured by Nurmi. Adapting the conventions of melodrama, Nurmi foolishly declines to immediately kill his opponents and instead provides a leisurely tour of his facilities and detailed description of his insane plan to create a new, perfect human race, with a being constructed by combining himself and Gomez as its ideal representative. Also in keeping with the genre, Halstead and his men overcome Nurmi and his henchmen by starting a fistfight, which leads to chaos within his headquarters and a disastrous flood of red liquid. While the evildoers perish in the flood, Halstead rescues Gomez and helps his colleagues escape within the cylinders used by Nurmi for his experiments. As a reward for their efforts, Halstead, Gomez, Ken, and Jake finally relax beside a swimming pool in swimsuits, again suggesting that no one really enjoys themselves in space. This may be the only other insight one might artfully extract from this generally mindless film.

The sequel *I Diafanoidi Portano la Morte* (*War of the Planets*) focuses more on space travel, as signaled by the sort of stirring narration that often begins the sillier spacesuit films: "The universe is endless and timeless. Who knows how it all began? With the advent of space travel, a greater dimension has been added to this small Earth. Man is exposed to new elements, harnessed and governed by an intelligence that is not his own." We immediately observe this other intelligence at work, as Captain DuBois (Carlo Giustini), arriving for his shift at a base on Earth, is overcome by strange green lights and gas. While his absence is noted, most people on Earth and in space are celebrating New Year's Eve; and festivities on Gamma 1 provide this film, like *I Criminali della Galassia*, with striking scenes of astronauts in space. Specifically, Halstead offers partygoers a spectacular show featuring astronauts floating in the station. As they fly around (on one occasion, a wire is visible), they join hands, rotate their bodies, stand on each other's shoulders, and run in place, all activities emphasizing with unusual force the complete freedom of movement available in space. Later, astronauts even spell out the words "HAPPY NEW YEAR" in space.

The party is interrupted by sobering news: Space station Delta 2 was mysteriously attacked, and residents have stopped responding to messages. Sent to investigate, spacesuited astronauts slowly land and walk on top of the station before entering to find everyone on board paralyzed, barely alive but motionless (though a few actors move slightly and blink their eyes). The cause is the same green lights and gas that vanquished DuBois and now attacks the visiting astronauts. As Delta 2 vanishes and other stations seem threatened, all are ordered to evacuate. Halstead decides to stay behind with a few crewmates to confront the coming aliens, prompting Gomez to call him a "space idiot." Unlike *I Criminali della Galassia*, there is no rhetoric about female equality, but the film makes a similar point by showing a space station headed by a woman and including a woman in the crew that investigates Delta 2.

When the green lights and gas arrive, Halstead drives them away. While their "lasers" (which resemble flame throwers) are ineffective, their .38s (later called "nucleonic pistols") are more effective. Halstead also figures out that the aliens cannot penetrate "lead titanium," presumably the screenwriters' way to describe some superstrong alloy of the two elements. Meanwhile, the aliens reveal their intentions by sending DuBois, now under their control, to meet Earth authorities, who describe the transformed captain by saying, "He's gone galaxy" and "The man is possessed." Evidently the aliens are a bodiless group intelligence that wishes humans to peacefully submit to possession. To persuade Earth's leaders to agree, DuBois offers to take representatives to the alien base as observers, and Halstead and his crewmates are selected for the assignment. They also bring Gomez and another woman, who are paralyzed after exposure to the aliens. (It is not explained why some humans are possessed by aliens while others are first frozen to prepare for this treatment.) In the spaceship, again wearing aviators' helmets, Halstead learns they are going to a uranium mine on Mars. Upon landing, they briefly endure the thin atmosphere of Mars (though we do not observe this) before entering the "artificial atmosphere" of the mine's interior.

Like Nurmi, the alien-dominated DuBois is not very bright, as he also fails to kill his visitors or put them under alien control and lets them stay in a chamber where they enjoy delicious food and drinks. He explains that the aliens originally came from Andromeda but were forced to relocate when their host species became extinct; now, humans can play that role. A horrified Halstead and the others find bodies of Delta 2 crew members—killed because they were not suited for alien control. After observing more people forced to choose between alien possession and death, a fed-up Halstead launches another fistfight, though in addition to fists and karate moves, the heroes also use nucleonic pistols. Grabbing the inert Gomez, they rush to a spaceship, gasping as they run through the Martian atmosphere, and leave the alien-controlled humans, now exposed to that atmosphere, to die. Some unexplained problem forces them to wait thirty minutes before launching, which is dangerous because a fleet from Earth is arriving to obliterate the base. Yet Halstead gets the spaceship up just as bombs begin exploding around them.

As flames from their spaceship cleverly dissolve into a shot of a fireplace cooking meat, the film comes to its celebratory conclusion: Halstead confirms that the aliens are dead, he learns he is both receiving a medal and being temporarily confined to quarters for disobeying orders, and Gomez first kisses him, slaps him when he makes a mildly critical comment, and allows him to kiss her as the film's final image. Most interestingly, the implication in *I*

Criminali della Galassia—that Earth is where everybody really wants to be—is made explicit when a crewmate remarks, "This is the life, all right—right here on old Mother Earth." The simple pleasures of barbequed food and alcohol, it seems, far outweigh the previously observed joys of weightless athleticism in space.

Il Pianeta Errante (*War Between the Planets*) (1966) and *La Morte Viene dal Pianeta Aytin* (*The Snow Devils*) (1967)

Sometimes called an imitation of *Yosei Gorasu* (to be discussed), *Il Pianeta Errante* is better regarded as a variation on Margheriti's *Il Pianeta degli Uomini Spenti*. The scientific nonsense begins immediately, for as Earth is inexplicably afflicted by landslides, earthquakes, and tidal waves, people theorize that they are caused by a "gravity disturbance in outer space never before encountered," though any body able to provoke such phenomena would be as large and close as the Moon. General Norton (Enzo Fiermonte) sends Commander Rod Jackson (Giacamo Rossi-Stuart) to take over Gamma 1 and find out what is responsible for Earth's problems. As in other Margheriti films, Jackson and two colleagues approach "good old Gamma 1," park their spaceship nearby, and float over to its upper platform, with wires sometimes visible.

Entering the station, Jackson is stern and grouchy while addressing beautiful communications officer Terry Sanchez (Ombretta Colli). He is evidently stressed by his assignment, and later apologizes for his "edginess." It emerges that they are lovers, even though Jackson is engaged to Norton's daughter Janet (Halina Zalewska). Others are worried as well, as Jackson orders newscasts from Earth, reporting on new disasters, to be blocked because "station morale is low." When "agitation" in the asteroid belt is noted, Jackson must investigate whether there is a "wild planet within Gamma 1's gravitational quadrant."

First, Jackson deals with a crisis in space: While on a spacewalk, crewmate Eric Dubrowski (Pietro Martellanza) reports feeling a strange wind that left three colleagues drifting away, so Jackson and others don spacesuits to rescue the men. Telling everyone to "link together" and "chain up," the team floats out to the stranded men, connected by two kinds of wires: the horizontal ones connecting everyone that are supposed to be seen, and the vertical supporting wires that are not supposed to be seen but often are. One man cannot be rescued, despite Jackson's efforts. Dubrowski later blames his death on Jackson's determination to engage in solitary heroics and provokes a furious fistfight between the two men. Sanchez intervenes, calling them "you idiots." Dubrowski also dislikes Jackson because he would not grant him a 48-hour pass to visit his wife and son on Earth, which becomes doubly significant when he learns a disaster on Earth killed his wife.

In an intimate conversation between Jackson and Sanchez, their displeasure about the impending arrival of Norton and his daughter is forgotten when Sanchez earnestly asks, "Are we trapped up here in space?" She worries that catastrophic events on Earth will destroy the entire planet, so "soon there'll be no Earth to go down to." As in other spacesuit films, people are willing to visit space, but are discomfited by the prospect of living there permanently. Then, when the station loses contact with an expedition searching for a "wild planet," Jackson guesses that they were captured by the unknown object's gravitational field. He plans to lead a mission to confirm its presence and, if possible, destroy it using "antimatter." Walking gingerly onto the platform in spacesuits, Jackson and others launch themselves to spaceships and depart, just missing Norton and his daughter, who also drift in spacesuits from a spaceship to the station. (Why no one in this future world develops a system for spaceships to dock at the station, eliminating the hazardous spacewalks, is not explained.)

Norton meets the man now heading the station, Frank Perkinson (Goffredo Unger), who informs the general he is busy with repairs that require a temporary period without gravity. People on the station briefly see small objects floating, though they remain on the ground (which would not occur in actual zero gravity).

Jackson discovers that an "oversized asteroid" with a "strange phosphorescent quality" is causing the disasters. After dealing with the sudden appearance of threatening asteroids, he observes that the asteroids are somehow being directed by the glowing world. Without discussing this astounding phenomenon, he decides to attempt a landing, though a crewmate who already landed was sucked into a pool of what looks like boiling lava (later described as a cold, jelly-like substance). Dubrowski also disobeys orders to arrive in the station's flagship, but upon landing is fatally entrapped by the deadly liquid.

The surface of this "wild planet" commands attention as another rare instance of an alien world that actually looks alien, with red and black pools of liquid and craters with thin tentacles emerging from them. When Jackson, Sanchez, and Perkinson enter a crater, the walls seem soft and resilient. Jackson describes the tentacles as "arteries," and other pulsating areas are termed "breathing valves." Evidently, the entire planet is an organic being, and its manipulation of asteroids suggests it is both intelligent and evil. Strikingly, no one comments on this amazing phenomenon or considers whether to try communicating with or studying this being, as they are solely intent on destroying it.

When shafts seem to close up around them, blocking their return to the surface, Jackson slices the arteries, which exude a red liquid resembling blood, to force the organism to open an escape route. But Sanchez drops the needed detonator in a pool of liquid, requiring the men to somehow use a device within their helmets to perform the same function. Despite warnings that the oxygen is too thin for survival, Jackson bravely takes off his helmet to effect this improvised solution, and when he visibly suffers from the exposure, Perkinson removes his own helmet and puts it on Jackson; later, he dons Jackson's helmet. In films like this, one rarely observes an awareness of the dangers of removing a space helmet, even temporarily, on a strange planet, or drama involving the need to quickly put a helmet back on. Finally, Jackson frees Sanchez when she is trapped by the arteries. Perkinson seems trapped on the ground but urges colleagues to flee while he stays behind to detonate the antimatter in his hands. After they reach the surface to be carried by crewmates back to the spaceships, Perkinson detonates the antimatter, destroying himself and the planet in a spectacular explosion.

Finally, the narrator announces that "peace and tranquility have returned" to Earth, and there is a memorial ceremony for Dubrowski and Perkinson; a plaque with their names bears the statement "Two Men — One Ideal." In a scene recalling how McCauley attempted to replace a dead crewmate by playing with his son in "A Handful of Hours," Jackson makes an effort to comfort Dubrowski's son. After the ceremony, the boy walks off holding the hands of Jackson and Sanchez, suggesting they will now become a family, while the rejected Janet leaves separately with her father. The scene interestingly contrasts with the lighthearted parties that ended Margheriti's last two films.

While of minimal value as a meditation on humanity's future in space, *La Morte Viene dal Pianeta Aytin* (*The Snow Devils*), the sequel to *Il Pianeta Errante*, can be celebrated as a pioneering warning about global warming, as it involves melting polar icecaps and the catastrophic flooding that results. Needless to say, in this sort of film, it is not caused by overproduction of greenhouse gases, but a sinister alien plot. Yet for much of the film's length, Stuart and new sidekick Frank Pulasky (Goffredo Unger) have seemingly abandoned all interest in space travel and alien life, since their new assignment is to investigate the destruction of a weather station in the Himalayas, and they must do so in the most primitive manner possible, by trekking through snowy mountains with a native guide, Sharu (Wilbert Bradley); the obligatory beautiful woman, Lisa Nielson (Ombretta Colli), seeking news of her missing husband, the station commander; and several porters who flee, fearing the Yeti, or "Snow Devils," presumed responsible for the attack on the station because a strange footprint was discovered there.

The story finally connects to space when the travelers are captured by the Yeti, who are blue-skinned, white-haired humans of normal dimensions. They identify themselves as aliens from a distant planet, forced to migrate because their world is passing through a deadly radioactive cloud. To make Earth their new home, they must make it frigid, which they plan to accomplish by first using advanced science to raise Earth's temperature and cause massive flooding, then reducing the temperature to freeze the flood waters and cover the planet with ice. After implausibly escaping through the ventilator shafts the aliens conveniently install in their underground headquarters, the humans use chemicals to make ether and overcome their adversaries. However, since the extreme weather conditions continue, Stuart must now locate and destroy the aliens' main base of operations.

To carry out this mission, Stuart and Pulasky return to Gamma 1, where extensive research pinpoints the Jovian moon Callisto as their probable headquarters. As they leave the station to participate in a massive attack on Callisto, Stuart, Pulasky, and another man are briefly observed in spacesuits, launching themselves toward a spaceship, perhaps a bit of footage borrowed from an earlier film. But one more activity in space is required when Stuart discovers that Callisto is surrounded by a force field which disables machinery. His solution is to fly to the asteroid belt, where he and others venture into space, again visibly supported by wires, to plant special devices on selected ferrous asteroids. Then, Stuart uses magnetic force to send them crashing into Callisto, completely destroying the alien base and ending the threat to Earth. A charitable commentator might detect another warning about a potential menace to Earth — a devastating asteroid impact — but the film conveys no point of this kind, as its conclusion again is comic: Planning on "going to the beach" for a break, Stuart and Pulasky find that "We're back to normal. It's going to rain," and drive through a rainstorm in a futuristic car.

Considering the "Gamma Quadrilogy" as a whole might lead someone to ponder an alternate history, for Margheriti's films do show, if nothing else, that spacesuits can be integrated into the sorts of melodramatic adventures involving mad scientists and aliens that filmmakers addressing space travel were increasingly coming to prefer. Perhaps, if *Star Trek* adopted the same approach, with characters regularly donning spacesuits to travel in space, spacesuits might have remained more prominent in films and television programs. But it is also striking that Margheriti's space scenes generally depict uneventful, routine business, while his genuine dramas — fistfights, chases, personal confrontations, and so on — occur in Earthlike environments. Indeed, Margheriti's persistent indifference to visible wires, and the antics in space observed in *I Diafanoidi Portano la Morte*, suggest that the director regarded sequences in space primarily as circus acts, entertaining interludes for stories, not unlike the dances Savage prepared for *I Criminali della Galassia*. Space is presented as a place to work, and place to play, but never a place where problems might develop. While one might regard this as an expression of confidence that humans can master the challenges of space, it is also, like so many other things in these films, not particularly realistic.

Raumpatrouille: Die Phantastischen Abenteuer des Raumschiffes Orion (*Space Patrol*) (1966)

The rarely seen German television series *Raumpatrouille: Die Phantastischen Abenteuer des Raumschiffes Orion* is regularly described as a "German *Star Trek*," and there are obvious similarities (though, since the two series debuted at almost exactly the same time, in September 1966, they did not influence each other). Both series involve spaceships with shuttlecrafts sent on missions to other planets; both spaceships have a charismatic young commander and internationally diverse crew; and both series reflect an effort to craft a consistent and visually interesting future world. Thus, among other striking features of *Raumpatrouille*, its spaceship *Orion* unusually takes off from an underwater base, where visitors relax in a lounge underneath a large dome where fish swim about; its spaceship lands by extending a thin column from underneath which contacts the surface and supports the ship while passengers exit from a door at the bottom; the series' robots are interestingly stylized, with rotund bodies supported by a slanting platform that hovers above the ground; and when characters converse in the lounge, extras engage in strange athletic dances in the background, a cheap and novel way to suggest a futuristic society. Clearly, as was true of *Star Trek*, much thought and planning went into the creation of this series.

There are also significant differences between the series. While *Star Trek* depicts an autonomous community traveling through interstellar space, only occasionally in contact with superiors, the scenario of *Raumpatrouille* more closely resembles *Tom Corbett, Space Cadet* and other early television series for young viewers. That is, the spaceship has a small crew (six people); they begin and end each mission on Earth and usually stay within the Solar System; and while astronauts engage in drinking and womanizing, they are considered too immature to be left unsupervised, so they are constantly under the scrutiny of superior officers on Earth who sometimes micromanage their activities, to their displeasure. Also, while *Star Trek* offers varied plots that only occasionally involve hostile aliens, *Raumpatrouille* has an overall story arc about efforts to defend Earth from an invasion by mysterious aliens called the Frogs. Finally, as the difference most relevant to this study, the German series is more realistic about the dangers of space in that it regularly depicts characters wearing spacesuits—with revelatory patterns in their appearances.

On board the *Orion*, none of the regular crew—Captain Cliff McLane (Dietmar Schönherr); crew members Mario (Wolfgang Völz), Hasso (Claus Holm), Atan (Friedrich G. Beckhaus), and Helga (Ursula Hillig); and watchdog Tamara Jagellovsk (Eva Pflug)—ever wear spacesuits or even contemplate wearing spacesuits; evidently, they improbably regard their craft, like the *Enterprise*, as secure enough to eliminate any concerns about contact with the vacuum of space, though there are times when spaceships are blasted out of the sky by enemies. However, while the *Orion* (unlike the *Enterprise*) lands on alien planets, the spaceship also has two shuttlecrafts, one called the *Lancet*, used for short journeys through space. When characters enter these vehicles in the first three episodes, they put on spacesuits, suggesting these smaller spaceships are considered more vulnerable. To keep characters' faces fully visible at all times, the helmets are huge glass enclosures resting upon a metal circle around each person's neck, with a well-noted flaw: a visible hole at the top of each helmet, which would be fatal in an actual vacuum. (The holes were added, according to reports, because actors became too hot inside the spacesuits and needed ventilation.)

An occasional need for spacesuits is illustrated by the first episode, "Angriff aus dem All" ("Attack from Space") (aired September 17, 1966). When a planetary station fails to respond to messages, Hasso and Atan are sent to investigate in the *Lancet*. They keep their spacesuits on after landing since they discover the facility has been drained of its oxygen supply, an easily anticipated hazard of living in space. Then, all cast members don spacesuits in the second episode, "Planet ausser Kurs" ("Planet Off Course") (aired October 1, 1966), wherein McLane and his crew board two shuttlecrafts and abandon the *Orion* before it is launched into a rogue planet approaching Earth, charged with energy, in what proves a successful effort to destroy the menace. Still wearing spacesuits, they enter a disabled spaceship, the *Hydra*, also suffering from a reduced oxygen supply, and fix the problem to revive its crew. Most interestingly, in a subplot of the third episode, "Hüter des Gesetzes" ("Guardian of the Law") (aired October 15, 1966), Atan and Helga are sent in the *Lancet* to retrieve data from space probes, and Atan engages in a well-staged spacewalk. Thus, spacesuits seem essential to the series' space travelers.

Then spacesuits completely vanish in the last four episodes. True, the fourth and seventh episodes, "Deserteure" ("Deserters") (October 29, 1966) and "Invasion" (December 10, 1966), did not involve shuttlecrafts, creating no need for spacesuits by the series' logic; and while Tamara and Helga board the *Lancet* in the fifth episode, "Der Kampf um die Sonne" "Battle for the Sun" (November 12, 1966), they only travel from one place on a planet's surface to another, so not wearing spacesuits is understandable. However, in the sixth episode, "Die Raumfalle" "The Space Trap" (November 26, 1966), science fiction writer Pieter-Paul Ibsen (Reinhard Glemnitz) is allowed to ride through space in the *Lancet* by a reluctant McLane, and the decision to send him out without a spacesuit cannot be justified. (Fortunately, when abducted by an evil scientist, he reaches an asteroid with a breathable atmosphere, so the absent spacesuit causes no problems.)

To account for the disappearance of spacesuits from *Raumpatrouille*, one must consider not the series' internal logic, but external factors. Perhaps the actors, despite the openings for ventilation, kept complaining about the burden of wearing the awkward and heavy costumes, and producers eventually gave in and removed spacesuits from later episodes. One can also speculate that, viewing early episodes, producers decided that, instead of cumbersome spacesuits, audience members would prefer to see characters in normal clothing. From this series, then, one might deduce two general reasons why space films avoid spacesuits: actors dislike them, and audiences dislike them. And such issues will always outweigh any concerns about scientific accuracy.

2 + 5: Missione Hydra (*Star Pilot*) (1966)

Despite an incongruously somber conclusion, *2 + 5: Missione Hydra* (*Star Pilot*) is a silly film, epitomized by its character Luisa Solmi (Leontine May), a woman who regards all events in the film, including her abduction into space and murderous foes, as jokes, while she wears skimpier and skimpier outfits to flirt with a handsome alien. Needless to say, its disregard for science is equally egregious, through spacesuits — and even Einstein's Theory of Relativity — make brief appearances.

An alien spaceship lands in Sardinia and immediately sinks into the ground, requiring its female commander Kaena (Leonora Ruffo) to place her crew of two male subordinates and "robots" (who look exactly like humans) into suspended animation. Two years later, scientist Dr. Solmi (Roland Lesaffre) is lecturing on Einstein's theories, the significance of which emerges later in the film; he is asked to go to Sardinia, along with daughter Luisa and assistants Belsy (Kirk Morris) and Artie (Alfio Caltabiano), to investigate strange radioactivity. Soon, after entering a cave and discovering the spaceship, they are confronted by Dr. Chang (John Sun) and two other Chinese agents, who are following Solmi due to reports of his amazing new invention, which they assume is the alien spaceship. But Kaena and her men emerge from the ship to take control of the situation with ray guns. She gives Solmi a piece of equipment he must repair so that her spaceship can take off, ensuring he will keep her presence a secret by holding Luisa hostage. After he returns with the repaired part, she forces the humans to become her crew, since her vehicle requires several different people in various locations to manipulate controls (a significant design flaw, to say the least).

Once they are in space, an Earth spaceship and space station endeavor to keep track of the fleeing alien craft, illustrated by footage borrowed from *Yosei Gorasu* (discussed below). (This pointless subplot is soon forgotten.) Inside the alien spaceship, Luisa floats to the ceiling because one of Kaena's subordinates, Paolo (Mario Novelli), did not properly adjust her "simulated weight," the film's novel description of artificial gravity. But the gravest breach of basic science comes when Paolo must go outside the spaceship for a familiar reason — to repair a broken antenna — so Kaena can receive both audio and video messages from her homeworld in the constellation Hydra. As he emerges from the spaceship, astonishingly, he does not wear a spacesuit, yet suffers no ill effects from the vacuum of space as he tumbles in the black void and replaces the bent antenna with a straight one. Later, during another impossible scene of this kind, we are told that the spacewalkers wear "space respirators," small objects positioned near their mouths that purportedly let them survive in space. With or without an oxygen supply, of course, any unprotected human in space would die instantly.

Kaena reports with alarm that the spacecraft has "been caught in a photon shower" (whatever that means), forcing aliens and humans to temporarily work together to make an emergency landing on a nearby planet. After landing, Kaena suddenly displays proper concern for the dangers of space by telling Luisa, "Go unstrap yourself. I have to get my spacesuit." Then, as the commander, she steps onto the planetary surface, wearing a spacesuit seemingly made of black leather, to conduct "preliminary reconnaissance." After briefly staring at predictably Earthlike scenery, she casually removes her helmet, and everyone else is soon walking around without protective garments. For a burst of drama, they are attacked by apelike creatures, easily defeated with ray guns, then immediately take off anyway to avoid them.

At this point, matters finally begin to seem serious, as the spaceship receives a mysterious message that Solmi deduces is either in Russian or Bulgarian. Kaena and a colleague go outside — again without spacesuits — to investigate the spaceship sending the message. Upon entering it, they discover a grim sight: two seated astronauts in spacesuits, obviously dead, their faces looking like skulls (they resemble the gruesome dead astronaut in *Riders to the Stars*). The endlessly repeating recorded message leads Solmi to a bold theory: While the captives traveled through space at relativistic speeds, many years elapsed on Earth, and during that time the planet was devastated by nuclear war. Further, when Kaena guides the spaceship to her own homeworld and sees only deserted ruins, the symbols on a large slab indicate that her own planet met a similar fate. The spaceship crew, now united, resolves to travel to another world to create a "perfect civilization."

Like *Frankenstein Meets the Spacemonster*, *2 + 5: Missione Hydra* indicates that pseudo-spacesuit films, by the mid–1960s, had reached a stage of exhaustion, with new ideas nowhere to be found, leading to feature films sustained solely by seemingly random borrowings from previous films. Here they range from *Destination Moon* and *Rocketship X-M* to *This Island Earth* and *Missile to the Moon*. And, while such films can be diverting in their own way, they have little to say about humanity's probable future in space.

...4...3...2...1...Morte *(Mission Stardust)* (1967)

It seems unlikely the Italian and Spanish filmmakers behind *...4...3...2...1...Morte* (also known as *Perry Rhodan— SOS aus dem Weltall, Alarm im Weltall, Órbita Mortal,* and *Mission Stardust*[4]) had seen *Radar Men from the Moon,* yet their story shares many similarities with that serial, since it also features aliens on the Moon improbably involved with criminals on Earth in adventures that include fistfights and a car chase. Even the shoddy special effects recall Saturday afternoon serials more than science fiction films of the 1960s. However, what entertained youngsters in 1952 could not please science fiction audiences in the late 1960s, making *...4...3...2...1...Morte* one of the era's most reviled genre films.

The film is based on early novels in the popular German "Perry Rhodan" series by K.H. Scheer and Clark Darlton (Walter Ernsting), and roughly follows their introductory story arc: Astronaut Rhodan encounters two aliens on the Moon and gradually masters their advanced technology to become Peacelord of the Universe (although he never assumes that title in the film). To update their story (which had Rhodan leading the first flight to the Moon in 1971), the film is set farther in the future. Here Rhodan (Lang Jeffries) is a veteran of several space flights, including a Mars flyby. At a conference of bureaucrats that opens the film, we learn that his upcoming Moon flight, officially for scientific purposes, will actually search for a valuable new mineral; Rhodan and his teammates were chosen for the mission because of their experience and compatibility. Master criminal Arkin (Pinkas Braun) discovers the mission's true intent from a source within the space agency and is monitoring developments, hoping to obtain the mineral for himself. Their brief flight to the Moon has one odd moment: Preparing to land, Rhodan advises crewmates to "restore your respiration pill and put your helmets on," vaguely suggesting some futuristic means of breathing.

As in *Kaijû Daisensô* (discussed below), there is a realistic Moon landing before the nonsense begins: Astronauts emerge from their capsule wearing spacesuits and lower a wheeled "exploration vehicle" to the surface to begin the expedition. But the colors are wrong—the surface of the Moon sometimes looks dark blue, not gray, and the Earth overhead is in a blue sky—and the spaceship and exploration vehicle are visibly tiny models, accompanied by one point by a tiny doll representing an astronaut. As the men proceed, one astronaut looks nostalgically at "old Mother Earth" while another recalls the excesses of pulp science fiction by exclaiming, "I'd prefer a twelve-headed, six-eyed, eight-foot monster to this blasted silence!" What they actually encounter is a large humanoid figure in a spacesuit who tells them (presumably via radio) to "Follow me" into an enormous spherical spaceship. Inside, their escort (a robot, making it strange that he wore a spacesuit) advises them, "You can take off your helmets. The atmosphere in here is quite safe to breathe," and they meet two human-looking aliens, the elderly and friendly Crest (John Karlsen) and beautiful and arrogant Thora (Essy Persson).

The aliens have a typically incredible story to tell. Though advanced beings (Thora identifies herself as a "ninth-level" intelligence, whereas Rhodan is only "fourth-level"), theirs is a dying race in desperate need of reinvigoration. The preferred plan is "uniting with a younger race"—interbreeding—though Thora doubts humans would be suitable. They are on the Moon because their spaceship is disabled.

Rhodan's physician determines that the ailing Crest suffers from leukemia. Fortunately, Rhodan knows of a Dr. Haggard (Stefano Sibaldi) in Mombasa, Kenya, who is perfecting a cure for leukemia, and he proposes a secret return to Earth (to keep humans from seeking the aliens' superior technology) in an alien shuttlecraft to persuade Haggard to treat Crest. From this point on, until a brief coda at the end, all the film's action takes place on Earth.

The interwoven threads of the contrived plot can be briefly summarized. Rhodan gradually succeeds in melting the heart of the initially contemptuous Thora; the blustering General Roon (John Bartha) vainly endeavors to have his troops seize control of Thora's spacecraft, though she easily resists his attacks; Rhodan and crewmate Mike Bull (Luis Dávila) must use diamonds, and some nifty weapons obtained from Thora, to obtain a car and drive to Mombasa; and Arkin, informed of events and now wishing to seize the alien spacecraft, has confederates pursue Rhodan and Bull in a frenzied car chase. The men eventually reach Haggard, who agrees to treat Crest as long as he can bring his own assistants; however, by means of secret confederates, Arkin infiltrates the medical team with a phony Haggard and gun-toting nurses who briefly commandeer Thora's ship, though they are overcome by Rhodan's heroics. Amidst these goings-on, Crest is cured, and Rhodan and the aliens fly back to the Moon.

Long after anyone with an interest in cinematic depictions of space flight would stop watching ...*4...3...2...1...Morte*, there is a brief, stunning scene which, like the upward space flight in *Captain Video: Master of the Stratosphere*, almost redeems the entire film. The journey to the Moon is disrupted by the reappearance of Arkin, who somehow survived his last battle with our heroes and used a teleportation device stolen from Thora to again attempt to take over the spaceship. Fortunately, a switch activates a device which expels Arkin into the "total void of space," and we see his body drifting away, getting smaller, against a dark backdrop of stars. The special effects, as always, are substandard, but like similar scenes in other films, the image reminds audiences that space really is a hazardous place. But the mood is immediately broken by a purportedly humorous conclusion wherein the aliens begin the process of "uniting" with humans by offering Rhodan his choice of comely alien women. Only one other incident from the film merits mention, a mildly amusing moment during the flight to Earth: An astronaut feels foolish playing poker with a robot who sees his cards with x-ray vision. There were also poker-playing astronauts in the *Men into Space* episode "Dateline: Moon," but this is another reminder that long periods of boredom, creating a need for games, will be characteristic of space travel.

Given the vast numbers of Perry Rhodan novels, there might have been countless sequels to ...*4...3...2...1...Morte*, but its savage reception by audiences ensured that no additional Rhodan films would appear. Simply put, the film's producers were twenty years too late in offering this sort of entertainment.

• EGYPT AND MEXICO •

Films from the Soviet Union and Eastern Europe, Italy and Western Europe, and Japan and Western Asia reached America in two ways: Classic films from admired directors were shown in art houses, and colorful science fiction films were dubbed and edited for American filmgoers or television viewers hungry for a type of film that American producers provided only sporadically. Films made outside those regions tended to remain unknown in America, so there may be many space films from other countries that Americans have not yet watched or discussed. Two exceptions to the pattern are a recently discovered film from Egypt, and science fiction films from Mexico, often seen in America because the country borders the United States and is home to many American immigrants. These films suggest that former colonies of Europe may have remained strongly influenced by the countries that governed them, since their visions of space travel resemble the melodramatic adventures and comedies of Western Europe and hence are best discussed in proximity to those films.

Rehla ilal Kamar (*Journey to the Moon*) (1959)

While described as an imitation of *Abbott and Costello Go to Mars*, the Egyptian film *Rehla ilal Kamar* (*Journey to the Moon*)[5] has few similarities to that film, though both follow the standard trope of spacesuit comedies, clearly becoming familiar throughout the world: the complete incompetent who joins a pioneering flight into space. And though its buffoon, Ismail Yasseen, is accompanied by a straight man, Rushdi Abaza, the men do not interact as a team in the manner of Abbott and Costello.

In crafting this film, writer-director Hamada Abdel Wahab could not reasonably posit that a nation like Egypt had an official space program or homegrown scientist capable of building a spaceship. To get Egyptians into space, he introduces a German scientist, Dr. Sharvin (Edmoun Toeima), who is assembling a rocket in Egypt, which makes sense since its location nearer the Equator would be better for spaceship launches (though the film offers no such rationale). Journalist Rushdi (Rushdi Abaza) and a photographer are taken to the rocket site by driver Ismail (Ismail Yasseen), but the photographer is detained because Sharvin wants no pictures taken. Interestingly, Sharvin is first observed wearing a spacesuit, with a man pounding on his head, presumably a method to firmly attach the helmet. Then, when Rushdi interviews Sharvin in the spaceship, Ismail sneaks on board to take photographs and use them to get a newspaper job. Reported as a spy when he cannot be located, Ismail is discovered by Sharvin, who prepares to shoot him despite Rushdi's pleas. As Ismail retreats, he accidentally pushes a lever to launch the spaceship.

Predictably, the flight is not particularly realistic, since the travelers endure only mild pressure upon liftoff and never experience weightlessness; it is also stunning to see Rushdi casually light a cigarette. But a shuttered window is periodically opened to show the receding Earth, approaching Moon and, in a topical reference, the Russian satellite with the dog Layka. But Ismail's antics are foregrounded. While Sharvin is temporarily unconscious and Rushdi sends Ismail to find a first aid kit, he discovers bottles of alcohol and begins drinking enthusiastically, becoming the first drunkard in space since *Himmelskibet*'s David Dane. Suggesting he is bored in the spaceship's cramped quarters, he asks, "Did you bring playing cards? Did you bring backgammon or domino[es]?" But he primarily wants to "return to

Egypt" and undertakes to do that all by himself. When Sharvin and Rushdi, working in the upper chamber, suddenly notice that the "cabin no longer has air," indicating the hull has been breached (which in reality would instantly kill them both), Rushdi hurries downstairs and sees that Ismail has vanished. A note explains, "I wore the rubber suit and went down [to Egypt]." Clearly, the loss of air came when Ismail opened the airlock door, but no one points that out; instead, they seek to retrieve the foolish man who went into space.

When they look out and see Ismail, floating in space in a standing position, Sharvin notes with bitter irony he has earned the honor of being "the first man to walk in the air" and tells Rushdi to put on a spacesuit and rescue him. His spacewalk, visibly staged in a film studio, is unimpressive, though Rushdi carefully crawls on the spaceship hull before throwing a rope to his comrade, and both men are observed standing sideways to suggest weightlessness. Since Ismail improbably drifted only a few feet, it is easy to toss him a rope and pull him in safely.

Once the spaceship reaches the Moon, any pretense of scientific accuracy vanishes. First, Ismail and Rushdi notice that objects are hovering in the air, strangely suggesting that weightlessness prevails not in space but on the Moon. Then, when the men don spacesuits to go outside, the Moon is appropriately barren, but the sky is blue, and clouds are later visible. Finally, after discovering a gear suggesting intelligent life, they encounter an enormous, childish-looking robot, which employs an invisible ray to hypnotize the men and force them to follow it into a cave. There, they remove their helmets (though we never see this — they wear them while entering the cave, and in the next shot, they are not wearing them) and, released from the robot's control, they meet an elderly man named Cosmo (Ibrahim Youness).

This lunar resident has many things to say. First, after probing their memories, he informs his visitors that his equipment also "makes you breathe everywhere, and tolerate any pressure," to explain why they are normally dressed, without spacesuits, when they take their next walk on the Moon. Cosmo says he is a survivor of a ruinous atomic war who avoided its damaging effects by retreating into this cave along with his daughter Stella (Safeya Tharwat) and other beautiful women. He shows the Earthmen an amazing telescope that provides close-up images of Earth, including Ismail's wife being passionately kissed by another man, naturally infuriating the driver. Rushdi is also falling in love with Stella, though his efforts to woo her, in the one scene that suggests the writer-director had seen *Abbott and Costello Go to Mars*, are complicated by a lunar machine that detects his lies. Sharvin had previously noted that he does not have enough fuel to return to Earth, so Cosmo says a powerful "atomic fuel" is available on the dark side of the Moon. In the meantime, Ismail employs a stupefying fluid resembling alcohol to make both him and the robot drunk, so the robot falls to pieces and cannot accompany the men on their journey to obtain fuel. Stella (who now loves Rushdi) must guide the Earthmen. Before their departure, for no reason whatsoever, the lunar ladies perform an extended athletic dance, presumably an Egyptian homage to *Cat-Women of the Moon*.

On the Moon's dark side, the travelers meet maimed and scarred survivors of the war, including a one-eyed general who brags about winning the war and companions without arms or legs. The general shows them where the fuel is, in containers that Sharvin cannot break open, but later events demonstrate the visitors did get the fuel. When a collapse in the cave apparently dooms Sharvin and Ismail, Rushdi and Stella reluctantly leave and, with Cosmo, the robot, and other Moon women, take off in the spaceship; but they spot their companions on the Moon and retrieve them. As the spaceship returns to Earth, it flies by the pyramids before landing. Emerging travelers are met by an enthusiastic crowd. As a final joke, the robot, preferring a more sedate reception, hypnotizes the greeters so they walk around like zombies.

As noted, spacesuit comedies can be defended as expressions, even vindications, of the common person's desire to be included in the conquest of space, instead of reserving such ventures for trained astronauts and scientists. Such stories might have special power in countries like Egypt and Mexico that cannot create their own space programs and hence may forever be excluded from space. Yet *Rehla ilal Kamar* provides surprisingly little support for such aspirations; for while Rushdi better represents his countrymen, Ismail suggests that a typical Egyptian who joins an expedition to the Moon would do little more than get drunk and cause trouble. His failure to display even the minimal heroism of *The Reluctant Astronaut*'s Roy Fleming indicates that, on reflection, it might be best to limit space travel to well-qualified individuals.

Conquistador de la Luna (*The Astronauts*) (1960)

It may seem to future film historians that an international law, passed in the early 1950s, required all film comedians to make films about space travel. Mexico inaugurated the tradition in 1946, when silent comedian Buster Keaton starred in in *El Moderno Barba Azul* (literally "The Modern Bluebeard," and released on videocassette as *Boom on the Moon*). In a story that would become typical, Keaton, an American soldier mistaken for a Mexican criminal, is released with another convict to fly a scientist's rocketship to the Moon. The spaceship really lands in Mexico, but Keaton fails to realize that, inspiring comic interludes with Mexicans mistaken for aliens. The astronauts wear wizards' robes, not spacesuits, so this reportedly execrable film demands no attention here.

In 1960, Mexican comedian Antonio "Clavillazo" Espino made another space journey in *Conquistador de la Luna*.[6] Though this flight predictably involves absurd circumstances and implausible aliens, he conducts himself with a bit more dignity than other comics, and his film intermingles the usual slapstick with a few interesting points about space travel. Also, the film apparently borrows footage from other films to provide persuasive special effects (some scenes seem grayer and fuzzier than the sharp footage featuring Clavillazo), but this is done artfully enough and contributes to the film's overall ambience. (Surprisingly, despite having watched so many of these films, I cannot identify the film or films that provided the recycled footage.)

After we see the Rube Goldberg–like devices of an eccentric electrician, Bartolo (Antonio "Clavillazo" Espino), a scientist (Andrés Soler) prepares to discuss his impending launch of a rocketship to the Moon. As he leaves home, his beautiful daughter (Ana Luisa Peluffo) tries to do some ironing, but when she plugs in the iron, sparks fly and the outlet is blackened. After calling Bartolo to repair the iron, she conducts a last-minute check of her father's spaceship. Rushing to proudly show her the repaired iron, Bartolo boards the spaceship, tries to plug it in, and hits a lever that launches the spaceship.

The usual business of spacesuit films then follows: The faces of Bartolo and the woman are distorted as they endure the pressure of liftoff (conveyed economically by warping the film while Clavillazo makes funny faces); then, Bartolo is comically distressed when he floats upward. The woman throws him magnetic boots so he can walk, upside down, on the ceiling. The woman contacts her father via radio, though they also see his image on a television screen, and a later scene suggests that people on Earth see the travelers on television as well. This film may qualify, then, as another science fiction work that anticipates television cameras on a Moon flight. As if fond of the effect, the director shows the distorted faces of Bartolo and the woman as they approach the Moon, though the pressure of decelerating near the Moon would be trivial compared to the strain of leaving Earth's gravity.

After they land and inform the professor, there is excited talk about how much this means to Mexico, though unlike American films like *Project Moon Base* and *Way...Way Out*, there are no moral concerns about having an unmarried man and woman together on the Moon. But demonstrating that some standard attitudes still prevail, Bartolo insists "Me first" as they prepare to leave the spaceship and touch the Moon, "because I'm the man." Although the daughter of the man who built the spaceship has a better claim to the honor than an accidental passenger, the woman agrees, so Bartolo drops to the surface and puts the ladder in place, gallantly, so the woman disembarks with more dignity.

For a moment of sobriety, Bartolo and the woman contemplate the stark lunar landscape, with a crescent Earth in the dark starry sky, and Bartolo makes large leaps in the weak gravity, exclaiming after his second jump — almost a brief flight through the sky — that he feels like Superman. A cylindrical chamber emerges from the ground, its door opens, and the humans enter to descend to an underground cavern. There, they meet the Moon's inhabitants, who resemble humanoid fish with four arms and fins on their heads, and their leader, an enormous brain with a projecting eye on a tentacle. Unusually aware of potential dangers, the Earth people resist alien efforts to remove their helmets, and when they do, both the man and woman hold their breath as long as possible before realizing that the cavern contains breathable air. Further enhancing the aura of unreality, the aliens can vanish and reappear at will, which later scenes suggest is achieved by special portals for teleportation.

The imprisoned Bartolo and the woman begin feeling hungry, and Bartolo indulges in an elaborate pantomime of eating a delicious meal. A female alien then materializes (her gender indicated by a ribbon of white hair on her head) carrying a platter with typical science fiction food: two pills, each on a small plate. After consuming the pills, Bartolo decides it might be advantageous to romance the alien, who proves receptive, as the two engage in a strange dance while the human woman is interrogated by the brain. When Bartolo meets the brain, he learns its sinister plan: A flying saucer will leave a space station and land in Earth's oceans to make sea levels rise, threatening billions of lives. Images indicate that the aliens will also make Earth animals like birds, dogs, and fish drop dead, explode buildings, and perhaps blow up the entire planet. Amidst these grandiose schemes, the brain falls in love with the woman and undertakes to forcibly marry her, outfitting her in a garish showgirl's costume while aliens solemnly surround her in a bizarre parody of a marriage ceremony.

Fortunately, Bartolo is making progress with the alien woman, who gives him a silver pill to make him invisible. This seems ineffective, since Bartolo keeps his spacesuit on and hence can still be seen (though apparently lacking a head and hands). As he surreptitiously grabs their spacesuits while alien guards fail to notice his presence, his head and hands are oddly visible, though he later becomes invisible again. He also gains the power to use the teleportation portals. Rushing into the brain's chamber to disrupt the wedding, he seizes the woman and pushes her and himself through a midair portal to get to a safe place where they don spacesuits and rush to their spaceship.

Before this occurs, though, Bartolo had previously visited the spaceship by himself, to inform Earth that they encountered "indigenous people" on the Moon who threaten to destroy Earth. This causes a panic, as illustrated by oddly disjointed scenes: a television announcer faints on camera when handed a paper with the news; a banker cannot interest people in his piles of money, and when bills fall to the ground, people step over them instead of picking them up; a bartender trying to attract customers places free drinks on the bar, which remain unclaimed; and a fat woman begins to embrace and fervently kiss her husband. The professor and his colleagues have heated discussions about how to respond to the alien menace.

Bartolo and his female companion are not as safe as they thought, because the aliens pursue their spaceship with their saucer. The brain's eye materializes menacingly from their spaceship's ceiling, and the space travelers throw objects at it. To deal with the saucer, Bartolo resolves to go on a spacewalk. Then, when the eye appears to send Bartolo drifting into space, cinematic history is made when his female companion, observing his plight, dons a spacesuit and goes out to rescue him, becoming the first woman on film to walk in space. Using an oxygen tank to maneuver around, she flies to him and carries him into the spaceship. Bartolo uses the rocket exhaust from the ship to destroy the saucer, apparently killing the alien brain and eliminating the threat.

Conquistador de la Luna concludes with celebrations, in the spaceship and on Earth, where the professor announces, "The human race has been saved." Life on Earth returns to normal: The announcer resumes his air of smug confidence, people scramble to pick up the money, the bartender takes the free drinks away, and the fat woman goes back to attacking her husband. Bartolo and the professor's daughter also announce on television they have fallen in love and show the world a passionate kiss. As in American space comedies, an Everyman figure improbably triumphs against all odds in space.

Gigantes Planetarios (*Planetary Giants*) (1965) and *El Planeta de las Mujeres Invasoras* (*Planet of the Female Invaders*) (1966)

Though routinely described as a comedy, there is not much buffoonery in *Gigantes Planetarios* (*Planetary Giants*); what little there is mostly involves the secondary characters of boxer Marcos Godoy (Rogelio Guerra) and trainer Rey Taquito (José Ángel "Ferrusquilla" Espinosa). It otherwise seems a melodramatic spacesuit film, recalling *Captain Video: Master of the Stratosphere* and *Flight to Mars*, employing a standard story: The evil ruler of another planet seeks to conquer Earth, requiring humans to fly to his world to oppose his efforts, whereupon they find and ally themselves with subjects opposed to his rule and join forces to overthrow him.

In opening scenes, a flying saucer lands in Africa, an unseen alien emerges, and he uses a ray gun to disintegrate a spear-toting tribesman. Precisely what the aliens gained from this attack is unclear, but it alerts authorities, including scientist Daniel Wolf (Guillermo Murray) and beautiful assistant Silvia (Adriana Roel), that Earth faces an alien invasion, as announced in dramatic newspaper headlines. But the aliens, who naturally look exactly like humans, have secretly infiltrated Earth institutions, including a gathering of experts who discuss the threat, attended by a bald alien named Espia (Nathanael "Frankenstein" Léon). (Aliens are distinguished solely by an electronic device on their stomachs, which Espia suspiciously touches during the meeting.) Wolf talks to scientist Professor Walter (Mario Orea), who designed a spaceship to visit the aliens' homeworld, known only as "the Planet of Eternal Night." To oppose this initiative, Espia first kills Walter, then attempts to bribe Wolf with one million dollars before falling into a bathtub and, due to his device, dying by electrocution. There are also time-consuming interchanges in a nightclub involving Wolf, Silvia, Godoy (whom Wolf calls "my friend"), Taquito, and a woman who is an alien agent.

Godoy and Taquito flee from an angry crowd after Godoy loses a fight. They find themselves in a hotel room with two spacesuits. They hastily put them on, as a disguise to elude pursuers, but the ploy backfires when officials enter the room and, believing they are astronauts scheduled to accompany Wolf, sedate them and carry them to the spaceship (a squat cylinder similar to Flash Gordon's craft). As the spaceship takes off (oddly, from inside a large building), Wolf discovers that Silvia is also on board, then notices that Godoy and Taquito are somehow his crewmates. He also fulfills a ritual of spacesuit films by painfully stretching his arm to reach a poorly located switch.

As the ship flies through space (which in this black-and-white film looks gray, not black), one man is briefly observed upside-down, but there are no other signs of weight-

South-of-the-Border Spacesuits: The poster promoting the Mexican film *Gigantes Planetarios* (*Planetary Giants*) (1965) features protagonists Daniel Wolf (Guillermo Murray), Silvia (Adriana Roel), and Marcos Godoy (Rogelio Guerra) in spacesuits, though they wear them only briefly in the film, suggesting that the garments were deemed an effective way to market a space adventure to potential filmgoers.

lessness. When a crisis makes the craft rock back and forth, Wolf takes a spacewalk to repair an engine. In a somewhat authentic sequence, he slowly floats through space to reach the faulty rocket, insert a wrench, and evidently get it working again, since a previously dark opening lights up to indicate functionality. The spaceship then glides to a landing on the rocky surface of its destination, and any further pretenses to scientific realism are abandoned.

Though astronauts put down their faceplates to land, and Wolf emerges from the spaceship with his helmet on, he immediately raises his faceplate, as if sure the atmosphere will be safe, perhaps because he already glimpsed human-like inhabitants approaching. The visitors are escorted underground, where these people live to avoid inhospitable surface conditions. Following a long tradition of aliens recalling Earth's ancient cultures, the alien costumes and building seem modeled upon classical Greece. The humans are brought before the world's Grand Protector, who resembles Ming the Merciless, and he reveals evil plans to conquer Earth with a death ray. He demonstrates his weapons' effectiveness by using a ray gun to disintegrate four countrymen. But visitors learn that many of the Grand Protector's subjects despise his rule and sympathize with their cause: A beautiful woman falls in love with Godoy, an unattractive chubby woman is attracted to Taquito, and an old man tells Wolf of his opposition to the ruler. After a dinner with the Grand Protector that turns violent, Godoy escapes. While others are taken to a prison cell, he dons the costume of a palace guard and, with the help of his new girlfriend, evades capture.

As the Grand Protector, about to carry out his scheme, again addresses his captives, Godoy sneaks into his chamber to overcome him, with the support of comrades and the dictator's rebellious followers. Godoy kills some aliens with their own ray gun, while Silvia, by throwing a ray gun and smashing a television screen showing alien confederates on Earth, somehow kills them as well. While the Grand Protector flees to the spaceship, he is confronted and defeated, and the old man takes control of the planet, clearly to seek peaceful relations with Earth. As the humans prepare to return, a final moment of comedy involves spacesuits: Taquito's homely girlfriend attempts to kiss him goodbye, but Taquito accidentally — or deliberately? — lowers his faceplate so she cannot.

Gigantes Planetarios was filmed simultaneously with another film, *El Planeta de las Mujeres Invasoras* (*Planet of the Female Invaders*), which again features Wolf, Silvia, Godoy, and Taquito as protagonists. It is fitting, as a matter of history, that the films were sequentially released to make *El Planeta de las Mujeres Invasoras* seem a sequel to the other film. For, while *Gigantes Planetarios* pays homage to the serials of the 1930s and early 1950s, *El Planeta de las Mujeres Invasoras* imitates the major innovation in melodramatic spacesuit films that dominated films of the 1950s: replacing menacing male aliens with beautiful females garbed in scanty outfits and high heels.

Again, the film begins with extended events on Earth: A flying saucer piloted by two women lands on Earth and, noticing an amusement park ride with a similar saucer, they replace its phony spacecraft with their real spacecraft to capture humans and take them to their homeworld. Meanwhile, Godoy is visited by gangsters who hand him a large sum of money, and subsequent events suggest that he was being bribed to lose an upcoming match; for after he wins the fight, the criminals attempt to shoot him. When Godoy visits the amusement park with Silvia, while Taquito waits outside, the gangsters also board the saucer, along with a couple, their child, and a fat man, and the alien women take off and subdue passengers by deploying a ray gun against a gun-wielding criminal. Alerted to the problem by Taquito, Wolf tracks the saucer's flight via television but takes no immediate action.

On the alien world, the humans are blinded by intense light, a problem requiring the alien women to wear visors on the surface and otherwise live underground. (Oddly, the visors are entirely clear, not tinted, so they appear useless.) The humans are brought to the world's evil queen, Adastrea (Lorena Velázquez), and learn of her insidious plot: She wishes to relocate her people to Earth, but they cannot breathe comfortably in our atmosphere; thus, she captured humans to obtain their lungs to solve the problem. The visitors also meet the queen's good twin sister Alburnia (also Velázquez), who becomes their ally. Alburnia sends a sympathizer in a saucer to Earth, to inform Wolf about her sister's plans, but she struggles to breathe, her informative note is destroyed by alien women pursuing her, and she can only gasp out a few words of warning to Taquito before dying. The men resolve to fly to the alien world and rescue Godoy, Silvia, and the other humans.

Using the spaceship from *Gigantes Planetarios*, Wolf and Taquito get on board wearing spacesuits. When they land and emerge from their craft, they again encounter human-looking aliens, and Taquito quickly lifts up his faceplate and can easily breathe (raising the question of why alien women cannot breathe our atmosphere). The main reason he lifts his visor, though, is to awkwardly don a protective visor provided by alien women. They are escorted to the evil queen holding their helmets, but they abandon them at some point, since they are not observed during the rest of the film.

Although the captive humans, joined by Wolf and Taquito, are treated with surprising civility, the queen's evil schemes demand an immediate response: After the aliens operated on two dead humans to obtain "adaptors" that worked only briefly for the alien women who visited Earth, the aliens attempt to operate on the little boy, believing children's lungs will be better. The humans are relieved when they decide to spare the boy and seek other children for their purposes. The queen unveils her death ray, which travels from her homeworld to an orbiting satellite resembling a gyroscope, which deflects the beam to a precise point on Earth and kills three adults supervising a class of children. The two alien women then escort the children into their saucer.

Godoy and Wolf, who tried to romance Adastrea, seize control of the ray and use it to kill the aliens on Earth, freeing the children, as well as the guards who rush to assist the queen. Alburnia now takes control, and she and her restrained evil twin accompany the humans to Wolf's spaceship, evidently so they can all travel to Earth (though the spaceship does not seem to have enough room). One criminal, who previously allied himself with Alastrea, tries to shoot Alburnia and apparently kills both twins.

Like their American counterparts, these films illustrate how spacesuits may be incorporated into melodramatic spacesuit films, but tend to be pushed to the sidelines. Thus, while the first film features extensive use of spacesuits, including a spacewalk, the second film reduces space flight and spacesuits to brief scenes, providing more time for unrealistic conflicts between humans and human-like aliens. The final stage of the process, observed in both America and Mexico, is eliminating spacesuits altogether.

• Japan and Western Asia •

Reflecting its reputation as a nation eager to embrace new technology, Japan in the 1950s plunged in science fiction films with great enthusiasm. Some films featured giant monsters rampaging through cities or battling each other, beginning with *Gojira* (1954); others involved aliens visiting Earth, usually with hostile intent, beginning with *Uchûjin*

Tôkyô ni Arawaru (*Warning from Space*) (1956). The latter films soon began to include human space travel, making them relevant to this study, and by the 1960s, all traditions merged in films with convoluted stories mingling monsters, aliens, and human astronauts.

Chikyu Boeigun (*The Mysterians*) (1957) and *Uchû Daisensô* (*Battle in Outer Space*) (1959)

While aliens in Japanese films rarely seem like genuine space travelers, as exemplified by the inept invaders in the 1959 film *Yusei Oji* (*The Prince of Space*), *Chikyu Boeigun* commands attention because its aliens, and one human ally, do wear spacesuits, though they seem rather flimsy. One wonders why they wear them, since they look exactly like humans. Perhaps it is because Mysterians are identified as weak beings, potentially susceptible to extreme heat, since they are survivors of an atomic war that destroyed their planet, which once orbited between Mars and Jupiter; thus, spacesuits might protect them against Earth's environment. Yet these aliens are ready to settle here, as they seek to establish a base on Earth, marry Earth women, and have children to revive their damaged race. Though this desire can be seen as another sign of their frailty, it also indicates they must be capable of surviving in conditions suitable for their future wives. (Manifestly, Mysterians will never have children if they always wear spacesuits on Earth, or if their human brides must wear spacesuits in alien-friendly environments.)

One might better theorize that the Mysterians' spacesuits serve primarily to denote social class: The spacesuit of their leader is orange, those of his associates are yellow, and those worn by menial guards are blue. This also explains why the human who briefly allies himself with the Mysterians (before learning of their evil intentions) wears a yellow spacesuit. While this can be the purpose of any uniform, *Chikyu Boeigun* may be the only film that employs spacesuits primarily for this reason.

A Raygun Wedding? The unidentified leader of the alien invaders from *Chikyu Boeigun* (*The Mysterians*) (1957) inspects the women recruited as their possible brides.

Sometimes described as a loose sequel to *Chikyu Boeigun*, *Uchû Daisensô* (*Battle in Outer Space*) makes no reference to the earlier film and involves another race of sinister aliens with a different plan: Instead of seeking to live on Earth, they remain in a base on the Moon and launch attacks from there, requiring the beleaguered human race to venture into space to destroy the base.

The aliens' evil designs are first demonstrated by scenes of spectacular destruction: A flying saucer beams energy at an orbiting space station and destroys it; a saucer hovers over a railroad bridge and, again using a ray, makes the bridge rise several feet in the air, sending a railroad plummeting into a river; finally, saucers touch the ocean to create huge "waterspouts" that raise ocean levels and lead to disastrous flooding. When scientists and diplomats meet under the auspices of the United Nations, a scientist explains that, since gravity depends upon the movement of atoms, the aliens use a "freeze ray" to counteract gravity and cause destruction. (This is a dubious "explanation" of gravity.)

Aliens can also take mental control of certain humans, though why they use this power on only two people, when it would be advantageous to have many agents, is another unanswered question. The first of their mental slaves, Dr. Achmed (Malcolm Pearce), attempts some sabotage before being teleported to a saucer, and through him people at the meeting learn that the aliens plan to colonize Earth. In response, Earth will send two spaceships to the Moon on what is initially described as a reconnaissance flight to locate the alien base, though its crew will actually endeavor to destroy the base. To assist them, scientists develop, as a logical answer to the freeze ray, a destructive "heat ray."

Before the spaceships leave, a crew member and his girlfriend lie in a field and contemplate the joys of nature; the man observes, "We humans will gradually lose such feelings of beauty." This intriguing suggestion that either scientific progress in general, or space travel in particular, will somehow dehumanize people is never developed in the film; rather, attention shifts to the man's friend, also part of the crew, who becomes the second alien slave.

The film then offers a reasonably realistic look at possible space travel at a time when large, spacious spacecraft were still considered feasible. Some images are genre clichés: As spaceships take off, astronauts' faces show the strain of acceleration, and once in space, a man unbuckles his belt and floats to the ceiling. There is an evocative moment when objects approaching one spaceship, thought to be enemy saucers, turn out to be fragments of the destroyed space station. Referencing its dead crew, the commander tells colleagues, "Better say a prayer for them." As spaceships get close to the Moon, the alien agent tries to sabotage his craft, but he is found and captured before any damage is done.

Once on the Moon, crew members rush to a room with space helmets on a table and don spacesuits. Advised to "check your oxygen" and "check the radio," two men are lowered to the surface by an enormous arm, while others in a hovercraft are lowered by wires. As standard developments, one spacesuited man makes an enormous leap in the low lunar gravity, though he is cautioned to be careful after a rough landing, and the sole female astronaut gazes up at Earth in the sky. The lunar surface is well rendered, though the colors are sometimes wrong: The sky is blue, not black, and parts of the ground are brown, not gray.

However, rather than contemplating the wonders of an alien world, these astronauts must prioritize their silly plot. Leaving the alien slave tightly bound, men in the hovercraft, alternately rolling and floating across the surface, approach the area of the alien base. Switching to foot travel, they stumble upon the entrance to a cave which they speculate will lead to the base. Inside, the woman is attacked by aliens; their features concealed by mask-like

Invaders in the Craters: To justify the title of their film, the people who prepared the poster for the American release of *Uchû Daisensô* (*Battle in Outer Space*) (1959) naturally had to depict the attack on the aliens' lunar base, along with spacesuited astronauts who look much more Caucasian than the Japanese adventurers in the film.

space helmets, they are smaller than humans and incessantly make chattering noises. They are also ineffectual foes, since all they do is stand around the woman and paw at her, so a man coming to her rescue easily walks into their midst and pulls her to safety. Why aliens who destroy space stations with destructive rays carry no hand weapons represents another inconsistency in the story.

The humans see the alien base (resting on the lunar surface, though they gained access to it through a cave) and set up the heat ray to destroy it; the aliens respond by unleashing their own destructive rays. The invaders also rouse their agent, who blows up one spaceship and makes his way into the other. After a seemingly endless exchange of destructive ray beams with no effect, the humans finally obliterate the base, freeing the saboteur from alien control. When the humans reach the surviving spaceship, he volunteers to stay behind and fire at the remaining saucers, allowing the spaceship to safely depart.

This appears to end the story, but there is an anticlimactic coda: Still feeling threatened, Earth's people urge national leaders to unite to protect the planet. At one rally filmed by someone with a poor understanding of English, protesters make their case with a sign reading, "All Earth Fight for Freedom — Mash the Monster!" All countries work together to create a fleet of space fighter planes to combat the aliens, and there is a lengthy final scene in which an armada of these planes (flown by men in standard pilot gear, not spacesuits) battle in space against a large flying saucer escorted by six smaller saucers. Gradually, as rays hit their targets, the humans prevail against their enemies. The sequence is yet another cinematic anticipation of similar scenes in George Lucas's *Star Wars* (1977), but like battles in that film, these resemble old films about aerial combat more than genuine efforts to depict plausible space combat.

Overall, this film may be of most value in first making the point, later observed in films as disparate as *Way...Way Out* and *Moon Zero Two*, that it is virtually impossible to stage conventional battles when opponents wear spacesuits; whether the weapons are handguns or fists, such fights seem incongruous. The solution devised by Ishirô Honda, director of *Uchû Daisensô,* is to exclusively employ magical ray guns in futuristic-seeming battles, but these are not dramatically involving. Another reason why this film was not as popular as its predecessor, *Chikyu Boeigun,* may be that the earlier film, occurring entirely on Earth, never had heroes in spacesuits or took them to alien worlds, eliminating disconcerting elements from a cosmic tale of cops and robbers.

Kyojin to Gangu (*Giants and Toys*) (1958)

A film unlike any others discussed here, *Kyojin to Gangu* is a realistic satire about business competitors that happens to involve the use of spacesuits in advertising. The film thus illustrates the point, documented in Megan Preminger's *Another Science Fiction: Advertising the Space Race 1957–1962,* that in the late 1950s advertisers aggressively employed the imagery of space travel to promote their products. However, as suggested by Preminger's time frame, the fad proved ephemeral, so *Kyojin to Gangu* might be termed predictive because it also suggests the appeal of space might prove limited.

We first meet two advertising executives for World Caramels, young Yousuke Nishi (Hiroshi Kawaguchi) and overstressed boss Goda (Hideo Takamatsu). Fiercely competing with rivals Giant and Apollo, they are pressured to come up with "something new. A totally new concept" for a vigorous ad campaign. As one response, they recruit a free-spirited young woman, Kyoko Shima (Hitomi Nozoe), to work as a model, sensing she has a quirky charm despite her bad teeth. As Nishi seeks information about his competitors by talking to a friend who works for Giant and a girlfriend who works for Apollo, the girlfriend provides an idea: spacesuits, which will be effective because "the kids will love it." They present the proposal at a meeting with bigwigs: After claiming "I've been looking into what interests children," Nishi announces, "A clear answer has emerged. Science! Space!" His specific suggestion is a contest in which prizes can be spacesuits and ray guns, because while this is "old hat to Americans," it is new to Japanese children. They also will exploit an upcoming Space Expo as a tie-in and "place space and science stories in the press." Despite an executive's protest ("You can't link caramels to space"), the plan is approved.

Nishi is worried because Apollo unveils an ad campaign based on cash prizes which may be more successful, because it appeals to adults as well as children; as he glumly notes, "Spacesuits don't eliminate poverty." Nevertheless, the company proceeds, placing Kyoko in a brown spacesuit with a spherical glass helmet for promotional photographs; one man compliments her by saying, "You could run for Miss Mars and you'd win." It is announced, "World Caramel is proud to present as prizes a set of spacesuits, space helmet and space gun, plus caramel-packed rockets. And free invitations to the planetarium." A man wearing a spacesuit also passes out free caramels on the street, and an elaborate commercial features Kyoko in her spacesuit dancing with beautiful women and other figures in spacesuits. Thus, in deliberately overstated fashion, director Yasuro Masumura shows the iconography of space travel crassly reduced to a marketing tool, with nothing conveyed about its true nature or purpose.

While Kyoko's personal popularity soars, the campaign proves ineffective. Though a fire at the Apollo factory temporarily weakens one rival, World Caramel's sales remain disappointing, and against a background of posters showing the spacesuited Kyoko by a rocketship, Nishi is told, "We need more publicity, more space shows." They pin their hopes on the upcoming Space Expo, where they want Kyoko to hand out caramels. The naïve and carefree Kyoko has grown cynical and manipulative, and she refuses to be a huckster for World Caramels, archly noting, "Handing out caramels in a spacesuit is not in my contract," which deals solely with media appearances. In desperation, the ailing Goda, whose ulcers are now making him spit up blood, orders Nishi to seduce Kyoko, noting she had once been attracted to him (though Nishi rejected her advances because he still preferred his girlfriend). After initially refusing, Nishi approaches her after she completes a garish production number in a nightclub. His blunt courtship is rebuffed, and he learns that her boyfriend and manager is none other than his old friend, who is more than willing to double-cross Nishi to advance his own interests.

Goda puts on the spacesuit to appear at the Space Expo but, as he is still spitting up blood, Nishi hits him to prevent him from proceeding. After recently announcing, "I won't sacrifice my dignity," Nishi dons the spacesuit and attends the Space Expo, incongruously wearing a tie that is visible through his helmet. His now-estranged girlfriend makes a brief, enigmatic appearance to say, "Give them a smile."

While *Kyojin to Gangu* foregrounds a general argument about the destructive effects of pursuing profits above all else, it also makes a point about space travel. While characters in science fiction films can wear spacesuits with dignity, these garments remained to most people objects associated exclusively with children—explaining why Nishi fretted that his campaign would not appeal to adults. Thus, in realistic films about everyday people, having to wear something childish like a spacesuit only represents a humiliation. The film's role reversal is that Kyoko, having fixed her teeth and adopted a glamourous wardrobe, has grown powerful enough to reject entreaties to market candy to children, whereas the previously dominant Nishi is reduced to doing so. Their changes in status are symbolized by the fact that Kyoko can now refuse to wear a spacesuit, while Nishi must wear one. If not a film about space travel, *Kyojin to Gangu* illustrates how the public perceived space travel in the 1950s: as child's play.

Yosei Gorasu (*Gorath*) (1962)

After producing other sorts of science fiction movies in the late 1950s, Toho Studios and director Honda were by the 1960s specializing in giant monster movies modeled on *Gojira* and its sequels. *Yosei Gorasu* (*Gorath*), focusing on a different sort of menace from space, was therefore surprising. After completing the film, Honda was pressured to add a brief appearance by a typical monster—a giant walrus—unearthed by earthquakes at the South Pole. Though the creature would seem an ideal device for promoting the film in America, these awkwardly interpolated scenes didn't make it into the U.S. version.

The film begins with odd occurrences in space, implausibly ranging from disturbances in the Van Allen radiation belts around Earth to a deviation in Pluto's orbit. These are soon attributed to the appearance of a new star, named Gorath, which is entering the Solar System on a collision course with Earth. This reddish body, resembling a planet covered with lava, has a "mass 6000 times that of the Earth" while only half the size of Earth, which suggests a white dwarf, though the film describes Gorath only as "a sun so dense a handful would weigh a ton." To investigate this menace, a Japanese spaceship named the *Hawk* is dispatched to its vicinity; indicating an ongoing tendency to employ familiar items in visualizing space travel, astronauts wear crash helmets like those of motorcycle or race car drivers. Its captain observes Gorath by ordering "Periscope up" and, after a device protrudes from the spaceship, looking through a periscope like those in a submarine. Captured by Gorath's gravity, the captain realizes they are doomed, but continues gathering information to assist Earth's people. This justifies their sacrifice, as the spaceship plummets to fiery destruction on Gorath; precisely what valuable data they garnered is not clear. All that is mentioned is the determination that Gorath will collide with Earth, but an approaching body's path can be deduced from observations on Earth, as in *Il Pianeta degli Uomini Spenti*.

The focus shifts to Earth, as another Japanese spaceship, the *Eagle*, is readied for takeoff. In a building where the crew prepares, astronauts wearing spacesuits float inside a chamber to train them to move in zero gravity. Failing to take their work seriously, the men playfully fight, prompting an observer to complain that they are in a "chamber for zero gravity research, not a nursery." Afterwards, they remove their spacesuits to undergo medical tests. Impetuous astronaut Tatsumi Kanai (Akira Kubo) breaks away from the test upon hearing that their commander has arrived. He and other crew members are disappointed to learn the flight has been cancelled, due to the spaceship's huge expense and uncertainty about its fate should it approach Gorath.

Scientists pursue two potential solutions to their dilemma: the possibility of destroying Gorath (to be determined, in some unspecified fashion, by sending the *Eagle* to study it), or the possibility of moving Earth out of Gorath's way with immense rocket engines to be constructed at the South Pole. This massive construction project causes destructive earthquakes and much damage, but repairs are effected and work seems to proceed satisfactorily. Meanwhile, in response to international pressure, the *Eagle* finally travels to Gorath, though what it is intended to accomplish, and what it actually accomplishes, are not explained. As the ship approaches the star, a few astronauts, led by Kanai, don spacesuits to pilot an auxiliary vehicle to its vicinity. This leads to a crisis, as the ship spins uncontrollably while Kanai stares in horror at Gorath. The vehicle soon returns to the safety of its mother ship, as spacesuited astronauts stand outside, using ropes to draw the vehicle into the spacecraft. The shocked Kanai now suffers from amnesia.

As Gorath approaches Earth, there is considerable doubt as to whether the Earth is being moved a sufficient distance to avoid its destruction; however, when Gorath sucks up Earth's moon, that helps to ensure that Earth is a safe distance away. When Kanai again gazes upon Gorath, that somehow cures his amnesia. After Gorath has passed, there is optimistic dialogue about the crisis's helpful effects (it brought the nations of the world together) and coming efforts to repair the damage done by Earth's celestial visitor. Also, throughout the film, three disparate space stations of different nations have functioned as observers and supporters of activities in space, and though they retreat to the ground and are apparently destroyed due to the catastrophic effects of Gorath, they reappear in space at the end, as if to symbolize that humanity will recover from this calamity.

Overall, *Gorath* conveys a surprisingly negative attitude toward space travel. While there is minimal value in the knowledge to be obtained, ventures into space otherwise seem useless, and this film's spaceships contribute nothing to the struggle to avoid a catastrophe. Astronauts themselves are either stoic but ineffectual (like the *Hawk*'s crew) or childish (like Kanai). While the film's conclusion suggests, among other things, that humanity will emerge from its crisis with a renewed space program, there is no assurance that astronauts will be better able to deal with another disaster, since they could not deal with Gorath. Indeed, when we next encounter Japanese space travelers, they are only helpless observers of the antics of enormous monsters.

Kaijû Daisensô (*Godzilla vs. Monster Zero*) (1965) and *Kaijû Sôshingeki* (*Destroy All Monsters*) (1968)

After a decade of movies about gigantic monsters, Japanese filmmakers clearly needed some new element to keep attracting audiences, and given their experience with other films, space travel was an obvious novelty to work into the stories. The trend began with *San Daikaijû: Chikyû Saidai no Kessen* (*Ghidrah, the Three-Headed Monster*) (1964), the fourth Godzilla movie, which features an enormous creature from space and a female prophet from Venus. The next Godzilla film, *Kaijû Daisensô* (*Godzilla vs. Monster Zero*), introduces space travelers. Still, by their nature, monsters, not astronauts, remain the center of attention, and concerns about space travel were inevitably peripheral to the problems raised by these implausible menaces.

A strange new planet has entered the Solar System, and two astronauts, Glenn Amer (Nick Adams) and K. Fuji (Akira Takarada), are sent to investigate. Scientists previously failed to observe Planet X, we are told, because it is "very dark" (though when they approach, it does not look particularly dark). Only after the recent detection of mysterious radio waves did they finally learn of its existence. The only noteworthy aspects of their flight are two disorienting scenes (Fuji is seen upside down, due to Amer's error in aligning the spaceship, and astronauts are sideways when they land), and the astronauts, after testing for radiation, begin exploring the planet's stark terrain wearing red spacesuits with white helmets. Momentarily, as I note elsewhere,[7] the scene resembles the lunar landing of *Destination Moon*, as Fuji scales a rugged hill with a staff bearing the combined flags of the United Nations, Japan, and the United States and prepares, one assumes, to claim the planet for his international sponsors.

Fuji is rudely interrupted by an abrupt descent into nonsense. First, there is "thunder and lightning"; then, when Fuji notices that Glenn and the spaceship have vanished, a mysterious voice summons him to a strange cylinder that rises to the surface from underground. Soon he and Amer have removed their helmets to talk with the residents of Planet X, who resemble humans except for black visors over their eyes. Their leader, the Controller (Yoshio Tsuchiya), explains they must live underground because Ghidrah, driven away from Earth in a previous film by the combined efforts of monsters Godzilla, Rodan, and Mothra, now ravages their planet; the only way to stop him, they believe, is to transport Godzilla and Rodan to their world to again defeat him. (Mothra, perhaps as a cost-cutting measure, is not mentioned or seen in the film.) Logically, beings who can carry dinosaurs from planet to planet in immense energy spheres should be able to kill monsters, especially since they also employ destructive rays, so Amer and Fuji should realize this is all a ruse; instead, they agree to return to Earth to obtain permission for the aliens to seize the monsters. In exchange, the aliens will provide Earth with a tape containing a cure for all diseases.

Godzilla and Rodan are soon carried to Planet X, accompanied by a flying saucer with Amer, Fuji, and scientist Dr. Sakurai (Jun Tazaki) on board. After Earth's monsters deal with Ghidrah, they receive the tape and a duplicate of their original spaceship to fly back to Earth. But the tape contains no cure, only an ultimatum: Earth must surrender to Planet X, or the aliens will destroy Earth by using magnetic beams to mentally control the three monsters in their possession and force them to relentlessly attack. Their story was simply a scheme to capture two additional monsters to aid in their conquest. The film now begins to resemble *Earth vs. the Flying Saucers*, the novelty being that the flying saucers shooting destructive rays are accompanied by monsters.

With space travel long forgotten, the rest of the plot unfolds: Amer is captured by aliens, who we learn are under computer control, but Amer first gets a note from an alien woman who somehow resisted her masters and fell in love with him. Her note reveals that the aliens are vulnerable to loud noises. Fortuitously, Amer is imprisoned with the nerdish boyfriend of Fuji's sister, Tetsuo Teri (Akira Kubo), who invented a device that emits a loud noise. While they escape, Fuji and Sakurai perfect a method to neutralize the magnetic beams controlling the monsters, and they join forces for a concerted assault on the invaders. The sound from Teri's invention is broadcast to disable the aliens, the monsters are freed from alien control, and Godzilla and Rodan battle Ghidrah and drive him away. (Their struggle goes underwater, leaving the monsters' fate unresolved at the end of the film.)

There is a final twist, intended as a joke, that is actually surprisingly sensible: Though he wants a vacation, Amer learns he must return to Planet X, because "you're to be our first ambassador." Given that the residents of Planet X are Earth's neighbors, and that their invasion was motivated by legitimate problems (a damaged environment and severe shortage of water) that might be solved peacefully, it seems reasonable to open diplomatic relations with Earth's would-be conquerors instead of preparing to resist their next attack, the usual conclusion of alien invasion films. Perhaps someone envisioned a sequel in which Earth and its new alien allies would team up to battle other aliens or other monsters, demonstrating the value of mending relations with former enemies — something Japanese filmmakers marketing films to Americans may have been especially cognizant of.

While the immediate sequels to *Kaijû Daisensô*, the undistinguished *Gojira, Ebirâ, Mosura: Nankai no Daiketto* (*Godzilla vs. the Sea Monster*) (1966) and *Kaijûtô no Kessen: Gojira no Musuko* (*Son of Godzilla*) (1967), involve no space travel, astronauts and spaceships figure in the all-star monster movie *Kaijû Sôshingeki* (*Destroy All Monsters*). To praise the film, one might say it unusually depicts a future world where space travel is such an accepted aspect of everyday life that it is taken for granted and receives no special attention. A more critical perspective would be that the film portrays space ventures in a bland, perfunctory manner while focusing on colorful aliens and giant monsters.

In opening scenes, the world of 1999 seems peaceful, perhaps even utopian, but only two specific advances are highlighted: Humanity has a permanent base on the Moon, with daily flights from Earth, and all Earth's monsters are safely confined by a force field on islands near Japan called Monsterland. But a mysterious gas surrounds Monsterland and causes residents of its underground base to fall unconscious. Soon, as shocked authorities learn, all monsters escape and attack the world's major cities. When they cannot contact Monsterland, officials of the United Nations Scientific Committee order a spaceship from the Moon to investigate, which is odd, since in such a crisis authorities might seek troops from a closer location who could reach the islands more quickly. But the decision allows the film's hero, Captain Tatsuo Yamabe (Toho stalwart Akira Kubo), to lead a team of astronauts to the scene, all wearing bright yellow spacesuits. As if to emphasize the routine nature of the activity, the only interior shots of the spaceship show space travelers seated in rows like riders on a bus.

After glimpsing a flying saucer, demonstrating that aliens are involved, astronauts land in Monsterland and find its staff members brainwashed by aliens, represented by a beautiful woman in a sparkling bodysuit (Kyôko Ai). To those who remember *Kaijû Daisensô*, they have a familiar story to tell: Humanoid aliens, here asteroid inhabitants called the Kilaaks, are taking control of Earth's monsters to conquer the planet. After politely explaining themselves, the aliens attempt to overcome the astronauts with their gas. Yamabe and his colleagues grab gas masks to escape with one alien-dominated human. During interrogation, he commits suicide by jumping out a window. After thwarting another effort to seize Yamabe and other humans, scientists find a device near his ear, explaining how aliens control human minds. Theorizing that the aliens are sending radio waves to similar devices to dominate the monsters, Yamabe and his astronauts search for radio transmitters while monsters converge on Tokyo. After freeing a woman from alien control by removing her earrings, Yamabe finds an alien base under Mount Fuji, fending off Godzilla and Rodan on the way, and learns the main source of alien rays is on the Moon.

As their spaceship lands on the Moon, aliens attack the vehicle with fire, but the astronauts escape by lowering themselves onto the surface in a moon tank and break down the base's defenses, and discover that aliens can be killed by extreme cold. When they disable the transmitter controlling the monsters, the creatures switch sides and attack the aliens under Mount Fuji; in response, the aliens borrow another subplot from *Kaijû Daisensô* by sending Ghidrah to battle Godzilla and his comrades. The three-headed monster is swiftly defeated. There is also a brief appearance by something that Yamabe assumes is a fire dragon, though it is an alien saucer. Then, after the aliens under Fuji are destroyed with a "cooling missile," the monsters return to Monsterland, and peace is restored to Earth.

As an indication of how unimportant space travel is to *Kaijû Daisensô*, one notes that its story could have been revised to eliminate this element altogether, since Yamabe could have flown from a regular airport, and the other alien base could have been located somewhere on Earth. Perhaps scenes of spaceships flying through the blackness of space, or a briefly glimpsed moonscape, added a little excitement, but for viewers presumably interested in monsters, they were surely perceived as little more than delaying tactics in a film that could not economically offer nonstop footage of its star attractions. One might be saddened to realize that audiences in the 1960s preferred to be entertained by imaginary monsters, not realistic space travelers, a point illustrated by many other films.

Taekoesu Yonggary (*Yongary, Monster from the Deep*) (1967)

Aware that Japanese filmmakers were profiting from movies about monsters, South Korean companies understandably thought of crafting a similar film, so South Korean company Kuk Dong joined Japan's Toei studios to produce *Taekoesu Yonggary* (*Yongary, Monster from the Deep*). In keeping with recent traditions, the film features both a monster and space travel, though strangely, its astronaut has almost nothing to do with the plot.

After we meet a just-married couple, the groom, an astronaut, is contacted on his wedding night and told he must report for duty immediately; there is an imminent nuclear test in the Middle East, and he must pilot an orbital reconnaissance flight to monitor the explosion. Since special effects show his space capsule traveling so far away from Earth as to make its entire sphere visible, one wonders how valuable such long-distance "reconnaissance" would be — surely, an airplane would be more useful — and the man never appears to see the test or say anything about it. Further, all we see of the entire mission is the liftoff; the separation of the manned capsule from the rest of the vehicle; one head shot of the astronaut in his space helmet, sometimes seen rightside up and sometimes seen upside down; and the landing of the space capsule, oddly using rockets instead of a parachute for a soft landing. Finally, the flight has a pointless moment of drama when the astronaut's radio temporarily fails, making him lose contact with Earth and driving his new wife to tears. Then the radio starts working again, with the reason for its malfunction unexplained.

Now there is an abrupt transition to the film's main story: During the flight, an earthquake is detected with a steadily moving epicenter, which as one scientist notes is "defying every natural law that man knows." This requires the astronaut to change his landing site. Upon landing, he essentially vanishes from the story, as the focus shifts to his bride's sister, her scientist boyfriend, and her precocious kid brother, all immersed in the plot of a typical monster movie. The earthquake is really a "gigantic reptile," the legendary monster Yongary, who soon rampages through a city, smashes buildings, and destroys vehicles with fiery breath. Except for a horn on the face (which later shoots laser beams), the monster resembles Godzilla. While a general insists that missiles will defeat Yongary, the scientist realizes (since the boy reported the monster was drinking oil) that Yongary absorbs and feeds upon sources of energy, making missiles useless, and instead guesses (based on another of the boy's observations) that a certain ammonia compound will destroy him. After an early version of the compound temporarily makes Yongary unconscious, the reawakened monster is killed when the scientist, riding a helicopter, drops the improved compound on Yongary.

Since the astronaut and his flight could have been edited out of the film without his absence being noted, one wonders why he was included at all. My theory is that, in making a very typical monster movie, filmmakers may have been anxious to convey this was a brand new film, not a recycled old film, and a spacesuited astronaut on posters and in previews could function as a convenient icon of modernity. If nothing else, the film illustrates that space travel has been and remains a symbol of the future, even as space travel becomes common in the present.

Uchû Daikaijû Girara (*The X from Outer Space*) (1967)

While *Taekoesu Yonggary* seems a monster movie with a short spacesuit film as its prologue, *Uchû Daikaijû Girara* (*The X from Outer Space*) seems a spacesuit film with a short monster movie as its epilogue. The film's first hour, about a flight to Mars, gives little indication the film will conclude with an enormous creature rampaging through the Japanese countryside.

After the fuel needed for the expedition is delivered via helicopter, we see the mission's astronauts — Captain Sano (Toshiya Wazaki), biologist Lisa (Peggy Neal), Dr. Shioda (Keisuke Sonoi), and communications officer Miyamoto (Shinichi Yanagisawa) — incongruously sitting in standard school desks while a man lectures about their impending flight. Six previous flights to Mars ended with a mysterious loss of communication apparently connected to an encounter with a UFO, but they are launching this seventh attempt with no additional precautions, it seems, other than a warning to Sano to be especially careful. During the last minute prior to liftoff, the astronauts sit sideways in their spaceship, wearing spacesuits, while monitors on the ground look nervously at instruments. Soon, in a scene recalling the capture of space capsules in *You Only Live Twice* in reverse, a large spaceship opens panels to disgorge a smaller spaceship resembling those in the Flash Gordon serials.

Inside the spaceship, there is a moment of weightlessness, as comic relief Miyamoto watches a clipboard floating away from him, but flipping a switch labeled "Stabilizer" somehow restores normal gravity. As Shioda succumbs to a strange fainting spell (described as "a form of space sickness"), a UFO appears. Sano resolves to accelerate away from the object despite Lisa's concerns for the frail Shioda. Though a noted biologist, Lisa adopts a standard feminine role by handing cups of coffee to male colleagues (and later serves prepared dinners as well). Instructed to return to the Lunar Base because of Shioda's illness, crew members put on spacesuits as they prepare to land, but they are not needed due to ingenious technology: After they land in a designated circle, two halves of a clear dome emerge from the ground to envelope the spaceship, creating a sealed environment allowing them to disembark without helmets.

There are now glimpses of daily life on the Moon: The astronauts are served dinner with a bowl of enormous apples as a resident explains that the Moon's lack of an atmosphere causes plants to grow larger (though one imagines the real cause would be low gravity). We also meet a beautiful woman named Michiko (Itoko Harada), obviously in love with Sano and jealous to see him in Lisa's company (though the women appear to become fast friends). There is a striking scene of two men in spacesuits bouncing up and down on the Moon's surface, like people on a trampoline, and when Sano and Miyamoto share a bath, Sano notes that the water is "man-made," synthesized out of lunar rocks. Finally, the women don evening gowns and drink cognac at a stylish party, making conditions on the Moon seem pleasant indeed, though one character insists, "Earth is man's home ground," not the Moon.

Lunar physician Dr. Stein (Mike Daneen) is unhappily drafted to replace Shioda on another effort to reach Mars. The flight involves some traditional hazards of spacesuit films — meteorites and interpersonal conflicts. Alerted to a meteorite shower by the sound of rocks striking the spaceship, Sano orders his crew to don "pressure suits" when a meteor penetrates the hull. For once, the effects of this event are portrayed realistically, as air furiously rushes out of the hole, drawing astronauts toward the breach until they can first block and then seal the hole. For some reason, Lisa also faints, causing concern until she is revived. Then, when the UFO reappears and traps the ship in a magnetic field, Sano decides that attempting to break away would only waste fuel and does nothing, leading a crazed Stein to seize the controls and fight the others while striving to fly away from the UFO. While they again elude the mysterious object, their ship is out of fuel, so they must wait for Michiko to fly a rescue rocket with additional fuel.

The astronauts now discover white deposits on the spaceship, apparently left either accidentally or deliberately by the UFO. (Where the material came from is regularly discussed but never resolved.) Sano and Lisa don spacesuits to float to the "strange substance." After Lisa places a sample, resembling a translucent egg, in a container, Sano blasts away the other "space matter" with a torch. Michiko soon arrives and, wearing her own spacesuit, floats to Sano's craft with a container of fuel.

When the astronauts return the sample to Earth and attend a celebratory party hosted by scientist Dr. Berman (Franz Gruber), the film finally shifts genres, as the party is interrupted by news of a lab accident where the sample was held. After puzzling over the absent sample, a footprint resembling a claw, and a hole in the floor, astronauts go to a hotel for drinks but are disturbed by a power failure, followed by the appearance of a huge reptilian monster with pointy ears, antennae, and glowing red eyes. Knowing the drill, the monster Guilala is immediately "bound for Tokyo." Ensuing scenes of spectacular destruction in the city and the country, interrupted by futile military attacks, require no detailed summary.

Interestingly, though, space travel is not entirely forgotten: Upon examining the remaining alien substance in the laboratory, Lisa determines it must be studied in its original airless environment, requiring them to use Lunar Base for experiments. After Sano, Lisa, Michiko, and Miyamoto fly to the Moon, Lisa identifies the substance as a new element, named "Guilalanium" (pronounced "Guilanium" in the English version), found on the Moon. She theorizes that this material kept the monster from emerging while in space, and hence might stop the monster on Earth. When the astronauts attempt to return to Earth with some Guilalanium, the element disables their rocket engine, threatening to make them "a permanent satellite" of Earth. Michiko suggests that the element might be isolated by a dangerous "nuclear shield," whatever that means, and her idea works. While the Guilalanium is delivered to waiting airplane crews, there is final drama as the monster, going "from one energy source to another" in a quest for energy to absorb, destructively approaches the spaceport, causing Lisa to be trapped underneath some rubble and requiring Sano and Miyamoto to lure the monster away with nuclear material in a car they frantically drive across the countryside. In the end, the airplanes coat Guilala with white Guilananium, causing him to become immobile, shrink, and again take the form of an egg, which Lisa retrieves and places in a container.

The closing scenes, tying up the loose ends, convey a conservative message with unusual clarity. First, since Guilala "cannot be destroyed on Earth," the spore will be sent into space "on an endless voyage ... to circle the sun." Lisa then stands on a cliff, looking distraught, as Berman approaches to ask if she revealed her love for Sano. While Berman urges her to do so, stating, "Love demands courage," Lisa declines, explaining, "That's the lesson that the monster taught me." She also specifies what the "lesson" is: "All things should remain where they belong." So, Sano and Michiko stand on a hillside and hold hands, the spaceship containing the spore rockets through space, and everything is clear: Space monsters should remain in space, Japanese men should remain with Japanese women, American women should remain with American men, and — presumably — humans born on Earth should remain on Earth, since nothing is said about an eighth mission to Mars. Whether the occupants of the saucer deliberately planted a monster on the spaceship to discourage space travel, or it was an accidental byproduct of an effort to destroy the spaceship, it seems that humans, at least the humans in this film, are now inclined to remain on Earth, "man's home ground," instead of furthering venturing into space.

Surveying these foreign-language spacesuit films, one must acknowledge impressive achievements and unusual perspectives offered by filmmakers from other cultural traditions. But the overall impression of someone familiar with English-language spacesuit films must be, "More of the same."

First, a few films from the Soviet Union and Eastern Europe recall the classic American and British spacesuit films. Perhaps only nations with active space programs, or their close allies, will have the motive and means to produce such films. Yet even those countries move away from realism to more entertaining depictions of colorful aliens and vast cosmic journeys. Next, in other countries, whether due to the influence of Anglophone films, or filmmakers independently reaching similar solutions to similar problems, one finds films following the same strategies developed by American and British filmmakers by employing familiar patterns of melodrama, comedy, and horror. Like their Anglophone counterparts, these films may offer unusual insights, especially the singular *Kyojin to Gangu*, but generally involve little more than routine heroics, slapstick, and monsters. While there may be additional films from other countries that merit a place in this study, the odds they will contribute anything new to the tradition of spacesuit films seem low indeed.

— 7 —

From Reel to Real: The Rebirth and Death of the Films

The revival of spacesuit films in the late 1960s can be attributed to two developments. First, all Russian and American space flights prior to 1967 had seemed routine successes, and even rare moments of drama — like the uncontrollable spinning that briefly threatened *Gemini 8* — were fiercely downplayed by officials who were eager to portray space missions as well-prepared, safety-conscious endeavors. The public was invited to conclude that actual space travel, despite the meteors, marauders, and monsters of films, was not dangerous and hence not a promising subject for realistic portrayals. That perception was shattered by two events in early 1967: the deaths of three *Apollo 1* astronauts on January 27, 1967, in a fire during a ground test, and the death of Soviet cosmonaut Vladimir Komarov on April 24, 1967, when his Soyuz capsule crashed upon returning to Earth. These tragedies reminded everyone that ventures into space remained perilous, and especially that even minor equipment problems might instantly kill astronauts. Space travel, as a result, again seemed suitable for dramatic entertainment.

Perhaps more significantly, Hollywood executives are always aware of what competitors are doing, and whenever expensive, heavily promoted films await release, producers may hastily create cheaper films along similar lines, hoping to exploit the free publicity generated by the eagerly anticipated blockbuster. This practice previously affected the spacesuit film in the 1950s, when *Rocketship X-M* was hurriedly filmed and released to capitalize on the expected popularity of the forthcoming *Destination Moon*. At the start of 1968, everyone in the industry knew Stanley Kubrick's epic film about future space travel, *2001: A Space Odyssey*, would soon appear, and knew that NASA was preparing the most expensive and spectacular spacesuit film of all time — the *Apollo 11* Moon landing, to be broadcast on live television worldwide. Such imminent developments would make it a propitious time to release spacesuit films.

As bases for new spacesuit films, producers mostly ignored films from the 1950s, which had largely been invalidated by events: Real footage could show what spaceship launches looked like, eliminating a need for the often unpersuasive special effects of earlier films, and everyone realized that astronauts would travel not in roomy spaceships but cramped capsules, and would not be menaced by swarms of meteors. Some executives turned to the realistic space novels that had started appearing in the early 1960s in response to public interest in America's space program: Hank Searls's *The Pilgrim Project* (1965) was adapted as *Countdown*, while Martin Caidin's *Marooned* (1964) inspired a film of that name. After discussing those films, I violate chronological order to conclude this study with the two greatest spacesuit films, made by more imaginative creators: *2001: A Space Odyssey* and television coverage of *Apollo 11*.

Countdown (1968)

The first thing to notice about *Countdown* is that it never refers to a meaningful purpose for space travel, whether it be securing a military advantage, expanding scientific knowledge, obtaining new resources, or preparing for space colonization. Instead, the sole motive behind its space program is boosting national prestige by beating the Russians to the Moon. With that goal in mind, America creates a secret program to hurriedly place an American on the Moon, should a Russian landing appear imminent, even if the technology needed to land men on the Moon and return them to Earth is not ready. A modified Gemini capsule with one astronaut will descend to the lunar surface, whereupon he will make his way to a previously launched shelter with necessary supplies. By periodically delivering such shelters, NASA will keep the astronaut alive until an Apollo capsule can retrieve him. During this waiting period — probably at least ten months — the astronaut will simply sit in his shelter, making no effort to explore the Moon or study its features, functioning solely as a symbol of America's technological superiority. Thus, when Russian cosmonauts orbit the Moon, seemingly to prepare for a subsequent landing, NASA activates its "Pilgrim Project," informing the projected pilot, veteran astronaut Chiz (Robert Duvall), that he will leave in three weeks.

Immediately, the desire to promote America's image that inspired this pointless mission also threatens its safety; for when the space program's leader, Ross Duellan (Steve Ihnat), is summoned to the White House, State Department officials explain that the Russians are manning Moon flights exclusively with civilians. Thus, to similarly demonstrate America's program has only peaceful purposes, he must replace military pilot Chiz with a civilian. When Duellan argues that he must make decisions based on practical considerations, not public relations, he is told that "Public relations is everybody's problem" because the space program requires public acceptance and public revenue. Given no alternative, Duellan reluctantly assigns an inexperienced civilian astronaut, Lee Stegler (James Caan). A furious Chiz must train Stegler even while doing everything he can to persuade superiors to reassign him to the mission.

There ensues the extended drama of preparing Stegler for the flight that explores what sort of person is best suited for space flight. To eliminate his rival and reclaim the mission, Chiz confronts Stegler with simultaneous problems during a flight simulation, and when he fails to immediately respond in the proper manner, Chiz submits a report documenting his purported incompetence and insists the experience proves Stegler is unsuitable. In a meeting with Stegler and Chiz, Duellan tells Chiz his report was futile — he will pass it on as "disapproved" to ensure it will be ignored, its probable fate in any event — and simply asks Stegler if he feels ready. Receiving a positive answer, Duellan keeps him assigned to the mission. Later, in a brief confrontation with Chiz, Stegler tells him, "You couldn't make this mission, Chiz. You got the guts but you haven't got the brains." His point, presumably, is that setting up the unfair test and writing the report was stupid, since it could not possibly persuade anyone to replace Stegler and could only damage Chiz's reputation. There is a novel implication here: If going into space is purely a matter of public relations and political pressure, then successful astronauts must have interpersonal skills as well as technical skills. Stegler is a better choice for the mission not only because he is a civilian, but also because, unlike the hot-headed Chiz, he can get along with colleagues and project a likable image.

Interestingly, after this argument, Chiz appears to accept that Stegler is the best man for the job and becomes more supportive, as shown during a later simulation. A spacesuited Stegler, wearing a harness called the "Peter Pan rig" to simulate the Moon's low gravity, attempts to enter the shelter. He falls off the ladder and dislodges an air hose, threatening his life in the simulation's airless chamber. Other observers want to stop the exercise to rescue Stegler, but Chiz insists he must be allowed to solve the problem himself, since he will have no one to assist him on the Moon. His confidence in Stegler is vindicated when the astronaut manages to get up and enter the chamber before his air supply is threatened.

Other sources of conflict are Gus (Charles Aidman), the project's physician, and Stegler's wife Mickey (Joanna Moore), who both worry about this improvised mission's extreme danger. Talking with Stegler and Mickey, Gus elaborates on the hazards involved: "Suppose you get hit by a meteor. Suppose you get a blast of radiation and you're cooked." Mickey, who previously accepted Stegler's assurances about safety, now stops being supportive like other astronauts' wives, in film and in real life; after he takes off, Mickey confesses, "I tried to stop him. I really did." But Stegler reminds Mickey what astronauts' wives are supposed to do: "Just smile. If it kills you, you just smile." To explain why he agreed to the mission, he says, "I got sucked in," but elaborates after a fashion: "I promised you caution, but ... but ... it's easy, it's really easy..." As if unable to articulate the motives that made him accept the assignment, he reveals, "I spent years thinking of myself taking that trip" and sums it up by saying, "That's who I am."

From this exchange, and recalling what we learned about Chiz, another essential trait in astronauts is revealed: a desperate desire for personal glory. Yet previous films foregrounded motives like patriotism (*Destination Moon*), scientific knowledge (*Riders to the Stars*), and signs of alien life (*Men into Space*), and criticized glory-seekers like Dan Prescott of *First Man into Space*. Perhaps reflecting the cynicism that characterizes director Robert Altman's other films, *Countdown* strips away other purported goals as high-minded pretense and insists that the conquest of space will be undertaken solely to gratify national and individual egos.

When word arrives that another Russian mission to the Moon was launched, apparently making the Pilgrim Project futile — since the Russians will land before Stegler arrives — there is talk of canceling the mission. Stegler successfully insists that it should proceed, apparently on the grounds that an American on the Moon a few days after the Russians is better than an American on the Moon a year later. As a favor to his son, previously observed playing catch with his father in a scene recalling McCauley and his son in *Men into Space*, Stegler will take his son's toy mouse with him to the Moon, stuffed into the package with an all-important item, a folded-up American flag. The mouse, named José, apparently references the character created by comedian Bill Dana, astronaut José Jimenez, who had become popular among American astronauts.

Stegler's flight is at first uneventful, but firing a necessary rocket leaves his capsule "shaking badly" like a "wild horse," and his capsule is slowing losing power. Monitors on the ground order Stegler to shut down all nonessential systems, including the radio, and sleep for four hours while technicians work on the problem. As if fulfilling another requirement of spacesuit films, a flashlight in Stegler's hands is released and it floats upward, a reminder of the weightlessness of space. Awakening to observe the Moon at close range,

Training for Touchdown: In a special harness that simulates the lower lunar gravity, astronaut Lee Stegler (James Caan) practices his eventual descent to the lunar surface in *Countdown* (1968).

Stegler says, "Fantastic," but he has a more practical reason for studying the landscape below: According to plans, he can land on the Moon only if he observes the shelter's red beacon. After repeated inquiries, he announces he sees it, but he is lying, something Chiz quickly figures out. This does not surprise one monitor, who says, "Anybody with the courage to go would have landed." Eager for the glory of being the first man on the Moon, Stegler risks not finding the shelter and dying when his oxygen runs out; Chiz, or another astronaut, would have done the same.

When Stegler lands, there are alternating scenes of Stegler walking across the lunar surface and observers on the ground, anxiously awaiting the signal indicating that Stegler has entered the shelter and hence is safe. (Stegler himself can no longer communicate with Earth, presumably due to the power problems, and never says a word on the Moon.) As Stegler wanders across a gray, barren Moon, wearing a white spacesuit, the scenes are so devoid of color as to sometimes resemble black-and-white footage. Altman may have deliberately toned down the color to achieve this effect: knowing previous television coverage of astronauts in space had been in black and white, he might have thought this would make his lunar footage seem more authentic.

As the first of two improbable coincidences, Stegler finds a crashed Russian spaceship and two dead cosmonauts — one lying some distance away, his visor apparently deliberately opened to commit suicide, and the other, stuck in the door, who must have died while emerging from his wrecked craft. In a cosmonaut's hand, he finds a folded-up Soviet flag, similar to his own American flag. To comment on the absurdity of national conflicts and the need for international cooperation in space, he drapes both flags on a lunar rock; but, demonstrating that he still feels some American pride, the American flag is above the Soviet flag.

Then, guided by the direction that José points when the mouse is dangled by its tail, Stegler starts walking again; and literally five minutes before his oxygen runs out, he sees a red glare on his spacesuit and looks up to see the shelter, close enough to reach in time. At this moment, in a strangely understated fashion, the movie ends, so audiences never see Stegler enter the shelter or see observers on Earth scream with joy when the shelter's signal is received. Altman's point, presumably, is that completion of this purposeless mission is not worth celebrating—another way in which *Countdown* may be the most iconoclastic of the spacesuit films.

Marooned (1969)

Watching *Marooned* when it was released in December, 1969, one might imagine spacesuit films had come of age. Along with a large budget, the film offers the star power of Oscar-winner Gregory Peck, future Oscar winners Gene Hackman and Lee Grant, and veteran television actors Richard Crenna, David Janssen, James Franciscus, and Mariette Hartley. Yet the performers seem oddly uncomfortable in this novel setting, suggesting that mainstream Hollywood still found it difficult to embrace such films.

The film's first thirty minutes depict what seems a routine space mission: astronauts Jim Pruett (Crenna), Buzz Floyd (Hackman), and Clayton Stone (Franciscus) are sent in an Apollo capsule for a seven-month stay at an orbiting space laboratory, anticipating the Skylab missions of the 1970s (and probably based on NASA's already-developed plans). The astronauts' personalities are established: the stoic but competent commander, Pruett; the irritable and sometimes uncooperative Floyd; and the always cheerful scientist, Stone, who smiles as he looks down on Earth and says, "Looks like a fine day down there." They wear realistic-looking spacesuits when they take off and rendezvous with the laboratory, and remove their helmets to relax when they reach orbit. Once in the laboratory, weightlessness is established with now-standard effects: An astronaut touching the ceiling, an astronaut apparently standing upside down and talking to a crewmate, a camera that floats away during a spacewalk. Like actual astronauts, they are constantly filmed and sometimes address the camera, aware that the job of American astronauts now involves being film stars as well.

Five months later, ground monitors become concerned: Based on footage of a fumbling astronaut during a spacewalk and Floyd's rambling report, they conclude there has been a "serious decline in the ability to perform even simple manual tasks." The program head, Charles Keith (Peck), briskly orders, "Bring them down." The crisis then occurs: After leaving the laboratory in the capsule, its retrorockets fail to fire, marooning them in orbit with limited oxygen. The astronauts are instructed "Get out of your hot suits" while scientists and technicians on the ground attempt to diagnose and correct what went wrong.

At this point, NASA policies which the film must emulate complicate the narrative: In genuine spacesuit films, all heroics involve both specialists on Earth, who employ their expertise and superior data to better understand events and offer helpful guidance, and astronauts in space, who contribute to and implement the solutions. But in earlier films, space travelers were allowed to sometimes disobey orders and save the day in a manner that preserved their image as true heroes, while NASA's astronauts lack that freedom. Thus, Pruett proposes a spacewalk to examine and possibly fix the malfunctioning rocket, as astronauts speculate that its failure to fire might be due to a stuck valve or meteor strike; that is how Colonel McCauley might have handled the situation. But supervisors on Earth, Keith and veteran astronaut Ted Dougherty (David Janssen), insist that, according to instruments, nothing they could repair in space caused the failure, so a spacewalk would only waste vital oxygen. Instead, astronauts are told, the wisest course is for them to sit quietly and sedate themselves with pills to make the oxygen supply last as long as possible; and like real astronauts, not cinematic heroes, that is what they do, just as Stegler received and followed similar advice. But this is dramatically unsatisfying for two reasons: The astronauts are revealed to be powerless, and they are instructed to be passive. Traditional heroes, whatever their other traits, are invariably dominant and active in everything they do.

Amidst this drama, there is a domestic interlude: Since supportive spouses have long figured in spacesuit films, we must meet the astronauts' wives, Celia Pruett (Lee Grant), Betty Lloyd (Mariette Hartley), and Teresa Stone (Nancy Kovack). Like Mrs. McCauley in the "Moon Probe" episode of *Men into Space* and Mickey Stegner in *Countdown*, they observe the mission's progress in a special section of the control center. When informed of their

A Rushed Rescue: After a potentially disastrous delay, astronaut Ted Dougherty (David Janssen) finally arrives in time to save crazed astronaut Buzz Floyd (Gene Hackman) in *Marooned* (1969).

husbands' plight, Celia and Betty, whose husbands are veteran astronauts, remain stoic, while Teresa, whose scientist husband is apparently on his first flight, is distraught. Betty advises her, "The best thing is for us girls to keep our feelings to ourselves and let the men get on with their jobs." Indeed, following NASA's pattern more than the pattern of previous spacesuit films, which at least occasionally introduce female astronauts and scientists, the astronauts, scientists, technicians, and officials of *Marooned*'s space program are exclusively male. Then, there is an interesting moment when scientist Stone looks down at Florida and notices a hurricane is developing, which soon become important to the story. Though *Destination Space*'s Benedict briefly mentions "weather forecasting" as a potential benefit of his space station, this may be the first time in spacesuit films that such a prediction actually occurs, though the film does not emphasize the point.

The issue dividing Keith and Pruett — whether to heed scientific facts and act appropriately, or rashly attempt heroic deeds despite daunting realities — comes up again when the drama shifts to the ground. Dougherty wishes to lead a rescue mission, piloting an untested spacecraft and madly rushing through procedures that normally take weeks to reach the stranded men within the next 42 hours, when their oxygen will run out. Keith, again the voice of reason, vetoes the idea, insisting the plans are unrealistic and would needlessly endanger lives. A defiant Dougherty angrily suggests that Keith lacks emotions, inappropriate behavior for an astronaut, who might urge a superior to do something but would never scream at the man.

Remarkably, Keith remains calm and responds, "I have feelings. That's why we live by the rules." Like the hero of Tom Godwin's "The Cold Equations" (1954), Keith rationally examines the situation and resolves to let people die because, according to the cold equations of space flight, there is no alternative. The administrator changes his mind only when pressured by the president, who tells him during a telephone call, "If we do it your way, 200 million people are going to start raising hell."

"Well, Mr. President, it's not my way," Keith replies. "There is data and there are certain facts that we have to deal with."

"Put away your slide rule for a minute," the president tells him, and advises him it would be a disaster for everyone if no rescue is attempted. As in *Project Moon Base* and *Countdown*, political considerations influence what should be scientific decisions: Keith must undertake to rescue the astronauts because *not* doing so would diminish the president's popularity and threaten future funding for NASA projects.

Another sort of conflict regularly observed in *Men into Space*, between professional astronauts and scientists who travel with them, emerges in the increasingly tense capsule. Based on previous patterns, one expects the veteran astronauts would keep their emotions under control while the neophyte Stone would get nervous and dangerously rebellious, like Merrity in *Satellite in the Sky*. Instead, following another stereotypical image of scientists, Stone remains preternaturally calm while Lloyd seems more and more jittery and eventually cracks up. To explain himself, Stone says he is simply doing what scientists do, which is to "observe systems under stress," and speaks of the scientist's constant "devotion to truth." His attitude angers Lloyd, who tells him, "Take that Ph.D. and shove it."

Next come some efforts to generate poignancy about the astronauts' plight: Asked to look out the window, Pruett sees a small light on Earth blinking on and off, which is the city of San Diego, Pruett's hometown, turning all its lights on and off to say hello to their orbiting hero. Then the wives talk with their husbands, the most striking comment being Celia's question to her husband, "Is it very lonely where you are?" Knowing full well that

Pruett is crammed into a small chamber with two other men, Celia cannot be referring to the "loneliness" of lacking human companionship and must instead be inquiring about the more cosmic sense of loneliness all space travelers might feel. However, like other aspects of these strangely abbreviated conversations, the point is not developed, and these fragmentary exchanges have no emotional impact. Previous spacesuit films, ranging from *Riders to the Stars* to *Countdown*, understood that one establishes genuine bonds between space travelers and the women they leave behind only by means of extended prologues on Earth; without such scenes, audiences cannot discern that these are men and women who love each other, making it difficult to really care about these astronauts' fate. (Another factor might be the acting skills on display, for despite their experience, Crenna seems bored, Franciscus overly glib, and even Hackman strangely unpersuasive as his character goes insane.)

Improbably, rushed preparations for the rescue mission go smoothly, and at the proper time Dougherty is seated sideways in his spacecraft—which resembles a space shuttle, already on NASA drawing boards and perhaps making its first appearance on film. But there is an intractable problem: the hurricane, now generating fierce winds faster than the 40 knots per hour needed for a safe launch. After nervously watching a dial indicating that wind speeds are increasing, Keith aborts the flight one minute before launch, knowing this will doom three astronauts; but it is necessary to save the life of Dougherty, who would surely die if he took off. A meeting with reporters after his decision prompts a brief, spirited debate about the value of space travel. A skeptical reporter anticipates that the disaster will bring about "a general examination of the purposes of space and the morality of putting men into space without adequate—"

Before he finishes, Keith angrily cuts him off and insists that he ask a question, which soon comes: "Are the results you gained worth the lives you lost?"

"You're damn right they are!" Keith exclaims. "Because of men like these, we've taken the first step off this little planet. A trip to the Moon is just a walk around the block. We're going to the stars, to other worlds, other civilizations." Because Keith's reference to "other worlds, other civilizations" obviously echoes the opening narration of *Star Trek*—"Its five-year mission: to explore strange, new worlds; to seek out new life, and new civilizations"—this may be the first explicit effort to link NASA's activities to the extravagant dreams of *Star Trek*, providing an odd but appealing new argument for supporting space exploration: so that someday, people like Kirk can travel across the galaxy to enjoy inspirational adventures with humanoid aliens. This logic later led NASA to exploit the popularity of *Star Trek* in the manners described above.

Hurrying away from the irksome reporters, Keith is handed new data by a subordinate: The eye of the hurricane will soon move over the launching area, providing a brief interval of low winds that would allow the rescue mission to proceed. He immediately orders the launch, but there remains a problem: Because it will take off too late, there will not be enough oxygen to keep three astronauts alive until Dougherty arrives. However, if one man sacrifices his own life, the other two might survive until help arrives. Unwilling to bluntly describe this grim reality, Keith contacts Pruett, explains the facts, and prods him to do some thinking and figure out what to do.

At this point, the wheels begin to fall off the plot, and a reasonably plausible story becomes downright silly. First, the debate over which astronaut should die becomes a debate about which astronaut will don his space helmet and leave the capsule to die. But this is nonsensical, since opening the hatch will remove all oxygen from the capsule's interior and doom the other astronauts, since they have only five minutes of oxygen in their spacesuits, which they will need to move from the capsule to the rescue vehicle. The distasteful but proper action, if no poison is available, is for one man to strangle the chosen victim.

Nevertheless, after rejecting Floyd's offer to leave, Pruett volunteers to go outside, purportedly to attempt repairs to the rocket (but this would be fruitless, since even if the rocket ignites, the astronauts do not have enough oxygen to survive the descent). He opens the hatch, leaves the space capsule, opens his spacesuit to release the remaining oxygen and quickly dies. The other astronauts don helmets as he departs, but they later close the hatch and find some oxygen has remained inside, since Stone deals with the unstable Floyd by giving him his spacesuit oxygen and taking off his helmet, announcing he's "going back on cabin air — must be some left." And somehow there is, since he does not immediately die, though he looks distressed.

How did any air remain in the capsule after the hatch opened? The only explanation to be deduced from the film is ludicrous: Apparently, screenwriter Mayo Simon believed there was a significant difference between merely opening the hatch and blowing the hatch. If one blows the hatch, opening it quickly and abruptly, the air inside will rush out; however, if one instead gently opens the hatch, like Pruett, most of the air will stay inside. As evidence that this was his belief, the film generates drama with an argument between Keith and Lloyd as rescue is imminent: Keith tells Lloyd to open the hatch, which would presumably be safe, but the deranged Lloyd is insanely bent upon blowing the hatch, which would prove disastrous. Yet the distinction is idiotic: If one opens the hatch of a spaceship, the air rushes out in a few seconds, regardless of how quickly or slowly one opens it. Perhaps Simon misinterpreted the scene in *2001* when Dave Bowman blows his pod's hatch to enter the *Discovery*'s airlock and thought Bowman used explosive bolts to generate a rush of escaping air to push him into the airlock, since opening the hatch in the normal fashion would not have that result. In fact, a rush of escaping air would occur no matter how Bowman opens his pod; he used explosive bolts merely to open the hatch as quickly as possible and minimize the time he would be perilously exposed to the vacuum of space.

Perhaps this dubious science bothered few viewers, but something else makes the conclusion of *Marooned* unsatisfactory even to the scientifically illiterate. When informed that some American astronauts are in trouble, and the Americans probably cannot assemble a rescue mission in time, anyone would ask an obvious question: What about the Soviet Union, the other nation with a manned space program? In fact, Keith considers this possibility and contacts a friend in Russia's space program but is told the only available cosmonaut cannot help because he is in a "different orbit." Thus, it comes as a surprise when, while astronauts wait for Dougherty, a Russian spacecraft approaches, as Keith belatedly learns the cosmonaut changed his orbit to attempt a rescue. (Why this surprises people is puzzling: That is, told that a potential rescuer is in a "different orbit," wouldn't Keith immediately ask, "Well, can he change his orbit?" and discover it was possible?) Briefly, it seems the cosmonaut will be the film's unexpected hero; indeed, the film might have dispensed with Dougherty's improbable heroics to focus on scientific and diplomatic efforts to arrange a Russian rescue, a more logical path to a happy ending.

Marooned now demonstrates the limits of acceptable internationalism in American films during the Cold War: It is all right to portray Russians as nice guys, which after all happened in two episodes of *Men into Space*, but they cannot be heroes. Thus, a Russian can show up and attempt a rescue, but he must prove a bumbler, unable to do anything significant until the real hero, Dougherty, arrives. Specifically, after Stone tries to push the crazed Lloyd toward the Russian spacecraft, the cosmonaut can leave his vehicle and, attached to a cord, reach out to Lloyd; but he must miss him and instead watch as he moves farther away. Then, he can enter the Apollo capsule and hover over the other astronaut, struggling to breathe in his spacesuit, but cannot help him until Dougherty arrives. This is dramatically awkward, to say the least: Why go to the trouble of bringing a character into the story if he cannot do anything?

The cosmonaut will finally play a role, albeit an extremely small one, in effecting a rescue: When Dougherty arrives, the cosmonaut flashes a light on the receding Floyd, alerting Dougherty to his plight and enabling him to use his jetpack to rendezvous with Floyd and hook a fresh oxygen tank onto his spacesuit. In addition, when Dougherty reaches the Apollo capsule, the cosmonaut helps him maneuver Stone out of the capsule and toward the rescue vehicle. Just as astronauts in realistic spacesuit films cannot succeed without assistance from people on the ground, they may also need help from others in space. The clumsy interactions of the two would-be rescuers, then, might be said to visualize the untraditional and necessarily collaborative nature of heroism in space.

To conclude the film, Dougherty informs Keith and others that he rescued the two men, inspiring shouts of joy, papers tossed into the air, and other forms of riotous celebration. This seems jarringly inappropriate because no one recalls that the third astronaut is dead, making it difficult to consider the mission a complete success. In contrast to the more somber joy better suited to the occasion, this incongruous scene seems a deliberate effort to impose a conventional happy ending on a story that, due to inherent tensions in spacesuit films, consistently resisted efforts to make it conventional.

Officially, though *Marooned* became the third spacesuit film to win an Oscar for special effects (following *Destination Moon* and *2001: A Space Odyssey*), the film was considered a failure, since it cost eight million dollars but earned less than five million dollars. Echoing a similar response to the disappointing reception of *Conquest of Space*, executives surely concluded that realistic space films were not a good way to profit; it would be wiser to make more films like the popular *Planet of the Apes*, and leave spacesuit films to the company now specializing in them — the National Aeronautics and Space Administration.

2001: A Space Odyssey (1968)

Stanley Kubrick and Arthur C. Clarke's *2001: A Space Odyssey* is widely celebrated as a masterpiece, voted by film critics as one of the ten best films ever made, and has been extensively analyzed by scores of scholars; and while I am qualified to discuss the film, one may wonder what I can profitably add to these commentaries. But I have one powerful advantage over my predecessors, for I alone can knowledgeably place the film within its proper context.

For whatever else one might say about *2001*, it represents the crowning achievement in the tradition of spacesuit films — as its creators understood. Kubrick prepared for this task by watching many of the films covered in this book, which undoubtedly influenced his film; as one example, having observed spacesuits from *Destination Moon* re-used in scores of lesser films, he ordered the spacesuits from *2001* destroyed after filming, so his handiwork would not suffer a similar fate, and one detects in his story explicit borrowings from earlier films. And while Clarke's only other contribution to spacesuit films was writing some lost episodes of the *Captain Video* television series, he had written both fiction and nonfiction involving speculations about future space flights and was surely aware of many previous space films, as shown by his omnibus of nonfiction, *Greetings, Carbon-Based Bipeds! Collected Essays 1934–1998* (1999), which includes reviews from the early 1950s of *Destination Moon* and *When Worlds Collide*, and references to the films *Rocketship X-M*, *The Day the Earth Stood Still*, and *Forbidden Planet*. Yet while *2001* magnificently summarizes its predecessors, it also makes significant new contributions to the spacesuit film, notably in its unique prologue and unique conclusion.

The opening sequence of *2001*, introduced as "The Dawn of Man," is interestingly the only part of the film taking place on Earth, and is ostensibly intended to explain human intelligence as the result of alien intervention in the form of a "black monolith" which appears near a tribe of struggling pre-humans. However, the scenes also respond to a major question addressed in other spacesuit films: namely, the reasons why humans should venture into space. Strangely, two explicit answers offered in Clarke's novel *2001: A Space Odyssey* (1968), presumably derived from earlier versions of the script, are muted in the film itself: The primate named Moon-Watcher, so named because he constantly stares at the nighttime sky, is not identified in the film, and his habits are represented solely by one upward glance at a crescent Moon. Thus, the notion that humans have an ancient impulse to reach for the stars, articulated in films like *Space Monster*, is almost imperceptible in the film. Then, after he learned to use bones as weapons, the novel's Moon-Watcher ponders his next step, and Clarke says only, "He would think of something," indicating that the ability to create tools, once developed, will inexorably lead humans to make more and more complex tools, culminating in spaceships. This relates to another implicit reason for space travel in previous films: It is something we should do simply because we can do it.

The striking manner in which the film conveys this message — the jump cut from the tossed bone to the spaceship — suggests a different message: that inspiring humans to build spaceships (the logical end result of their initial tool-making) was the *purpose* behind the alien intervention. A desire to travel into space, then, may have been deliberately implanted in our species along with enhanced intelligence. Thus, the argument would go, humans must venture into space to follow ancient alien instructions. This is further suggested by the aliens' placement of a monolith on the Moon to monitor human progress: They had no interest in other achievements of this uplifted species, but they wanted to know if it ever reached the Moon.

Yet whether caused by an inherent human desire, an inclination to tinker for tinkering's sake, or alien marching orders, the prologue also establishes that mastering the technology needed for space travel will have negative as well as positive effects; for immediately after using bones to kill a tapir and enjoy a hearty meal, the primates use their new tool to kill a member of an opposing tribe, drive others away, and seize control of a watering hole. The competitive urge that will inspire innumerable inventions, then, will also cause ruinous conflicts between people, as illustrated by developments in *2001*; for the root cause of the *Discovery* mission's problems is the American decision to keep the lunar monolith a secret, and while Dr. Heywood R. Floyd (William Sylvester) talks in a high-minded manner about the need to avoid "cultural shock" and "social disorientation" by concealing its existence, it seems clear the real motive is gaining an advantage over the Soviet Union, since there remains tension between the superpowers.

Before exploring the drawbacks of tools, *2001* must first, in the manner of genuine spacesuit films, convey to audiences the strangeness of humanity's new environment. One central problem — weightlessness — is illustrated immediately, as our first glimpse of the sleeping Floyd, traveling to the Moon to investigate the monolith, shows his pen floating

Monument on the Moon: Heywood R. Floyd (William Sylvester) and unidentified lunar colleagues stand before the alien monolith which is the driving force behind events in *2001: A Space Odyssey* (1968).

away from his pocket, to be retrieved by a stewardess. However, she must move carefully to keep her feet attached to the floor with "grip shoes." Many previous films showed floating objects in space, and astronauts using special shoes to remain on the floor; the innovation here is that Velcro, not magnetism, makes the shoes effective. The stewardess also has her hair entirely covered by a cap, to keep it from flying around uncontrollably in space, a problem not addressed in other films. Another concession to weightlessness, observed on Floyd's flight from the space station to the Moon, is liquefied food, kept in sealed containers with identifying pictures and sucked up with straws. (Floyd has a brief problem with his meal when he fails to hold his tray tightly and it floats upward.) Also, while delivering trays of food, the stewardess famously enters a circular chamber, walks entirely around until she is, from the audience's perspective, standing on the ceiling, and enters the pilots' cabin, oriented opposite to the passenger compartment, where she greets them still apparently upside down until the camera rotates to her new viewpoint. (The sequence recalls a scene in *Project Moon Base*, though it is more artfully staged.)

These relatively conventional depictions of weightlessness are augmented by another theme: that the ultimate way to combat weightlessness is placing people in rotating chambers so the so-called centrifugal force will push them outward and simulate gravity. This is first observed when Floyd arrives at the space station, which unlike those observed in *Conquest of Space* and other films consists of two connected wheels in space. The second wheel, "the new section," is still under construction, with some parts of the wheel open gridworks in the vacuum of space, suggesting that Kubrick is almost literally building on the work of predecessors to add a second wheel to their designs. Its interior is seen as a long rounded corridor which Floyd walks through, conveying that its rotation keeps his feet on the ground. The same principle is employed on the *Discovery*, where astronaut Frank Poole (Gary Lockwood) runs laps around a similar rotating torus, while also practicing boxing jabs (a reminder of human hostility, seen earlier at the watering hole).

The broader point is that while life on Earth involves flat plains and rectangular construction, life in space will involve curved surfaces and buildings that are spheres, cylinders, or toruses — a fundamental change in perspective providing some of the film's most striking effects. Also, the way the stewardess walks in a circle to enter a chamber apparently upside down, an action later duplicated by astronauts Poole and Dave Bowman (Keir Dullea) on their spaceship, is not directly related to any effort to create artificial gravity, but reinforces the notion that space travel demands circular motion, in contrast to the linear motion characteristic of travel on Earth's surface. (The choice of Johann Strauss's "Blue Danube Waltz" to accompany early scenes of space travel may be relevant, since the waltz is a dance involving graceful circular movements around a room.)

In other respects, scenes featuring Floyd make intriguing points about space travel. In a later interview, Bowman notes that the "life support capability" required to keep people alive in space is "basically food and air," and while the need for air is emphasized only in scenes of astronauts in space, accompanied solely by breathing sounds, the film constantly depicts the human need for food with several meals. Such sequences are usually rare, since film classes advise aspiring screenwriters that eating scenes are essentially a way to kill time, so they are clearly ubiquitous here to convey a message about our basic nature (shown also in opening scenes, since the pre-humans' priority is visibly getting enough food to eat). Thus, Floyd is walking to a restaurant when he meets Russian colleagues, he consumes the aforementioned liquefied food on his way to the Moon, and he eats a sandwich with two companions while traveling to the monolith. This film also uniquely notes that the elimination of food requires technological adjustments, as Floyd in the spaceship's bathroom studies detailed instructions for using the "zero gravity toilet." Finally, when Floyd talks to the Russians, we learn that the discovery of the monolith is being concealed with a leaked cover story about a virulent epidemic at the base, explaining why there has been no contact with it. The rumor is credible because, as other spacesuit films demonstrate, infectious diseases are a real danger in the confined quarters of space.

After Floyd lands on the Moon (accompanied by the film's first use of spacesuits, as astronauts on the Moon look up at the descending spacecraft), he proceeds to a briefing and delivers a dull, insipid speech about the need for "complete security" regarding the monolith. Yet a colleague bizarrely compliments him for his "excellent speech" that "beefed up morale a hell of a lot." Clearly, people in the future do not understand what true communication involves, and repeatedly seem unable to communicate. Thus, Floyd cannot really talk to Russian colleagues, carries on a stilted conversation with his daughter, and delivers a meaningless speech. It is as if, surrounded and supported by machinery as never before in history, humans are becoming like machines themselves, unable to function as genuine people who convey genuine feelings. This is not an unusual observation to make about *2001*, particularly while explaining Kubrick's decision to employ actors of limited ability and provide them with banal dialogue. But while this problem might afflict all humans in 2001, it is exacerbated by space travel, since people in space are constantly and completely dependent upon technology to stay alive in this harsh environment.

After the briefing, Floyd and a few lunar residents fly to the monolith and walk in spacesuits down to where the uncovered artifact stands. (Despite the focus on weightlessness during Floyd's flights, Kubrick makes no effort to depict the Moon's low gravity.) In a deliberately humorous scene, they gather in front of the monolith to be photographed — which is absurd, because no one can recognize them in their spacesuits, a point long ago made in *Destination Moon*. Here, it reinforces the idea that space travel dehumanizes its participants. The way they gather around it, and the way Floyd touches the monolith like Moon-Watcher, also suggest that humans, despite their accomplishments, have not advanced very far beyond their distant ancestors — and after all, since there was no title to begin the section of the film featuring Floyd, the entire film from its beginning up to the encounter with the monolith is technically all part of "The Dawn of Man." Strangely, while the fact that the film, after its prologue, takes place entirely in space seemingly indicates that space is becoming humanity's proper home, there are numerous hints that people remain basically the same as they were when the monolith first visited four million years ago, and perhaps have even become worse due to the baleful effects of tools. Hence, a strong radio blast to Jupiter, which briefly deafens Floyd and his colleagues, signals that humanity has reached the monolith — and is ready for another upgrade.

The next part, "Jupiter Mission: Eighteen Months Later," features astronauts Bowman and Poole flying to Jupiter to investigate why the monolith sent its message there, though that is known only to the three crewmates in hibernation and the spaceship's computer, HAL 9000 (voiced by Douglas Rain). Much of this sequence reinforces observations about life in space already made: Bowman and Poole enjoy another artificial meal of homogenized though solid food, there are insipid conversations between astronauts and people on Earth, and Poole runs around the rotating cylinder to convey the characteristic nature of buildings in space. The major new feature is humanity's most advanced and sophisticated tool, HAL, officially the sixth member of the crew though in some ways its true commander, given its complete command of the spaceship and superior intelligence, demonstrated when it beats Bowman at chess.

We become aware there may be a flaw in this machine when HAL announces a flaw in another machine, the AE-35 unit which maintains the antenna used to communicate with Earth. This requires Bowman to enter a spherical shuttlecraft called a "pod" to venture into space, leave the pod to float to the antenna, and replace the part that, according to HAL, will soon fail. This is an overt homage to *Destination Moon*, since an antenna problem also inspires a spacewalk in that film; while spacesuits on the Moon were silver, Bowman's spacesuit is red and Poole's is yellow, referencing the brightly colored spacesuits of *Destination Moon*. And while never a threat, two meteors zooming through space precede Bowman's mission to remind audiences of menaces from earlier spacesuit films.

When Bowman returns to the *Discovery* and finds nothing wrong with the replaced unit, the astronauts realize something may be wrong with HAL, though it requires considerable attentiveness to the film to figure out the precise origins of the problem. After HAL is disabled, a recorded message reveals that the computer, unlike Bowman and Poole, had been told the true reason for the mission; yet in a previous conversation with Bowman, HAL pretends to know as little as the astronauts did. Instructed to keep its knowledge a secret, while mandated to respond to the astronauts' needs and desires, HAL received conflicting instructions that eventually caused the malfunction of detecting a nonexistent flaw. Like humanity's first tool, the bone, this highly advanced tool has been misused, and the results will again be lethal. For after Bowman and Poole decide, during a conversation inside a sealed pod, that HAL must be turned off if it is in error, the computer learns of this threat by reading their lips and engages in more flawed reasoning: If they disable this essential tool, the all-important mission will be jeopardized, so I must kill them to stop that from happening.

The film's second spacewalk — Poole going into space to reinstall the original part and see if HAL's predicted failure occurs — and its aftermath illustrate with terrible force just how vulnerable humans are in space, as one faulty tool quickly leads to four deaths. First, when Poole leaves the pod, HAL seizes control of the shuttlecraft and, advancing menacingly toward Poole, uses its arm to cut the air hose and send him hurtling into the void of space. As in *Quatermass II* and the *Men into Space* episode "Moon Probe," an astronaut helplessly drifts in space, first frantically clutching his hose but later making no motions, evidently dead. Though Bowman rushes to another pod to attempt a rescue, the effort will not succeed. Then, while Bowman is in space, HAL recognizes that, when the other astronauts wake up to find their colleagues missing, they might also decide to disable the computer; hence, he must kill them too, which he accomplishes by turning off the machinery keeping them alive, as conveyed by flashing signs stating "Computer Malfunction," "Life Functions Critical," and "Life Functions Terminated." The impersonality of the murders is chilling, but HAL's actions show what might happen to any astronauts in a spaceship: If life support systems fail, they will quickly die.

In the drama that ensues, *2001* takes the spacesuit film into entirely new territory, offering an innovative response to a basic question that is always central to its narrative: How can humans survive in the constantly threatening environment of space? The standard answer is to build machines that protect humans from space and provide needed oxygen — spaceships and spacesuits — and, like McCauley, to be constantly vigilant in checking the machines, to see they are working properly, and proceeding with extreme caution on all missions. But Bowman failed to follow these procedures: He did not realize until too late that a vital machine was malfunctioning and, rushing to rescue a comrade, he forgot some essential equipment — his spacesuit's helmet — that he might need to survive. Thus, Bowman seems doomed: HAL will not permit him to reenter the *Discovery* in his pod, and he cannot use the emergency airlock because he lacks a helmet to protect him outside his pod. In desperation, Bowman devises a new answer to the question: Humans must learn to live in the vacuum of space, without technological support.

Specifically, he will move his pod near the airlock, open its door, hold his breath, and use the pod's explosive bolts to quickly release him from the pod and propel him into the airlock; then, if he can stay alive for several seconds in the vacuum, he can turn a lever, close the airlock door, and fill the chamber with oxygen. The scheme is not unprecedented, since an imperiled astronaut did the same thing in Clarke's story "The Other Side of the Sky" (1957), which led to a "Vacuum-Breathers' Club" with members who eventually achieve a "record time in space" of two minutes (34). But Bowman will be the first cinematic astronaut to come into contact with space and survive.

When his efforts succeed, an emboldened Bowman essentially takes additional steps to achieve human independence in space: He turns off HAL, leaving him without any support from computers, and also seems to remove himself from all contact with Earth, since the only further communication we see is a pre-recorded message about the monolith, triggered by HAL's demise. (Perhaps HAL was correct, and the antenna unit did fail; perhaps HAL deliberately disabled the antenna so he would not have to report his actions to Earth.) Lacking these forms of support, however, Bowman remains dependent on his spaceship and spacesuit when he reaches Jupiter and must investigate the huge monolith he observes in its orbit (as a further sign of the disorienting absence of an "up" and "down" in space, it is observed sideways); he travels toward it inside of a pod, wearing his spacesuit (and space helmet). The subsequent actions of the unseen aliens then suggest they also wish to help humanity live in space without the help of tools.

The celebrated "trip" sequence that follows, apparently a chaotic series of bizarre images, actually has a three-part structure, the first two parts separated by close-up images of Bowman's eye in strange colors (the third part is frequently interrupted by similar images). First,

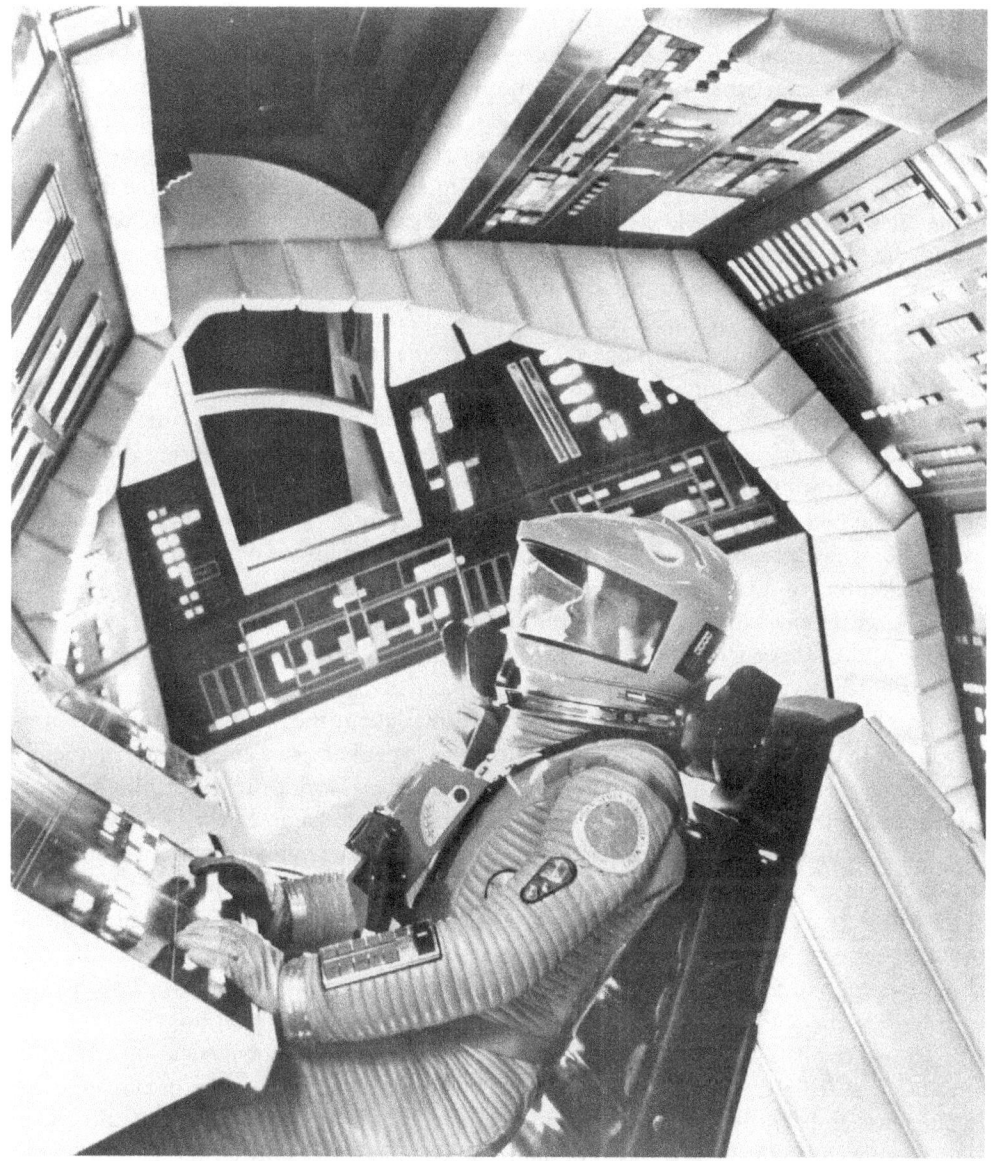

Doomed by *Discovery*: Astronaut David Poole (Gary Lockwood) is ready to venture outside the *Discovery*, where he will be unceremoniously slaughtered by the spaceship's deranged computer HAL 9000, in a scene cut from *2001: A Space Odyssey* (1968).

Bowman sees himself seemingly falling down between two walls of brightly colored light, first seen vertically and then seen horizontally, corresponding to a presumed trip through hyperspace to a distant locale. Second, we observe objects in space — clusters and filaments of stars, colorful nebulas — indicating that Bowman reached a different region of space, perhaps near the center of the galaxy where stars and star formations are packed together. Finally, we see a planetary surface, shown in unusual colors, suggesting that Bowman is landing on an alien world. Part of the aliens' scheme is now apparent: The human discovery of the monolith on the Moon, proving they mastered space travel, would trigger a radio signal pointing humans to Jupiter, when a representative of the species could be lured into hyperspace and brought in for observation — and further improvement.

The final scenes, when Bowman finds himself inside a suite with elegant, old-fashioned furniture, are confusingly staged. First, Bowman inside the pod observes himself in a spacesuit, visibly aged. Then the film shifts to *that* Bowman's perspective as he surveys his surroundings and sees a more elderly version of himself, eating dinner at a table; then, as the film shifts to the diner's perspective, he looks around to see an incredibly old Bowman lying on the bed; finally, the film shifts to that man's perspective as he observes a monolith inside the room. One might interpret this as Kubrick's abbreviated way of showing that Bowman lived out his life in this chamber while aliens studied him; alternatively, this alien observation may be causing him to rapidly age. However explained, the scenes clearly show Bowman being weaned away from tools, significantly within a room that recalls the eighteenth century (the era before the Industrial Revolution began and provided new tools that both led to space travel and had deleterious effects on the human psyche). First, Bowman is inside a spacecraft; then the spacecraft vanishes and he only wears a spacesuit; then the spacesuit vanishes and he is dressed in a robe, using only simple utensils to eat his meal; and finally, he lies in bed wearing only a white robe, with no tools in sight. Thus, by means of tools, humans could enter space; but to master space, they must become beings who no longer need tools.

The aged Bowman is transformed into a fetus-like creature, usually termed the Star Child, and the film concludes ostensibly by providing little information about his character and attributes, save for a close look at his preternaturally wise and staring eyes as he gazes down on Earth. But we do learn two important things about the Star Child: First, whereas Bowman originally had to approach a monolith and experience a cosmic journey, evidently effected by advanced technology, before reaching an alien world, the Star Child instantly returns to his home world; apparently, he has the power to transport himself to any position in space, eliminating the need for spaceships. Second, he floats in the vacuum of space, protected only by a sort of ethereal amniotic sac, indicating that he can live in this environment, eliminating the need for spacesuits. Whatever else he is, the Star Child is a true inhabitant of space, perfectly adapted to its conditions. Clarke's novel adds that he possesses vast mental abilities employed to destroy Earth's nuclear weapons; but even without this data, the film conveys that the Star Child is an advanced, and very powerful, form of life.

In two respects, *2001* brings the spacesuit film to certain logical conclusions. First, as already suggested by *Men into Space*, one ultimate purpose of space travel is contacting alien intelligence, and even if the contact proves tantalizingly enigmatic, it will be transformative. More significantly, *2001* suggests that humans can conquer space only if they become beings who can inhabit space. Spaceships and spacesuits are flawed and incomplete methods for making humans residents of space; no matter how advanced they become, they can still malfunction, and humans will always feel threatened in space and, hence, never fully comfortable there, contributing to the belief, expressed in many spacesuit films, that Earth remains humanity's true home. However, if humans can easily survive in space, then they can comfortably become its permanent inhabitants.

The problem, from the perspective of human storytelling, is that such beings would be so different from, and so far beyond, humans that no present-day human can imagine what they would be like; thus, the point at which *2001* ends, with the birth of the new species, represents precisely how far this narrative can proceed. As I document in "The Endless Odyssey," all efforts to extend the original story of *2001* have faltered for precisely this reason. Yet even if a spacesuit film cannot complete the story that it begins, it remains an important genre, because it conveys a message that other forms of human narrative never acknowledge: that humanity is capable of becoming something utterly different from what it is now, and the challenging new environment of space will most likely provoke this alteration.

Television Coverage of the *Apollo 11* Moon Landing (1969)

Since there are vast amounts of film documenting the American and Soviet space programs, a thorough survey is beyond this study's scope (and this author's expertise). Thus, I focus on events so widely and repeatedly viewed (first spacewalks and Moon landings) that they entered the realm of popular culture.

Other film of astronauts in flight, including live television coverage, attracted little attention, since all they could show was astronauts sitting in cramped space capsules, images of Earth seen from space, and small objects floating in the capsule—all familiar images in spacesuit films. But there was genuine drama in the pioneering spacewalks of Alexei Leonov and Ed White, for this was when humans actually began living in space, a process that entered a second phase when astronauts first walked on the surface of another world.

The footage of Leonov and White in space offers a striking contrast. We first observe Leonov facing the camera and clinging to his capsule, as if hesitant to let go; then, he finally launches himself into space, still facing the camera while receding away from it. This, in miniature, is the classic image (seen in several films) of the distressed astronaut who drifts away from his spaceship to possibly experience a slow, agonizing death, lost in the vastness of space. The aura of potential peril is reinforced by Leonov's next actions: He constantly fiddles with the tubes connecting him to his spacecraft, as if fearful they might get tangled or break. While he never ventures more than several feet away, his movements suggest worries about losing contact with his spacecraft and being unable to return. These images surely influenced the scene in *2001* when Poole, his oxygen cord cut by HAL, helplessly grapples with the broken cord while rushing further and further away from the *Discovery*.

White, however, takes a different approach. On the edge of his capsule, he faces toward space, not looking back at the camera, and pushes himself outward with an air of confidence, keeping his back to the camera, until he gets about ten feet away and slowly turns around to face the camera, indicating complete control over his movements. As a further indication of calm assurance, White never plays with lifelines and instead holds a camera to film the experience from his own perspective, recalling the cameramen observed in *Nebo Zovyot* and other films. White thus exemplifies the other sort of spacewalking astronaut in films, the capable veteran who moves purposefully through space to accomplish tasks or reach a destination. As he keeps hovering and moving around in space, White further suggests he is, in his own modest way, attempting to emulate the spectacular space gymnastics of *I Diafanoidi Portano la Morte*, and there is a final sign that he, unlike Leonov, thoroughly enjoys space, for we hear the impatient voice of Mission Control telling White, "The flight director says get back in!" Evidently, White lingered in space longer than superiors on the ground wished.

Still, in spacesuit films, spacewalks generally function as the prelude to the climax of actually reaching another planet, and NASA in the 1960s worked hard to provide audiences with precisely that sort of drama. An important innovation came with the 1968 flight of

White Flight: Astronaut Edward White waits outside of the *Gemini 4* space capsule in June 1965, preparing to become the first American to walk in space.

Apollo 7, the first with a live television broadcast. The footage is not particularly interesting—floating objects, images of Earth, a look at instrument panels—but it indicated that NASA, as was not true of its spacewalks, was preparing to show the world its astronauts taking humanity's first steps on another world at the moment the event occurred.

While it can be observed differently, the best way to experience the grainy footage of Neil Armstrong and Buzz Aldrin on the Moon is to watch it precisely as most Americans watched it on July 20, 1969—on CBS, with anchorman Walter Cronkite and astronaut Wally Schirra as commentators. (Their coverage is available on YouTube.) As they and viewers witnessed the historic moment, it is evident that NASA carefully planned and scripted its television show, making it a spacesuit film: After landing, astronauts would first lower a camera from their Lunar Excursion Module (LEM) into position to record Armstrong descending a ladder to the surface; then, when he and Aldrin were outside, Armstrong would hold the camera to offer panoramic views of the lunar landscape; finally, he would place the camera to show the LEM and its surroundings, where astronauts would conduct ceremonies in front of their vehicle before setting up scientific experiments and gathering lunar rocks. With only a few moments of spontaneity, Armstrong and Aldrin, like all dutiful astronauts, precisely followed NASA's instructions.

Waiting for the show to begin, CBS entertains viewers with a studio simulation of an actor playing Armstrong preparing to emerge from the LEM; but this is interrupted to provide the first images from the lowered camera, which initially shows only the ladder and its surroundings. However, in an ironic reminder that space may defy expectations of "up" and "down," Cronkite notes that the scene is "upside down on our monitor"—a problem soon corrected, though it occurs again later. The audience now sees Armstrong slowly descending the ladder, already engaged in what becomes a recurring activity—commenting on the nature of the lunar surface: "Very fine-grained, almost like a powder."

When he touches the surface, there are two conspicuous glitches in following the script. First, since NASA anticipated that the LEM would sink deeper into lunar dust than it actually did, the ladder ended a few feet above the surface, so moving from its lowest rung to the ground required a significant leap. This made Armstrong's carefully prepared first words on the Moon—"That's one small step for a man, one giant leap for all mankind"—rather silly, since he really took a very large step. More significantly, a nervous Armstrong omitted a key word—"a"—so his statement was clearly heard as "That's one small step for man, one giant leap for all mankind"—which is nonsensical, since "man" without an indefinite article and "mankind" were synonymous in the terminology of the era (now regarded as sexist—if written today, it would be "one small step for a human, one giant leap for all humanity"). Later, NASA claimed that Armstrong did say "a," but it was not heard due to faulty radio transmission. However, while there are annoying omissions in Aldrin's later statements—ground controllers keep asking him to repeat himself, complaining he was "breaking up"—there were no similar problems with Armstrong's statements.

On the ground, Armstrong describes the Moon's surface as "like powdered charcoal," and says he "can see the footprints of my boots." Photographs of those footprints would become iconic images of the Moon landing. Soon, though, as he struggles to scrape up lunar material for his "contingency sample," he notes the Moon's "very hard surface" with "very cohesive material of the same sort." Strangely, the lunar surface proves both powdery and firm. He also begins discussing the experience of walking on the Moon: He has "no difficulty in moving around," and the task is "perhaps easier than the simulations of one-sixth G." The ease of astronauts' movements in low lunar gravity would soon be conveyed by scenes of the men taking bounding steps while rapidly crossing in front of the camera. In these comments and movements, the astronauts fulfill a priority of spacesuit films, conveying that conditions in space are significantly different from those of Earth.

After obtaining the contingency sample and taking a few photographs—planned as his first tasks in case some emergency required a premature departure—Armstrong now advises Aldrin as he begins descending the ladder. He reinforces two major themes of Armstrong's comments — that the Moon offers "very very fine powder" and "walking is also very comfortable"— but Aldrin's first words on the Moon add a third element to humanity's response to this alien world: He says the Moon is "beautiful, beautiful" and speaks of its "magnificent desolation." Indeed, unlike the stoic Armstrong, Aldrin seems to enjoy being on the Moon more than his crewmate, as he jumps up and down and even offers the only joke during this first sojourn to the Moon when he pretends to "see some purple rocks." This also suggests that the uniform grayness of the Moon is disappointingly undramatic, generating a desire for bright colors. Still, the men remain focused on business, offering another observation about lunar movements: Due to a "slight tendency" to move "backward," astronauts must "lean in the direction you want to go."

Their next task is ceremonial: After cameraman Armstrong announces he is "gonna change lenses on ya," presumably to provide better images of what will follow, he begins "unveiling the plaque" on the LEM, which he reads: "Here men from the planet Earth first set foot upon the Moon, July 1969 A.D. We came in peace for all mankind." But there are already signs this pioneering Moon walk is becoming less involving, as astronauts are reduced

Aldrin, a Day's Work: *Apollo 11* astronaut Buzz Aldrin stands near the lunar module and the solar wind collector he and Neil Armstrong deployed during their famous sojourn on the Moon in July, 1969.

to repetitious comments about the surface material which is "like very finely powdered carbon"; and while one man observes there is "something interesting in this little crater," we are not told what it is. Armstrong swings around the camera to provide panoramic views of the landscape, which is monotonously flat in all directions, unlike the jagged mountains typically depicted in cinematic lunar landings. This is because an understandably risk-adverse NASA directed astronauts to a lunar region without potentially dangerous mountains or craters. Then, showing how important television coverage was to NASA, Armstrong is nagged several times to position the camera in precisely the right position to show viewers the LEM and its environs in the most desirable manner.

At this point, commentator Cronkite expresses his own sense that NASA's spacesuit film is insufficiently interesting. To inject excitement, he repeats the comment of Armstrong's wife: "I can't believe it! I can't believe it!" Then, as astronauts proceed to the next chore on their checklist — planting the American flag on the Moon — his resonant remark about the significance of seeing "the Stars and Stripes on the lunar surface" accompanies the observation that there "ought to be some music" to accompany this event. Unintentionally, Cronkite references another significant difference between space and Earth — the vacuum ensures constant silence, other than radio messages — and suggests the event needs a musical score to be truly dramatic. Finally, as the astronauts are taking pictures of each other, Cronkite sardonically describes them as the "first tourists on the Moon." In spacesuit films, the first astronauts on the Moon are bold adventurers, constantly ready to face unexpected challenges; but actual astronauts, who follow careful plans to avoid all dangers and eliminate surprises, seem more like tourists, sedately making their way through a safe environment and calmly observing the sights.

There are more comments about the special characteristics of lunar motion: One must "keep track of where your center of mass is," and their bouncing steps are a "so-called kangaroo hop" that "would get rather tiring," though this "may be a function of this suit" along with "lack of gravity." But there is one final ceremony to complete: Astronauts are told to move to where the camera can see them to receive a phone call from the president of the United States. "That would be an honor," one replies, as the television screen offers a split image of astronauts near their flag while Richard Nixon, sitting in the Oval Office holding a phone, seems to look at them. This intrusion of politics into humanity's first visit to the Moon is mercifully brief, as Nixon self-aggrandizingly describes his action as "the most historic phone call ever made from the White House" and congratulates the astronauts because, due to their work, "the heavens have become a part of man's world." Recalling what the plaque said about "peace for all mankind," Nixon hopes the landing will inspire everyone to "redouble our efforts to bring peace and tranquility to Earth." Picking up on this theme, the astronauts respond they feel honored to be "representing not only the United States" but *all* nations.

Now that this expensive mission has been justified as a noble effort to bring about world peace, a motive expressed in previous spacesuit films, the astronauts spend the rest of their time on the Moon fulfilling another traditional purpose for space travel: scientific research. Specifically, they collect rocks for later study on Earth; they obtain a "core sample" with a device that retrieves material from sixteen inches below the surface; and they set up a "seismic experiment" and "laser reflector" to determine the Moon's precise distance from the Earth. As the camera focuses on the LEM, with astronauts sometimes outside camera range as they perform tasks, this spacesuit film inexorably becomes less and less involving, although Cronkite does observe that the entire scene resembles "early movies of science fiction of man on the Moon." In a sense, he is correct, since one can liken Armstrong and Aldrin's work to activities observed in, say, *Destination Moon* or episodes of *Men into Space*. Yet more so than those films, this lunar landing lacks even the minimal drama of insufficient fuel or a mechanical problem. As one further task, the astronauts inspect their LEM for signs of damage, but everything looks fine, with nothing to require emergency repair. And so, reminded by ground controllers that it is time to return to the module, Armstrong and Aldrin climb back inside, leaving the camera to show nothing but their motionless spacecraft.

Overall, even in this first film about an actual Moon landing, one can tell that such adventures will quickly cease to interest audiences. This carefully planned, meticulously executed mission lacks all the usual characteristics of entertaining space films — no color, no music, no unexpected developments or crises, no exotic aliens, no sinister stowaways, and no Russian saboteurs sneaking up on the astronauts from the far side of the Moon. All NASA can offer is the Moon itself, which Cronkite notes has a "stark beauty all its own," and the spectacle of humans adjusting to life in low gravity. Properly appreciated, this is truly dramatic in ways that are entirely beyond the entirety of human experience; but to typical viewers it is boring, unlike *Planet of the Apes* or *Star Trek*.

To do a better job the second time, NASA provided its next lunar mission, *Apollo 12*, with a color camera, and astronauts Charles "Pete" Conrad and Alan Bean seemed better prepared to offer lively and entertaining commentary than the laconic Armstrong and Aldrin. Indeed, humanity's second visit to the Moon begins with a joke that, unlike Aldrin's, is genuinely amusing: Reaching the lunar surface, Conrad mocks Armstrong's first words on the Moon, and his short height, by saying, "Whoopee! Man, that may have been a short one for Neil, but that's a long one for me." He also reinforces comments previously made by Armstrong and Aldrin about the proper way to walk on the Moon by noting he "can walk pretty well" but needs to "take it easy and watch what I'm doing." Unfortunately, when Bean took over Armstrong's task of placing the camera in precisely the right position for later coverage, nagging from Earth led the astronaut to accidentally aim the camera directly at the Sun, damaging the camera and prematurely ending the television coverage. A concern about achieving the best spacesuit film possible, in other words, actually ruined the entire film.

Pondering the twin triumphs of *2001: A Space Odyssey* and the Moon landing, one can argue the tradition of spacesuit films had been taken as far as it could go: Kubrick's film fully develops the implicit messages of all spacesuit films — that the ultimate effect of humanity's ventures into space and probable contact with alien intelligence would be a transformation of our species present-day humans cannot imagine — while images of actual astronauts on the Moon convey the authentic experience of space in ways that could not be improved upon. Yet there remained areas for exploration: Films could have crafted other scenarios for further human evolution in response to space travel, perhaps emulating classic novels like Olaf Stapledon's *Last and First Men* (1930), George Zebrowski's *Macrolife* (1979), and Clarke's *Childhood's End* (1953) — long optioned but never filmed. And NASA could have developed projects to send astronauts to other worlds with new wonders for audiences on Earth, like a nearby asteroid, Mercury, or Mars. Indeed, during television coverage of the Moon landing, Cronkite reports rumors that the American government would use this moment to announce its next goal: a mission to Mars. As it happens, those visionary spacesuit films, and voyages to new worlds, never occurred; and this book's final task is to ponder why this happened.

— 8 —
Return to Earth: Spacesuit Films After 1969

Nineteen sixty-nine was a heady year for space enthusiasts: There were two landings on the Moon, eight additional lunar flights were planned, and excited talk of a forthcoming mission to Mars. Yet the future of human space exploration looked very different only a few years later: The next lunar mission, *Apollo 13*, ended disastrously, three of the next seven flights were cancelled, and instead of Mars, NASA pursued a more modest goal, a reusable space shuttle which could only reach near–Earth orbit. All other ambitions — a permanent space station, return to the Moon, or flights to other worlds — were postponed indefinitely.

What went wrong? Certainly, the *Apollo 13* accident reminded everyone that space travel remained difficult and dangerous, and preliminary work on a Mars mission surely revealed daunting obstacles: an immense cost, the challenge of keeping astronauts alive in space for several months, and the danger that long-term exposure to weightlessness would make it impossible for astronauts to again live in Earth's gravity. Yet such problems might have been overcome with sufficient resources and effort. The real reason progress in space stagnated was quite simple: American citizens were no longer interested.

This became evident to policymakers in several ways. In providing television coverage of later lunar missions, NASA strived to make the shows more attractive to viewers, including color cameras, landing sites with more varied terrain, a lunar rover allowing astronauts to travel about, and a camera left behind to display the liftoff from the lunar surface. Individual astronauts tried to be entertaining: *Apollo 14*'s Alan Shepard brought a golf club and golf ball to spectacularly demonstrate the Moon's low gravity with a stroke that sent the ball soaring to an immense height and distance; *Apollo 15*'s David Scott and James Irwin restaged Galileo's famous experiment, showing a falling feather and hammer striking the Moon simultaneously; *Apollo 17*'s Eugene Cernan and Harrison Schmidt broke into song with parody lyrics: "I was strolling on the Moon one day..." But ratings for subsequent missions steadily declined, and when three flights were cancelled, there was no public outcry which might have reversed the decision. As a final production, NASA employed a leftover Apollo capsule for a purely political mission: a 1975 rendezvous with a Soviet capsule in Earth orbit, producing a symbolically important image of American Thomas Stafford and Russian Alexei Leonov shaking hands after their capsules docked. This gesture inspired no further collaborations in space and instead ended American space flights for six years, until the space shuttle flew in 1981.

Since that time, NASA continued offering spacesuit films of its own, though one elaborately planned effort, science lessons from "Teacher in Space" Christa McAuliffe, ended tragically. There were many scenes of astronauts inside the space shuttle or engaged in spacewalks, usually working to construct the space station, as well as two unusual missions to repair the Hubble Space Telescope. But the shows, not deemed worthy of live television coverage, were generally watched only by space enthusiasts on NASA's website.

What did become popular in the early 1970s, and remained popular ever since, was a cancelled television series called *Star Trek*, watched by a constantly growing audience while airing every day in syndication. In contrast to spacesuited astronauts lumbering around barren landscapes or attaching widgets in space, the series offered attractive men and women in skin-tight outfits visiting worlds that looked almost exactly like Earth, to have exciting adventures with good and evil aliens who looked almost exactly like humans. And unlike previous melodramatic spacesuit films, *Star Trek* overcame the scientific absurdity of such scenarios by setting the action far in the future and positing scientific advances that were improbable, but not impossible, to justify space travel without spacesuits and regular visits to Earth-like planets. An episode of the successor series *Star Trek: The Next Generation*, "The Chase" (aired April 24, 1993), even explained implausible numbers of human-like aliens as the work of an ancient race that seeded the Galaxy with beings resembling themselves.

With successful, conventional melodrama transplanted into space with arguable scientific underpinnings, *Star Trek* became the pattern for the overwhelming majority of future space films and television programs, prominently including the *Star Wars* films, the later *Star Trek* series and films, and the series *Babylon 5* (1994–1999). In effect, people in America and abroad rejected the realities of space travel to embrace this attractive fantasy of space travel. In such imagined futures, spacesuits would be employed rarely if at all, but exceptional cases might for that reason have special impact. One noteworthy example occurs in the first *Star Trek* film, *Star Trek: The Motion Picture* (1979), when Spock makes a lonely journey through space, in a spacesuit with a jetpack, to explore the alien spaceship V'ger. The image of a tiny Spock, racing through space toward the immense construct, unusually conveys the vastness of space and potential mysteries it offers; indeed, in a film that consistently strives to be breathtaking, it is the only genuinely impressive scene. However, to dispel any notion that the *Star Trek* franchise might be rethinking its general attitude toward spacesuits, *Enterprise* crew members later walk on the structure in the vacuum of space, magically protected by an atmosphere generated by V'Ger, to confront the original space probe that merged with an alien intelligence.

This is not to say that spacesuit films entirely vanished, only that they became infrequent and, usually, not particularly interesting. The films fell into standard categories: a few genuine spacesuit films, including films based on actual space flights, and larger numbers of melodramatic spacesuit films, humorous spacesuit films, and horrific spacesuit films.

It is hard to find films that perform the typical function of classic spacesuit films: to portray humanity's near-future life in space without introducing aliens or spectacular disasters. Example include *Outland* (1981), a tale of conflict and corruption on a Jovian moon that might have been more admirable were it not so explicitly modeled on the Western *High Noon* (1952); a 1998 episode of *The Outer Limits*, "Phobos Rising," depicting tension between the Mars bases of rival powers when Earth may have been destroyed; and *Moon* (2009), about the lone inhabitant of a lunar base who discovers he is not the man he believes himself to be, but rather one in a series of clones of that man, continually created and destroyed as an economical way to maintain mining operations. These stories, in their own ways, empha-

Seeking Out New Life: A spacesuited Mr. Spock (Leonard Nimoy) is dwarfed by the immense alien spacecraft he is investigating in the only really impressive sequence of *Star Trek: The Motion Picture* (1979).

size that residents of space, constantly confined either to their quarters or spacesuits, will feel lonely, isolated, and inclined to mental instability.

Other films, like *Countdown* and *Marooned*, work within the framework of past or present NASA technology to provide fictional but potentially true stories about present-day space flights. These include: *Stowaway to the Moon* (1975), a television movie about a boy who sneaks on board an Apollo flight to the Moon and ends up helping astronauts complete their mission; two episodes of the television series *Salvage 1*, "Salvage" (aired January 20, 1979) and the two-part episode "Golden Orbit" (aired March 12 and March 19, 1979), involving an enterprising businessman's use of leftover space technology to make profitable flights; the television miniseries *Space* (1985), based on James Michener's novel, that foregrounds fictional characters against the backdrop of NASA's historical achievements and depicts the imaginary flight of *Apollo 18*; and *SpaceCamp* (1986), which features young attendees at NASA's actual Space Camp who are accidentally launched on a space shuttle to face a crisis involving their oxygen supply. Except for necessary updating to include Apollo capsules or space shuttles, these remain stories that might have been episodes of *Men into Space*, with superior special effects but no additional insights about the experience of living in space.

As if in keeping with J.G. Ballard's singular prediction that space travel would become an abandoned activity nostalgically recalled,[1] a small subgenre of films featured former astronauts, dealing with Earthbound lives and perhaps dreaming of recapturing old glories. In *Terms of Endearment* (1983), retired astronaut Garrett Breedlove (Jack Nicholson) has seemingly come to terms with his past, with spacesuits observed only in photographs. But in *Space Cowboys* (2000), four elderly astronauts who never reached space implausibly fly the space shuttle to a Soviet satellite, based on one astronaut's antiquated design, that harbors nuclear weapons; and in *The Astronaut Farmer* (2002), a former astronaut plans to launch himself into space in his own experimental rocket.

In a category all its own is the lamentable sequel to *2001, 2010: The Year We Make Contact* (1984), which follows Clarke's 1982 novel *2010: Odyssey Two* in entirely contradicting the first film's central premise — that the transformed Bowman is the progenitor of a new super-race — to recast the Star Child as merely a messenger and errand boy for the monolith builders, who no longer wish to further advance humanity and instead have a new project, the impossible transformation of Jupiter into a star to provide a stable environment for promising creatures in the subterranean seas of the Jovian moon Europa. While the film replicates the spacesuit designs of *2001* (with inferior special effects), it fails to recapture its enigmatic power or add to its unsettling message.

Except for *Salvage 1* and *The Astronaut Farmer*, wherein government officials may seem like villains attempting to thwart an upstart's efforts, these films generally project a positive image of America's space program. But a few films built upon suspicions that the Apollo landings were faked to depict NASA bureaucrats conspiring to conceal unpalatable facts. In *The Astronaut* (1972), the first man to reach Mars dies; unwilling to reveal that news, officials recruit a duplicate to replace him first in faked footage of Mars, and later as a returning hero. *Alternative 3* (1977) posits that purported Soviet-American competition to reach the Moon concealed their joint efforts to colonize Mars; in *Capricorn One* (1977), a future NASA, unable to complete an actual Mars mission, stages a phony landing; and an elusive short film, *Sea of Tranquility* (2008), apparently questions the achievements of Armstrong and Aldrin. By suggesting that actual space achievements may have been fraudulent, such films validate America's rejection of its space program in favor of *Star Trek* as its choice between two fantasies.

Sea of Tranquility also brings to mind the one genuinely new type of spacesuit film that appeared after 1969: factual accounts of real American astronauts, strangely still regarded as science fiction films though they are based on real events. Two offered revisionist looks at the real personalities of astronauts who were uniformly portrayed by NASA as bland paragons: *Return to Earth* (1976), based on Buzz Aldrin's memoir, focuses on his nervous breakdown following the flight of *Apollo 11*; and *The Right Stuff* (1983), based on Tom Wolfe's book, portrays test pilot Chuck Yeager and colleagues who became Mercury astronauts as rambunctious mavericks. But other films offered more conventional accounts of famous heroics in space: *Apollo 13* (1995), the story of that imperiled flight (also dramatized in an inferior 1974 television movie, *Houston, We've Got a Problem*); two films about Armstrong and Aldrin's mission, *Apollo 11* (1996) and *Moonshot* (2009); and the miniseries *From the Earth to the Moon* (1998), chronicling American space achievements during the 1960s.

While some of these films were reasonably successful, there remained little interest in what American and Russian astronauts actually achieved in their space travels. Consider, as evidence, two recent movies involving Armstrong and Aldrin as characters: *Fly Me to the*

Moon (2008), an animated story about three talking flies that stow away on the *Apollo 11* mission, slightly dignified by a filmed epilogue featuring Aldrin himself; and *Transformers: Dark of the Moon* (2011), which posits that after their televised sojourn on the Moon, Armstrong and Aldrin took a secret side trip to investigate a crashed alien spacecraft. The lesson could not be clearer: To get audiences to pay attention to real space travelers, you must incorporate large doses of colorful fantasy.

Melodramatic spacesuit films include the lighthearted James Bond adventure *Moonraker* (1979), wherein the famous spy eventually dons a spacesuit and ascends to Earth orbit to counter an absurd terrorist threat, and *Fortress 2* (1999), where a wrongly imprisoned man struggles to escape from an oppressive prison in space. There were also two films, released the same year, about huge objects approaching Earth with human villainy in their subplots, *Deep Impact* (1998) and *Armageddon* (1998). In both, heroic astronauts rendezvous with the object and destroy it with explosives before it can collide with Earth. Another sort of disaster—falling into a black hole—threatens the crew of a medical spaceship in *Supernova* (2000), while two other films featured improbable threats from the Sun: In *Solar Crisis* (1990), astronauts must set off bombs to prevent a deadly solar flare from devastating Earth,

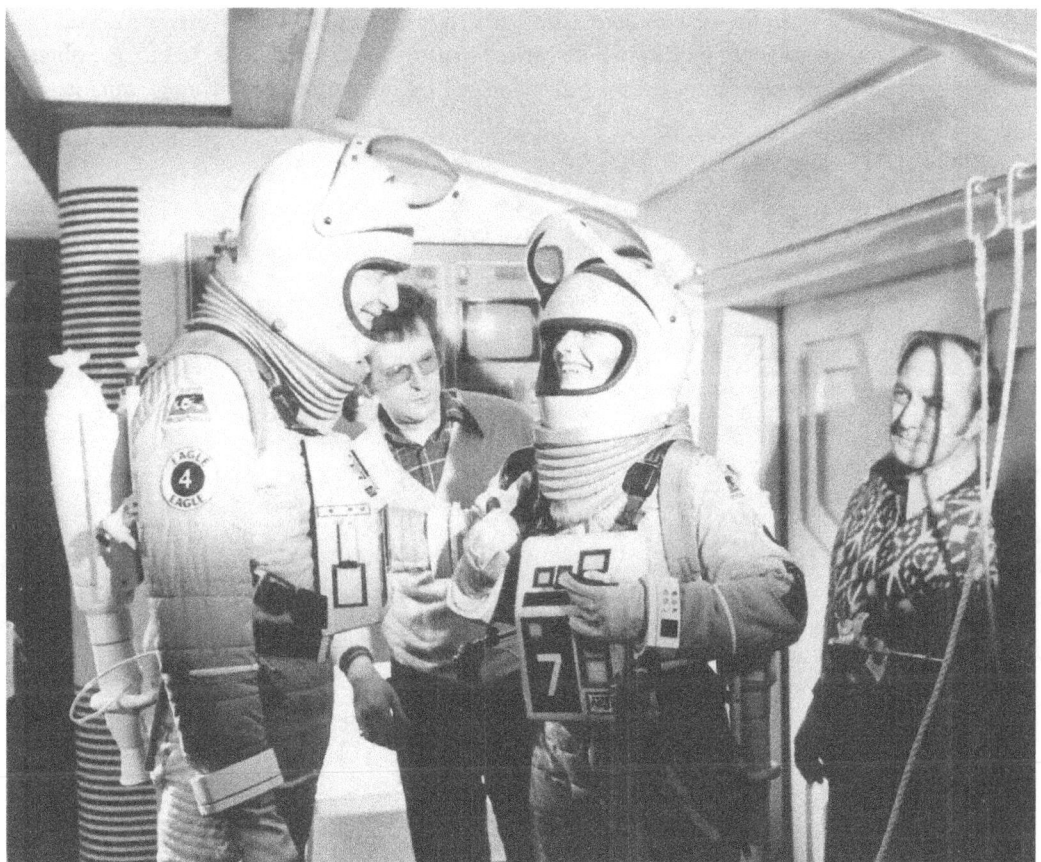

Prudence Amidst the Preposterousness: While his space adventures were generally far more ludicrous than those in *Star Trek*, Commander John Koenig (Martin Landau) of *Space: 1999* (1975–1977) would at least regularly wear a spacesuit. Here he is observed off-camera with an unidentified female companion and two members of the series' crew.

and in *Sunshine* (2007), astronauts must, in some poorly explained fashion, reignite a dying Sun.

More commonly, such films feature sinister aliens. As one example, after *Döppelganger*, Gerry and Sylvia Anderson launched two risible television series that sporadically featured spacesuits: *UFO* (1970–1973), about an international defense force opposing aliens in flying saucers attempting to invade Earth, and *Space: 1999* (1975–1977), about an explosion that impossibly sends the Moon careening through interstellar space, carrying the crew of a moon base. *Superman II* (1980) briefly shows superpowered criminals from Krypton confronting astronauts on the Moon. Stories set further in the future involve all-out space wars against aliens recalling *Starship Troopers* (1997), including the television series *Space: Above and Beyond* (1995–1996) and *Battle Planet* (2008).

Several movies about Mars, respecting current knowledge, properly feature astronauts wearing spacesuits on its surface amidst other improbable developments. Examples include the television miniseries *The Martian Chronicles* (1980), based on Ray Bradbury's famous collection of that name, and the Arnold Schwarzenegger epic *Total Recall* (1990), which absurdly concludes with the hero turning on an ancient alien machine to quickly provide the planet with a breathable atmosphere. A third film, *Mission to Mars* (2000), explicitly emulates *2001* by sending spacesuited astronauts to the Red Planet to investigate a strange alien artifact. In its most interesting sequence, a spaceship dispatched to rescue members of an earlier Mars expedition has its hull damaged by meteorites, requiring astronauts to

Martian Melodrama: Unaware of the trite encounters that await them on the Martian surface, three astronauts in *Mission to Mars* (2000) — Jim McConnell (Gary Sinise), Terri Fisher (Connie Nielsen), and Phil Ohlmyer (Jerry O'Connell) — face more plausible challenges outside their spaceship in Martian orbit.

don spacesuits and attempt emergency repairs. To save his colleagues, an astronaut launches himself into space without the possibility of return, creating the familiar but still haunting image of a doomed astronaut receding from the camera into the depths of space. Unfortunately, when they land and enter a large building in the shape of a face, they discover no daunting mysteries, only the hologram of a sobbing Martian with a trite story to tell about an asteroid that devastated her verdant world and forced inhabitants to abandon their home, though not before seeding the Earth with organisms that eventually evolved into humans. Another film about Mars released the same time, *Red Planet* (2000), for much of its length portrays a grim struggle to survive in a harsh Martian environment, but as in *Robinson Crusoe on Mars*, the situation becomes more hospitable as astronauts incredibly discover that Mars has a thin but breathable atmosphere; and native insect life, now revived and feeding on algae brought from Earth, promises to enrich the Martian atmosphere with oxygen. Finally, *Stranded* (2001) similarly begins with astronauts, crash-landed on Mars, who struggle to survive before experiencing alien contact by entering an ancient Martian structure.

In the manner of *World Without End*, the *Outer Limits* episode "The Man Who Was Never Born," and the series *It's About Time*, some melodramatic spacesuit films depict journeys through time effected through space travel, providing introductory or concluding images of spacesuited astronauts. Two examples are the second sequel to *Planet of the Apes* (1968), *Escape from the Planet of the Apes* (1971), wherein intelligent apes survive the destruction of their future Earth by flying back to 20th-century Earth, and the series *Odyssey 5* (2002–2004), in which aliens transport astronauts five years back in time to avert a global catastrophe.

Humorous spacesuit films include the children's television series *Far Out Space Nuts* (1975–1976), employing the familiar scenario of bumbling incompetents accidentally launched into space; two telemovies that endeavored to revive the *I Dream of Jeannie* TV series, *I Dream of Jeannie ... Fifteen Years Later* (1985) and *I Still Dream of Jeannie* (1991); the Turkish comedy *Fehmi the Astronaut* (1978); the bizarre musical *The American Astronaut* (2001); Eddie Murphy's *The Adventures of Pluto Nash* (2002), which invites consideration as a humorous version of *Moon Zero Two*; and a few whimsical fantasies primarily aimed at children: *Zathura: A Space Adventure* (2005), wherein game-playing space travelers encounter a spacesuited astronaut; *Ella and the Astronaut* (2008), offering a child's perspective on space travel; and *Space Buddies* (2009), featuring talking dogs in spacesuits who travel to the Moon.

Finally, there were horrific spacesuit films. Astronauts who return to Earth transformed by alien contact range from the monstrous *The Incredible Melting Man* (1977) to the more subtly altered astronauts of *The Astronaut's Wife* (1999); astronauts also bring back deadly alien spores in *Contamination* (1981). Moving further into the future, spacesuits are occasionally worn by space travelers in the *Alien* films — *Alien* (1979), *Aliens* (1986), *Alien³* (1992), and *Alien Resurrection* (1997) — though most encounters with monsters occur inside spaceships or on habitable planets; the title characters in *Space Truckers* (1986) struggle against a horde of homicidal robots that were secretly their latest cargo; and in *Event Horizon* (1997), the perils in space involve a damaged spaceship that somehow comes into contact with another, evil dimension. Episodes of the revived *The Outer Limits* feature astronauts confronting alien menaces, including "The Voyage Home" (aired June 30, 1995), "Joyride" (aired February 26, 1999), and "The Vessel" (aired April 13, 2001).

I have not watched, or have not recently watched, many of these films, so their use of spacesuits is not always confirmed, and I surely omit some relevant items for other researchers to chronicle. Perhaps films mentioned here, and not mentioned here, are brimming with

Space Men at Work: When not battling monsters, astronauts in the *Alien* films would sometimes wear spacesuits, like Lambert (Veronica Cartwright), Dallas (Tom Skerritt), and Kane (John Hurt), who investigate a crashed alien spaceship in the original *Alien* (1979).

overlooked insights about our future life in space. But as this book approaches its 200,000th word, I will be forgiven for rushing through this survey of recent films to offer provisional conclusions about the history of spacesuit films, which I suspect would be unaffected by additional study.

As intimated, the cinematic spacesuit conveys key messages about humanity's future in space. Space is an environment unlike anything people have encountered, and its forbidding nature, and potential presence of enigmatic aliens, will require significant changes in human attitudes and, ultimately, human nature itself. As most fully presented in *2001*, these truths can take narratives into strange, unsettling territory, perhaps until further exploration is impossible, as humans may be incapable of imagining the characteristics of a transformed humanity. However, since this represents our likely future, one can readily justify further efforts to tell this story; yet science fiction films usually ignore this imperative.

Instead, filmmakers deal with the challenge of space by falsely positing that space will be just like Earth and limiting visions of future space travel to beings and places much like those on our world. Spacesuits may fleetingly appear in such films, but they become icons of a different sort: In places where special protection is not needed, a superfluous spacesuit symbolizes childishness, because it is silly to wear spacesuits in such circumstances. Thus, spacesuits appear in works like *My Favorite Martian* and *The Terrornauts* solely as outfits worn by children at play, and *Kyojin to Gangu* singularly makes the connection explicit: If one refuses to acknowledge the special nature of space, spacesuits are only of interest to children, and if adults don spacesuits, it is humiliating. Seeking a powerful concluding image to convey that advertiser Tousuke Nishi totally sold his soul to the mad pursuit of financial success, director Yasuro Masumura could think of nothing better than to show him wearing a spacesuit to promote his company's product.

Yet one can turn this argument on its head to maintain that spacesuits should properly be regarded as childish, and that filmmakers' gradual abandonment of that icon represents a process of maturation. From this perspective, the primary responsibility of storytellers is to ponder the human condition. If characters are placed in cumbersome spacesuits and odd environments without air or gravity, that goal is compromised, as the result is flat characters engaged in meaningless dramas about menacing meteors and grim contemplation of an emptying oxygen cylinder. When programs like *Star Trek* eschew spacesuits to focus on normal-looking people in normal-looking places, they can correctly devote themselves to fully developed characters, analyses of age-old human dilemmas, and profound commentary on contemporary social problems. This is the viewpoint of critic David Thomson, who argues in *A Biographical Dictionary of Film* that *Metropolis* (1927) is a better film that *2001* because the former film's story is "subordinated to the human aspect of the film" and is "about society," whereas *2001* is only "an elaborate, academic toy" ("Stanley Kubrick" 493). A film which fails to emphasize "the human aspect," as is necessarily the case in true spacesuit films, is thus immature and valueless, like a "toy," almost as a matter of definition.

But there is an obvious flaw in this argument. Humanity today essentially faces two possible futures: We can either permanently remain on Earth, and permanently remain the same, or colonize space, and transform ourselves into inhabitants of space. It may be, as I argue elsewhere, that the second option will prove far more challenging than science fiction writers imagined, and that genuine progress in conquering space may require another few decades, or centuries, until the appropriate technology is developed. But eventually, if not now, humans will face that choice, and we should actively ponder the ultimate consequences of permanently living in the fundamentally different realm we have only begun to explore. *Star Trek* falsely argues that no choice need be made: We can conquer the universe, and we can also remain exactly the same as we are now. But this prevalent attitude is truly silly, and genuinely childish.

True, in some science fiction stories, there appears the comforting, and theoretically possible, notion that future humans may have the power to transform space into an environment resembling Earth, perhaps rendering concerns about its presently forbidding nature unnecessary. This is the idea of terraforming, scientifically making a barren planet into a paradise, which impossibly occurs instantaneously in *Total Recall*. But through centuries of labor involving the introduction of massive amounts of chemicals and organisms, as most thoroughly described in Kim Stanley Robinson's Mars trilogy, such transformations might be achieved. It is indeed delightful to imagine that someday, humans might sail on Martian canals or Venusian oceans as in old science fiction stories. Yet as long as humans travel from planet to planet, spacesuits and the daunting environment of space will forever remain part of their experience, since endless space cannot be provided with breathable air and comfortable temperatures; and terraforming demands technology on a scale many factors beyond any project humans have undertaken, raising doubts about its plausibility.

A better and more practical answer to the problem of colonizing other worlds, termed pantropy, is to transform humans so they can safely inhabit diverse environments, imaginatively depicted in the James Blish stories collected in *The Seedling Stars* (1957); A. E. van Vogt's *The Silkie* (1969) even envisions a humanlike creature who can survive in the vacuum of space. A near-future story along these lines, Frederik Pohl's *Man-Plus* (1976), might be viewed as a counterargument to Robinson's Mars trilogy, as it describes a future man who is bioengineered to become a bizarre being capable of living on the present-day Martian surface, hopefully the progenitor of a new Martian race. Or, if we cannot transform ourselves into beings that can live in space, we may someday construct such a race — one underlying theme in the remarkable *Wall-E* (2008). While barely qualifying for inclusion in my bibliography — due to a few images of a live actor and a brief scene where residents of a space ark have protective glass helmets cover their faces during a crisis, arguably sorts of spacesuit — it remains one of the most heterodox spacesuit films, since it explicitly argues that humans belong on Earth; while a soaring dance in space featuring robots Wall-E and Eva demonstrates, as previously argued in *Gog*, that robots might prove the ideal inhabitants of space.[2]

But relatively few science fiction stories ponder how space might mandate transforming humanity, or replacing humanity, so it might seem uncharitable to berate science fiction films for so militantly refusing to explore such possibilities. Certainly, to producers seeking profits, mimicking *Star Trek* invariably seems wiser than trying something original. Yet films and their effects have a special power to evoke unfamiliar environments and experiences: Reading a description of an astronaut plummeting through endless space in Heinlein's "Ordeal in Space" lacks the impact of watching a doomed astronaut receding into the distance in *2001* and *Mission to Mars*. But instead of portraying realistic space environments and potential superhumans in the manner of *2001*— whose special effects remain unmatched today — science fiction filmmakers generally employ special-effects artists solely to craft grotesque alien monsters drawn from ancient human legends and nightmares.

Thus, it would be interesting indeed to see a filmmaker attempt a genuine sequel to *2001*, jettisoning the disheartening contrivances of Clarke's sequels to begin with the Star Child in Earth orbit, having destroyed all of Earth's nuclear weapons, proceeding to take further actions to transform and elevate his former race. A filmmaker might build upon intriguing ideas in works like Fritz Leiber's "The Beat Cluster" (1961) and *A Specter Is Haunting Texas* (1968) to offer a thorough picture of the unusual activities and physical transformations that might emerge in weightless societies. Someone might adapt a novel like *Man-Plus* or finally film Clarke's long-optioned *Childhood's End* (1953), wherein alien invaders oversee the transformation of humanity into a disturbing group intelligence which finally destroys the Earth to obtain energy and collectively soars into the cosmos to fulfill its destiny within a community of such collective beings. There are surely other stories to add to the tradition of spacesuit films that have not yet been made, because no one has had the vision or courage to produce them.

So, we are left to cherish what filmmakers have actually accomplished: a series of fascinating films that culminated with *2001* and the *Apollo 11* moon landing to offer a good start in relating the saga of humanity's possible futures in space. There is much to learn from these films, as I trust this study has conveyed. I bring this journey through space to a close with the hope that other scholars, and other filmmakers, will undertake similar voyages of discovery into this strange and still largely unexplored realm.

A Filmography of Spacesuit Films

This filmography has three parts: a comprehensive list of spacesuit films and series from 1918 to 1969, which I have personally verified involve spacesuits; a list of films and series of probable relevance from that period I have not seen (some of which are lost); and a provisional list of spacesuit films and series from 1970 to the present.

I. Spacesuit Films, 1918–1969

1918

Himmelskibet. (*A Trip to Mars, A Ship to Heaven*) Danish. Nordisk, 1918. Director Holger-Madsen. Writers Sophus Michaelis (novel); Michaelis and Ole Olsen (screenplay).

1929

Die Frau im Mond. (*Woman in the Moon*) German. Fritz Lang-Film, 1929. Director Fritz Lang. Writers Thea von Harbou (novel); Lang (screenplay).

1935

Kosmicheskiy Reys: Fantasticheskaya Novella. (*The Space Voyage, The Space Ship*) Russian. Mosfilm, 1935. Director Vasili Zhuravlev. Writers Konstantin Tsiolkovsky (novel); Aleksandr Filimonov (screenplay).

1950

Destination Moon. George Pal, 1950. Director Irving Pichel. Writers Robert A. Heinlein (novel); Alford Van Ronkel, Heinlein, and James O'Hanlon (screenplay).

Rocketship X-M. Lippert, 1950. Director Kurt Neumann. Writers Neumann, Orville Hampton, and Dalton Trumbo (uncredited).

Space Patrol. [TV series] ABC-TV, 1950–1955. Episodes involving spacesuits are separately cited.

Tom Corbett, Space Cadet. [TV series] CBS-TV, 1950; ABC-TV, 1951–1952; NBC-TV, 1951, 1954–1955; Dumont, 1953–1954. Episodes involving spacesuits are separately cited.

1951

Captain Video: Master of the Stratosphere. [serial] Columbia, 1951. Directors Spencer Gordon Bennet and Wallace Grissell. Writers George Plympton (story); Royal Cole, Sherman Lowe, and Joseph Poland (screenplay).

The Day the Earth Stood Still. Twentieth Century–Fox, 1951. Director Robert Wise. Writers Harry Bates (story); Edmund North (screenplay).

Flight to Mars. Monogram, 1951. Director Lesley Selander. Writer Arthur Strawn.

The Man from Planet X. Mid-Century, 1951. Director Edgar G. Ulmer. Writers Aubrey Wisberg and Jack Pollexfen.

"The Space Patrol Code Belt." *Space Patrol.* ABC-TV, October 20, 1951. Director Dik Darley. Writer Norman Jolley.

"Space Patrol Kids Visit." *The George Burns and Gracie Allen Show.* CBS-TV, August 16, 1951. Director Ralph Levy. Writers Paul Henning, Sid Dorfman, Harvey Helm, and William Burns.

1952

"Hit by a Meteorite." *Space Patrol.* ABC-TV, February 9, 1952. Director Dik Darley. Writer Norman Jolley.

"Plague from Space." *Tales of Tomorrow.* ABC-TV, April 25, 1952. Director Don Medford. Writers Harry Guth (story); Mann Rubin (teleplay).

Radar Men from the Moon. [serial] Republic, 1952. Director Fred Brannon. Writer Ronald Davidson.

1953

Abbott and Costello Go to Mars. Universal, 1953. Director Charles Lamont. Writers D.D. Beauchamp and Howard Christie (story); Beauchamp and John Grant (screenplay).

Cat-Women of the Moon. (*Rocket to the Moon*) Z-M, 1953. Director Arthur Hilton. Writers Jack Rabin and Al Zimbalist (story); Roy Hamilton (screenplay).

"Contact Has Been Established." *The Quatermass Experiment.* London: BBC-TV, July 18, 1953. Director Rudolph Cartier. Writer Nigel Kneale.

"Persons Reported Missing." *The Quatermass Experiment.* London: BBC-TV, July 18, 1953. Director Rudolph Cartier. Writer Nigel Kneale.

Phantom from Space. Planet Filmways, 1953. Director W. Lee Wilder. Writers Myles Wilder (story); William Raynor and Myles Wilder (screenplay).

Project Moon Base. Galaxy, 1953. Director Richard Talmadge. Writers Robert A. Heinlein and Jack Seaman.

The Quatermass Experiment. [TV miniseries] London: BBC-TV, July 18 through August 22, 1953. Director Rudolph Cartier. Writer Nigel Kneale. The first two episodes (the only surviving episodes), both involving spacesuits, are separately cited.

Robot Monster. Three Dimension, 1953. Director Phil Tucker. Writer Wyott Ordung.

Spaceways. British. Hammer, 1953. Director Terence Fisher. Writers Charles Eric Maine (play); Richard Landau and Paul Tabori (screenplay).

1954

"Beyond the Curtain of Space." [three-part episode] *Rocky Jones, Space Ranger.* Syndicated: February 23, March 2 and March 9, 1954. Director Hollingsworth Morse. Writer Warren Wilson. Reedited as *Beyond the Moon* (1956).

"Bobby's Comet." [three-part episode] *Rocky Jones, Space Ranger.* Syndicated: April 6, 13 and 20, 1954. Director Hollingsworth Morse. Writer Warren Wilson. Reedited as *Menace from Outer Space* (1956).

"The Breath of Death." *Flash Gordon.* Syndicated: November 26, 1954. Director Wallace Worsley, Jr. Writers Earl Markham and Bruce Elliot.

"The Claim Jumpers." *Flash Gordon.* Syndicated: November 12, 1954. Director Wallace Worsley, Jr. Writers Earl Markham and Bruce Elliot.

"Escape into Space." *Rocky Jones, Space Ranger.* Syndicated: May 1, 1954. Director Hollingsworth Morse. Writer Warren Wilson.

Flash Gordon. [TV series] Syndicated, 1954–1955. Episodes involving spacesuits are separately cited.

Gog. Ivan Tors, 1954. Director Herbert L. Strock. Writers Ivan Tors (story); Tom Taggart and Richard Taylor (screenplay).

"The Moon or Bust." *The Mickey Rooney Show.* NBC-TV, September 4, 1954. Director Leslie Martinson. Writers Benedict Freedman and John Fenton Murray.

Riders to the Stars. A-Men, 1954. Director Richard Carlson. Writers Ivan Tors (story); Curt Siodmak (screenplay).

Rocky Jones, Space Ranger. [TV series] Syndicated, 1954. Episodes involving spacesuits are separately cited.

1955

"Ambush in Space." *Tom Corbett, Space Cadet.* NBC-TV, May 21, 1955. Director Ralph Ward. Writers Willie Gilbert and Jack Weinstock.

"Assignment: Mercury." *Tom Corbett, Space Cadet.* NBC-TV, February 26, 1955. Director Ralph Ward. Writer unknown.

Conquest of Space. Paramount, 1955. Director Byron Haskin. Writers Chesley Bonestell and Willy Ley (book); Barré Lyndon, George Worthing Yates and Philip Yordan (adaptation); James O'Hanlon (screenplay).

"The Destroyers." *Quatermass II.* London: BBC-TV, November 26, 1955. Director Rudolph Cartier. Writer Nigel Kneale.

"Fight for Survival." *Tom Corbett, Space Cadet.* NBC-TV, June 4, 1955. Director Ralph Ward. Writer Albert Aley.

King Dinosaur. Zimgor, 1955. Director Bert I. Gordon. Writers Gordon and Al Zimbalist (story); Tom Gries (screenplay).

"Man and the Moon." *Disneyland.* ABC, December 28, 1955. Director Ward Kimball. Writers William Bosche, John W. Dunn and Kimball.

"The Mystery of the Missing Mail Ship." *Tom Corbett, Space Cadet.* NBC-TV, March 12, 1955. Director Ralph Ward. Writer Albert Aley.

"Pursuit of the Deep Space Projectile." *Tom Corbett, Space Cadet.* NBC-TV, April 30, 1955. Director Ralph Ward. Writer Richard Jessup.

Quatermass II. [TV miniseries] London: BBC-TV, October 22 through November 26, 1955. Director Rudolph Cartier. Writer Nigel Kneale. The sixth episode is separately cited.

The Quatermass Xperiment. (*The Creeping Unknown*) British. Hammer, 1955. Director Val Guest. Writers Nigel Kneale (TV play); Guest and Richard Landau (screenplay).

1956

Earth vs. the Flying Saucers. Clover, 1956. Director Fred F. Sears. Writers Donald Keyhoe (book); Curt Siodmak (story); George Worthing Yates and Bernard Gordon (screenplay).

Forbidden Planet. MGM, 1956. Director Fred Wilcox. Writers Allen Adler and Irving Block (story); Cyril Hume (screenplay).

Satellite in the Sky. British. Tridelta, 1956. Director Paul Dickson. Writers Edith Dell, John Mather and J. T. McIntosh.

World Without End. Allied Artists, 1956. Director Edward Bernds. Writer Bernds.

1957

Chikyu Boeigun. (*The Mysterians*) Japanese. Toho, 1957. Director Ishirô Honda. Writers Shigeru Kayama and Jojiro Okami (story); Takeshi Kimura (screenplay).

Doroga k Zvezdam. (*Road to the Stars*) [documentary] Russian. Leningrad Popular Science, 1957. Director Pavel Klushantsev. Writers Boris Lyapunov and Vasili Solovyov.

Outer Space Jitters. [short] Columbia, 1957. Director Jules White. Writer Jack White.

Space Ship Sappy. [short] Columbia, 1957. Director Jules White. Writer Jack White.

Totò nella Luna. (*Totò in the Moon*) Italian-Spanish. Maxima, 1957. Director Steno [Stefano Vanzina]. Writers Lucio Fulci and Steno (story); Sandro Continenza, Ettore Scola and Steno (screenplay).

20 Million Miles to Earth. Morningside, 1957. Director Nathan Juran. Writers Charlotte Knight (story); Christopher Knopf and Robert Creighton Williams (screenplay).

1958

From the Earth to the Moon. Waverly, 1958. Director Byron Haskin. Writers Jules Verne (novel); Robert Blees and James Leicester (screenplay).

It! The Terror from Beyond Space. Vogue, 1958. Director Edward L. Cahn. Writer Jerome Bixby.

Kyojin to Gangu. (*Giants and Toys*) Japanese. Daiei, 1958. Director Yasuro Masumura. Writers Takeshi Kaikô (novel); Yoshio Shirasaka (screenplay).

Missile to the Moon. Astor, 1958. Director Richard Cunha. Writers H. E. Barrie and Vincent Fotre.

La Morte Viene dallo Spazio. (*The Day the Sky Exploded*) Italian-French. Lux, 1958. Director Paolo Heusch. Writers Virgilio Sabel (story); Sondra Continenza and Marcello Coscia (screenplay).

Queen of Outer Space. Allied Artists, 1958. Director Edward Bernds. Writers Ben Hecht (story); Charles Beaumont (screenplay).

1959

The Angry Red Planet. Sino, 1959. Director Ib Melchior. Writers Sidney Pink (story); Melchior and Pink (screenplay).

"**Asteroid.**" *Men into Space.* CBS-TV, November 25, 1959. Director Lee Sholem. Writer Ted Sherdeman.

"**Building a Space Station.**" *Men into Space.* CBS-TV, October 14, 1959. Director Otto Lang. Writer Meyer Dolinsky.

"**Burnout.**" *Men into Space.* CBS-TV, December 9, 1959. Director Alvin Ganzer. Writer Donald Duncan.

"**Christmas on the Moon.**" *Men into Space.* CBS-TV, December 23, 1959. Director Richard Carlson. Writers Lawrence Louis Goldman (story); David Duncan (teleplay).

Destination Space. Paramount, 1959. Director Joseph Pevney. Writer Rip Van Ronkel.

"**Edge of Eternity.**" *Men into Space.* CBS-TV, December 2, 1959. Director Nathan Juran. Writer Kalman Phillips.

First Man into Space. British. Anglo-Amalgamated, 1959. Director Robert Day. Writers Wyott Ordung (story); John Croydon and Charles Vetter (screenplay).

"First Woman on the Moon." *Men into Space.* CBS-TV, December 16, 1959. Director Herman Hoffman. Writer James Clavell.

Have Rocket, Will Travel. Columbia, 1959. Director David Lowell Rich. Writer Raphael Hayes.

"Lost Missile." *Men into Space.* CBS-TV, November 4, 1959. Director Walter Doniger. Writer Michael Plant.

Men into Space. [TV series] CBS-TV, 1959–1960. Its thirty-nine episodes — all involving spacesuits — are separately cited.

"Moon Landing." *Men into Space.* CBS-TV, October 7, 1959. Director Walter Doniger. Writer James Clavell.

"Moon Probe." *Men into Space.* CBS-TV, September 30, 1959. Director Walter Doniger. Writer Arthur Weiss.

"Moonquake." *Men into Space.* CBS-TV, November 11, 1959. Director Lee Sholem. Writer William Templeton.

Nebo Zovyot. (*The Sky Calls*) Russian. Dovzhenko, 1959. Directors Mikhail Karzhukov and Aleksandr Kozyr. Writers Karzhukov, Yevgeni Pomeshchikov, and Aleksei Sazanov. Reissued with new footage as *Battle Beyond the Sun* (1962) (q.v.).

"Quarantine." *Men into Space.* CBS-TV, December 30, 1959. Director Walter Doniger. Writer Stuart James Byrne.

Rehla ilal Kamar. (*Journey to the Moon*) Egyptian. Delta, 1959. Director Hamada Abdel Wahab. Writer Wahab.

"Space Trap." *Men into Space.* CBS-TV, November 18, 1959. Director Charles Haas. Writers Marianne Mosner and Francis Rosenwald.

Teenagers from Outer Space. Tom Graeff, 1959. Director Tom Graeff. Writer Graeff.

The Twilight Zone. [TV series] CBS-TV, 1959–1964. Episodes involving spacesuits are separately cited.

Uchu Daisenso. (*Battle in Outer Space*) Japanese. Toho, 1959. Director Ishirô Honda. Writers Jojiri Okami (story); Shinichi Sekizawa (screenplay).

"Water Tank Rescue." *Men into Space.* CBS-TV, October 28, 1959. Director Otto Lang. Writer Ib Melchior.

1960

"Beyond the Stars." *Men into Space.* CBS-TV, May 11, 1960. Director Jack Herzberg. Writer David Duncan.

"Caves of the Moon." *Men into Space.* CBS-TV, February 3, 1960. Director Lee Sholem. Writer Meyer Dolinsky.

Conquistador de la Luna. (*The Astronauts*) Mexican. Sotomayor, 1960. Director Rogelio González. Writers José Maria Fernández Unsáin and Francisco Verala.

"Contraband." *Men into Space.* CBS-TV, March 2, 1960. Director Alvin Ganzer. Writers Stuart James Byrne (story); David Duncan (teleplay).

"Dark of the Sun." *Men into Space.* CBS-TV, March 9, 1960. Director Alvin Ganzer. Writer David Duncan.

"Dateline: Moon." *Men into Space.* CBS-TV, February 10, 1960. Director Alan Crosland, Jr. Writers Mike Adams (story); Robert Warnes Leach (teleplay).

"Earthbound." *Men into Space.* CBS-TV, January 27, 1960. Director Nathan Juran. Writers Robert Hecker (story); Hecker and David Duncan (teleplay).

"Emergency Mission." *Men into Space.* CBS-TV, May 4, 1960. Director Alvin Ganzer. Writer Kalman Phillips.

"Flare Up." *Men into Space.* CBS-TV, August 17, 1960. Director Herman Hoffman. Writers Sidney Kalcheim (story); Donald Duncan (teleplay).

"Flash in the Sky." *Men into Space.* CBS-TV, April 4, 1960. Director Walter Doniger. Writer David Duncan.

"Flight to the Red Planet." *Men into Space.* CBS-TV, September 14, 1960 [by some reports never aired]. Director David Friedkin. Writer Lewis Jay [Jerome Bixby].

"From Another World." *Men into Space.* CBS-TV, April 27, 1960. Director Herman Hoffman. Writer Beirne Lay, Jr.

"A Handful of Hours." *Men into Space.* CBS-TV, January 20, 1960. Director Alvin Ganzer. Writer Michael Plant.

"Into the Sun." *Men into Space.* CBS-TV, August 24, 1960. Director Jack Herzberg. Writer Fred Freiberger (story); Lewis Jay [Jerome Bixby] (teleplay).

"Is There Another Civilization?" *Men into Space.* CBS-TV, March 23, 1960. Director Nathan Juran. Writers Jerome Bixby (story); Robert Warnes Leach (teleplay).

"Lunar Secret." *Men into Space.* CBS-TV, April 13, 1960. Director Franklin Adreon. Writer Michael Plant.

Man in the Moon. British. Allied, 1960. Director Basil Dearden. Writers John Foley (novel, uncredited); Bryan Forbes, Michael Relph, and Dearden (uncredited) (screenplay).

"Mission to Mars." *Men into Space.* CBS-TV, May 25, 1960. Director William Conrad. Writer Lewis Jay [Jerome Bixby].

"Moon Cloud." *Men into Space.* CBS-TV, February 17, 1960. Director Otto Lang. Writers Sidney Kalcheim (story); Michael Plant (teleplay).

"Moon Trap." *Men into Space.* CBS-TV, June 1, 1960. Director Otto Lang. Writer Lewis Jay [Jerome Bixby].

"Mystery Satellite." *Men into Space.* CBS-TV, September 7, 1960. Director William Conrad. Writer Lewis Jay [Jerome Bixby].

Die Schweigende Stern. (*First Spaceship on Venus*) East German-Polish. Deutsche, 1960. Director Kurt Maetzig. Writers Stanislaw Lem (novel); Jan Fethke, Wolfgang Kohlhaase, Maetzig, Günter Reisch, Günther Rucker, Alexander Stenbock-Fermor, and J. Barkhauer (uncredited) (screenplay).

"Sea of Stars." *Men into Space.* CBS-TV, January 13, 1960. Director Lee Sholem. Writers Marianne Mosner and Francis Rosenwald (story); Mosner, Rosenwald, and Kalman Phillips (teleplay).

"Shadows on the Moon." *Men into Space.* CBS-TV, March 30, 1960. Director Alvin Ganzer. Writer David Duncan.

Space Men. (*Assignment Outer Space*) Italian. Titanus/Ultra, 1960. Director Antonio Margheriti. Writers Ennio De Concini and Jack Wallace.

"The Sun Never Sets." *Men into Space.* CBS-TV, August 31, 1960. Director Alvin Ganzer. Writer Lewis Jay [Jerome Bixby].

"Tankers in Space." *Men into Space.* CBS-TV, January 6, 1960. Director Alvin Ganzer. Writer Arthur Weiss.

12 to the Moon. Luna, 1960. Director David Bradley. Writers Fred Gebhardt (story); DeWitt Bodeen (screenplay).

"Verdict in Orbit." *Men into Space.* CBS-TV, March 16, 1960. Director Nathan Juran. Writers Sidney Kalcheim (story); Michael Plant (teleplay).

"Voice of Infinity." *Men into Space.* CBS-TV, April 20, 1960. Director Alan Crosland Jr. Writer Ib Melchior.

1961

Baron Prášil. (*The Fabulous Baron Munchausen*) Czechoslovakian. Gottwaldov, 1961. Director Karel Zeman. Writers Rudolph Erich Raspe, Gottfried August Bürger (books); Jirí Brdecka, Josef Kainar, and Zeman (screenplay).

"The Invaders." *The Twilight Zone.* CBS-TV, January 27, 1961. Director Douglas Heyes. Writer Richard Matheson.

Nude on the Moon. Moon, 1961. Directors Raymond Phelan and Doris Wishman. Writers Phelan and Wishman.

The Phantom Planet. Four Crown, 1961. Director William Marshall. Writers Fred Gebhardt (story); Fred De Gorter, Gebhardt, William Telaak, and Marshall (screenplay).

Il Pianeta degli Uomini Spenti. (*Battle of the Worlds*) Italian. Ultra, 1961. Director Antonio Margheriti. Writer Ennio De Concini.

1962

Battle Beyond the Sun. American version of *Nebo Zovyot* (1959) (q.v.) with new footage. Filmgroup, 1962. American director: Thomas Colchart [Francis Ford Coppola].

Journey to the Seventh Planet. Swedish-American. Cinemagic, 1961. Director Sidney Pink. Writers Pink (story); Ib Melchior and Pink (screenplay).

Moon Pilot. Walt Disney, 1962. Director James Neilson. Writers Robert Buckner (story); Maurice Tombragel (screenplay).

Planeta Bur. (*Planet of Storms*) Soviet. Leningrad Popular Science, 1962. Director Pavel Klushantsev. Writers Aleksandr Kazantsev and Klushantsev. Reissued with new footage as *Voyage to the Prehistoric Planet* (1965) (q.v.) and *Voyage to the Planet of Prehistoric Women* (1967) (q.v.).

The Road to Hong Kong. British. Melnor, 1962. Director Norman Panama. Writers Melvin Frank and Panama.

Yosei Gorasu. (*Gorath*) Japanese. Toho, 1962. Director Ishirô Honda. Writers Jojiri Okami (story); Takeshi Kimura (screenplay).

1963

The Crawling Hand. Joseph F. Robertson, 1963. Director Herbert L. Strock. Writers Joseph Cranston, Bill Idelson, and Robert Young (story); Idelson and Strock (screenplay).

"Death Ship." *The Twilight Zone.* CBS-TV, February 7, 1963. Director Alan Crosland, Jr. Writer Rod Serling.

"How to Be a Hero Without Really Trying." *My Favorite Martian.* CBS-TV, December 29, 1963. Director Sidney Miller. Writers Ed James and Seaman Jacobs.

Ikarie XB-1. (*Icarus XB-1*) Czechoslovakian. Barrandov, 1963. Director Jindrich Polák. Writers Pavel Jurácek, Polák, and Stanislaw Lem (uncredited). Reissued with new footage as *Voyage to the End of the Universe* (1964) (q.v.).

"The Man Who Was Never Born." *The Outer Limits.* ABC-TV, October 28, 1963. Director Leonard Horn. Writer Anthony Lawrence.

Mechte Navstrechu. (*A Dream Come True, Encounter in Space*) Soviet. Odessa, 1963. Directors Mikhail Karzhukov and Otar Koberidze. Writers A. Berdnik and Ivan Bondin (draft screenplay); Karzhukov and Koberidze (final screenplay). Reissued with new footage as *Queen of Blood* (1966) (q.v.).

The Mouse on the Moon. British. Walter Shenson, 1963. Director Richard Lester. Writers Leonard Wibberley (novel); Michael Pertwee (screenplay).

My Favorite Martian. [TV series] CBS-TV, 1963–1965. An episode involving spacesuits is separately cited.

The Outer Limits. [TV series] ABC-TV, 1963–1965. Episodes involving spacesuits are separately cited.

"The Parallel." *The Twilight Zone.* CBS-TV, March 14, 1963. Director Alan Crosland, Jr. Writer Rod Serling.

1964

"Cold Hands, Warm Heart." *The Outer Limits.* ABC-TV, September 26, 1964. Director Charles Haas. Writer Milton Krims.

First Men in the Moon. British-American. Columbia, 1964. Director Nathan Juran. Writer H. G. Wells (novel); Nigel Kneale and Jan Read (screenplay).

"The Invisible Enemy." *The Outer Limits.* ABC-TV, October 31, 1964. Director Byron Haskin. Writer Jerry Sohl (story); Sohl, Haskin, Seeleg Lester, and Ben Brady (the latter three uncredited) (teleplay).

"Moonstone." *The Outer Limits.* ABC-TV, March 9, 1964. Director Robert Florey. Writer William Bast, Joseph Stefano, and Lou Morheim (story); Bast (teleplay).

Robinson Crusoe on Mars. Schenck-Zabel, 1964. Director Byron Haskin. Writers Daniel Defoe (novel); John Higgins and Ib Melchior (screenplay).

"Specimen Unknown." *The Outer Limits.* ABC-TV, February 24, 1964. Director Gert Oswald. Writers Stephen Lord (story); Lord and Joseph Stefano (teleplay).

Voyage to the End of the Universe. American version of *Ikarie XB 1* (1963) (q.v.) with new footage. American International, 1964. American director and writer unknown.

1965

"Anybody Here See Jeannie?" *I Dream of Jeannie.* NBC-TV, October 30, 1965. Director Gene Nelson. Writer Andrew Horwltt.

Dos Cosmonautas a la Fuerza. (*002 Operazione Luna*) Spanish-Italian. IMA, 1965. Director Lucio Fulci. Writers Vittorio Metz and Amedeo Sollazzo (story); José Luis Dibildos, Metz, and Sollazzo (screenplay).

I Criminali della Galassia. (*The Wild, Wild Planet*) Italian. Mercury, 1965. Director Antonio Margheriti. Writers Renato Moretti and Ivan Reiner.

"The Derelict." *Lost in Space.* CBS-TV, September 22, 1965. Director Alexander Singer. Writer Shimon Wincelberg (story); Peter Packer (teleplay).

Frankenstein Meets the Spacemonster. Vernon-Seleca, 1965. Director Robert Gaffney. Writers R.H.W. Dillard, George Garrett, and John Rodenbeck.

Gemini 4, Film of Edward White spacewalk. Taken June 3, 1965.

Gigantes Planetarios. (*Planetary Giants*) Mexico. Corsa, 1965. Director Alfredo Crevenna. Writers Alfredo Ruanova (story); Emilio Goméz Muriel (screenplay).

I Dream of Jeannie. [TV series] NBC-TV, 1965–1970. Episodes involving spacesuits are separately cited.

"Island in the Sky." *Lost in Space.* CBS-TV, September 29, 1965. Director Anton Leader. Writer Shimon Wincelberg (story); Norman Lessing (teleplay).

Kaijû Daisensô. (*Godzilla vs. Monster Zero, Monster Zero*) Toho, 1965. Director Ishirô Honda. Writer Shinichi Sekizawa.

"The Lady in the Bottle." *I Dream of Jeannie.* NBC-TV, September 18, 1965. Director Gene Nelson. Writer Sidney Sheldon.

Lost in Space. [TV series] CBS-TV, 1965–1968. Episodes involving spacesuits are separately cited.

Luna. (*The Moon*) [documentary] Russian. Leningrad Popular Science, 1965. Director Pavel Klushantsev.

Mutiny in Outer Space. Hugo Grimaldi, 1965. Directors Hugo Grimaldi and Arthur Pierce (uncredited). Writer Pierce.

"Nyet, Nyet, Not Yet." *Gilligan's Island.* CBS-TV, November 18, 1965. Director Jack Arnold. Writers Robert Riordan and Adele T. Strassfield.

"The Reluctant Stowaway." *Lost in Space.* CBS-TV, September 15, 1965. Director Anton Leader. Writer Shimon Wincelberg.

Sergeant Dead Head. American International, 1965. Director Norman Taurog. Writer Louis M. Heyward.

Space Monster. American International TV, 1965. Director Leonard Katzman. Writer Katzman.

Terrore nello Spazio. (*Planet of the Vampires*) American-Italian-Spanish. American International, 1965. Director Mario Bava. Writers Renato Pestriniero (story); Bava, Alberto Bevilacqua, Callisto Cosulich, Antonio Román, and Rafael Salvia (original screenplay); Louis M. Heyward and Ib Melchior (English screenplay).

Voskhod 2, Film of Alexei Leonov spacewalk. Taken March 19, 1965.

Voyage to the Prehistoric Planet. American version of *Planeta Bur* (1962) (q.v.) with new footage. American International, 1965. American director Curtis Harrington. American writer Harrington.

The Wizard of Mars. American General, 1965. Director David L. Hewitt. Writers L. Frank Baum (novels, uncredited); Armando Busick and Hewitt (story); Hewitt (screenplay).

1966

"Angriff aus dem All." ("Attack from Space") *Raumpatrouille: Die Phantastischen Abenteuer des Raumschiffes Orion.* (*Space Patrol*) Munich: ARD, September 17, 1966. Director Michael Braun. Writers Rolf Honold, Braun, Hans Gottschalk, Helmut Krapp, Theo Mezger, and Oliver Storz (the latter five collectively cited as W.G. Larsen).

I Diafanoidi Portano la Morte. (*War of the Planets*) Italian. Mercury, 1966. Director Antonio Margheriti. Writers Renato Moretti and Ivan Reiner.

"Happy Anniversary." *I Dream of Jeannie.* NBC-TV, September 12, 1966. Director Claudio Guzman. Writer Sidney Sheldon.

"Hüter des Gesetzes." ("Guardian of the Law") *Raumpatrouille: Die Phantastischen Abenteuer des Raumschiffes Orion.* (*Space Patrol*) Munich: ARD, October 15, 1966. Director Theo Mezger. Writers Rolf Honold, Michael Braun, Hans Gottschalk, Helmut Krapp, Mezger, and Oliver Storz (the latter five collectively cited as W.G. Larsen).

"One Way to the Moon." *The Time Tunnel.* ABC-TV, September 16, 1966. Director Harry Harris. Writer William Welch.

Il Pianeta Errante. (*War Between the Planets*) Italian. Mercury, 1966. Director Antonio Margheriti. Writers Renato Moretti and Ivan Reiner.

"Planet ausser Kurs." ("Planet Off Course") *Raumpatrouille: Die Phantastischen Abenteuer des Raumschiffes Orion.* (*Space Patrol*) Munich: ARD, October 1, 1966. Director Theo Mezger. Writers Rolf

Honold, Michael Braun, Hans Gottschalk, Helmut Krapp, Mezger, and Oliver Storz (the latter five collectively cited as W.G. Larsen).

El Planeta de las Mujeres Invasoras. (*Planet of the Female Invaders*) Mexican. Corsa, 1966. Director Alfredo Crevenna. Writers Emilio Gómez Muriel and Alfredo Ruanova.

Queen of Blood. American version of *Mechte Navstrechu* (1963) (q.v.) with new footage. Cinema West, 1966. American director Curtis Harrington. American writer Harrington.

Raumpatrouille: Die Phantastischen Abenteuer des Raumschiffes Orion. (*Space Patrol*) [TV series] Munich: ARD, 1966. Episodes involving spacesuits are separately cited.

Star Trek. [TV series] NBC-TV, 1966–1969. An episode involving spacesuits is separately cited.

2 + 5: Missione Hydra. (*Star Pilot*) Italian. Golden, 1966. Director Pietro Francisci. Writers Fernando Paolo Girolami (story); Francisci (screenplay); Ian Danby (English screenplay).

Way...Way Out. Coldwater, 1966. Director Gordon Douglas. Writers William Bowers and László Vadnay.

"Wild Adventure." *Lost in Space.* CBS-TV, September 21, 1966. Director Don Richardson. Writers Allan Balter and Walter Read Woodfield.

1967

Automat na Prání. (*The Wishing Machine*) Czechoslovakian. Gottwaldov, 1967. Director Josef Pinkava. Writer Pinkava.

"Condemned of Space." *Lost in Space.* CBS-TV, September 6, 1967. Director Nathan Juran. Writer Peter Packer.

...4...3...2...1...Morte. (*Perry Rhodan—SOS aus dem Weltall, Alarm im Weltall, Órbita Mortal, Mission Stardust*) Spanish-Italian. Aitor, 1967. Director Primo Zeglio. Writers K.H. Scheer and Clark Darlton [Walter Ernsting] (novels); Kurt Vogelmann (story); Federico De Urrutia, Sergio Donati, Karlheinz Scheer, Vogelmann, and Zeglio (screenplay).

In Like Flint. Twentieth Century–Fox, 1967. Director Gordon Douglas. Writer Hal Fimberg.

Jules Verne's Rocket to the Moon. (*Those Fantastic Flying Fools*) Jules Verne, 1967. Director Don Sharp. Writers Jules Verne ("writings"); Harry Alan Towers (story); Dave Freeman (screenplay).

La Morte Viene dal Pianeta Aytin. (*The Snow Devils*) Italian. Mercury, 1967. Director Antonio Margheriti. Writers Renato Moretti, Ivan Reiner, Bill Finger (uncredited), and Audrey Wisberg (uncredited) (story); Moretti, Reiner and Margheriti (screenplay).

The Reluctant Astronaut. Universal, 1967. Director Edward Montagne. Writers James Fritzell and Everett Greenbaum.

Taekoesu Yonggary. (*Yongary, Monster from the Deep*) South Korean-Japanese. Kuk Dong and Toei, 1967. Director Yi-Duk Kim. Writers Kim and Yun-Sung Seo.

The Terrornauts. Amicus, 1967. Director Montgomery Tully. Writers Murray Leinster (novel); John Brunner (screenplay).

Tumannost Andromedy. (*The Andromeda Nebula*) Russian. Dovzhenko, 1967. Director Yevgeny Sherstobitov. Writers Ivan Efremov (novel); Sherstobitov (screenplay).

Uchû Daikaijû Girara. (*The X from Outer Space*) Japanese. Shôchiku Eiga, 1967. Director Kazui Nihonmatsu. Writers Moriyoshi Ishida, Eibi Motomochi, and Nihonmatsu.

Voyage to the Planet of Prehistoric Women. Second American version of *Planeta Bur* (1962) (q.v.), with footage from *Nebo Zovyot* (1959) (q.v.) and new footage. Filmgroup, 1967. American director Peter Bogdanovich. American writer Henry Nye.

You Only Live Twice. United Artists, 1967. Director Lewis Gilbert. Writers Ian Fleming (uncredited) (novel); Harold Jack Bloom (story); Roald Dahl (screenplay).

1968

Barbarella. Dino de Laurentiis, 1968. Director Roger Vadim. Writers Claude Brulé and Jean-Claude Forest (comic); Vittorio Bonicelli, Brian Degas, Forest, Tudor Gates, Terry Southern, Vadim, and Clement Biddle Wood (screenplay).

Countdown. Warner Brothers, 1968. Director Robert Altman. Writers Hank Searls (novel); Loring Mandel (screenplay).

The Green Slime. MGM/Toei, 1968. Director Kinji Fukasaku. Writers Bill Finger and Ivan Reiner (story); Tom Rowe and Charles Sinclair (screenplay).

"Haven't I Seen Me Someplace Before?" *I Dream of Jeannie.* NBC-TV, March 23, 1968. Director Claudio Guzman. Writer Martin Roth.

Kaijû Sôshingeki. (*Destroy All Monsters*) Toho, 1968. Director Ishirô Honda. Writers Honda and Takeshi Kimura.

Mission Mars. Red Ram, 1968. Director Nicholas Webster. Writers Aubrey Wisberg (story); Michael St. Clair (screenplay).

"Operation: First Couple on the Moon." *I Dream of Jeannie.* NBC-TV, March 16, 1968. Director Claudio Guzman. Writer Arthur Julian.

"The Tholian Web." *Star Trek.* NBC-TV, November 15, 1968. Director Herb Wallenstein. Writers Judy Burns and Chet Richards.

2001: A Space Odyssey. MGM, 1968. Director Stanley Kubrick. Writers Kubrick and Arthur C. Clarke.

1969

Apollo 11*,* Television coverage of Neil Armstrong and Buzz Aldrin moon walk. Shown on all major networks on July 20, 1969.

Apollo 12*,* Television coverage of Charles Conrad and Alan Bean moon walk. Shown on all major networks on November 19, 1969.

"Around the World in 80 Blinks." *I Dream of Jeannie.* NBC-TV, March 24, 1969. Director Claudio Guzman. Writer James Henerson.

Döppelganger. (*Journey to the Far Side of the Sun*) British. Century 21, 1969. Director Robert Parrish. Writers Gerry Anderson and Sylvia Anderson (story); Gerry Anderson, Sylvia Anderson, and Donald James (screenplay).

Marooned. Columbia, 1969. Director John Sturges. Writers Martin Caidin (novel); Mayo Simon (screenplay).

Moon Zero Two. Warner Brothers, 1969. Director Roy Ward Baker. Writers Martin Davison, Frank Hardman, and Gavin Lyall (story); Michael Carreras (screenplay).

II. UNSEEN SPACESUIT FILMS, 1918–1969

"The Astronaut." *R3.* London: BBC-TV, February 6, 1964. Director Terence Williams. Writer N. J. Crisp.

"The Case of the Angry Astronaut." *Perry Mason.* CBS-TV, April 7, 1962. Director Francis Lyon. Writer Samuel Newman.

The Clear Horizon. [TV series] CBS-TV, 1960–1961, 1962.

"Clem and the Satellite." *The Red Skelton Hour.* CBS-TV, October 7, 1958.

Commando Cody: Sky Marshal of the Universe. [serial] Republic, 1953. [Whether this serial actually appeared in theaters is debated.] Later aired on television as *Commander Cody: Sky Marshal of the Universe.* NBC-TV, 1955.

It's About Time. [TV series] CBS-TV, 1966–1967.

"José, the Astronaut." *The Bill Dana Show.* NBC-TV, December, 1, 1963. Director Coby Ruskin. Writer Don Hinkley.

"Junior Astronaut." *Dennis the Menace.* CBS-TV, January 13, 1963. Director Jeffrey Hayden. Writers Jay Sommers and Joe Bigelow.

Klaun Ferdinand a Raketa. (*Clown Ferdinand and the Rocket*) Czechoslovakian. Barrandov, 1962. Director Jindrich Polák. Writers Ota Hofman and Polák.

"Lucy Becomes an Astronaut." *The Lucy Show.* CBS-TV, November 5, 1962. Director Jack Donohue. Writers Madelyn Pugh, Bob Schiller, Bob Carroll, Jr., and Bob Weiskopf.

"McKeever's Astronaut." *McKeever and the Colonel.* NBC-TV, January 13, 1963. Director John Rich. Writer unknown.

"Meteor." *Captain Z-Ro.* Syndicated: April 15, 1956. Director David Butler. Writer unknown.

Muz z Prvniho Stoleti. (*The Man from the First Century*) Czechoslovakian. Barrandov, 1961. Director Oldrich Lipský. Writers Lipský (story); Lipský, Zdenek Bláha, Milos Fiola, and Jan Fiser (screenplay).

Pasi Spre Luna. (*Steps to the Moon*) Romanian. Bucuresti, 1963. Director Ion Popescu-Gopo. Writer Popescu-Gopo.

Pathfinders to Mars. [TV miniseries] London: ABC Weekend Entertainment, 1960–1961.

Pathfinders to Space. [TV miniseries] London: ABC Weekend Entertainment, 1960.

Pathfinders to Venus. [TV miniseries] London: ABC Weekend Entertainment, 1961.

"Pop the Astronaut." *The Red Skelton Hour.* CBS-TV, September 30, 1969. Director unknown. Writers George Balzer, Fred Fox, Mort Greene, Seaman Jacobs, Bob Mott, Dave O'Brien, Robert Orben, Arthur Phillips, Mike Settle, and Skelton.

"Queen of Mars." *The Red Skelton Hour.* CBS-TV, February 1, 1955. Director and writer unknown.

"Robotic Astronaut." *My Living Doll.* CBS-TV, February 3, 1965. Director Ezra Stone. Writer unknown.

Rod Brown of the Rocket Rangers. [TV series] CBS-TV, 1953–1954.

Space School. [TV miniseries] London: BBC-TV, 1956.

"Spaceville." *The Many Loves of Dobie Gillis.* ABC-TV, April 25, 1961. Director Rod Amateau. Writer Arnold Horwitt.

Target Luna. [TV miniseries] London: ABC Weekend Entertainment, 1960.

III. SPACESUIT FILMS, 1970 TO THE PRESENT

1970

UFO. [TV series] London: ITV, 1970–1973.

1971

Apollo 14, Television coverage of Alan Shepard and Edgar Mitchell moon walks. Shown on all major networks on February 5 and 6, 1971.

Apollo 15, Television coverage of David Scott and James Irwin moon walks. Shown on all major networks on July 31, August 1 and August 2, 1971.

Earth II. [TV movie] ABC-TV, November 28, 1971. Director Tom Gries. Writers Allan Balter and William Read Woodfield.

Escape from the Planet of the Apes. Twentieth Century–Fox, 1971. Director Don Taylor. Writer Paul Dehn.

1972

Apollo 16, Television coverage of John Young and Charles Duke moon walks. Shown on all major networks on April 21, 22 and 23, 1972.

Apollo 17, Television coverage of Eugene Cernan and Harrison Schmidt moon walks. Shown on all major networks on December 11, 12 and 13, 1972.

The Astronaut. [TV movie] ABC-TV, 1972. Director Robert Michael Lewis. Writers Robert Biheller and Charles Kuenstle (story); Biheller, Gerald Di Pego, and Kuenstle (screenplay).

Solaris. Mosfilms, 1971. Director Andrey Tarkovskiy. Writers Stanislaw Lem (novel); Fridrikh Gorenshtein, and Tarkovskiy (screenplay).

1974

Houston, We've Got a Problem. [TV movie] ABC-TV, March 2, 1974. Director Lawrence Doheny. Writer Dick Nelson.

1975

Far Out Space Nuts. [TV series] CBS-TV, 1975–1976.

Space: 1999. [TV series] ITC: 1975–1977.

Stowaway to the Moon. [TV movie] CBS-TV, January 10, 1975. Director Andrew McLaglen. Writers William Shelton (novel); Jon Boothe (screenplay).

1976

Return to Earth. [TV movie] ABC-TV, May 14, 1976. Director Jud Taylor. Writers Buzz Aldrin and Wayne Warga (book); George Malko (screenplay).

1977

Alternative 3. [TV movie] London: Anglia, June 20, 1977. Director Christopher Miles. Writers David Ambrose and Miles.

Capricorn One. Associated General, 1977. Director Peter Hyams. Writer Hyams.

Space Academy. [TV series] CBS-TV, 1977.

The Incredible Melting Man. American International, 1977. Director William Sachs. Writer Sachs.

1978

Fehmi the Astronaut. Turkish, 1978. Director Naki Yurter. Writer Recep Filiz.

1979

Alien. Brandywine, 1979. Director Ridley Scott. Writers Dan O'Bannon and Ronald Shusett (story); O'Bannon (screenplay).

"Golden Orbit." [two-part episode] *Salvage 1.* ABC-TV, March 12 and March 19, 1979. Director Ron Satlof. Writer Robert Swanson.

Moonraker. United Artists, 1979. Director Lewis Gilbert. Writers Ian Fleming (novel, uncredited); Christopher Wood (screenplay).

"Salvage." *Salvage 1.* ABC-TV, January 20, 1979. Director Lee Phillips. Writer Mike Lloyd Ross.

Salvage 1. [TV series] ABC-TV, 1979. Episodes involving spacesuits are separately cited.

Star Trek: The Motion Picture. Paramount, 1979. Director Robert Wise. Writers Alan Dean Foster (story); Harold Livingston (screenplay).

1980

Contamination. (*Alien Contamination*) Italian-West German. Alex, 1980. Director Luigi Cozzi. Writers Cozzi (story); Cozzi and Erich Tomek (screenplay).

The Martian Chronicles. [TV miniseries] NBC-TV, January 27–29, 1980. Director Michael Anderson. Writer Richard Matheson.

Superman II. Warner Brothers, 1980. Directors Richard Lester and Richard Donner (uncredited). Writers Mario Puzo (story); David Newman, Leslie Newman, Puzo, and Tom Mankiewicz (uncredited) (screenplay).

1981

Outland. Ladd, 1981. Director Peter Hyams. Writer Hyams.

1983

The Right Stuff. Ladd, 1983. Director Philip Kaufman. Writers Tom Wolfe (book); Kaufman (screenplay).

Terms of Endearment. Paramount, 1983. Director James Brooks. Writers Larry McMurtry (novel); Brooks (screenplay).

1984

Space. [TV miniseries] CBS-TV, April 14, 1985. Directors Lee Phillips and Joseph Sargent. Writers James Michener (novel); Richard Berg and Stirling Silliphant (screenplay).

2010: The Year We Make Contact. MGM, 1984. Director Peter Hyams. Writers Arthur C. Clarke (novel); Hyams (screenplay).

1985

I Dream of Jeannie...Fifteen Years Later. [TV movie] NBC-TV, October 20, 1985. Director William Asher. Writers Irma Kalish, Dinah Kirgo, and Julie Kirgo (story); Kalish (teleplay).

1986

Aliens. Brandywine, 1986. Director James Cameron. Writers Cameron, David Giler, and Walter Hill (story); Cameron (screenplay).

Space Truckers. Goldcrest, 1986. Director Stuart Gordon. Writers Gordon and Ted Mann (story); Mann (screenplay).

SpaceCamp. ABC-TV, 1986. Director Harry Winer. Writers Patrick Bailey and Larry Williams (story); Clifford Green and Casey Mitchell (screenplay).

1987

Star Cops. [TV series] BBC-TV, 1987.

1990

Solar Crisis. Japan America, 1990. Director Richard Safarian (as Alan Smithee). Writers Takeshi Kawata (novel); Joe Gannon and Crispan Bolt (screenplay).

Total Recall. Carolco, 1990. Director Paul Verhoeven. Writers Philip K. Dick (story); Ronald Shusett, Dan O'Bannon, and Jon Povill (screen story); Shusett, O'Bannon, and Gary Goldman (screenplay).

1991

I Still Dream of Jeannie. [TV movie] NBC-TV, October 20, 1991. Director Joseph Scanlan. Writer April Kelly.

1992

Alien³. Brandywine, 1992. Director David Fincher. Writers Vincent Ward (story); David Giler, Walter Hill, and Larry Ferguson (screenplay).

1993

Living and Working in Space: The Countdown Has Begun. [TV documentary] PBS, March 31, 1993.

1995

Apollo 13. Universal, 1995. Director Ron Howard. Writers Jim Lovell and Jeffrey Kluger (book); William Broyles, Jr., and Al Reinert (screenplay).

The Outer Limits. [TV series] Showtime, 1995–2002. Episodes probably involving spacesuits are separately cited.

Space: Above and Beyond [TV series] Fox, 1995–1996.

"**The Voyage Home.**" *The Outer Limits.* Showtime, June 30, 1995. Director Tibor Takács. Writer Grant Rosenberg.

1996

Apollo 11. [TV movie] Family Channel, November 17, 1996. Director Norberto Barba. Writer Phil Penningroth.

The Cape. [TV series] Syndicated, 1996–1997.

1997

Alien Resurrection. Brandywine, 1997. Director Jean-Pierre Jeunet. Writer Joss Whedon.

Event Horizon. Golar, 1997. Director Paul W.S. Anderson. Writer Philip Eisner.

RocketMan. Caravan Pictures, 1997. Director Stuart Gillard. Writers Oren Aviv, Greg Erb, and Craig Mazin (story); Erb and Mazin (screenplay).

1998

Armageddon. Touchstone, 1998. Director Michael Bay. Writers Jonathan Hensleigh and Robert Roy Pool (story); Tony Gilroy and Shane Salerno (adaptation); J.J. Abrams and Hensleigh (screenplay).

Deep Impact. Paramount, 1998. Director Mimi Leder. Writers Bruce Joel Rubin and Michael Tolkin.

From the Earth to the Moon. [TV miniseries] HBO, April 5–May 10, 1998.

"**Phobos Rising.**" *The Outer Limits.* Showtime, December 4, 1998. Director Helen Shaver. Writer Garth Gerald Wilson.

1999

The Astronaut's Wife. New Line, 1999. Director Rand Ravich. Writer Ravich.

Fortress 2: Re-Entry. TriStar, 1999. Director Geoff Murphy. Writers Steven Feinberg and Troy Neighbors (story); John Flock and Peter Doyle (screenplay).

"Joyride." *The Outer Limits.* Showtime, February 26, 1999. Director James Head. Writers Dan Wright, David Alexander, and Sam Egan (story); Egan (teleplay).

2000

Mission to Mars. Touchstone, 2000. Director Brian De Palma. Writers Lowell Cannon, Jim Thomas and John Thomas (story); Jim Thomas, John Thomas, and Graham Yost (screenplay).

Red Planet. Warner Brothers, 2000. Director Anthony Hoffman. Writer Chuck Pfarrer (story); Pfarrer and Jonathan Lemkin (screenplay).

Space Cowboys. Clipsal, 2000. Director Clint Eastwood. Writers Ken Kaufman and Howard Klausner.

Supernova. United Artists, 2000. Director Walter Hill (as Thomas Lee), Francis Ford Coppola (uncredited), and Jack Sholder (uncredited). Writers William Malone and Daniel Chuba (story); David Wilson (screenplay).

2001

The American Astronaut. BNS, 2001. Director Cory McAbee. Writer McAbee.

Star Trek: Enterprise. [TV series] UPN, 2001–2005.

Stranded. Niggeman IndieFilms, 2001. Director María Lidón. Writer Juan Miguel Aguilera.

"The Vessel." *The Outer Limits.* Showtime, April 13, 2001. Director Jimmy Kaufman. Writer Sam Egan.

2002

The Adventures of Pluto Nash. Warner Brothers, 2002. Director Ron Underwood. Writer Neil Cuthbert.

"Human Trials." *The Outer Limits.* Showtime, January 18, 2002. Director Brad Turner. Writers Harlan Ellison and A. E. van Vogt (original story); Grady Hall and Brian Nohr (television story); Mark Stern (teleplay); Chris Ruppenthal, Michael Sadowski, Naren Shankar, and Tracy Tormé (excerpts).

Odyssey 5. [TV series] Science Fiction Channel, 2002–2004.

Solaris. Twentieth Century–Fox, 2002. Director Steven Soderbergh. Writer Soderbergh.

2004

Battlestar Galactica. [TV series] Sci-Fi Channel, 2004–2009.

2005

The Quatermass Experiment. [TV movie] London: BBC-4, April 2, 2005. Director Sam Miller. Writers Nigel Kneale (original teleplay); Richard Fell (adaptation).

Zathura: A Space Adventure. Columbia, 2005. Director Jon Favreau. Writers Chris Van Allsburg (book); David Koepp and John Kamps (screenplay).

2006

The Astronaut Farmer. Warner Brothers, 2006. Director Michael Polish. Writers Mark Polish and Michael Polish.

2007

Sunshine. DNA, 2007. Director Danny Boyle. Writer Alex Garland.

2008

Battle Planet. NightLight, 2008. Director Zach Ward. Writer Ward.

Ella and the Astronaut. [short] 2008. Directors Robert Machoian and Rodrigo Ojeda-Beck. Writers Machoian and Ojeda-Beck.

Fly Me to the Moon. nWave, 2008. Director Ben Stassen. Writer Domonic Paris.

Sea of Tranquility. [short] 2008. Director J.P. Bolles. Writers Ryan Sheffer (story); Bolles and Lex White (story and screenplay).

Wall-E. Pixar/Disney, 2008. Director Andrew Stanton. Writers Pete Docter and Stanton (story); Jim Reardon and Stanton (screenplay).

2009

Defying Gravity. [TV miniseries] ABC-TV, 2009.

Moon. British. Liberty UK, 2009. Director Duncan Jones. Writers Jones (story); Nathan Parker (screenplay).

Moonshot. [TV movie] History Channel, 2009. Director Richard Dale. Writer Tony Basgallop.

Space Buddies. Disney, 2009. Director Robert Vince. Writers Vince, Anna McRoberts, and Phil Hanley.

Virtuality. [TV movie] Fox Channel, June 26, 2009.

2011

Apollo 18. Apollo 18 Productions, 2011. Director Gonzalo López-Gallego. Writers Cory Goodman and Brian Miller.

Green Lantern. Warner Brothers, 2011. Director Martin Campbell. Writers Greg Berlanti, Michael Green, and Marc Guggenheim (story); Berlanti, Green, Guggenheim, and Michael Goldenberg (screenplay).

Transformers: Dark of the Moon. Paramount, 2011. Director Michael Bay. Writer Ehren Kruger.

Chapter Notes

CHAPTER 1

1. Hugo Gernsback, "The $500 Cover Prize Contest," 213.
2. I discuss Méliès's film in "Celebrating a Century of Science Fiction Columns with *A Trip to the Moon*."
3. I viewed the Edition Filmmuseum DVD, with *Himmelskibet* and *Verdens Undergang* (*The End of the World*) (1916), evidently the same version released by the Danish Film Institute in 2006. (As a rule, I will not identify the precise way I watched a film unless it might affect my perceptions of the film.)
4. Like most silent films, *Frau im Mond* exists in several versions of various lengths; I viewed the 2004 Kino DVD release, which is longer (169 minutes) than previously available versions, with English titles by Ingrid Scheib-Rothbart.

CHAPTER 2

1. I discuss links between "Ordeal in Space," *Destination Moon,* and later science fiction films and novels in "Robert A. Heinlein's *2001: A Space Odyssey*."
2. I analyze this film at greater length in "The Dark Side of the Moon: Robert A. Heinlein's *Project Moonbase*."
3. The videotape copy of *Riders to the Stars* (a color movie) that I viewed was in black-and-white, possibly influencing my assessment of the film.
4. Three instances come to mind: During his Mercury flight, Scott Carpenter irresponsibly wasted fuel on unnecessary maneuvers, threatening his safe return, and was immediately informed he would never fly again. The crew of *Apollo 7*— Wally Schirra, Donn Eisele, and Walter Cunningham — were consistently uncooperative during their flight, and they were not assigned to another mission. Finally, the crew of the third Skylab mission — Gerald Carr, William Pogue, and Edward Gibson — maddened by a daunting schedule of one task after another, squeezed into the final Skylab flight, openly rebelled and refused to obey orders, ensuring they would never work as astronauts again.
5. The episodes of *Men into Space* I watched — in the undated DVD set issued by Vintage Popcorn Theater Television — came from sources of differing quality. Some episodes must have been taped by someone when the series aired in syndication, since one regularly sees the logo of a Channel 12 in the lower right-hand corner. These episodes may be slightly edited, like most programs shown in syndication, to make room for additional commercials. Yet at least three episodes must come directly from the CBS vaults, since they include original commercials for Lucky Strike cigarettes and Gulf Crest gasoline (one with a concluding message from Lundigan himself, praising and puffing on a Lucky Strike), and these are presumably complete and unedited.

CHAPTER 3

1. While "Hit by a Meteorite" was available in a high-quality version on YouTube, "The Space Patrol Code Belt" (aired October 20, 1951), "Threat of the Thormanoids" (aired May 25, 1952), and "The Laughing Alien" (aired March 28, 1953), viewed at the Internet Archive, were of an extraordinarily poor quality, with blurry and sometimes distorted images, and occasionally inaudible or improperly synchronized sound.
2. This situation represents poor planning: Since no one would have a commercial jet fly from New York to Washington with only one pilot on board, it is hard to believe anyone would send a spaceship to Alpha Centauri

with only one pilot. But spacesuit films often employ dubious pretexts to generate drama, and precisely the same problem — having only one crew member who can carry out a vital operation — occurs in a later spacesuit film, *Sunshine* (2007).

3. Among Freiberger's other positive contributions, he retired two of Roddenberry's weakest tropes — voyages to planets that are exactly like past eras of Earth history, and Kirk outwitting a computer — and experimented with surrealistically staged episodes like "Spectre of the Gun" (aired October 25, 1968) and "The Empath" (aired December 6, 1968).

4. Two examples: When Bob Cummings could no longer abide co-star Julie Newmar in the comedy *My Living Doll* (1964–1965), he quit near the end of its only season, and Jack Mullaney's character assumed the lead role; and when Dean Jagger became too ill to play Principal Albert Vane in the drama *Mr. Novak* (1963–1965), an episode wherein he ran unsuccessfully for state superintendent of schools was re-edited to have him win the election, so that Martin Woodbridge (Burgess Meredith) could take his position.

5. An obvious example would be Reagan, who regularly employed quotations from old movies to justify his decisions.

Chapter 4

1. The title "Space Patrol Kids Visit" was surely created after the fact for purposes of identification, since the title appears nowhere in the episode and is inaccurate: Perhaps to avoid complaints from the producers of *Space Patrol*, the episode's space enthusiasts call themselves the Rocket Patrol.

2. In 1954, some three-dimensional comic books were actually published, but none with this exact title. In any event, the publication observed looks more like a tabloid newspaper than a comic book.

3. Another episode of *Love That Bob*, aired November 18, 1958, was entitled "Bob in Orbit," but included no references to space flight.

4. The DVD of this film irksomely cropped off the sign that provided the full name of this institute, otherwise identified only as NARSTI, so the only visible part of the fourth word was "ST." That the missing word is "Studies" is only my conjecture.

Chapter 5

1. This relates to an ongoing issue in spacesuit films: the need to make astronauts seem human and sympathetic, requiring helmets with large, clear visors to keep facial features visible. Sometimes they are even huge transparent spheres. Interestingly, in footage of actual astronauts in spacesuits, the visors tend to be reflective and entirely conceal their features, which may be one reason why support for the space program diminished as such images, not photographs of astronauts on Earth, came to dominate perceptions of space travel.

2. What the man actually says is "some new vary looms up," which is nonsensical unless one assumes he inadvertently omitted syllables from the more logical "variable."

Chapter 6

1. *Automat Na Přání* was released in an English-language version as *The Wishing Machine* in 1971, but that version no longer seems to be available, so I watched the film in its original language, without subtitles. After reviewing several print and online summaries that, based on the evidence of my eyes, were manifestly inaccurate, I am grateful to the Kiddie Matinee website (http://www.kiddiematinee.com/w-wishing.html), which provides a thorough summary that uniquely corresponded to what I watched and cleared up some storyline issues.

2. After its 1963 Czechoslovakian release, this film was severely edited and released in America in 1964 as *Voyage to the End of the Universe*. For recent DVD release, the English-language version restored deleted footage but retained the altered ending. This discussion is based on that version, which sources indicate is faithful to the original story with noted exceptions.

3. Though the Internet Movie Database indicates the film was originally 110 minutes long, the only version I found was 80 minutes, with dubbed English dialogue.

4. The film has so many titles that it is sometimes cited as two separate Perry Rhodan films.

5. Though its title is often translated as *A Trip to the Moon*, the film's actual English title, observed in the opening credits, is *Journey to the Moon*. (As a lingering effect of Egypt's former status as a British colony, Egyptian films of the era routinely provided an "official" English title.)

6. This and a later Mexican film, *Gigantes Planetarios*, were apparently never released with English dubbing or subtitles, so I could only watch them in Spanish. While my limited knowledge of Spanish made these more comprehensible than other foreign-language films I watched in their original languages, my understanding of their stories remains necessarily limited. The brief (and no doubt crude) translations of dialogue are my own.

7. See Gary Westfahl, "Godzilla's Travels: The Evolution of a Globalized Gargantuan."

CHAPTER 8

1. Ballard's stories about space travel in *Memories of the Space Age* (1982) are discussed in my "The Man Who Didn't Need to Walk on the Moon."

2. As discussed at greater length in my "Aye, Robot."

Bibliography

This bibliography lists cited films and television programs that are not spacesuit films, and other cited books and articles.

Aelita: Queen of Mars. Russian. Mezhrabpom-Rus, 1924. Director Yakov Protazanov. Writers Aleksei Tolstoy (play); Aleksei Fajco and Fyodor Otsep (screenplay).
"And When the Sky Was Opened." *The Twilight Zone.* CBS-TV, December 11, 1959. Director Douglas Heyes. Writers Richard Matheson (story); Rod Serling (teleplay).
"Apollo." *I Spy.* NBC-TV, November 20, 1967. Director Earl Bellamy. Writer Ernest Frankel.
"Appointment on Mars." *Tales of Tomorrow.* ABC-TV, June 27, 1952. Director Don Medford. Writer S.A. Lombino.
Around the World in Eighty Days. Michael Todd, 1956. Director Michael Anderson. Writers Jules Verne (novel); James Poe, John Farrow and S.J. Perelman (screenplay).
Asimov, Isaac. "For the Birds." *Isaac Asimov's Science Fiction Magazine*, 4 (May 1980), 82–90.
The Atomic Man. Merton Park, 1955. Director Ken Hughes. Writer Charles Eric Maine (novel and screenplay).
"The Atomic Vault." *Space Patrol.* ABC-TV, February 26, 1955. Director Dik Darley. Writer Norman Jolley.
"Balance of Terror." *Star Trek.* NBC-TV, December 15, 1966. Director Vincent McEveety. Writer Paul Schneider.
"Battle Beyond the Sun." *American Film Institute Catalog: Feature Films, 1961–1970.* Editor Kenneth W. Munden. 1976. Berkeley and Los Angeles: University of California, 1997, 66–67.
Baum, L. Frank. *The Wonderful Wizard of Oz.* 1900. Signet, 1969.
Beneath the Planet of the Apes. Twentieth Century–Fox, 1969. Director Ted Post. Writers Paul Dehn and Mort Abrahams (story); Dehn (screenplay).
"Blast Off into Space." *Lost in Space.* CBS-TV, September 14, 1966. Director Nathan Juran. Writer Peter Packer.
Blish, James. *The Seedling Stars.* 1957. Signet, 1959.
The Blob. Fairview, 1958. Directors Irvin Yeaworth. Writers Irvine Millgate (idea); Theodore Simonson and Kate Phillips (screenplay).
"Bob Goes to the Moon." *Love That Bob.* NBC-TV, April 1, 1958. Director Bob Cummings. Writers Paul Henning, Shirley Gordon and Dick Wesson.
"Bob in Orbit." *Love That Bob.* NBC-TV, November 18, 1958. Director Bob Cummings. Writers Paul Henning and Dick Wesson.
"The Bolts." *Quatermass II.* London: BBC-TV, October 22, 1955. Director Rudolph Cartier. Writer Nigel Kneale.
Bradbury, Ray. *The Martian Chronicles.* 1950. Bantam, 1951.
"The Brain of Colonel Barham." *The Outer Limits.* ABC-TV, January 2, 1965. Director Charles Haas. Writers Sidney Ellis (story); Robert Dennis (teleplay).
Brick Bradford. [serial] Columbia, 1947. Directors Spencer Gordon Bennet and Thomas Carr. Writers Clarence Gray and William Ritt (comic strip); Lewis Clay, Arthur Hoerl, and George Plympton (screenplay).
Buck Rogers. [serial] Universal, 1939. Directors Ford Beebe and Saul Goodkind. Writers Philip Francis Nowlan (comic strip); Dick Calkins, Norman Hall, and Ray Trampe (screenplay).
The Cage. [video] Desilu, 1986. Director Robert Butler. Writer Gene Roddenberry. [original *Star Trek* pilot]
Captain Video and His Video Rangers. [TV series] Dumont, 1949–1955.
"The Chase." *Star Trek: The Next Generation.* Syndicated: April 24, 1993. Director Jonathan Frakes. Writers Joe Menosky and Ronald D. Moore (story); Menosky (teleplay).
Clarke, Arthur C. *Childhood's End.* Ballantine, 1953.
_____. *A Fall of Moondust.* Harcourt, Brace & World, 1961.

———. *Greetings, Carbon-Based Bipeds!: Collected Essays, 1934–1998*. St. Martin's, 1999.
———. "The Other Side of the Sky." 1957. *The Other Side of the Sky*. By Clarke. 1958. Signet, 1959, 26–44.
———. *2001: A Space Odyssey*. Signet, 1968.
———. *2010: Odyssey Two*. Del Rey/Ballantine, 1982.
Clute, John, and Peter Nicholls, eds. *The Encyclopedia of Science Fiction*. St. Martin's, 1993.
"Controlled Experiment." *The Outer Limits*. ABC-TV, January 13, 1964. Director Leslie Stevens. Writer Stevens.
Creature from the Black Lagoon. Universal International, 1954. Director Jack Arnold. Writers Maurice Zimm (story); Harry Essex and Arthur Ross (screenplay).
Crouching Tiger, Hidden Dragon. Asia Union, 2000. Director Ang Lee. Writers Du Lu Wang (book); Hui-Ling Wang, James Schamus, and Kuo Jung Tsai (screenplay).
Davin, Eric Leif. *Pioneers of Wonder: Conversations with the Founders of Science Fiction*. Prometheus, 1999.
The Day of the Triffids. Security, 1962. Directors Steve Sekely and Freddie Francis (uncredited). Writers John Wyndham (novel); Bernard Gordon (screenplay).
Devil Girl from Mars. British. Danziger, 1954. Director David MacDonald. Writers John Mather (play); James Eastwood (screenplay).
Doin' Time on Planet Earth. Cannon, 1988. Director Charles Matthau. Writers Darren Star, Andrew Licht, and Jeffrey Mueller (story); Star (screenplay).
E.T.: The Extra-Terrestrial. Universal, 1982. Director Steven Spielberg. Writer Melissa Mathison.
"Elegy." *The Twilight Zone*. CBS-TV, February 19, 1960. Director Douglas Heyes. Writer Charles Beaumont.
Ellison, Harlan. "That Moon Plaque: Comments from Science Fiction Writers." *Men on the Moon*. Ed. Donald A. Wollheim. Ace Books, 1969, 189–91.
"The Empath." *Star Trek*. NBC-TV, December 6, 1968. Director John Erman. Writer Joyce Muskat.
"Errand of Mercy." *Star Trek*. NBC-TV, March 23, 1967. Director John Newland. Writer Gene L. Coon.
Excursion dans la Lune. (*Excursion to the Moon*) Pathé Frères, 1908. Director Segundo de Chomón. Writer de Chomón.
"The Exploding Stars." *Space Patrol*. ABC-TV, November 13, 1954. Director Dik Darley. Writer Norman Jolley.
Fantastic Voyage. Twentieth Century-Fox, 1966. Director Richard Fleischer. Writers Jerome Bixby and Otto Klement (story); David Duncan (adaptation); Harry Kleiner (screenplay).
Fire Maidens of Outer Space. British. Criterion, 1956. Director Cy Roth. Writer Roth.
Flash Gordon. [serial] Universal, 1936. Directors Frederick Stephani and Ray Taylor. Writers Alex Raymond (comic strip); Basil Dickey, Ella O'Neill, George Plympton, and Stephani (screenplay).
Flash Gordon Conquers the Universe. [serial] Universal, 1940. Directors Ford Beebe and Ray Taylor. Writers Alex Raymond (comic strip); Basil Dickey, George Plympton, and Barry Shipman (screenplay).
Flash Gordon's Trip to Mars. [serial] Universal, 1938. Directors Ford Beebe and Robert Hill. Writers Alex Raymond (comic strip); Herbert Dalmas, Wyndham Gittens, Norman Hall, and Ray Trampe (screenplay).
"Flight Overdue." *Tales of Tomorrow*. ABC-TV, May 28, 1952. Director Don Medford. Writers Jim Lister (story); David Davidson (teleplay).
"The Forbidden World." *Lost in Space*. CBS-TV, September 14, 1966. Director Don Richardson. Writer Barney Slater.
Frankenstein. Universal, 1931. Director James Whale. Writers Mary Shelley (novel); Peggy Webling (play); John L. Balderston (adaptation); Garrett Fort and Francis Edward Faragoh (screenplay).
Franklin, H. Bruce. *Robert A. Heinlein: America as Science Fiction*. Oxford University Press, 1980.
"The Galaxy Being." *The Outer Limits*. ABC-TV, September 16, 1963. Director Leslie Stevens. Writer Stevens.
Gernsback, Hugo. "The $500 Cover Prize Contest." *Amazing Stories*, 2 (June 1927), 213.
———. *Ralph 124C 41+: A Romance of the Year 2660*. 1911–1912. Boston: Stratford, 1925.
———. "Results of $300.00 Scientifiction Prize Contest." *Amazing Stories*, 3 (September 1928), 519 [unsigned].
"The Ghost Planet." *Lost in Space*. CBS-TV, September 28, 1966. Director Nathan Juran. Writer Peter Packer.
Godwin, Tom. "The Cold Equations." 1954. *The Science Fiction Hall of Fame, Volume I*. Ed. Robert Silverberg. 1970. Avon Books, 1971, 543–69.
Godzilla, King of the Monsters! American version of *Gojira* (1954) (q.v.) with new footage. Jewell, 1956. American director Terry Morse. American writer Al Ward.
Gojira. Toho, 1954. Director Ishirô Honda. Writers Shigeru Kayama (story); Honda and Takeo Murata (screenplay). Reedited with new footage as *Godzilla, King of the Monsters!* (1956) (q.v.).
Gojira, Ebirâ, Mosura: Nankai no Daiketto. (*Godzilla vs. the Sea Monster*) Toho, 1966. Director Jun Fukuda. Writer Shinichi Sekizawa.
Goldfinger. United Artists, 1964. Director Guy Hamilton. Writers Ian Fleming (novel); Richard Maibaum and Paul Dehn (screenplay).
Hardy, Phil. *The Encyclopedia of Science Fiction Movies*. 1984. Minneapolis: Woodbury, 1986.
Heinlein, Robert A. *Have Space Suit—Will Travel*. 1958. Ace, 1969.
———. *The Moon Is a Harsh Mistress*. 1966. Berkley, 1968.
———. "Ordeal in Space." 1948. *The Green Hills of Earth*. By Heinlein. 1951. Signet, 1952, 111–24.
———. *Rocket Ship Galileo*. 1947. Ace, 1969.

_____. "Shooting *Destination Moon.*" 1950. *Requiem: New Collected Works by Robert A. Heinlein and Tributes to the Master.* Ed. Yoji Kondo. Tor, 1992, 117–131.
_____. *Space Cadet.* 1948. Ace, 1969.
_____. *Stranger in a Strange Land.* Putnam, 1961.
High Noon. United Artists, 1952. Director Fred Zinnemann Writers John Cunningham (story); Carl Foreman (screenplay).
Invasion of the Body Snatchers. Walter Wanger, 1956. Director Don Siegel. Writers Jack Finney (novel); Donald Mainwaring and Richard Collins (uncredited) (screenplay).
The Invisible Ray. Universal, 1936. Director Lambert Hillyer. Writers Howard Higgin and Douglas Hodges (story); John Colton (screenplay).
Island of Lost Souls. Paramount, 1932. Director Erle C. Kenton. Writers H.G. Wells (novel); Waldemar Young and Philip Wylie (screenplay).
It Came from Outer Space. Universal, 1953. Director Jack Arnold. Writers Ray Bradbury (story); Harry Essex (screenplay).
The Jetsons. [TV series] ABC-TV, 1962–1963; Syndicated, 1985–1987.
Johnny Jupiter. [TV series] ABC-TV, 1953–1954.
Journey to the Center of the Earth. Twentieth Century–Fox, 1959. Director Henry Levin. Writers Jules Verne (novel); Walter Reisch and Charles Brackett (screenplay).
Just Imagine. Fox, 1930. Director David Butler. Writers Lew Brown, Buddy DeSylva and Ray Henderson.
Kaijûtô no Kessen: Gojira no Musuko. (*Son of Godzilla*) Toho, 1967. Director Jun Fukuda. Writers Shinichi Sekizawa and Kazue Shiba.
"The Laughing Alien." *Space Patrol.* ABC-TV, March 28, 1953. Director Dik Darley. Writer Norman Jolley.
Leiber, Fritz. "The Beat Cluster." 1961. *The Seventh Galaxy Reader.* Ed. Frederik Pohl. Doubleday, 1964, 199–214.
_____. *A Specter Is Haunting Texas.* Walker, 1968.
Lem, Stanislaw. *Solaris.* 1961. Trans. Joanna Kilmartin and Steve Cox. Faber & Faber, 1971.
Lewis, C.S. "On Science Fiction." *Of Other Worlds: Essays and Stories.* By Lewis. Ed. Walter Hooper. 1966. Harcourt Brace Jovanovich, 1975, 59–73.
"The Lonely." *The Twilight Zone.* CBS-TV, November 13, 1959. Director Jack Smight. Writer Rod Serling.
The Lost Planet. [serial] Columbia, 1953. Director Spencer Gordon Bennet. Writers George Plympton and Arthur Hoerl (story).
The Lost World. Twentieth Century–Fox, 1960. Director Irwin Allen. Writers Arthur Conan Doyle (novel); Allen and Charles Bennett (screenplay).
"Man in Space." *Disneyland.* ABC-TV, March 9, 1955. Director Ward Kimball. Writers Heinz Haber (book, uncredited); William Bosche and Kimball (teleplay).
"The Man with the Power." *The Outer Limits.* ABC-TV, October 7, 1963. Director Laslo Benedek. Writer Jerome Ross.
"Mars and Beyond." *Disneyland.* ABC, December 4, 1957. Director Ward Kimball. Writers William Bosche, Chuck Downs, John Dunn, Kimball, and Con Pederson.
Un Matrimonio Interplanetario. Italian. Latium, 1910. Director Enrico Novelli. Writer Novelli.
Metropolis. Universum, 1927. Director Fritz Lang. Writers Thea von Harbou (novel); von Harbou and Lang (uncredited) (screenplay).
"The Mice." *The Outer Limits.* ABC-TV, January 6, 1964. Director Alan Crosland, Jr. Writers Bill Ballinger and Lou Morheim (story); Ballinger and Joseph Stefano (teleplay).
Michener, James. *Space.* Random House, 1982.
El Moderno Barba Azul. (*Boom in the Moon*) Mexican. Alsa, 1946. Director Jaime Salvador. Writers Salvador and Victor Trivas.
The Mouse That Roared. Columbia, 1959. Director Jack Arnold. Writers Leonard Wibberley (novel); Roger MacDougall and Stanley Mann (screenplay).
"The Mutant." *The Outer Limits.* ABC-TV, March 16, 1964. Director Alan Crosland, Jr. Writers Jerome Thomas (story); Allan Balter and Robert Mintz (teleplay).
Mysterious Island. Columbia, 1961. Director Cy Endfield. Writers Jules Verne (novel); John Prebble, Daniel Ullman, and Crane Wilbur (screenplay).
"Nightmare." *The Outer Limits.* ABC-TV, December 2, 1963. Director John Erman. Writer Joseph Stefano.
"Obsession." *Star Trek.* NBC-TV, December 15, 1967. Director Ralph Senensky. Writer Art Wallace.
"On Thursday We Leave for Home." *The Twilight Zone.* CBS-TV, May 2, 1963. Director Buzz Kulik. Writer Rod Serling.
Pajama Party. American International, 1964. Director Don Weis. Writer Louis M. Heyward.
"People Are Alike All Over." *The Twilight Zone.* CBS-TV, March 25, 1960. Director Mitchell Leisen. Writers Paul Fairman (story); Rod Serling (teleplay).
A Pied, à Cheval et en Spoutnik. (*A Dog, a Mouse, and a Sputnik, Sputnik*) French. Films Around the World, 1958. Director Jean Dréville. Writers Noël-Noël and Jean-Jacques Vital (story); Jacques Grello, Noël-Noël, and Robert Rocca (screenplay).

Planet of the Apes. Twentieth Century–Fox, 1968. Director Franklin J. Schaffner. Writers Pierre Boulle (novel); Michael Wilson and Rod Serling (screenplay).
Pohl, Frederik. *Man-Plus*. 1976. Bantam, 1977.
Preminger, Megan. *Another Science Fiction: Advertising the Space Race 1957–1962*. Blast, 2010.
"Probe 7 — Over and Out." *The Twilight Zone*. CBS-TV, November 29, 1963. Director Ted Post. Writer Rod Serling.
The Producers. Crossbow, 1968. Director Mel Brooks. Writer Brooks.
Quatermass II. (*Enemy from Space*) Hammer, 1957. Director Val Guest. Writers Nigel Kneale and Guest.
San Daikaijû: Chikyû Saidai no Kessen. (*Ghidrah, the Three-Headed Monster*) Toho, 1964. Director Ishirô Honda. Writer Shinichi Sekizawa.
Schow, David J., and Jeffrey Frentzen. *The Outer Limits: The Official Companion*. Ace, 1986.
"The Sixth Finger." *The Outer Limits*. ABC-TV, October 14, 1963. Director James Goldstone. Writer Ellis St. Joseph.
Spaceflight IC-1: An Adventure in Space. Lippert, 1965. Director Bernard Knowles. Writer Harry Spalding.
"Spectre of the Gun." *Star Trek*. NBC-TV, October 25, 1968. Director Vincent McEveety. Writer Gene L. Coon.
Stapledon, Olaf. *Last and First Men*. 1930. London: Methuen, 1978.
Star Trek II: The Wrath of Khan. Paramount, 1982. Director Nicolas Meyer. Writers Harve Bennett, Jack Sowards, and Samuel Peeples (uncredited) (story); Sowards and Meyer (uncredited) (screenplay).
Star Wars. Twentieth Century–Fox, 1977. Director George Lucas. Writer Lucas.
Steele, Allan. *Orbital Decay*. Ace, 1989.
Stranger from Venus. British. Rich and Rich, 1954. Director Burt Balaban. Writers Desmond Leslie (story); Hans Jacoby (screenplay).
Swift, Jonathan. *Gulliver's Travels*. 1721. Lancer, 1968.
"Test Flight." *Tales of Tomorrow*. ABC-TV, October 26, 1951. Director Charles Dubin. Writers Nelson Bond (story); Mel Goldberg (teleplay).
The Thing (from Another World). Winchester, 1951. Directors Christian Nyby and Howard Hawks (uncredited). Writers John W. Campbell, Jr. (story); Charles Lederer, Hawks (uncredited), and Ben Hecht (uncredited) (screenplay).
Things to Come. British. London, 1936. Director William Cameron Menzies. Writer H.G. Wells (novel and screenplay).
"Third from the Sun." *The Twilight Zone*. CBS-TV, January 8, 1960. Director Richard Bare. Writers Richard Matheson (story); Rod Serling (teleplay).
This Island Earth. Universal, 1955. Directors Joseph Newman. Writer Raymond F. Jones (novel); Franklin Coen and Edward O'Callaghan (screenplay).
Thomson, David. *The New Biographical Dictionary of Film*. Alfred A. Knopf, 2004.
Those Magnificent Men in Their Flying Machines. Twentieth Century–Fox, 1965. Director Ken Annakin. Writers Annakin and Jack Davies.
"Threat of the Thormanoids." *Space Patrol*. ABC-TV, May 25, 1952. Director Dik Darley. Writer Norman Jolley.
The Three Stooges in Orbit. Normandy, 1962. Director Edward Bernds. Writers Norman Maurer (story); Elwood Ullman (screenplay).
The Time Machine. MGM, 1960. Director George Pal. Writers H. G. Wells (novel); David Duncan (screenplay).
The Trollenberg Terror. (*The Crawling Eye*) Tempean, 1958. Director Quentin Lawrence. Writers Peter Key (story); Jimmy Sangster (screenplay).
Tsiolkovsky, Konstantin. *Beyond the Planet Earth*. [*Outside the Earth*] 1920. Trans. V. Talmy. *The Call of the Cosmos*. By Tsiolkovsky. Ed. V. Dutt. Foreign Languages Publishing House, [1960], 161–332.
20,000 Leagues Under the Sea. Walt Disney, 1954. Director Richard Fleischer. Writers Jules Verne (novel); Earl Fenton (screenplay).
Uchûjin Tôkyô ni Arawaru. (*Warning from Space*) Japanese. Daiei, 1956. Director Koji Shima. Writers Gentaro Nakajima (novel); Hideo Oguni (screenplay).
van Vogt, A. E. *The Silkie*. Ace, 1969.
Verdens Undergang. (*The End of the World*) Nordisk, 1916. Director August Blom. Writer Otto Rung.
Verne, Jules. *From the Earth to the Moon*. 1865. Trans. Lowell Bair. Bantam, 1993.
Visit to a Small Planet. Paramount, 1960. Director Norman Taurog. Writers Gore Vidal (play); Edmund Beloin and Henry Garson (screenplay).
Le Voyage à Travers l'Impossible. (*The Impossible Voyage*) French. Georges Méliès, 1904. Director Georges Méliès. Writers Jules Verne and Adolphe d'Ennery (play); Méliès (screenplay).
Le Voyage dans la Lune. (*A Trip to the Moon*) French. Georges Méliès, 1902. Director Georges Méliès. Writers Jules Verne and H.G. Wells (novels); Méliès (screenplay).
Voyage sur Jupiter. (*Voyage to Jupiter*) Spanish. Pathé Frères, 1909. Director Segundo de Chomón. Writer de Chomón.
Voyage to the Bottom of the Sea. [TV series] ABC-TV, 1964–1968.
The War of the Worlds. Paramount, 1953. Director Byron Haskin. Writers H.G. Wells (novel); Barré Lyndon (screenplay).

Wells, H. G. *The First Men in the Moon*. 1901. Ballantine, 1964.
_____. *The Time Machine*. 1895. Bantam, 1968.
_____. *The War of the Worlds*. 1898. Berkley, 1964.
Westfahl, Gary. "Aye, Robot: A Review of *Wall-E*." Locus Online, posted June 29, 2008, http://locusmag.com/2008/Westfahl_Wall-E.html.
_____. "Celebrating a Century of Science Fiction Columns with *A Trip to the Moon*." *Interzone*, No. 176 (February 2002), 47–48.
_____. "*Columbia*, and the Dreams of Science Fiction." Locus Online, posted February 2, 2003, http://locusmag.com/2003/Commentary/Westfahl02.html.
_____. "The Dark Side of the Moon: Robert A. Heinlein's *Project Moon Base*." *Extrapolation*, 36 (Summer, 1995), 126–35.
_____. "The Endless Odyssey: The *2001* Saga and Its Inability to Predict Humanity's Future." *Science Fiction and the Prediction of the Future: Essays on Foresight and Fallacy*. Ed. Westfahl, Wong Kin Yuen and Amy Chan Kit-sze. McFarland, 2011, 135–70.
_____. "Godzilla's Travels: The Evolution of a Globalized Gargantuan." *World Weavers: Globalization, Science Fiction, and the Cybernetic Revolution*. Ed. Wong Kin Yuen, Westfahl and Amy Chan Kit-sze. Hong Kong University Press, 2005, 167–88.
_____. *Islands in the Sky: The Space Station Theme in Science Fiction Literature*. Second Edition, Revised and Updated. Borgo Press/Wildside Press, 2009.
_____. "The Man Who Didn't Need to Walk on the Moon: J.G. Ballard and 'The Vanished Age of Space.'" The Internet Review of Science Fiction, posted July 2, 2009, http://irosf.com/q/zine/article/10561.
_____. "Not-So-Close Encounters: *Men into Space* and Their Search for Extraterrestrial Life." The Internet Review of Science Fiction, posted December 11, 2009, http://www.irosf.com/q/zine/article/10614.
_____. "The Odyssey Continues: Relevance of *2001* Resounds in 2001." *Florida Today* (February 11, 2001), 15A.
_____. "Robert A. Heinlein's *2001: A Space Odyssey*." *Interzone*, No. 163 (January 2001), 54–55.
_____. "The True Frontier: Confronting and Avoiding the Realities of Space in American Science Fiction Films." *Space and Beyond: The Frontier Theme in Science Fiction*. Ed. Westfahl. Westport, CT: Greenwood Press, 2000), 55–65.
Wingrove, David. *The Science Fiction Film Source Book*. London: Longman, 1985.
The Wizard of Oz. MGM, 1939. Director Victor Fleming. Writers L. Frank Baum (novel); Noel Langley, Florence Ryerson, and Edgar Allan Woolf (screenplay).
Wolfe, Tom. *The Right Stuff*. Farrar, Straus, Giroux, 1979.
Wright, Bruce Lanier. *Yesterday's Tomorrows: The Golden Age of Science Fiction Movie Posters, 1950–1964*. Dallas: Taylor, 1993.
Yusei Oji. (*The Prince of Space*) Japanese. Toei, 1959. Director Eijiro Wakabayashi. Writers Masaru Igami (story); Shin Morita (screenplay).
"The Zanti Misfits." *The Outer Limits*. ABC-TV, December 30, 1964. Director Leonard Horn. Writer Joseph Stefano.
Zebrowski, George. *Macrolife*. Harper & Row, 1979.

Index

À Pied, à Cheval, et en Spoutnik! 247, 342ch6n3
Abaza, Rushdi 270
Abbott, Bud 11, 140, 144, 146, 147, 151, 164, 169, 171, 173, 246–247, 257, 270
Abbott, Philip 109
Abbott and Costello Go to Mars 144–147, 149, 172, 270, 271
Abbott and Costello Meet Frankenstein 144
Abbott and Costello Meet the Invisible Man 144
Abbott and Costello Meet the Killer, Boris Karloff 144
Ackerman, Forrest J. 245
Adams, Nick 214, 284
Adrian, Max 126
The Adventures of Baron Munchausen 140
The Adventures of Pluto Nash 319
Aelita: Queen of Mars 10, 88, 101
Agar, John 52, 53
Ai, Kyôko 286
Aidman, Charles 52, 292
Alarm in Weltall see ...4...3...2...1...Morte
Albertson, Frank 11
Aldiss, Brian W. 54; Billion Year Spree 54
Aldrin, Buzz 7, 26, 35, 308–312, 316–317; Return to Earth (with Warga) 316
Aletter, Frank 109
Alien 187, 188, 219, 255, 319, 320
Alien films 319, 320
Alien Resurrection 319
Alien³ 319
Aliens 319
Allen, Gracie 141–142, 145
Allen, Irwin 115, 121, 123
Allen Quatermain stories (Haggard) 3
Alternative 3 316
Altman, Robert 292, 293, 294
"Ambush in Space" (Tom Corbett, Space Cadet) 79–80
The American Astronaut 319
American Film Institute Catalog: Feature Films 1961–1970 226–227

Amundsen, Roald 148
Analog: Science Fiction/Science Fact 23
"And When the Sky Was Opened" (The Twilight Zone) 108
Anders, Rudolph 178
Anderson, Gerry 134, 137, 218
Anderson, Sylvia 134, 137, 318
Anderson, Warner 32
The Andromeda Nebula see Tumannost Andromedy
"Angriff aus dem All" (Raumpatrouille) 266
The Angry Red Planet 193–195, 197, 219
Ankrum, Morris 91, 102
Anna-Lisa 110, 148–149
Another Science Fiction: Advertising the Space Race 1957–1962 (Preminger) 281
Ansara, Michael 161
"Apollo" (I Spy) 123
Apollo 11 316; television coverage 7, 26, 290–291, 307–312, 322
Apollo 12 television coverage 7, 312
Apollo 13 316
Apollo 14 television coverage 7, 313
Apollo 15 television coverage 7, 313
Apollo 16 television coverage 7
Apollo 17 television coverage 7, 313
"Appointment on Mars" (Tales of Tomorrow) 80–81
Aranda, Ángel 257
Archer, John 21
Arden, Eve 162–163
Armageddon 317
Armstrong, Neil 7, 26, 57, 58, 132, 308–312, 316–317
Arnold, Jack 179
"Around the World in Eighty Blinks" (I Dream of Jeannie) 161–162
Around the World in Eighty Days 102
Asimov, Isaac 147, 172, 237; "For the Birds" 172
"Assignment: Mercury" (Tom Corbett, Space Cadet) 79
Assignment: Outer Space see Space Men
"Asteroid" (Men into Space) 56, 58–59, 61, 69, 184

"Astray in the Stratosphere" (Captain Video: Master of the Stratosphere) 82
The Astronaut 316
The Astronaut Farmer 316
The Astronauts (East Germany) see Die Schweigende Stern
The Astronauts (Mexico) see Conquistador de la Luna
The Astronaut's Wife 319
Ates, Roscoe 143
The Atomic Man 238
"The Atomic Vault" (Space Patrol) 76
"Attack from Space" (Raumpatrouille) see "Angriff aus dem All"
Automat Na Práni 232–233, 234–236, 342ch6n1
Avalon, Frankie 162, 163
"Aye, Robot" (Westfahl) 343n2

Babylon 5 314
Backus, Jim 158–159
Baird, Philip 110
Baker, Roy Ward 134
Bakewell, William 84
"Balance of Terror" (Star Trek) 139
Ball, Frank P. 56
Ball, Lucille 159
Ballard, J.G. 137, 316, 343n1; Memories of the Space Age 343n1
Bara, Nina 76, 97
Barbarella 131–132
Baron Prášil 232–234
Barrat, Robert 91
Barrie, J.M. 18, 292; Peter Pan 18, 292
Barron, Baynes 210
Barrows, George 176–177
Bartashevich, Konstantin 225
Bartha, John 269
Bartok, Eva 28
Battle Beyond the Sun 225, 228–229, 243
"Battle for the Sun" (Raumpatrouille) see "Der Kampf um die Sonne"
Battle in Outer Space see Uchû Daisensô

Battle of the Worlds see *Il Pianeta degli Uomini Spenti*
Battle Planet 318
Baum, L. Frank 205, 206; *The Wonderful Wizard of Oz* 205, 206
Bava, Mario 256
Bean, Alan 312
"The Beat Cluster" (Leiber) 322
Beaumont, Charles 98
Beck, Vincent 158
Beckett, Scotty 77–78
Beckhaus, Friedrich G. 265
Beery, Noah, Jr. 86
Beir, Fredrick 108
Bender, Russ 210
Beneath the Planet of the Apes 96
Bennett, Joan Sterndale 167
Bernath, Shari Lee 109
Bernhardt, Eve 205
Berry, Charles A. 56
Berserker stories (Saberhagen) 255
Besser, Joe 148
Bey, Tema 110
"Beyond the Curtain of Space" (*Rocky Jones, Space Ranger*) 77–78
Beyond the Planet Earth (Tsiolovsky) 17
"Beyond the Stars" (*Men into Space*) 59–60, 62, 71–72
The Bill Dana Show 159; "José, the Astronaut" 159
Billion Year Spree (Aldiss) 54
A Biographical Dictionary of Film (Thomson) 321
Birch, Paul 98
Bissell, Whit 66
Bixby, Bill 159
Bixby, Jerome 10, 187, 189
Blake, Whitney 52
Blanchard, Mari 147
"Blast Off into Space" (*Lost in Space*) 120
Blish, James 322; *The Seedling Stars* 322
The Blob 232
Blutecher, Alf 12
"Bob Goes to the Moon" (*Love That Bob*) 144
"Bob in Orbit" (*Love That Bob*) 342ch4n3
"Bobby's Comet" (*Rocky Jones, Space Ranger*) 78
"The Bolts" (*Quatermass II*) 183
Bonestell, Chesley 56, 93
Boom on the Moon see *El Moderno Barba Azul*
Boon, Robert 244
Booth, Walter 11
Borisenko, Boris 243
Bradley, David 111
Bradbury, Ray 318; *The Martian Chronicles* 318
Bradley, Wilbert 264
"The Brain of Colonel Barham" (*The Outer Limits*) 199
Brannon, Fred C. 84
Braun, Pinkas 268

Braverman, Bart 186–187
"The Breath of Death" (*Flash Gordon*) 77
Breck, Peter 198
Brejchová, Jana 233
Brick Bradford 81
"Bridge of Death" (*Radar Men from the Moon*) 84–85
Bridges, Lloyd 86
Brocco, Peter 84
Brooke, Walter 42
Brooks, Geraldine 203
Brooks, Mel 168–169
Brown, James 210
Brown, Lester 99
Brunner, John 126, 127
Bryant, Bill 185
Buck Rogers (serial) 10, 75
Buck Rogers (tv series) 75
"Building a Space Station" (*Men into Space*) 55, 56, 59
"Burnout" (*Men into Space*) 55, 56, 62, 67
Burns, George 141–142, 145
Burroughs, Edgar Rice 2, 3; Tarzan stories 3
Bushman, Francis X. 110, 114
Buttram, Pat 163–164

Caan, James 291, 293
Caesar, Julius 105–106
"The Cage" (*Star Trek*) 34
Caidin, Martin 290; *Marooned* 290
Callahan, James T. 122
Caltabiano, Alfio 267
Capricorn One 316
Captain Video and His Video Rangers 75–76, 231, 299–300
Captain Video: Master of the Stratosphere 75–76, 81–83, 131, 269, 274; "Astray in the Stratosphere" 82; "Captain Video's Peril" 82; "Entombed in Ice" 82; "Flames of Atoma" 82; "Invisible Menace" 83; "Journey into Space" 81–82; "Menace of Atoma" 82; "Video vs. Vultura" 83
"Captain Video's Peril" (*Captain Video: Master of the Stratosphere*) 82
Carleton, Claire 143
Carlson, Richard 36, 57
Carpenter, Scott 341ch2n4
Carr, Gerald 341ch2n4
Carradine, John 141, 206, 207
Carreras, Michael 27
Cartwright, Angela 118
Cartwright, Veronica 320
Cass, Maurice 78, 142–143
Cassutt, Mark 1
Cassutt, Michael 1–2
Cat-Women of the Moon 26, 56, 80, 92–94, 95, 96, 97, 99, 106, 112, 132, 143, 147, 148, 193, 206, 240, 251, 271
"Caves of the Moon" (*Men into Space*) 58, 60, 68
Cernan, Eugene 313
Champlin, Irene 76

Chapman, Edward 11
Chapman, Marguerite 91
"The Chase" (*Star Trek: The Next Generation*) 314
Chernyak, V. 226, 228
Chevreau, Cecile 28
Chikyu Boeigun 278–279, 281
Childhood's End (Clarke) 312, 322
Chomon, Segundo de 11
"Christmas on the Moon" (*Men into Space*) 44, 57, 58, 66, 68, 252
"The Claim Jumpers" (*Flash Gordon*) 77
Clark, Fred 162–163
Clark, Ken 110
Clarke, Arthur C. 59, 213, 232, 254, 299–300, 304, 306, 312, 316, 322; *Childhood's End* 312, 322; *A Fall of Moondust* 59; *Greetings, Carbon-Based Bipeds!: Collected Essays 1934–1998* 299–300; "The Other Side of the Sky" 304; *2001: A Space Odyssey* 300, 306; *2010: Odyssey Two* 213, 316
Clarke, Gary 96
Clavillazo see Antonio "Clavillazo" Espino
The Clear Horizon 49
"Clem and the Satellite" (*The Red Skelton Show*) 141
Clitheroe, Jimmy 168
Clute, John 27; *The Encyclopedia of Science Fiction* (with Nicholls) 27
Cobb, Lee J. 80, 124
Coburn, James 123
Colbert, Robert 122 149
"The Cold Equations" (Godwin) 296
"Cold Hands, Warm Heart" (*The Outer Limits*) 198, 202–203
Coleman, Dabney 200
Colin, Ian 180
Colli, Ombretta 262, 264
Collins, Joan 154
Colman, Booth 95
"*Columbia*, and the Dreams of Science Fiction" (Westfahl) 138
Columbus, Christopher 11, 12, 148, 248
Commando Cody: Sky Marshal of the Universe 75
"Condemned of Space" (*Lost in Space*) 120–121
Connery, Sean 125, 126
Connor, Frank 45–46
Conquest of Space 5, 6, 8, 17, 20, 23, 26, 33, 34, 38, 41–45, 47, 49, 51, 52, 53, 55, 56, 61, 66, 85, 87, 88, 94, 103, 115, 188, 207, 232, 252, 299, 301
Conquistador de la Luna 118–119, 272–274, 343n6
Conrad, Charles "Pete" 312
Considine, John 199
"Contact Has Been Established" (*The Quatermass Experiment*) 179–180

Contamination 319
"Contraband" (*Men into Space*) 60, 67, 68
"Controlled Experiment" (*The Outer Limits*) 199
Conway, Tom 110
Coogan, Richard 75
Cook, Tommy 96
Coon, Gene L. 127
Cooper, Ben 122
Cooper, Gordon 108
Coppola, Francis Ford 228–229, 245
Corby, Ellen 143
Corman, Roger 227, 228
Corrigan, Ray 187
Cosby, Bill 123
Dos Cosmonautas a la Fuerza 257–258
Cosmonauts on Venus see *Planeta Bur*
Costello, Anthony 204
Costello, Lou 11, 140, 144, 146, 147, 151, 164, 169, 171, 173, 246–247, 257, 270
Cotten, Joseph 102
Countdown 5, 7, 49, 214, 290, 291–294, 295, 296, 297
Cowan, Jerome 149
Crane, Richard 77–78
The Crawling Hand 197–198, 214, 219
Creature from the Black Lagoon 211
The Creeping Unknown see *The Quatermass Xperiment*
Crenna, Richard 294, 297
Cribbens, Bernard 155
I Criminali della Galassia 258–260, 261–262, 264–265
Cronkite, Walter 308–309, 311, 312
Crosby, Bing 151, 153–154, 164, 246–247
Crouching Tiger, Hidden Dragon 218
Crow, Carl 207
Culp, Robert 123
Cummings, Bob 144, 342*ch3n4*
Curran, Pamela 207
Curtis, Wanda 185
Cutell, Lou 212
Cuthbertson, Allan 168

Daily, Bill 160
Dana, Bill 159, 292
Daneen, Mike 288
"Dark of the Sun" (*Men into Space*) 60, 65, 68
Darlton, Clark 268, 269; "Perry Rhodan" novels (with Scheer) 268, 269
Darren, James 122
"Dateline: Moon" (*Men into Space*) 60, 69, 70, 269
Dauphin, Claude 131
Dávila, Luis 269
Davin, Eric Leif 88; *Pioneers of Wonder* 88
Dawson, Anthony see Margheriti, Antonio

The Day of the Triffids 201
The Day the Earth Stood Still 175–176, 177, 219, 299–300
The Day the Sky Exploded see *La Morte Viene dallo Spazio*
Dean, Isabel 179–180
Dean, Margia 182
"Death Ship" (*The Twilight Zone*) 108–109
DeBeausset, Michael 214
de Bergerac, Cyrano 233, 234
Deep Impact 317
Defoe, Daniel 54, 117, 227; *Robinson Crusoe* 54, 117, 227
Dennis the Menace 159; "Junior Astronaut" 159
Denver, Bob 158, 159
"The Derelict" (*Lost in Space*) 119
DeRita, Joe 149
"Deserters" (*Raumpatrouille*) see "Deserteure"
"Deserteure" (*Raumpatrouille*) 266
Destination Moon 1, 4, 5, 7, 16, 17, 20–26, 27, 28, 32, 33, 38, 43, 45, 50, 51, 52, 55, 56, 58, 59, 67, 68, 75, 79–80, 85–86, 87, 89, 90, 93, 103, 109–110, 121–122, 127, 131, 132, 143, 145, 180, 181, 188, 191, 230, 268, 284, 290, 292, 299–300, 302, 303, 312, 341*ch2n1*
Destination Space 20, 41, 51–54, 55, 56, 58, 61, 296
Destroy All Monsters see *Kaijû Soshingeki*
"The Destroyers" (*Quatermass II*) 183–184
Devil Girl from Mars 32, 179
Devlin, Cory 110
De Vries, George 214
Dexter, Anthony 110, 114
I Diafanoidi Portano la Morte 258, 260–262, 264–265, 307
Dickinson, Angie 61, 62
Dijon, Alain 251
Disneyland 8, 20, 45–47, 69, 70, 221, 223, 230–231, 233; "Man and the Moon" 8, 20, 45–47, 69, 70, 221, 223, 230–231, 233; "Man in Space" 45; "Mars and Beyond" 45
Dobson, James 208
Doin' Time on Planet Earth 153
Domergue, Faith 236, 238
Donahue, Troy 167
Donlevy, Brian 181
Doohan, James 128
Döppelganger 102, 134–137, 318
DoQui, Robert 204
Doran, Ann 187
Doroga k Zvezdam 8, 221–223, 224, 234
Douglas, Gordon 124
Dowling, Constance 39
Downs, Cathy 96
A Dream Come True see *Mechte Navstrechu*
Dubbins, Don 103
Duel of the Space Monsters see

Frankenstein Meets the Spacemonster
Duff, Howard 27
Duggan, Andrew 124
Dullea, Keir 302
Duncan, David 110
Dunskus, Erich 77
Duvall, Robert 291

Earle, Edward 91
Earth vs. the Flying Saucers 176, 285
"Earthbound" (*Men into Space*) 58, 60, 173, 251
Eden, Barbara 160, 161
"Edge of Eternity" (*Men into Space*) 56–57, 58, 62
Edwards, Bill 189, 190
Efremov, Ivan 246; *Tumannost Andromedy* 246
Egan, Richard 39
Einstein, Albert 95, 266–267
Eisele, Donn 341*ch2n4*
Eitner, Don 244
Ekberg, Anita 165
Eldredge, George 81
"Elegy" (*The Twilight Zone*) 108
Ella the Astronaut 319
Ellison, Harlan 157; "That Moon Plaque" 157
Ely, Lawrence D. 56
"Emergency Mission" (*Men into Space*) 56, 57
Emery, John 86
Emory, Richard 45–46
"The Empath" (*Star Trek*) 342*ch3n3*
Encounter in Space see *Mechte Navstrechu*
The Encyclopedia of Science Fiction (Clute and Nicholls) 27
Encyclopedia of Science Fiction Movies (Hardy) 23, 209
The End of the World see *Verdens Undergang*
Enemy from Space see *Quatermass II*
"The Enemy Planet" (*Radar Men from the Moon*) 85
"The Enemy Within" (*Star Trek*) 128
"Entombed in Ice" (*Captain Video: Master of the Stratosphere*) 82
Ernsting, Walter see K.H. Scheer and Clark Darlton
"Errand of Mercy" (*Star Trek*) 130
Escape from the Planet of the Apes 319
"Escape into Space" (*Rocky Jones, Space Ranger*) 78
Espino, Antonio "Clavillazo" 272
Espinoza, José Ángel "Ferresquilla" 274
E.T.: The Extra-Terrestrial 175
Event Horizon 319
Excursion dans la Lune 11
Excursion to the Moon see *Excursion dans la Lune*
"The Exploding Stars" (*Space Patrol*) 76

354   INDEX

The Fabulous Baron Munchausen see *Baron Prášil*
Faith, Dolores 114, 207
A Fall of Moondust (Clarke) 59
Fantastic 193
Fantastic Voyage 245
Far Out Space Nuts 319
Farinon, Gabriella 251
Fehmi the Astronaut 319
Field, Margaret 178
Field, Shirley Anne 150
Fiermonte, Enzo 262
"Fight for Survival" (*Tom Corbett, Space Cadet*) 80
Filimonov, S. 224
Filipovský, František 234
Fine, Larry 148, 149
Fire Maidens from Outer Space 8, 32, 96
First Man into Space 189–193, 208, 214, 249, 292
First Men in the Moon 102, 103, 104–107, 156, 167
The First Men in the Moon (Wells) 102, 104, 105, 106, 107
First Spaceship on Venus see *Die Schweigende Stern*
"First Woman on the Moon" (*Men into Space*) 55, 60, 62–65, 66, 68, 161, 184, 224, 251
Fischer, Madeleine 250
Fisher, Terence 27
"Flames of Atoma" (*Captain Video: Master of the Stratosphere*) 82
"Flare Up" (*Men into Space*) 67–68
Flash Gordon (comic strip) 147
Flash Gordon (serial) 10, 83
Flash Gordon (tv series) 75, 76–77; "The Breath of Death" 77; "The Claim Jumpers" 77
Flash Gordon Conquers the Universe 10
Flash Gordon serials 10, 11, 75, 109–110, 207, 247, 275, 276, 287
Flash Gordon's Trip to Mars 10
"Flash in the Sky" (*Men into Space*) 59, 60–61, 68
Fleming, Eric 42, 98
Flesh Gordon 131
"Flight Overdue" (*Tales of Tomorrow*) 80–81
Flight to Mars 63–64, 88–92, 95, 113, 114, 115, 274
"Flight to the Red Planet" (*Men into Space*) 58, 68, 72
Fly Me to the Moon 316–317
Flying Disc Man from Mars 81
Fonda, Jane 131
Fong, Benson 43
"For the Birds" (Asimov) 172
Forbidden Planet 7–8, 94–95, 108, 121, 138, 230, 231, 232, 299–300
"The Forbidden World" (*Lost in Space*) 120
Ford, Ross 33
Forman, Joey 142
Forrest, Steve 108

Fortress 2 317
Foster, Phil 43
…4…3…2…1…Morte 268–269, 342*ch*6*n*4
Fox, Michael 39
Franchi, Franco 257
Franciscus, James 294, 297
Frankenstein 18–19, 163
Frankenstein Meets the Space Monster 7, 211–214, 219, 268
Franklin, H. Bruce 22–23
Franz, Arthur 89
Frau im Mond 6, 9, 10, 13, 14–17, 18, 19, 20, 22, 24, 26, 29, 33, 45, 58, 62, 65, 87, 93, 100, 103, 341*ch*1*n*4
Fredericks, Dean 113, 114
Freeman, Joan 169
Freiberger, Fred 127–128, 342*ch*3*n*3
Frentzen, Jeffrey 200, 201, 202, 204–205; *The Outer Limits Companion* (with Schow) 200, 201, 202, 204–205
Fritsch, Willy 14–15
Frobe, Gert 167
"From Another World" (*Men into Space*) 61, 68, 69, 71
From the Earth to the Moon (film) 102–104, 107, 156, 167
From the Earth to the Moon (miniseries) 316
From the Earth to the Moon (Verne) 102, 233
Frydberg, Wera 77
Fukasaku, Kinji 218

Gabor, Zsa Zsa 99
Gaines, Richard 89
"The Galaxy Being" (*The Outer Limits*) 199
Galileo, Galilei 313
Gallagher, Patti 185
"Gamma Quadrilogy" 258–259, 264
Gaponenko, Vassili 17
Garland, Richard 207
Garrick, John 11
Gastoni, Lisa 259–260
Gentry, Roger 205
The George Burns and Gracie Allen Show 140, 141–142, 160; "Space Patrol Kids Visit" 141–142, 342*ch*4*n*1
Gernsback, Hugo 10, 18–19, 22, 142, 180, 220, 247; *Ralph 124C 41+: A Romance of the Year 2660* 22; "Results of $300.00 Scientifiction Prize Contest" 247
Gerstle, Frank 45–46
Ghidrah, the Three-Headed Monster see *San Daikaijû: Chikyu Saidai no Kessen*
"The Ghost Planet" (*Lost in Space*) 120
Giants and Toys see *Kyojin to Gangu*
Gibson, Edward 341*ch*2*n*4
Gigantes Planetarios 274–276, 277, 343*n*6

Gilligan's Island 158–159; "Nyet, Nyet, Not Yet" 158–159
Giustini, Carlo 260
Glass, Everett 95
Glemnitz, Reinhard 266
Glenn, John 108
Goddard, Mark 118
Goddard, Robert 9, 165–166
Godwin, Tom 296; "The Cold Equations" 296
Godzilla vs. Monster Zero see *Kaijû Daisensô*
Godzilla vs. the Sea Monster see *Gojira, Ebirâ, Mosura: Nankai no Daiketto*
"Godzilla's Travels: The Evolution of a Globalized Gargantuan" (Westfahl) 343*n*7
Gog 20, 33, 39–41, 173, 322
Gojira 277–278, 282
Gojira, Ebirâ, Mosura: Nankai no Daiketto 284
Goldberg, Rube 272
"Golden Orbit" (*Salvage 1*) 315
Goldfinger 123
Gorath see *Yosei Gorasu*
Gordeichik, Larisa 243
Gordon, Bert I. 185
Grant, Lee 294, 295
Gray, Charles 150
Gray, Colleen 114
The Green Slime 8, 207, 216–219
Greetings, Carbon-Based Bipeds! Collected Essays 1934–1998 (Clarke) 299–300
Gregory, Thea 49
Grey, Monica 183
Griffith, Hugh 183
Grissom, Gus 35–36
Gruber, Franz 288
Gstettenbaur, Gustl 14–15
"Guardian of the Law" (*Raumpatrouille*) see "Hüter des Gesetzes"
Guerra, Rogelio 274, 275
Guest, Val 181
Gulliver's Travels (Swift) 113

Hackman, Gene 294, 295, 297
Haggard, H. Rider 3; Allen Quatermain stories 3
Hagman, Larry 160
Hale, Alan, Jr. 198
Hama, Mie 125
Hamilton, Roy 93
"A Handful of Hours" (*Men into Space*) 57, 58, 62, 68
Hanley, Jimmy 48, 49
Hanold, Marilyn 212
"Happy Anniversary" (*I Dream of Jeannie*) 161
Harada, Itoko 288
Hardy, Phil 23, 209; *Encyclopedia of Science Fiction Movies* 23, 209
Harrington, Curtis 244, 245
Harris, Jonathan 117
Harryhausen, Ray 106, 185, 186
Hartley, Mariette 294, 295
Harvey, Don 83

"Has Anybody Seen Jeannie?" (*I Dream of Jeannie*) 160–161
Haskin, Byron 116, 203, 204–205
Have Rocket, Will Travel 148–149, 172, 173
Have Space Suit—Will Travel (Heinlein) 1, 23
"Haven't I Seen Me Someplace Before?" (*I Dream of Jeannie*) 161
Hawkins, Frank 180
Hawks, Howard 218
Hawtrey, Charles 126
Hayden, Naura 193, 194
Hayes, Patricia 126
Hecht, Ben 98
Heinlein, Robert A. 1, 10, 19, 20–23, 24–25, 27, 30, 32, 33–34, 79, 155, 165, 322, 341*ch*2*n*1, 341*ch*2*n*2; *Have Space Suit—Will Travel* 1, 23; *The Moon Is a Harsh Mistress* 155; "Ordeal in Space" 24–26, 322, 341*ch*2*n*1; *Rocket Ship Galileo* 21–22, 23; "Shooting *Destination Moon*" 20–21, 22, 23; *Space Cadet* 79; *Stranger in a Strange Land* 165
Held, Karl 199
Hemmings, David 131
Henderson, Douglas 185
Hendry, Ian 136
Henry, Emmaline 162
Herbert, Charles 61
Hewitt, Heather 214
Hewitt, Virginia 76
Hickman, Dwayne 159
High Noon 314
Hillig, Ursula 265
"Hills of Death" (*Radar Men from the Moon*) 85
Hilton, Arthur 93
Himmelskibet 6, 9, 10, 12–14, 16, 18, 19, 20, 22, 101, 270, 341*ch*1*n*3
"Hit by a Meteorite" (*Space Patrol*) 76
Ho, Don 37
Hodge, Al 75
Holdren, Judd 81
Holger-Madsen 6, 9, 12, 13, 14, 140
Holland, Steve 76
Holm, Claus 265
Honda, Ishirô 281, 282
Hope, Bob 151, 153–154, 164, 246–247
Hopper, Dennis 244
Hordren, Michael 150
Horne, David 27
Horton, Robert 216, 217, 219
Houston, We've Got a Problem 316
"How to Be a Hero Without Really Trying" (*My Favorite Martian*) 160
Howard, Moe 148, 149
Hoyle, Les 198
Hubenaková, Svatava 240
Hubschmid, Paul 250
Hurt, John 320
Huston, Virginia 89, 90

"Hüter des Gesetzes" (*Raumpatrouille*) 266
Hyer, Martha 35, 105, 144

I Dream of Jeannie 120, 160–162, 319; "Around the World in Eighty Blinks" 161–162; "Happy Anniversary" 161; "Has Anybody Seen Jeannie?" 160–161; "Haven't I Seen Me Someplace Before?" 161; "The Lady in the Bottle" 160; "Operation: First Couple on the Moon" 161
I Dream of Jeannie ... Fifteen Years Later 319
I Spy 123; "Apollo" 123
I Still Dream of Jeannie 319
Ignatova, Kyunna 236
Ihnat, Steve 124, 291
Ikarie XB-1 240–242, 342*ch*6*n*2
The Impossible Voyage see *Le Voyage à Travers l'Impossible*
In Like Flint 123–125
The Incredible Melting Man 319
Ingrassia, Ciccio 257
"Into the Sun" (*Men into Space*) 55, 57
"The Invaders" (*The Twilight Zone*) 108–109
"Invasion" (*Raumpatrouille*) 266
Invasion of the Body Snatchers 248
"The Invisible Enemy" (*The Outer Limits*) 198, 203–205, 215
"Invisible Menace" (*Captain Video: Master of the Stratosphere*) 83
The Invisible Ray 11
Ireland, Anthony 27
Irwin, James 313
"Is There Another Civilization?" (*Men into Space*) 71
"Island in the Sky" (*Lost in Space*) 119
Island of Lost Souls 18–19
Islands in the Sky (Westfahl) 58
It Came from Beneath the Sea 238
It Came from Outer Space 179
It! The Terror from Beyond Space 187–189, 208, 212, 213
It's About Time 159, 319
Ives, Burl 167

Jacobsen, Frederik 12
Jacobson, Lilly 14
Jaeckel, Richard 200, 218
Jaffe, Carl 189
Jagger, Dean 342*ch*3*n*4
Janssen, David 294, 295
Jeffries, Lang 268
Jeffries, Lionel 105, 106, 167
Jelinek, Rudolf 233
The Jetsons 159
Johansson, Scarlett 2
Johnny Jupiter 75
Johns, Larry 33
Johnson, Russell 158
Jory, Victor 93
"José, the Astronaut" (*The Bill Dana Show*) 159
"Journey into Space" (*Captain Video: Master of the Stratosphere*) 81–82
Journey to the Center of the Earth 102
Journey to the Moon see *Rehla ilal Kamar*
Journey to the Seventh Planet 195–197
"Joyride" (*The Outer Limits*) 319
Judd, Edward 105, 106
Judge, Arline 198
Jules Verne's Rocket to the Moon 156, 167–169
"Junior Astronaut" (*Dennis the Menace*) 159
Just Imagine 11, 12, 140, 251–252

Kaijû Daisensô 158, 268, 284–285, 286
Kaijû Soshingeki 285–286
Kaijûtô no Kessen: Gojira no Musuko 284
"Der Kampf um die Sonne" (*Raumpatrouille*) 266
Karen, James 212
Karloff, Boris 149
Karlsen, John 269
Karnes, Robert 38
Karzhukov, Mikhail 243
Katzman, Leonard 209–210, 211
Kawaguchi, Hiroshi 281
Keaton, Buster 272
Keegan, Barry 50
Keith, Brian 152, 166
Kelley, DeForest 128, 129
Kemmer, Ed 76
Kennedy, John F. 52, 54, 109
Kerman, David 212
Kersh, Kathy 160
Kiddie Matinee website 342*ch*6*n*1
Kiel, Richard 114
King Dinosaur 185–186, 188
King of the Rocket Men 83, 84
Kirk, Joe 144
Kirk, Tommy 152, 162
Klega, Danny 158
Klugman, Jack 108
Klushantsev, Pavel 221, 223
Kneale, Nigel 179, 180, 181, 183, 184
Knight, Shirley 199
Knotts, Don 151, 169, 170
Kobe, Gail 52, 200
Kobi, Michi 110
Koenig, Walter 128, 129
Komarov, Sergei 17
Komarov, Vladimir 7, 290
Kornbech, Svend 13
Koscina, Sylva 247
Kosmicheskiy Reys 6, 10, 13, 17–18, 19, 20, 22, 24, 26, 55, 59, 157, 221
Kossoff, David 155, 156
Kovack, Nancy 295
Kristen, Marta 118
Kruschen, Jack 145, 193, 194
Kubo, Akira 283, 285
Kubrick, Stanley 254, 290, 299, 301, 302, 306, 312, 321
Kulp, Nancy 144
Kyojin to Gangu 281–282, 289, 321

LaBeouf, Shia 2
Lackovic, Otto 240
"The Lady in the Bottle" (*I Dream of Jeannie*) 160
Lake, Veronica 80
Lamont, Duncan 180
Lamour, Dorothy 154
Landau, Martin 199, 317
Landau, Richard 181
Landi, Maria 191
Lang, Fritz 6–7, 9, 12, 15, 17, 18, 19, 25, 140
Langan, Glenn 207
Langton, Paul 188
Last and First Men (Stapledon) 312
"The Laughing Alien" (*Space Patrol*) 76
Lauren, Rod 198
Lauter, Harry 70
Lavi, Daliah 167
Law, John Philip 131
Leaver, Philip 27
Lee, Ang 218
Leiber, Fritz 322; "The Beat Cluster" 322; *A Specter Is Haunting Texas* 322
Leinster, Murray 126
Lem, Stanislaw 72, 196; *Solaris* 72, 196
Lembeck, Harvey 163
Leon, Nathanael "Frankenstein" 274
Leonov, Alexei 1, 160, 223, 307, 313
Lesaffre, Roland 267
Leslie, William 207
Lester, Seeleg 204–205
Levy, Ori 132
Lewis, Bobo 165
Lewis, C.S. 4
Lewis, Jerry 164, 165, 246–247, 257
Ley, Willy 79
Liberace 154
Lindbergh, Charles 191
Lindsey, Erin 180–181
Litel, John 89
Lockhart, June 118
Lockwood, Gary 301, 305
Lom, Herbert 135
"The Lonely" (*The Twilight Zone*) 108
Loring, Lynn 135
Lost in Space 8, 117–121, 159, 341–342*ch*3*n*2; "Blast Off into Space" 120; "Condemned of Space" 120–121; "The Derelict" 119; "The Forbidden World" 120; "The Ghost Planet" 120; "Island in the Sky" 119; "No Place to Hide" 117–118; "The Reluctant Stowaway" 118–119; "Wild Adventure" 120
"Lost Missile" (*Men into Space*) 56, 57, 58, 59, 68
The Lost Planet 81
The Lost World 121
Love, David 176
Love That Bob 144, 342*ch*4*n*3;

"Bob Goes to the Moon" 144; "Bob in Orbit" 342*ch*4*n*3
Lucas, George 281
"Lucy Becomes an Astronaut" (*The Lucy Show*) 159
The Lucy Show 159; "Lucy Becomes an Astronaut" 159
Lukavská, Radovan 240
Lukes, Oldrich 230
Luna 223–224
"Lunar Secret" (*Men into Space*) 70, 88
Lundigan, William 36, 37, 63, 341*n*5
Lundin, Victor 116
Lyden, Robert 78

Machowski, Ignacy 230
Macrolife (Zebrowski) 312
Magellan, Ferdinand 148
Maine, Charles Eric 27
Malleson, Miles 104
"Man and the Moon" (*Disneyland*) 8, 20, 45–47, 69, 70, 221, 223, 230–231, 233
The Man from Planet X 178, 179, 237
"Man in Space" (*Disneyland*) 45
Man in the Moon 32, 149–151, 155, 164, 342*ch*4*n*4
Man-Plus (Pohl) 322
"The Man Who Didn't Need to Walk on the Moon" (Westfahl) 343*n*1
"The Man Who Was Never Born" (*The Outer Limits*) 96, 198, 199–200, 319
"The Man with the Power" (*The Outer Limits*) 199
Mansfield, Sally 78
Mantee, Paul 115
The Many Loves of Dobie Gillis 159; "Spaceville" 159
Marceau, Marcel 131
Marcus, Vitina 120
Margheriti, Antonio 251, 254, 258, 262, 264–265
Marietta 99, 100
Marlowe, Hugh 95, 176
Marooned 7, 290, 294–299
Marooned (Caidin) 290
"Mars and Beyond" (*Disneyland*) 45
Mars Invades Puerto Rico see *Frankenstein Meets the Spacemonster*
Mars Needs Women 213
Mars trilogy (Robinson) 321, 322
Marshall, Herbert 35, 36, 39
Marshall, Nancy 212
Marshall, Zena 126
Martell, Donna 32
Martellanza, Pietro 262
The Martian Chronicles 318
The Martian Chronicles (Bradbury) 318
Martin, Dean 154
Martin, Lock 177
Martin, Ross 43, 108

Martinková, Marcela 240
Massen, Osa 86
Massey, Raymond 11
Masumura, Yasuro 282, 321
Maurus, Gerda 14–15
Maxwell, Lois 47
May, Leontine 266
McAuliffe, Christa 138, 173, 313–314
McGavin, Darren 214
McGee, Vic 205
McIntosh, J.T. 50
McKeever and the Colonel 159; "McKeever's Astronaut" 159
"McKeever's Astronaut" (*McKeever and the Colonel*) 159
McMahon, Horace 145
McNally, Stephen 200
Meadows, Stanley 126
Mechte Navstrechu 243–244
Medwin, Michael 29–30
Melchior, Ib 193, 195
Méliès, George 11, 140, 341*ch*1*n*2
Memories of the Space Age (Ballard) 343*n*1
Men into Space 2, 5–6, 8, 20, 24, 34, 37, 41, 44, 47, 49–50, 51, 52, 54–73, 79–80, 81, 88, 89, 97, 103, 126, 139, 158, 161, 166, 173, 184, 191, 195, 200, 202, 216, 224, 226–227, 229, 251, 252, 263, 269, 292, 295, 296, 298, 304, 306, 312, 315, 341*n*5; "Asteroid" 56, 58–59, 61, 69, 184, 216; "Beyond the Stars" 59–60, 62, 71–72, 126; "Building a Space Station" 55, 56, 59; "Burnout" 55, 56, 62, 67; "Caves of the Moon" 58, 60, 68; "Christmas on the Moon" 44, 57, 58, 66, 68, 252; "Contraband" 60, 67, 68, 89; "Dark of the Sun" 60, 65, 68; "Dateline: Moon" 60, 69, 70, 269; "Earthbound" 58, 60, 173, 251; "Edge of Eternity" 56–57, 58; "Emergency Mission" 56, 57; "First Woman on the Moon" 55, 60, 62–65, 66, 68, 161, 184, 224, 251; "Flare Up" 67–68; "Flash in the Sky" 59, 60–61, 68; "Flight to the Red Planet" 58, 68, 72; "From Another World" 61, 68, 69, 71; "A Handful of Hours" 57, 58, 62, 68, 263; "Into the Sun" 55, 57; "Is There Another Civilization?" 71; "Lost Missile" 56, 57, 58, 59, 68; "Lunar Secret" 70, 88; "Mission to Mars" 57, 64, 67, 158, 166, 226–227, 229; "Moon Cloud" 58, 60, 68; "Moon Landing" 58, 67, 68, 69; "Moon Probe" 54–55, 56, 59, 61, 66–67, 79–80, 184, 295, 304; "Moon Trap" 55, 64–65, 68; "Moonquake" 58, 60, 62; "Mystery Satellite" 69, 70–71; "Quarantine" 58, 60, 68; "Sea of Stars" 57; "Shadows on the

Moon" 70, 72–73; "Space Trap" 56, 57, 68, 69; "The Sun Never Sets" 55, 56, 57, 59, 67; "Tankers in Space" 55, 59; "Verdict in Orbit" 60, 62, 68; "Voice of Infinity" 57, 61, 68; "Water Tank Rescue" 55, 58
"Menace of Atoma" (*Captain Video: Master of the Stratosphere*) 82
Menzies, William Cameron 11
Meredith, Burgess 342*ch3n*4
Meredith, Judi 244
Metropolis 19, 321
Meyer, Walter 99
"The Mice" (*The Outer Limits*) 199
Michener, James 315; *Space* 315
The Mickey Rooney Show 141, 142–144; "The Moon or Bust" 141, 142–144
Milczaca Gwiazda see *Die Schweigende Stern*
Missile to the Moon 94, 96–98, 268
Mission Mars 214–216
Mission Stardust see *...4...3...2...1...Morte*
Mission to Mars 207, 318–319, 322
"Mission to Mars" (*Men into Space*) 57, 64, 67, 158, 166, 226–227, 229
Mr. Novak 342*ch3n*4
Mitchell, Cameron 89
Mitchell, Gerald 193, 194
Mitchell, Laurie 99
El Moderno Barba Azul 272
Moffett, Gregory 178
Mohr, Gerald 193, 194
Monch, Peter 196
Montgomery, Robert, Jr. 110
Montressor, David 251
Moody, Ron 155
The Moon see *Luna*
"Moon Cloud" (*Men into Space*) 58, 60, 68
The Moon Is a Harsh Mistress (Heinlein) 155
"Moon Landing" (*Men into Space*) 58, 67, 68, 69
"The Moon or Bust" (*The Mickey Rooney Show*) 141, 142–144
Moon Pilot 151–153, 166
"Moon Probe" (*Men into Space*) 54–55, 56, 59, 61, 66–67, 79–80, 184, 295, 304
"Moon Rocket" (*Radar Men from the Moon*) 83
"Moon Trap" (*Men into Space*) 55, 64–65, 68
Moon Zero Two 132–134, 208, 281, 319
"Moonquake" (*Men into Space*) 58, 60, 62
Moonraker 126, 316
Moonshot 316
"Moonstone" (*The Outer Limits*) 198, 201, 202, 205
Moore, Clayton 84
Moore, Joanna 292
Moore, Kieron 47, 48
Moorhead, Agnes 108

More, Kenneth 149
Morgan, Barbara 173
Morley, Robert 154, 165
Morris, Howard 165
Morris, Kirk 267
Morrison, Barbara 33
La Morte Viene dal Pianeta Aytin 258, 263–264
La Morte Viene dallo Spazio 158, 184, 216, 249–250
Moskalenko, K. 17
The Mouse on the Moon 155–158
The Mouse on the Moon (Wibberley) 155
The Mouse That Roared 155
The Mouse That Roared (Wibberley) 155
Mullaney, Jack 342*ch3n*4
Mulligan, Richard 16
Mumy, Billy 117
Murray, Guillermo 274, 275
"The Mutant" (*The Outer Limits*) 199
Mutiny in Outer Space 207–209, 342*ch5n*2
My Favorite Martian 8, 159–160, 321; "How to Be a Hero Without Really Trying" 160; "My Favorite Martian" 159
"My Favorite Martian" (*My Favorite Martian*) 159
My Living Doll 159, 342*ch3n*4; "Robotic Astronaut" 159
The Mysterians see *Chikyu Boeigun*
Mysterious Island 102
"Mystery Satellite" (*Men into Space*) 69, 70–71

"The Naked Time" (*Star Trek*) 128
Nash, Joseph 76
Nash, Noreen 178
Neal, Peggy 287
Nebo Zovyot 224–229, 238, 243, 307
Needham, Leo 45–46
Neiiendam, Nicolai 12
Nero, Franco 260
Neumann, Kurt 85–86, 87, 88
Newmar, Julie 159, 342*ch3n*4
Nicholls, Peter 27; *The Encyclopedia of Science Fiction* (with Clute) 27
Nichols, Nichelle 130, 138
Nicholson, Jack 316
Nicol, Alex 201, 202
Nielsen, Leslie 94–95, 169
"Nightmare" (*The Outer Limits*) 199
Nimoy, Leonard 128, 129, 315
Nixon, Richard 7, 34, 111, 166, 311
"No Place to Hide" (*Lost in Space*) 117–118
Noël-Noël 247
North, Jay 159
Nostradamus 48
Novelli, Mario 267
Nozoe, Hitomi 281
Nude on the Moon 99–102
"Nyet, Nyet, Not Yet" (*Gilligan's Island*) 158–159

Oates, Simon 126
Oberth, Hermann 9, 15, 16, 19
O'Brian, Hugh 86
O'Brien, Edmond 152–153
O'Brien, Willis 185
"Obsession" (*Star Trek*) 111
O'Connell, Arthur 169
O'Connor, Tim 201, 202
Odyssey 5 319
002 Operazione Luna see *Dos Cosmonautas a la Fuerza*
Ohmart, Carol 65
Olson, James 132, 133
"On Thursday We Leave for Home" (*The Twilight Zone*) 108
"One Way to the Moon" (*The Time Tunnel*) 121–123
Ongewe, Julius 230
"Operation: First Couple on the Moon" (*I Dream of Jeannie*) 161
Órbita Mortal see *...4...3...2...1...Morte*
Orbital Decay (Steele) 119
"Ordeal in Space" (Heinlein) 24–26, 322, 341*ch2n*1
Orea, Mario 275
Osborn, Andrew 28
Osborn, Lyn 76
O'Shea, Milo 131
"The Other Side of the Sky" (Clarke) 304
Ottosen, Carl 196
The Outer Limits (1963–1965) 8, 96, 198–205, 207, 215, 319; "The Brain of Colonel Barham" 199; "Cold Hands, Warm Heart" 198, 202–203; "Controlled Experiment" 199; "The Galaxy Being" 199; "The Invisible Enemy" 198, 203–205, 215; "The Man Who Was Never Born" 96, 198, 199–200, 319; "The Man with the Power" 199; "The Mice" 199; "Moonstone" 198, 201, 202; "The Mutant" 199; "Nightmare" 199; "The Sixth Finger" 210; "Specimen: Unknown" 8, 198, 200–202, 207, 216; "The Zanti Misfits" 199
The Outer Limits (1995–2002) 314, 319; "Joyride" 319; "Phobos Rising" 314; "The Vessel" 319; "The Voyage Home" 319
The Outer Limits Companion (Schow and Frentzen) 200, 201, 202, 204–205
Outer Space Jitters 147, 148
Outland 314

Paget, Debra 103
Paige, Robert 144
Pajama Party 162
Pal, George 19, 20, 96
Pallenberg, Anita 131
Paluzzi, Luciana 218
"The Parallel" (*The Twilight Zone*) 108–109, 134–135, 136, 137
Parker, Shirley 214

Patrick, Butch 160
Pearce, Malcolm 279
Peary, Robert 148
Peck, Gregory 294
Peluffo, Ana Luisa 272
"People Are Alike All Over" (*The Twilight Zone*) 108
Pereverzev, Ivan 224, 225
"Perry Rhodan" novels (Scheer and Darlton) 268, 269
Perry Rhodan—SOS aus dem Weltall see *...4...3...2...1...Morte*
"Persons Reported Missing" (*The Quatermass Experiment*) 180–181
Persson, Essy 269
Peter Pan (Barrie) 18, 292
Peterson, Zanny 12
Pflug, Eva 265
Phantom from Space 94, 178–179, 237
The Phantom Planet 113–115
"Phobos Rising" (*The Outer Limits*) 314
Il Pianeta degli Uomini Spenti 254–255, 258, 262, 283
Il Pianeta Errante 258, 259, 262–264
Pichel, Irving 20, 21, 23
The Pilgrim Project (Searls) 290
Pink, Sidney 193, 195
Pinkava, Josef 236
Pioneers of Wonder (Davin) 88
"Plague from Space" (*Tales of Tomorrow*) 81
"Planet ausser Kurs" (*Raumpatrouille*) 266
Planet of Storms see *Planeta Bur*
Planet of the Apes 96, 299, 312, 319
Planet of the Female Invaders see *El Planeta de las Mujeres Invasoras*
Planet of the Vampires see *Terrore nello Spazio*
"Planet Off Course" (*Rampatrouille*) see "Planet ausser Kurs"
Planeta Bur 236–237, 238, 243–244
El Planeta de las Mujeres Invasoras 276–277
Planetary Giants see *Gigantes Planetarios*
Platt, Edward 51
Pleasence, Donald 125
Pober, Leon 37; "Tiny Bubbles" 37
Pogue, William 341*ch*2*n*4
Pohl, Frederick 322; *Man-Plus* 322
Pohl, Klaus 14–15
"Pop the Astronaut" (*The Red Skelton Hour*) 159
Postnikow, Michail N. 230
Powers, Tom 21, 25
Preminger, Megan 281; *Another Science Fiction: Advertising the Space Race 1957-1962* 281
Price, Dennis 167
The Prince of Space see *Yusei Oji*
"Probe 7—Over and Out" (*The Twilight Zone*) 108

The Producers 168–169
Project Moon Base 5, 20, 23, 30, 32–35, 36, 38, 40–41, 43, 44, 53, 55, 56, 58, 59, 61, 63–64, 65, 68, 88, 124, 142, 145,165, 166, 207, 273, 296, 301, 341*ch*2*n*2
Protazanov, Yakov 10
Puglia, Frank 186–187
"Pursuit of the Deep Space Projectile" (*Tom Corbett, Space Cadet*) 79

"Quarantine" (*Men into Space*) 58, 60, 68
The Quatermass Experiment 179–181, 184–185, 197, 198, 212, 214; "Contact Has Been Established" 179–180; "Persons Reported Missing" 180–181
The Quatermass Xperiment 32, 181–183, 186, 189, 219, 250
Quatermass II (film) 184–185
Quatermass II (miniseries) 32, 183–185, 304; "The Bolts" 183; "The Destroyers" 183–184
Queen of Blood 243, 244–245
"Queen of Mars" (*The Red Skelton Show*) 141
Queen of Outer Space 8, 98–99, 149
The ? Motorist 11

Rabin, Jack 93
Rackelmann, Kurt 230
Radar Men from the Moon 43–44, 81, 83–85, 137–138, 212, 268; "Bridge of Death" 84–85; "The Enemy Planet" 85; "Hills of Death" 85; "Moon Rocket" 83
Rain, Douglas 303
Rains, Claude 254
Ralph 124C 41+: A Romance of the Year 2660 (Gernsback) 22
Rannow, Jerry 205
Rasp, Fritz 14–15
Rathbone, Basil 236, 237–238, 244
"Die Raumfalle" (*Raumpatrouille*) 266
Raumpatrouille: Die Phantastischen Abenteuer des Raumschiffes Orion 265–266; "Angriff aus dem All" 266; "Deserteure" 266; "Hüter des Gesetzes" 266; "Invasion" 266; "Kampf um die Sonne, Der" 266; "Planet ausser Kurs" 266; "Die Raumfalle" 266
Raumschiff Venus Antwortet Nicht see *Die Schweigende Stern*
Raycroft, Roy 83
Raynor, William 179
Reagan, Ronald 138, 342*ch*3*n*5
Red Planet 319
The Red Skelton Hour 159; "Pop the Astronaut" 159
The Red Skelton Show 141; "Clem and the Satellite" 141; "Queen of Mars" 141
Redfield, William 42

Rehla ilal Kamar 270–272, 342*ch*6*n*5
Reilly, Robert 212
The Reluctant Astronaut 141, 164, 169–173, 272
"The Reluctant Stowaway" (*Lost in Space*) 118–119
Rennie, Michael 175–176, 177
"Results of $300.00 Scientifiction Prize Contest" (Gernsback) 247
Return to Earth 316
Return to Earth (Aldrin and Warga) 316
Reynolds, Kay 161
Rhodes, Christopher 181
Ride, Sally 38
Riders to the Stars 5, 20, 24, 26, 35–39, 40, 41–42, 43–44, 45, 49, 53, 54, 56, 57, 61, 68, 79, 88, 97, 98, 134, 144, 149, 152, 173, 189, 191, 238, 267, 292, 297, 341*ch*2*n*3
The Right Stuff 316
The Right Stuff (Wolfe) 316
Ritchie, June 155
The Road to Hong Kong 124, 125, 153–155, 173
Road to the Stars see *Doroga k Zvezdam*
"Robert A. Heinlein's *2001: A Space Odyssey*" (Westfahl) 341*ch*2*n*1
Robertson, Cliff 80
Robinson, Kim Stanley 321, 322; Mars trilogy 321, 322
Robinson, John 183
Robinson Crusoe (Defoe) 54, 117, 227
Robinson Crusoe on Mars 7, 18, 113, 115–117, 203, 205–206, 319
Robot Monster 148, 176–178
"Robotic Astronaut" (*My Living Doll*) 159
Rocket Ship Galileo (Heinlein) 21–22, 23
Rocketship X-M 7, 26, 31, 42, 63–64, 85–88, 91, 95, 230, 232, 239, 250, 268, 290, 299–300
Rocky Jones, Space Ranger 75, 77–79, 94; "Beyond the Curtain of Space" 77–78; "Bobby's Comet" 78; "Escape into Space" 78
Rod Brown of the Rocket Rangers 75, 80; "The Suits of Peril" 80
Roddenberry, Gene 34, 127–128, 342*ch*3*n*3
Roel, Adriana 274, 275
Roman, Ruth 202
Rooney, Mickey 142
Rorke, Hayden 33, 160
Rossi-Stuart, Giacomo 258–259, 262
Roth, Gene 81, 148
Rubin, Benny 148
Ruffo, Leonora 267
"The Runaway Rocket" (*Tom Corbett, Space Cadet*) 79
Russel, Tony 258–259

Saberhagen, Fred 255; Berserker stories 255
Salce, Luciano 248
"Salvage" (*Salvage 1*) 315
Salvage 1 315, 316; "Golden Orbit" 315; "Salvage" 315
San Daikaijû: Chikyû Saidai no Kessen 284
Sanders, George 102
Sandler, Tony 99
Sarantsev, Yuri 236
Satellite in the Sky 20, 32, 47–51, 61, 149, 151, 155, 186, 296
Savage, Archie 251, 260, 264–265
Saval, Dany 152
Saxon, John 244
Schallert, William 178
Scheer, K.H. 268, 269; "Perry Rhodan" novels (with Darlton) 268, 269
Schell, Catherine 133
Schirra, Walter 108, 308–309, 341*ch*2*n*4
Schmidt, Harrison 313
Schönherr, Dietmar 265
Schow, David, J. 200, 201, 202, 204–205; *The Outer Limits Companion* (with Frentzen) 200, 201, 202, 204–205
Schwarzenegger, Arnold 318
Die Schweigende Stern 158, 230–232, 251
Science Fiction Theater 81
Scott, David 313
Scott, Jacqueline 109
Scott, Ridley 187, 219, 255
"Sea of Stars" (*Men into Space*) 57
Sea of Tranquility 316
Seamans, Jack 32
Searls, Hank 290; *The Pilgrim Project* 290
The Seedling Stars (Blish) 322
Selander, Lesley 88
Selby, Sarah 152
Serato, Massimo 259–260
Sergeant Dead Head 162–164
Serling, Rod 108, 109
"Shadows on the Moon" (*Men into Space*) 70, 72–73
Shatner, William 128, 129, 130, 202, 203
Shaughnessy, Mickey 43
Shawn, Dick 164, 165
Shepard, Alan 35–36, 189, 191, 313
"Shooting *Destination Moon*" (Heinlein) 20–21, 22, 23
Shvorin, Aleksandr 226
Sibaldi, Stefano 269
The Silent Star see *Die Schweigende Stern*
The Silkie (van Vogt) 192, 322
Simon, Günther 230
Simon, Mayo 298
Sinatra, Frank 154
Sini, Linda 257
Siodmak, Curt 10, 36
Sitka, Emil 148
"The Sixth Finger" (*The Outer Limits*) 210

Skelton, Red 141, 159
Skerritt, Tom 320
The Sky Calls see *Nebo Zovyot*
Smith, Shawn 95, 187
Smyrner, Ann 197
The Snow Devils see *La Morte Viene dal Pianeta Aytin*
Sohl, Jerry 203, 204–205
Solar Crisis 317–318
Solari, Rudy 204
Solaris (1972) 72
Solaris (2002) 72
Solaris (Lem) 72, 196
Soler, Andrés 272
Solovyov, Georgi 221
Son of Godzilla see *Kaijûtô no Kessen: Gojira no Musuko*
Son of Hercules movies 1
Sonoi, Keisuke 287
Space 315
Space (Michener) 315
Space: Above and Beyond 318
Space Buddies 319
Space Cadet (Heinlein) 79
Space Cowboys 316
Space Men 39, 60, 92, 173, 230, 251–254, 255, 258, 260
Space Monster 209–211, 219, 300
Space: 1999 159, 317, 318
Space Patrol (1950–1955) 75, 76, 341*ch*3*n*1, 342*ch*4*n*1; "The Atomic Vault" 76; "The Exploding Stars" 76; "Hit by a Meteorite" 76; "The Laughing Alien" 76; "The Space Patrol Code Belt" 76; "Threat of the Thormanoids" 76
Space Patrol (1966) see *Raumpatrouille: Die Phantastischen Abenteuer des Raumschiffes Orion*
"The Space Patrol Code Belt" (*Space Patrol*) 76
"Space Patrol Kids Visit" (*The George Burns and Gracie Allen Show*) 141–142, 342*ch*4*n*1
Space Suit Sappy 147–148
"Space Trap" (*Men into Space*) 56, 57, 68, 69
"The Space Trap" (*Raumpatrouille*) see "Die Raumfalle"
Space Truckers 319
The Space Voyage see *Kosmicheskiy Reys*
SpaceCamp 315
Spaceflight IC-1: An Adventure in Space 118, 240–241
"Spaceville" (*The Many Loves of Dobie Gillis*) 159
Spaceways 5, 20, 27–32, 33, 35, 38, 40, 43, 47, 48, 51, 61, 132, 149, 151, 155, 181, 182
Spalding, Kim 187
"Specimen: Unknown" (*The Outer Limits*) 8, 198, 200–202, 207, 216
A Specter Is Haunting Texas (Leiber) 322
"Spectre of the Gun" (*Star Trek*) 342*ch*3*n*3

Spielberg, Steven 175
Stacy, John 254
Stafford, Thomas 313
Stalin, Josef 17
Stapledon, Olaf 312; *Last and First Men* 312
Star Pilot see *2 + 5: Missione Hydra*
Star Trek 7–8, 10, 34, 65, 87, 102, 121, 127–130, 138–139, 173, 209, 230, 264, 265, 297, 312, 314, 316, 317, 321, 322, 342*ch*3*n*3; "Balance of Terror" 139; "The Cage" 34; "The Empath" 342*ch*3*n*3; "The Enemy Within" 128; "Errand of Mercy" 130; "The Naked Time" 128, 209; "Obsession" 111; "Spectre of the Gun" 342*ch*3*n*3; "The Tholian Web" 128–130
Star Trek films 314
Star Trek: The Motion Picture 314, 315
Star Trek: The Next Generation 314; "The Chase" 314
Star Trek II: The Wrath of Khan 43–44, 85
Star Wars 8, 10, 131, 281
Star Wars films 314
Starship Troopers 318
Steele, Allan 119; *Orbital Decay* 119
Steffen, Sirry 198
Stepánek, Zdenek 240
Stevens, Connie 165
Stevens, K.T. 97
Stevenson, Robert R. 84
Stewart, Larry 82
Stone, John 183
Stowaway to the Moon 315
Stranded 319
Stranger from Venus 179
Stranger in a Strange Land (Heinlein) 165
Strawn, Arthur 88
"Suit Up for Death" (*Tom Corbett, Space Cadet*) 79
"The Suits of Peril" (*Rod Brown of the Rocket Rangers*) 80
Sukman, Harry 37
Sullivan, Barry 255
Sun, John 267
"The Sun Never Sets" (*Men into Space*) 55, 56, 57, 59, 67
Sunshine 317–318, 341–342*ch*3*n*2
Superman II 318
Supernova 317–318
Sweeney, Bob 152
Swift, Jonathan 113; *Gulliver's Travels* 113
Sylvester, William 300, 301

Taekoesu Yonggary 286–287
Takamatsu, Hideo 281
Takarada, Akira 284
Tales of Tomorrow 80–81; "Appointment on Mars" 80–81; "Flight Overdue" 80–81; "Plague from Space" 81; "Test Flight" 80–81
Tanba, Tetsurô 125

Tang Hua-Ta 230
Tani, Toko 230, 231
"Tankers in Space" (*Men into Space*) 55, 59
Tarzan stories (Burroughs) 3
Tate, Reginald 179–180, 183
Taylor, Joan 187
Taylor, Kent 198
Taylor, Rod 95, 96
Tazaki, Jun 284
Teege, Joachim 168
Teenagers from Outer Space 176
Tejkh, Georgi 236
Temple, Shirley 53
Terms of Endearment 316
Terrore nello Spazio 255–257
The Terrornauts 126–127, 321
Terry-Thomas 167
"Test Flight" (*Tales of Tomorrow*) 80–81
Tharwat, Safeya 271
"That Moon Plaque" (Ellison) 157
The Thing (from Another World) 218, 244
Things to Come 11, 12, 17, 207
Thinnes, Roy 135
"Third from the Sun" (*The Twilight Zone*) 108
This Island Earth 94, 113, 114, 238, 268
"The Tholian Web" (*Star Trek*) 128–130
Thomas, Frankie 79
Thompson, Marshall 187, 189
Thomson, David 321; *A Biographical Dictionary of Film* 321
Those Fantastic Flying Fools see *Jules Verne's Rocket to the Moon*
Those Magnificent Men in Their Flying Machines 167
"Threat of the Thormanoids" (*Space Patrol*) 76
The Three Stooges 11, 140, 147, 151, 153, 163, 164, 169, 171, 173, 246–247
The Three Stooges in Orbit 149
Throne, Malachi 203
Til, Roger 110
The Time Machine 96, 102
The Time Machine (Wells) 96, 106
The Time Tunnel 121–123; "One Way to the Moon" 121–123
"Tiny Bubbles" (Pober) 37
Toeima, Edmoun 270
Tognassi, Ugo 247
Tolnaes, Gunnar 12
Tom Corbett, Space Cadet 75, 79–80, 265; "Ambush in Space" 79–80; "Assignment: Mercury" 79; "Fight for Survival" 80; "Pursuit of the Deep Space Projectile" 79; "The Runaway Rocket" 79; "Suit Up for Death" 79
Tom Swift novels (Appleton) 211
Tonuuts, Gurgen 225
Toomey, Regis 142
Tors, Ivan 36, 37, 39, 40
Total Recall 318, 321
Totò 247

Totò in the Moon see *Totò nella Luna*
Totò nella Luna 125, 154, 247–249
Towne, Aline 85
Townes, Harry 51, 58
Transformers: Dark of the Moon 316–317
Travis, Richard 96
Tremayne, Les 193, 194
A Trip to Mars see *Himmelskibet*
A Trip to the Moon see *Le Voyage dans la Lune*
The Trollenberg Terror 32
Tryon, Tom 152
Tsiolkovsky 9, 17, 220, 221–222, 223, 224; *Beyond the Planet Earth* 17
Tsuchiya, Yoshio 284
Tucker, Phil 176–177
Tufts, Sonny 93
Tumannost Andromedy 245–246
Tumannost Andromedy (Efremov) 246
12 to the Moon 13, 109–113, 230, 251
Twenty Million Miles to Earth 186–187
20,000 Leagues Under the Sea 102
Twenty Thousand Leagues Under the Sea (Verne) 214
The Twilight Zone 81, 108–109, 134–135, 136, 137, 198; "And When the Sky Was Opened" 108; "Death Ship" 108–109; "Elegy" 108; "The Invaders" 108–109; "The Lonely" 108; "On Thursday We Leave for Home" 108; "The Parallel" 108–109, 134–135, 136, 137; "People Are Alike All Over" 108; "Probe 7—Over and Out" 108; "Third from the Sun" 108
2 + 5: Missione Hydra 268–270
2001: A Space Odyssey 4–5, 6, 7, 26, 33, 39, 72, 92, 132, 134, 135–136, 175, 184, 191, 207, 212–213, 216, 219, 252, 254, 255, 290–291, 298, 299–307, 312, 316, 318, 320, 321, 322
2001: A Space Odyssey (Clarke) 300, 306
2010: Odyssey Two (Clarke) 213, 316
2010: The Year We Make Contact 316

Uchû Daikaijû Girara 287–289
Uchû Daisensô 279–281
Uchûjin Tôkyô ni Arawaru 277–278
UFO 318
Unger, Goffredo 263, 264
Urbanova, Ruzena 240

Vadim, Roger 131
Vance, Vivian 159
Van Doren, Mamie 236, 238–239, 240
Van Nutter, Rik 251
Van Ronkel, Rip 51

van Vogt, A.E. 192, 322; *The Silkie* 192, 322
Velásquez, Lorena 277
Verdens Undergang 341ch1n3
"Verdict in Orbit" (*Men into Space*) 60, 62, 68
Verne, Jules 102, 103, 104, 107, 142–143, 214, 233, 234; *From the Earth to the Moon* 102, 233; *Twenty Thousand Leagues Under the Sea* 214
Vernov, Gennadi 236
Vespucci, Amerigo 248
"The Vessel" (*The Outer Limits*) 319
Victoria, Queen 104, 105–106
Vidal, Gore 164; *Visit to a Small Planet* 164
"Video vs. Vultura" (*Captain Video: Master of the Stratosphere*) 83
Villena, Fernando 255–256
Visit to a Small Planet 164
Visit to a Small Planet (Vidal) 164
"Voice of Infinity" (*Men into Space*) 57, 61, 68
Völz, Wolfgang 265
von Braun, Wernher 45, 46, 221, 248
von Harbou, Thea 19
von Wangenheim, Gustav 14–15
Le Voyage à Travers l'Impossible 11
Le Voyage dans la Lune 11
"The Voyage Home" (*The Outer Limits*) 319
Voyage to the Bottom of the Sea 121
Voyage to the End of the Universe 241, 242, 342ch6n2
Voyage to the Planet of Prehistoric Women 99, 236, 238–240
Voyage to the Prehistoric Planet 236, 237–238, 239, 243

Wahab, Hamada Abdel 270
Wall-E 322
Wallace, George 83, 84
Walley, Deborah 163
Walston, Ray 159
Waltz, Patrick 98
War Between the Planets see *Il Pianeta Errante*
War of the Planets see *I Diafanoidi Portano la Morte*
The War of the Worlds 102, 116
The War of the Worlds (Wells) 107
Ward, Larry 122
Warner, Jack 181
Warning from Space see *Uchûjin Tôkyô ni Arawaru*
"Water Tank Rescue" (*Men into Space*) 55, 58
Way...Way Out 164–167, 273, 281
Wazaki, Toshiya 287
Weaver, Dennis 165
Weber, Richard 110, 113, 114
Weingartner, Vit 234
Wells, H.G. 11, 96, 102, 104, 105, 106, 107, 142–143; *The First Men in the Moon* 102, 104, 105, 106, 107; *The Time Machine* 96, 106; *The War of the Worlds* 107

Wengraf, John 39, 110
Wesson, Dick 21, 24
West, Adam 115, 203
Westfahl, Gary 2, 58, 138, 306, 341*ch*1*n*2, 343*n*7; "Aye, Robot" 343*n*2; "Celebrating a Century of Science Fiction Columns with *A Trip to the Moon*" 341*ch*1*n*2; "*Columbia*, and the Dreams of Science Fiction" 138; "The Endless Odyssey" 306; "Godzilla's Travels: The Evolution of a Globalized Gargantuan" 343*n*7; *Islands in the Sky* 58; "The Man Who Didn't Need to Walk on the Moon" 343*n*1
Whalen, Michael 96
Wheatley, Alan 28
When Worlds Collide 299–300
White, Ed 1, 160, 307, 308
White, Jesse 170
White, Kitty 37
Whitsun-Jones, Paul 181
Wibberley, Leonard 155; *The Mouse on the Moon* 155; *The Mouse That Roared* 155
"Wild Adventure" (*Lost in Space*) 120
The Wild, Wild Planet see *I Criminali della Galassia*

Wilder, Myles 179
Wilder, W. Lee 179
Williams, Guy 118
Willock, Dave 98
Wilson, Neil 180
Windsor, Marie 92–93
Wingrove, David 39
The Wishing Machine see *Automat Na Prání*
Wishman, Doris 99, 100
The Wizard of Mars 205–207
The Wizard of Oz 205
Wolfe, Tom 316; *The Right Stuff* 316
Wolfit, Donald 48, 49
Woman in the Moon see *Frau im Mond*
The Wonderful Wizard of Oz (Baum) 205, 206
Woodbury, Doreen 148
Wordsworth, Richard 181
World Without End 95–96, 137, 186, 319
Wright, Bruce Lanier 33; *Yesterday's Tomorrows* 33
Wright, Orville 191
Wright, Wilbur 191
Wymark, Patrick 135

The X from Outer Space see *Uchû Daikaijû Girara*

Yanagisawa, Shinichi 287
Yasseen, Ismail 270
Yeager, Chuck 316
Yemelyanov, Vladimir 236
Yesterday's Tomorrows (Wright) 33
Yongary, Monster from the Deep see *Taekoesu Yonggary*
York, Francine 210
Yosei Gorasu 262, 267, 282–284
You Only Live Twice 125, 287
Youness, Ibrahim 271
Young, Ralph 99
Yusei Oji 278

Zalewska, Halina 262
"The Zanti Misfits" (*The Outer Limits*) 199
Zathura: A Space Adventure 319
Zebrowski, George 312; *Macrolife* 312
Zeman, Karel 234
Zeman, Milan 234
Zhuravlev, Vasili 6–7, 10, 12, 17, 18, 140
Zhzhyonov, Georgi 236
Zimbalist, Al 93
Zombies of the Stratosphere 81

www.ingramcontent.com/pod-product-compliance
Lightning Source LLC
Chambersburg PA
CBHW081536300426
44116CB00015B/2646